CARING FOR

OUR CHILDREN

**National Health and Safety
Performance Standards:
Guidelines for Out-of-Home
Child Care Programs**

CARING FOR

OUR CHILDREN

National Health and Safety Performance Standards: Guidelines for Out-of-Home Child Care Programs

A Joint Collaborative Project of the

American Public Health Association
1015 Fifteenth Street, N.W.
Washington, DC 20005

and the

American Academy of Pediatrics
141 Northwest Point Blvd.
P.O. Box 927
Elk Grove Village, IL 60009

Support for this project was provided by the
Maternal and Child Health Bureau,
Health Resources and Services Administration,
Department of Health and Human Services
(Grant # MCJ 113001)

5M1/92

ISBN 0-87553-205-5

Printed and bound in the United States of America
    Design: Gail M. Peck, Silver Spring, MD
    Photography: Daniel Peck, Silver Spring, MD
    Typesetting: Litho Comp, Bethesda, MD
    Set in: Garamond
    Printing and Binding: Edwards Brothers, Ann Arbor, MI

PREAMBLE

In 1984, Cecil Sheps, MD, MPH, recently appointed chair of the American Public Health Association (APHA) Program Development Board, asked the APHA's Sections to identify gaps and needs. In response to this request, the APHA Maternal and Child Health (MCH) Section suggested the development of health and safety standards for out-of-home child care facilities. At that time, Linda Randolph, MD, MPH, was chair of the MCH Section and Patricia Schloesser, MD, was chair-elect. It was recognized that the MCH Section, through its Child Development and Day Care Committee, had been involved in the promotion of the health of children in out-of-home child care settings since the early 1960s.

Simultaneously, the Minnesota Public Health Association submitted a resolution stating that child care standards, especially in the area of prevention of communicable diseases, were needed. Dr. Sheps felt that it would be beneficial if such standards were developed jointly with the American Academy of Pediatrics (AAP). The Academy also has had a long-standing interest and involvement in this area. In 1987, the Committee on Early Childhood, Adoption, and Dependent Care published *Health in Day Care: A Manual for Health Professionals,* which was a successor to *Standards for Day Care Centers,* initially published in 1971. The Committee's work was completed under the leadership of Selma Deitch, MD, MPH, editor of the manual and immediate past chair of the committee. Thus, a proposal was developed jointly by the APHA and the AAP for a collaborative project to be housed at the APHA headquarters. Funding for this collaborative project, "Development of National Health and Safety Performance Standards in Out-of-Home Child Care Programs," was awarded by the then Bureau of Maternal and Child Health and Resources Development (now called the Bureau of Maternal and Child Health), Department of Health and Human Services, effective July 1, 1987.

Contents

PROJECT WORK GROUPS

This report was prepared by the following individuals:

Central Steering Committee

Albert Chang, MD, MPH
Co-chair, APHA, Los Angeles, CA

George Sterne, MD
Co-chair, AAP, New Orleans, LA

Susan Aronson, MD, Philadelphia, PA
David Beard, MSW, Austin, TX
Helen Blank, BS, Washington, DC
Gwen Morgan, MS, Boston, MA
Linda Randolph, MD, MPH, Albany, NY
Cecil Sheps, MD, MPH, Chapel Hill, NC
Patricia Wise, RN, MEd, Holyoke, MA

Technical Panel Chairs

Environmental Quality
George Kupfer, MS, Ann Arbor, MI
Prevention and Control of Infectious Diseases
G. Scott Giebink, MD, Minneapolis, MN
Injury Prevention and Control
Albert Chang, MD, MPH, Los Angeles, CA
General Health
Selma Deitch, MD, MPH, Manchester, NH
Nutrition
Catherine Cowell, PhD, New York, NY
Prevention and Management of Child Abuse
David Chadwick, MD, San Diego, CA

Staff Health
Stacey Graville, RN, MN, Bellingham, WA
Children With Special Needs
Herbert J. Cohen, MD, Bronx, NY
Health Concerns Related to Social Environment and Child Development
Albert J. Solnit, MD, New Haven, CT
Health and Safety Organization and Administration
Patricia T. Schloesser, MD, Topeka, KS

Project Support

Geraldine Norris-Funke, RN, MS
Phyllis E. Stubbs, MD, MPH
   Bureau of MCH, DHHS, Project Officers
Susan Campbell, MPH
Randolph S. Moore, MA
   AAP, Staff Liaisons

Seiko Baba Brodbeck, APHA Associate
   Executive Director, Project Administrator
Debra Hawks Peabody, MPH, Project Director
   and Editor
Olivia Alegre-Ipanag, MD, MPH, Project Analyst
Deborah Jackson, Senior Office Assistant

Technical Panel Members and Resource Persons

Environmental Quality

Arthur L. Banks, RS, Washington, DC
Sallye Skipper Blake, EdS, Montgomery, AL
Robert E. Brewster, RS, MPA, Wheaton, IL
Jack L. Mayer, MD, New York, NY
Eric W. Mood, MPH, New Haven, CT

Bliss Moore, MPH, RS, Olympia, WA
Thomas A. Reardon, RS, Pasadena, CA
Ellen Schroth, RS, Washington, DC
Key Vaughn, RS, Austin, TX

Additional comments were provided by the following resource persons:

Albert H. Brunswasser, MPH, MBA, Pittsburgh, PA
David Goff, PE, MS, Hamden, CT

Robert Shane, PhD, Wynnewood, PA

Prevention and Control of Infectious Diseases

Janice Boase, RN, Seattle, WA
Albert Chang, MD, MPH, Los Angeles, CA
Steven Cochi, MD, Atlanta, GA
Steven Hadler, MD, Atlanta, GA
Frederick W. Henderson, MD, Chapel Hill, NC
Helene Gayle, MD, MPH, Atlanta, GA
Dennis O. Juranek, DVM, MSc, Atlanta, GA
Pauline D. Koch, MS, Wilmington, DE
Edgar O. Ledbetter, MD, Elk Grove Village, IL

Michael Osterholm, PhD, Minneapolis, MN
Robert F. Pass, MD, Birmingham, AL
Georges Peter, MD, Providence, RI
Larry Pickering, MD, Houston, TX
Martha Rodgers, MD, Atlanta, GA
Lawrence Schonberger, MD, MPH, Atlanta, GA
Ethel Seiderman, MA, Fairfax, CA
Carol S. Stevenson, JD, San Francisco, CA
Harry T. Wright, Jr, MD, MPH, Los Angeles, CA

Injury Prevention and Control

Brenda Coakley, MA, Washington, DC
Julianne Crevatin, MPH, Seattle, WA
Dee Cuney, MEd, Napa, CA
Leslie Fisher, MPH, Albany, NY
Judith Garrard, PhD, Minneapolis, MN
Nancy Ellen Jones, PNP, DrPH, New York, NY
Letty Lie, MPH, Minneapolis, MN

Mary Ann Mateo, Pine Hill, NM
Mary Ann O'Connor, MA, Hanover, NH
Carol W. Runyan, PhD, Chapel Hill, NC
Robert Shane, PhD, Wynnewood, PA
Sam Sheps, MD, Vancouver, BC, Canada
Mark Widome, MD, MPH, Hershey, PA

Additional comments were provided by the following resource persons:

Judy Blanding, MSN, San Jose, CA
Janet Braunstein, RN, MPH, Halifax, NS, Canada

Emily H. Gates, MD, Jacksonville, FL
Andrea Gielen, MPH, Baltimore, MD

General Health

Joanne Ascheim, MSN, CPNP, Concord, NH
Judy Coughlan, RN, Auburn, NH
Sheila Dobbin, MSW, Boston, MA
Patricia Fosarelli, MD, Baltimore, MD
Elmer Green, DDS, MPH, Albany, NY

Kathleen Malloy, MD, MPH, Martinez, CA
Linda Morgan, MD, Lynn, MA
Sally Reid, Esq, Dedham, MA
Mary Jane Wallner, MEd, Concord, NH

Nutrition

Maryrose J. Baiano, MS, RD, Dobbs Ferry, NY
Elizabeth Brannon, MS, RD, Rockville, MD
Mojdeh Bruss, MPH, RD, Albuquerque, NM
Doris F. Clements, MS, RD, Richmond, VA
Terry S. Hatch, MD, Champaign-Urbana, IL

Brearley B. Karsch, MS, RD, Philadelphia, PA
Margaret Phillips, EdD, RD, Rockville, MD
Ann Prendergast, MPH, RD, Rockville, MD
Marion N. Scarborough, MPH, RD, Jacksonville, FL
Clotilde Zayas (Deceased), MA, New York, NY

Prevention and Management of Child Abuse

Barbara Chernofsky, La Mesa, CA
David Finkelhor, PhD, Durham, NH
Kee MacFarlane, MSW, Los Angeles, CA
Cheri Robertson, Temecula, CA

Susan Russell, MS, Chapel Hill, NC
Hector Sanchez, MSW, Washington, DC
Siubhan Stevens, San Jose, CA

Staff Health

Judy Calder, RN, Oakland, CA
Bria Chakofsky, RN, Seattle, WA
Barry Fibel, MSW, Olympia, WA
Maxine Hayes, MD, Olympia, WA
Lynn Manfredi, BS, Decatur, GA
Pamela Mangu, MA, Washington, DC
Marcia K. McDonnell, MN, CANP, Atlanta, GA

Karen Patjens, BA, Tacoma, WA
Patricia St. Clair, RN, ScD, Seattle, WA
Jeanne Stellman, PhD, Brooklyn, NY
Rosemary Totten, BA, CDA, Tacoma, WA
Elaine Trate, Burke, VA
Cynthia Vlasich, RN, Washington, DC

Children with Special Needs

Madeline Appell, MA, New York, NY
Rebecca Fewell, PhD, New Orleans, LA
Meredith Harris-Copp, EdD, Boston, MA
Ruth K. Kaminer, MD, Bronx, NY

Patricia M. Pierce, PhD, Gainesville, FL
Peggy Pizzo, MEd, Arlington, VA
Anne Riley, RN, Iowa City, IA
Patricia Wagner, EdD, Brooklyn, NY

Health Concerns Related to Social Environment and Child Development

Jean Adnopoz, MPH, New Haven, CT
Angela Crowley, MA, RN-C, PNP, New Haven, CT
Cynthia Farrar, PhD, New Haven, CT

Lola Nash, MA, New Haven, CT
Sally Provence, MD, New Haven, CT
Kathryn Young, PhD, Westport, CT

Health and Safety Organization and Administration

Norris Class, MS, Topeka, KS
Ed Ehlinger, MD, MPH, Minneapolis, MN
Karen Juola, Topeka, KS
Kay Kent, RN, Lawrence, KS

Shirley Norris, MA, Topeka, KS
Peggy Scally, RN, Lawrence, KS
Helen Wallace, MD, MPH, San Diego, CA
Aileen Whitfill, Arlington, VA

Major assistance in the development of the standards was provided by Chris Pressey-Murray of Hanover, New Hampshire; the Children's Foundation, the National Association for Child Care Resource and Referral Agencies, the National Association for the Education of Young Children, the National Association for Family Day Care, and the National Association for Regulatory Administration in Human Services; and the state maternal and child health directors and state licensing directors who participated in two national surveys conducted during the standards development. The hosts of the field assessment sites were Glenda Bean of the Governor's office in Arkansas; Martha Daley of the Denver City Child Care Office; Dr. Benjamin Gitterman, the American Academy of Pediatrics State Child Care Contact in Colorado; Joyce Borgmeyer and Dr. Darryl Leong of the Iowa Health Department; Robert Lettelier of the New Hampshire Licensing Department; Dr. Jon Tillinghast and Valerie Marr of the City-County Health Department of Oklahoma County; Jack Thompson of the Seattle-King County Health Department; and Cris Ros-Dukler of the Texas Licensing Department. Local and state organizations and individuals in Arkansas, Colorado, Iowa, New Hampshire, Oklahoma City, Seattle, and Texas assisted in the field assessment of the draft standards. Hundreds of other individuals and organizations in the public and private sector were helpful in developing the standards.

INTRODUCTION

In an MCH panel discussion at the APHA meeting in 1943, Dr. Leona Baumgartner said it was important that

> . . . Health standards [in child care centers] be maintained in the new centers and that these standards include a safe and clean environment [and] a medical and nutritional program that safeguards the health of the young child, and a staff of warm, friendly adults who will allow children to make the best of their innate possibilities and recognize the marked differences in the mental, physical and emotional make-up and needs in individual children and in children of various ages.

The principles enunciated by Dr. Baumgartner, a pediatrician and public health administrator, apply just as much today as they did almost 50 years ago. At present, no set of health standards that can be applied to child care programs on a national level exists. The set of standards contained in this monograph, which was jointly developed by the American Public Health Association and the American Academy of Pediatrics, addresses this important need. These standards have been conceived through an interdisciplinary approach and have been broadly developed, widely reviewed, and extensively disseminated to caregivers, regulators, and health professionals who are intimately involved in the field of out-of-home child care.

Before standards are defined or discussed, the terms *recommendation, guideline,* and *regulation* should be defined and discussed.

A *recommendation* is a statement of practice that potentially provides a health benefit to the population served. It is usually initiated by an organization or a group of individuals with expertise or broad experience in the subject matter. It may originate within the group or be solicited by individuals outside of the organization. A current recommendation is that the *Haemophilus influenzae* type b conjugate vaccine be administered to childen 2 months to 5 years old who are in facilities. A recommendation is not binding on the practitioner; that is, there is no obligation to carry it out. A statement may be issued as a recommendation because it addresses a fairly new topic or

issue, because scientific supporting evidence may not yet exist, or because the practice may not yet enjoy widespread acceptance by the members of the organization.

A *guideline* is a statement of advice or instruction pertaining to practice. Like a recommendation, it originates in an organization with acknowledged professional standing. Although it may be unsolicited, a guideline is developed in response to a stated request or perceived need for such advice or instruction. Examples of guidelines are contained in the American Academy of Pediatrics' *Manual on Guidelines for Perinatal Care,* 2nd Edition, which provides comprehensive instructions on the health delivery practices to be followed around the time of pregnancy and birth.

A *regulation* takes a previous recommendation or guideline and makes it a requirement for compliance by an operating agency. A regulation originates in an agency with either governmental or official authority and has the power of law. Such authority is usually accompanied by an enforcement activity. Examples of regulations are state regulations pertaining to health and safety requirements for caregivers and children in a licensed child care center: immunizations required of preschool-age children, annual tuberculosis screening of caregivers, and so on. The components of the regulation, of course, will vary by topic addressed as well as by area of jurisdiction (e.g., municipality or state). Because a regulation prescribes a practice that every agency or program must comply with, it usually is the minimum or the floor below which no agency or program should operate.

A *standard* is a statement that defines a goal of practice. It differs from a recommendation or a guideline in that it carries a great incentive for universal compliance. It differs from a regulation in that compliance is not always required. It usually has a base of legitimacy or validity based on scientific or epidemiological data or, when this evidence is lacking, it represents the widely agreed upon, state-of-the-art, high-quality level of practice. Thus the agency, program, or health practitioner that does not meet the standard may incur disapproval or sanctions from within or outside the organization. Two examples of standards may be cited: all children should be immunized against diphtheria, tetanus, pertussis, polio, measles, mumps, and rubella on entry into first grade, and all pregnant women should begin prenatal care as early as possible in the first trimester of pregnancy. Given this definition, standards are indeed the strongest criteria for practice set by a health organization or association.

The National Research Council's recent report, *Who Cares for America's Children? Child Care Policy for the 1990's*,[1] calls for "uniform national child care standards—based on current knowledge from child development research and best practice from the fields of public health, child care, and early childhood education—as a necessary... condition for achieving quality in out-of-home child care. Such standards should be established as a guide to be adopted by all states as a basis for improving the regulation and licensing of child care and preschool education programs.... Based on existing knowledge, it is possible to specify reasonable ranges for standards to govern many important features of child care, including staff:child ratios, group size, caregiver qualifications, and the configuration of physical space."

What are the basic health and safety considerations in out-of-home child care programs? First, a child must be safe and protected from hazards and potential injuries. These include both unintentional injuries (e.g., falls from swings and slides) and intentional injuries (e.g., aggressive acts such as biting and hitting). A child must also be protected from potentially serious infectious diseases, such as measles, meningitis, hepatitis, and gastroenteritis. It must be acknowledged that it may be impossible to prevent the spread of infections such as upper respiratory infections and colds. Child care settings cannot be and should not be aseptic and germ-free environments, but the potential for serious infectious diseases should be reduced to a minimum. Caregivers can be active partners with the child's parents and health professionals in primary prevention, early detection, and prompt treatment of illness or disease.

Facilities must also provide a setting for nurturing and affection. They should not only protect a child, but should also promote the achievement of his or her fullest potential in both physical and psychological health.

The standards contained in this monograph were initially formulated by 10 technical panels composed of experts in each area: Environmental Quality, Prevention and Control of Infectious Diseases, Injury Prevention and Control, General Health, Nutrition, Prevention and Management of Child Abuse, Staff Health, Children with Special Needs, Health Concerns Related to Social Environment and Child Development, and Health and Safety Organization and Administration. Over 130 individuals with professional backgrounds in medicine, nursing, social work, health education, nutrition, sanitation, psychology, early childhood education, law, and other related fields were involved in the development of the standards. This group was ethnically and geographically diverse. Under the guidance of an editorial committee, the standards have been arranged in an order that facilitates their use by providers and regulators of child care programs.

Two constituency-building activities were conducted with drafts of the standards in order to develop a consensus about what constitutes good practice in child care. In a national review of the standards, hundreds of individuals across the country who were representative of the intended users reviewed the standards' content. In a field assessment of the standards, caregivers and advocates, legislators, educators, health professionals, and health and regulatory agencies in five states and two cities reviewed the standards in terms of implementability, acceptability, and usability. The comments from both review activities, including comments critical of the draft standards, were considered and evaluated and the standards revised, as deemed appropriate by the technical panels based on their scientific and professional judgment. The use of the word *national* in the title reflects this gathering of input from large numbers of experts to reflect the field and this consensus of good practice. Because these are national guidelines, local variability cannot be addressed. However, some standards may need to be modified to be more appropriate for a given locality (e.g., urban/rural), climate, or geography.

It should be noted that two concurrent activities took place during the development of the standards. One was a survey of selected state/municipal licensing regulations for out-of-home child care facilities as they were in effect in the summer of 1988. The objective of that survey was to provide a national perspective on the content and level of current regulations as they pertain to standards in each area of health and safety

---

[1] *Who Cares for America's Children? Child Care Policy in the 1990's.* National Research Council Report. National Academy of Sciences, Washington, DC, 1990.

addressed by the APHA/AAP project. A wide range of coverage was found, with many states lacking basic standards in prevention of infectious disease and injuries, and other states having very detailed standards covering many aspects of child care. Many gaps were also found in the areas of children with special needs, staff health, and nutrition. These were areas of new knowledge and new concern, and had not yet been addressed by many states.

The other activity was a survey of model health and safety program practices in the 10 technical panel areas. These practices were identified by various individuals and agencies closely involved in the child care field, and the practices were described by the staff of the facilities identified. Although a number of innovative practices were described in areas such as injury prevention, prevention of infectious disease, staff health, and prevention of child abuse and neglect, there was relatively little mention of collaboration between facilities and health professionals and agencies.

The intended audience of these standards is the general child care system in the United States. The system includes both privately and publicly funded facilities, such as child care centers, large and small family-child-care homes, before- and after-school programs, public schools, Head Start, and organized part-time programs. Individuals who direct or work in facilities should be the ones most concerned with the intent and content of these standards. Individuals and agencies involved in licensing and regulation of facilities should also use these standards frequently. Health professionals involved as caregivers or consultants to facilities should find these standards pertinent and relevant to their activities. Lastly, developers, sponsors, policymakers, and advocates for facilities also will find these standards useful.

These standards should be used to plan and establish a quality program of child care. The project leadership intended these standards to serve as goals for practice and as guidelines for implementation. It is readily recognized that some standards are more easily implemented than others for cost or other considerations. In addition, implementation of certain of these standards may be prohibited in some jurisdictions by state or local laws. Thus the standards should not be used as rigid criteria to evaluate the quality of the programs or facilities. They were developed to represent neither the minimal acceptable level of performance nor a platonic ideal, but rather to occupy the area between minimal acceptable practice and the ceiling beyond which additional effort and expertise would not yield commensurate improvements in health and safety. As new knowledge and innovative practices evolve, the standards themselves should be modified and updated.

Elsewhere in this monograph are listed the many contributors to the development of these standards. The project leadership owes each and every one of these individuals a profound debt of appreciation and gratitude.

The financial resources that are necessary to make child care a healthful experience may not be available or forthcoming in the near future. Nevertheless, we must continue our efforts to create in every child care setting a healthful, safe, and nurturing environment for our children, our most valuable natural resource and our future. We also must focus attention on the caregivers themselves, and must set standards that promote work environments that support them so that they may provide care that fosters child growth and development. We realize that the setting of these standards will require a greater financial commitment than our society has previously been willing to provide. It is not realistic to assume that this additional cost can or should be borne solely by parents. In other developed countries, considerable government funds pay for much of the cost of child care. In our pluralistic society, it is reasonable to expect not only government but voluntary agencies as well to invest more in our future. Employers are increasingly involved in providing or subsidizing this service for their employees' children.

We would be remiss if we failed to note that one of the major deterrents to improving heath and safety in out-of-home child care settings is the rapid turnover of caregivers. This turnover is largely due to the extremely low levels of income earned doing this vital work. Funds must be found to improve the income and working conditions of caregivers so that the tremendous expense of constantly training new caregivers can be minimized, and so that our children will have the continuity of caregivers so vital to their emotional development as well as their physical health and safety.

Albert Chang, MD, MPH
George Sterne, MD
Co-Chairs, Central Steering
    Committee

ADVISORY TO THE USER

The standards that follow are the result of an extensive process jointly organized by the American Public Health Association (APHA) and the American Academy of Pediatrics (AAP). Technical panels worked on particular subject matter areas for more than 2 years, after which time their recommendations were merged into a single set of recommended standards and widely reviewed by the public. The final document represents a consensus of the various disciplines involved with child care, with particular emphasis on the health specializations.

We recognize that many other organizations have developed standards and recommendations concerning out-of-home child care. The National Association for the Education of Young Children (NAEYC) has developed standards concerning developmentally appropriate practices; Head Start has published performance standards; the AAP has published *Health in Day Care: A Manual for Health Professionals;* and the Child Welfare League of America has published *Standards for Day Care Service.* All of these are valuable resources, as are many excellent state publications. It is not our intent to duplicate or supplant the efforts of others, but to supplement them from the particular perspective of health and safety. We do not mean to imply that these are the only or even the most important issues in child care; we mean to say only that these health and safety issues needed to be addressed.

Because of continuing concerns about health and safety issues, especially injuries and infections occurring in out-of-home child care settings, the APHA and the AAP have developed this set of standards. Health involves more than the absence of illness and injury. Many child development issues are related to mental health, and many of the more global issues important to mental health and development are also addressed in detailed publications on developmentally appropriate practices by early childhood educators. Some overlap is inevitable and indeed desirable.

Child:staff ratios serve as an example of this overlap. NAEYC has pointed out the need for low infant-to-staff ratios for implementation of developmentally appropriate practices. The need of infants for a consistent, nurturing caregiver is both a mental health issue and a physical health and safety issue. Infants need a primary caregiving relationship to develop trust and the ability to make emotional attachments. Sufficient staff must be able to evacuate infants from the building in case of fire or other emergencies and to allow sufficient time to practice health and safety routines (e.g., handwashing and other hygiene practices). Caregivers must be recognized as performing a job for groups of children that parents of twins, triplets, or quadruplets would rarely be considered able to handle alone. Caring for a group of three infants is the same as caring for infant triplets; four toddlers are equivalent to a set of quadruplets.

This set of standards is intended to be useful guidance material for a number of different purposes. However, these standards (unless codified by federal, state, or local law) are not mandated by law. Although this document reflects the best information available at the time of publication, updating the material to reflect changes in knowledge affecting child care will be required from time to time.

Definitions

Child care offers developmental care and education for children who live at home with their families. Several types of facilities are covered by the general definition of child care. Although states vary greatly in their legal definitions, the facilities are generally defined as follows:

Center

Provides care and education for any number of children in a nonresidential setting if open on a regular basis (i.e., it is not a drop-in facility).

Full-day centers usually enroll infants, toddlers, and preschool children for 4 hours or more per day.

Part-day centers, including nursery schools, Head Start programs, and preschools, usually enroll preschool children for less than 4 hours per day. Before- and after-school facilities usually enroll children for a few hours a day during the hours when they are not in school, and may offer full-day care during vacations.

Large Family-Child-Care Home

Usually offers care and education for 7 to 12 children (including preschool children of the caregiver) in the home of the caregiver, who employs one or more qualified adult assistants to meet the staff:child ratio requirements. This type of care is likely to resemble center care in its organization of activities. Applicable terms are abbreviated here to *large family home* or *large family home caregiver.*

Small Family-Child-Care Home

Usually offers care and education for one to six children (including preschool children of the caregiver) in the home of the caregiver. Caregivers model their programs either on a nursery school or on a skilled parenting model. Applicable terms are abbreviated here to *small family home* or *small family home caregiver.*

Special Facility for Ill Children

Not the same as child care for ill children provided by the child's regular center, large family-child-care home, or small family-child care-home. This is a facility that cares only for ill children or a facility that cares for more than six ill children at a time (see *Special Facilities for Ill Children*, p. 100).

Facility for Children with Special Needs

Usually offers care and education in a residential or nonresidential setting for one or more children with developmental disabilities, mental retardation, emotional disturbance, sensory or motor impairment, or significant chronic illness who require special health surveillance or specialized programs, interventions, technologies, or facilities (see *Children with Special Needs*, p. 237).

School-Age-Child Care Facility

Offers a program of activities before and after school and/or during vacations.

Drop-in Facility

Usually offers care and education for one or more children in a residential or nonresidential setting for less than 10 hours per day, no more than once a week, to any child.

Note that children with special needs can be, and wherever appropriate should be, mainstreamed in general child care centers and family-child-care homes. Specialized centers serving only children with special needs deal with children with more disabilities and often with more serious disabling conditions, therefore requiring more specialized standards.

Several terms are commonly used to describe the child care setting, but the term *facility* is used in this document for consistency to describe the child care center and small and large family-child-care home. Facility has a legal definition: the buildings, the grounds, the equipment, the people, and the activities that are involved in providing child care of any type. The term *caregiver* is used for consistency to represent staff in child care centers (i.e., director, teacher, etc.) and family-child-care homes. The term *family-child-care home* refers to both small and large family-child-care homes. The term *family home caregiver* refers to both small and large family home caregivers.

A distinction has been made in these standards about the type of facility to which the standard applies. If a standard applies only to a center, the symbol 𝄞 will appear directly above the standard. If a standard applies only to a large family-child-care home, the symbol [A] will appear above the standard. If a standard is relevant to only a small family-child-care home, the symbol 🍎 will appear above the standard. If no symbol appears above the standard, it is understood that the standard applies to centers, large family-child-care homes, and small family-child-care homes.

The following age categories are used in these standards:

Age Category		Functional Definition
Infant	0–12 months	Birth to ambulation
Toddler	13–35 months	Ambulation to toilet training
Preschooler	36–59 months	Toilet training to entry in regular school
School-Age	5–12 years	Entry in regular school, including kindergarten

Basic Orientation

Like any standard-writing group, the panelists for the APHA/AAP project had to decide whether to set their standards at the optimal level of the ideal or at the level of the absolutely necessary. In many cases the two are not different. In the material that follows, if a standard is recommended as optimal practice but is not feasible to require, the Comments section will identify it and discuss the reasoning behind it.

Standards directed to the facility appear in chapters 1 through 8, whereas Recommendations to federal, state, and local organizations and to entities other than the facility are in chapter 9. In chapters 1 through 8, the Rationale section cites the scientific reference and/or epidemiologic evidence for the standard. References for the rationales are given at the end of each chapter. If these are not available, the best professional opinion to support the standard is cited. The rationale not only explains the intent of and the need for the standard, but serves as an educational tool. The Comments section includes other explanatory information relevant to the standard, such as applicability of the standard and, whenever possible, ways to measure compliance with the standard.

The standards represent the consensus of many people about good practice in child care. All of the standards are attainable. Some may have already been attained in individual settings; others can be implemented over time. It should be understood, however, that the panelists did not intend to establish standards which would come to be regarded, solely by their having been published, as the community standard by which the actions of a particular facility and its staff might be judged in the context of legal liability. Each community and each facility must consider its own specific and particular circumstances in making judgments about whether the standards should be applied.

Those judgments should be based on the same kinds of scientific and professional opinions as were considered by the panels. These standards, therefore, provide guidance as to the scientific and professional knowledge that is available as of the publication date. The panelists hope, and have made every effort to assure, that they have presented the best available scientific and professional information.

Whether it is feasible to adopt the standards in their entirety or to modify them will depend on the purpose for which they are used. For example, any organization that funds child care should, in our opinion, adopt these standards as funding requirements and should set a payment rate that covers the cost of meeting them.

The following are some of the ways in which this guidance material may be used:

1. As guidance material for caregivers. Anyone operating a facility on any level, from a chain of centers to a small family-child-care home, needs information on good practice. These standards will, we hope, prove useful to administrators, caregivers, and those who teach courses to caregivers.

2. As a reference for public health professionals, pediatricians, and others who provide consultation to caregivers. Many local and state health departments have developed child care guidance material that public health nurses, sanitarians, and nutritionists, among others, use in consulting with caregivers. The American Academy of Pediatrics published *Health in Day Care: A Manual for Health Professionals* for pediatricians providing guidance to their patients or consultation to caregivers. The APHA/ AAP standards will serve as a comprehensive, national reference to enhance existing guidance material as well as to address gaps.

3. As guidance to citizens' groups in states revising their licensing requirements. Because licensing has the force of law, caregivers and facilities must meet any requirements set by licensing agencies. Cost feasibility may delay full implementation of some of the recommended standards, particularly in states where family incomes are not high and child care is not subsidized. Nevertheless, requirement-writing committees will want to know the best thinking in the field as they discuss what can be required in their states.

4. As guidance material to state Departments of Education (DOEs) and local school administrations. Public schools and private schools are beginning to offer programs for 4-year-olds and even younger children. A few schools have even included infant programs. Organized school systems, whether public or private, are seldom covered by licensing requirements. Few state DOEs have written standards for such programs. School codes have no provisions for younger children, and often inadequately address such aspects as child handwashing, location of bathrooms, child:staff ratios and group size, teacher qualifications for working with preschool children, and injury prevention. As state DOEs begin to write standards for school-operated child care and preschool facilities, and as principals begin to investigate the meaning of good practice in early childhood and child care facilities, guidance material will be important.

5. As guidance material for funding standards of subsidized facilities. States and localities contract for child care for eligible families through purchase-of-service contracts and individual vendor/voucher mechanisms. There is a new interest in purchasing child development services to contribute to the growth and development of at-risk children under a new federal welfare reform program. For the first time in many states, it will be possible for welfare mothers to use the same sources for

child care/development facilities that other parents in the community use. Subsidized child care/development services will also be offered for children with special needs. Schools and other agencies may set up specialized facilities serving only children with special needs, but they may also pay for mainstreamed education provided in the community by local nursery schools, child care centers, and Head Start.

When states and localities purchase services, the guidance material on standards should offer them important information on the level of service they should require, and the level of funding they should offer, to meet the needs of the children for whom they are assuming a purchase responsibility.

6. As guidance material to other national private organizations that write standards. Several other national organizations have strong interest in child care and will continue to write standards for accreditation or guidance for the field. This APHA/AAP project has drawn on the expertise of these other organizations in developing these standards, and anticipates that the work done on these standards will be equally useful to other organizations.

7. As guidance material for parents and the general public. Parents need consumer information in selecting quality child care for their childen. This material should serve as a reference guide for parents and the organizations that serve them, such as resource and referral counselors. The material should also be a reference for local health departments and even for the media or any other source of information to the general public.

It should be noted that the technical panels were unable to consider all local laws and ordinances and persons using these materials or involved in the child care system are cautioned to be alert to any applicable laws and regulations that may apply to facilities in particular locales.

Multiple Uses

Because this guidance material will have multiple uses, it has not been written from the perspective of a single use. Many of the standards may well be used as licensing requirements; therefore, to the extent possible they have been written to be measurable and enforceable. This measurability will also be important when the standards are used as performance standards in a contractual relationship by a funding source. Concrete and specific language is helpful to the caregivers and facilities that will put the standards into practice. Where an intangible is difficult to measure, an attempt has been made to describe it in order to provide guidance that is as specific as possible. At times the language is highly technical and will need to be interpreted by specialists. Whenever feasible, the standards have been written to be understood by readers from a wide variety of backgrounds.

It will be important to avoid duplication of inspectors as these standards are implemented. In general, child care is regulated by at least three different legal systems. The first is the building code system. Building inspectors enforce building codes to protect life and property in all buildings, not just child care facilities. Some of the recommended standards should be written into state or local building codes, rather than into the licensing requirements.

The second major legal system that regulates child care is the health system. A number of different codes are applied to prevent the spread of disease in restaurants, hospitals, and other institutions where hazards might exist. Health codes are not specific to child care; however, specific provisions for child care might be found in a health code. Some of the provisions in the recommended standards might be appropriate for a health code revision.

The third legal system applied to child care is the actual licensing system. Approvals from health and building safety authorities are usually required before a license can be granted. Sometimes a standard is not included as a licensing requirement because it is covered in another code. Sometimes, however, it is not covered in any code, as is the case for some of the standards that follow. It is important that children be fully protected, and the issues addressed in the recommended standards should be addressed in public policy. However, it is important to an effective regulatory system that different inspectors not try to regulate the same thing. Advocates should decide which codes to review in adding these standards to their regulatory systems. Although the licensing requirements are most usually affected, it may be more appropriate to revise the health or building codes to include certain standards.

Continuing Improvement

Standards are never static. Each year the knowledge base increases, and new scientific findings become available. New areas of concern and interest arise. This is why standards are frequently revised and improved. Twenty-five states wrote new licensing requirements between 1987 and 1989.

These recommended standards will assist citizens who are involved in the continuing work of standards improvement at every level: in the field of practice, in the field of regulatory requirements, and in the professional goals of the relevant disciplines.

Each of these areas affects the others in the ongoing process of improving the way we meet the needs of children. Possibly the most important use of these standards will be to raise the level of understanding among the general public about what those needs are, and to contribute to a greater willingness to commit more resources to achieve a level of quality that is necessary for children to grow in a healthy and safe environment.

GUIDING PRINCIPLES FOR THE STANDARDS

The following are the guiding principles from which these standards have been developed:

1. Child care for infants, young children, and school-age children is anchored in a respect for the developmental needs, characteristics, and cultures of the children themselves; it recognizes the unique qualities of each individual.

2. To the extent possible, program activities should be geared to the needs of the individual child, as well as to the group as a whole.

3. The relationship between parent and child is of utmost importance for the child's current and future development, and should be supported by caregivers. The parent/legal guardian is the primary decision maker regarding the child's day-to-day care. A cornerstone of out-of-home child care is planned communication and involvement between the parent/legal guardian and the child's caregiver.

4. The nurturing of a child's development, based on a knowledge of general health and growth and the unique characteristics of the individual child, enhances the enjoyment of both child and parent as maturation and adaptation take place.

5. Trustworthy relationships with a small number of adults and an encircling, benevolent, affective atmosphere are essential to the healthy development of children. Staff selection, training, and support should be directed to the following goals:
   a) promoting continuity of affective relationships;
   b) encouraging staff capacity for identification and empathy with the child; and
   c) emphasizing an attitude of playfulness while maintaining the stance of an adult.

6. Programs and care should be based on a child's functional status, and the child's needs should be described in behavioral or functional terms. Rigid categorical labeling of children should be avoided as much as possible.

7. Written policies and procedures shall identify facility requirements and persons and/or entities responsible for implementing such requirements. Processes, however, should never become more important than the care and education of children.

8. Confidentiality of records must be maintained to protect the child, family, and staff. The information obtained in the course of child care is used to plan for a child's safe and appropriate participation, and parents/legal guardians must be assured of the vigilance of the staff in protecting such information.

9. The health record is the written profile of the health of the child. Unlike the situation in the child's household, in the child care setting there is no one who has a memory of the unique characteristics and details of the individual child's health. The health record documents health status, steps for management of known minor or chronic disease, and who, when, and where to call should a situation arise that requires a medical decision.

10. The care of ill children in groups should provide emotional support, attention to physical needs, and respect for the developmental needs of the children. Mildly ill children can often be cared for in their regular child care arrangements. Definitions of levels of care and types of illness served in the regular child care facility suggest there is also a need for alternative special facilities. Facility policies should clearly identify when an ill child
    a) can be excluded from a facility;
    b) can be included in the facility but kept outside the regular group; or
    c) can be included in the group, with the facility required to modify the child's activities.

11. Parents should be requested to
    a) inform the facility when a child is ill with a communicable condition; and
    b) inform their health care provider that the child is enrolled in child care and request the provider's cooperation in consulting

with the facility in the event of an illness that excludes the child from care.

12. The acquisition and transmission of infection among children in out-of-home child care is influenced by
   a) child-specific procedures;
   b) immunizations of children against vaccine-preventable childhood diseases;
   c) parental access to, and utilization of, educational materials; and
   d) staff training, awareness, and supervision (including employee-specific counseling as necessary).

13. State and community activities undertaken to reduce the acquisition and transmission of communicable diseases in child care settings include, but are not limited to, the following:
   a) established liaisons to provide timely reporting of communicable disease between child care settings and state and local health agencies;
   b) notification procedures between parents and child care settings regarding communicable disease exposure and prophylaxes; and
   c) state and local health department policies for prevention and control of communicable disease.

14. The health status of staff is an important component of job performance. For this reason, staff health should be assessed prior to employment and at regular intervals thereafter to promote good health and job performance. Facility policies must include criteria for excluding staff from the facility in the event of illness and for the return of excluded staff.

15. Offering workers' benefits to staff members contributes to the continuity of care of children, minimizes the spread of communicable disease, and improves morale, all of which help promote a nurturing environment for children.

16. Staff members need to know how to prevent illness and injury to children and themselves, and how to protect their own and the children's rights to a safe and healthful facility environment.

17. Health education for the toddler and for the preschool- and school-age child is an investment in a lifetime of good health practices and contributes to a healthier childhood and adult life. The child care setting offers many opportunities for incorporating health education into everyday activities.

18. The health of children in child care includes safety concerns (prevention of harm) as well as attention to healthy physical, emotional, cognitive, and social growth. Child abuse occurring in the home may be recognized first in child care settings. Child abuse may occur in child care settings. Child abuse may be prevented by the positive modeling of good care of children in care and by dissemination of knowledge of good practice by caregivers. These guidelines attempt to define the feasible measures available to caregivers and supervisory agencies that will ameliorate and interrupt child maltreatment.

19. Injury prevention and control efforts (including emergency preparedness) must be an integral and organized part of facility operations and activities.

20. Supervision and developmentally appropriate interaction by adults with children are key components of safety practices.

21. All indoor and outdoor facility equipment (including swimming and wading pools) must be maintained to ensure safety and to minimize the spread of infectious disease.

22. Planning and maintenance of plumbing, sanitary facilities, heating, cooling, ventilation, lighting, and electrical services are necessary for the proper operation of facilities. Space should be well organized, orderly, differentiated, and designed for children's use.

23. The use of toxic substances must be either prohibited or controlled through proper storage, handling, use, and disposal.

24. The transportation of children must be in vehicles that meet basic state licensure and registration requirements. The operators of such vehicles must be appropriately licensed, must be trained in safety precautions and emergency situations, and must understand their supervisory responsibilities.

25. The facility's nutrition activities complement and supplement those of home and community. Food provided in a child care setting should help to meet the child's daily nutritional needs while reflecting individual and cultural differences and providing an opportunity for learning. Facilities can contribute to overall child development goals by helping the child and family understand the

relationship of nutrition to health, the factors that influence food practices, and the variety of ways to provide for nutritional needs.

26. Food service planning in centers and large family-child-care homes involving a Nutrition Specialist (see Appendix B-1, on page 328, and Appendix B-2, on p. 329) or food services expert must be carried out to ensure that layout, equipment, storage areas, work flow, dining space, and all other aspects of an efficient and cost-effective food service are addressed.

27. Properly equipped food preparation areas and proper food-handling practices are required for the prevention of foodborne illness.

28. No child with special needs should be denied access to child care because of his/her disabilities, unless the child's extreme special needs make it unsafe for the child to be cared for in a community child care setting.

29. The facility chosen for each child should be one that is geared to meet the developmental needs of that child. Whenever possible, children with special needs should be cared for and provided services in settings including children without disabilities. If care in an integrated setting is not feasible (due to the particular nature of the child's needs and level of care required; the physical limitations of the site; limited resources in the community; or the unavailability of specialized, trained staff), a segregated setting is the next best alternative.

30. Care for children with special needs should be provided by staff trained to offer specialized services where required.

31. Families should be involved in determining the kind, amount, location, and method of delivery of care and services for children with special needs, preferably as a part of the development and implementation of a formal Individualized Family Service Plan.

32. The expression of, and exposure to, cultural and ethnic diversity enriches the experience of all children.

33. Community resources should be identified and utilized as much as possible to provide consultation and related services as needed.

CHAPTER 1
STAFFING

1.1 Child:Staff Ratio and Group Size

STANDARDS

ST1. One small family home caregiver (without an assistant) shall not care for more than six children, including no more than two children under age 2. These numbers include the caregiver's own children under the age of 6. If any child under age 3 is in care, there shall be no more than four children, including the caregiver's children under the age of 6. If only children under age 2 are in care, there shall be no more than three children, including those of the caregiver.

ST2. Child:staff ratios for centers and large family-child-care homes shall be maintained as follows during all hours of operation:

Age	Child:Staff Ratio	Maximum Group Size
Birth–12 mos.	3:1	6
13–24 mos.	3:1	6
25–30 mos.	4:1	8
31–35 mos.	5:1	10
Three-year-olds	7:1	14
Four-year-olds	8:1	16
Five-year-olds	8:1	16
6–8-year-olds	10:1	20
9–12-year-olds	12:1	24

When there are mixed age groups in the same room, the child:staff ratio and group size shall be consistent with the age of the majority of the children when no infants or toddlers are in the mixed age group. When infants or toddlers are in the mixed age group, the child:staff ratio and group size for infants and toddlers shall be maintained.

RATIONALE

The 101 Life Safety Code 1988 of the National Fire Protection Association stipulates a child:staff ratio in small family-child-care homes of one staff for up to six children, including the caregiver's own children under age 6, with no more than two children under the age of 2.[1] (See also rationale for Standard ST2.)

These child:staff ratios are the more stringent ratios for each age group used by the National Association for the Education of Young Children (NAEYC) in its accreditation program.[2] NAEYC uses a range because it is able to apply a less stringent ratio in centers where the director and staff are more highly trained. The APHA/AAP collaborative project (see Preamble) supports NAEYC's use of child:staff ratios maintained in relation to group size used as the basis for accreditation. The APHA/AAP standard for child:staff ratios uses a single ratio rather than a range.

Also, these child:staff ratios and group sizes are within the acceptable ranges, and in some cases are the more stringent ratios and group sizes recommended in the National Research Council's report *Who Cares for America's Children? Child Care Policy for the 1990's.*[4] Child:staff ratios and group size are two of the four most critical areas needing to be addressed in national standards, according to this report.[4]

COMMENTS

Unscheduled inspections are required to confirm compliance with this standard.

The *child:staff ratio* indicates the maximum number of children permitted per caregiver (e.g., 3:1—three children to one caregiver). A *group* is the number of children assigned to a caregiver or team of caregivers occupying an individual classroom or well-defined space within a larger room.[3]

These ratios assume caregivers who have limited bookkeeping and housekeeping duties, so that they may be free to provide direct care for children.

These ratios do not include other personnel (e.g., bus drivers) necessary for specialized functions (e.g., transportation).

These standards are based on what children need in order to have a reasonable amount of quality nurturant care. Those who question whether these ratios are affordable overlook the basic needs of young children in order to limit costs, which clearly reflects a lower priority for children than is acceptable.

 applies to a small family-child-care home applies to a large family-child-care home applies to a center. If no symbol appears, the standard applies to all three.

STANDARDS

In large family-child-care homes with two or more caregivers caring for no more than 12 children, there shall be no more than three children under the age of 2.

RATIONALE

Low child:staff ratios for nonambulatory children are essential for fire safety. The National Fire Protection Association, in its *1988 Life Safety Code 101,* recommends no more than three children under 2 years of age in large family-child-care homes with two staff members caring for up to 12 children.[1]

Children benefit from social interactions with peers; however, larger groups are generally associated with less positive interactions and developmental outcomes.

Group size and ratio of children to adults are limited to allow for one-to-one interaction, intimate knowledge of individual children, and consistent caregiving.[5] Child:staff ratios are not predictors of quality of care, but direct, warm, social interaction between adults and children is more common and more likely with lower child:staff ratios.

Caregivers must be recognized as performing a job for groups of children that parents of twins, triplets, or quadruplets would rarely be considered able to handle alone. Caring for a group of three infants is the same as caring for infant triplets; four toddlers are equivalent to a set of quadruplets.

Research shows that the child:staff ratio is most critical for infants and young toddlers (0 to 24 months).[4] There is evidence that infant development will be impaired if large numbers of infants are permitted per caregiver.[6]

The overall size of the group of children was found by the National Day Care Center Study to have a powerful effect on the quality of a facility without a concomitant effect on cost.[6] For 3- and 4-year-olds, the size of the group proved even more important than ratios.

The recommended group size and child:staff ratio allow 3- to 5-year-olds continued adult support and guidance while encouraging independent, self-initiated play and other activities.[7] In addition, the children's physical safety and the

COMMENTS

Unscheduled inspections are required to confirm compliance with this standard.

Small family-child-care homes for infants may offer lower chances of acquiring an infectious disease.

The cost of child care must be increased to pay for enough staff to nurture the emotional and physical development of children.

Favorable group sizes allow for appropriate activities geared to the growing competence and complexity of the 3- to 5-year-old.

maintenance of sanitation routines require staff who are not fragmented by excessive demands.

The "group" represents the "homeroom" for the child 6 to 12 years old; it is the psychological base that the child identifies with and from which the child gains continual guidance and support as he/she moves into and among various activities. This standard does not prohibit larger numbers of children from joining in collective activities as long as child:staff ratios and the concept of "homeroom" are maintained.

Child:staff ratios in child care settings should be sufficiently low to keep staff stress below levels that might endanger children. Excessive numbers of young children increase the danger of high caregiver stress and loss of control.

ST3. Child:staff ratios established for out-of-home child care (see standards ST1 and ST2 on p. 1) shall be maintained on all transportation provided or arranged by the facility. No child of any age shall be left unattended in a vehicle.

This standard is necessary to ensure that children continue to receive adequate supervision while in care. Placement of a child in a vehicle does not eliminate the need for supervision during this time.

These ratios do not include other personnel (e.g., bus drivers) necessary for specialized functions (e.g., transportation).

ST4. The following child:staff ratios shall apply while children are wading or swimming:

Similar Developmental Level	Children	Adults
Infants	1	1
Toddlers	2	1
Preschoolers	4	1
School-age children	6	1
Mixed Developmental Level*	Children	Adults
Infants/toddlers	2	1
Infants/toddlers/ preschoolers	3	1
Infants/toddlers/ preschoolers/ school-age children	3	1
Infants/toddlers/ school-age children	4	1
Preschoolers/ school-age children	5	1

This standard is needed to ensure safety and proper supervision. Our knowledge of the circumstances surrounding drownings and water-related injuries of young children suggests environmental modifications that will reduce the risk presented by common water sources. These modifications include fences and self-locking gates around all swimming/wading pools, hot tubs, and spas,[8] and special "safety covers"[9] on pools when they are not in use. Children must be under the constant supervision of qualified personnel while playing in or with water.[3]

These ratios do not include other personnel (e.g., bus drivers) necessary for specialized functions (e.g., transportation).

*There shall be a minimum of two adults present during any swimming/wading activity involving mixed developmental levels when two or more infants and/or toddlers are swimming or wading. (See also *Swimming, Wading, and Water*, p. 192.)

For additional information on child:staff ratio and group size, see also standard HP96 in chapter 3 on p. 93, *Child:Staff Ratio*, on p. 105, and standard CSN37 in chapter 7, on p. 250, on child:staff ratios for facilities serving children with special needs.

1.2 Licensure/Certification of Qualified Individuals

ST5. Any individual who will be alone with children or who will be responsible for a group shall hold an official credential as specified in *Individual Licensure/Certification*, on p. 301.

The term *credential* means a license, certificate, or other official recognition of an individual's qualifications.

1.3 Qualifications

For additional information on qualifications, see Appendix A, Qualifications and Responsibilities of Caregivers by Age Groups of Children on p. 323.

The states use various terms for facility staff; we have attempted to use the most common terms for staff positions.

QUALIFICATIONS BY ROLE

For additional information on qualifications by role, see also Appendix A, on p. 323; *General Qualifications for All Staff,* on p. 16, and *Training*, on p. 18.

Qualifications of Directors
Qualifications of Directors of Centers

ST6. The director of a center enrolling fewer than 60 children shall be at least 21 years old and shall have an undergraduate degree in early childhood education, child development, social work, nursing, or other child-related field, or a combination of college coursework and experience under qualified supervision. Education shall include a course in business administration or equivalent on-the-job training in an administrative position; a minimum of four courses in child devel-

The director of the facility is the team leader of a small business. Both administrative and child development skills are essential for this individual to manage the facility and set appropriate expectations. Research has shown that college-level coursework has a measurable, positive effect on quality child care, but experience per se does not.[7, 10]

The director of a center plays a pivotal role in ensuring the day-to-day smooth functioning of the

The profession of early childhood is changing. The exact combination of college coursework and supervised experience is still being developed. For example, the National Association for the Education of Young Children has developed a draft titled "NAEYC Model of Early Childhood Professional Development." For information, contact

NAEYC
1834 Connecticut Ave., NW
Washington, DC 20009

STANDARDS

opment and early childhood education; and 2 years' experience as a teacher of children of the age group(s) in care.

ST7. The director of a center enrolling 60 or more children shall be at least 21 years old and shall have an undergraduate degree in early childhood education, child development, social work, nursing, or other child-related field, or a combination of college coursework and experience under qualified supervision. Education shall include one course in administration or at least 6 months' experience in administration, and 3 years' experience as a teacher of children of the age group(s) in care.

ST8. Centers enrolling 30 or more children must employ a nonteaching director. Centers with fewer than 30 children may employ a director who teaches as well.

ST9. In addition to the credentials listed in Appendix A, on p. 323, a director of a center or a small family-child-care-home system enrolling 30 or more children shall provide documentation of one course or 26 to 30 clock hours of training in health and safety issues for out-of-home facilities, in addition to other educational qualifications, upon employment.

RATIONALE

facility within the framework of appropriate child development principles and knowledge of family relationships. The well-being of the children, the confidence of the parents of children in the facility's care, and the high morale and consistent professional growth of the staff depend largely upon the knowledge, skills, and dependable presence of a director who is able to respond to long-range and immediate needs. Management skills are important but should be viewed primarily as a means of support for the key role of educational leadership a director provides. A skilled director should know how to use community resources and to identify specialized personnel to enrich the staff's understanding of behavior and curriculum content. Past experience working in an early childhood setting is essential to running a facility.

See rationale for standard ST6.

The director is the person accountable for all center policies. A basic entry-level knowledge of health and safety is essential in order for the director to administer the facility. It is important for directors to be knowledgeable about infectious disease because properly implemented health policies can reduce the spread of disease not only among the children but

COMMENTS

Additional information on the early childhood profession is contained in *Challenge to the Profession: The Dynamic Model of Staffing* by Gwen Morgan (1988), which may be obtained from:

Center for Career Development in Early Care and Education Wheelock College 200 The Riverway Boston, MA 02215

See comment for standard ST6.

A small family-child-care-home system is a group of small family-child-care homes in one management system.

The American Red Cross offers a 27-hour course on health issues specific to child care for entry-level caregivers in its Child Care Course.[11] This course consists of four health and

STANDARDS

This training requirement shall be reduced to a minimum of 17 clock hours for directors of facilities caring for fewer than 30 children. This training shall include at least the following content:

a) Mechanisms of communicable disease spread.
b) Procedures for preventing the spread of communicable disease, including handwashing, sanitation, diaper changing, health department notification of reportable disease, equipment/toy selection and proper washing/disinfecting to reduce disease and injury risk, and health-related aspects of pets in the facility.
c) Immunization requirements for children and staff.
d) Common childhood illnesses and their management, including child care exclusion policies.
e) Organization of the facility to reduce illness and injury risks.
f) Training child care staff and children in infection and injury control.
g) Emergency procedures.
h) Promotion of health in the child care setting.

Additional qualifications for directors are given below for centers serving children under 5, school-age child care facilities, facilities serving children with special needs, and special facilities for ill children.

For additional qualifications and responsibilities of directors of centers, see also Appendix A, on p. 323; *General Requirements for All Staff,* on p. 16; *Training,* on p. 18; and *Identifiable Governing Body/Accountable Individual,* on p. 269.

RATIONALE

also among the staff, in the families, and in the community at large.

A knowledge of injury prevention measures in child care is essential to control known risks.

Pediatric first aid training is important because the director is fully responsible for the health of children in care.

COMMENTS

safety units (total 17 hours) and three child development units (total 9 hours). Each unit may be taken separately, with a certificate issued for each and a course certificate issued when all four health and safety units have been taken. The health and safety certificates are valid for 3 years. At a minimum, directors should have taken this course or its equivalent. It is more likely that directors of larger centers may be able to fulfill this training requirement because they usually have more training opportunities. Additional training in infectious disease control and injury prevention is desirable. Such training can be arranged with health professional preparatory schools, health institutions, or individual health professionals in the community. For more information about the Red Cross course, telephone the local chapter of the American Red Cross or write to

American Red Cross
National Headquarters
Health and Safety
18th and F Streets, N.W.
Washington, DC 20006

STANDARDS	COMMENTS	RATIONALE

Additional Requirements for Directors of Centers for Children Under 5

ST10. In addition to the general requirements in *Qualifications of Directors of Centers*, p. 4, the director of a facility for children under 5 years of age shall have not less than 2 to 3 years of experience, depending on the size of the center, as a teacher of infants, toddlers, and preschoolers. Directors of facilities for children ages 0 to 35 months shall have their 2 to 3 years of experience with infants and toddlers. Directors of facilities for children ages 3 to 5 years shall have their 2 to 3 years of experience with preschoolers.

The director must relate positively to the staff and parents, and must have an in-depth understanding of child development and be capable of applying this understanding in the design of the curriculum.[12]

Additional Requirements for Directors of School-Age Child Care Facilities

ST11. In addition to the general requirements in *Qualifications of Directors of Centers*, p. 4, the director of a school-age child care facility shall hold an undergraduate degree in early childhood education, elementary education, child development, recreation, or other child-related field, or a combination of college coursework and experience under qualified supervision, and not less than 2 years' experience working with school-age children.

These requirements are consistent with *Standards for Licensure or Approval of School-Age Child Care Programs* by the Commonwealth of Massachusetts Office for Children and *School-Age Child Care: An Action Manual*.[13, 14]

See comment for standard ST6.

Additional Requirements for Directors of Centers for Children with Special Needs

In addition to the general requirements in *Qualifications of Directors of Centers*, on p. 4, see *Center-based Administration*, on p. 249.

Additional Requirements for Directors of Special Facilities for Ill Children

In addition to the general requirements in *Qualifications of Directors of Centers*, on p. 4, see standard HP140 in chapter 3 on p. 103.

Qualifications of Teaching/Caregiving Staff

ST12. Caregivers shall have knowledge of child development and early childhood education; an undergraduate degree in early childhood education, child development, social work, nursing, or other child-related field, or a combination of experience under qualified supervision and college coursework; 1 year's experience (or the equivalent as specified in Appendix A); and on-the-job training to provide a nurturing environment and to meet the child's out-of-home needs.

For additional qualifications and responsibilities of teaching/caregiving staff, see also Appendix A, on p. 323; *General Qualifications for All Staff*, on p. 16; and *Training*, on p. 18.

Qualifications for Differentiated Roles

ST13. Centers shall employ licensed/certified teaching/caregiving staff (see *Individual Licensure/Certification*, on p. 301) for direct work with children in a progression of roles such as the following:
a) aides,
b) assistant teachers,
c) associate teachers,
d) teachers,
e) lead teachers, and
f) education coordinators

Each role with increased responsibility shall have increased educational qualifications as outlined in Appendix A, on p. 323. See also *General Qualifications for All Staff*, on p. 16, and *Training*, on p. 18.

Child care that promotes healthy development is based on the developmental needs of infants, toddlers, and preschool children. Caregivers are chosen for their knowledge of, and ability to respond appropriately to, the needs of children of this age generally and the unique characteristics of individual children.[5,7,10,12]

A progression of roles enables centers to offer career ladders rather than dead-end jobs. (Refer to Appendix A.) It promotes a mix of college-trained staff with other members of a child's own community who might have entered at the aide level and moved into higher roles through college training offered on the job.

Professional education and preprofessional inservice training programs provide an opportunity for career progression and job and pay upgrading, and lead to less turnover. Turnover rates in the late 1980's were 40 percent in centers and 60 percent in large and small family-child-care homes.[15,16]

See comment for standard ST6.

Early childhood professional knowledge must be required whether programs are in private centers, public schools, or other settings.

The National Association for the Education of Young Children's (NAEYC) National Academy of Early Childhood Programs has proposed a multi-level training program that addresses preemployment educational requirements and continuing education requirements for entry-level assistants, teachers, and administrators; it also establishes a table of qualifications for accredited programs.[2] This table is being reviewed and NAEYC has stated its intention to change it. The APHA/AAP standards will refer to the recommendations of this professional organization. NAEYC's table guided the development of the APHA/AAP standards in Appendix A.

STANDARDS	RATIONALE	COMMENTS

Qualifications of Teachers for Centers Serving Children from Birth to 35 Months

ST14. Every center, regardless of setting, shall have at least one licensed/certified lead teacher (or mentor teacher) who has a Bachelor of Arts, Bachelor of Science, Bachelor of Education, or Master of Education degree in early childhood education, child development, social work, nursing, or other child-related field, in addition to at least 1 year of experience working in child care serving this age group. All teachers in charge of a group shall be licensed/certified as lead teachers, teachers, or associate teachers, with education and experience related to the care and development of infants and toddlers, as well as supervised experience with this age group. (See *Individual Licensure/Certification*, on p. 301.)

Infant caregiving requires skills to promote development and learning of children whose needs and abilities change at a rapid rate.

See also the rationale for standard ST12.

Adequate compensation for skilled workers will not be given priority until the skills required are recognized and valued.

ST15. Caregivers shall want to work with infants and toddlers when asked and shall know what the job entails—fostering interaction, diapering, bathing, feeding, holding, comforting, and responding.

For additional qualifications and responsibilities of teachers for centers serving children from birth to 35 months, see also *Qualifications of Teaching/Caregiving Staff*, on p. 8; Appendix A, on p. 323, *General Qualifications for All Staff*, on p. 16; and *Training*, on p. 18.

Qualifications of Teachers for Centers Serving Children Between 3 and 5 Years Old

ST16. Every center, regardless of setting, shall have at least one licensed/certified lead teacher (or mentor teacher) who has a Bachelor of Arts, Bachelor of Science, Bachelor of Education, or Master of Education degree in early childhood

The quality of the staff is the most important determinant of the quality of an early childhood program. Research has found that staff training in child development or early childhood education, or both, is related to positive outcomes for children.[2, 10]

education, child development, social work, nursing, or other child-related field, as well as at least 1 year of experience working in child care with this age group. All teachers in charge of a group shall be licensed/certified as lead teachers, teachers, or associate teachers, with education in child development and early childhood education specific to this age group, as well as supervised experience with preschool children. (See *Individual Licensure/Certification*, on p. 301.)

ST17. Caregivers shall demonstrate an ability to apply their understanding of the developmental characteristics of 3- to 5-year-olds. Caregivers shall demonstrate knowledge and understanding of these children's independence and social competence, more complex inner lives, and increasing ability to adapt to their environment and cope with stress.

Three- to 4-year-olds continue to be dependent on the affection, physical care, intellectual guidance, and emotional support of their teachers.[5,12]

A supportive, nurturing setting that supports a demonstration of feelings and accepts regression as part of development continues to be vital for preschool children. A preschool child needs to be helped to build a positive self-image, a sense of self as a person of value from a family and a culture to be proud of. Children should be enabled to view themselves as coping, problem-solving, passionate, expressive individuals.

For additional qualifications and responsibilities of teachers for centers serving children between 3 and 5 years old, see also *Qualifications of Teaching/Caregiving Staff*, on p. 8; Appendix A, on p. 323; *General Qualifications for All Staff*, on p. 16; and *Training*, on p. 18.

Qualifications of Teachers for Centers Serving School-Age Children

ST18. Every center, regardless of setting, shall have at least one licensed/certified group leader (or mentor teacher) who has a Bachelor of Arts, Bachelor of Science, Bachelor of Education, or Master of Arts degree in child development or early childhood education covering ages newborn to 8 or 3 to 8, elementary education, recreation, or a related field, as well as at least 1 year of experience working in child care. Teachers in charge of a group shall

See the rationale for ST16.

STANDARDS	RATIONALE	COMMENTS

be licensed/certified as lead teacher, teacher, or associate teacher with education in child development and programming specific to this age group; they shall also have supervised experience with school-age children. Caregivers shall have training and supervised experiences in child development and education. (See *Individual Licensure/Certification*, on p. 301.)

ST19. Caregivers shall demonstrate knowledge about the social and emotional needs and developmental tasks of 5- to 12-year-old children, and shall know how to implement a nonacademic, enriching program.

A school-age child develops a strong, secure sense of identity through positive experiences with adults and peers.[17]

An informal, enriching environment that encourages the cultivation of interests and relationships at a self-paced rate promotes the self-worth of school-age children.

For additional qualifications and responsibilities of teachers for centers serving school-age children, see also *Qualifications of Teaching/Caregiving Staff*, on p. 8; Appendix A, on p. 323; *General Qualifications for All Staff*, on p. 16; and *Training*, on p. 18.

Qualifications of Teachers for Centers Serving Children with Special Needs

See *Direct Care and Provisional Staff*, on p. 250.

For additional qualifications and responsibilities of teachers for centers serving children with special needs, see also *Qualifications of Teaching/Caregiving Staff*, on p. 8; Appendix A, on p. 323; *General Qualifications for All Staff*, on p. 16; and *Training*, on p. 18.

Qualifications of Teachers for Special Facilities for Ill Children

See standard HP141 in chapter 3 on p. 104.

For additional qualifications and responsibilities of teachers for special facilities for ill children, see also *Qualifications of Teaching/ Caregiving Staff*, on p. 8; Appendix A, on p. 323; *General Qualifications for All Staff*, on p. 16; and *Training*, on p. 18.

Qualifications of Assistant Teachers and Associate Teachers

ST20. For all age groups, assistant teachers in centers who are counted in ratio requirements shall be 18 years old, shall be high school graduates or equivalent, shall participate in ongoing training, shall demonstrate competence in assigned tasks, and shall demonstrate responsiveness to group needs.

ST21. Associate teachers shall have a Childhood Development Associate (CDA) credential or an Associate degree in early childhood education or child development, shall have more than 6 months' related work experience, and shall be enrolled in coursework preparatory to becoming qualified as a teacher.

ST22. Staff below the age of 18 can be volunteers but cannot be employed in the role of assistant teacher until they reach age 18.

For additional qualifications and responsibilities of assistant teachers and associate teachers, see also Appendix A, on p. 323; *General Qualifications for All Staff*, on p. 16; and *Training*, on p. 18.

Qualifications of Aides

ST23. Aides shall be at least 18 years old and shall receive on-the-job training to carry out assigned tasks under the supervision of another staff member.

For additional qualifications and responsibilities of aides, see also Appendix A, on p. 323; *General Qualifications for All Staff*, on p. 16; and *Training*, on p. 18.

STANDARDS	RATIONALE	COMMENTS

Qualifications of Health Advocates

ST24. Each facility shall designate a person as health advocate to be responsible for policies and day-to-day issues related to health and safety of individual children, children as a group, staff, and parents.

An internal advocate for issues related to health and safety can help integrate these concerns with other factors involved in formulating facility plans.

The health advocate role should be assigned by the director to the staff member who seems to have an interest in this area. This person need not perform all the health and safety tasks in the facility, but should serve as the person who raises health and safety concerns and has designated responsibility for seeing to it that plans are implemented to ensure a safe and healthful facility.[18]

ST25. A designated, trained caregiver shall be the health advocate, to be the primary parent contact about health concerns, health-related parent/staff observations, health-related information, and provision of resources. For a center and school-age child care facility, this person shall be an assigned caregiver (this could be the director). This person shall be licensed/certified (see *Individual Licensure/Certification*, on p. 301) as a lead teacher, teacher, or associate teacher (for centers) or shall be a health professional or social worker who works at the facility on a regular basis (at least weekly). The health advocate shall have documented health training that includes Sudden Infant Death Syndrome (SIDS) for facilities caring for infants and toddlers, infectious disease control, how to handle an emergency, recognition and handling of seizures, safety/hazard recognition, and how to help parents, caregivers, and children cope when death, severe injury, or a natural or man-made catastrophe has been or will be experienced. (See *Emergency Plan*, on p. 280.)

The effectiveness of an intentionally designated health advocate in improving the quality of facility performance has been demonstrated in all types of early childhood settings.[18]

A designated caregiver with health training is effective for parent teaching through development of a personal interest in the child and an ongoing relationship with the parent.[3,19]

Caregivers who are better trained are more able to prevent, recognize, and correct health and safety problems.

A health advocate is a regular member of the staff of a center or large or small family-child-care home system, and is not the same as the health consultant recommended in *Health Consultants*, on p. 33. It is necessary to realize the importance of the child's actual caregiver, who is very familiar with the child and will recognize atypical behavior.

A plan for personal contact with parents should be made, even though this contact will not be possible on a daily basis. A plan for personal contact and documentation of a designated caregiver as "health advocate" will ensure that specific attempts are made to have the health advocate communicate directly with caregivers and families on health-related matters. For small family-child-care homes, the health advocate will usually be the caregiver.

A good source for SIDS information is a booklet for caregivers that can be obtained from

California Sudden Infant Death
   Syndrome Program
Room 400
2151 Berkeley Way Annex 4
Berkeley, CA 94704

ST26. At least one caregiver shall have knowledge of childhood immunization requirements and shall have responsibility for periodically reviewing the children's immunization records to ensure they are current. (See *Immunizations and Preventive Health Care*, on p. 86.)

Children require frequent boosters and immunizations in early childhood. Although they may be current with required immunizations when they enroll, they can miss scheduled immunizations thereafter. Since the risk of vaccine-preventable disease is increased in group settings, assuring appropriate immunization is an essential responsibility in child care.

For additional qualifications and responsibilities of health advocates, see also Appendix A, on p. 323; *General Qualifications for All Staff*, on p. 16; and *Training*, on p. 18.

Qualifications of Nurses

See *Direct Care and Provisional Staff*, on p. 250.

Qualifications for Large and Small Family Home Caregivers

ST27. Caregivers in large and small family-child-care homes shall meet the age and other general requirements in *General Qualifications for All Staff*, on p. 16, and the education and experience requireements in Appendix A based on ages of children served.

Small family home caregivers often work alone and are solely responsible for the health and safety of small numbers of children in care.

A large family home caregiver caring for more than six children and employing one or more assistants is a facility director in a sense. An operator of a large family-child-care home should be offered training relevant to the management of a small facility.

ST28. Caregivers in small family-child-care homes with 3 years' experience and substantial approved training shall be licensed or registered as meeting a higher educational level, so that the license or registration serves as a credential. (See *Individual Licensure/Certification*, on p. 301.)

ST29. The license/certificate (see *Individual Licensure/Certification*, on p. 301) for a caregiver in a small family-child-care home shall have two levels identified by number, Level 1 and Level 2. Level 1 shall

The National Association for Family Day Care has established an accreditation process to enhance the level of quality and professionalism in small family-child-care homes.[20]

For information, contact

National Association for
Family Day Care
725 15th Street, N.W.
Suite 505
Washington, DC 20005

include caregivers who meet the entry-level qualifications, participate in training, and are accredited by the National Association for Family Day Care. Level 2 caregivers either shall have a small family-child-care home Child Development Associate credential or shall be accredited by the National Association for Family Day Care and have a college certificate representing 3 credit hours of family child care leadership training or master caregiver training.

ST30. Small family home caregivers shall provide documentation of at least 6 hours of training in health management for out-of-home facilities prior to initiating operation. This training shall include at least the content specified in standard ST9 on p. 5.

It is important for caregivers to be knowledgeable about infectious disease because properly implemented health policies can reduce the spread of disease not only among the children but also among the staff, among the families, and in the community at large.

The American Red Cross offers training on health issues specific to child care in its *Child Care Course.*[11] This course includes a 3-hour unit on preventing infectious diseases and a 3-hour unit on caring for ill children; these units include the basic information every caregiver should know. For more information about this course, telephone the local chapter of the American Red Cross or write to

American Red Cross
National Headquarters
Health and Safety
18th and F Streets, N.W.
Washington, DC 20006

ST31. Large and small family home caregivers shall be encouraged to have active membership in local or state Family Day Care Associations (if such associations exist) or in the National Association for Family Day Care. (See also *Networking for Small Family-Child-Care Homes*, on p. 316.)

For additional qualifications and responsibilities of large and small family home caregivers, see also Appendix A, on p. 323; *General Qualifications for All Staff*, on p. 16, and *Training*, on p. 18.

These activities demonstrate a commitment to quality child care; membership in the Family Day Care Association and attendance at meetings indicate the desire to gain new knowledge about how to work with children.

For the reasons noted in the rationale, it is clearly beneficial for small family home caregivers to be active members of the local Family Day Care Association, the National Association for Family Day Care, or family child care support groups or similar groups organized by local resource and referral agencies, if these are available in their communities.

Additional Requirements for Large and Small Family Home Caregivers Who Provide Child Care for Childen with Special Needs

See *Small Family-Child-Care Homes*, on p. 285.

For additional qualifications and responsibilities of large and small family home caregivers who provide child care for children with special needs, see also Appendix A, on p. 323; *General Qualifications for All Staff,* on p. 16; and *Training*, on p. 18.

GENERAL QUALIFICATIONS FOR ALL STAFF

For additional qualifications and responsibilities of all staff, see also *Qualifications by Role*, on p. 4; Appendix A, on p. 323; and *Training*, on p. 18.

Requirements for All Staff

ST32. Center directors and small and large family home caregivers shall ask applicants for all positions whether they have abused children in any way in the past. Persons who acknowledge the past abuse of children shall not be hired in centers or to assist in small or large family-child-care homes even when they are licensed/certified. (See *Individual Licensure/Certification*, on p. 301.)

To ensure their safety and physical and mental health, children must be protected from any risk of abuse.

Although few persons will acknowledge past child abuse to another person, the obvious attention directed to the question by the licensing agency or caregiver may discourage some potentially abusive individuals from seeking employment in child care. In addition, this measure is very inexpensive.

ST33. Center directors and large family home caregivers shall ask all prospective employees if they are sexually oriented to children. Persons who acknowledge a sexual orientation to children shall not be hired for child care positions even if they are licensed/certified. (See *Individual Licensure/Certification*, on p. 301.)

See rationale for standard ST32.

Questions about sexual orientation or questions specifically about orientation to children should be included on preemployment questionnaires supplied by the licensing agency.

Because it is a difficult question to ask, the following question can be included on the preemployment form: "Do you ever think that you would like a sexual experience with a child?"

STANDARDS	RATIONALE	COMMENTS

ST34. Directors and large family home caregivers shall check references and examine employment history before employing any staff, including substitutes, who will be alone with a child or a group of children in child care.

ST35. The staff recruitment policy shall be to include men as well as women in staff positions. (See also standard ST37.)

Staff positions should be open to both men and women so that both sex roles can be observed by the children.

Reasonable efforts to recruit staff of both sexes should be demonstrated via nonsexist public advertising and may be confirmed by a review of responses to the ads.

For additional information on general requirements for all staff, see also *Individual Licensure/Certification* on p. 301, and *Qualifications of Drivers*, on p. 200.

Minimum Age for All Staff

ST36. All caregivers included in the child:staff ratio (see *Child:Staff Ratio and Group Size*, on p. 1) shall be at least 18 years of age. Directors, at least one caregiver in each large family home, and all small family home caregivers shall be 21 years of age or older. Assistants and aides shall be at least 18 years of age.

Age 18 is the earliest age of legal consent. Mature leadership is clearly preferable. Age 21 allows for the maturity level necessary to meet the responsibilities of managing a center or independently caring for a group of children who are not one's own.

It is unlikely that an individual could meet the education and experience requirements in Appendix A, on p. 323, by the age of 18, but 18 years is the minimum age of legal consent.

Preservice Education and/ or Experience for All Staff

ST37. All staff, including caregivers, transportation staff, and food service staff, shall meet the following preservice education and/or experience qualifications:
a) Caregivers providing direct services to children without immediate and continuous supervision by another qualified staff member shall have child development-related courses and/or in some cases (see Appendix A on p. 323) at least 1 year of experience in child care, an early childhood education degree, or a Child Development Associate (CDA) credential.
b) Staff shall meet all preservice education requirements for their assigned roles.

Research demonstrates that staff training in child development and/ or early childhood education is related to positive outcomes for children.[10] This training enables staff to provide children with a variety of learning and social experiences appropriate to the age of the child.

Experience and qualifications used by the CDA program and included in degree programs with field placement are valued above didactic teaching alone.

Early childhood professional knowledge must be required whether programs are in private centers, public schools, or other settings. The National Association for the Education of Young Children's (NAEYC) National Academy of Early Childhood Programs has established a table of qualifications for accredited programs.[2] This table is being reviewed and NAEYC has stated its intention to change it.[14] The APHA/AAP standards will refer to the recommendations of this professional organization.

STANDARDS

c) Staff shall display sound judgment, emotional maturity, and an understanding of children.
d) Staff members shall reflect the cultural and ethnic diversity of the community in which the enrolled children live. Facilities shall recruit staff from the communities of the children enrolled.

ST38. Staff shall also meet preservice qualifications as specified in *Preservice Qualifications*, on p. 18.

RATIONALE

A democratic pluralistic society rests on valuing cultural diversity.[21,22]

Young children's identities cannot be separated from family and culture. They need to see successful role models from their own cultural groups and to develop the ability to relate to others different from themselves.

COMMENTS

NAEYC's table guided the development of APHA/AAP standards in Appendix A, on p. 323.

Since a center can serve fewer than six children in some states, the licensing requirements for educational qualifications of staff should consider the size of the center.

In staff recruiting, the community pool to be tapped should extend beyond the immediate neighborhood of the child's residence or the location of the facility to reflect the diversity of people with whom the child can be expected to have contact as a part of life experience.

Caregivers may be employed who lack educational qualifications but have personal characteristics, experience, and skills required in working with parents and children, and potential for development on the job or in a training program. Application of quotas for ethnic groups should not determine hiring of unqualified staff when recruiting staff from the communities of the children enrolled.

1.4 Training

GENERAL TRAINING

ST39. Caregivers shall be educationally qualified in advance for the role they are entering and shall receive orientation training (see *Orientation Training*, on p. 19) during the week immediately following employment. Caregivers shall also receive continuing education each year (see *Continuing Education*, on p. 24). In centers, directors shall ensure that 12 hours of staff meetings are held, in addition to the continuing education specified in *Continuing Education*, on p. 24.

Many states have preservice education and experience qualifications for caregivers by role and function. Orientation and ongoing training are especially important for aides and assistant teachers, for whom preservice educational requirements are limited. Entry into the field at the level of aide or assistant teacher should not be made difficult, because it is important to enable members of the families and cultural groups of the children in care to enter the field.

Ongoing training ensures that staff are challenged and stimulated, have access to current knowledge, and have access to education that will qualify them for new roles. It is important to offer a career ladder to

Child care staff are important figures in the lives of the young children in their care. Caregivers should be educated and supported so they can interact at optimum levels with children in care.

All training for child care staff in the future should include increased attention to health issues. It is axiomatic that full-day programs require competence in all aspects of child development, not just learning aspects. Full-day programs for preschool children are growing rapidly; many part-day nursery schools now offer extended hours so that parents have the option of a full-day program. It is less well known that part-day programs, too, require a holistic approach to the

attract individuals into the child care field, where labor is in short supply. Ongoing training in one role becomes preservice training to qualify for another role.

care of young children. Many public and private schools have begun to offer programs for younger children without adapting their traditional teacher requirements, health and safety provisions, and programming to these new needs. States are beginning to include ongoing health training in their licensing requirements, and the broader skills have proved important and necessary to teachers in both part-day and full-day programs.

In addition to the growth of full-day programs, there are an increasing number of children younger than 3 enrolled in centers and in small family-child-care homes, for whom sanitation practices are critical to the community. Because of all these changing needs, it is recommended that colleges and accrediting bodies examine teacher preparation guidelines and substantially increase the health content of early childhood professional preparation.

PRESERVICE QUALIFICATIONS

For preservice qualifications of directors, see standard ST9 on p. 5.

For preservice qualifications of small family home caregivers, see standard ST30 on p. 15.

For additional information on preservice qualifications, see also *General Qualifications for All Staff*, on p. 15, and *Training*, on p. 316.

ORIENTATION TRAINING

ST40. All new full- and part-time staff shall be oriented to, and demonstrate knowledge of, the following items a through o. The director of any center or large family-child-care home shall provide this training to newly hired caregivers. Small family home caregivers shall avail themselves of orientation training offered by the licensing agency, a resource and referral agency, or other such agency. This training shall include evaluation and a repeat demonstration of the training lesson. The orientation shall address, at a minimum:

Upon employment, staff members should be able to carry out basic sanitation, disinfection, and emergency procedures. Orientation ensures that all staff receive specific and basic training for the work they will be doing and are oriented to their new responsibilities.

All facilities and the children enrolled vary. Facility-specific orientation programs for new employees that address the health and safety of the children enrolled as well as those of the employees that are specific to the site can be most productive.[23,24]

This standard applies to all facilities, including special facilities for ill children, facilities for children with special needs, and large family-child-care homes where assistants are employed.

a) The goals and philosophy of the facility.

b) The names and ages of the children for whom the caregiver will be responsible, and their specific developmental needs.

c) Any special adaptation(s) of the facility required for a child with special needs.

d) Any special health or nutrition need(s) of the children assigned to the caregiver.

e) The planned program of activities at the facility. (See *Program of Developmental Activities*, on p. 45.)

f) Routines and transitions.

g) Acceptable methods of discipline (See *Discipline*, on p. 52.)

h) Policies of the facility about relating to parents. (See *Parent Relationships*, on p. 55.)

i) Meal patterns and food-handling policies of the facility. (See *Nutrition Plan and Policy*, on p. 284, *Food Service Records*, on p. 295, and chapter 4, *Nutrition and Food Service*, on p. 115.)

j) Occupational health hazards for caregivers. (See *Occupational Hazards*, on p. 38.)

k) Emergency health and safety procedures. (See *Emergency Plan*, on p. 279, and *Emergency Procedures*, on p. 95.)

l) General health policies and procedures, including but not limited to the following:

1) Handwashing techniques, including indications for handwashing. (See *Handwashing*, on p. 72.)

2) Diapering technique and toileting, if care is provided to children in diapers and/or needing help with toileting, including appropriate diaper disposal and diaper-changing techniques. (See *Toilet, Diapering, and Bath*, on p. 168, *Toileting, Diapering, and Toilet Training*, on p. 68, *Toilet Training Equipment, Toilets, and Bathrooms*, on p. 76, and *Diaper-Changing Areas*, on p. 77.)

3) Correct food preparation, serving, and storage techniques if employee prepares food. (See *Food Safety*, p. 130.)

Because of frequent turnover, it is the obligation of centers to institute orientation programs that protect the health and safety of children and new staff.

4) Formula preparation, if formula is handled. (See *Nutrition Plan and Policy*, on p. 284, and *Nutrition for Infants*, on p. 117.)

m) Child abuse detection, prevention, and reporting. (See *Child Abuse and Neglect*, on p. 93.)

n) Teaching health promotion concepts to children and parents as part of the daily care provided to children. (See *Health Education for Children*, on p. 60.)

o) Recognizing symptoms of illness. (See *Daily Health Assessment*, on p. 65.)

ST41. Orientation training in centers shall be documented. The director shall document the topics covered and the dates on which the orientation was provided (see standard ST40, on the employee's training records.)

See rationale for standard ST40.

ST42. During the first 3 months of employment, the center director or large family home caregiver shall document, for all full-time and part-time staff, additional orientation in and the employee's satisfactory knowledge of the following topics for the purpose of noting and responding to illness in the facility. Staff shall not be assigned to tasks involving these topic areas before receiving the orientation training.

a) Recognition of symptoms of illness and correct documentation procedures for recording illness symptoms.

b) Exclusion and readmission procedures.

c) Cleaning, sanitation, and disinfection procedures.

d) Procedures for administering medication to children and for documenting medication administered to children.

e) Procedures for notifying parents or legal guardians of communicable disease occurring in children or staff within the facility.

f) Procedures for performing the daily health assessment of children (see *Daily Health Assessment*, p. 65) to determine whether they are ill and whether they need to be excluded from the facility.

ST43. Staff members shall not be expected to take responsibility for any aspect of care for which they have not been oriented and trained.

For additional information on orientation training, see also *Substitutes*, on p. 31, *Training*, p. 316, for staff in special facilities for ill children, *Preservice, Orientation, and Training Standards*, p. 252, for caregivers serving children with special needs, and *Training*, p. 316, on state and local training and technical assistance.

FIRST AID AND CPR

ST44. The director of a center or a large family-child-care home shall ensure that all staff involved in the provision of direct care are certified in pediatric first aid that includes rescue breathing and first aid for choking. At least one certified staff person shall be in attendance at all times and in all places that children are in care.

To ensure the health and safety of children in a child care setting, there must be someone in attendance at all times to respond to common life-threatening emergencies. With staff trained in pediatric first aid, including rescue breathing and first aid for choking, coupled with a facility that has been modified and designed to ensure the safety of children, the potential for childhood injury can be reduced. Knowledge of pediatric first aid, including rescue breathing and first aid for choking, and the confidence to utilize these skills are critically important to the outcome of any emergency situation. In a recent study of incidence of injuries in centers, it was noted that of 423 injuries, first aid was sufficient treatment for 84.4 percent.[25]

A first aid certificate issued by the American Red Cross is valid for 3 years.

States that have developed rules regulating facilities have recognized the need for training in medical emergency management. CPR training is not considered essential for the care of healthy children in child care because cessation of breathing almost always precedes cardiac arrest in children by a period that makes it unlikely that cardiac resuscitation would save lives. See the CPR training requirements in standards ST47 and ST48, p. 23, in this chapter for swimming activities and for care of children with special needs.

ST45. Small family home caregivers should be certified in pediatric first aid training that includes rescue breathing and first aid for choking.

Small family home caregivers often work alone and are solely responsible for the health and safety of small numbers of children in care.

ST46. Pediatric first aid training, including rescue breathing and first aid for choking, shall be consistent with pediatric first aid training developed by the American Red Cross, the American Heart Association, or the National Safety Council for First Aid Training Institute, or the equivalent of one of the three. The offered first aid instruction shall

First aid for children in the child care setting requires a more child-specific approach than standard first aid offers.

Usually, other children will have to be supervised while the injury is managed. Parental notification and communication with emergency medical services must be carefully planned. The American Red Cross *Child Care Course* includes training on infant and child first aid, of which rescue breathing and first aid for choking are components. For

STANDARDS	RATIONALE	COMMENTS

STANDARDS

include, but not be limited to, the emergency management of
a) Bleeding.
b) Burns.
c) Poisoning.
d) Choking.
e) Injuries, including insect, animal, and human bites.
f) Shock.
g) Convulsions or nonconvulsive seizures.
h) Musculoskeletal injury (e.g., sprains, fractures).
i) Dental emergencies.
j) Head injuries.
k) Allergic reactions.
l) Eye injuries.
m) Loss of consciousness.
n) Electric shock.
o) Drowning.

ST47. Facilities that have a swimming pool or built-in wading pool shall require infant and child CPR training for caregivers. At least one of the caregivers, volunteers, and other adults who are counted in the child:staff ratio for wading and swimming (see standard ST4, p. 3) shall be trained in basic water safety and certified in infant and child CPR each year by a person certified as an instructor in water safety and in CPR. (For small family-child-care homes, the person trained in water safety and CPR shall be the caregiver.) Written verification of CPR and lifesaving certification, water safety instructions, and emergency procedures shall be kept on file. (See also *Safety Rules for Swimming/ Wading Pools*, p. 195, and *Water Safety*, p. 96.)

ST48. Facilities that serve children with special needs shall have at least one caregiver certified in infant and child CPR. Written verification of CPR certification shall be kept on file.

RATIONALE

Statistics on the frequency of occurrence of circumstances that require CPR (not just rescue breathing or first aid for choking) are not available in the literature. However, it is probably a rare event. Drowning involves cessation of breathing, and rarely requires cardiac resuscitation of salvageable victims. Nevertheless, because of the increased risk for cardiopulmonary arrest related to wading and swimming, the facility should have personnel trained to deal promptly with a life-threatening emergency. Children have drowned in as little as 3 to 4 inches of water or less.

Studies have consistently documented that both lay and professional students quickly forget critical elements of CPR skills. Yearly recertification is necessary to ensure that skills are maintained.[26,27]

Although no statistics exist on the need for infant and child CPR, health professionals are concerned by the potential need for CPR measures when children with special needs are under care.

COMMENTS

more information about this course, telephone the local chapter of the American Red Cross or write to

American Red Cross
National Headquarters
Health and Safety
18th and F Streets, N.W.
Washington, DC 20006

A CPR certificate is valid for 1 year.

This standard is primarily intended to protect the child with seizures, pulmonary or cardiac difficulties, or problems managing oral secretions. Children with mild disabilities (e.g., deafness, mild mental retardation, speech and language deficits) may not require the presence of someone trained in CPR at the facility site.

A CPR certificate is valid for 1 year.

STANDARDS	RATIONALE	COMMENTS

ST49. Records of current certification of pediatric first aid including rescue breathing and first aid for choking (and infant and child CPR, when indicated) shall be maintained in the files of the facility.

For additional information on first aid and CPR, see also *Field Trips*, p. 52, on first aid training requirements and *Training*, p. 316, on state and local training and technical assistance.

CONTINUING EDUCATION

ST50. Directors and all caregivers shall have at least 30 clock hours per year of continuing education in the first year of employment, 16 clock hours of which shall be in child development programming and 14 of which shall be in child health, safety, and staff health; and 24 clock hours of continuing education based on individual competency needs (see standards ST85 and ST86 on p. 42) each year thereafter, 16 of which shall be in child development programming and 8 of which shall be in child health, safety, and staff health.

Copies of such records in the facility assist in implementation and in monitoring for proof of compliance.

Caregivers must, because of the nature of their caregiving tasks, attain knowledge and skills that are multi-faceted. Child health and employee health are an integral part of any education/training curriculum and program management plan. Twenty-seven states require ongoing training for directors and/or teaching/care-giving staff.[6]

In addition to low child:staff ratio, group size, age mix of children, and stability of caregiver, the training/education of caregivers is a specific indicator of child care quality.[7]

Most states require training for child care staff depending upon their functions and responsibilities. Staff who are better trained are better able to prevent, recognize, and correct health and safety problems.

Training needs are based on knowledge needs rather than on a required number of hours. The number of hours in training recommended here reflects the focus of caregivers on *child development*, supplemented by health and safety. The total of 24 clock hours of annual training is used by leading organizations in child care and early childhood education. NAEYC recommends that every early childhood professional complete a minimum of 24 clock hours of inservice training annually and includes in its recommendation training in child growth and development, curriculum, discipline, communication with parents, health,

The first aid certificate issued by the American Red Cross is valid for 3 years. A CPR certificate is valid for 1 year.

The following are suggested topics for directors and caregivers to select in meeting their 16 hours of continuing education in child development programming.
a) Child growth and development.
b) Appropriate services for infants, preschool and school-age children, children with disabilities, migrant children, and children with limited English proficiency.
c) Mainstreaming children with special needs into child care.
d) Child development activities for children who are ill.
e) Child observation.
f) Acceptable methods of discipline.
g) Planning learning activities.
h) Scheduling, pacing, and transitions.
i) Design of space.
j) Communicating with families.
k) Opportunities to reinforce learning through talking.
l) Techniques for group development.
m) Child care administration and policies.
n) Death, dying, and the grief cycle.
o) Methods of effective communication with children, parents, and coworkers.

The following are suggested topics for directors and caregivers to select in meeting their 8 hours of continuing education in child health, child safety, and staff health.
a) Communicable disease management:
  • handwashing.

ST50. *continued*

safety, nutrition, multicultural aspects, and professional issues.[28] Twenty-four hours of continuing education are recommended in NAEYC's publication, *Accreditation Criteria and Procedures.*[13] The American Red Cross has a 27-hour course on health issues specific to child care for entry-level caregivers in its *Child Care Course.*[11]

There are very few illnesses for which children need to be excluded from child care. Decisions about management of ill children are facilitated by the increased skill in assessing the degree to which the behavior suggesting illness requires special management.[29] Continuing education on communicable disease management helps prepare caregivers to make these decisions. The American Red Cross *Child Care Course* requires 3 hours of training in preventing infectious diseases.[11]

Nutrition education and information are among the recommendations for improving the health of the nation.[30]

All caregivers should be trained to prevent, assess, and treat injuries common in child care settings and to comfort an injured child.

- handling contaminated items.
- using disinfectants.
- avoiding contact with urine, saliva, secretions.
- preventing transmission of blood-borne diseases.
- routes of Human Immunodeficiency Virus (HIV) transmission and prevention.
- food handling.
- formula preparation, if applicable.
- Cytomegalovirus (MV) infection.
- knowledge of immunization requirements.
- policies for exclusion/admission.
- assessing the health of children.
- recognizing symptoms of illness.
- temperature taking.
- ability to describe minor illness.
- documenting and managing minor illness.
- caring for ill children.
- when and how to call for medical assistance.
- administering medication.

b) Occupational health and safety.
c) Injury prevention.
d) Transportation safety.
e) Emergency response procedures/first aid.
f) Child abuse detection, prevention, and reporting.
g) Linkages with community services, including facilities that enroll children with special needs.
h) Nutrition:
   - foods and nutrition.
   - application of foods and nutrition to child development and family health.
   - information and behavioral skills to use in selecting and preparing more healthful diets.
   - more effective means of communicating nutrition information to people in different age and ethnic groups.
   - the creation of a physical, social, and emotional environment that supports and promotes development of sound food habits, and the role of the caregiver in helping child and family achieve adequate nutrition.
   - healthy food choices in the home, in schools, and at the worksite, by health care providers as part of government food service programs (such as State Maternal and Child Health Nutrition, Project Head Start,

ST50. *continued*

National School Lunch Program, and Women, Infants and Children Supplemental Food (WIC) Programs).

There should be an annual emphasis on continuing education in infection control, as outlined in item a above, and in nutrition, as outlined in item h above. Guidance should be sought from the Nutrition Specialist (see Appendices B-1 and B-2, on pp. 328–329).

For some facilities, more than 8 hours in health and safety training and fewer than 16 hours in child development training may be required to bring caregivers up to a basic level of minimum knowledge in health and safety.

Although training priorities should be given to those topics that protect life, care must be taken to ensure that these topics are not favored to the exclusion of those topics that improve the quality of daily life in a child care setting. Training should be based on competency needs.

Resources to contact to obtain training on health issues include state and local health departments (especially the public health nursing department), resource and referral agencies, and the state and local chapters of the American Academy of Pediatrics, the American Academy of Family Physicians, the American Nurses' Association, the Visiting Nurse Association, the National Association of Pediatric Nurse Associates and Practitioners, the National Association for the Education of Young Children, and the National Association for Family Day Care. The American Red Cross offers a *Child Care Course* on health and safety.[11] For more information about this course, telephone the local chapter of the American Red Cross or write to

American Red Cross
National Headquarters
Health and Safety
18th and F Streets, N.W.
Washington, DC 200006

(See also *Technical Assistance and Consultation to Caregivers and Families*, p. 313, and *Training*, p. 316.)

STANDARDS	RATIONALE	COMMENTS

ST50. *continued*

There are many resources for facilities to contact for possible Nutrition Specialists (see Appendices B-1 and B-2, on pp. 328–329). Most state maternal and child health departments have a Nutrition Specialist on staff. If this Nutrition Specialist has knowledge and experience in child care, a facility might negotiate for him/her to be its Nutrition Specialist. Other resources to contact for possible Nutrition Specialists are state and local health department nutritionists, the state department's maternal and child health director and children with special health care needs director, state university and college nutrition departments, the home economists at utility companies, state affiliates of the American Dietetic Association, state and regional affiliates of the American Public Health Association, the American Home Economics Association, the registered dietitian at a hospital, high school home economics teachers, the Dairy Council, the local American Heart Association affiliate, the local Cancer Society, the Society for Nutrition Education, and the local Cooperative Extension.

Nutrition education resources may be obtained from

Food and Nutrition
    Information Center
National Agricultural Library
    Building, Room 304
10301 Baltimore Boulevard
Beltsville, MD 20705

The staff's continuing education in nutrition may be supplemented by periodic newsletters and/or literature or audiovisual materials prepared or recommended by the Nutrition Specialist (see Appendixes B-1 and B-2, on pp. 328–329).

Financial support and accessible training programs need to be made available through the creation of national, state, and local planning consortia. The arguments for and against financial support and training programs have been made in the Federal Register FIDCR 1980 proposed regulations.[23]

Home study, video courses, workshops, training newsletters, telecommunications, and lectures can be used to meet

STANDARDS	RATIONALE	COMMENTS

ST50. *continued*

the training hours requirement as well as more formally conducted training. Completion of training may be documented by self-declaration or by submitting self-tests.

A sample form to help plan, evaluate, and document staff training is provided in Appendix VII.1 in *Health in Day Care: A Manual for Health Professionals.* To obtain this publication, contact

American Academy of Pediatrics
141 Northwest Point Blvd.
P.O. Box 927
Elk Grove Village, IL 60009-0927

ST51. Small family home caregivers shall have at least 12 clock hours of continuing education based on staff competency needs (see standards ST85 and ST86, on p 42.)

Small family home caregivers often work alone and are solely responsible for the health and safety of small numbers of children in care.

See also rationale for standard ST50.

The content of continuing education for small family home caregivers may include, but is not required to include, the following topics:
a) Child growth and development.
b) Infant care.
c) Recognizing and managing minor illness.
d) Business aspects of the small family child care home.
e) Planning developmentally appropriate activities in mixed-age groupings.
f) Nutrition for children.
g) Acceptable methods of discipline.
h) Organizing the home for child care.
i) Preventing unintentional injuries in the home.
j) Available community services.
k) Detecting, preventing, and reporting child abuse.
l) Pediatric first aid, including rescue breathing and first aid for choking. (See *First Aid and CPR*, on p. 22.)
m) CPR (if the caregiver takes care of children with special needs or has a swimming/wading pool). (See *First Aid and CPR*, on p. 22.)
n) Methods of effective communication with children and parents.
o) Evacuation drill procedures as specified in *Evacuation Plan and Drills*, on p. 280.
p) Occupational health hazards. (See *Occupational Hazards*, on p. 38.)
q) Death, dying, and the grief cycle.

There are in-home training alternatives for small family home caregivers, such as listening to audiotapes or videotapes with self-check lists.

There is still concern in the field that mandated training for small family home caregivers may act as a disincentive for them to enter the system. This would adversely affect the supply of child care services at a time when there is a severe shortage.

ST52. All staff members with food-handling responsibilities shall be trained in proper food handling.

Foodborne illness outbreaks have occurred in many settings, including facilities. Because large centers serve more meals on a daily basis than many restaurants, food handlers in these settings should take courses on appropriate food handling.

Child Care Food Program sponsors have to provide this training for small family home caregivers.

Resources to contact to obtain training in food handling include the regional Food and Drug Administration offices and state and local health department nutrition and environmental health programs.

ST53. Caregivers shall avail themselves of child abuse prevention education materials from the licensing agency for use by the children, caregivers, and parents.

Centers and large and small family-child-care homes are strategic locations in which to distribute materials for the prevention of abuse.

States will need to learn to select from the many available media that can be employed in child abuse prevention activities.

ST54. Caregivers shall be trained in the symptoms and signs caused by sexually transmitted diseases in children as specified in standard HP104 in chapter 3, on p. 94.

ST55. Staff in facilities for ill children shall meet continuing education requirements as specified in *Training*, on p. 104.

For additional information on continuing education, see also *Consultation Records*, on p. 295, on documentation of training by health consultants; *General Training*, on p. 18, on continuing education; standard ID21 in chapter 6 on p. 214 for continuing education on infections of the intestines (often with diarrhea) or liver; *Continuing Education*, on p. 254, for caregivers serving children with special needs; and *Training*, on p. 316, on state and local training and technical assistance.

SPECIAL NEEDS TRAINING

In addition to *General Training, Preservice Qualifications, Orientation Training,* and *First Aid and CPR,* on pp. 18–22, see *Preservice, Orienta-*

tion, and Training Standards and *Continuing Education,* on pp. 252–254.

TRAINING RECORD

ST56. The director of a center or a large family-child-care home shall provide and maintain documentation of training received by, or provided for, staff. For centers, the date of the training, the number of hours, the names of staff participants, the name(s) and qualification(s) of the trainer(s), and the content of the training (both orientation and continuing education) shall be recorded in each staff person's file or in a separate training file.

The training record shall be used to assess each employee's need for additional training and to provide regulators with a tool to monitor compliance. Continuing education with course credit shall be recorded and the records made available to staff to document their applications for licenses/certificates or for license upgrading.[31] (See *Individual Licensure/Certification,* on p. 301.)

Colleges issue transcripts, workshops can issue certificates, and facility administrators can maintain individual training logs.

RELEASED TIME AND EDUCATIONAL LEAVE

ST57. The facility shall make provisions for paid released time for staff to participate in required training during work hours, or reimburse staff for time spent attending training.

Most caregivers work long hours and most are poorly paid.[7,23]

Education in child care often takes place a few hours a week during time when the participant is not released from other work-related duties, such as answering phones or caring for children. It would be very helpful to staff if centers would provide substitutes and released time during work hours for such training.

ST58. Directors of centers and large family-child-care homes shall arrange for continuing education that is paid for by government, by charitable organizations, or by the facility, rather than by the employee. Small family home caregivers shall avail themselves of training opportunities offered in their communities.

Caregivers often make low wages and may not be able to pay for mandated training. Forty percent of child care workers earn close to or less than minimum wage.[10]

ST59. Directors shall make provisions for staff who request unpaid educational leave of up to 1 year to return to their jobs.

Precedents for educational leave exist in other professions, such as nursing and law enforcement.

Educational leave usually means a paid or unpaid leave of absence (e.g., 1 year) to acquire further education.

1.5 Substitutes

STANDARDS

RATIONALE

COMMENTS

ST60. Substitutes shall be employed to ensure that child:staff ratios (as specified in *Child:Staff Ratio and Group Size*, on p. 1) are maintained at all times. Substitutes and volunteers without licenses/certificates shall work under direct supervision and shall not be alone with a group of children. (See *Individual Licensure/ Certification*, on p. 301.)

ST61. All substitutes, during the first week of employment, shall be oriented to, and shall demonstrate knowledge of, the following items. The director of any center or large family-child-care home shall provide this training to newly hired substitutes. This training shall include the opportunity for an evaluation and a repeat demonstration of the training lesson. In centers, this orientation training shall be documented. The orientation shall address, at a minimum

a) The names of the children for whom the caregiver will be responsible, and their specific developmental needs.
b) Any special health or nutrition need(s) of the children assigned to the caregiver.
c) The planned program of activities at the facility. (See *Program of Activities*, on p. 286, and *Program of Developmental Activities*, on p. 45.)
d) Routines and transitions.
e) Acceptable methods of discipline. (See *Discipline*, on p. 52.)
f) Meal patterns and food-handling policies of the facility. (See *Nutrition Plan and Policy*, on p. 284, *Food Service Records*, on p. 295, and chapter 4, *Nutrition and Food Service*, on p. 115.)
g) Emergency health and safety procedures. (See *Emergency Plan*, on p. 290, and *Emergency Procedures*, on p. 95.)
h) General health policies and procedures as appropriate for the ages of

Upon employment, staff members should be able to carry out basic sanitation and emergency procedures.

Orientation ensures that all staff receive specific and basic training for the work they will be doing and are oriented to their new responsibilities.

All facilities and the children enrolled in them vary. Orientation programs for new employees that address the health and safety of the children enrolled as well as employees' health and safety concerns that are specific to the site can be most productive.[23,24]

Because of frequent turnover, it is the obligation of centers and large family-child-care homes to institute orientation programs that protect the health and safety of children and new staff.

This standard applies to all centers, including special facilities for ill children, facilities for children with special needs, and large family-child-care homes where assistants are employed.

See also comment for standard ST60.

the children cared for, including but not limited to the following:

1) Handwashing techniques, including indications for handwashing. (See *Handwashing*, on p. 72.)

2) Diapering technique, if care is provided to children in diapers, including appropriate diaper disposal and diaper-changing techniques. (See *Toilet, Diapering, and Bath Areas*, on p. 168, *Toileting, Diapering, and Toilet Training*, on p. 68, *Sanitation, Disinfection, and Maintenance of Toilet Training Equipment, Toilets, and Bathrooms*, on p. 76, and *Diaper Changing Areas*, on pp. 77.)

3) Correct food preparation and storage techniques, if employee prepares food. (See *Nutrition Plan and Policy*, on p. 284, and *Food Safety*, on p. 130.)

4) Formula preparation if formula is handled (See *Nutrition Plan and Policy*, on p. 77 and *Nutrition for Infants*, p. 117.)

ST62. A short-term substitute caregiver in a small family-child-care home shall be oriented to emergency response practices, including how to call for emergency medical assistance, how to reach parents or emergency contacts, how to arrange for transfer to medical care, and the evacuation plan. (See specifics for the aforementioned items in *Emergency Plan*, on p. 280, *Evacuation Plan and Drills*, on p. 280, and Appendix C, item A on p. 330.) A regularly used substitute shall have the same clearances as the small family home caregiver, (i.e., criminal record check, child abuse history, medical assessment, etc.). (See *Qualifications of Large and Small Family Home Caregivers*, on p. 14, *Staff Health*, on p. 35, and *Individual Licensure/ Certification*, on p. 301.)

See rationale for standard ST61.

It is recommended that substitute caregivers possess current CPR (if the small family-child-care home has a swimming/wading pool) and first aid certification (see *First Aid and CPR*, on p. 22). However, small family-child-care home substitutes are very difficult to find, especially at the last minute. Requiring first aid and CPR (if needed) training for small family-child-care home substitutes would force small family home caregivers to close during the times they could not cover. This would have a negative impact on the families and children they serve.

See also comment for standard ST60.

1.6 Health Consultants

STANDARDS

ST63. Each center and organized small family-child-care-home system shall utilize the services of a health consultant. Large and small family home caregivers shall avail themselves of community resources established for health consultation to child care.

ST64. The health consultant shall be a physician, certified pediatric or family nurse practitioner, or registered nurse with pediatric or out-of-home child care experience, and shall be knowledgeable about out-of-home child care, community child care licensing requirements, and available health resources.

RATIONALE

Child care staff are rarely trained health professionals. Since staff and time are often limited, caregivers should have access to consultation on available resources in a variety of fields (physical and mental health care, nutrition, safety, oral health care, developmental disabilities, etc.).[32,33]

The specific health and safety policies for an individual facility depend on the resources available to that facility.[34] To be effective, a health consultant should know the available resources in the community and should involve staff and parents in the policy-setting process. Setting health and safety policies in cooperation with both staff and parents will better ensure successful implementation.[3]

COMMENTS

When physical, mental, social, or health concerns are raised for the child or for the family, they should be addressed appropriately, often through referral to resources available in the community. If a resource file is maintained, it must be updated regularly and used by a caregiver knowledgeable about health and about the community. Local resource and referral agencies may maintain such information.

If they are not provided through a public health system, a health consultant's services are very difficult to obtain—particularly for small family-child-care homes. Caregivers should seek the volunteer services of a health consultant through state and local professional organizations, such as the local chapters of the American Academy of Pediatrics, the American Nurses' Association, the Visiting Nurse Association, the American Academy of Family Physicians, the National Association of Pediatric Nurse Associates and Practitioners, the National Association for the Education of Young Children, and the National Association for Family Day Care, or through the state and local health departments (especially the public health nursing departments and the state communicable disease specialist's or epidemiologist's office). Caregivers also should not overlook health professionals who are parents of children enrolled in their facility.

A health consultant should be a person who has an interest in and experience with children, has a knowledge of resources, and is comfortable working with facilities outside the medical system.

Programs with a significant number of non–English-speaking families need to provide materials on community health resources in the parents' native languages.[2]

STANDARDS	RATIONALE	COMMENTS

ST65. The health consultant shall visit each facility regularly to review and give advice on the facility's health component. Facilities that serve any child under 2 years of age shall be visited at least once a month. Facilities that are not open every day or that serve only children 2 years of age or older shall be visited quarterly on a schedule that meets the needs of the composite group of children. (See *Consultation Records*, on p. 295.)

Almost everything that goes on in a center and almost everything about the center itself affects the health of the children it serves.[35] Caregivers acknowledge the lack of availability of staff trained in infant care and a high turnover rate of staff. Infants are more vulnerable to injuries and infections. Their rapid changes in behavior make regular and frequent visits by the health consultant extremely important.

Nursery schools are examples of facilities that might not be open every day.

ST66. The health consultant shall define the aspects of care, activity, physical maintenance, and administration in the facility that relate to prevention and management of illness and injury and to the enhancement of the child's development. The health consultant shall have contact with the facility's administrative authority (see *Identifiable Governing Body/Accountable Individual*, on p. 269) in the facility so that the health consultant's recommendations can be reviewed, revised, and implemented. A health consultant shall be used by each facility for advice about the health plan and about specific problems as they arise, and as a source for contacts with the health care community.

A health consultant who only provides direct consultation to child care staff is unlikely to make any change in child care policy.[3]

ST67. The health consultant shall assist in the development and implementation of written policies (see chapter 8, *Administration*, p. 269) for the prevention and control of communicable diseases, injuries, and child abuse; in the integration of children with special needs; and in providing related health education to children, staff, and parents (see *Health Consultants*, on p. 33).

Child care health consultants can help develop and implement written policies for the prevention and management of communicable diseases. Planning in this area can reduce stress for staff, parents, and health professionals when an outbreak of communicable disease occurs in a facility. Licensing requirements for facilities increasingly require specific arrangements with a health consultant to assist in the development of written policies for the prevention and control of communicable diseases.

ST68. The health consultant shall be given the responsibility for approving all policies and procedures addressed in these APHA/AAP standards.

See rationale for standard ST67.

The common policies and procedures reviewed by health consultants should include, but not be limited to, the following:
a) Admission and readmission after illness, including inclusion/exclusion criteria.

ST68. *continued*

b) Health evaluation and observation procedures on intake, including physical assessment of the child and other criteria used to determine the appropriateness of a child's attendance.
c) Plans for health care and management of children with communicable disease.
d) Plans for surveillance of illnesses and injuries cared for and problems that arise in the care of children.
e) Plans for caregiver training and for communication with parents and health care providers.

ST69. The health consultant shall review the policies as specified in standard AD51 in chapter 8 on p. 285.

ST70. The health consultant shall inspect the injury log as specified in *Incidence Logs of Illness, Injury, and Other Problems,* on p. 290.

This monitoring will help in identifying patterns of injuries that are potentially preventable or that may indicate signs of child abuse.

For health consultants to facilities serving children with special needs, see also *Direct Care and Provisional Staff*, on p. 250. For health consultants serving special facilities for children who are ill, see also *Health Consultants*, on p. 106. For nutrition staffing and consultation, see *Staffing*, on p. 122.

For additional information on health consultants, see also *Health Consultation*, on p. 278, *Consultation Records*, on p. 295, on documentation of health consultant training and visits, and *Consultants*, on p. 314.

1.7 Staff Health

PREEMPLOYMENT STAFF HEALTH APPRAISAL, INCLUDING IMMUNIZATION

Please note that if a staff member has no contact with the children or with anything that the children come into contact with, these standards do not apply to that staff member.

STANDARDS

ST71. All staff (volunteer and paid) shall have a health appraisal within the 3 months prior to employment or within the first month of employment. A record of this health appraisal shall be on file at the facility. The staff health appraisal shall include, at a minimum
a) Health history.
b) Physical exam.
c) Vision and hearing screening.
d) Tuberculosis (Tb) screening by the Mantoux method.
e) A review of immunization status (measles, mumps, rubella, diphtheria, tetanus, and polio).[38,39]
f) A review of occupational health concerns.
g) Assessment of need for vaccines against influenza, pneumococcus, and hepatitis B, and of risk from exposure to common childhood infections, such as parvovirus, CMV, and chicken pox.[39-41]
h) Assessment of orthopedic, psychological, neurological, or sensory limitations or communicable diseases that may impair the staff member's ability to perform the job.

ST72. The Tb test shall be repeated as recommended by local health authorities. A record of test results shall be on file in the facility. (See *Tuberculosis*, on p. 207.)

ST73. Staff shall be current for immunizations as specified in standard ID31 in chapter 6 on p. 221.

RATIONALE

All employees must demonstrate that they are in good health, for their protection as well as for the protection of others at the facility.[3,36,37]

Since tuberculosis is on the increase[42] and incidence varies, monitoring frequency should be determined locally.

COMMENTS

A health professional may need to assess the staff member's ability to do the following things that are typically required of caregivers
a) Move quickly to supervise and assist young children.
b) Lift children, equipment, and supplies.
c) Sit on the floor and on child-sized furniture.
d) Practice frequent handwashing.
e) Eat the same food served to the children (i.e., does the staff member have dietary restrictions?).
f) Hear and see at a distance for playground supervision or driving.

Currently there are no screening tools or self-appraisals to identify specific health conditions that may be a hazard in child care settings. The "Staff Health Appraisal" in the AAP's *Health in Day Care: A Manual for Health Professionals,* Appendix II.5, and the NAEYC's *Healthy Young Children: A Manual for Programs* provide good models for an assessment by a health professional. Contact the AAP about its publication at the following address:

American Academy of Pediatrics
141 Northwest Point Blvd.
P.O. Box 927
Elk Grove Village, IL 60009-0927

Contact the NAEYC about its publication at the following address:

National Association for the
  Education of Young Children
1834 Connecticut Avenue, N.W.
Washington, DC 20009

Concern about the cost of health exams (particularly when many caregivers do not receive health benefits and many earn minimum wages) is a barrier to meeting this standard.

STANDARDS	**RATIONALE**	**COMMENTS**

ONGOING STAFF HEALTH APPRAISALS

Please note that if a staff member has no contact with the children or with anything that the children come into contact with, these standards do not apply to that staff member.

ST74. After the preemployment health appraisal, staff shall have health appraisals as recommended by their health care provider or by supervisory or regulatory/certifying personnel.

Current medical guidelines regarding the value of testing indicate that an annual exam is not necessary.[43,44]

ST75. On a daily basis, the administrator of the facility shall assess (visually and verbally) staff and volunteers for obvious signs of ill health. Staff and volunteers shall be responsible for reporting immediately to their supervisor any injuries or illnesses they experience at the facility or elsewhere, especially those that might affect their health or the health and safety of the children.

Sometimes adults may report to work when feeling ill, or may become ill during the day but feel it is their responsibility to stay. The administrator's gross assessment may prevent the spread of illness.

Guidelines need to be developed to ensure proper use of this standard.

HEALTH LIMITATIONS OF STAFF

Please note that if a staff member has no contact with the children or with anything that the children come into contact with, these standards do not apply to that staff member.

ST76. If a staff member is found unable to do his/her job due to health limitations
1) The staff member's duties shall be limited until he/she can meet them; or
2) The staff member's duties shall be modified.

See rationale for standard ST71.

ST77. Staff and volunteers must have a health care provider's release to return to work in the following situations:
a) When they have experienced conditions that may affect their ability to do their job (e.g., pregnancy, specific injuries, infectious diseases).

It is the responsibility of the director to decide when this release is necessary.

STANDARDS	RATIONALE	COMMENTS

b) After serious or prolonged illness.

c) When promotion or reassignment to another role could be affected by health.

d) Before return from a job-related injury.

e) If there are workers' compensation issues or if the facility is at risk of liability related to the employee's or volunteer's health problem.

For additional information on health limitations of staff, see also standards ID49 in chapter 6 on p. 230 for staff with acute or chronic hepatitis B and standard ID59 in chapter 6 on p. 232 for staff with asymptomatic HIV.

OCCUPATIONAL HAZARDS

Please note that if a staff member has no contact with the children or with anything that the children come into contact with, these standards do not apply to that staff member.

ST78. The center's written personnel policies shall address the major occupational health hazards for child care outlined in Appendix D, on p. 337.

Stress

ST79. Measures to decrease stress for staff shall be implemented and shall include the following:

a) Wages and benefits that adequately compensate the skills, knowledge, and performance required of caregivers, and that approximate the levels of wages and benefits paid for other jobs that require comparable skills, knowledge, and performance.

b) Job security.

c) Training to improve skills and hazard recognition.

d) Stress management training.

e) Regular work breaks.

f) Appropriate child:staff ratios. (See *Child:Staff Ratio and Group Size*, on p. 1.)

g) Liability insurance for caregivers.

h) Staff lounge separate from child care area.

One of the best indicators of quality child care is consistent staff with low turnover rates. The National Child Care Staffing Study[16] found that staff turnover has nearly tripled in the past decade, from 15 percent in 1977 to 41 percent in 1988, and that despite having higher levels of formal education than the average American worker, child care teaching staff earn an average of $5.35 an hour, scarcely more than minimum wage. Stress reduction measures (particularly adequate wages) are essential to decrease staff turnover and thus promote quality care.[7, 15, 24, 36] Staff health, welfare, and safety are determinants of their ability to provide care for the children.

Serious physical abuse usually occurs at a time of high stress for the caregiver.

Documentation of implementation of such measures shall be on file in the facility.

STANDARDS	RATIONALE	COMMENTS
i) The use of sound-absorbing materials.	The use of sound-absorbing materials and the provision of breaks and a separate lounge allow for respite from noise and from nonauditory stress. Noise, or unwanted sound, can be damaging to hearing as well as to psychosocial well-being. The stress effects of noise will potentiate the other stress factors present in the facility. In addition, uncontrolled noise will force the caregiver to speak continually at levels above those normally used for conversation and thus may increase the risk of throat irritation. Throat irritation may be a particularly serious consequence when the staff are exposed to infectious agents.	

Infectious Diseases/Injuries

Please note that if a staff member has no contact with the children or with anything that the children come into contact with, these standards do not apply to that staff member.

See standard AD14 in chapter 8 on p. 273 on staff injuries from acts of aggression by children; *Care of Ill Children*, on p. 274; standard FA104 on prevention of back injuries in chapter 5, on p. 158; *Toilet, Diapering, and Bath Areas*, on p. 168, *Toileting, Diapering, and Toilet Training*, on p. 68, and *Sanitation, Disinfection, and Maintenance of Toilet Training Equipment, Toilets, and Bathrooms*, on p. 76; *Hygiene*, on p. 72; and chapter 6, *Infectious Diseases*, on p. 207.

Injury-preventive and hygienic activities recommended for children also protect staff.

Toxic Exposures

See *Toxic Substances*, on p. 163.

Noise

See *Stress*, on p. 38.

1.8 Staff Benefits

STANDARDS

ST80. The following basic benefits shall be offered to staff:
a) Health insurance.
b) Sick leave.
c) Vacation leave.
d) Social Security or other retirement plan.
e) Workers' compensation.
f) Holidays.
g) Parental leave.
h) Educational benefits.

RATIONALE

The quality and continuity of the caregiving workforce is the primary determiner of the quality of care. Nurturing the nurturers is essential to prevent burnout and excessive staff turnover. Fair labor practices should apply to child care as well as to other work settings.

Child care workers should be considered as worthy of benefits as workers in other career areas. Medical coverage is especially important, due to the health evaluation required of child care workers, and the potential for increased incidence of communicable disease and stress-related conditions in this work setting. Sick leave is important to minimize the spread of communicable disease and maintain the health of staff. Sick leave for staff is another measure to promote recovery from illness and thus decrease further illness spread or recurrence. Other benefits contribute to improved morale and decreased staff turnover, and thus promote quality child care. Lack of benefits is a major reason reported for high turnover of child care staff.[10,16]

The potential for acquiring injuries and infections when caring for young children is a health and safety hazard for child care workers. There is extensive information about the risk of infectious disease for children in child care settings. Staff come into close and frequent contact with children and their excretions and secretions and are vulnerable to these illnesses as well, since children are reservoirs for many infectious agents. Additionally, many child care workers are women who are planning pregnancy or who are pregnant, and they may be vulnerable to potentially serious effects of infection on pregnancy outcome.

Most states require training for caregivers depending upon their functions and responsibilities. Caregiver training has been found to correlate with quality in child care.[7,16] Caregiver training and monitoring have

COMMENTS

Staff benefits may be appropriately addressed in center personnel policies and in state and federal labor standards. Not all the material needed to be addressed in such policies is necessarily appropriate for state child care licensing requirements.

As facilities strive to be able to offer all of these benefits, just having facilities acknowledge which benefits they do provide will help to enhance the general awareness of staff benefits among child care workers and other concerned parties.

Currently, this standard is difficult to achieve. There are many options for providing leave benefits and education reimbursements, ranging from partial to full, based on time employed with the facility, etc. Health benefits can include full coverage, partial coverage, or merely access to group rates. Staff could join the local or state Child Care Association to get reduced group rates for health insurance. This applies to center staff as well.

ST80. *continued.*

been shown to reduce the spread of infections of the intestines (often with diarrhea) or liver.[18, 45-47] In a study of four centers, caregiver training in hygiene combined with close monitoring of caregivers' compliance was associated with a significant decrease in infant-toddler diarrhea.[45] In another study, periodic evaluation of caregivers trained in hygiene was associated with significant improvement in the practices under study. When training was combined with periodic evaluation, additional improvement was observed.[18] In a study of 12 centers, continuous surveillance without training was associated with a significant decrease in diarrheal illness during the course of a longitudinal study. One-time staff training without subsequent monitoring did not result in an additional decrease.[46] A similar decline in diarrhea rates during the course of surveillance without training was observed in a longitudinal study of 60 centers.[47] These studies suggest that training combined with outside monitoring of child care practices can modify caregiver behavior as well as disease occurrence.

ST81. Small and large family home caregivers shall have policies, including
a) Sick leave.
b) Vacation leave.
c) Holidays.
d) Personal leave.
For large family homes, these policies shall be in writing.

See rationale for standard ST80.

For additional information on staff benefits, see also *Personnel Policies*, on p. 287.

1.9 Performance Evaluation

ST82. All caregivers shall be familiar with the provisions of the facility's policies, plans, and procedures as described in *Administration*, on p. 269. Their compliance with these

---

policies, plans, and procedures shall be used in performance evaluations and documented in the personnel file.

ST83. All caregivers shall sign an agreement on the discipline policy as specified in standard AD13 in chapter 8 on p. 273.

ST84. Periodic evaluations of staff shall include an evaluation of their adherence to the policies and procedures of the facility (see *Sanitation Plan*, on p. 283, *Interior Maintenance*, on p. 197, *Hygiene*, on p. 72, and chapter 6, *Infectious Diseases*, on p. 207.

ST85. The competency of personnel and their continuing education needs shall be assessed annually through a systematic process and shall be documented.

Staff who are better trained are better able to prevent, recognize, and correct health and safety problems.[48]

Compliance with this standard may be determined by licensing requirements set by the state and local regulatory processes.

ST86. For each employee, there shall be a written annual self-evaluation, a performance review from the personnel supervisor, and a continuing education plan based on the needs assessment of continuing education described in standard ST85.

A system for evaluation of employees is a basic component of any personnel policy.

Formal evaluation is not a substitute for continuing feedback on day-to-day performance. See also the above comment for standard ST85.

ST87. Successful completion of requirements for a current teaching or professional certificate (if available) shall be required of each professional.

Maintenance and upgrading of skills is viewed as essential.

State licensure/certification requirements may apply.

ST88. When a staff member does not meet the minimum competency level, the center's director shall place said employee on probation and assist the person to achieve the necessary skills.

The minimum competency level is related to the director's assessment of the caregiver's performance.

For additional information on performance evaluation, see also *Personnel Records,* on p. 290.

References

1. *NFPA 101 Life Safety Code 1988.* Quincy, Mass: National Fire Protection Association; 1988.

2. *Accreditation and Criteria Procedures of the National Academy of Early Childhood Programs.* Washington, DC: National Association for the Education of Young Children; 1984.

3. Deitch S, ed. *Health in Day Care: A Manual for Health Professionals.* Elk Grove Village, Ill: American Academy of Pediatrics; 1987.

4. National Research Council. *Who Cares for America's Children? Child Care Policy in the 1990's.* Washington, DC: National Academy Press; 1990.

5. Bredekamp S, ed. *Developmentally Appropriate Practice in Early Childhood Programs Serving Children From Birth Through Age 8.* Washington, DC: National Association for the Education of Young Children; 1987. 17–46.

6. Morgan G. *The National State of Child Care Regulation 1986.* Boston, Mass: Work/Family Directions Inc.; 1987.

7. Ruopp R, Travers J, Glantz F, et al. *Children at the Center: Final Report of the National Day Care Study. Vol 1.* Cambridge, Mass: Abt Associates; 1979.

8. Save a Child's Life! [brochure]. Elk Grove Village, Ill: American Academy of Pediatrics; 1988.

9. Personal correspondence. Consumer Product Safety Commission; 1988.

10. Phillips D, ed. *Quality in Child Care: What Does Research Tell Us?* Washington, DC: National Association for the Education of Young Children; 1987.

11. *Child Care Course.* Washington, DC: American Red Cross; 1990.

12. Almy M. Day care and early childhood education. In: Zigler E, Gordon E, eds. *Day Care: Scientific and Social Policy Issues.* Boston, Mass: Auburn House; 1982. 476–495.

13. *Standards for Licensure or Approval of School-Age Child Care Programs.* Boston: Commonwealth of Massachusetts Office for Children; 1987.

14. Baden R, Genser RA, Levine JA, et al. *School-Age Child Care: An Action Manual.* Dover, Mass: Auburn House; 1982. 214–217.

15. Whitebook M, Howes C, Friedman J, et al. Caring for the caregivers: Burn-out in child care. Norwood, NJ: Early Childhood Education. 1982;4.

16. Whitebook M, Howes C, Phillips D. *Who Cares: Child Care Teachers and the Quality of Care in America.* Oakland, Calif: Child Care Employee Project; 1989.

17. *School Age Child Technical Assistance Paper (2 and 8).* Boston: Commonwealth of Massachusetts Office for Children; 1988.

18. Aronson S, Aiken L. Compliance of child care programs with health and safety standards: impact of program evaluation and advocate training. *Pediatrics.* 1980; 65:318–325.

19. Yogman M. Child care as a setting for parent education. Group Care for Young Children. Pediatric Round Table 12. Skillman, NJ: Johnson & Johnson; 1986.

20. *Accreditation Profile.* Washington, DC: National Association for Family Day Care; 1988.

21. Ramsey PG. Multicultural education in early childhood. *Young Children.* 1982; 38(2):13–24.

22. Saracho O, Spodek B, eds. Understanding the multicultural experience in early childhood education. *Children's Environmental Quarterly.* 1983. 1–2.

23. *Federal Interagency Day Care Requirements.* Washington, DC: US Department of Health, Education and Welfare; 1980.

24. *Twenty Facts on Women Workers.* Washington, DC: US Department of Labor; 1986.

25. Chang A, Lugg M, Nebedum A. Injuries among preschool children enrolled in day care centers. *Pediatrics.* 1989; 83:272–277.

26. Wilson E, Brooks B, Tweed WA. CPR skill retention of lay basic rescuers. *Ann Emerg Med.* 12:8; 482–484.

27. William K, Mancini M. Retention of cardiopulmonary skills by physicians, nurses and the general public. *Critical Care Med.* 1986; 14(7): 620–622.

28. *Don't Shortchange America's Future: The Full Cost of Quality Must Be Paid.* Washington, DC: National Association for the Education of Young Children; 1990.

29. *Protocol for Management of Infections in Child Care Facilities.* Charlotte, NC: Mecklenberg County Health Department; 1983.

30. *Promoting Health/Preventing Disease: Objectives for the Nation.* Washington, DC: US Department of Health and Human Services; 1980.

31. Ard L. Where to find training. *Texas Child Care Quarterly.* Fall 1985; 11–15.

32. Committee on Early Childhood, Adoption and Dependent Care. Pediatrician's role in promoting the health of a patient in day care. *Pediatrics.* 1984; 74(1).

33. Introduction of S-1885. *Congressional Record.* November 19, 1987.

34. Aronson SS, Gilsdorf JR. Prevention and management of infectious diseases in day care. *Pediatr in Rev.* 1986;7:259–268.

35. Aronson SS. Health consultation in child care. *Day Care and Early Education.* Fall 1983; 26–32.

36. Kendrick A, Kauffmann R, Messenger K, eds. *Healthy Young Children: A Manual for Programs.* Washington DC: National Association for the Education of Young Children; 1991.

37. *School Health: A Guide for Health Professionals.* Elk Grove Village, Ill: American Academy of Pediatrics; 1987.

38. Aronson SS, Osterholm MT. Infectious diseases in child day care: management and prevention, summary of the symposium and recommendations. *Rev Infect Dis.* 1986; 8:677.

39. Haskins R, Kotch J. Day care and illness: evidence, costs and public policy. *Pediatrics.* 1986; 77(6) (suppl) (2).

40. Food and Drug Administration. Shots adults should not do without. FDA Consumer Publication 86–3161. Washington, DC: Food and Drug Administration; June 1986.

41. McGregor JA, Mark S, Crawford G, et al. Varicella-zoster antibody testing in the care of pregnant women exposed to varicella. *Amer J Obstet Gynecol.* 1987; 157:281–284.

42. US Department of Health and Human Services. Tuberculosis, Final Data: United States, 1986. *MMWR.* 1988; 36(50 & 51):817–819.

43. Branch WT. *Office Practice of Medicine.* Philadelphia, Pa: Saunders; 1987.

44. Lindberg S. Adult preventive health screening: 1987 update. *Nurse Practitioner.* 1987; 19–45.

45. Black RE, Dykes AC, Anderson KD, et al. Handwashing to prevent diarrhea in day care centers. *Amer J Epidemiol.* 1981;113:445–451.

46. Bartlett AV, Jarvis BA, Ross V, et al. Diarrheal illness among infants and toddlers in day care centers: effects of active surveillance and staff training without subsequent monitoring. *Amer J Epidemiol.* 1988;127:808–817.

47. Sullivan P, Woodward WE, Pickering LK, et al. A longitudinal study of the occurrence of diarrheal disease in day care centers. *Amer J Public Health.* 1984;74:987–991.

48. Beer M. Note on performance appraisal. Boston, Mass: Intercollegiate Case Clearinghouse; 1977.

CHAPTER 2

Program:
Activities for Healthy
Developement

CHAPTER 2
PROGRAM: ACTIVITIES FOR HEALTHY DEVELOPMENT

This chapter is not intended to address the program in its entirety, but only the aspects of the program that are most relevant to health and safety.

2.1 Program of Developmental Activities

STANDARDS	RATIONALE	COMMENTS

GENERAL PROGRAM ACTIVITIES

PR1. Facilities shall establish a planned program of activities based on the development of the child at each stage of early childhood to encourage normal developmental progress.

Centers shall develop a written plan that sets out the basic elements from which the daily program is to be built. The elements to be included are those specified in this chapter.

Reviews of children's performance after attending out-of-home child care indicate that children attending centers with well-developed curricula achieve appropriate levels of development.[1]

Early childhood specialists agree on the inseparability of cognitive, physical, emotional, and social development; the influence of the child's health on all areas; the central importance of continuity of affectionate care; the relevance of the phase or stage concept; and the importance of action (including play) as a mode of learning.[2]

Those who provide child care and education must require of themselves that they be clear about their program.

Child care is a "delivery of service" involving a contractual relationship between provider and consumer. A written plan helps to particularize the service and contributes to specific and responsible operations that are conducive to sound child development and safety practices and to positive consumer relations.

Plans can ensure that some thought goes into programming for children. They also allow for monitoring and for accountability.

A written plan can provide a basis for staff orientation.

The NAEYC publication *Accreditation Criteria and Procedures* can serve as a resource. To obtain this publication, write to

National Association for the Education of Young Children
1834 Connecticut Avenue, N.W.
Washington, DC 20009

PR2. The facility activities shall include structured and unstructured times and teacher-directed and child-initiated experiences.

A planned but flexible program that allows children the opportunity to make decisions about their activities fosters independence and creative expression.

PR3. The child must be helped to cope with the experience of separation and loss. This shall be accomplished by
a) Encouraging parents to spend time in the facility with the child.

In childhood, some separation experiences facilitate psychological growth by mobilizing new approaches for learning and adaptation. Other separations are painful and traumatic. The way in which

Parents, too, experience pain at separation, and the younger the child, the more intense the pain. The facility should help parents with separation by
a) Validating their feelings as a

🍎 applies to a small family-child-care home   Ⓐ applies to a large family-child-care home   🛝 applies to a center.
If no symbol appears, the standard applies to all three.

b) Enabling the child to bring tangible reminders of home/family to child care (e.g., a favorite toy or a picture of self and parent).
c) Helping child to play out themes of separation and reunion.
d) Frequently exchanging information between parent and caregiver.
e) Reassuring the child about his/her parent's return.

PR4. At least one member of the staff shall be able to communicate in the primary language of the parents and children, or the facility shall have arrangements to provide an adult translator to communicate with parents.

PR5. Facilities must work to increase understanding of cultural, ethnic, and other differences by enrolling children who reflect the cultural and ethnic diversity of the community. (See also standard ST37 in chapter 1 on p. 17.)

influential adults provide support and understanding, or fail to do so, will shape the child's experience.[3]

The future development of the child depends in no small degree on his/her command of language.[4] Richness of language increases as it is nurtured by verbal interaction of the child with adults and peers.

Basic communication with parents and children requires an ability to speak their language.

A democratic pluralistic society rests on valuing cultural diversity.[5, 6]

universal human experience.
b) Providing parents with information about the positive effects on children of high-quality facilities with strong parent participation.
c) Encouraging parents to discuss their feelings.
d) Providing parents with evidence, such as photographs, that their child is enjoying the activities of the facility.

By facilitating the expression of cultural or ethnic identity and by encouraging familiarity with different groups and practices through ordinary interaction and activities integrated into a developmentally appropriate curriculum, a facility can foster the children's ability to relate to others different from themselves, their sense of possibility, and their ability to succeed in a diverse society, while also promoting feelings of belonging and identification with a tradition.

Holidays and other events of the cultural and ethnic groups found in the community may be celebrated to provide opportunities to introduce children to a range of customs and beliefs. Materials and displays must represent the cultural heritages of the children and staff to instill a sense of pride and positive feelings of identification in all children and staff.

PROGRAM ACTIVITIES
FROM BIRTH TO 35 MONTHS

PR6. Ordinarily, no child will be considered eligible for out-of-home care before 6 weeks of age.

It takes at least 6 weeks for parents to be able to form a lasting attachment to their baby. It requires much longer than that for the baby, but if the parent has not been able to form such an attachment it will be impossible for the baby to do so.

Many parents may have no other option than to place their children in out-of-home child care before 6 weeks of age, because many employers do not provide parental leave. In most other industrialized countries (e.g., France, Sweden, Norway,

STANDARDS	RATIONALE	COMMENTS

<table>
<tr><td></td><td></td><td>Finland, Denmark, and Holland) family leave with pay is a minimum of 6 months and can be taken by either mother or father or in some combination.</td></tr>
<tr><td>

PR7. Opportunities shall be provided for each child to develop a personal and affectionate relationship with and attachment to one or a small number of caregivers whose care for and responsiveness to the child ensure relief of distress, experiences of comfort and stimulation, and satisfaction of the need for a social partner. The caregivers shall
a) Hold and comfort the child who is upset;
b) Engage in social interchanges such as smiling, talking, and touching; and
c) Be play partners as well as protectors.

</td><td>

Kissing, hugging, and cuddling infants and children are expressions of wholesome love that should be encouraged. Caregivers should be advised that it is all right to demonstrate affection for children of both sexes. The wishes of children, regardless of their ages, should always be respected with regard to physical contact and their comfort/discomfort with it. Even "friendly contact" (e.g., touching the shoulder or arm) with a child should be avoided if he or she is uncomfortable with it. This is especially true of the school-age child.[7]

The presence of trustworthy adults who are able to give of themselves as they provide care and learning experiences can hardly be overemphasized in its significance for a child's development as an active, self-respecting, thinking, feeling, and loving person.[8, 9]

</td><td></td></tr>
<tr><td>

PR8. A speaking social partner shall be provided who engages the child in verbal exchanges linked to daily events and experiences. To encourage the development of language, the caregiver shall be skilled in verbal communication, as observed in interactions between caregiver and child. Communication starts with the response to and encouragement of soft infant sounds.

</td><td>

The speech of the adult is one of the principal channels through which the child learns about himself/herself, others, and the world he/she lives in. Although adults speaking to children teach the children facts, the social and emotional communications and the atmosphere of the exchange are equally important. Reciprocity of expression and response and the initiation and enrichment of dialogue are the hallmarks of such conversations' essentially social function and significance.[8, 10, 11]

See also rationale for standard PR4, on p. 46.

</td><td></td></tr>
<tr><td>

PR9. Caregivers shall talk to young infants as they feed, change, and cuddle them.

</td><td>

See rationale for standard PR8.

</td><td></td></tr>
<tr><td>

PR10. Caregivers shall name objects and sing rhymes to all children.

</td><td>

Richness of language increases as it is nurtured by verbal interaction of the child with adults and peers.

</td><td>

Children's stories and poems presented on records or tapes with a fixed speed for sing-along can actually interfere with a child's ability to participate in the singing or recitation. For some children the pace will

</td></tr>
</table>

STANDARDS

RATIONALE

COMMENTS

be too fast and the activity will require repetition in order to be learned. Live, real-time interaction with caregivers is preferred.

PR11. The facility shall provide space, colorful materials, and equipment, indoors and outdoors, arranged to support learning and optimize
a) Opportunities for the child to act upon the environment; to confront new opportunities; to experience obstacles, frustrations, and dangers; and thereby to learn to manage both inner feelings and resources and the occurrences and demands of the outer world.
b) Opportunities for play that serve to reduce anxiety and to help the child adapt to reality, resolve conflicts, bind together the inner and outer worlds, and construct systems of symbols.

Such opportunities to be active are vitally important for the development of motor competence and awareness of one's own body and person; the development of sensory motor intelligence; the ability and motivation to mobilize physical and mental initiative; and the feelings of mastery and of successful coping. Coping involves original, imaginative, and innovative behavior as well as previously learned strategies. A physical and social environment that provides opportunities for active mastery and coping enhances the child's adaptive abilities.[12-14]

The importance of play for cognitive development, for maintaining an affective and intellectual equilibrium, and for creating and testing new capacities is well recognized. Play involves a balance of action and symbolization and of feeling and thinking.[15, 16]

Compliance should be measured by attestation of an expert in child development who is recognized by the credentialing body and who visits the facility to observe, document, and give advice about the extent to which the facility's written plan (see standard PR1, on p. 45) meets the standard and whether the facility's performance complies with the standard as well. Involvement of outside experts is a method of quality assurance and program improvement employed in many human service and industrial settings.

PR12. Except in family-style, small closed groups of mixed-aged children, infants and toddlers younger than 2 years of age shall be cared for in a closed room(s) that separates them from older children. Activities that bring children younger than 2 years of age in contact with older children, except in small groups, shall be prohibited in facilities caring for three or more children younger than 2 years. Caregivers of infants shall not be responsible for the care of older children who are not a part of the infants' closed child care group.

Infants need quiet, calm environments, away from the stimulation of older children. The younger babies should be cared for in rooms separate from the more boisterous toddlers. In addition to the developmental needs of infants, there are important disease-prevention reasons for separation. Rates of hospitalization for all forms of acute infectious respiratory diseases are highest during the first year of life, indicating that respiratory illness severity is inversely related to age. Therefore infants should be a principal focus for interventions to reduce the incidence of respiratory disease. Most respiratory infections are spread from older children or adults to infants. Therefore exposure of infants to older children should be restricted to limit exposure of infants to respiratory viruses and bacteria.

Although this separation deprives the younger and older children of a desirable socialization experience, the risk of exposure to infections justifies the separation. The immune systems of younger children may not be prepared for the risk of exposure to infections experienced by older children. This separation of younger children from older children ideally should be implemented in all facilities, but may be less feasible in small or large family-child-care-homes.

A group of children of different ages receiving care together from one or two caregivers may experience increased risk of transmission of infection among the members of the group, but the developmental and curricular advantage of such mixed-age groupings may offset this risk. Mixing of children from different groups during arrival and departure times or for specialized activities during the day should be discouraged, as this practice pools the infectious disease exposure of all the children.

For additional information on program activities from birth to 35 months, see also standard PR20, on p. 50.

PROGRAM ACTIVITIES FOR 3- TO 5-YEAR-OLDS

PR13. Opportunities for each child to build long-term, trusting relationships with a few caring caregivers shall be provided by limiting the number of adults who are assigned to care for any one child during his/her experience in child care to a maximum of six to eight adults in a given year.

Children learn best from adults who know and respect them; who act as guides, facilitators, and supporters of a rich learning environment; and with whom they have established a trusting relationship. [17]

Compliance should be measured by staff and parent interviews.

PR14. Opportunities shall be provided for children to observe, explore, order and reorder, make mistakes and find solutions, and move from the concrete to the abstract in learning.

The most meaningful learning is that which has its source in the child's own self-initiated activities. The learning environment that supports individual differences, learning styles, abilities, and cultural values will foster confidence and curiosity in the learner. [17]

PR15. Age-appropriate equipment for both indoor and outdoor play shall be selected for safety, for its ability to provide large and small motor experiences, and for its adaptability to serve many different ideas, functions, and forms of creative expression. (See also *Play Equipment*, on p. 160, and *Additional Indoor Requirements for Infants, Toddlers, and Preschoolers*, on p. 181.)

An aesthetic, orderly, appropriately stimulating, child-oriented environment contributes to the preschooler's sense of well-being and control. [18]

PR16. There shall be encouragement and enhancement of expressive activities that include play, painting, drawing, story telling, music, and dancing.

Expressive activities serve as vehicles for socialization, conflict resolution, and language development. They are, in addition, vital energizers and organizers for cognitive development. Too early stifling of the preschooler's need to play damages a natural integration of thinking and feeling. [19]

PR17. A cooperative rather than competitive atmosphere shall be fostered. There shall be encouragement of verbal skills and attentiveness to the needs of individuals and the group as a whole.

As 3-, 4-, and 5-year-olds play and work together, they shift from almost total dependence on the adult to seeking support from peers. The rules and responsibilities of a well-functioning group help children of this age to internalize impulse control and to become increasingly responsible for managing their behavior. A dynamic curriculum designed to include the ideas and values of a broad socioeconomic group of children will promote socialization. The inevitable clashes and disagreements that occur are more easily resolved when there is a positive influence of the group on each child.[19]

PR18. There shall be particular opportunities for language development in a facility rich in first-hand experience. There shall also be an abundance of books of fantasy, fiction, and nonfiction, and chances for the children to relate stories. Caregivers shall foster language development by
a) Speaking with children rather than at them.
b) Encouraging children to talk to each other by helping them to listen and respond.
c) Giving children models of verbal expression.
d) Reading books about the here and now and also about imaginative themes.

Language reflects and shapes thinking. A curriculum created to match the needs and interests of preschoolers enhances language skills. First-hand experiences encourage children to talk to each other and to adults, to seek increasingly more complex vocabulary, and to use language to express thinking, feeling, and curiosity.[10, 20]

Measure compliance by structured observation.

Examples of encouragement of verbal expression are ''Ask Johnny if you can play with him,'' ''Tell him you don't like being hit,'' ''Tell Sara what you saw downtown yesterday,'' and ''Tell Mommy about what you and Johnny played this morning.''

PR19. Opportunities for helping the child learn about his or her body and how it functions shall be encouraged in the context of socializing with others. Curiosity and body mastery, consistent with parental expectations and cultural preferences, shall be facilitated and practiced. Body mastery includes feeding oneself, toilet training, running, skipping, climbing, balancing, playing with peers, and using and manipulating space.

Socializing with others and achieving the pleasure and gratification of feeling physically competent on a voluntary basis is a basic component of realistic self-esteem and of the ability to use socializing opportunities in being with adults and other children inside and outside the family.[7, 12, 13, 19, 21]

PR20. In order to help children achieve bowel and bladder control, caregivers shall enable children to take an active role in using toileting facilities when it is appropriate physically and when efforts to encourage toileting are supported by the parents. Caregivers shall take into account the preferences and customs of the child's family. (See *Toilets and Toilet Training Equipment*, on p. 168, and *Sanitation, Disinfection, and Maintenance of Toilet Training Equipment, Toilets, and Bathrooms*, on p. 76.)

Caregivers should enable children to take an active part in controlling the functions of their bodies in a manner that gives them a sense of pride and confidence.[22-24]

For further information on toilet training, see *Toilet Training: A Parent's Guide*. To obtain this publication write to

American Academy of Pediatrics
141 Northwest Point Blvd.
P.O. Box 927
Elk Grove Village, IL
60009-0927

PR21. Health, nutrition, and safety awareness shall be addressed as an integral part of the overall program by including in program planning the health, nutrition, and safety aspects of each formally structured activity documented in a curriculum plan.

The curriculum that best meets the needs of preschool children is one in which the daily events of their living together provide the raw materials for an integrated approach. Children are able to accept and enforce rules about health and safety when they have personal experience of why these rules were created, for example, when they are taught why they should eat balanced meals, or why they must wash their hands after using the toilet.[2,25,26]

PROGRAM ACTIVITIES FOR SCHOOL-AGE CHILDREN

PR22. The facility shall have a program of supervised activities designed especially for school-age children, to include
a) Free choice of play.
b) Opportunities to run, climb, and jump.
c) Opportunities for concentration, alone or in a group.
d) Time to read or do homework.
e) Opportunities to be creative, to explore the arts, sciences, and social studies, and to solve problems.

Whether they can be run in separate facilities or not, programs for older children after school or during vacation time require additional skills and interests of the staff members beyond the personal qualities that all good caregivers share.[25]

A good resource is *Recommended Standards for School-Age Child Care Programs.* To obtain this publication write to

Project Home Safe
1555 King Street
Alexandria, VA 22314

PR23. A space for indoor and outdoor activities shall be provided.

A safe and secure environment that fosters the growing independence of school-age children is essential for their development[27, 28]

Children should become partners with staff and peers in understanding and implementing safety measures.

PR24. Opportunities for developing trusting, supportive relationships with staff and peers shall be provided.

Although school-age children require more independent experiences, they continue to need the guidance and support of adults. Peer relationships take on increasing importance for this age group.

PR25. An organized, informal, and nonscholastic program based on the needs and interests of the age group as well as of the individuals shall be offered.

A school-age child care facility should provide an enriching contrast to the formal school program. Facilities that offer a wide range of activities (e.g., team sports, cooking, dramatics, art, music, crafts, games, open time, and quiet time) allow children to explore new interests and relationships.

PR26. Opportunities for community outreach and involvement, such as field trips and community improvement projects, shall be provided. (See *Field Trips*, on p. 52.)

As the world of the school-age child encompasses the larger community, facility activities should reflect this stage of development. Field trips and other opportunities to explore the community should enrich the child's experience.

PR27. Facilities that accept school-age children directly from school shall develop a system of communication with the child's school teacher.

Activities that have gone on during the day may be very important in anticipating and understanding after-school behavior.

2.2 Supervision

PR28. Facilities shall maintain supervision of children at all times as specified in *Supervision Policy,* on p. 272.

For additional information on supervision, see standard FA141 in chapter 5 on p. 168 on children using toilet training equipment and standard FA186 in chapter 5 on p. 176 on children sleeping on futons.

2.3 Field Trips

PR29. An adult holding a valid pediatric first aid certificate (see *First Aid and CPR,* on p. 22) shall accompany children at all times for field trips and out-of-facility activities, including during transportation. The facility's emergency plan (see *Emergency Plan,* on p. 280) shall be reviewed and understood by the adult chaperone to ensure that policies and procedures are followed in the event of an emergency. Child: staff ratios shall be maintained as specified in chapter 1.1.

Injuries are more likely to occur when a child's surroundings change or when there is a change in routine. Dispersed activities outside the facility may have the potential for increasing a child's risk of injury. When children are excited or busy playing in unfamiliar areas, they are likely to forget safety measures unless they are supervised at all times.

PR30. First aid kits shall be taken on field trips as specified in standard FA116 in chapter 5 on p. 161.

For additional information on field trips, see also Appendix X, on p. 389, and standard etc. in Appendix C, on p. 330, for information on written authorization and records.

2.4 Discipline

PR31. Discipline shall include positive guidance, redirection, and the setting of clear-cut limits that foster the child's ability to become self-disciplined. Disciplinary meas-

The word *discipline* has fallen into ill repute. It has respectable origins in a Latin root that establishes its connection with learning and education. It still retains its connections with edu-

Discipline should be an ongoing process to help children develop inner control so that they can manage their own behavior in a socially approved manner. Positive discipline

STANDARDS

ures shall be clear and understandable to the child, shall be consistent, and shall be explained to the child before and at the time of any disciplinary action.

PR32. Caregivers shall guide the child to develop self-control and orderly conduct in his/her relationships with peers and adults. Caregivers shall show children positive alternatives rather than just telling children "no." Good behavior shall be rewarded. Caregivers shall work with children without recourse to physical punishment or abusive language.

PR33. The facility shall use the teaching method described in standard PR32 immediately when it is important to show that aggressive physical behavior toward staff or children is unacceptable. Caregivers shall intervene immediately when children become physically aggressive.

PR34. Disciplinary practices established by the facility shall be designed to encourage the child to be fair, to respect property, and to assume personal responsibility and responsibility for others.

RATIONALE

cation in the dictionary definition—"training that develops self-control, character, or orderliness and efficiency"—but common usage has corrupted the word so that *discipline* today is synonymous with punishment, most particularly corporal punishment.[29]

The word *discipline* should be restored to its ancient and honorable sense. When employed in the context of child-rearing, it should imply education of character. In discussing methods of discipline, we should then hew closely to the real significance of this term and speak of those methods that instruct, making learning possible.

Children have to be given understandable guidelines for their behavior if they are to develop internal control of their actions. The aim is to develop personal standards in self-discipline, not to enforce a set of institutional rules.

Children in centers in the United States have demonstrated more aggressive behavior than children reared at home or children in centers in other countries. Children will mimic adult behavior; adults who demonstrate loud or violent behavior will serve as models for children.[30]

Caregiver intervention protects children and encourages more acceptable behavior of children.

To foster social development, a facility should have a clearly defined code of behavior and a disciplinary policy to support it.

Behavioral goals and disciplinary methods established for the facility should be explained to new caregivers and to parents, because not everyone shares the same opinion about what is "right." It is important for staff members to be consistent in their approach, and the best results are achieved with family cooperation.

COMMENTS

may include brief, supervised separation from the group, or withdrawal of special privileges, such as play time with other children. Logical consequences of an action (e.g., not being able to play in the sandbox for a time if one throws sand) are effective methods of positive discipline.

The following publications provide further information on discipline:

The Magic Years by Selma H. Fraiberg, published by Charles Scribner's Sons, 1959; pages 244-250.

Health in Day Care: A Manual for Health Professionals. To order, write to

American Academy of Pediatrics
141 Northwest Point Blvd.
P.O. Box 927
Elk Grove Village, IL 60009-0927

Children could assist in the rule-making to develop this sense of responsibility.

STANDARDS

PR35. The following behavior shall be prohibited in all child care settings and by all caregivers:
a) Corporal punishment, including hitting, spanking, beating, shaking, pinching, and other measures that produce physical pain.
b) Withdrawal or the threat of withdrawal of food, rest, or bathroom opportunities.
c) Abusive or profane language.
d) Any form of public or private humiliation, including threats of physical punishment.
e) Any form of emotional abuse, including rejecting, terrorizing, ignoring, isolating, or corrupting a child.

PR36. Children shall not be physically restrained except as necessary to ensure their own safety or that of others, and then only for as long as is necessary for control of the situation. Children shall not be given medicines or drugs that will affect their behavior except as prescribed by their health care provider and with specific written instructions from their health care provider for the use of the medicine (see *Medications*, on p. 88).

PR37. "Time out" that enables the child to regain control of himself or herself and that keeps the child in visual contact with a caregiver shall be used selectively, taking into account the child's developmental stage and the usefulness of "time out" for the particular child.

For additional requirements related to discipline, see also *Management Plan and Statement of Services*, on p. 271,

RATIONALE

Child care administrators and caregivers can facilitate good behavior by creating an environment responsive to the children's needs. A good "fit" between the temperament of the caregiver and the child always helps.[25]

Corporal punishment may be physical abuse or may become abusive very easily. Emotional abuse can be extremely harmful to children, but, unlike physical or sexual abuse, it is not adequately defined in most state child abuse reporting laws. Corporal punishment is clearly prohibited in small family-child-care homes in 32 states, and is prohibited in centers in 39 states.[31] Research links corporal punishment with negative effects such as later criminal behavior and impairment of learning.[31]

Primary factors supporting the prohibition of certain methods of punishment include current child development theory and practice, legal aspects (namely that a caregiver is not in an *in loco parentis* relationship with the child), and increasing liability suits.

The AAP is opposed to the use of corporal punishment.[32] Physicians, educators, and caregivers should neither inflict nor sanction corporal punishment.[33]

Undue restraint can be abusive, as can the use of drugs to control children's behavior.

See rationale for standard PR31 on p. 52.

COMMENTS

Examples of appropriate alternatives to corporal punishment for infants and toddlers include brief verbal expressions of disapproval; for preschoolers, "time out" (i.e., out-of-group activity) under adult supervision; for school-age children, denial of privileges.

on signed parent agreements, *Discipline Policy*, on p. 272, on dealing with acts of aggression and fighting by children, *Posting Documents*, on p. 296, on posting discipline policies, and *Child Abuse and Neglect*, on p. 93.

2.5 Parent Relationships

GENERAL

PR38. All aspects of child care programs shall be designed to facilitate parental input and involvement.

Research, practice, and accumulated wisdom attest to the crucially important influence on the development of the infant and young child of the child's relationship with those closest to him/her.

The child's experience in child care will be most beneficial when his/her parents and caregivers can develop feelings of mutual respect and trust. In such a situation the child feels a continuity of affection and concern, which facilitates the child's adjustment to separation and his/her use of the facility. For the infant and young child, separation from those whom he/she loves and on whom he/she is dependent is an ongoing source of stress. Of the various programmatic elements in the facility that can help to alleviate that stress, by far the most important is the comfort created by the fact that his/her parents and caregivers know the child and his/her needs and wishes very well, are in contact with each other, and can respond in ways that enable the child to deal with separation experiences. The encouragement and involvement of parents in the social and cognitive leaps of preschoolers provide parents with the confidence vital for their sense of competence. The parent/caregiver partnership models a positive adult endeavor for the school-age child and demonstrates a mutual concern for the child's well-being. [12, 34-46]

PR39. Information about the child's daily needs and activities shall be shared with parents on a daily informal basis.

See rationale for standard PR38.

STANDARDS	RATIONALE	COMMENTS

PR40. Consenting parents shall be given a list of names and phone numbers of other (consenting) parents whose children attend the same facility. The list shall include an annotation encouraging parents whose children attend the same facility to communicate with one another about the service. The list shall be updated at least annually.

If parents communicate with each other about a caregiver, patterns of action that may be associated with abuse can be identified. Encouraging parents' communication is simple, inexpensive, and beneficial.

PR41. Caregivers shall inform all parents that they may visit the site at any time when their child is there, and that they will be admitted immediately without delay. This open-door policy shall be part of the "admission agreement" (see *Management Plan and Statement of Services*, on p. 271) or other contract between the parent and the caregiver.

This provision may be the single most important method for preventing the abuse of children in child care. Requiring unrestricted access of parents to their children is essential to preventing the abuse of children in child care.[25] When access is restricted, areas observable by the parents may not reflect the care the children actually receive.

See also rationale for standard PR38.

The caregiver needs to know how to handle an unstable (e.g., intoxicated) parent who wants admittance but whose behavior poses a risk to the children.

Parents can be interviewed to see if the open-door policy is enthusiastically implemented.

For additional information on general parent relationships, see also standard PR4 on p. 46 on primary language of the parents.

REGULAR COMMUNICATION

PR42. Planned communication (e.g., parent conferences) shall be scheduled with at least one parent of every child in care to review the child's development and adjustment to care; to reach agreement on appropriate, nonviolent disciplinary measures; and to discuss specific health issues and such concerns as persistent behavior problems, developmental delays, special needs, overweight, underweight, or eating or sleeping problems. (See *Child Health Services*, on p. 276, on health assessment and standard HP5 in chapter 3 on p. 66 on nutrition assessment and follow-up.) At these planned communications, the child's medical report (item B in Appendix C on p. 331) and the health record (item F in Appendix C on p. 335) shall be reviewed by a staff member with the parent to identify medical and developmental issues that require follow-up or adjustment of the facility. Each review shall be documented by the signature of the parent and staff reviewer in the child's facility health record (see item F in Appendix C on

Both parents and caregivers should be aware of, and should have arrived at an agreement on, each other's beliefs and knowledge about how to deal with children.

Reviewing the health record with parents ensures correct information and can be a valuable teaching and motivational tool.[47] It can also be a staff learning experience, through insight gained from parents on a child's special circumstances.

A health history is the basis for meeting the child's health, mental, and social needs in the child care setting.[25] Review of the health record can be a valuable educational tool for parents, through better understanding of the medical report and immunization requirements.[25, 47]

A goal of out-of-home care of infants and children is to identify parents in need of instruction so preventive health/nutrition care can be provided at a critical time during the child's growth and development.

Follow-up on needed intervention is increased when an understanding of the need and motivation for the intervention has been achieved through personal contact.

A health history is most useful if the health advocate (see *Qualifications of Health Advocates*, on p. 13) personally reviews the records and updates the parent. A health history ensures that all information needed to care for the child is available to appropriate staff. Special instructions, such as diet, can be copied for use on a daily basis.

p. 335). These planned communications shall be as follows:
a) As part of the intake process.
b) At each health update interval as follows:
  1) Every 6 months for children under 6;
  2) Every year for children over 6.
c) Whenever new information is added to the child's facility health record.

Notes about these planned communications shall be maintained in each child's record at the facility and shall be available for review. (See item F in Appendix C on p. 335.)

It is in the child's best interest that staff communicate with parents about the child's needs and progress. Parent support groups and parent involvement at every level of facility planning and delivery are usually beneficial to the children, parents, and staff of the facility.

Communication among parents whose children attend the same facility helps the parents to share useful information and to be mutually supportive.

Compliance can be assessed by reviewing records of these planned communications.

PR43. The facility shall assign a specific staff member to each parent to ensure contact between the designated staff member and parent that may take place at the beginning and end of the day or when a parent can drop in. The contact shall consist of
a) Discussions between the parent and staff member regarding observations about the child.
b) Providing an opportunity for the parents to observe the child's playmates and surroundings.

For additional information on regular communication, see also standard AD54 in chapter 8 on p. 287 on transition contacts with parents.

A designated staff member with health training is helpful for parent teaching through development of a personal interest in the child and an ongoing relationship with the parent(s).[48, 49] A plan for personal contact and documentation of a designated staff person will ensure that specific attempts are made to communicate directly with families on health-related matters.

A plan for personal contact with parents should be made, even though such contact may not be possible on a daily basis.

Compliance can be documented by spot observations or self-reporting.

In larger facilities, this designated staff person may be the "health advocate" (See *Qualifications of Health Advocates*, on p. 13.)

LOG FOR INFANTS, TODDLERS, AND PRESCHOOLERS

PR44. For infants, toddlers, and preschoolers, there shall be a method for parents and staff to share observations, concerns, and comments, such as a daily log or notebook entry.

Notebooks can substitute, in part, for direct parent contact, when the latter is not possible.[25]
a) They can also be an effective means for parents to express their concerns and wishes when they might feel intimidated in a face-to-face "conference" setting.
b) They can be educational for parents by pointing out concerns, or need for special considerations in the child care setting, and by including health information or resources as appropriate.

Alternative methods (e.g., regular phone contact, daily face-to-face conversation) may be recommended and more effective for parents or caregivers who have difficulty with written communication.

The daily log is maintained by staff at the facility for review by staff and parents. The notebook is maintained by staff and parents and is carried to and from the facility by the parent.

STANDARDS	RATIONALE	COMMENTS

PARENTAL INVOLVEMENT

PR45. Each caregiver shall, at least twice a year (or, at a parent's request, more often), seek the views of parents of the children cared for by the caregiver about the strengths and needs of the facility.

This standard strengthens both parent and caregiver recognition that parents have essential rights in helping to shape the kind of child care service their children receive.

Small and large family home caregivers should have group meetings of all parents once or twice a year.

This standard avoids mention of procedures inappropriate to small family-child-care, as it does not require any explicit mechanism (e.g., a parent advisory council) for obtaining or offering parental input.

Individual or group meetings with parents would suffice to meet this standard.

Seeking consumer input is a cornerstone of facility planning and evaluation.

PR46. There shall be an open-door policy whereby parents are welcomed and encouraged to speak freely to administrators and caregivers about concerns and suggestions.

See rationale for standard PR45.

Parents who use child care services should be regarded as active participants and partners in facilities that should meet their needs as well as their children's.

Compliance can be measured by interviewing parents and staff.

PR47. Arrangements shall be made for joint resolution with parents of any problems that may arise. The arrangements for the resolutions shall be documented. In centers, mechanisms for ad hoc meetings between staff and groups of parents shall be developed.

Coordination between the facility and the parents is essential to promote their respective child care roles and to avoid value confusion or conflicts.

In addition to routine meetings, special meetings can deal with crises and special problems.

This ad hoc group could identify facility needs, assist in developing resources, and recommend facility and policy changes to the governing body (see *Identifiable Governing Body/Accountable Individual*, on p. 269.

It is most helpful to document the proceedings of these meetings to facilitate future communications and to ensure continuity of service delivery.

There could be facility-sponsored activities outside facility hours.

PR48. Parental participation in the process of evaluating the child and making decisions about services shall be required by the facility and shall be documented. Parents shall be explicitly invited to participate in all such decision-making activities and their presence at these meetings, or invitations to attend, shall be documented in writing.

Parental observations and reports about the child and their expectations for the child, as well as the family's need for child care services, must be recognized in order to provide services effectively.

A marked discrepancy between professional and parental observations of or expectations for a child necessitates further discussion and development of a consensus on a plan of action.

Parental participation in the planning of the developmental and educational program for the child should be integral to the process of evaluation by professionals and in the formulation of any plans for the child.

STANDARDS	RATIONALE	COMMENTS

PR49. Parental participation shall include caregivers' learning about parental expectations and goals and integrating this information into the child's care.

See comment for standard PR48.

PR50. When an assessment of a child is conducted at the facility, the parents shall be informed of the results and given an opportunity to discuss them and present alternative perspectives. The exchange shall be documented.

Parents need to have accurate information about their children.

An evaluation of a child is completed only when the information has been discussed with the parent.

Results must be sensitively and honestly explained to parents without using technical jargon.[50]

Parents need to be included in the process of shaping decisions about their children. They have both the motive and the legal right to be included in the decision-making process and to seek other opinions.

Parents' input should be considered by those conducting an evaluation and when subsequently discussing the findings with the family. A second independent opinion can also be offered to the family to confirm the original evaluation, though extensive "shopping" for a more desirable or favorable opinion should be discouraged.

For additional information on parental involvement, see also standard AD29 in chapter 8 on p. 280, standard ST25 in chapter 1 on p. 13, and *Child Abuse and Neglect*, on p. 93 on parent involvement and communication. See also *Parental Participation*, on p. 241, and *The Informing Process*, on p. 242 on communication and participation of parents of children with special needs.

HEALTH INFORMATION SHARING

PR51. The facility shall ask parents to share information regarding the child's health status with a caregiver, especially information about the child's health since the last attendance in the facility.

Admission of children without this information will leave the facility unprepared to deal with the daily and emergent health needs of the child as well as those of other children and staff if there is a question of communicability of disease.

Parents may balk at providing this information; if so, they should be invited to view this exchange of information as an opportunity to express their own concerns about the facility.

USE OF COMMUNITY HEALTH RESOURCES

PR52. The facility shall help families who have no provider of health care to locate such a resource. (See also standard AD24 in chapter 8 on p. 278 on the family's health care provider.)

Primary care and preventive health services for children will assist their healthy growth and development and can identify problems early for intervention.

Linking families to the health care system (a well-child clinic, public health department, private physician, etc.) is a primary prevention goal. As a last resort, the family should know what emergency room is closest to their home. Emergency rooms are not designed to provide primary, preventive health care for children.

PR53. The center shall make available to parents and staff information about human service resources in the community.

In order for the facility to have as comprehensive a program as possible to meet the individual needs of the families, community resources need to be tapped.

Local resource and referral agencies, mental health services, social services, community health centers, hospitals, private physicians, public health nurses, Head Start, clinic groups, the American Red Cross, and county extension services are but a few examples of potential resources.

Parents and caregivers will be more aware of these community resources when the center calls their attention to them, for example, by providing resource directories and by inviting personnel from community agencies to participate in staff meetings, parent meetings, and "open houses."

Potential barriers to the use of community resources are the lack of training of health care providers in working with facilities, the frequent requirement that a parent accompany a child using these resources, and the lack of coordination of resources.

2.6 Health Education

HEALTH EDUCATION FOR CHILDREN

PR54. Caregivers shall talk about healthful behaviors while carrying out routine daily activities. Activities shall be accompanied by words of encouragement and praise for achievement.

This is an important way to demonstrate and reinforce health behaviors of both caregivers and children.

Caregivers are important in the lives of the young children in care. They should be educated and supported to be able to interact at optimum levels with children in their care.

Compliance shall be documented by observation.

PR55. Centers and school-age child care facilities shall use age-appropriate health education materials in the children's projects, which, when taken home, will educate parents as well as the children.

Messages conveyed in children's artwork have been shown to be an effective way to provide educational materials that parents "notice."[51]

PR56. All health education activities shall be geared to the developmental age of the child and shall take into account individual personalities and interests.

Young children learn better through experiencing an activity and observing behavior rather than through didactic training.[52] There may be a reciprocal relationship between

An extensive education program to make such experiential learning possible must be supported by strong community resources—in the form of both consultation and materials learning and play, so that play experiences are closely related to learning.[16]

from such sources as the health department, nutrition councils, and so forth. Suggestions for topics and methods of presentation are widely available; see, for example, Georgetown University's *Health in Day Care: A Manual for Day Care Providers*. To order this publication, write to

Georgetown University Child Development Center
3800 Reservoir Road, N.W.
Washington, DC 20007

PR57. Health education shall include physical, oral, mental, and social health and shall be integrated daily in the program of activities. See the content in standard APP10 in Appendix E, on p. 338. (See also *Program of Activities*, on p. 286.)

For young children, health and education are inseparable. Children learn about health and safety by experiencing risk taking and risk control fostered by adults. Education to promote healthy behaviors should be integrated whenever opportunities for learning occur. Health education should be seen not as a structured curriculum but as a daily component of the planned program that is part of child development.

Caregivers can cover physical, oral, mental, and social health on an informal basis (see standard PR54).

PR58. The facility shall prepare caregivers to discuss with the children anatomical facts related to gender identity and sexual differences.

Open discussions among adults concerning childhood sexuality increase their comfort with the subject. The adults' comfort may reduce children's anxiety about sexuality.

Developing a common approach to matters involving sexuality and gender identity is not always easy because the views of facility administrators, caregivers, parents, and community leaders do not always coincide.[53]

PR59. The facility shall require all staff members to model healthy behaviors and attitudes in their contacts with children in the facility, including eating nutritious foods (see *Requirements for Special Groups or Ages of Children*, on p. 47) and complying with "No Smoking" policies (see *Smoking and Prohibited Substances*, on p. 98) and handwashing protocols (see *Hygiene*, on p. 72).

Modeling is a most effective way of confirming a behavior as one to be imitated.

Modeling of healthy behavior and attitudes can be specified in the plan as compliance with "No Smoking" policies, handwashing protocols, and so forth.

For additional information on health education for children, see also Appendix C, on p. 330.

HEALTH EDUCATION FOR STAFF

PR60. Health education shall include physical, oral, mental, and social health. See the content in standard APP9 in Appendix E on p. 338.

See rationales for standards PR56 and PR57.

STANDARDS	RATIONALE	COMMENTS

For additional information on health education for staff, see also *Training*, on p. 18, for a comprehensive description of staff training topics.

HEALTH EDUCATION FOR PARENTS

PR61. Parents shall be given opportunities to observe staff modeling of healthy behavior and child development facilitation and have opportunities to both ask questions and describe how effective the modeling has been. This also applies to school-age child care facilities.

Modeling can be an effective educational tool.[49]

By providing a one-way observation area or other opportunities for parents to learn by example, the facility can avoid intimidating parents.

PR62. The facility shall schedule regular health education programs for parents designed to meet the unique characteristics of the enrolled families. These programs may be in the form of "open house" meetings with guest speakers or opportunities for discussion, newsletters, etc.

If done well, didactic teaching can be effective for educating parents. If not done well, there is a danger of demeaning parents and making them feel less, rather than more, capable.[49, 54]

Even small family-child-care homes can plan for these meetings. Frequently, those parents who might benefit most may not attend. There are severe time constraints on many families that preclude their participation.

Community resources that may provide help with these programs include the Women, Infants and Children (WIC) Supplemental Food Program; medical and dental societies; departments of social services; mental health, drug, and alcohol programs; child development specialists; public health departments; and Visiting Nurse Associations.

PR63. The content of a parent education plan shall be individualized to meet each parent's and/or child's needs. See the content in standard APP10 in Appendix E on p. 338.

Individualized content and approach are needed for successful intervention.

Parent attitudes, beliefs, fears, and educational and socioeconomic levels all need to be given consideration in planning and conducting parent education.[49]

Knowing the family will help the health advocate (see *Qualifications of Health Advocates*, on p. 13) to determine content and method of the parent education plan.

Specific attention should be paid to the parents' need for support and consultation or help with resources for their own problems. If a referral is made or resource suggested to the parent, this should be documented in the child's record. Specifics of what the parent shared need not be recorded.

For additional information on health education for parents, see also standard PR43, on p. 57 on parent communication; standard PR55, on p. 60 on parent health education; and *Technical Assistance from the Licensing Agency,* on p. 313.

References

1. Constantine LL, Martinson FM. *Children and Sex: New Findings, New Perspectives.* Boston, Mass: Little, Brown, and Co; 1981.

2. *Head Start Program Performance Standards.* Washington, DC: DHHS, Head Start Bureau; 1984.

3. Murphy LB. *The Widening World of Childhood: Path Toward Mastery.* New York, NY: Basic Books; 1962.

4. Ramey CT, Finklestein NW. Contingent stimulation and infant competence. *J Pediatr Psychol.* 1978; 3:89–96.

5. Ramsey PG. Multicultural education in early childhood. *Young Children.* 1982;38(2):13–24.

6. Saracho O, Spodek B, eds. Understanding the multicultural experience in early childhood education. *Children's Environmental Quarterly.* 1983;1–2.

7. Zigler E, Hall NW. Day care and its effect on children: an overview for pediatric health professionals. *J Dev & Behav Pediatr.* 1988;9:38–46.

8. Provence S, Lipton R. *Infants in Institutions.* New Haven, Conn: Yale University Press; 1962.

9. Gonzalez MJ, Eyer EW. *Infancy and Caregiving.* Palo Alto, Calif: Mayfield Pub Co; 1980.

10. Cazden C, ed. *Language in Early Childhood Education.* Washington DC: National Association for the Education of Young Children; 1981.

11. Reilly AB. *The Communication Game: Perspectives on the Development of Speech, Language and Non-Verbal Communication Skills.* Piscataway, NJ: Johnson and Johnson Co; 1980.

12. Provence S, Naylor A, Patterson J. *The Challenge of Daycare.* New Haven, Conn: Yale University Press; 1977.

13. Murphy LB. Coping, vulnerability and resilience in childhood. In: Coehlo GV, Humburg DA, Adams JE, eds. *Coping and Adaptation.* New York, NY: Basic Books; 1974.

14 Murphy LB, Moriarty AE. *Vulnerability, Coping and Growth.* New Haven, Conn: Yale University Press; 1976.

15. Welles A, Ricciuti H. *A Good Beginning for Babies: Guidelines for Group Care.* Washington, DC: National Association for the Education of Young Children; 1975.

16. Chance P. *Learning Through Play.* New Brunswick, NJ: The Company; 1979.

17. Biber B, Shapiro E, Wickens D. *Promoting Cognitive Growth: A Developmental Interaction Point of View.* Washington DC: National Association for the Education of Young Children; 1977.

18. Greenman J. *Caring Spaces, Learning Places.* New York, NY: Columbia University Press; 1984.

19. Biber B. *Early Education and Psychological Development.* New Haven, Conn: Yale University Press; 1984.

20. Cohen D, Stern V, Balaban N. *Observing and Recording the Behavior of Young Children.* New York, NY: New York Teachers, College Press, Columbia University; 1983.

21. Freud A. *Normality and Pathology in Childhood.* New York, NY: International Universities Press; 1965.

22. Comer JP, Poussaint AF. *Black Child Care.* New York, NY: Simon and Schuster; 1975.

23. Weisberger E. *When Your Child Needs You.* Bethesda, Md: Adler and Adler; 1987.

24. Spock B. *Baby and Child Care.* 16th ed. New York, NY: EP Dutton; 1985.

25. Deitch S, ed. *Health in Day Care: A Manual for Health Professionals.* Elk Grove Village, Ill: American Academy of Pediatrics; 1987.

26. Dittman L. *Children in Day Care With Focus on Health.* Washington, DC: Children's Bureau No. 444; 1967.

27. Baden R, Genser RA, Levine JA, et al. *School-Age Child Care: An Action Manual.* Medfield, Mass: Auburn House Pub. Co; 1982:380–424.

28. School Age Child Care Technical Assistance Paper (2). Boston, Mass: Massachusetts Office for Children; 1988.

29. Fraiberg SH. *The Magic Years.* New York, NY: Charles Scribner's Sons; 1959:244–250.

30. Haskins, R. Public school aggression among children with varying day care experience. *Child Dev.* 1985; 56:669–703.

31. Morgan G. *The National State of Child Care Regulation 1986.* Boston, Mass: Work/Family Directions Inc.; 1987.

32. American Academy of Pediatrics Committee on School Health. Corporal punishment in schools. *Pediatrics.* 1984;73:258.

33. Christopherson E. The pediatrician and parental discipline. *Pediatrics.* 1980;66:641–642.

34. Dittmann L. *The Infants We Care For.* Washington, DC: National Association for the Education of Young Children; 1984.

35. Weissbourd B. Supporting parents as people. In: Weisbourd B, Musick J, eds. *Infants: Their Social Environments.* Washington, DC: National Association for the Education of Young Children; 1981.

36. Croft DJ. *Parents and Teachers: A Resource Book for Home, School and Community Relations.* Belmont, Calif: Wadsworth; 1979.

37. Gazda GM. *Human Relations Development: A Manual for Educators.* Boston, Mass: Allyn & Bacon; 1973.

38. Honig A. Parent involvement in early childhood education. In: Spodek B, ed. *Handbook of Research in Early Childhood Education.* New York, NY: Free Press; 1982.

39. Katz L. Mothering and teaching: some significant distinctions. In: Katz L, ed. *Current Topics in Early Childhood Education.* Norwood, NJ: Ablex; 1980; 3:47–64.

40. Lightfoot S. *Worlds Apart: Relationships Between Families and Schools.* New York, NY: Basic Books; 1978.

41. Becher RM. Parent involvement and reading achievement: a review of research. *Childhood Education.* 1985; 62(1):44–50.

42. Bjorklund G, Burger C. Making conferences work for parents, teachers, and children. *Young Children.* 1987; 42(2):26–31.

43. Hymes JL Jr. *Effective Home-School Relations.* Carmel, Calif: Hacienda Press; 1975.

44. Lyons P, Robbins A, Smith A. *Involving Parents: A Handbook for Participation in Schools.* Ypsilanti, Mich: High Scope; 1983.

45. Powell DR. Research in review: parent education and support programs. *Young Children.* 1986:41(3):47–53.

46. Readdick CA, Golbeck SL, Klein EL, et al. The child-parent-teacher conference: a setting for child development. *Young Children.* 1984: 39(5):67–73.

47. Aronson SS, Aiken LS. Compliance of child care programs with health and safety standards: impact of program evaluation and advocate training. *Pediatrics.* 1980;65:318–325.

48. Kendrick AS, Kaufmann R, Messenger KP, eds. *Healthy Young Children: A Manual for Programs.* Washington, DC: National Association for the Education of Young Children; 1991.

49. Yogman M. Child care as a setting for parent education. Group Care for Young Children. Pediatric Round Table 12. Skillman, NJ: Johnson & Johnson; 1986.

50. Kaminer R, Cohen HJ. Informing parents about their child's mental retardation: *Contemp Pediatr.* 1988;5:39–49.

51. Personal communication, Nadina Riggsbee, Drowning Prevention Foundation, P.O. Box 202, Alamo, CA 94507.

52. *Health in Day Care.* Washington, DC: Georgetown University; 1987.

53. Gordon S, Gordon J. *Raising a Child Conservatively in a Sexually Permissive World.* New York, NY: Simon and Schuster; 1983: chaps 3 and 4.

54. Powell S. The interpersonal relationship between parents and caregivers in day care settings. *Amer J Orthopsychol.* 1978;48:680–689.

CHAPTER 3

Program: Health Protection and Promotion

CHAPTER 3
PROGRAM: HEALTH PROTECTION AND PROMOTION

3.1 Health Protection and Health Promotion in All Child Care

STANDARDS

RATIONALE

COMMENTS

DAILY HEALTH ASSESSMENT

HP1. Every day, upon entry or as soon as possible after entry, and during continual observation of the child at play, a health assessment of each child shall be performed by a trained staff member. The assessment shall include the following:

a) Changes in behavior or appearance from those observed during the previous day's attendance.

b) Skin rashes, itchy skin, or itchy scalp.

c) Increase in body temperature, determined by taking the child's temperature, if there is a change in the child's behavior or appearance.

d) Complaints of pain or of not feeling well.

Daily intake procedures to appraise each child's health and ascertain recent illness in the child and family reduce the acquisition and transmission of communicable diseases in child care settings.

This assessment should be performed in a manner that is comfortable to the child and respects the child's body and feelings.

The health consultant (see *Health Consultants,* on p. 33) should train the caregiver(s) in conducting a health assessment, preferably using a checklist for assessment. (See Appendix G, on p. 341 for a sample symptom record.)

A sample symptom record is also provided in *Healthy Young Children.* To obtain this publication, contact

> National Association for the
> Education of Young Children
> 1834 Connecticut Avenue, N.W.
> Washington, DC 20009

HP2. Every day, or as often as possible, and during observation of the child at play, the small family home caregiver shall conduct a health assessment of each child. The assessment shall include the items specified in standard HP1.

See rationale for standard HP1.

See comment for standard HP1.

HP3. Information to complete the assessment may be obtained by direct personal observation of the child, by querying the parent or legal guardian, and/or by conversation with the child.

Assessment by querying the parent should take place at the time of transfer of care of the child from the parent to the facility. If this takes place outside the center (e.g., when the child is put on a bus or in a car pool), some means of communication about the child's status must be used. Examples of these means might include written notes, checklists, conversations held by the driver with the parent, and daily log books.

---

 applies to a small family-child-care home    applies to a large family-child-care home   applies to a center.
If no symbol appears, the standard applies to all three.

HP4. The written record of concerns identified during the daily health assessment shall be kept for at least 3 weeks by the facility.

The vast majority of communicable diseases of concern in child care have incubation periods of less than 21 days.

For additional information on daily health assessment, see also *Incidence Logs of Illness, Injury, and Other Problems*, on p. 290, and Appendix C, on p. 330.

GROWTH DATA

HP5. The facility shall require that the children have routine health supervision that includes documentation of height and weight assessment and head circumference (if less than 24 months old) according to the standards of the American Academy of Pediatrics (see Appendix F, on p. 340). (See standards AD25, on p. 278 and PR42, on p. 56 follow-up for nutrition and growth problems and nutrition assessment data and item B(3) on growth assessment in Appendix C, on p. 331.

The plotting of height and weight measurements by health care providers on a reference growth chart will show how the child is growing over time and how he/she compares with other children of the same chronological age and sex.[1, 2] Growth charts are based on data from national probability samples representative of children in the general population. Their use by health care providers will direct attention to unusual body size, which may be due to disease or poor nutrition that requires modification of feeding practices in the child care setting.[3, 4]

Some infants and toddlers identified as showing signs of neglect and failure to thrive due to lack of food or inconsistent feeding practices are enrolled in facilities for both promotional and preventive health services. Periodic height and weight measurements by a trained staff person are easily obtainable indicators of health status. The data could then be shared with the designated health care provider. Staff training on growth assessment can be provided by the health consultant (see *Health Consultants*, on p. 33).

SLEEP

HP6. The facility shall provide an opportunity for, but shall not require, sleep and rest. A regular rest period shall be made available for school-aged children, if desired by the child. For children unable to sleep, time and space shall be provided for quiet play.

Conditions conducive to sleep and rest for younger children include a consistent caregiver, a routine quiet place, and a regular time for rest.[5]

Most preschool children in all-day care benefit from scheduled periods of rest. This rest may take the form of actual napping, a quiet time, or a change of pace between activities. The times of naps will affect behavior at home.[6]

In the young infant, favorable conditions for sleep and rest include being dry, well-fed, and comfortable.

Board games and other forms of quiet play should be available in a school-age child care facility.

HP7. Children shall be supervised while sleeping as specified in *Supervision Policy*, on p. 272.

For additional information on sleep, see also *Supervision Policy*, on p. 272, *Sleeping*, on p. 175, on sleeping/napping bedding and equipment, and *Sanitation, Disinfection, and Maintenance of Bedding*, on p. 79.

STANDARDS	**RATIONALE**	**COMMENTS**

ORAL HEALTH

HP8. Children older than 2 years shall brush their teeth with fluoride toothpaste after each meal or snack. Children aged 4 years and older shall brush their own teeth, with direct supervision of the caregiver if necessary. Otherwise, the caregiver shall do it. The caregiver shall be knowledgeable about the correct brushing method. If children do their own brushing, the caregiver shall demonstrate step by step.

Regular toothbrushing with fluoride toothpaste is encouraged to reinforce oral health habits and prevent gingivitis and tooth decay.

Use a small dab of toothpaste (about the size of a pea) and rinse well. Flossing should be done only if necessary (e.g., if food is caught between the teeth). The children can also rinse and spit out after a snack if their teeth have already been brushed after a meal.

HP9. In facilities where toothbrushing is an activity, each child shall have a personally labeled toothbrush. Toothbrushes shall be replaced when bristles have lost their tone.

This standard prevents contamination, misuse, and injury. Toothbrushes become contaminated with infectious agents from the mouth and must not be allowed to serve as a conduit of infection from one individual to another. Individually labeling the toothbrushes will prevent sharing of the same toothbrush among different children.

See *Supplies*, on p. 116.

HP10. Toothbrushes shall be stored so that they do not drip on other toothbrushes, and shall be separate from one another, bristles up exposed to the air to dry, and not in contact with any surface.

See rationale for standard HP9.

Storage of toothbrushes is a problem in some child care settings. Test tube racks, wall pockets, and so forth have been suggested.

HP11. All children 2 years of age or older shall receive oral health education and practice as a part of the daily facility activities. Oral health education shall include information on prevention of oral disease and promotion of oral health (toothbrushing [see standard HP10], flossing, water fluoridation, use of dietary fluoride supplements and dental sealants, regular dental visits, avoidance of tobacco, and a healthy diet). Oral health shall be included as a part of health education. (See *Health Education*, on p. 60.)

Studies have reported that the oral health of participants improved as a result of educational programs.[7, 8]

The following ages for education and preventive dental services are suggested:
Dental visits and fluoridation—all ages.
Topical fluorides—at first dental visit (3 years).
Dental sealants—generally at 6 or 7 years of age for permanent molars, and for primary molars if decay has started (seal undecayed molars or if grooves in teeth are deep).

Compliance with these activities would be facilitated by yearly staff training and oral health presentations to the children by local dental health professionals.

HP12. The cavity-causing effect of frequent exposure to food shall be counterbalanced by offering the children drinking water after snacks when brushing is not possible.

Rinsing with water helps to remove food particles from teeth and prevent cavities.

For additional information on oral health, see also chapter 8.2 on emergency plan and Appendix C on child records.

TOILETING, DIAPERING, AND TOILET TRAINING

HP13. Diapers worn by children shall be able to contain urine and stool and minimize fecal contamination of the children, caregivers, environmental surfaces, and objects of the child care setting. The diaper shall have an absorbent inner lining completely contained within an outer covering made of waterproof material that prevents the escape of feces and urine. The outer covering and inner lining shall be changed together at the same time as a unit and shall not be reused unless both are cleaned and disinfected.

Gastrointestinal disease caused by bacteria, viruses, and parasites and hepatitis A virus infection of the liver are spread from infected persons through fecal contamination of objects in the environment and hands of caregivers and children. Procedures that reduce fecal contamination, such as handwashing, proper personal hygiene, and fecal containment in diapered children, control the spread of these diseases.

Diapering practices that require increased manipulation of the diaper and waterproof covering, particularly reuse of the covering before it is cleaned and disinfected, provide increased opportunities for fecal contamination of the caregivers' hands, the child, and consequently, objects and surfaces in the environment. One study demonstrated that fecal contamination in the center environment was less when paper diapers were used than when cloth diapers worn with pull-on pants were used.[9] When clothes are worn over either paper[10] or cloth diapers with pull-on pants,[9] there is a reduction in contamination; in this case, the difference in contamination between cloth and paper diapers is not statistically significant.[9]

Diaper dermatitis occurs frequently in diapered children. Theoretically, diapering practices that reduce the frequency and severity of diaper dermatitis will result in reduced application of skin creams, ointments, and drug treatments, thereby decreasing the likelihood for fecal contamination of caregivers' hands. Most common diaper dermatitis represents an irritant contact dermatitis; the source of irritation is prolonged contact of the skin with urine, feces, or both.[11] The action of fecal digestive enzymes on urinary urea and the resulting production of ammonia make the diapered area more alkaline, which has been shown to damage skin.[12, 13] Damaged skin is more susceptible to other biological, chemical, and physical insults that can cause or aggravate

Four types of diapers or diapering systems are currently available: disposable paper diapers, reusable cloth diapers worn with pull-on pants, reusable cloth diapers worn with a modern front closure waterproof cover, and single unit reusable diaper systems with an inner cotton lining attached to an outer waterproof covering. Two types of diapers meet the physical requirements of the standard: modern disposable paper diapers with absorbent gelling material or carboxymethyl cellulose and single unit reusable diaper systems with an inner cotton lining attached to an outer waterproof covering. A third type, reusable cloth diapers worn with a modern front closure waterproof cover, meet the standard only: 1) if the cloth diaper and cover are removed simultaneously as a unit and are not removed as two separate pieces, and 2) if the cloth diaper and outer cover are not reused until both are cleaned and disinfected. Reusable cloth diapers worn either without a covering or with pull-on pants made of waterproof material do not meet the physical requirements of the standard. Whichever diapering system is used in the facility, it is recommended that clothes be worn over diapers while the child is in the facility. Rigorous protocols should be implemented for diaper handling and changing, personal hygiene, and environmental decontamination.

The use of modern disposable paper diapers with absorbent gelling material or carboxymethyl cellulose is associated with less fecal contamination of the child care environment than occurs when cloth diapers with pull-on pants made of waterproof material are used.[9] Therefore, reusable cloth diapers worn alone or worn with pull-on pants are not recommended in facilities.

While single unit reusable diaper systems with an inner cloth lining attached to an outer waterproof covering and reusable cloth diapers

STANDARDS

HP13 *continued.*

RATIONALE

diaper dermatitis.[11] Frequency and severity of diaper dermatitis are lower when diapers are changed more often, regardless of the diaper used.[14]

COMMENTS

worn with a modern front closure waterproof cover meet the physical criteria of this standard, if used as described, they have not been evaluated for their ability to reduce fecal contamination, or for their association with diaper dermatitis. Moreover, it has not been demonstrated that the waterproof covering materials remain waterproof with repeated cleaning and disinfecting. If these reusable diaper products are used in child care, the user should take care to determine the waterproof characteristics of the covering material at frequent intervals.

The use of modern disposable paper diapers with absorbent gelling material or carboxymethyl cellulose has been associated with less frequent and severe diaper dermatitis in some children than occurs when cloth diapers and pull-on pants made of a waterproof material are used.[14–18]

All major brands of disposable diapers contain absorbent gelling material. There may be one or two diaper marketers who make a disposable diaper without absorbent gelling material.

Concern has arisen over the potential risk for injury and disease associated with the use of disposable and other diapers. This includes flammability of the diaper, the potential for ingestion, the potential for insertion into body cavities*, and the potential for aspiration.** The possibility of creating a "hot house" effect or a culture medium for microbial growth also theoretically exists, but should be reduced by the recommended frequency of checking and changing the diaper (see standard HP14).

The stated purpose of these standards is health and safety in out-of-home child care settings. With respect to this particular standard, the reduction of contamination in facilities was identified as a significant objective by the Technical Panel on Prevention and Control of Infectious Diseases (see Introduction for a description of the Technical Panel). Issues not directly related to this objective or the purposes of this publication were therefore regarded as tangential and were not addressed in the Panel's

---

*Rimsza ME, Chun JJ. Vaginal discharge of "beads" and the new diapers. *Pediatr* 1988; 81:332.

**National Injury Information Clearinghouse. Reported incident file. Diapers, accident investigation. Printout of file. Washington, DC: US Consumer Product Safety Commission; Nov. 1985.

---

deliberations. In particular, the Panel did not consider the following concerns: (i) environmental impact of cloth and disposable diapers, which has fueled a controversy over their relative merits,[19] and (ii) potential for increased health risks for sanitation workers who work at landfills where disposable diapers are dumped.

For additional information on decreasing contamination when diapering, see also *Toileting, Diapering, and Toilet Training*, on p. 68. *Handwashing*, on p. 72; and *Sanitation, Disinfection, and Maintenance of Handwashing Sinks*, on p. 77.

HP14. Diapers shall be checked for wetness or feces at least hourly and whenever the child indicates discomfort or exhibits behavior that suggests a soiled or wet diaper, and shall be changed when found to be wet or soiled.

Frequency and severity of diaper dermatitis are lower when diapers are changed more often, regardless of the type of diaper used.[11]

See the rationale for standard HP13 for further information on diaper dermatitis.

HP15. Diaper changing procedures consistent with those recommended by the Centers for Disease Control in the publication *What to Do to Stop Disease in Child Day Care Centers* shall be posted in the changing area.

See rationale for standard HP14.

To obtain the publication *What to Do to Stop Disease in Child Day Care Centers,* contact

    Centers for Disease Control
    1600 Clifton Road, N.E.
    Atlanta, GA 30333

HP16. Children shall be diapered or have soiled underwear changed in the diaper-changing area. See *Diaper Changing Areas*, on p. 171.

The use of a separate area for diaper-changing prevents disease transmission.

HP17. Children shall be discouraged from remaining in or entering the diaper-changing area.

Children should be kept away from the area to avoid contact with waste containers and to prevent contamination.

HP18. Diapering shall not be conducted on surfaces used for other purposes.

This measure is to control and prevent the spread of disease and contamination.

HP19. If cloth diapers are used (see standard HP13 above), soiled cloth diapers and/or soiled training pants shall be stored in a labeled container with a tight-fitting lid provided by an accredited commercial diaper service (see standard HP27 on p. 72 of this chapter), or in a sealed plastic bag. The sealed plastic bag shall be sent home with the child at the end of the day. The containers or sealed diaper bags of soiled cloth diapers shall not be accessible to any child.

See rationale for standard HP18. This standard is also based on the accreditation standards of the Diaper Service Accreditation Council.[20]

STANDARDS	RATIONALE	COMMENTS

HP20. If cloth diapers are used (see standard HP13 above), soiled cloth diapers and/or soiled training pants shall never be rinsed. The fecal contents of cloth and disposable diapers may be placed in a toilet, but diapers shall not be rinsed in the toilet.

See rationale for standard HP24.

Disposing of the fecal contents in the toilet may reduce the load on the solid waste stream.

HP21. The child's perineal (urinary and anal) area shall be cleaned with disposable wipes

See rationale for standard HP18.

HP22. After removing a soiled diaper and before putting a fresh diaper on a child, staff members shall wipe their own hands with a premoistened towelette or a damp paper towel and dispose of it in a plastic bag or plastic-lined receptacle as specified in *Waste and Diaper Storage and Disposal*, on p. 154.

This measure is to control and prevent contamination.

HP23. The child's hands shall be washed after every diaper change regardless of the presence or absence of perianal fecal material or irritation.

Children's hands often stray into the diaper area (the area of the child's body covered by diaper) during the diapering process and can then transfer fecal organisms to the environment. Washing the child's hands will reduce the number or organisms carried into the environment in this way. Infectious organisms are present on the skin and diaper even though they are not seen. These organisms may be present from earlier diaper changes.

HP24. Changing tables shall be kept in good repair and shall be cleaned and disinfected after each use by cleaning to remove visible soil, followed by wiping with an approved disinfectant solution, whether or not disposable, nonabsorbent paper is used. If disposable, nonabsorbent paper is used, it shall be approved by the health department for this purpose and shall be discarded immediately after each diapering.

Many communicable diseases can be prevented through appropriate hygiene, sanitation, and disinfection methods. Bacterial cultures of environmental surfaces in facilities have demonstrated evidence of fecal contamination, which has been used to gauge the adequacy of sanitation, disinfection, and hygiene measures practiced at the facility.

HP25. Staff members shall wash their hands after each diaper change as specified in *Handwashing*, p. 72.

HP26. If disposable gloves are used, they must be discarded immediately and hands washed. (See *Prevention of Exposure to Blood*, p. 74.)

STANDARDS

HP27. If cloth diapers are used (see standard HP13 on p. 68), the diapers shall be cleaned and laundered/disinfected by a commercial diaper service accredited by the Diaper Service Accreditation Council.[20] If caregivers launder cloth diapers, they shall do so only while not caring for children and only in an environment accredited by the Diaper Service Accreditation Council[20] on or away from the facility.

HP28. Diapers shall be disposed of as specified in *Waste and Diaper Storage and Disposal*, on p. 154.

For additional information on toileting, diapering, and toilet training, see also *Diaper Changing Areas*, p. 171, on physical requirements and standard NU70, p. 130.

HYGIENE

Handwashing

HP29. Staff and children shall wash their hands at least at the following times, and whenever hands are contaminated with body fluids:
a) Before food preparation, handling, or serving.
b) After toileting or changing diapers.
c) After assisting a child with toilet use.
d) Before handling food.
e) Before any food service activity (including setting the table).
f) Before and after eating meals or snacks.
g) After handling pets or other animals.

RATIONALE

This standard provides for adequate supervision of children and prevents contamination of the environment.

Thorough handwashing with soap for at least 10 seconds using warm, running water, which lifts the organisms off the skin and allows them to be rinsed away, has been effective in preventing disease transmission.[21] Washing hands after eating is especially important for children (who eat with their hands) in order to decrease the amount of saliva (which may contain bacteria) on the hands.

Illnesses may be spread in a variety of ways: in human waste (urine, stool); in body fluids (saliva; nasal discharge; secretions from open injuries, cuts or skin sores; eye discharge; blood); by direct skin-to-skin contact; by touching an object that has germs on it; and in drops of water, such as those produced by sneezing and coughing, that travel through the air. Since many infected people carry communicable diseases without having symptoms and many are contagious before they experience a symptom, staff need to protect themselves and the children they serve by carrying out, on a routine basis, sanitation and disinfection procedures that approach

COMMENTS

To obtain *Standards for Accrediting Diaper Services,* by the Diaper Service Accreditation Council, contact

National Association of Diaper Services
2017 Walnut Street
Philadephia, PA 19103

STANDARDS	RATIONALE	COMMENTS

every potential illness-spreading condition in the same way.[6]

Animals, including pets, are a source of illness for people, and people may be a source of illness for animals.[22]

HP30. Children and staff shall wash and scrub their hands for at least 10 seconds with soap and warm running water.

See rationale for standard HP29.

Warm running water in sinks is optimal to promote handwashing.

Soap does not have to be antibacterial. Bar soap or liquid soap may be used by staff, as both are equally effective. However, liquid soap should be used by children, as they do not have the dexterity to handle a bar of soap. It is the physical action of handwashing, not the type of soap, that removes soil. Bar soap does not transmit bacteria.

HP31. The facility shall ensure that staff and children are instructed in, and monitored on, the use of running water, soap, and single-use or disposable towels in handwashing as specified in this chapter.

Education of staff regarding handwashing and other cleaning procedures can reduce the occurrence of illness in the group of children with whom they work.[23] Staff training and monitoring have been shown to reduce spread of infections of the intestine (often with diarrhea) or liver.[23-26] In a study of four centers, staff training in hygiene combined with close monitoring of staff compliance was associated with a significant decrease in infant-toddler diarrhea.[23] In another study, periodic evaluation of caregivers trained in hygiene was associated with significant improvement in the practices under study. Training combined with evaluation was associated with additional significant improvement.[24] In a study of 12 centers, continuous surveillance without training was associated with a significant decrease in diarrheal illness during the course of longitudinal study. One-time staff training without subsequent monitoring did not result in additional decreases.[25] A similar decline in diarrhea rates during the course of surveillance without training was observed in a longitudinal study of 60 centers.[26] These studies suggest that training combined with outside monitoring of child care practices can modify staff behavior as well as disease occurrence.

STANDARDS	RATIONALE	COMMENTS

HP32. Weekly monitoring by the center director shall ensure that handwashing and cleaning procedures are followed as specified in this chapter and in *Sanitation Plan*, on p. 283. (See also *Enteric (Diarrheal) and Hepatitis A Virus Infections*, on p. 214.

For additional information on handwashing, see *Sanitation Plan*, on p. 283, and *Handwashing Sinks*, on p. 77.

See rationale above.

Compliance with weekly monitoring should be measured by observations and interviewing of staff.

Cuts and Sores

HP33. Cuts or sores shall be covered whenever possible.

See rationale for standard HP 38, on p. 75.

It is not usually possible to cover lips and eyes effectively.

Nose-Blowing

HP34. Noses shall be blown or wiped with disposable, one-use tissues that are discarded in a plastic-lined and covered garbage container. Hands shall be washed after blowing as specified in *Handwashing*, on p. 72.

See rationale for HP33.

Prevention of Exposure to Blood

HP35. Staff shall adopt universal precautions as outlined in standard HP 38, on p. 75 below and as may be recommended by the Centers for Disease Control in the future to handle potential exposure to blood and blood-containing body fluids and injury discharges of all children in the setting.

Bacteria and viruses carried in the blood, such as hepatitis B virus, may pose a small but finite hazard in the child care setting.[27-38] In such settings, blood and direct blood-derived fluids (such as watery discharges from injuries) pose the highest potential risk, by virtue of containing the highest concentration of viruses. In addition, hepatitis B virus can survive in dried state in the environment for at least a week and perhaps even longer. Some other body fluids—such as saliva contaminated with blood or blood-associated fluids—may contain live virus (with hepatitis B virus) but at lower concentrations than are found in blood itself. Other body fluids, including urine and feces, do not pose a risk with these bloodborne diseases unless they are visibly contaminated with blood, although these fluids do pose a risk with other infectious diseases, and should be dealt with as described in *Hygiene*, on p. 72, and chapter 6, *Infectious Diseases,* on p. 207.

STANDARDS	RATIONALE	COMMENTS

Some children may unknowingly be infected with HIV or other infectious agents, such as hepatitis B virus; these agents may be present in blood or body fluids. Thus, staff in all facilities should adopt universal precautions for blood spills from all children[39] as described in standard HP38 below.

HP36. Handwashing after exposure to blood or blood-containing body fluids and tissue discharges as specified in *Handwashing*, p. 72, shall be observed.

See rationale for standard HP35.

HP37. Staff shall avoid contact with blood or blood-containing body fluids and tissue discharges. Gloves shall be worn if there is contact with blood or blood-containing body fluids or tissue discharges.

See rationale for standard HP35.

Either single-use disposable gloves or utility gloves should be used. Single-use disposable gloves should be used only once and then discarded immediately without being handled. If utility gloves are used, they should be cleaned after every use with soap and water and then dipped in the bleach solution (see "Disinfect" in the Glossary) up to the wrist; the gloves should then be taken off and hung to dry. The utility gloves themselves should be worn, not handled, during this cleaning and disinfecting procedure.

HP38. Spills of body fluids (i.e., urine, feces, blood, saliva, nasal discharge, eye discharge, and injury or tissue discharges) shall be cleaned up immediately, as follows:
a) For spills of vomitus, urine, and feces, floors, walls, bathrooms, table tops, toys, kitchen countertops, and diaper-changing tables shall be cleaned and disinfected.
b) For spills of blood or blood-containing body fluids and injury and tissue discharges, the area shall be cleaned and disinfected. Gloves shall be used in these situations unless the amount of blood or body fluid is so small that it can easily be contained by the material used for cleaning.
c) Persons involved in cleaning contaminated surfaces shall avoid exposure of open skin sores or mucous membranes to blood or blood-containing body fluids and injury or tissue discharges by using gloves to protect hands

Illnesses may be spread in a variety of ways, such as by coughing, sneezing, direct skin-to-skin contact, or touching an object or surface with germs on it. Infectious germs may be contained in human waste (urine, feces) and body fluids (saliva, nasal discharge, tissue and injury discharges, eye discharges, and blood). Since many infected people carry communicable diseases without having symptoms, and many are contagious before they experience a symptom, staff need to protect themselves and the children they serve by carrying out, on a routine basis, sanitation and disinfection procedures that approach every potential illness-spreading condition in the same way.

Education of staff regarding cleaning procedures can reduce the occurrence of illness in the group of children with whom they work.[23]

A solution of ¼ cup household liquid chlorine bleach in one gallon of tap

See comment in standard HP37 on gloves.

See also comment for standard HP63, on p. 80.

when cleaning contaminated surfaces.

d) Mops shall be cleaned, rinsed in sanitizing solution (see standard HP63, on p. 80), and then wrung as dry as possible and hung to dry.

e) Blood-contaminated material and diapers shall be disposed of in a plastic bag with a secure tie.

water prepared fresh daily (see "Disinfect" in the Glossary) is an effective surface disinfectant for environmental surfaces and other inanimate objects that have first been thoroughly cleaned of organic soil.[40]

Gloves are used primarily when people knowingly contact or suspect they may contact blood, blood-containing body fluids, or tissue or injury discharges. These fluids may contain the viruses that transmit HIV and hepatitis B.

See also rationale for standard HP38, on p. 75.

SANITATION, DISINFECTION, AND MAINTENANCE

HP39. The frequency of cleaning, sanitation, and disinfection in the facility shall be increased from baseline routine frequencies specified in *Maintenance for Safety*, p. 197, and *Hygiene*, p. 72, to the frequency specified by the local health department when necessary to control certain infectious diseases.

See rationale for standard HP38, on p. 75.

For additional information on sanitation, disinfection, and maintenance, see also *Interior Maintenance*, p. 197.

Sanitation, Disinfection, and Maintenance of Toilet Training Equipment, Toilets, and Bathrooms

HP40. Toilet rooms, flush toilets, toilet training equipment, and fixtures shall be cleaned and sanitized at least daily and when obviously soiled, and shall be in good repair.

See rationale for standard HP24, on p. 71.

Measure compliance by staff interviews and by observation of practice when a contamination of toilet rooms and equipment occurs.

HP41. If potty chairs are used (see standard FA146 in chapter 5, on p. 169), they shall be emptied into a toilet, cleaned in a utility sink, sanitized after each use, and stored in the bathroom.

Sanitary handling of potty chairs is very difficult.

See also rationale for standard HP24, on p. 71.

HP42. Utility gloves and equipment designated for cleaning and sanitizing toilet training equipment and flush toilets shall be used for each cleaning and shall not be used for other cleaning purposes.

Contamination of hands and equipment in the room has appeared to play a role in the transmission of disease.[41, 42]

STANDARDS	RATIONALE	COMMENTS

HP43. Disposable towels or clean reusable towels laundered between uses shall be used for cleaning. Disposable towels shall be sealed in a plastic bag and removed to outside garbage. Cloth towels shall be placed in a closed, foot operated receptacle until laundering

See rationale for standard HP24, on p. 71.

HP44. Toilet and bathroom odors shall be controlled by ventilation and sanitation. Chemical air fresheners shall not be used.

Chemical air fresheners may cause nausea or an allergic response in some children.

Ventilation and sanitation help control and prevent the spread of disease and contamination.

HP45. Waste receptacles in toilet rooms shall be kept clean and in good repair.

This practice prevents the spread of disease and filth.

For additional information on sanitation, disinfection, and maintenance of toilet training equipment, toilets, and bathrooms, see also *Toilets and Toilet Training Equipment*, on p. 168.

Sanitation, Disinfection, and Maintenance of Diaper-Changing Areas

See *Toileting, Diapering, and Toilet Training*, p. 68.

Sanitation, Disinfection, and Maintenance of Handwashing Sinks

HP46. Handwashing sinks shall be cleaned and sanitized at least daily and when soiled.

See rationale for standard HP45.

Sanitation, Disinfection, and Maintenance of Surfaces

HP47. Indoor environmental surfaces associated with children's activities, such as table tops, shall be cleaned and disinfected when they are soiled or at least once weekly.

Respiratory secretions that contaminate environmental surfaces remain infectious for variable periods of time, and infection can be acquired by touching articles and surfaces contaminated with infectious respiratory secretions.[43-46] Respiratory syncytial virus and rhinoviruses have both been shown to survive on environmental surfaces, and infection with these viruses has been transmitted by contact with secretion-contaminated fomites. Therefore, a reasonable effort should be made to clean respiratory secretions from environmental surfaces. However, continuously maintained table tops and toys free of contamination from respiratory secretions is an unrealistic goal.

HP48. Surfaces contaminated with blood or blood-containing body fluid shall be first cleaned and then disinfected as specified in standard HP38, on p. 75.

HP49. Walls, ceilings, floors, and other surfaces shall be maintained free from visible soil and in a clean condition.

One way to measure compliance is to wipe the surface with a mop and then insert it in cold rinse water; if the surface is clean, no residue will appear in the rinse water.

Sanitation, Disinfection, and Maintenance of Toys and Objects

HP50. Toys that are placed in children's mouths or are otherwise contaminated by body secretions or excretions shall be set aside to be cleaned with water and detergent, disinfected, and rinsed before handling by another child. Machine-washable cloth toys can be used and shall be machine-washed when contaminated.

Contamination of hands, toys, and other objects in the room has appeared to play a role in the transmission of diseases in child care settings.[41, 42]

This cleaning can be accomplished by having a dishpan labeled "soiled toys" into which mouthed toys can be dropped for later cleaning. This pan can contain soapy water to start to remove soil or can be a container used to bring the soiled toys to a toy-cleaning area later in the day. Having enough toys to rotate through the cleaning makes this method possible.

HP51. All frequently touched toys in rooms in which infants and toddlers are cared for shall be cleaned and disinfected daily.

See rationale for standard HP50.

See comment for standard HP50.

HP52. Toys in rooms in which older (nondiapered) children are cared for shall be cleaned weekly and when soiled.

See rationale for standard HP50.

See comment for standard HP50.

HP53. The use of soft, nonwashable toys in the infant/toddler areas of facilities shall be limited to personal use articles that are not shared between childen.

See rationale for standard HP50.

HP54. Thermometers, pacifiers, and other such objects shall be cleaned and disinfected between uses by different children.

See rationale for standard HP50.

HP55. The children's personal items, such as individual cloth towels used for bathing, washcloths, combs, and hairbrushes, shall be returned home for cleaning and disinfecting or

See rationale for standard HP50 and rationale in *Sanitation, Disinfection, and Maintenance of Bedding*, p. 79.

cleaned and disinfected by the staff weekly (or more often as needed).

HP56. Equipment provided by the caregiver for use by the children shall be maintained in a clean and disinfected condition and in good repair.

See rationale for standard HP50.

HP57. Staff shall be assigned to check all play equipment at least monthly to ensure that it is safe for children.

Sanitation, Disinfection, and Maintenance of Bedding

HP58. Each bed, mattress, cot, and mat and all bedding shall be cleaned and sanitized prior to assignment to another child.

Lice infestation, scabies, and ringworm are among the most common infectious diseases in child care. These diseases are transmitted by direct skin-to-skin contact or by the sharing of personal articles such as combs, brushes, towels, clothing, and bedding. Prohibiting people from sharing personal articles helps prevent the spread of these diseases.

HP59. All bedding (i.e., sheets, pillowcases, and blankets) shall be cleaned and sanitized when soiled or wet; infant bedding shall be changed daily. All linens shall be cleaned and sanitized at least weekly or more often if soiled. All blankets shall be changed and laundered routinely at least once each month.

This practice prevents contamination and the spread of disease.

Caregivers may ask parents to provide bedding, which will be sent home weekly for washing.

Compliance can be measured by interviewing the staff about laundry procedures used.

HP60. Crib mattresses shall be cleaned and sanitized at least weekly and when soiled or wet.

See rationale for standard HP50.

For additional information on sanitation, disinfection, and maintenance of bedding, see also *Laundry*, on p. 174, and standard FA194, on p. 178.

Sanitation, Disinfection, and Maintenance of Carpets, Rugs, and Floors

HP61. Carpets and floors shall be maintained in good repair.

Poorly maintained carpets and floors may cause people to trip or slip.

HP62. Floors, except those carpeted, shall be vacuumed or swept and mopped with a sanitizing solution at least daily and when soiled.

Contamination of hands, toys, and other equipment in the room has appeared to play a role in the transmission of diseases in child care settings.[41, 42] Regular and thorough cleaning of rooms prevents disease transmission.[47]

See also the rationale for standard HP24, on p. 71.

HP63. Mops shall be cleaned thoroughly in fresh water and soap and rinsed in a sanitizing dilution of bleach before and after a day of use. Mops shall be wrung as dry as possible and hung to dry.

This procedure minimizes bacterial growth in mops.

The bleach dilution used for disinfecting (see Glossary) is more than adequate to sanitize mops.

Detachable mop heads may be cleaned in a washing machine.

HP64. Carpeting shall be maintained free from visible soil. Carpeted areas shall be vacuumed daily and shampooed at least every 6 months, or as often as necessary to remain visibly free of soil that can be removed by shampooing. Carpets shall be cleaned when children are not present. Only products warranted by the manufacturer to be nonhyperallergenic products may be used for cleaning. The use of carpet deodorizers shall be prohibited unless they are approved as safe by the local health authority.

See rationale for standard HP62.

Measure compliance by staff interviews.

HP65. Rugs shall be spot-cleaned, shampooed, or steam-cleaned whenever body fluids contaminate such surfaces.

See rationale for standard HP62.

Measure compliance by staff interviews and by observation of practice when such contamination occurs.

HP66. Large throw rugs that cannot be washed shall be vacuumed at least daily and shampooed at least every 6 months and when soiled.

See rationale for standard HP62.

HP67. Small rugs that can be washed shall be shaken or vacuumed at least daily and washed at least weekly and when soiled.

See rationale for standard HP62.

MANAGEMENT AND PREVENTION OF ILLNESS

Inclusion/Exclusion/ Dismissal

Child inclusion/exclusion/ dismissal

HP68. A facility shall not deny admission to or send home a child because of illness unless one or more of the following conditions exists. The parent, legal guardian, or other person authorized by the parent shall

Exclusion of children with many mild infectious diseases is likely to have only a minor impact on the incidence of infection among other children in the group. Thus, when formulating exclusion policies, it is

A child may be included in the regular facility and his/her activities may be modified if the child is comfortable and the facility has enough caregivers to accommodate the adaptation. No child should be forced to

be notified immediately when a child has a sign or symptom requiring exclusion from the facility, as described below:

a) The illness prevents the child from participating comfortably in facility activities;

b) The illness results in a greater care need than the child care staff can provide without compromising the health and safety of the other children; or

c) The child has any of the following conditions:

1) *Temperature:* Oral temperature 101° or greater; rectal temperature 102° or greater; axillary (armpit) temperature 100° or greater; accompanied by behavior changes or other signs or symptoms of illness–until medical evaluation indicates inclusion in the facility. Oral temperature shall not be taken on children younger than 4 years (or younger than 3 years if a digital thermometer is used). Rectal temperature shall be taken only by persons with specific health training.

2) *Symptoms and signs of possible severe illness* (such as unusual lethargy, uncontrolled coughing, irritability, persistent crying, difficult breathing, wheezing, or other unusual signs)–until medical evaluation allows inclusion.

3) *Uncontrolled diarrhea,* that is, increased number of stools, increased stool water, and/or decreased form that is not contained by the diaper– until diarrhea stops. (See also *Child-Specific Procedures for Enteric (Diarrheal) and Hepatitis A Virus Infections,* p. 215, on additional separation and exclusion standards for children with diarrhea; standard HP70, on p. 83 on separate care for these children; and standard HP90, on p. 91 on notifying parents.)

4) *Vomiting illness* (two or more episodes of vomiting in the previous 24 hours) until vomiting resolves or until a

reasonable to focus on the needs and behavior of the ill child and the ability of staff in the out-of-home child care setting to meet those needs without compromising the care of other children in the group.[48]

Chicken pox, measles, rubella, mumps, and pertussis are highly communicable illnesses for which routine exclusion of infected children is warranted. It is also appropriate to exclude children with treatable illnesses until treatment is received and until treatment has reduced the risk of transmission. The presence of diarrhea, particularly in diapered children, and the presence of vomiting increase the likelihood of exposure of other children to the infectious agents that cause these illnesses. It may not be reasonable to routinely culture children who present with fever and sore throat or diarrhea. However, in some outbreak settings, identifying infected children and excluding or treating them may be necessary.

Fever is defined as an elevation of body temperature above normal (see Glossary). Fever may or may not preclude a child's participation in the facility. The height of the fever does not necessarily indicate the severity of the child's illness. A child's over-exertion in a hot, dry climate may produce a fever. Generally, young infants show less fever with serious illness than older children. Infants and children older than 4 months should be excluded whenever fever is accompanied by behavior change, signs, or symptoms of illness. Infants 4 months old and younger should be excluded for rectal temperature above 101° or axillary (armpit) temperature above 100°, even if there has not been a change in their behavior.

Children with fever are managed differently in child care. The presence of fever alone has little relevance to the spread of disease and may not preclude a child's participation in child care. A small proportion of childhood illness with fever is caused by life-threatening diseases, such as meningitis. It is unreasonable and inappropriate for child care staff

participate in facility activities when in ill health. Exclusion/dismissal should be for the child's comfort and safety if the facility cannot meet the child's needs.[53]

For all treated infectious diseases, continued inclusion after treatment has been initiated should be conditional on completion of the prescribed course of therapy and (clinical) improvement of the child's illness.

When the following diseases are diagnosed for a child in the facility, children in the facility not immunized for the disease must be excluded if exposed:[54] measles, rubella, mumps, and pertussis.

Instructions on how to take a child's temperature and a sample symptom record are provided in *Healthy Young Children.* To obtain this publication, contact

National Association for the Education of Young Children
1834 Connecticut Avenue, N.W.
Washington, DC 20009

See a sample symptom record in Appendix G.

Protocols for the management of these symptoms of illness and a symptom record are provided in the American Red Cross *Child Care Course.*[55] For more information about this course, telephone the local chapter of the American Red Cross or write to

American Red Cross
National Headquarters
Health and Safety
18th and F Streets, N.W.
Washington, DC 20006

Protocols for the management of illness are also provided in the *Child Care Health Handbook.* To obtain this publication, contact

Child Care Health Program
Seattle–King County Department of Public Health
110 Prefontaine Place South, #500
Seattle, WA 98104

Vomiting with symptoms such as lethargy and/or dry skin or mucus membranes may indicate dehydration.

health care provider determines the illness to be noncommunicable, and the child is not in danger of dehydration. (See also standard HP70 and standard HP89, on p. 83 and p. 91.)

5) *Mouth sores with drooling,* unless a health care provider or health official determines the condition is noninfectious.

6) *Rash with fever or behavior change,* until a health care provider determines that these symptoms do not indicate a communicable disease.

7) *Purulent conjunctivitis* (defined as pink or red conjunctiva with white or yellow eye discharge), until 24 hours after treatment has been initiated.

8) *Scabies, head lice, or other infestation,* until 24 hours after treatment has been initiated.

9) *Tuberculosis,* until a health care provider or health official states that the child can attend child care.

10) *Impetigo,* until 24 hours after treatment has been initiated.

11) *Strep throat or other streptococcal infection,* until 24 hours after initial antibiotic treatment and cessation of fever. (See also *Streptococcal Infection,* p. 211.)

12) *Chicken pox,* until 6 days after onset of rash or until all sores have dried and crusted. (See also standard ID33 in chapter 6, on p. 222.)

13) *Pertussis,* until 5 days of appropriate antibiotic treatment (currently, erythromycin) to prevent an infection have been completed

14) *Mumps,* until 9 days after onset of parotid gland swelling.

15) *Hepatitis A virus,* until 1 week after onset of illness or as directed by the health department when passive immunoprophylaxis (currently, immune serum globulin) has been administered to appropriate children and staff.

to attempt to determine which illnesses with fevers may be serious. The child's parents or legal guardians, with the help of their child's health care provider, are responsible for these decisions;[49] therefore, parents should be informed promptly when their child is found to have a fever while attending child care.

Exclusion of children with diarrhea may not prevent the spread of disease, but is for the child's welfare.[50-52]

Exclusion of children with a vomiting illness may not prevent the spread of the disease.[51]

Conjunctivitis, which is usually associated with viral upper respiratory and intestinal infection, is most often transmitted by the respiratory route (e.g., coughing, sneezing, nasal discharge, and saliva). This type of conjunctivitis is usually nonpurulent, defined as pink conjunctiva with a clear, watery eye discharge and without fever, eye pain, or eyelid redness. This type of conjunctivitis usually can be managed without excluding a child from a facility, as in the case of children with mild respiratory infection. Such a case, however, might require exclusion if a responsible health department authority, the child's health care provider, or the facility's health consultant (see *Health Consultants,* p. 33) determines that the child's conjunctivitis was contributing to transmission of the infection within or outside the facility.

Purulent conjunctivitis, defined as pink or red conjunctiva with white or yellow eye discharge, often with matted eyelids after sleep, and including eye pain or redness of the eyelids or skin surrounding the eye, is more often caused by a bacterial infection, which may require antibiotic treatment. Children with purulent conjunctivitis, therefore, should be excluded until they have been examined by the child's health care provider and cleared for readmission to the facility, with or without treatment, as determined by the health care provider.

Children in child care who develop signs and symptoms of a severe

A child with these symptoms should be evaluated medically.[50]

A child who vomits should be observed carefully for other signs of illness. If none are present, the child may continue to attend the facility.

Any skin rash that has open, seeping wounds and/or is not healing should be evaluated medically.

The lay term *pink eye* is used interchangeably to describe purulent and nonpurulent conjunctivitis. The infectious characteristics of purulent and nonpurulent conjunctivitis, however, are quite different.

Lice and scabies are highly contagious and all parents should be notified to watch for signs of infestation.[50]

16) *Measles*, until 6 days after onset of rash.
17) *Rubella*, until 6 days after onset of rash.
18) *Unspecified respiratory illness* (see standard ID19 in chapter 6 on p. 212).
19) *Shingles* (see standard ID35 in chapter 6 on p. 223).
20) *Herpetic gingivostomatitis* (see standard ID36 in chapter 6 on p. 223).

HP69. A child whose illness requires that the child be sent home from the facility shall be given appropriate attention to his/her needs, so long as this attention does not compromise the care of other children in the facility, until the ill child's parent arrives to remove the child.

HP70. A child with uncontrolled vomiting or diarrhea (see standard HP68) shall be provided separate care apart from the other children, with extra attention given to hygiene and sanitation, until the child's parent arrives to remove the child.

HP71. During the course of an identified outbreak of any communicable illness at the facility, a child shall be excluded if the local health official or health care provider determines that the child is contributing to the transmission of the illness at the facility. The child shall be readmitted when the local health official or health care provider who made the initial determination decides that the risk of transmission is no longer present.

HP72. Certain conditions do not constitute an a priori reason for denying admission to, or sending a child home from, child care, unless the child would be excluded by the above criteria or the child is determined by a health authority to contribute to transmission of the illness at the facility. These conditions include
a) Presence of germs in urine or feces in the absence of illness symptoms, as described in standard ID23 in chapter 6 on p. 215.

illness, even though fever is absent, should not be managed as are children with mild to moderate illness. Standard HP68 in this section describes exclusion criteria for more seriously ill children.

Exclusion of children with many mild infectious diseases is likely to have only a minor impact on the incidence of infection among other children in the group and the staff.[48] Thus, when formulating exclusion policies, it is reasonable to focus on the needs and behavior of the ill child and the ability of staff in the out-of-home child care setting to meet those needs without compromising the care of other children in the group.[48]

STANDARDS

b) Nonpurulent conjunctivitis, defined in the rationale for standard HP68, on p. 80.

c) Rash without fever and without behavior changes.

d) CMV infection, as described in standard ID39 in chapter 6 on p. 227.

e) Hepatitis B virus carrier state as described in standard ID41 in chapter 6 on p. 227.

f) HIV infection, as described in standard ID55 in chapter 6 on p. 231.

For additional information on child inclusion, exclusion, and dismissal, see also *When to Call a Doctor*, on p. 88; standard ID6 in chapter 6, on p. 209 on exclusion during antibiotic treatment of *Haemophilus influenzae* type b (Hib); standard ID10 in chapter 6, on p. 210 on exclusion during antibiotic treatment of meningococcal infection; standard ID15 in chapter 6, on p. 211 on exclusion during antibiotic treatment of pertussis; standard ID56 in chapter 6, on p. 231 on excluding children with immune systems that do not function properly to prevent infection; *Emergency Plan*, on p. 280; *Health Department Plan*, on p. 309; *The Health Department's Role*, on p. 310; and Appendix C, on p. 330.

Staff Exclusion

Please note that if a staff member has no contact with the children, or with anything that the children come into contact with, these standards do not apply to that member.

HP73. A facility shall not deny admission to or send home a staff member or substitute with illness unless one or more of the following conditions exist. The staff member shall be excluded as follows:

a) *Chicken pox*, until 6 days after onset of the rash or until all sores have dried and crusted over.

b) *Shingles*, only if the sores cannot be covered by clothing or a dressing until the sores have crusted.

RATIONALE

See the rationale for standard HP68, on p. 82 on purulent and nonpurulent conjunctivitis.

Adults are as capable of spreading infectious disease as children.

See also rationale for *Child Inclusion/Exclusion/Dismissal*, on p. 80.

COMMENTS

See the comment for standard HP68, on p. 82 on pink eye.

Other management procedures should be followed as stated in *Child Inclusion/Exclusion/Dismissal*, on p. 80.

See also comments for *Child Inclusion/Exclusion/Dismissal*, on p. 80.

c) *Rash with fever or joint pain*, until diagnosed not to be measles or rubella.

d) *Measles or rubella*, until 5 days after rash onset.

e) *Diarrheal illness*, three or more episodes of diarrhea during the previous 24 hours, until diarrhea resolves.

f) *Vomiting illness*, two or more episodes of vomiting during the previous 24 hours, until vomiting resolves or is determined to be due to such noncommunicable conditions as pregnancy or a digestive disorder.

g) *Hepatitis A virus*, for 1 week after onset or as directed by the health department when immunoglobulin has been given to appropriate children and staff in the facility.

h) *Pertussis*, until after 5 days of antibiotic therapy as specified in *Pertussis*, on p. 210.

i) *Skin infection (e.g., impetigo)*, until 24 hours after treatment has been initiated.

j) *Tuberculosis*, until noninfectious or as determined by a health care provider or health official.

k) *Strep throat or other streptococcal infection*, until 24 hours after initial antibiotic treatment and cessation of fever.

l) *Scabies, head lice, or other infestation*, until 24 hours after treatment has been initiated.

m) *Purulent conjunctivitis* (defined in the rationale for standard HP68, on p. 80), until 24 hours after treatment has been initiated.

n) *Haemophilus influenzae* type b (Hib), as specified in standard ID6 in chapter 6 on p. 207.

o) *Meningococcal infection*, as specified in standard ID5 in chapter 6 on p. 209.

p) *Respiratory illness*, as specified in *Unspecified Respiratory Infection*, p. 212.

HP74. During the course of an identified outbreak of any communicable illness in the out-of-home child care setting, a staff member may be excluded if the health department or health consultant (see *Health Consultants*, on p. 33) determines that he/she is contributing to the transmission of the illness at the facility. The staff member may be readmitted when the health department determines that the risk of transmission is no longer present.

For additional information on staff exclusion, see also *Staff Health*, on p. 35 and *Health Department Plan*, on p. 309, and *The Health Department's Role*, on p. 310.

Immunizations and Preventive Health Care

HP75. If immunizations are contraindicated because of a medical condition, a statement from the child's health care provider shall be on file (see sample in comments). This standard also applies to school-age child care facilities.

Immunizations must be up to date for children in child care to reduce the incidence of diseases preventable by immunization. Involving large numbers of our youngest children, who are now enrolled in facilities, in updating immunizations is an opportunity to significantly improve the health of our nation. National surveys document that child care has a positive influence on protection from vaccine-preventable illness.[56] Immunizations should be required for all children in child care settings, should be documented, and should follow the recommendations in the most current report of the Committee for Infectious Disease, American Academy of Pediatrics, and the Advisory Committee on Immunization Practices of the U.S. Public Health Service.

Sample:

This is to inform you that ___name___ should not be immunized with ___(vaccine)___ due to ___(condition)___ (e.g., immunosuppression).

                    Signed,
                    (Physician)

HP76. If immunizations are not given because of parents' religious or other beliefs, a waiver signed by the parent shall be on file. If a significant number (more than 10 percent) of all children in care are not immunized at all, parents must be notified that the risk of spread of preventable disease exists.

See rational for standard HP75.

HP77. Infants and children, including infants and children who were not immunized at the recommended time in early infancy, shall be immunized as specified in *Vaccine-Preventable Diseases*, on p. 219.

For additional information on immunizations and preventive health care, see also Appendix C, on p. 330.

Reporting Illness

HP78. Each facility shall, upon registration of each child, inform parents of the need to notify the facility within 24 hours after the child has developed a known or suspected communicable disease, or if any member of the immediate household has a communicable disease, and to inform the facility of any other illness that is not a communicable disease or other absence experienced by the child when the child returns to the facility. When the child has a disease requiring exclusion or dismissal (see *Child Inclusion/Exclusion/Dismissal*, on p. 80), the parents shall inform the facility of the diagnosis.

This requirement will facilitate prompt reporting of disease and prepare the caregiver to care for the child better. Disease surveillance and reporting to local health authorities are critical to the prevention and control of diseases in the child care setting. The major purpose of surveillance is to allow early detection of disease and prompt implementation of control measures. Ascertaining whether an ill child attends a facility is important when evaluating childhood illnesses; ascertaining whether an adult with illness either works in a facility or is a parent of a child attending a facility is important when considering a diagnosis of hepatitis A or other disease transmitted by the route of infections of the intestine (often with diarrhea) or liver. Cases of infections of the intestine (often with diarrhea) or liver in household contacts may necessitate questioning about illness in the child attending child care and testing the child for infection. Information concerning communicable disease in a child care attendee, staff, or household contact should be communicated to public health authorities, to the child care director, and to parents of the child.

The state health department's list of communicable diseases should be posted as a reference.

HP79. A written list of conditions for which exclusion and dismissal are required, as specified in HP68 on p. 80, shall be given to each parent.

HP80. The facility shall comply with the state's reporting requirements for ill children. All communicable diseases shall be reported to the public health agency.

HP81. The facility shall have a list of reportable diseases provided by the local or state health authorities and shall provide a copy to each parent. The facility shall have the telephone number of the responsible local or state health authority to

Effective control and prevention of infectious diseases in child care depend on affirmative relationships between parents, caregivers, public health authorities, and primary health care providers.

whom confirmed or suspected cases of these diseases, or outbreaks of other communicable diseases, shall be reported, and shall have a staff member who is responsible for reporting the disease.

For additional information on reporting illness, see also *Disease Surveillance of Enteric (Diarrheal) and Hepatitis A Virus Infections*, on p. 218, standard ID50 in chapter 6 on p. 230 on reporting hepatitis B, *Health Department Plan*, on p. 309, and *The Health Department's Role*, on p. 310, Appendix C, on p. 330, on child records, and Appendices I-1–I-4, on pp. 343–351.

When to Call a Doctor

Emergency Plan, on p. 280, and Appendix H, "Get Medical Help Immediately," on p. 342, for a checklist from the American Red Cross *Child Care Course*.[55] (See also the comments in *Child Inclusion/Exclusion/Dismissal/*, on p. 80, on when to seek medical evaluation, and standard HP104, on p. 94 on STDs in children.)

Medications

HP82. The administration of medicines at the facility shall be limited to
a) Those prescribed medications ordered by a health care provider for a specific child.
b) Those nonprescription medications recommended by a health care provider for a specific child, with written permission of the parent or legal guardian referencing a written or telephone instruction received by the facility from the health care provider.

Facilities must have clear, accurate instruction and medical confirmation of the child's need for medication while in the facility before assuming responsibility for administration of medicine. Caregivers should not be involved in inappropriate use of drugs based solely on a parent's desire to give the child medication. Excessive use of over-the-counter medications is suggested by the results of the National Center for Health Statistics' survey of the incidence of medicated respiratory infection, which showed that 29.5 percent of children under 5 in the survey were reported by their parents to have had a medicated respiratory illness in the 2 weeks before the interview.[57]

Decongestants and antihistamines have been shown to prolong the retenion of secretions in the middle ear rather than helping children get well.[58] No evidence exists that decon-

For more information about this course, telephone the local chapter of the American Red Cross or write to

American Red Cross
National Headquarters
Health and Safety
18th and F Streets, N.W.
Washington, DC 20006

An example of written permission, as described in item b, is as follows: "My child can receive acetaminophen when the child's rectal temperature is 101°F or greater. See attached note from the child's health care provider."

Standing orders for commonly used medications (e.g., acetaminophen) may be used to avoid the need for a health care provider's instruction or parents' written permission for every instance for every child. Parents should always be notified in every instance when medication is used. Telephone instructions from a health care provider are acceptable if fully documented by the caregiver and if the request for health care provider instruction is initiated by the parent.

Advance notification of the parent (before medication is given) is ideal, but may not be appropriate if a child needs medication urgently (e.g., to stop an allergic reaction) or when

gestants or antihistamines, alone or in combination, prevent inner ear infections; therefore, the use of such medications for common colds is not recommended.[58]

contacting the parent will delay appropriate care unreasonably.

Safeguards against liability for accepting telephone instructions for medication administration should be checked with an attorney.

Nonprescription medications should be given according to the manufacturers' instructions unless a health care provider gives written instructions otherwise.

A sample form for parental consent to administer medication is in *Healthy Young Children*. To obtain this publication, contact

National Association for the
  Education of Young Children
1834 Connecticut Avenue, N.W.
Washington, DC 20009

HP83. Any prescribed medication brought into the facility by the parent, legal guardian, or responsible relative of a child shall be dated, and shall be kept in the original container labeled by a pharmacist with the child's first and last names; the date the prescription was filled; the name of the health care provider who wrote the prescription; the medication's expiration date; and specific, legible instructions for administration, storage, and disposal (i.e., the manufacturer's instructions or prescription label).

See rationale for standard HP82.

A small lock box can be kept in the refrigerator to hold medications.

HP84. Any over-the-counter medication brought into the facility for use by a specific child shall be labeled with the following information: the date; the child's first and last names; specific, legible instructions for administration and storage (i.e., manufacturer's instructions); and the name of the health care provider who made the recommendation.

See rationale for standard HP82.

HP85. All medications, refrigerated or unrefrigerated, shall have child-protective caps, shall be kept in an orderly fashion, shall be stored away from food at the proper temperature, and shall be inaccessible to children. Medication shall not be used beyond the date of expiration.

Child-resistant safety packaging was shown to decrease poisonings by about 38 percent from 1973 to 1976 among children aged 0–4 years, while poisonings from non-regulated products increased by 20 percent during this period for this age group.[59, 60] In addition, should the medication leak or spill, it will not contaminate food.

HP86. There shall be a written policy for the use of any commonly used, nonprescription medication as specified in *Medication Policy*, on p. 280.

The health consultant (see *Health Consultants*, on p. 33) could be helpful in preparing such a policy as it relates to acetaminophen, sunscreen, syrup of ipecac, and so forth. It is recommended that all children have sunscreen applied when exposed to the sun. Syrup of ipecac should be on hand in the facility in case of an emergency (see standard HP106, on p. 95).

HP87. Any caregiver who administers medication shall be trained to check for the name of the child; to read the label/prescription directions in relation to the measured dose, frequency, and other circumstances relative to administration (e.g., relation to meals); and to document properly that the medication was administered (see Appendix C, item E, on p. 335).

Caregivers need to be aware of what medication the child is receiving, who prescribed the medicine and when, and what the known reactions or side effects may be in the event that a child has a negative reaction to the medicine.[61] A child's reaction to medication may occasionally be extreme enough to initiate the protocol developed for emergencies. The medication record is especially important if medications are frequently prescribed or if long-term medications are being used.

For additional information on medications, see also Appendix C, item E, on p. 335.

Notification of Parents

HP88. The center director or large or small family home caregiver, after consulting with the facility's health consultant (see *Health Consultants*, on p. 33) or the responsible public health authority, shall follow the recommendations of the consultant or authority regarding notification of parents of children who attend the facility about exposure of their child to a communicable disease. When notification is recommended, it shall be oral or written and shall include the following information:

a) The disease to which the child was exposed, and whether there is one case or an outbreak.

b) Signs and symptoms of the disease that the parent should watch for in the child.

c) Mode of transmission for the disease.

d) Period of communicability.

e) Disease-prevention measures recommended by the public health department (if appropriate).

Licensing requirements for facilities increasingly require specific arrangements with a health consultant to assist in the development of written policies for the prevention and control of communicable diseases.

Effective control and prevention of infectious diseases in child care depends on affirmative relationships between parents, caregivers, public health authorities, and primary health care providers.

For a sample letter to parents notifying them of illness of their child or other enrolled children, see Appendix V.4 in *Health in Day Care: A Manual for Health Professionals*. To order this publication, contact

American Academy of Pediatrics
141 Northwest Point Blvd.
P.O. Box 927
Elk Grove Village, IL 60009-0927

For sample letters to parents about infectious diseases that their children may have contracted or may have been exposed to, see *Healthy Young Children*. To order this publication, contact

National Association for the
    Education of Young Children
1834 Connecticut Avenue, N.W.
Washington, DC 20009

f) Control measures implemented at the facility.

HP89. If a child appears ill after a vomiting episode, the parents shall be told to have the child seen by a health care provider.

Vomiting with symptoms such as lethargy and/or dry skin or mucus membranes may indicate dehydration, and the child should be evaluated medically.

If there is more than one case of vomiting in the facility, it may indicate contagious illness or food poisoning.

HP90. If a child has diarrhea with blood or mucus in diarrheic stool(s), the parents shall be told to have the child seen by a health care provider.

Diarrhea with fever or other symptoms usually indicates the presence of infection. Blood and/or mucus may indicate shigellosis, which should be treated.[50-52]

HP91. For the child with persistent abdominal pain (i.e., continues for more than 2 hours) or intermittent pain associated with fever or other symptoms, the parents shall be told to obtain medical consultation.

If the facility is unable to contact the parent, medical advice should be sought until the parents can be located.

If a child with abdominal pain is extremely drowsy, irritable, and unhappy; has no appetite; and is unwilling to participate in usual activities, the child should be seen by his/her health care provider.

Abdominal pain may be associated with viral gastrointestinal illness, which is contagious, or with food poisoning. It may also indicate kidney disease or other conditions and should be referred for medical consultation (by telephone if necessary) if severe or persistent.

HP92. In cooperation with the local health department, parents of other children who attend the facility shall be informed by the facility and/or the health department that their child may have been exposed at the facility to the following diseases or conditions (see chapter 6, *Infectious Diseases*, on p. 207):

Neisseria Meningitidis (Meningococcal) on p. 209.
Pertussis, on p. 210.
Streptococcal infections and scarlet fever (see *Streptococcal Infection*, on p. 211).
Chicken pox (see *Disease Recognition and Control of Herpes Simplex and Chicken Pox Viruses*, on p. 222).
Ectoparasites (lice and scabies).
Giardia lamblia diarrhea.
Infections of the intestines (often with diarrhea) or liver (see *Enteric (Diarrheal) and Hepatitis A Virus Infections*, on p. 214).

See the comment for standard HP88.

Hepatitis A (see *Enteric
(Diarrheal) and Hepatitis A
Virus Infections*, on p. 214).
*Haemophilus Influenzae type
B*, on p. 207).
Campylobacter gastroenteritis.
Salmonella diarrhea.
Shigella diarrhea.

Notification of the Health Department

See *Reporting Illness*, on p. 87; and
standards APP11, on p. 343; APP15,
on p. 346; and APP20, on p. 349, in
Appendices I-1, I-2, and I-3, respec-
tively. See also *Health Department
Plan*, on p. 309; *The Health Department's Role*, on p. 310, on the health
department's responsibility in communicable diseases; and Appendix
I-4, on p. 351.

Death, SIDS and Other

HP93. If a facility experiences the
death of a child, the following shall
be done:
a) If the child dies while at the
facility:
  1) Immediately notify emergency
  medical personnel.
  2) Immediately notify the child's
  parents.
  3) Notify the licensing agency.
  4) Provide age-appropriate information for children and parents.
b) For a Sudden Infant Death Syndrome (SIDS) death:
  1) Seek support and SIDS information from local, state, or
  national SIDS resources.
  2) Provide SIDS information to
  the parents of the other children in the facility.
  3) Provide age-appropriate information to the other children in
  the facility.
c) If the child dies while not at the
facility:
  1) Provide age-appropriate information for children and parents.
  2) Make resources for support
  available to parents and children.

For additional information on death,
SIDS and other, see also standard
AD29 in chapter 8, on p. 280 and
standard ST25, on p. 13 on coping
with death.

The licensing agency and a SIDS
program can offer support and counseling to caregivers. These agencies
know that in such cases caregivers
are not at fault; therefore caregivers
should not fear license/certificate (see
Individual Licensure/Certification,
on p. 301) revocation or punitive
actions. Following the described
steps would constitute prudent
action.[6] Accurate information given
to the other parents and children will
help them understand the event and
facilitate their support of the
caregiver.

It is important that caregivers be
knowledgeable about SIDS and that
they take proper steps so that they
are not falsely accused of child abuse.
For information and support, contact

National SIDS Clearinghouse
8201 Greensboro Drive, Suite 600
McLean, VA 22102

SIDS Alliance
10500 Little Patuxent Parkway
Suite 402
Columbia, MD 21044

STANDARDS	RATIONALE	COMMENTS

CHILD ABUSE AND NEGLECT

HP94. The facility shall report to the department of social services, child protective services, or police any instance where there is reasonable cause to believe that child abuse, neglect, or exploitation may have occurred.

HP95. Caregivers and health professionals shall establish linkages with physicians, child psychiatrists, nurses, nurse practitioners, physicians' assistants, and child protective services who are willing to provide them with consultation about suspicious injuries or other circumstances that may indicate abuse or neglect. The names of these consultants shall be available for inspection. (See also *Health Consultation*, on p. 278, and *Health Consultants*, on p. 33.)

Many mistakes in reporting can be avoided by consulting with an experienced consultant before a decision is made about what to do.

Many health departments will be willing to provide this service. The American Academy of Pediatrics can also assist in recruiting and identifying physicians who are skilled in this work. Contact

> American Academy of Pediatrics
> 141 Northwest Point Blvd.
> P.O. Box 927
> Elk Grove Village, IL 60009-0927

HP96. Caregivers must be aware of the common behaviors shown by abused children and, if many such children are in the center, make special provisions for them by the addition of staff.

Abused children are likely to be more needy and to require more individual staff time and attention than children who are not abused.

A quantitative standard for this case is difficult to establish at present.

HP97. Caregivers who report abuse in the settings where they work shall be immune from discharge, retaliation, or other disciplinary action for that reason alone, unless it is proven that the report was malicious.

Reports of child abuse in child care settings are infrequently made by workers. Reported cases suggest that sometimes workers are intimidated by superiors in the centers where they work and fail to report abuse for that reason.[62]

HP98. Employees and volunteers in centers shall receive an instruction sheet about child abuse reporting that contains a summary of the state child abuse reporting statute and a statement that they will not be discharged solely because they have made a child abuse report.

See rationale for standard HP97.

HP99. All caregivers in all settings and at all levels of employment shall know the definitions of the four forms of child abuse (see the Glossary) and

If caregivers know something about child abuse, they will be better able to prevent it and to deal with it appropriately if they see it.

The four forms of child abuse are emotional abuse, neglect, physical abuse, and sexual abuse. Definitions are provided in the Glossary.

shall be able to give examples. They shall know the child abuse reporting requirements as they apply to themselves, and how to make a report.

HP100. Caregivers with a year of experience in child care, and all small family home caregivers, shall know the symptoms and indicators of abuse that abused children may show. They shall know the common factors, both chronic and situational, that lead to abuse, and some ways of helping persons who are prone to abuse to avoid committing abuse. These symptoms and indicators shall be listed in the written policies.

See rationale for standard HP99.

For information on common factors that lead to abuse, see Appendix IV.1, "Summary of Clues to Child Abuse," and Appendix IV.2, "Characteristics of Abusive Adult Family Members," in the publication *Health in Day Care: A Manual for Health Professionals.* This publication may be obtained from

American Academy of Pediatrics
141 Northwest Point Blvd.
P.O. Box 927
Elk Grove Village, IL 60009-0927

HP101. Center directors shall know methods for reducing the risks of child abuse. They shall know how to recognize common symptoms and signs of child abuse.

The director is in a position of authority and responsibility for a large number of children.

HP102. Caregivers shall have ways of taking breaks and finding relief at times of high stress (e.g., they shall be allowed 15 minutes of break time every four hours, in addition to a lunch break of at least 30 minutes). (See also *Stress*, on p. 38.)

Serious physical abuse usually occurs at a time of high stress for the caregiver.

HP103. The physical layout of facilities shall be arranged so that all areas can be viewed by at least one other adult in addition to the caregiver at all times to reduce the likelihood of isolation or privacy for individual caregivers with children, especially in areas where children may be undressed or have their genitals exposed. (See also *Bathrooms*, on p. 172.)

Abuse tends to occur in privacy and isolation, and especially in toileting areas.[62] A significant number of cases of abuse have been found involving young children being diapered in diaper-changing areas.[62]

This standard does not mean to disallow privacy for older children who may need privacy for independent toileting.

HP104. Caregivers shall be knowledgeable about the symptoms and signs caused by sexually transmitted diseases (STDs) in children. They

Sexually transmitted diseases often indicate that children have been sexually abused; however, when a caregiver suspects that a child has an

The occurrence of STDs in child care is uncommon, but suspected cases pose a major challenge to the caregiver. Consultation with the

must refer such children for care by calling the health care provider as well as the parent in order to be certain that the child is taken for care. They must determine from the health care provider when the child may return to the site and what precautions, if any, are needed to protect other children. Caregiver training on these items shall be documented.

For additional information on child abuse and neglect, see also *Discipline*, on p. 52; standard PR40 in chapter 2, on p. 56 on contact information for other parents; *Technical Assistance from the Licensing Agency*, on p. 313; and recommendation REC73 on state collaboration to prevent and control child abuse in chapter 9, on p. 319.

EMERGENCY PROCEDURES

HP105. When an immediate response is required, the following emergency procedures shall be utilized:
a) First aid and CPR care shall be employed, and the emergency medical response team shall be called, as indicated.
b) The facility shall have a plan for emergency transportation to a local hospital or health care facility.
c) The parent or parent's emergency contact person shall be called.

HP106. Syrup of ipecac shall be available for administration as a vomiting agent, but shall be used only under the direction of the poison control center or physician.

STD, the child must be diagnosed by a health care provider, who then takes responsibility for the decision to report the situation.[57]

Staff must know the plan for dealing with emergency situations when a child requires immediate care and a parent is not available.

An emetic (vomiting agent), such as syrup of ipecac, limits the absorption of certain toxins. However, emetics should not be used without the direction of a physician or poison control center, because certain toxic substances (e.g., petroleum distillates) can cause damage to breathing passages when vomited.[63]

health consultant (see *Health Consultation*, on p. 278 and *Health Consultants*, on p. 33) and the health department is advisable in all such cases.

A description of the symptoms, diagnosis, and treatment of major STDs is provided in *Healthy Young Children*. To obtain this publication, contact

> National Association for the
> Education of Young Children
> 1834 Connecticut Ave., N.W.
> Washington, DC 20009

First aid instructions are provided in Appendix VI.6 in *Health in Day Care: A Manual for Health Professionals*. To order this publication, contact

> American Academy of Pediatrics
> 141 Northwest Point Blvd.
> P.O. Box 927
> Elk Grove Village, IL 60007-0927

Emergency and first aid procedures are provided in *Healthy Young Children*. To obtain this publication, contact

> National Association for the
> Education of Young Children
> 1834 Connecticut Avenue, N.W.
> Washington, DC 20009

HP107. The staff shall demonstrate the ability to locate and operate the fire extinguishers.

A fire extinguisher may be used to put out a small fire or to clear an escape path.[64]

HP108. Children shall be instructed to drop and roll when garments catch fire. Cold water shall be applied to burns immediately. The injury shall be covered with a loose bandage or clean cloth. Children shall be instructed to crawl under smoke.

Running when garments have been ignited will fan the fire. The removal of heat from the affected area will prevent continued burning and deepening of tissue damage. Asphyxiation causes more deaths in house fires than does thermal injury.[65]

For additional information on emergency procedures, see also *Emergency Plan*, on p. 280, *Evacuation Plan and Drills*, on p. 280, and recommendation REC59 in chapter 9 on p. 315.

WATER SAFETY

HP109. Children shall not be permitted to play without constant supervision in areas where there is any body of water, including swimming pools, built-in wading pools, tubs, pails, sinks, or toilets. (See also *Safety Rules for Swimming/Wading Pools*, on p. 195.)

Any body of water, including swimming and wading pools, hot tubs, pails, and toilets, presents a drowning risk to young children.[6, 23, 66]

HP110. All young children shall be supervised while using bathroom facilities, but children under 3 shall be supervised especially closely.

This supervision will prevent drowning.[63, 67–79]

HP111. Preschool children and children with special needs shall not be left unattended in a bathtub or shower.

There is a significant risk of injury or aspiration in these populations so that supervision is needed.

The need for constant supervision is of particular concern in dealing with very young children or those children with significant motor dysfunction or mental retardation.

HP112. At least one of the caregivers, volunteers, or other adults who are counted in the child:staff ratio for wading and swimming shall be certified in CPR and basic water safety as specified in *First Aid and CPR*, on p. 22.

It is necessary that an adult be present who can provide lifesaving techniques in the event of an emergency.

HP113. Caregivers shall prohibit dangerous behavior. Children shall not be permitted to push each other, hold each other under water, or run at poolside. Children shall be instructed to call for help only in a genuine emergency.

Such behavior is dangerous and will distract caregivers from other children, thereby placing the other children at greater risk.

HP114. Tricycles, wagons, and other nonwater toys shall not be permitted on the pool deck. Use of flotation devices shall be prohibited.

Playing with non-water toys such as tricycles or wagons on the pool deck may result in unintentional falls into the water. Reliance on flotation devices may give children false confidence in their ability to protect themselves in deep water. Flotation devices may also promote complacency among caregivers who believe that the child is safe.

HP115. Child:staff ratios shall be followed while children are swimming or wading as specified in standard ST4 in chapter 1 on p. 24.

For additional information on water safety, see also standard FA271 in chapter 5 on p. 194, requiring that an adult who knows the pump location be present when children are in the pool.

ANIMALS

HP116. Any pet or animal present at the facility, indoors or outdoors, shall be in good health, show no evidence of carrying any disease, and be a friendly companion for the children.

This standard helps to protect the children's health and safety.

HP117. Dogs or cats, where allowed, shall be immunized for any disease that can be transmitted to humans and shall be maintained on a flea, tick, and worm control program.

This standard aids in the control of transmittable diseases.

HP118. There shall be no ferrets, turtles, psittacine birds (birds of the parrot family), or any wild or dangerous animals kept in a facility.

Animals, including pets, are a source of illness for people, and people may be a source of illness for animals.[22]

HP119. All pets shall be cared for as recommended by the regulating health agency. When pets are kept on the premises, procedures for their care and maintenance shall be written and followed. When immunizations are required, proof of current compliance signed by a veterinarian shall be on file at the facility where the pet is kept.

Compliance with this standard helps to prevent the spread of filth, disease, and odor.

HP120. Animal cages shall be of an approved type with removable bottoms and shall be kept clean and sanitary.

See rationale for standard HP119.

HP121. The living quarters of animals shall be enclosed and kept clean of waste to reduce the risk of human contact with this waste.

See rationale for standard HP118.

HP122. Animal litter boxes shall not be located in areas accessible to children.

See rationale for standard HP118.

HP123. All animal litter must be immediately removed from children's areas and properly disposed of.

See rationale for standard HP118.

HP124. Caregivers shall always be present when children are exposed to domestic animals (including dogs and cats). Children shall be instructed on safe procedures to follow when in close proximity to these animals (e.g., not to provoke or startle them or remove their food). Potentially very aggressive animals (pit bulls, boxers, etc.) shall not be in the same physical space with the children.

Injuries by household pets are very common.[80] Approximately one of every 200 emergency room visits at a children's hospital was for a dog bite injury.[81] Dog bites to children under 4 years usually occur at home, and the most common injury sites are the head, face, and neck.

HP125. Animal food supplies shall be kept out of reach of the children.

Just as food intended for human consumption may become contaminated, a pet's food can become contaminated by standing at room temperature, or by animals, insects, or people.

HP126. Live animals and fowl shall be prohibited from food preparation, food storage, and eating areas.

See rationale for standard HP125.

HP127. Hands shall be washed after handling animals or animal wastes as specified in *Handwashing*, on p. 72.

Thorough handwashing with soap for at least 10 seconds using warm, running water, which lifts the organisms off the skin and allows them to be rinsed away, has been effective in preventing disease transmission.[23]

SMOKING AND PROHIBITED SUBSTANCES

HP128. The use of tobacco (in any form), alcohol, and illegal drugs shall be prohibited on the facility premises during the hours of operation.

Recent scientific evidence has linked respiratory health risks to ''passive'' smoke. No children, especially those with respiratory problems, should be exposed to an additional risk in the air they breathe.[82]

Infants and young children exposed passively to environmental tobacco smoke are at increased risk of developing bronchitis, pneumonia, and otitis media when they experience common respiratory infections.[83, 84]

Separation of smokers and non-smokers within the same air space may reduce, but does not eliminate,

The age, defenselessness, and lack of discretion of the children under care make this prohibition an absolute requirement.

exposure of nonsmokers to environmental tobacco smoke.

The U.S. Fire Administration estimates that 22 percent of all residential fire deaths can be attributed to smoking.[85] A study of fire fatalities in Maryland, 1971–1977, indicated that 45 percent were caused by cigarettes.[81, 86-88]

Cigarettes used by adults are the leading cause of ignition of fatal house fires. Cigarettes are responsible for 30–45 percent of these deaths.[64]

LEVELS OF SEVERITY OF ILLNESS FOR WHICH THE FACILITY CAN PROVIDE

HP129. The facility shall specify in its procedures what severity level(s) of illness it can handle and how much and what types of illness will be addressed. The plan of care shall be approved by the facility's health consultant (see *Health Consultation*, on p. 278, and *Health Consultants*, on p. 33. (See also recommendation REC4 in chapter 9 on p. 301 on different sick care facilities.)

a) *Severity Level 1* includes children whose health condition is accompanied by high interest and complete involvement and activity due to an absence of symptoms of illness (e.g., children recovering from pink eye, a treated rash, or chicken pox), but who still need further recuperation time. Appropriate activities for this level include most of the normal activities for the child's particular age and developmental level, including both indoor and outdoor play.

b) *Severity Level 2* includes children whose health condition is accompanied by a medium activity level due to symptoms (e.g., children with low-grade fever, those at the beginning of an illness, or those in the recovery period of an illness). Appropriate activites for this level include crafts, puzzles, table games, fantasy play, and opportunities to move about the room freely.

c) *Severity Level 3* includes children whose health condition is accompanied by a low activity level due to symptoms that preclude much involvement. Appropriate activities for this level are sleep and rest; light meals and liquids; passive activities such as stories, music, and records; and being held and rocked (especially for children under 3 years of age).

3.2 Special Facilities for Ill Children

GENERAL REQUIREMENTS

HP130. Individuals and public and private organizations that provide child care shall acknowledge the need for and shall develop guidelines for facilities for ill children.

Children enrolled in child care are of an age that places them at increased risk for acquiring infectious diseases. Many children with illness (particularly mild respiratory illness without fever) can continue to attend their usual facility; exclusion of these children from child care is often counterproductive.[89] This perspective is reflected in the standards for excluding children from child care attendance (see *Management and Prevention of Illness*, on p. 80). Current state regulations concerning exclusion of children from facilities for illness may be more restrictive than these standards. At least 75 percent of states currently require isolation of a child who becomes ill during the day while attending the facility, and an ill child is not expected to return to the facility the following day.[90] The most common type of alternative care arrangement is for a parent of the ill child to stay home from work and care for the child, but this introduces considerable hardship in some families.[91] Recently, a few states have begun to investigate issues involving child care for sick children, and progress is being made toward permitting these children to continue in child care.[90]

There are inadequate data on which to judge the impact of group care of ill children on their subsequent health and on the health of their families and community. The principles and standards proposed herein represent the most current views of pediatric and infectious disease experts on provid-

Technical expertise and guidance can be obtained from the health consultant (see *Inclusion/Exclusion/Dismissal*, on p. 80, *Health Consultants*, on p. 33 and on p. 106).

STANDARDS

RATIONALE

COMMENTS

ing this special type of child care. These standards will require revision as new information on disease transmission in these facilities becomes available.

HP131. Individuals and public and private organizations who provide care for children with illness in a variety of settings shall adhere to the administrative procedures and staff policies that have been formulated to reduce the introduction and transmission of communicable diseases as specified in these APHA/AAP standards.

Young children enrolled in facilities experience a high incidence of illness (upper respiratory infections, otitis media, etc.) and other temporary disability (exacerbation of asthma, eczema, etc.) that often preclude their participation in the usual facility activities. Because many state regulations now require that childen with these conditions be excluded from their usual care arrangements,[92] several alternative care arrangements have been established. These alternatives include (1) care in the child's own home,[93] (2) care in a small family-child-care home,[94] (3) care in the child's own center with special provisions designed for the care of ill children (sometimes called the infirmary model),[95] and (4) care in a separate center that serves only children with illness or temporary disability.[96] Clearly, when children with possible communicable diseases are present in the alternative care arrangements, emphasis on preventing the further spread of disease is as important as in the usual facilities. Although most facilities claim to adhere to general principles of prevention and control of communicable disease, a recent study found that only one facility followed strict isolation procedures[97] and another demonstrated no additional transmission of communicable disease from the children served to the rest of the well children attending the usual facilities.[98]

Prevention of additional cases of communicable disease should be an important objective in these alternative care arrangements for children with minor illness and temporary disability.

For additional information on general requirements for special facilities for ill children, see *Program of Activities*, on p. 286, and *Program of Developmental Activities*, on p. 45 for the developmental aspects to consider in special facilities for ill children. Only the health aspects of this facility are addressed in *Special Facilities for Ill Children*, on p. 100. See also *The Health Department's Role*, on p. 310.

SPACE IN SPECIAL FACILITIES FOR ILL CHILDREN

HP132. Environmental space utilized for the care of children who are ill with infectious diseases and cannot receive care in their usual child care group shall be defined as follows:

a) If the program for ill children is in the same facility as the well-child program, then no furniture, fixtures, equipment, or supplies designated for use in caring for ill children or for use by ill children shall be shared with or used by children in the facility for well children.

b) Indoor space utilized by the facility for ill children, including hallways, bathrooms, and kitchens, shall be separate from indoor space utilized by the well-child facility, thereby reducing the likelihood of commingling supplies, toys, and equipment. A single kitchen may be shared by the facilities for ill and well children if the kitchen is staffed by a cook who has no other child care responsibilities.

c) Children whose symptoms are primarily those of infections of the intestine (often with diarrhea) or liver, or with diarrheal illness, who are cared for in special facilities for ill children shall receive this care in a space separate from other children with other illnesses to reduce the likelihood of disease transmission between children by limiting child-to-child interaction, separating staff responsibilities, and limiting the commingling of supplies, toys, and equipment.

d) If children with chicken pox are cared for in a facility, care shall be provided in a separate room that is externally ventilated.

HP133. A handwashing sink shall be present in each child care room.

Transmission of infectious diseases in child care settings may be influenced by the design, construction, and maintenance of the physical environment.[99]

The population that uses centers is usually quite susceptible to chicken pox, which is readily spread by airborne droplets.[100] Although there are no scientific studies on the space required to reduce disease transmission in child care, most health authorities believe that adequate space and ventilation reduce the transmission of disease.[99] Airborne transmission of measles in elementary schools and physicians' offices has been documented.[101-103] The Minnesota Department of Health reported no transmission of chicken pox to other children in its evaluation of a free-standing sick-child care facility that accepted children with chicken pox into a room with a separate entrance and external air ventilation.[98]

Handwashing sinks should be stationed in each room not only to provide the opportunity to maintain cleanliness, but also to give the caregivers an opportunity for continuous supervision of the other children in care.

Some facilities may have staffed get-well rooms typically caring for fewer than six ill children.

HP134. Each room in which children who wear diapers are cared for shall have its own diaper-changing area placed adjacent to the hand-washing sink.

Diaper-changing areas should be adjacent to sinks not only to provide the opportunity to maintain cleanliness, but also to enable caregivers to provide continuous supervision of the other children in care.

HP135. In a facility for ill children, there shall be a minimum of one toilet for 10 children. Toileting areas shall provide for privacy.

Toileting areas should be easily available to handle the needs of ill children, especially those with gastro-intestinal illnesses.[104]

The same ratio of toilets to children is suggested for the care of well (see *Toilets and Toilet Training Equipment*, on p. 168) and ill children. If an area is designed for use by toilet-trained children with diarrhea, more toilets are desirable.

HP136. Children shall have access to rest or nap areas without distraction or disturbance from other activities whenever the child desires. (See also *Sleep*, on p. 66, on additional sleep requirements.)

Children who are ill need more opportunity for rest or quiet activities.

HP137. There shall be at least 35 square feet of useable indoor floor space per child as specified in *Play Indoors*, on p. 168.

Although no data are available to address space requirements for out-of-home care of ill children, it is reasonable to assume that this care is optimum in a space at least as large as that required for well children of the same age.

HP138. Each facility shall use paper cups and plates and plastic utensils, which shall be disposed of after use, or shall use a mechanical dishwasher meeting local sanitation standards, or shall use a three-compartment sink that meets local sanitation standards. (See also *Kitchens and Equipment*, on p. 127.)

Eating utensils, bedding, and towels that are not thoroughly cleaned between uses pose a health threat to users of these items.

HP139. Each facility shall have a mechanical washing machine and dryer on site, or contract with a laundry service as specified in *Laundry*, on p. 174.

See rationale for standard HP138.

STAFFING IN SPECIAL FACILITIES FOR ILL CHILDREN

HP140. The director of a facility that cares for ill children shall have the following qualifications, in addition to the general qualifications described *Qualifications of Directors*, on p. 4.
a) A total of at least 40 hours of training in prevention and control of communicable diseases and

The director shall be college-prepared in early childhood education and have a college-level course in illness prevention and control, as this is the person responsible for establishing the facility's policies and procedures and for meeting the training needs of new staff members.

and care of ill children, including subjects listed in standard HP142.

b) At least 2 prior years' successful experience as a director of a regular facility.

c) At least 12 credit hours of college-level training in child development or early childhood education.

HP141. Each staff member of a special facility that cares for ill children shall have at least 2 years' successful work experience as a caregiver in a regular well-child facility prior to employment in the special facility, in addition to the general qualifications described in *Qualifications of Teaching/Caregiving Staff*, on p. 8.

Since meeting the physical and psychological needs of ill children requires a higher degree of skill and understanding than caring for well children, a commitment to children and an understanding of their general needs is imperative. Work experience will help the caregiver develop these skills. States that have developed rules regulating facilities have recognized the need for training in illness prevention and control and medical emergency management. First and foremost, people working with children should have an understanding of children and should always create an environment for children that is developmentally appropriate, healthful, and safe.

Staff caring for ill children in special facilities or in a get-well room in a regular center shall meet the staff qualifications that are applied to centers generally. These qualifications will include training in preventing the spread of disease, recognizing symptoms of illness, and caring for ill children. Knowledge of childhood immunization requirements is essential in limiting the spread of vaccine-preventable diseases in child care.

TRAINING IN SPECIAL FACILITIES FOR ILL CHILDREN

HP142. The facility that cares for ill children shall document 20 hours of orientation training (in addition to the orientation training specified in *General Training*, on p. 18, and *Orientation Training*, on p. 19) for each new staff member upon employment or within 3 months of employment, including training in each of the following subjects. (See recommendation REC42 in chapter 9 on p. 312 on health department assistance in developing such training.)

a) Pediatric first aid, including rescue breathing and first aid for choking (see *First Aid and CPR*, on p. 22).

b) General infection control procedures, including
   1) Handwashing.
   2) Handling of contaminated items.

Caregivers need to be prepared for handling illness and must have an understanding of their scope of work. Special training is required of teachers who work in special facilities for ill children because both the director and the caregivers are dealing with communicable diseases and need to know how to prevent the spread of infection. Each caregiver should have training to decrease the risk of transmission of disease.

The potential for medical emergencies due to illness is greater in facilities for ill children than in regular well-child facilities and preparedness is appropriate.

States that have developed rules regulating facilities have recognized the need for training in illness prevention and control, aseptic technique, and medical emergency management.

3) Use of disinfectants.
4) Food handling.
5) Washing and disinfection of toys.
c) Care of children with common mild childhood illnesses, including
   1) Recognition and documentation of illness signs and symptoms.
   2) Administration of medications.
   3) Temperature-taking.
   4) Nutrition of ill children.
   5) Communication with parents of ill children.
   6) Knowledge of immunization requirements.
   7) When and how to call for medical assistance or notify the local public health department of communicable diseases.
   8) Emergency procedures.
d) Child development activities for children who are ill.

HP143. Upon employment, each employee of a facility that cares for ill children shall begin a thorough orientation to the facility and to its policies; documentation of this orientation shall be kept in the employee's employment file. (See also recommendation REC42 on health department assistance on developing such training in chapter 9 on p. 312.)

Staff need to be prepared for handling illness and must have an understanding of their scope of work.

HP144. Each director and staff member of a facility that cares for ill children shall have at least 3 clock hours of continuing education annually related to the care of ill children and the prevention and control of communicable disease, in addition to the continued training in general aspects of infection control in child care specified in standard ST50 in chapter 1 on p. 24.

Special training is required for staff who work in special facilities for ill children because both the director and staff are dealing with communicable diseases and need to know how to prevent the spread of infection.

CHILD: STAFF RATIO IN SPECIAL FACILITIES FOR ILL CHILDREN

HP145. Each facility for ill children shall maintain a child:staff ratio no greater than the following:

No studies exist that substantiate appropriate staffing levels. Most staffing requirements made by state licensing authorities are stated in terms of what number of staff are required to remove children from a

These ratios do not include other personnel (e.g., bus drivers) necessary for specialized functions (e.g., transportation).

Age of Children	Ratio of Children to Staff
2–24 months	3 children to 1 staff member
25–71 months	4 children to 1 staff member
72 months and older	6 children to 1 staff member

building quickly in the event of fire or other emergency. Certainly, ill children require more intensive and personalized care; therefore, the lowest ratios used per age group seem appropriate.

When there are mixed age groups in the same room, the child:staff ratio shall be consistent with the age of the youngest child.

HEALTH CONSULTANTS IN SPECIAL FACILITIES FOR ILL CHILDREN

HP146. Each special facility for the care of ill children shall utilize the services of a health consultant to provide ongoing consultation to the facility in its overall operation and to assist in the development of written policies relating to health care. The facility shall involve the consultant in the development, review, and sign-off of the written policies and procedures for the management of specific illnesses, and shall review and update the process annually.

Appropriate involvement of health consultants is especially important for facilities for the care of ill children. Facilities must utilize the expertise of health professionals to design and provide a child care environment with sufficient staff and facilities to meet the needs of ill children.[105] The best interests of the child and family must be given primary consideration in the care of ill children. Some health care experts feel that consultation by physicians, especially pediatricians, is critical in the planning of facilities for the care of ill children.[96]

Unless provided through a public health system, the health consultant's services are very difficult to obtain, particularly for small family-child-care homes. Caregivers should seek the volunteer services of a health consultant through state and local professional organizations, such as the local chapters of the American Academy of Pediatrics, the American Nurses' Association, the Visiting Nurse Association, the American Academy of Family Physicians, the National Association of Pediatric Nurse Associates and Practitioners, the National Association for the Education of Young Children, and the National Association for Family Day Care, or through the state and local health departments (especially the public health nursing departments and the state communicable disease specialist's or epidemiologist's office). Caregivers also should not overlook health professionals who are parents of children enrolled in their facility.

HP147. The health consultant shall have training and experience with children; optimally, the health consultant will be a public health nurse, a pediatric or family nurse practitioner, or a pediatrician licensed in the state.

See rationale for standard HP46.

HP148. The facility shall assign the health consultant the responsibility for developing written policies and procedures for the following:

See rationale for standard HP46.

a) Admission and readmission after illness, including inclusion/exclusion criteria.

b) Health evaluation procedures on intake, including physical assessment of the child and other criteria used to determine the appropriateness of a child's attendance.

c) Plans for health care and for managing children with communicable diseases.

d) Plans for surveillance of illnesses cared for and problems that arise in the care of children.

e) Plans for staff training and communication with parents and health care providers.

f) Plans for injury prevention and emergency care.

For additional information on health consultants in special facilities for ill children, see also *Health Consultation*, on p. 278; *Consultation Records*, on p. 295, on documentation of health consultant visits; *Health Consultants*, on p. 33, on general health consultant qualifications and responsibilities; and recommendation REC44 in chapter 9 on p. 313 on health consultants for special facilities for ill children.

LICENSING SPECIAL FACILITIES FOR ILL CHILDREN

HP149. Special facilities that care for ill children shall be required to comply with specific licensing requirements, which shall address the unique regulatory needs of service to children with illness cared for in out-of-home settings.

Facilities for ill children are generally required to meet the licensing requirements that apply to all facilities of a specific type, for example, small or large family-child-care homes or centers.

For additional information on licensing special facilities for ill children, see also *The Regulatory Policy*, on p. 299, on licensing requirements.

PROCEDURES FOR CARE IN SPECIAL FACILITIES FOR ILL CHILDREN

HP150. For each day of care in a special facility that cares for ill children, the caregiver shall have the following additional information on each child:
a) The child's specific diagnosis and the individual providing the diagnosis, that is, the doctor, parent, or legal guardian.
b) Current status of the illness, including potential for contagion, diet, activity level, and illness duration.
c) Health care, diet, and medication plan, including an appropriate release form to obtain emergency health care and administer medication.
d) Communications with the parent on the child's progress.

The caregiver needs child-specific information to provide optimum care for each ill child and to make appropriate decisions regarding the inclusion or exclusion of a given child for the facility.

HP151. Inclusion and exclusion policies shall be considered by facilities that care for ill children for conditions requiring extra attention from the caregiver. (See *Child Inclusion/ Exclusion/Dismissal*, on p. 80.)
a) Ill children may be included in a special facility if they have symptoms and signs of illness that exclude them from a regular well-child facility.
b) Ill children with any of the following signs and symptoms shall be excluded from care in the special facility for ill children:
1) Fever with stiff neck, lethargy, irritability, or persistent crying.

These signs may indicate a significant systemic infection that requires professional medical management and parental care.

2) Diarrhea (i.e., five or more stools in an 8-hour period or an increased number of stools compared to the child's normal pattern, and with increased stool water and/or decreased form) in addition to one or more of the following:
   a) Signs of dehydration.
   b) Blood or mucus in the stool, unless at least one stool culture demonstrates absence of shigella, salmonella, campylobacter, and E. coli 015:H57.
3) Diarrhea due to shigella, salmonella, campylobacter, or giardia. However, a child with diarrhea due to shigella, salmonella, giardia may be readmitted 24 hours after treatment has been initiated if cleared by his/her physician.
4) Vomiting three or more times, or with signs of dehydration.
5) Contagious stages of pertussis, measles, mumps, chicken pox, rubella, or diphtheria, unless the child is appropriately isolated from children with other illnesses and cared for only with children having the same illness.
6) Untreated infestation (e.g., scabies, head lice).
7) Untreated tuberculosis.
8) Undiagnosed rash.
9) Abdominal pain that is intermittent or persistent.
10) Difficulty in breathing.
11) Lethargy such that the child does not play.
12) Other conditions as may be determined by the director or health consultant (see *Health Consultants*, on p. 106) on an individual basis.

HP152. A facility may care for children with symptoms requiring exclusion provided there is licensing authority approval of written plans describing symptoms to be cared for, justification for doing so, and procedures for daily care. (See also recommendation REC4 in chapter 9 on p. 301 for different ill care facilities.)

Because diarrheal illness caused by shigella, salmonella, campylobacter and giardia may spread from child to child or from child to staff, children and staff with these infections, when accompanied by diarrhea, should be excluded from child care until 24 hours after treatment has been initiated. Antibiotic therapy of campylobacter may not alter symptoms, but it does decrease shedding of the organism, and therefore lowers the infectivity of these children. Antibiotic therapy for salmonella gastroenteritis is generally not recommended unless diarrhea is severe, sepsis is present, or the child has a specific underlying medical condition making this illness problematic. Therefore, most children with salmonella gastroenteritis will not be treated with antibiotics, and should not be included in regular or special child care until the diarrheal illness has resolved.

HP153. In a facility that cares for ill children, equipment and materials shall be available that are varied, that stimulate the child's interest and involvement, and that provide a match between the child and his/her level of development and condition of health or illness, as defined by the facility's health consultant (see *Health Consultants*, on p. 106) and the child's health care provider.

Frequent mild illness is a normal condition of childhood, and the activity level of ill children is age dependent. Ill children, like well children, need to engage in activities that are suitable to their age and developmental level and consistent with their state of health or illness and their accompanying level of interest or responsiveness. A low level of responsiveness in the school-age child usually leads to his/her sleeping and resting for much of the day, requiring a minimum of activities and stimulation. Infants, toddlers, and preschool-age children tend to be unable to rest for such long periods of time, and therefore require more attention from the caregiver in terms of providing activities and guidance.

For additional information on procedures for care in special facilities for ill children, see also *Emergency Plan*, on p. 280.

References

1. Paige DM. *Manual of Clinical Nutrition.* Pleasantville, NJ: Nutrition Publications; 1983.

2. Cook R, Davis SB, Radke FH, et al. Nutritional status of Head Start and nursery school children. *J Amer Diet Assoc.* 1976;68:120–126.

3. *Pediatric Nutrition Handbook.* Elk Grove Village, Ill: American Academy of Pediatrics; 1985:326.

4. Marotz LR, Ruch JM, Cross MZ. *Health, Safety and Nutrition for the Young Child.* Albany, NY: Delmar; 1985.

5. Provence L. *Guide for the Care of Infants in Groups.* New York, NY: Child Welfare League of America; 1967.

6. Deitch S, ed. *Health in Day Care: A Manual for Health Professionals.* Elk Grove Village, Ill: American Academy of Pediatrics; 1987.

7. Embler B, Windahy A, Zaino SW, et al. The value of repetition and reinforcement in improving oral health performance and oral hygiene performance. *J Periodontol.* 1980;51:4.

8. Kleinman PR, Rose C, Rogers EW, et al. An assessment of the Alabama smile keeper school dental health education programs. *J Amer Dent Assoc.* 1979:98(1):51–54.

9. Van R, Wun C-C, Morrow AL, et al. The effect of fecal containment on fecal coliform contamination in the day care center environment. *J Amer Med Assoc.* 1991;265:1840–1844.

10. Van R, Morrow AL, Reves RR, et al. Environmental contamination in child day care centers. *Amer J Epidemiol.* 1991;133:460–470.

11. Berg RW. Etiology and pathophysiology of diaper dermatitis. *Adv Dermatol.* 1988;3:75–98.

12. Berg RW, Buckingham KW, Stewart RL. Etiologic factors in diaper dermatitis: the role of urine. *Pediatr Dermatol.* 1986;3:102–106.

13. Buckingham KW, Berg RW. Etiologic factors in diaper dermatitis: the role of feces. *Pediatr Dermatol.* 1986;3:107–112.

14. Jordan WE, Lawson KD, Berg RW, et al. Diaper dermatitis: frequency and severity among a general infant population. *Pediatr Dermatol.* 1986;3:198–207.

15. Zimmerer RE, Lawson KD, Calvert CJ. The effects of wearing diapers on skin. *Pediatr Dermatol.* 1986;3:95–101.

16. Seymour JL, Keswick BH, Hanifin JM, et al. Clinical effects of diaper types on the skin of normal infants and infants with atopic dermatitis. *J Amer Acad Dermatol.* 1987; 17:988–997.

17. Campbell RL, Seymour JL, Stone LC, et al. Clinical studies with disposable diapers containing absorbent gelling materials: evaluation of effects on infant skin condition. *J Amer Acad Dermatol.* 1987;17:978–987.

18. Campbell RL, Bartlett AV, Sarbaugh FC, et al. Effects of diaper types on diaper dermatitis associated with diarrhea and antibiotic use in children in day-care centers. *Pediatr Dermatol.* 1988;5:83–87.

19. Koshland DE Jr. The dirty air act. *Science.* 1990;249:1481.

20. Diaper Service Accreditation Council. *Standards for Accrediting Diaper Services.* Philadelphia, Pa: National Association of Diaper Services; 1979.

21. Simmons BP. Centers for Disease Control guidelines for the prevention and control of nosocomial infections. *Amer J Infect Control.* 1983;11:97–124.

22. Benenson A. *Control of Communicable Diseases in Man.* Washington, DC: American Public Health Association; 1985.

23. Black RE, Dykes AC, Anderson KE. Handwashing to prevent diarrhea in day care centers. *Amer J Epidemiol.* 1981;113:445–451.

24. Aronson SS, Aiken LS. Compliance of child care programs with health and safety standards: impact of program evaluation and advocate training. *Pediatrics.* 1980;65:318–325.

25. Bartlett AV, Jarvis BA, Ross V, et al. Diarrheal illness among infants and toddlers in day care centers: effects of active surveillance and staff training without subsequent monitoring. *Amer J Epidemiol.* 1988;127:808–817.

26. Sullivan P, Woodward WE, Pickering LK, et al. A longitudinal study of the occurrence of diarrheal disease in day care centers. *Amer J Public Health.* 1984;74:987–991.

27. Hadler SC, McFarland L. Hepatitis in day care centers: epidemiology and prevention. *Rev Infect Dis.* 1986;8:548–557.

28. Hershow RC, Hadler SC, Kane MA. Adoption of children from countries with endemic hepatitis B: transmission risks and medical issues. *Pediatr Infect Dis.* 1987;6:431–437.

29. Francis DP, Favero MS, Maynard JE. Transmission of hepatitis B virus. *Sem Liver Disease.* 1981;1: 127–137.

30. Shapiro ED. Lack of transmission of hepatitis B in a day care center. *J Pediatr.* 1987;110:90–92.

31. Jenison SA, Lemon SM, Baker LN, et al. Quantitative analysis of hepatitis B virus in saliva and semen of chronically infected homosexual men. *J Infect Dis.* 1987;156:299–307.

32. Scott RM, Snitbhan R, Bancroft WH, et al. Experimental transmission of hepatitis B virus by semen and saliva. *J Infect Dis.* 1980;142:67–71.

33. Maynard JL. Modes of hepatitis transmission. In: Japan Medical Research Foundation, ed. *Hepatitis Viruses* (Proceeding of the 1976 International Symposium on Hepatitis Viruses, Tokyo, 18–20 November 1976). Tokyo, Japan: University of Tokyo Press; 1978:125–137.

34. MacQuarrie MB, Forghani B, Wolochow DA. Hepatitis B transmitted by a human bite. *JAMA.* 1974;230:723–724.

35. Hamilton JD, Larke B, Qizilbash A. Transmission of hepatitis B by a human bite: an occupational hazard. *Can Med Assoc J.* 1976;115:439–440.

36. Cancio-Bello TP, de Medina M, Shorey J, et al. An institutional outbreak of hepatitis B related to a human biting carrier. *J Infect Dis.* 1982;146:652–656.

37. MacDonald KL, Danila RN, Osterholm MT. Infection with human T-lymphotrophic virus type III/lymphadenopathy-associated virus: considerations for transmission in the child day care setting. *Rev Infect Dis.* 1986;8:606–612.

38. Davis LG, Weber DJ, Lemon SM. Horizontal transmission of hepatitis B virus. *Lancet.* 1989;I:889–893.

39. Centers for Disease Control. Education and foster care of children infected with human T-lymphotrophic virus type III/lymphadenopathy-association virus. *MMWR.* 1985;34:517–521.

40. Favero MS, Petersen NJ, Bond WW. *Laboratory Safety Principles and Practices.* Washington, DC: American Society for Microbiology; 1986:49–58.

41. Ekanem EE, DuPont HL, Pickering LK, et al. Transmission dynamics of enteric bacteria in day care centers. *Amer J Epidemiol.* 1983; 118:562–572.

42. Weniger BG, Ruttenber AJ, Goodman RA, et al. Fecal coliforms on environmental surfaces in two day care centers. *Appl Environ Microbiol.* 1983; 45:733–735.

43. Gwaltney JM Jr. Rhinovirus colds: epidemiology, clinical characteristics and transmission. *Eur J Resp Dis.* 1983;128:336–339.

44. Hall CB. The nosocomial spread of respiratory syncytial viral infections. *Annual Rev Med.* 1983; 34:311–319.

45. Hall CB, Douglas RG Jr, Schnable KC, Geiman JM. Infectivity of respiratory syncytial virus by various routes of inoculation. *Infect Immun.* 1981;33:779–783.

46. Murphy TV, Clements JF, Petroni M, et al. *Haemophilus influenzae* type b in respiratory secretions. *Pediatr Infect Dis J.* 1989;8:151.

47. Taylor MRH, Keane CT, Kerrrison IM, et al. Simple and effective measures for control of enteric cross-infection in a children's hospital. *Lancet.* 1979;1:865–867.

48. Shapiro ED, Kuribby J, Potter J. Policies for the exclusion of ill children from group day care: an unresolved dilemma. *Rev Infect Dis.* Jul/Aug 1986; 8(4).

49. Landis S, Earp JL, Sharp M. Day-care center exclusion of sick children: comparison of opinions of day-care staff, working mothers, and pediatricians. *Pediatrics.* 1988;81(5):662–667.

50. Brunell P. Infections in day care centers. *Amer J Dis Child.* 1987;141(4):404–405.

51. St. Gene J. Pickering L, Granoff D. Symposium—Day care diseases: focusing on GI illness and care. *Contemp Pediatr.* 1986;3:108–122.

52. *Report of the Committee on Infectious Diseases.* Elk Grove Village, Ill: American Academy of Pediatrics; 1986.

53. Child Day Care Infectious Disease Study Group, Centers for Disease Control. Public health considerations of infectious diseases in child day care centers. *J Pediatr.* 1984;105(5):683–701.

54. Calder J. Daily health care issues in child care. Admission, exclusions, hygiene, training. In: *Child Care: The Role of the Health Care Provider.* Presented at California Health Office and the American Academy of Pediatrics Northern California Chapter 1 Conference; November 8–9, 1985; San Rafael, Calif.

55. American Red Cross. *American Red Cross Child Care Course Instructor's Manual.* Washington, DC: American Red Cross; 1990.

56. Aronson S. Maintaining health in child care settings. *Group Care for Young Children. Pediatric Round Table 12.* 1986;10:24.

57. Presser B. Place of child care and medicated respiratory illness among young American children. *J Marriage and the Family.* 1988;50:995–1005.

58. Bluestone D. Modern management of otitis media. *Pediat Clin North Amer.* 1989;36:1371–1387.

59. Fisher L, VanBuren J, Lawrence RA. Genesee regional poison prevention project, phase II. *Vet and Human Toxicol.* 1986;28:123–126.

60. Fisher L, VanBuren J. An integrated model for childhood injury preventive programs. *Vet and Human Toxicol.* 1981;23:261–263.

61. Aronson S, Smith, H. Medication administration in child care. *Exchange.* 1985;41:27–29.

62. Finkelhor D, William LM, Burns N. *Nursery Crimes: Sexual Abuse in Day Care.* Beverly Hills, Calif: Sage Publications; 1988.

63. Robertson WO. Syrup of ipecac, a slow or fast emetic? *Amer J Dis Child.* 1962;103:136–139.

64. McLoughlin E, Crawford JD. Burns. *Pediat Clin North Amer.* 1985;32:61–75.

65. Massachusetts Department of Public Health. *Safe Home Checklist.* Boston, Mass; 1987.

66. Tron VA, Baldwin VJ, Pirie GE. Hot tub drownings. *Pediatrics.* 1985;75:4.

67. Walker S, Middlekamp JN. Pail immersion accidents. *Clin Pediatr.* 1981;20:5.

68. American Academy of Pediatrics. *Injury Control for Children and Youth.* Elk Grove Village, Ill: AAP; 1987.

69. Rowe MI, Abelardo A, Allington G. Profile of pediatric drowning victims in a water-oriented society. *J Trauma.* 1977;17:8.

70. Plueckhahn VD. Drowning: community aspects. *Med J Aust.* 1979;2:226–228.

71. American Academy of Pediatrics. *Save a Child's Life!* [brochure]. Available from Accident Prevention Committee, California Chapter 2, American Academy of Pediatrics, P.O. Box 2134, Inglewood, Calif 90305.

72. Consumer Product Safety Commission Medical Examiners and Coroners Alert Project. *MECAP News.* August 1987;12(3).

73. Emergency standard (ES) 13. Standard performance specifications for safety covers and labeling requirements for covers for pools, spas, and hot tubs. Philadelphia, Pa: American Society for Testing and Materials; April 4, 1989.

74. Spyker DA. Submersion injury: epidemiology, prevention and management. *Pediat Clin North Amer.* 1985;32:1.

75. Wintemute GJ, Kraus JF, Teret SP, et al. Drowning in childhood and adolescence: a population-based study. *Amer J Public Health.* 1987;77:830–832.

76. Webster DP. Pool drownings and their prevention. *Public Health Rep.* 1967;82:599.

77. Stitt VJ. Drowning in North Carolina. *North Carolina Med J.* 1982;43:6.

78. Wintemute GJ, Kraus JF, Teret SP, et al. Letters to the editor. *Amer J. Public Health.* 1988;78:98.

79. Pearn J, Nixon J. Bathtub immersion accidents involving children. *Med J Aust.* 1977;1:211–213.

80. Lauer EA, White WC, Lauer BA. Dog bites: a neglected problem in accident prevention. *Amer J Dis Child.* 1982;136:202.

81. Chun YT, Berkelhamer JE. Dog bites in children less than 4 years old. *Pediatrics.* 1982;69:119–120.

82. Office on Smoking and Health. *The Health Consequences of Involuntary Smoking: A Report of the Surgeon General.* Rockville, Md: Office on Smoking and Health, US Department of Health and Human Services, Centers for Disease Control; 1986.

83. Harlap S, Davies AM. Infant admissions to hospital and maternal smoking. *Lancet.* 1974;1:529–532.

84. Fleming DW, Cochi SL, Hightower AW, et al. Childhood upper respiratory tract infections: to what degree is incidence affected by day-care attendance? *Pediatrics.* 1987;79:55–60.

85. US Fire Administration. *Fire in the US: Deaths, Injuries, Dollar Loss, and Incidents at the National, State, and Local Levels in 1981.* 4th ed. Washington, DC: Federal Emergency Management Administration; 1982.

86. Birkey MM, et al. Fire fatality study, fire and materials. *JAMA.* 1979;3:211–217.

87. *Environmental Tobacco Smoke—Measuring Exposures and Assessing Health Effects.* Washington, DC: National Academy Press; 1986.

88. Garfinkel L, Auerback O, Joubert L. Involuntary smoking and lung cancer: a case-control study. *J Nat Cancer Inst.* 1985;75:463–469.

89. Pickering LK, Hadler SC. Management and prevention of infectious diseases in day care. In: RD Feigin, JD Cherry, eds. *Textbook of Pediatric Infectious Diseases.* Philadelphia, Pa: Saunders Co; 1987:2343–2361.

90. Fredericks B, Hardman B, Morgan G, et al. *A Little Bit Under the Weather: A Look at Care for Mildly Ill Children.* Boston, Mass: Work/Family Directions Inc; 1985.

91. Hershaw RC, Hadler SC, Kane MA. Adoption of children from countries with endemic hepatitis B: transmission risks and medical issues. *Pediatr Infec Dis.* 1987;6:431–437.

92. Morgan GG, Stevenson CS, Fiene R, et al. Gaps and excesses in the regulation of child care: Report of a panel. In: MT Osterholm, JO Klein, SS Aronson, et al., eds. *Infectious Diseases in Child Day Care: Management and Prevention.* Chicago, Ill: University of Chicago Press; 1987:122–131.

93. Chang A, Kelson G, Harris M, et al. Care of mildly ill children enrolled in day care centers: management by parents and by trained home workers. *Western J Med.* 1981;134:181–185.

94. Wilson DA, Bess CR. Establishing a community-based sick child center. *Pediatr Nurs.* 1985; 12:439–441.

95. Chiles DW. Help sick kids? we had to beat the bureaucracy first. *Medical Economics.* 1981; 58:133–142.

96. Chang A, Zeledon-Friendly A, Britt A, et al. Management of illness and temporary disability in children enrolled in day care centers. *Amer J Dis Child.* 1988;142:651–655.

97. Tauxe RV, Johnson KE, Boase JC, et al. Control of day care shigellosis: a trial of convalescent day care in isolation. *Amer J Public Health.* 1986; 76:627–630.

98. McDonald KL, White KA, Heiser JL, et al. Lack of detected increased risk of subsequent illness for children attending a sick-child day care center. *Pediatr Infect Dis J.* 1991;9:15.

99. Peterson JJ, Bressler GK. Design and modification of the day care environment. *Rev Infect Dis.* 1986; 8:618–621.

100. Brunell PA, Taylor-Wiedeman J, Lievens A. Varicella in day care centers. *Rev Infect Dis.* 1986; 8:589–590.

101. Riley EC, Murphy G, Riley RL. Airborne spread of measles in a suburban elementary school. *Amer J Epidemiol.* 1978;107:421–432.

102. Remington PL, Hall WN, Davis IH, et al. Airborne transmission of measles in a physician's office. *JAMA.* 1985;253:1574–1577.

103. Bloch AB, Orenstein WA, Ewing WM, et al. Measles outbreak in a pediatric practice: airborne transmission in an office setting. *Pediatrics.* 1985; 75:676–683.

104. Klein JO. Infectious diseases and day care. *Rev Infect Dis.* 1986;8:521–526.

105. Aronson SS, Osterholm MT. Infectious diseases in child day care: management and prevention, summary of the symposium and recommendations. *Rev Infect Dis.* 1986;8:677.

CHAPTER 4

Nutrition and
Food Service

CHAPTER 4
NUTRITION AND FOOD SERVICE

4.1 General Requirements

STANDARDS

NU1. Children shall be provided nourishing and attractive food according to a written plan (see standard AD45, on p. 284 developed by a qualified child care Nutrition Specialist (see Appendices B-1 and B-2 on pp. 328–329). Carrying out the plan shall be the shared responsibility of all caregivers, directors, and food service personnel. (See also *Nutrition Learning Experiences for Children*, on p. 136, for nutrition learning experiences with this plan.)

NU2. All meals and supplements (snacks) and their preparation, service, and storage shall meet the requirements for meals of the child care component of the U.S. Department of Agriculture (USDA) Child Care Food Program (CCFP)[1] and the Code of Federal Regulations (CFR) Part 226.20.[2] (See Appendices J and K on p. 352–353.)

NU3. The facility shall ensure that
a) Children in care for 8 hours or less shall be offered at least one meal and two supplements (snacks) or two meals and one supplement (snack).
b) Children in care for 9 hours or more shall be offered at least two meals and two supplements (snacks) or three supplements (snacks) and one meal.
c) A nutritious supplement (snack) shall be offered to all children in midmorning and in midafternoon.
d) Children shall be offered food at intervals not less than 2 hours and not more than 3 hours apart unless the child is asleep.

RATIONALE

Nourishing and attractive food is a foundation for developmentally appropriate learning experiences.[1-4] Nutrition and feeding are fundamental and required activities in every facility. Since the growth and development of children is more rapid during the first few years of life than at any other time, the child's home and the facility together must provide food adequate in amount and kind to meet the metabolic, growth, and energy needs of each child. Meals and supplements (snacks) provide opportunities for observation and conversation, which aids in the conceptual, sensory, and language, development of children.

The CCFP[6] and the CFR Part 226.20[7] provide the basic guidelines for good nutrition and sanitation practices. Meals offered to young children should provide a variety of nourishing foods on a frequent basis to meet the nutritional needs of young children.

Young children need frequently offered, nutritious meals as they may choose to eat well at any one time but may be uninterested in eating at another time. To ensure that the child's daily nutritional needs are met, small feedings of nourishing food should be scheduled over the course of a day.[1, 2] Snacks should be nutritious as they often are a significant part of a child's daily life.

Children in care for more than 9 hours need additional food, as this period represents a majority of the waking hours of a young child.

COMMENTS

Staff should use information on the child's growth in developing individual feeding plans. (See *Growth Data,* on p. 66.)

Caloric needs vary greatly from one child to another. More intake may be required during growth spurts.

Some states have regulations indicating the suggested times for meals and supplements (snacks).

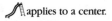 applies to a small family-child-care home applies to a large family-child-care home applies to a center. If no symbol appears, the standard applies to all three.

STANDARDS

NU4. A minimum of one serving of a fruit, vegetable, or juice high in vitamin C must be provided daily, and a food high in vitamin A must be served at least three times a week. Foods that are good sources of iron shall be served daily.

NU5. Supplements (snacks) that have a high sugar content or that are sticky (e.g., raisins) shall be avoided. Only full-strength (100 percent) fruit juice shall be served.

NU6. Dietary modifications shall be made under the direction of a trained health care provider. The caregiver shall modify and/or supplement the child's diet because of food allergies or special dietary needs only with written permission from the child's parent or legal guardian and from the child's health care provider. The caregiver shall obtain a list of foods that the child can and cannot consume from the parent/legal guardian or the child's health care provider. Menus shall be approved by the child care Nutrition Specialist (see Appendices B-1 and B-2, on pp. 328–329). Dietary modifications shall be recorded as specified in Appendix C, on p. 330.

RATIONALE

It is not sufficient to serve fruits and vegetables without focusing on particular nutrients, not only for the health of the child, but also for the education of the child.

This practice will reduce acids in the mouth that cause tooth decay. The frequency of exposure, rather than the quantity of food, is an important factor in whether foods cause tooth decay. Studies have shown that eating sweets and other refined carbohydrates causes tooth decay.[8] Sticky foods continue acid production in the mouth over a prolonged period of time.

Although sugar is not the only dietary factor likely to cause tooth decay, it is a major factor in the prevalence of tooth decay.[9] There are reports of a strong relationship between the reported consumption of sugar between meals and (D)ecayed (M)issing (F)illed values, but there seems to be practically no relationship between total consumption of sugar (which would include that eaten with meals) and DMF values.[10]

Drinks that are called *fruit juice drinks* have added sugar and are less than 100 percent juice.

Dietary modification under the guidance of a trained health professional ensures that the child's health will not be jeopardized. Consultation with a child care Nutrition Specialist (see Appendices B-1 and B-2, on pp. 328–329) is necessary to plan meals correctly.

COMMENTS

Staff should provide an example to children by eating the same foods as well as discussing the food being eaten as part of nutrition education for the children.

There is a relationship between food eaten and tooth decay that many parents and caregivers need to understand and accept.

STANDARDS	RATIONALE	COMMENTS

NU7. Written menus showing all foods to be served shall be prepared at least 1 month in advance and shall be dated, amended to reflect any changes in the food actually served, made available to parents, and retained for 3 years. Any substitutions shall be of equal nutrient value. (See *Posting Documents*, on p. 296 on posting menus.)

Planning menus in advance helps to ensure that food will be on hand. Parents need to be informed about food served in the facility to know how to complement it with the food served at home. If a child has difficulty with any food served at the facility, parents can address this issue with appropriate staff. Menus are required for up to 3 years by some regulatory agencies as a part of the licensing and auditing process.[1, 2]

Making the menus available to parents helps to educate parents about proper nutrition.

4.2 Requirements for Special Groups or Ages of Children

NUTRITION FOR INFANTS

NU8. Meals and supplements (snacks) provided by the facility for infants shall contain at a minimum the food components shown in Appendix J, on p. 352. Food shall be appropriate for infants' individual nutrition requirements and developmental stages as determined by written instructions obtained from the child's parent or health care provider.

Breast milk or iron-fortified formula is the first food and has been shown to support the rapid growth in both weight and length that occurs during the first year of life. The nutrient content of breast milk or iron-fortified formula is best suited to meet the nutritional needs of an infant from birth until 4 to 6 months of age. Breast milk is the ideal nutrient source for term infants.[11] Breast-feeding gives infants complete nutrition and helps provide them with resistance to infections.[11] An adequately nourished infant is more likely to achieve normal physical and mental development, which will have long-term positive consequences on health.[12, 13]

NU9. The introduction of solid foods shall be accomplished routinely between 4 and 6 months of age, as indicated by an individual child's nutritional and developmental needs after consultation with the parents. Modification of basic food patterns shall be provided in writing by the child's health care provider.

Early introduction (i.e., prior to 4 to 6 months of age) of solid food interferes with the intake of breast milk or iron-fortified formula that is needed to promote growth. Solid food given before an infant is developmentally ready may be associated with allergies and digestive problems. Growth data suggest that after the age of 4 to 6 months, infants fed exclusively on milk may develop nutritional problems including failure to thrive and iron-deficiency anemia.[6]

NU10. Infants shall be fed on demand unless the parent provides written instructions otherwise.

Demand feeding meets the infant's nutritional and emotional needs better than does following a rigid feeding schedule that does not take into account growth spurts, appetite, and activity level. Demand feeding provides an immediate response to the infant, which helps ensure trust and a feeling of security.

NU11. Infants shall either be held or be fed sitting up for bottle feeding. Infants unable to sit shall always be held for bottle feeding. Bottle propping and carrying of bottles by young children throughout the day and/or night shall not be permitted.

The manner in which food is given is conducive to the development of sound eating habits for life. Bottle propping may cause choking, aspiration, and increased risk for development of ear infections, tooth decay, and tooth trauma.

A pattern of extensive tooth decay called "baby bottle tooth decay" may be caused by giving an infant or toddler a bottle of milk or juice as a pacifier at bedtime and throughout the night.[14] Baby bottle tooth decay is characterized by severe dental caries in the primary teeth that may have significant short-term and long-term implications for the health of the child.[15] Any liquid except plain water can cause baby bottle tooth decay.[16] Long-term ramifications of bedtime and prolonged bottle feeding may include otitis media, orthodontic problems, speech disorders, and possible psychological problems.[17]

Carrying glass bottles creates a safety hazard if the child drops the bottle and it breaks. Milk may curdle if a child carries the bottle for extended periods.

At around 7 to 8 months of age, beverages (including milk and fruit juices) should be offered from a cup. The child of this age is usually developmentally and neurologically ready to handle the cup.

Caregivers and parents need to understand that there is a relationship between tooth decay and the milk or juice in a bottle used as a pacifier.

Bottle propping is the practice of allowing an infant too young to hold a bottle to feed unattended from one that is supported (propped) against objects adjacent to the infant, such as a pillow or rolled blanket.

NU12. Formula shall preferably be provided by the parents; if provided by the facility, formula shall be in a factory-sealed container. The formula shall be of ready-to-feed strength or shall be prepared from powder or concentrate at the child care site and diluted according to the instructions provided by the manufacturer, using water from a source approved by the local health department.

This standard promotes the feeding of a formula familiar to the infant, and supports family feeding practice. By following this standard, staff are able when necessary to prepare formula and feed an infant safely, thus reducing the risk of inaccuracy.

NU13. Only cleaned and disinfected bottles and nipples shall be used. All filled bottles of breast milk or iron-fortified formula shall be refrigerated until immediately before feeding. Any contents remaining after a feeding shall be discarded. Prepared bottles of formula from powder or concentrate or ready-to-feed formula

Bottles with formula that have been fed should not be reused because the milk will have been contaminated with saliva and bacteria, which could grow to spoil the formula before the bottle is refed; this is especially true if the bottle is out of refrigeration for the first feeding for an hour or more and then reheated. Open containers shall be refrigerated, and shall be discarded after 24 hours if not used. An open container of ready-to-feed or concentrated formula shall be covered, refrigerated, and discarded after 48 hours if not used. Unused expressed breast milk shall be discarded after 48 hours if refrigerated, or after 2 weeks if frozen.

of formula are not safe to use beyond the stated shelf period.[6]

NU14. Bottles of breast milk and formula shall be dated. When there is more than one bottle-fed infant, all bottles shall be labeled with the child's name. All formula and breast milk shall be used only for the intended child.

Identification of the bottles prevents cross-infection when there is more than one bottle-fed infant.

NU15. Frozen breast milk shall be thawed under running cold water or in the refrigerator.

NU16. If breast milk or formula is to be warmed, bottles shall be placed in a pan of hot (not boiling) water for 5 minutes, after which the bottle shall be shaken well and the milk temperature tested before feeding. Bottles of formula or breast milk shall never be warmed in a microwave oven.

Bottles of formula or breast milk warmed in a microwave oven heat unevenly and may cause a severe burn upon feeding, even after being shaken. Bottles of formula or milk that are warmed at room temperature or in warm water for extended periods provide an ideal medium for bacterial growth.

NU17. Bottles, bottle caps, and nipples reused by the facility shall be cleaned and disinfected by washing in a dishwasher or by boiling for 5 minutes or more just prior to filling.

NU18. For children requiring bottles, but no longer on formula, milk (see standard NU19) shall be poured from the original container into cleaned, disinfected, and labeled bottles or disposable, sterile bottle liners.

NU19. Only whole, pasteurized milk shall be served to children younger than 24 months of age who are not on formula or breast milk. Skim milk, reconstituted nonfat dry milk, and milk containing 1 percent or 2 percent butterfat shall not be used for drinking purposes by any child less than 24 months of age, except with the written direction of a parent and the child's health care provider.

Low-fat milk does not provide enough calories and nutrients for children under the age of 2.

NU20. Commercially packaged baby food shall be served from a bowl or cup and not directly from the commercial container. Solid food shall be fed by spoon only. Uneaten food in dishes shall be discarded.

The external surface of a commercial container may be contaminated with disease-causing microorganisms during shipment or storage and may contaminate the food product during feeding. A bowl or cup should be cleaned and disinfected before use, thereby reducing the likelihood of surface contamination. Uneaten food should not be put back into its original container for storage because it may contain potentially harmful bacteria from the infant's saliva. Solid food should not be fed in a bottle or infant feeder apparatus because at worst, the infant can choke; at best, the infant is taught to eat solid foods incorrectly.

For additional information on nutrition for infants, see also standard AD47, on p. 285; Appendix L, on p. 354, on bottle feeding and storage and handling of breast milk, formula, and baby food; and *Meal Service, Seating, and Supervision,* on p. 123 on the size of food pieces to serve infants and on supervision of feeding.

NUTRITION FOR TODDLERS AND PRESCHOOLERS

NU21. Meals and supplements (snacks) provided by the facility for toddlers and preschoolers shall contain at a minimum the food components shown for these age groups in Appendix K, on p. 353.

A nutritional analysis was conducted of the requirements in Appendix K, on p. 353, to ensure that a supplement (snack) and lunch meet two-thirds of the Recommended Dietary Allowances.[18]

Numerous and excellent guidelines can be found in references 19 to 24 following this chapter.

NU22. Toddlers and preschoolers shall be served small-sized portions and permitted to have one or more additional servings to meet the needs of the individual child.

Gradual extension of the diet begun in infancy should continue throughout the preschool period. A child will not eat the same amount each day because appetites vary and food "jags" are common. If normal variations in eating patterns are accepted without comment, feeding problems usually do not develop. Requiring that a specified food or amount of food be eaten may lead to eating problems. It is possible that eating habits established in infancy and early childhood may contribute to problems later in life. Inclusion of

It is important to continue to meet the child's needs for growth and activity. During the second and third years of life the child grows much less rapidly than during the first year of life.

nutritious supplements (snacks) in the daily meal plan will help to ensure that the child's nutrient needs are met. The quality of supplements (snacks) for young children is especially important, and small, frequent feedings are recommended to achieve the total desired daily intake.

NU23. Toddlers shall be encouraged to hold and drink from a cup, to use a spoon, and to use their fingers for self-feeding.

As children enter the second year of life, they are interested in doing things for themselves. Self-feeding appropriately separates the responsibilities of the adults and children. The adult is responsible for providing nutritious food, the child for deciding how much of it to eat.[25] In order to allow for the proper development of motor skills and eating habits, children need to be allowed to practice learning to feed themselves.

Foods served need to be appropriate for the developmental ability of the toddler.

For additional information on nutrition for toddlers and preschoolers, see also standard NU11 on p. 118 on bottle feeding, and *Meal Service, Seating, and Supervision*, on p. 123 on the size of food pieces to serve toddlers and preschoolers and on supervision of feeding.

NUTRITION FOR SCHOOL-AGE CHILDREN

NU24. Meals and supplements (snacks) provided by the facility for school-age children (including those in school-age child care facilities) shall contain at a minimum the food components shown for this age group in Appendix K, on p. 353. Children attending facilities for 2 or more hours after school need at least one supplement (snack); those attending for more than 2½ hours need an additional supplement (snack).

The principles of providing adequate, nourishing food for younger children apply to this group. At this age, there is a rapid rate of growth that increases the need for energy and essential nutrients to support optimal growth. Food intake may vary considerably because this is a time when children express strong food likes and dislikes. The quality of food provided should contribute toward meeting nutritional needs for the day and should not dull the appetite.[19-24]

A nutritional analysis was conducted of the requirements in Appendix K, on p. 353, to ensure that a supplement (snack) and lunch meet two-thirds of the Recommended Dietary Allowances.[18]

NUTRITION FOR CHILDREN WITH SPECIAL NEEDS

See *Special Feeding Techniques, Nutrition, and Diets,* on p. 259.

4.3 Staffing

NU25. The center director shall be responsible for the administrative aspects of the food service unit unless the facility is large enough to justify employment of a full-time child care Nutrition Specialist (see Appendices B-1 and B-2, on pp. 328–329) or child care food service manager (see Appendices B-2, on p. 329 and M, on p. 356), in which case the responsibility is delegated.

NU26. Each facility shall employ trained staff and provide ongoing supervision and consultation in accordance with individual site needs as determined by the child care Nutrition Specialist (see Appendices B-1 and B-2, on pp. 328–329). Prior work experience in food service shall be required for the solitary worker responsible for food preparation and so forth without the continuous on-site supervision of a food service manager. (See Appendix B-2, on p. 329.)

The need for trained personnel to work in the food service component of facilities has been identified as mandatory for meeting the nutrition standards in these facilities.[26–29]

The type of food service, type of equipment, number of children to be fed, location of the facility, and food budget determine the staffing patterns.

Several excellent sources of valuable information can be found in references 26 through 29 following this chapter.

NU27. A local child care Nutrition Specialist (see Appendices B-1 and B-2, on pp. 328–329) or food service expert (see Appendix M, on p. 356) shall be employed to work with the architect or engineer in development and implementation of the facility's nutrition plan (see standard AD45 in chapter 8 on p. 284) and to prepare the initial food service budget. The nutrition plan (see standard AD45 in chapter 8 on p. 284) encompasses kitchen layout; food procurement, preparation, and service; staffing; and nutrition education.

Efficient and cost-effective food service in a facility begins with a plan and evaluation of the physical aspects of the facility. Planning for the food service unit includes consideration of location and adequacy of space for receiving, storage, preparation, serving and cleanup, dishwashing, and dining areas, plus space for desk, telephone, records, and employee facilities (e.g., handwashing sinks, toilets, and lockers). All facets must be considered for new or existing sites, including remodeling or renovation of the unit.[29, 30]

NU28. When alterations in the nutrition plan (see standard AD45 in chapter 8 on p. 284) are contemplated, such as installing a new dishwasher or expanding storage or dining areas,

the procedure to be followed shall be the same as for new construction or renovation. The food service expert shall be involved in the decision-making process and oversee carrying out completion of the plan.

NU29. For facilities operating 6 or more hours a day and/or preparing and serving food on the premises, the food service staff requirements shown in Appendix M, on p. 356 shall apply.

For additional information on staffing, see also Appendix A, on p. 327, on nutrition staffing requirements and Appendices B-1 and B-2, on pp. 328–329 on local and state nutrition personnel and food service staff.

See rationale above.

An adequate number of food service personnel is essential to meet the goals and objectives of the facility and ensure that children are fed according to the facility's schedule.

The food service staff may not necessarily consist of full-time or regular staff members, but may include some workers hired on a consulting or contractual basis.

Resources for food service staff include vocational high school food preparation programs, university and community college food preparation programs, and trade schools that train cooks and chefs.

See Appendices B-1 and B-2, on pp. 328–329 for a description of qualifications and responsibilities.

4.4 Meal Service, Seating, and Supervision

NU30. Child care staff shall ensure that children who do not require high chairs are comfortably seated at tables that are between waist and mid-chest level and allow the child's feet to rest on a firm surface while seated for eating.

Proper seating while eating reduces the risk of food aspiration[31] and improves comfort in eating.

Measure compliance by observation of fit of furniture for children.

NU31. All furniture and eating utensils shall be age-appropriate and developmentally suitable for children, with special equipment provided for children with disabilities.

Suitable furniture and utensils provide comfort and enable the children to develop skill and coordination in handling food and utensils.

Eating utensils should be attractive, durable, and suitable in size and shape for small hands. Dining areas should be clean and cheerful. Numerous and excellent guidelines can be found in references 2, 19, 21, 24, 28, and 32 following this chapter.

NU32. Child care staff shall ensure that children do not eat when walking, running, playing, lying down, or riding in vehicles.

Children should be seated when eating.[30, 32] This reduces the risk of aspiration injury.[31]

NU33. Caregivers shall sit at the table and shall eat the meal or supplement (snack) with the children. Family-style meal service shall be encouraged. The adult(s) shall

The presence of an adult or adults will help prevent behaviors that increase risk: fighting, feeding each other, stuffing food into the mouth, and so forth.

Measure compliance by structured observation.

encourage social interaction and conversation about the concepts of color, quantity, number, and temperature of food; eating behaviors; and events of the day.

Conversation at the table adds to the pleasant meal-time environment.[23] The future development of children depends in no small degree on their command of language, and richness of language increases as it is nurtured by verbal interaction of the child with adults and peers.[33] Family-style meals encourage children to serve themselves.

In addition to being nourished by food, infants and young children are helped through the act of feeding to establish warm human relationships. Eating should be an enjoyable experience at the facility and at home.

NU34. Children shall be actively involved in serving food and other mealtime activities, such as setting and cleaning the table.

Children develop new motor skills and practice increases their dexterity.

See comment on standard NU33.

NU35. Children shall be offered familiar foods that are typical of the children's culture and shall also be introduced to unfamiliar foods.

By learning about new food, children increase their knowledge of the world around them and increase the likelihood that they will choose a more varied, better balanced diet in later life. Eating habits and attitudes about food formed in the early years may well last a lifetime.

NU36. Children and staff shall wash their hands as specified in *Handwashing*, on p. 72.

NU37. Adults shall not consume hot liquids in child care areas. Coffee and other hot liquids and hot foods shall be placed out of the reach of infants, toddlers, and preschoolers. Hot liquids shall not be placed at the edge of a counter or table, or on a tablecloth that could be yanked down, while the adult is holding or working with a child. Pot handled shall be positioned toward the back of the stove.

The most common burn in young children is scalding from hot liquids tipped over in the kitchen.[34, 35]

NU38. Children's food shall be served on plates or other disinfected holders and shall not be placed on a bare table.

Tables are often used for many purposes in child care. Although the tables should be washed before meal time, they will still bear a heavier load of infecting organisms than plates or dsinfected food holders.

NU39. One adult shall not feed more than three children at the same time.

Cross-contamination among children being simultaneously fed by one adult is a significant risk. In addition, mealtime should be a socializing occasion. If more than three children are being fed at the same time, feeding resembles an impersonal production line. Children with special needs may require assistance in being fed.

NU40. Midinfancy children just learning to feed themselves shall be supervised by an adult who is seated at the same table or adjacent to the child's feeding chair.

A supervising adult should watch for several common problems that occur when midinfancy children begin to feed themselves. "Squirreling" of several pieces of food in the mouth increases the likelihood of choking. Supervised eating also ensures that the child does not eat while talking, crying, laughing, or playing, and thus prevents choking.

The presence of molars is a good indication of a healthy child's ability to chew hard foods (e.g., raw carrots) that are likely to cause choking. These foods are to be avoided when molars are not yet present[36]

NU41. Foods that are round, hard, small, thick and sticky, smooth, or slippery shall not be offered to children under 4 years of age. Examples of such foods include hot dogs (sliced into rounds), whole grapes, hard candy, nuts, seeds, raw peas, dried fruit, pretzels, chips, peanuts, popcorn, marshmallows, spoonfuls of peanut butter, and chunks of meat larger than can be swallowed whole.

These are high-risk foods, often implicated in choking incidents.[37] Ninety percent of fatal chokings occur in children younger than 4.[31, 34, 37]

Peanuts may occlude the lower airway. A chunk of hot dog or grape may completely occlude the upper airway.[37]

Menus should reflect the developmental abilities of the age of children served to reduce the risk of choking. Lists of high-risk foods should be made available.

See also comment for standard NU40.

NU42. For infants, foods shall be cut up in small pieces no larger than ¼-inch cubes.

Infants usually swallow pieces of food whole without chewing.

NU43. For toddlers, foods shall be cut up in small pieces no larger than ½-inch cubes.

Toddlers often swallow pieces of food whole without chewing.

See the comment for standard NU41.

NU44. The nutrition plan (see standard AD45, on p. 384) shall include steps to take when problems occur that require rapid response on the part of the staff (e.g., when a child chokes during mealtime). The completed plan shall be on file and accessible to staff.

Staff must know ahead of time what procedures to follow, as well as their designated roles during an emergency.

NU45. A child shall be encouraged, but not forced, to eat.

Children who are forced to eat or for whom food is used to modify behavior come to view eating as a tug-of-war and are more likely to develop lasting food dislikes and unhealthy eating behaviors.

NU46. Food shall not be used as a reward or punishment.

Offering food as a reward or punishment places undue importance on food for the child and may have negative effects by promoting "clean the plate" responses that may lead to obesity or poor eating behavior.[1, 2]

STANDARDS	RATIONALE	COMMENTS

For additional information on meal service, seating, and supervision, see also standards NU106 and NU107, on pp. 136 and 137.

4.5 Food Brought from Home

NU47. Meals may be provided by the parent or legal guardian upon written agreement between the parent and the staff. Lunches and supplements (snacks) provided by the parent or legal guardian shall not be shared with other children. Potentially hazardous and perishable foods shall be refrigerated properly (as specified in *Food Safety*, on p. 130) and all foods shall be protected against contamination.

There is a long history of foodborne illness and poisoning from food that has not been properly refrigerated and/or covered.

NU48. Food brought into the facility shall have a label showing the child's name, the date, and the type of food.

NU49. The facility shall inform the parents of the nutritional requirements established by the facility and suggest ways to meet them. The facility shall have food available to supplement a child's food brought from home if it is deficient in meeting the child's nutrient requirements. If the food provided by the parent consistently does not meet the nutritional or food safety requirements, the facility shall provide the food or refer the parent for consultation to a child care Nutrition Specialist (see Appendices B-1 and B-2, on pp. 328–329) or to the child's primary source of health care. (See nutrition requirements in *General Requirements,* on p. 115, and *Requirements for Special Groups of Children*, on p. 117.)

The facility has a responsibility to avoid negligent feeding practices if it recognizes them, even if parents want these practices followed. Such behavior is a form of child abuse and neglect, even if it is done unwittingly.

For additional information on food brought from home, see also standard ST52 in chapter 1 on p. 29 on training for food handlers and *Nutrition for Infants,* on p. 117.

4.6 Kitchen and Equipment

STANDARDS	**RATIONALE**	**COMMENTS**

NU50. The food preparation area of the kitchen shall be separate from the eating, play, toilet, and bathroom areas and from areas where animals are kept, and shall not be used as a passageway while food is being prepared. Food preparation areas shall be separated from areas used by the children for activities unrelated to food by a door, gate, counter, or room divider, except in small family-child-care homes when separation may limit child supervision.

This standard protects food from contamination and children from fire and burns.

NU51. All food-contact-area surfaces (including tables and counter-tops) and floors and shelving in the food preparation area shall be in good repair and shall be made of smooth, nonporous material that may be easily sanitized and kept clean.

This standard protects food from contamination.

NU52. All kitchen equipment shall be clean and in good operable condition and shall be properly maintained.

NU53. Food service equipment shall be designed, installed, operated, and maintained to meet the performance and health standards of the National Sanitation Foundation and the United States Department of Agriculture (USDA) food program and sanitation codes as determined by the regulatory public health authority.

Proper design and materials ensure proper cleanability and safety.[38]

Inspectors with appropriate training must check this equipment and provide technical assistance to facilities. Manufacturers can attest to their compliance with equipment standards.

Standards can be obtained from

National Sanitation Foundation
3475 Plymouth Rd.
P.O. Box 1468
Ann Arbor, MI 48106

The Code of Federal Regulations Part 200, Section 354.210 (revised January 1990) on sanitary requirements is available from

USDA Food Safety and Inspection Service
Facilities and Equipment Sanitation Division
14th and Independence Ave., S.W.
South Building, Room 1142
Washington, DC 20250

NU54. There shall be a handwashing sink(s) separate from the sink(s) used for food preparation. Handwashing sinks shall not be used for food preparation.

Separation of handwashing and food preparation sinks prevents contamination of food.

NU55. Centers shall provide a separate handwashing sink in the facility with a minimum 8-inch-high splash guard or with 18 inches of space between the handwashing sink and any open food zones (preparation tables, food sink, etc.).

See rationale for standard NU54 above.

NU56. All sinks shall be supplied with hot and cold running water under pressure. (See *Hot Water*, on p. 173.)

Hot and cold running water are essential for thorough cleaning and disinfecting of equipment and utensils, cleaning of the facility, and proper handwashing.

NU57. Refrigerators shall be used that maintain temperatures of 40°F or less in all parts of the food storage areas, and freezers shall maintain temperatures of 0°F or less in food storage areas.

Storage of food at proper temperatures minimizes bacterial growth.

NU58. Thermometers shall be provided in all refrigerators, freezers, ovens, and cold and hot food holding areas. Thermometers shall be clearly visible, easy to read, and accurate, and shall be kept in working condition and regularly checked.

The use of accurate thermometers to monitor temperatures at which food is cooked and stored helps to ensure food safety.

NU59. In centers using commercial cooking equipment to prepare meals, ventilation shall be provided with an exhaust system capable of providing a capture velocity of 50 feet per minute[39] 6 inches above the outer edges of the cooking surfaces at the prescribed filter velocities.

Such an exhaust system properly collects fumes and grease-laden vapors at their source.

Refer to the exhaust system owner's manual for a description of capture velocity.

NU60. All gas ranges in centers shall be mechanically vented and fumes filtered prior to discharge to the outside. All vents and filters shall be maintained free of grease buildup, in a sanitary condition, and in good repair.

Properly maintained vents and filters control odorous and dangerous fumes.

NU61. Microwave ovens shall be so located as to be inaccessible to, and unable to be used by, children

This standard protects the children from getting their faces near the heat vent and from being exposed to possible microwave radiation from a malfunctioning oven.

STANDARDS	**RATIONALE**	**COMMENTS**
NU62. Heating units for warming bottles and food shall be accessible to adults but not to children. Microwave ovens shall not be used for warming infant bottles or infant food.	Food heated in microwave ovens can easily reach scalding temperature. Bottles of formula heated in microwave ovens have caused burns to infants when the contents reach a higher temperature than the exterior of the bottle.[40, 41]	Some manufacturers of prepackaged food provide specific instructions regarding the use of microwaves for heating food. Caregivers should be aware that (1) initial temperature of the food is an important factor, as food at room temperature requires less heating time than refrigerated food to reach the desired temperature, and (2) smaller initial volumes reach higher core temperatures.
NU63. Dishes shall have smooth, hard-glazed surfaces and shall be free from cracks or chips. If imported dishes are purchased, they must carry a certificate of compliance with U.S. standards. Imported ceramic dishware or pottery shall be tested by the local health authority for lead or other heavy metals before use.	Imported dishware may be improperly fired and may release toxic levels of lead into food. U.S. government standards prevent the marketing of domestic dishes with lead in their glazes.	If in doubt, consult the local health department. There is no safe level of lead in dishware.
NU64. Disposable plates and cups and plastic utensils of food-grade, medium weight, may be used for single service. They are to be discarded after use. *Styrofoam cups and plates shall not be used.*	The use of disposable items eliminates the spread of contamination and disease and provides for safety and injury prevention. Swallowed styrofoam pieces may cause choking.	
NU65. Single-service articles such as napkins, bibs, dishes, and utensils shall be discarded after each use.	Single-service dishware is generally porous or otherwise unable to be cleaned and disinfected for reuse.	
For additional information on kitchen and equipment, see also *Diaper-Changing Areas*, on p. 171, and *Maintenance*, on p. 133.		

4.7 Access to Kitchen

NU66. In centers, access to the kitchen by infants and toddlers shall be restricted. Access by older children shall be permitted if supervised by staff who have been certified by the child care Nutrition Specialist (see Appendices B-1 and B-2, on pp. 328–329) or center director as qualified to follow the sanitation, disinfection, and safety procedures of the facility.	Kitchens are hazardous places for young children.	

STANDARDS	**RATIONALE**	**COMMENTS**

NU67. Children younger than school age shall be restricted from hot food preparation areas during meal preparation.

See rationale for NU37 in chapter 4 on p. 124.

For additional information on access to kitchen, see also standard HP126 in chapter 3 on p. 98 on restricting animals from food areas.

4.8 Food Safety

NU68. The facility shall conform to the applicable standards for centers and small and large family-child-care homes of the U.S. Food and Drug Administration model food sanitation standards and all applicable state and local food service rules and regulations for centers and small and large family-child-care homes regarding safe food protection and sanitation/disinfection practices.[42]

To obtain the U.S. Food and Drug Administration's *Food Service Sanitation Manual,* contact

The Superintendent of Documents
Government Printing Office
Washington, DC 20402

NU69. No one who has signs or symptoms of illness, including vomiting, diarrhea, and infectious skin sores that cannot be covered, or who is potentially or actually infected with bacteria or viruses that can be carried in food, shall be responsible for food handling. No one with open or infected injuries shall work in the food preparation area unless the injuries are covered with nonporous (e.g., latex) gloves.

Food handlers who are ill can easily communicate their illness to others by contaminating the food they prepare with infectious agents they are carrying.

NU70. Staff who prepare food shall not change diapers. Staff who work with diapered children shall not prepare or serve food for older groups of children. When it is not possible to observe these restrictions, staff who are responsible for changing diapers shall prepare or serve food to the infants and toddlers in their groups only after thoroughly washing their hands. Caregivers who prepare food for infants shall practice careful handwashing before handling food, including infant bottles of formula or breast milk. (See also *Handwashing,* on p. 72.)

Caregivers who work with infants and toddlers are frequently exposed to feces and to children with infections of the intestines (often with diarrhea) or liver, and should not carry this potential contamination outside the group they work with.

Education of child care staff regarding handwashing and other cleaning procedures can reduce the occurrence of illness in the group of children with whom they work.[43]

Cooking food for a large group of children is different from cooking for one's family. Whenever possible cooks shall not be assigned child care or janitorial duties, so as to reduce the risk of illness in a cook who may infect the food served in the facility.

NU71. All food stored, prepared, or served must be microbiologically, chemically, and physically safe for human consumption.[23]

NU72. Foods shall be inspected daily for spoilage.

NU73. Meat shall be from government-inspected sources or otherwise approved by the governing health authority.[44]

NU74. All dairy products shall be pasteurized and Grade A where applicable.

The use of dairy products fortified with Vitamins A and D is recommended.

NU75. Raw, unpasteurized milk or milk products shall not be used.

Several states allow the sale of raw milk or milk products. These products have been implicated in outbreaks of salmonellosis, listeriosis, toxoplasmosis, and campylobacteriosis,[45, 46] and should never be served in facilities. Only pasteurized milk should be served.

NU76. Dry milk and milk products may be reconstituted in the facility for cooking purposes only, provided they are prepared, refrigerated, and stored in a sanitary manner, labeled with the date of preparation, and used or discarded within 24 hours of preparation.

NU77. Home-canned food, food from dented, rusted, bulging, or leaking cans, and food from cans without labels shall not be used.

NU78. Fruits and vegetables shall be washed thoroughly with water prior to use.

Soil particles and contaminants that adhere to fruits and vegetables can cause illness.

NU79. Frozen foods shall be defrosted in the refrigerator, under cold running water, as part of the cooking process, or by using the defrost setting of a microwave oven; they shall never be defrosted by leaving them at room temperature or in standing water, as in a pan or bowl.

Food thawed at room temperature promotes the growth of harmful bacteria.

NU80. Meat, fish, poultry, milk, and egg products shall be refrigerated until immediately before use.

This practice prevents bacterial growth and foodborne illness.

STANDARDS	RATIONALE	COMMENTS

NU81. Food shall be served promptly after preparation or cooking and/or maintained at temperatures of not less than 140°F for hot foods and not more than 40°F for cold foods.

This practice prevents bacterial growth.[42] Food intended for human consumption can be contaminated if it is left at room temperature.

NU82. Hot foods shall be steamed for no longer than 30 minutes before being covered and refrigerated.

Excessive heating of foods results in loss of nutritional content.

NU83. Food returned from individual plates and family-style serving bowls and potentially hazardous food (as described in *Food Safety*, on p. 130) that is not refrigerated shall be discarded.

Served foods have a high probability of contamination during serving. Bacterial multiplication proceeds rapidly in perishable foods out of refrigeration, as much as doubling the numbers of bacteria every 15 to 20 minutes.

It is most desirable to discard all food once served. It is understood that some food, such as bread, may not become contaminated or spoil as a result of the way it is served and could be used safely again.

NU84. Unserved food shall be promptly covered for protection from contamination, shall be refrigerated immediately, and shall be used within 24 hours. Perishable foods that have been served and/or otherwise not maintained at safe temperatures for 2 hours or more shall be discarded.

This practice prevents bacterial growth and foodborne illness.

NU85. All opened and spoilable potentially hazardous foods shall be dated, covered, and maintained at a temperature of 40°F or lower in the refrigerator or 0°F or lower in the freezer.

See rationale for standard NU84.

NU86. All food stored in the refrigerator shall be covered, wrapped, or otherwise protected from contamination. Hot foods to be refrigerated and stored shall be transferred to shallow containers in food layers less than 3 inches deep and shall not be covered until cool.

Covering food protects it from contamination and keeps other food particles from falling into it. Hot food cools more quickly in a shallow container, thus decreasing the time when the food would be susceptible to contamination. Foods should be covered only after they have cooled; leaving hot food uncovered allows it to cool more quickly, thus decreasing the time when bacteria may be produced.

NU87. In the refrigerator, raw foods shall be stored below cooked or ready-to-eat foods.

This practice reduces the possibility that spills from raw foods might contaminate the ready-to-eat food.

NU88. Refrigerators and freezers shall be maintained in a clean and sanitary condition.

NU89. Foods not requiring refrigeration shall be stored at least 6 inches above the floor in clean, dry, well-ventilated storerooms or other

Storage of food off the floor in a safe and sanitary manner helps prevent food contamination and keeps insects and rodents from entering the

It is most desirable to have food stored 12 inches above the floor, to facilitate cleaning. Food should be stored in nonporous containers.

approved areas. Storage shall facilitate cleaning. Food products shall be stored in such a way (e.g., in nonporous containers off the floor) as to prevent insects and rodents from entering the products.

products. This practice also facilitates cleaning.

NU90. Dry, bulk foods that are not in their original, unopened containers shall be stored off the floor in clean metal, glass, or food-grade plastic containers with tight-fitting covers, and shall be labeled and dated.

This practice prevents contamination and misuse.

NU91. Garbage shall be placed in containers inaccessible to children and shall be removed from the kitchen daily. The containers shall be labeled and covered with tight-fitting lids between deposits.

This practice minimizes odors, controls insects and rodents, and protects children and premises from contamination.

NU92. When cleaning agents cannot be stored separately and must be stored in the same room with food, these supplies shall be clearly labeled and kept separated from food items in separate cabinets that are inaccessible to children.

Food products should be stored away from cleaning products to prevent accidental poisoning, potential leakage problems, and contamination.

NU93. Poisonous or toxic materials shall be stored in an area separate from the food storage area and shall be inaccessible to children.

Separate storage of poisonous or toxic materials prevents contamination of food.

NU94. Medications requiring refrigeration shall be stored as specified in *Medications*, on p. 88.

For additional information on food safety, see also standard ST52, in chapter 1, on p. 29 on training for food handlers.

4.9 Maintenance

NU95. Areas and equipment used for the storage, preparation, and service of food shall be kept clean. All of the food preparation, food service, and dining areas shall be cleaned and sanitized between uses and before and after each meal. Food preparation equipment shall be cleaned and sanitized after each use and stored in a clean and sanitary manner.

Foodborne illness outbreaks have occurred in many settings, including child care settings. Many of these communicable diseases can be prevented through appropriate hygiene and sanitation methods.

Education of child care staff regarding handwashing and other cleaning procedures can reduce the occurrence of illness in the group of children with which they work.[43]

STANDARDS

NU96. Cutting boards shall be made of nonporous material and shall be scrubbed with hot water and detergent and sanitized between use for different foods. Boards with crevices and cuts shall not be used.

NU97. Centers shall provide a three-compartment dishwashing area with dual integral drainboards and/or an approved dishwasher capable of disinfecting multiuse utensils. If a dishwasher is installed, at least a two-compartment sink with a spray unit shall be provided. If a dishwasher or a three-compartment sink is not used, paper cups and plates and plastic utensils shall be used and shall be disposed of after every use.

NU98. Small and large family-child-care homes shall provide a three-compartment dishwashing area or a dishwasher. At least a two-compartment sink shall be installed to be used in conjunction with a dishwasher to wash, rinse, and disinfect dishes. The dishwashing machine must be chemically or heat-disinfected. If a dishwasher or a three-compartment dishwashing area is not used, paper cups and plates and plastic utensils shall be used and shall be disposed of after every use.

NU99. If a dishwasher is not used (see standards NU97 and NU98), reusable food service equipment and eating utensils shall be scraped of food when necessary, thoroughly washed in hot water containing a detergent solution, rinsed, and then disinfected by one of the following methods:
a) Complete immersion in hot water and maintenance at a temperature of 170°F for not less than 30 seconds. The items shall be air-dried.
b) Immersion for at least 1 minute in a lukewarm (not less than 75°F) chemical disinfecting solution equivalent to a chlorine bath containing a minimum of 50 to 100 ppm of available chlorine at all times. (Three-fourths to 1½ table-

RATIONALE

Cracks and crevices harbor food material that can grow bacteria that contaminate the next food cut on the surface.

These are minimum requirements for proper cleaning and disinfecting of dishes and utensils.[42]

See rationale for standard NU97.

These procedures provide for proper disinfection and control of bacteria.[42]

COMMENTS

A three-compartment sink is ideal. Where only a single- or double-compartment sink is available, three free-standing dishpans or two sinks and one dishpan may be used as the compartments needed to wash, rinse, and disinfect dishes.

See comment for standard NU97.

STANDARDS	RATIONALE	COMMENTS

spoons of fresh liquid chlorine bleach in 1 gallon of water will usually provide the proper mixture.) The disinfected items shall be air-dried.

Other methods may be used if approved by the governing health agency.

NU100. Bottles, bottlecaps, and nipples shall not be reused without first being cleaned and disinfected.

See rationale for standard NU99.

NU101. Washable napkins (when allowed by the regulatory agency) and bibs shall be laundered after each use. Tablecloths, if approved for use, shall be kept clean.

Clean napkins, bibs, and tablecloths maintain cleanliness and prevent the spread of microorganisms and filth.

4.10 Meals from Outside Vendors or Central Kitchens

NU102. Food provided by a central kitchen or vendor to off-site locations shall be obtained from sources approved and inspected by the local health authority.

This standard ensures safe food.

NU103. After preparation, food shall be transported promptly in clean, covered, and temperature-controlled containers. Hot potentially hazardous foods shall be maintained at temperatures of not less than 140°F, and cold potentially hazardous foods shall be maintained at temperatures of 40°F or less until the food is served.

Served foods have a high probability of contamination during serving. Bacterial multiplication proceeds rapidly in perishable foods out of refrigeration, as much as doubling the numbers of bacteria every 15 to 20 minutes.

NU104. Centers receiving food from an off-site food service facility shall have provisions for the proper holding and serving of food and washing of utensils (see *Kitchen and Equipment*, on p. 127, *Food Safety*, on p. 130, and *Maintenance*, on p. 133) to meet the requirements of the Food and Drug Administration's *Retail Food Sanitation Code* and the standards approved by the state or local health authority.[42]

See rationale for standard NU103.

To obtain the FDA's *Retail Food Sanitation Code*, contact

The Association of Food and
   Drug Officials
P. O. Box 3425
York, PA 17402-3425

For additional information on meals from outside vendors or central kitchen, see also standard ST52 in chapter 1 on p. 29 on training for food handlers.

4.11 Nutrition Learning Experiences and Education

STANDARDS

NUTRITION LEARNING EXPERIENCES FOR CHILDREN

NU105. The facility shall have a nutrition plan (see standard AD45, in chapter 2, on p. 284 that integrates the introduction of food and feeding experiences with facility activities and home feeding. The plan shall include opportunities for children to develop the knowledge and skills necessary to make appropriate food choices. This plan shall be the shared responsibility of all staff, including directors and food service personnel.

NU106. The nutrition plan (see standard NU105 above) shall be developed in advance with guidance from, and shall be approved by, the child care Nutrition Specialist (see Appendices B-1 and B-2, on pp. 328–329.) For centers, this shall be a written plan.

RATIONALE

Nourishing and attractive food is a foundation for developmentally appropriate learning experiences and contributes to health and well-being.[1-5]

Coordinating the learning experiences with food service staff maximizes effectiveness of the education.

In addition to the nutritive value of food, infants and young children are helped through the act of feeding to establish warm human relationships. Eating should be an enjoyable experience in the facility and at home.

COMMENTS

It is important that parents not relinquish all feeding of the child to the facility. Eating together at home provides a pleasurable interaction between parent and child. Caregivers must take care that teaching children about new foods does not interfere with the pleasure of eating and is a natural by-product of feeding.

The following are nutrition education resources: Nutrition Specialists with state maternal and child health departments and divisions of children with special health care needs, local health departments, university and college nutrition departments, the home economists at utility companies, the registered dietitians at hospitals, high school home economics teachers, and other groups, such as state affiliates of the American Dietetic Association, state and regional affiliates of the American Public Health Association, the American Home Economics Association, the Dairy Council, local American Heart Association affiliates, local branches of the American Cancer Society, the Society for Nutrition Education, and local Cooperative Extensions.

Additional nutrition education resources may be obtained from

Food and Nutrition Information Center
National Agricultural Library Bldg.
Room 304
10301 Baltimore Boulevard
Beltsville, MD 20705

STANDARDS	RATIONALE	COMMENTS

NU107. Children shall be taught about the taste and smell of foods, and shall feel the textures and learn the different colors and shapes of foods. This teaching shall be evident in mealtime and curricular activities, without interfering with the pleasure of eating.

For additional information on nutrition learning experiences for children, see also standards NU34 and NU35, on p. 124 on mealtime activities.

NUTRITION EDUCATION FOR STAFF

See standards ST52 on p. 29 and ST50 on p. 24 for these standards.

NUTRITION EDUCATION FOR PARENTS

NU108. Parents shall be informed of the scope of nutrition learning activities provided in the facility. Nutrition information/education programs shall be conducted at least twice a year under the guidance of the child care Nutrition Specialist (see Appendices B-1 and B-2, on pp. 328–329), based on a needs assessment for nutrition information/education as perceived by families and staff.

Rationale (NU108): One goal of a facility is to provide a positive environment for the entire family. Informing parents about nutrition, food, food preparation, and mealtime enhances nutrition and mealtime interactions in the home, which helps to mold a child's food habits and eating behavior.[2, 21] Nutrition education directed at parents complements and enhances the nutrition education provided to their children.

Comments (NU107): Measure compliance by structured observation.

Comments (NUTRITION EDUCATION FOR STAFF): For resources in obtaining nutrition education, see comment for standard NU105 on p. 136.

Comments (NU108): The educational programs may be supplemented by periodic newsletters and/or literature.

For resources in obtaining nutrition education, see comment for standard NU105 on p. 136.

References

1. *Head Start Program Performance Standards.* Washington, DC: US Dept of Health and Human Services; Nov 1984.

2. Marotz LR, Rush J, Cross MZ. *Health, Safety and Nutrition for the Young Child.* Albany, NY: Delmar Publishers Inc; 1989.

3. Goodwin MT, Pollen G. *Creative Food Experiences for Children.* Washington, DC: Center for Science in the Public Interest; 1980.

4. *A Fresh Approach to Nutrition for Head Start Directors.* New York, NY: Administration for Children, Youth and Families, Public Health Service, US Dept of Health and Human Services; 1980.

5. *Head Start Nutrition Education Curriculum.* Washington, DC: US Dept of Health and Human Services, Office of Human Development Services, Administration for Children, Youth and Families and the Head Start Bureau; 1988.

6. *Feeding Infants— A Guide for Use in the Child Care Food Program.* Washington, DC: US Dept of Agriculture; 1988. Food and Nutrition Service publication FNS-258.

7. Code of Federal Regulations Part 226.20. *Federal Register,* July 6, 1988;53:129.

8. Newbrun E. *Cariology.* Baltimore, Md: Williams and Wilkins; 1978:229.

9. Schamschula RG et al. *WHO Study of Dental Caries Etiology in Papua, New Guinea.* Geneva, Switzerland: World Health Organization; 1978:199.

10. Bogert JA. The American Academy of Pediatric Dentistry, its scope and function. *NYS Dent J.* 1988; 54(2):36–38.

11. *Report of the Surgeon General's Workshop on Breastfeeding and Human Lactation.* Washington, DC: US Dept of Health and Human Services; 1984.

12. *Pediatric Nutrition Handbook.* Elk Grove Village, Ill: American Academy of Pediatrics; 1985.

13. Fomon SJ. *Infant Nutrition.* Philadelphia, Pa: WB Saunders Company; 1974:472–482.

14. Ripa LW. *Baby Bottle Tooth Decay (Nursing Caries): A Comprehensive Review.* Atlanta, Ga: Centers for Disease Control, CPS Dental Disease Prevention Activity; Sept 1988.

15. Kelly K, Bruerd B. The prevalence of baby bottle tooth decay among two Native American populations. *J Public Health Dent.* 1987;47(2):94–97.

16. Johnson DC. Characteristics and backgrounds of children with "nursing caries." *Pediatr Dent.* 1982; 4(3):218–224.

17. Nowak AJ. *Public Health Currents.* Columbus, Ohio: Ross Laboratories; 1985.

18. National Research Council. *Recommended Dietary Allowances.* 10th ed. Washington, DC: National Academy Press; 1989.

19. Kendrick AS, Kaufman R, Messenger KP, eds. *Healthy Young Children: A Manual for Programs.* Washington, DC: National Association for the Education of Young Children; 1991.

20. Guthrie HA. *Introductory Nutrition.* St. Louis, Mo: Times, Mirror/Mosby; 1986;526:544–551.

21. Endres JB, Rockwell RE. *Food, Nutrition, and the Young Child.* Columbus, Ohio. Charles E Merrill Publishing Co; 1984.

22. Beal, VA. *Nutrition in the Life Span.* New York, NY: John Wiley and Sons; 1980;211–258.

23. Deitch S, ed. *Health in Day Care: A Manual for Health Professionals.* Elk Grove Village, Ill: American Academy of Pediatrics; 1987.

24. Pipes P. *Nutrition in Infancy and Childhood.* St. Louis, Mo: Times, Mirror/Mosby; 1989.

25. Satter E. *How to Get Your Kid to Eat. . . But Not Too Much.* Palo Alto, Calif: Bull Publishing Co; 1987.

26. *Personnel in Public Health Nutrition for the 1980's.* McLean, Va: Association of State and Territorial Health Officials Foundation; 1982.

27. Report of the California Child Nutrition Advisory Council. San Francisco, Calif: California Department of Health; 1987.

28. *Handbook for Local Head Start Nutrition Specialists.* Washington, DC: US Dept of Health, Education and Welfare; 1975.

29. *Training Programs for Food Service Personnel in Programs for Young Children.* Washington, DC: US Dept of Health and Human Services, Jul 1980; Publication No. (OHDS) 80-31142.

30. Baiano MJ. *Handbook for Day Care Centers.* White Plains, NY: Westchester County Department of Health; 1973.

31. Harris CS, Baker SP, Smith GA, et al. Childhood asphyxiation by food. *JAMA.* 1984;251:2231–2235.

32. *Equipment Guide for Preschool and School-Age Child Service Institutions.* Washington, DC: US Dept of Agriculture, Food and Nutrition Service, Child Nutrition Division; 1972.

33. Bettelheim B. *Food to Nurture the Mind.* Washington, DC: The Children's Foundation; 1970.

34. McIntire MS, ed. *Injury Control for Children and Youth.* Elk Grove Village, Ill: American Academy of Pediatrics Committee on Accident and Poison Prevention; 1987.

35. McLoughlin E, Crawford JD. Burns. *Pediatr Clin North Amer.* 1985; 32:61–75.

36. Johnson DC, Nowjack-Raymer R. Baby bottle tooth decay (BBTD): issues, assessment, and an opportunity for the nutritionist. *J Amer Diet Assoc.* 1989; 8:1112–1116.

37. *Food and Choking in Children. A Report to the Food and Drug Administration on a Conference Held in Elkridge, Maryland, August 4–5, 1983.* Evanston, Ill: American Academy of Pediatrics; Dec 1983.

38. *Standard #4. Cooking and Hot Food Storage Equipment.* Ann Arbor, Mich: National Sanitation Foundation; 1986.

39. *Heating, Ventilation and Air Conditioning Systems and Applications Handbook.* Atlanta, Ga: American Society of Heating, Refrigerating and Air Conditioning Engineers; 1987;19:19.6.

40. Sando WC, Gallagher KJ, Rodgers BM. Risk factors for microwaves scald injuries in infants. *J Pediatr.* 1984;105:864–867.

41. Puczynski M, Rademaker D, Gatson R. Burn injury related to the improper use of a microwave oven. *Pediatrics.* 1983;32:714–715.

42. Food and Drug Administration. *Retail Food Sanitation Code.* Washington, DC: US Dept of Health and Human Services, Public Health Service, Food and Drug Administration, Center for Food and Safety and Applied Nutrition; 1988.

43. Black RE, Dykes AC, Anderson KE. Handwashing to prevent diarrhea in day care centers. *Amer J Epidemiol.* 1981;113:445–451.

44. Food and Drug Administration. From the chicken to the egg. *FDA Consumer.* 1990;24:3,7–10.

45. Potter ME. Unpasteurized milk—the hazards of a health fetish. *JAMA.* 1984;252:2048–2052.

46. Sacks JJ. Toxoplasmosis infection associated with raw goat's milk. *JAMA.* 1982;248:1728–1732.

CHAPTER 5

Facilities, Supplies, Equipment, and Transportation

CHAPTER 5
FACILITIES, SUPPLIES, EQUIPMENT, AND TRANSPORTATION

5.1 Overall Space and Equipment Requirements

STANDARDS   **RATIONALE**   **COMMENTS**

GENERAL LOCATION, LAYOUT, AND CONSTRUCTION OF THE FACILITY

FA1. A center shall not be located in a private residence unless that portion of the residence is used exclusively for the children during the hours of operation.

Special sanitation and design are needed to protect children from injury and prevent transmission of disease. Undivided attention must be given to these purposes during child care operations.

FA2. Facilities shall be located in areas not subject to high air pollution, loud or constant noises, or heavy traffic, and away from unsafe buildings, deep excavations, radiation, and any other unsafe or harmful environmental elements.

This requirement will reduce exposure to conditions that cause injury or adversely affect health.

FA3. The facility shall be located on a well-drained site free from hazards.

Risk of injury and risk of disease from insects, which breed in poorly drained areas, must be controlled to have a safe facility.

FA4. Every exterior wall, roof, and foundation shall be weathertight and watertight. Every floor, wall, and ceiling shall be structurally sound and tight.

Children must be protected from the elements and from the unhealthy effects of exposure to the elements on buildings (e.g., mold, dust, insects).

FA5. Finished basements may be used for children 2½ years or older. Basements shall be dry and well-ventilated; shall be well-lighted; shall be maintained at required temperatures and humidity; and shall be free of radon in excess of 4 picocuries per liter of air. (See standard FA22, on p. 144 on requirements for exits; *Heating, Cooling, and Ventilation*, on p. 146; *Lighting*, on p. 148; and *Toxic Substances*, on p. 163.)

Basement areas can be quite habitable and should be usable as long as environmental quality is satisfactory.

🍎 applies to a small family-child-care home   Ⓐ applies to a large family-child-care home   🛝 applies to a center. If no symbol appears, the standard applies to all three.

STANDARDS	RATIONALE	COMMENTS

FA6. In buildings of wood construction, children, including infants and toddlers, shall be housed and cared for only on the ground floor. Rooms shall have a door to the exterior that is easy to open.

Fire and building safety experts recommend that children, including infants, be permitted above ground level only in certain types of construction.

FA7. Child care areas shall not be used for any business or purpose unrelated to child care when children are present in these areas.

Child care requires child-oriented, child-safe areas where the child's needs are primary.

FA8. Office space separate from child care areas shall be provided for administration and staff in centers.

For the efficient and effective operation of a center, office areas where activities that are incompatible with the care of young children are conducted should be separate from child care areas. These office areas can be expected to contain supplies and equipment that should be kept inaccessible to children. In addition, where records and documents, some of them confidential, are kept, staff should be free from the distractions of child care.[1, 2]

FA9. Rooms or spaces containing a commercial-type kitchen, boiler, maintenance shop, janitor closet, laundry, woodworking shop, flammable or combustible storage, or painting operation, or that are used for any purpose involving the presence of toxic substances, shall be separated from the child care areas and from the means of exit. The exit and the fire-resistive separation shall be approved by the appropriate regulatory agency responsible for building inspections. In small and large family-child-care homes, a fire-resistive separation shall not be required where the food preparation kitchen contains only a domestic cooking range and the preparation of food does not result in the escape of smoke or grease-laden vapors into indoor areas.

Toxic and hazardous substances must be kept separate from rooms used for longer term care to prevent children's and staff members' exposure to noxious substances.

FA10. Play, dining, and napping may be carried on in the same room (exclusive of bathrooms, hallways, and closets), provided the room is of sufficient size to have a defined area

Multipurpose use is permissible as long as bathrooms, exit routes, and uninhabitable spaces are not included in multipurpose activities areas.

Measure compliance by structured observation.

for each of the activities allowed there at the time when the activity (play, dining, or napping) is under way and meets other building requirements, and programming is such that use of the room for one purpose does not interfere with the use of the room for other purposes. (See also *Sleeping*, on p. 175, on napping requirements and *Additional Indoor Requirements for Special Groups or Ages of Children*, on p. 180.)

FA11. The physical layout of the facility shall be arranged to prevent child abuse as specified in standard HP103 in chapter 3 on p. 94.

For additional information on general location, layout, and construction of the facility, see also standard FA205 on environmental hazards on p. 180.

Openings

FA12. Each window, exterior door, and basement or cellar hatchway shall be weathertight and watertight.

Children's environments must be protected from exposure to moisture, dust, and excessive temperatures.

FA13. Rooms utilized by children shall have a total window area of at least 8 percent of the floor area of the room if the windows face directly to the outdoors and at least 15 percent if they do not, except for bathrooms and kitchens. Rooms without openable windows and kitchens and bathrooms shall be provided with mechanical ventilation.

Good ventilation is needed to provide fresh, temperate air and to remove odors and contaminants. This is standard practice.

As with other standards, the regulatory agency may grant waivers when it is clear that the intent of the regulation is being met by alternative means. (See *Waivers*, on p. 304.)

FA14. All windows above ground level in areas used by children under 5 years of age shall be constructed, adapted, or adjusted to limit the exit opening accessible to children to less than 6 inches, or be otherwise protected with guards that do not block outdoor light.

This standard is to prevent children from falling out of windows.

FA15. Openable windows shall be of a safety type (not wide-openable) that are childproofed and screened when open. When there are no openable windows or when windows

See rationale for standard FA14.

are not kept open, rooms shall be ventilated.

FA16. All openings used for ventilation shall be screened. (See also FA33, on p. 146.)

Screens prevent the entry of insects.

FA17. Glass windows and glass door panels within 36 inches of the floor shall have safety guards (e.g., rails or mesh) or be of safety-grade glass or polymer (e.g., Lexan®) and equipped with a vision strip.

Glass panels can be invisible to an active child or adult. When collisions occur, serious injury can result.

FA18. The width of doors shall accommodate wheelchairs and the needs of individuals with physical disabilities.

Facilities must be accessible to individuals with physical disabilities.

FA19. Interior doors shall swing in the direction of most frequent travel and exit doors shall swing to the exterior. Exception: boiler room doors shall swing inward.

This standard is to provide easy, quick passage and prevention of injuries. Boiler room doors should swing inward to contain explosions.

This provision should not apply to large or small family-child-care homes or to centers located in a private residence. Doors in homes usually open inward.

This provision may be addressed in local building codes.

FA20. Doorways and exits shall be free of debris and equipment to allow unobstructed traffic from the room.

This provision permits fast exit in the event of an emergency.

FA21. The hand contact and splash areas of doors and walls shall be coved with an easily cleanable finish, at least as cleanable as an epoxy finish or enamel paint.

Easily cleanable surfaces facilitate removal of filth and disease-producing germs.

Exits

FA22. Each building or structure, new or old, shall be provided with unobstructed exits to allow occupants to escape to an outside door or fire tower in case of fire or other emergency. Each floor above or below ground level used for child care shall have at least two unobstructed exits that lead to an open area at ground level that meets safety requirements for an outdoor play area (see *Layout, Location, and Size*, on p. 183). Entrance and exit routes shall be reviewed and approved by the local fire inspection authority.

This standard helps to prevent injuries.

STANDARDS	RATIONALE	COMMENTS

FA23. A facility shall have a minimum of two exits, at different sides of the building or home, leading to an open space at ground level. If the basement in a small family-child-care home is being used, one exit must be from the basement.

See rationale for standard FA22.

FA24. The minimum width of an exit shall be 36 inches.

This standard is that set by the National Fire Protection Agency (NFPA) in *NFPA 101 Life Safety Code, 1988.*[3]

Exceptions should be permitted as specified in *NFPA 101 Life Safety Code, 1988,* which is available from

National Fire Protection
   Association
Battery March Park
Quincy, MA 02269

FA25. Where exits are not immediately accessible from an open floor area, safe and continuous passageways, aisles, or corridors shall be maintained leading to every exit and shall be so arranged as to provide access for each occupant to at least two exits by separate ways of travel.

See rationale for standard FA24.

FA26. No lock or fastening that prevents free escape from the interior of any building shall be installed. All door hardware in areas used by school-age children shall be within the reach of children. In centers, only panic hardware (hardware that can be opened by pressure in the direction of travel) or single-action hardware (hardware that allows a door to open either way but keeps it from swinging back past the center point) shall be permitted on exterior doors.

FA27. Exits shall be clearly visible and the paths of escape shall be so arranged or marked that the path to safety outside is unmistakable.

FA28. An exit to the outside or a common hallway leading to the outside shall be directly accessible without passage through another room. If the other room does not have a fixed partition and a door that can be latched, then passage through such room shall be allowed.

STANDARDS	RATIONALE	COMMENTS

FA29. No obstructions shall be placed in the corridors or passageways leading to the exits.

FA30. Exits or exit markers or signs shall be visible during all periods of operation.

Visible exits or exit markers are required by fire codes.

Ask local fire marshal for fire safety code requirements.

For additional information on exits, see also standard FA52, on p. 149.

Heating, Cooling, and Ventilation

FA31. A draft-free temperature of 65°F to 75°F shall be maintained at 30 to 70 percent relative humidity during the winter months and a draft-free temperature of 68°F to 82°F shall be maintained at 30 to 70 percent relative humidity during the summer months. (See also *Humidity*, on p. 148.)

These requirements are based on the American Society of Heating, Refrigerating and Air Conditioning Engineers (ASHRAE) comfort chart,[4] which was developed taking both comfort and health into consideration.

To obtain the ASHRAE comfort chart, contact the American Society of Heating, Refrigerating and Air Conditioning Engineers as specified in standard FA32.

FA32. All rooms used by children shall be heated, cooled, and ventilated to maintain the required temperatures, humidity, and air exchange (see standard FA31) and to avoid accumulation of objectionable odors and harmful fumes.

These precautions are essential to the health and well-being of both the staff and the children.

To obtain further information, contact

American Society of Heating, Refrigerating and Air Conditioning Engineers 1791 Tullic Circle, N.E. Atlanta, GA 30329

FA33. Ventilation may be in the form of openable windows as specified in *Openings*, on p. 143.

FA34. Areas where arts and crafts activities are conducted shall be well ventilated. In areas where substances are used that create toxic fumes, exhaust hood systems or other devices shall be installed.

Exhaust hood systems keep toxic fumes from the breathing area of children.

FA35. Electric fans, if used, shall be mounted high on the wall or ceiling or shall be guarded to limit the size of the opening in the bladeguard to less than ½ inch.

This provision is to control and prevent injury.

Most fans have bladeguard openings of ½ inch, but openings of ¼ inch are more protective and desirable and should be utilized if such fans are available.

STANDARDS	RATIONALE	COMMENTS

FA36. When air cooling is needed, draft-free cooling units shall be used. They shall present no safety hazard to the children.

This provision is to enhance personal health and comfort.

FA37. Filters on recirculation systems shall be checked and cleaned or replaced monthly.

FA38. All heating and ventilating equipment shall be inspected annually by a heating/air conditioning contractor, who shall verify in writing that the equipment is properly installed, cleaned, and maintained to operate efficiently and effectively without emitting chemical or microbiological substances. The system shall be operated in accordance with operating instructions.

Annual inspections and proper operation control the growth and spread of microorganisms that may cause disease, and prevent emissions that might endanger children.

Emissions are measured on a sample of air coming from the heating or ventilating system. This test is done by a professional laboratory based on microscopic and chemical testing. To prevent harmful emissions, the system must be operated strictly in accordance with the operating instructions that the manufacturer warrants safe.

FA39. Window draft deflectors shall be provided.

Window draft deflectors eliminate drafts on children.

FA40. Thermometers that do not present a hazard to children shall be placed on interior walls in every indoor activity area at children's height.

Mercury, glass, or similar materials in thermometers can cause injury and poisoning of children. Placing the thermometer at the children's height allows proper monitoring of temperature where the children are in the room.

FA41. Portable, open-flame, and kerosene space heaters shall be prohibited. Portable gas stoves shall not be used for space heating.

Kerosene and other open-flame heaters discharge fumes into the living area. The potential for carbon monoxide poisoning from incomplete combustion of fuels exists if there is no proper outside ventilation.[5, 6] Some space heaters are easily tipped over and do not shut off when tipped over. Many become hot enough to start fires in adjacent objects. Electrical heaters can come in contact with water, causing shock. Many burns have been caused by contact with space heaters and other hot surfaces.

Any exceptions shall be approved by the local health and fire departments before use.

FA42. Electric space heaters shall be UL-approved, inaccessible to children, and stable; shall have protective covering; and shall be placed at least 3 feet from curtains, papers, and furniture.

This standard is based on the *Safe Home Checklist.*[7]

FA43. Heating systems, including the stove, stovepipe, and chimney, shall be inspected and cleaned yearly by a heating contractor, who shall furnish a letter or certificate warrant-

Heating equipment is the second leading cause of ignition of fatal house fires.[8]

STANDARDS	RATIONALE	COMMENTS

ing the heating system to be safe and sound. A protective screen shall be used for the stove. The heating systems shall be checked at the beginning of each cold season by a certified heating contractor. Documentation of these inspections and certification of safety shall be kept on file in the facility.

FA44. Fireplaces and fireplace inserts shall be screened securely or equipped with protective guards while in use. They shall be properly drafted. The facility shall provide evidence of cleaning the chimney at least once a year, or as frequently as necessary to prevent excessive build-up of combustibles in the chimney.

This standard is based on state and local building and fire codes for fire prevention.

See also rationale for standard FA43.

FA45. Heating units that utilize flame shall be vented properly to the outside and shall be supplied with sufficient combustion air.

When possible, fresh air should be used to supply combustion air.

FA46. Heating units, including water pipes and baseboard heaters hotter than 110°F, shall be made inaccessible to children by barriers such as guards or other devices.

A mechanical barrier separating the child from the source of heat can reduce the likelihood of burns.[9-17]

For additional information on heating, cooling, and ventilation, see also *Openings*, on p. 143.

Humidity

FA47. Humidifiers or dehumidifiers shall be used to maintain humidity as specified in standard FA31 on p. 146.

This requirement is based on best professional experience.

Lighting

FA48. All areas of the facility shall be lighted to meet the following levels of illumination:
a) Reading, painting, and other close work areas: 50 to 100 footcandles on the work surface.
b) Work and play areas: 30 to 50 footcandles on the surface.
c) Stairs, walkways, landings, driveways, and entrances: at least 20 footcandles on the surface.
d) Sleeping, napping areas: no more than 5 footcandles during sleeping or napping.[7]

These levels of illumination facilitate cleaning, reading, comfort, completion of projects, and safety.[18]

50–75–100 footcandles are recommended for general classroom illumination on task for performance of usual tasks of medium contrast or small size, such as reading.

20 to 50 footcandles illuminance (category D) on task is the recommended illumination for classroom areas for performance of visual tasks of high contrast or large size where

For further information, contact American National Standards Institute/Illuminating Engineers Society 1430 Broadway New York, NY 10018

A footcandle is defined as a unit of illuminance on a surface that is everywhere 1 foot from a uniform point source of light of one candle and equal to 1 lumen per square foot.

Contact the lighting or home service department of the local electric

STANDARDS	RATIONALE	COMMENTS

reading, grooming, table games, or conferring is performed.

The category A range of illumination is recommended for public spaces with dark surroundings.[18]

utility company to have footcandles measured.

FA49. Glare-free lighting shall be provided in all areas of a facility.

FA50. Light fixtures containing shielded or shatterproof bulbs shall be used in food preparation areas and other areas as deemed necessary by the regulatory authority.

Use of shielded or shatterproof bulbs prevents injury and contamination of food.

FA51. Sodium and mercury vapor lamps shall not be used for lighting the interiors of centers.

FA52. Emergency lighting shall be provided at building exits.

Emergency lighting at exits is a fire code requirement.

Ask the local fire marshal for fire safety code requirements.

For additional information on lighting, see also *Additional Indoor Requirements for School-Age Children*, on p. 182, and standard FA286, on p. 196.

Noise

FA53. Workplaces shall be equipped with space-dividing noise enclosures and/or sound-absorbing materials.

Noise, or unwanted sound, can be damaging to hearing as well as to psychosocial well-being. The stressful effects of noise will (minimally) add to and (maximally) potentiate other stress factors present in the facility. In addition, uncontrolled noise will continually force the caregiver to speak at levels above those normally used for conversation, and may increase the risk of throat irritation. This may be a particularly serious consequence when the caregiver's concurrent exposure to infectious agents is considered.

FA54. All rooms or areas accommodating more than one group of children, as defined in the child:staff ratio and group size provisions of *Child:Staff Ratio and Group Size*, on p. 1, shall be provided with an acoustical ceiling, carpeting, wall coverings, partitions, or draperies or

This standard is intended to reduce harmful noise and facilitate better hearing and communication.

Thirty-five db is the loss of hearing commonly experienced by children with serious otitis, which correlates with decreased language development skills.

Noise measurement should be made according to the Code of Federal Regulations (CFR), Title 16, Section 1500.47. To obtain this publication, contact

Superintendent of Documents
U.S. Government Printing Office
Washington, DC 20402

a combination thereof. Such measures shall maintain the decibel level at or below 35 to 40 db for at least 80 percent of the time as measured by acoustical engineers or, more practically, by the ability to be clearly heard and understood in a normal conversation without raising one's voice.

See also rationale for standard FA53.

Sound control measures should follow the pertinent American Society for Testing and Materials (ASTM) standards for noise, acoustics, and so forth as indicated below:

E477   Acoustical air flow performance

E1042 Classification of acoustic cells, absorptive materials (applied by towel/ spray)

E1264 Classification of acoustical ceiling products

E1124 Field measurement of sound power level—test

E1007 Sound transmission in floor-ceiling assemblies

E1050 Test for impedance/absorption of acoustical materials

C384   Test method for impedance and absorption of acoustical materials by the impedance tube method

E1130 Measurement of speech privacy in open offices

E1014 Outdoor noise, measuring outdoor A-weighted sound levels

E597   Determining a single number rating of airborne sound isolation for use in multiunit building specifications

E1041 Guide to masking sound in open offices

E596   Measuring noise reduction

EH13   Classification of airborne sound transmission in building partitions

For further information, contact

American Society for Testing and Materials
1916 Race St.
Philadelphia, PA 19103

Electrical Fixtures and Outlets

FA55. Facilities shall be supplied with electric service. Outlets and fixtures shall be installed properly and shall be connected to the source of electric energy in a manner that meets local electrical codes, as certified by an electrical code inspector.

Proper installation of outlets and fixtures helps to prevent injury.

State or local electrical codes may apply. For further information, see the *NFPA 101 Life Safety Code, 1988,* which is available from

National Fire Protection Association
Battery March Park
Quincy, MA 02269

FA56. Electrical outlets accessible to children shall be covered with child-resistant covers or be of the child-proof type. Shock stops (safety plugs) shall be installed on all unused outlets.

Shock stops and outlet covers prevent children from sticking objects into exposed outlets or sucking on exposed extension cord outlets.[7]

STANDARDS

FA57. No electrical outlet shall be located within reach of a water source unless it is protected by an approved ground fault circuit interrupter, which shall be tested at least every 3 months using the test button located on the device.

FA58. No electrical device or apparatus accessible to children shall be located so that it could be plugged into an electrical outlet while in contact with a water source, such as a sink, tub, shower area, or swimming/wading pool.

FA59. The use of extension cords shall be discouraged; however, when used, they shall not be placed under carpeting or across water-source areas. Electrical cords (extension and appliance) shall not be frayed or overloaded.

FA60. Electrical cords shall be placed beyond children's reach.[9-17]

Fire Warning Systems

FA61. Smoke detectors shall be placed on each floor, no more than 40 feet apart, installed on or 6 to 12 inches below the ceiling. Smoke detectors shall be tested monthly, and the batteries replaced at least yearly.

FA62. Fire extinguisher(s) shall be installed and maintained. The fire extinguisher shall be of the A-B-C type. Size and number of fire extinguishers shall be determined after a survey by the fire marshal or by an insurance company fire loss prevention representative. Instructions for the use of the fire extinguisher shall be posted on or near the fire extinguisher.

RATIONALE

This provision eliminates shock hazards.

Electrical malfunction is the third most frequent cause of ignition of fatal house fires.[3] The Consumer Product Safety Commission reports that in 1983, extension cords were the ignition sources of fires that caused 80 deaths and burn injuries requiring hospitalization of 260 persons.[8]

Children under 5 years are at greatest risk of injury from extension and appliance cords.[8]

A review of death certificates indicates that house fires are responsible for the great majority of fire and burn deaths, with children under 5 at highest risk.[8-19] Smoke detectors provide early warning to exit before toxic fumes make escape impossible. Fire statistics suggest that as a county approaches more complete detector coverage, the risk of residential fire deaths decreases significantly.[8]

A fire extinguisher may be used to put out a small fire or to clear an escape path.[7]

COMMENTS

Some state and local building codes specify the installation and maintenance of smoke detectors and fire alarm systems.

See codes of the following:

National Fire Protection
   Association
Battery March Park
Quincy, MA 02269

and

Building Officials and Code
   Administrators International
4051 W. Flossmoor Road
Country Club Hills, IL 60477

Plumbing and Sanitary Facilities

Clean water and plumbing

FA63. Every facility shall be supplied with piped running water under pressure, from a source approved by the Environmental Protection Agency (EPA) and/or the state or local health authority, to provide an adequate water supply to every fixture connected with the water supply and drainage system. When water is supplied by a well or other private source, it shall meet all applicable federal, state, and local health standards and shall be approved by the local health department or its designee prior to use. Any facility not served by a public water supply shall keep documentation of approval of the water supply on file.

This ensures a water supply that is safe, that is, one that does not spread disease or filth or contain dangerous substances.[20]

Contact

Environmental Protection Agency
401 M St., S.W.
Washington, DC 20460

FA64. The water shall be sufficient in quantity and pressure to supply water for cooking, cleaning, drinking, toilets, and outside uses.

FA65. Newly installed water handling and treatment equipment shall meet applicable National Sanitation Foundation (NSF) standards and shall be inspected and approved by the state or local health department or its designee.

Adherence to NSF standards will help ensure a safe water supply.

State and local codes vary, but generally protect against toxins or sewage entering the water supply.

Model codes are available from

National Sanitation Foundation
3475 Plymouth Road
Ann Arbor, MI 48106

FA66. There shall be no cross-connections that could permit contamination of the potable water supply.
a) Back-flow preventers, vacuum breakers, or strategic air gaps shall be provided for all boiler units in which chemicals are used.
b) Vacuum breakers shall be installed on all threaded hose bibs.
c) Nonsubmersible, antisiphon ball-cocks shall be provided on all flush-tank-type toilets.

Pressure differentials may allow contamination of drinking water if cross-connections or submerged inlets exist.

Water must be protected from cross-connections with possible sources of contamination.

FA67. Each gas pipe, water pipe, gas-burning fixture, plumbing fixture and apparatus, or any other similar fixture and all connections to water, sewer, or gas lines shall be installed and free from defects, leaks, and obstructions in accordance with the requirements of the state or local regulatory agency for buildings.

This standard prevents accidents and hazardous and unsanitary conditions.

STANDARDS	RATIONALE	COMMENTS

WATER TESTING

FA68. Drinking water shall be tested by the local health department or its designee no less than once a year for bacteriological quality and no less than once in 3 years for chemical quality. Testing shall be in compliance with procedures established by the National Sanitation Foundation.

This standard prevents the use of unsafe water supplies.

Tests could include analyses for radon and gross alpha radiation. The need for these tests is still being researched, but it is recommended that they be done.

Contact

National Sanitation Foundation
3475 Plymouth Road
Ann Arbor, MI 48106

FA69. When plumbing is unavailable to provide a handwashing sink (see *Sinks*, on p. 170), the facility shall provide a handwashing sink using a portable water supply and a sanitary catch system approved by a local sanitarian.

A diagram of an alternative to running water using a portable (bubbler) tank, a sink tap, and a cabinet is provided in *Healthy Young Children*. To obtain this publication, contact

National Association for the
Education of Young Children
1834 Connecticut Avenue, N.W.
Washington, DC 20009

FA70. In both private and public drinking water supplies where interior or service piping or joint seals contain lead or other toxic materials, water shall be evaluated at the beginning of operation and at least every 2 years by the local health authority to determine safe lead levels. Such samples shall consist of the first draw of water in the facility after at least a 6-hour lapse in use.

FA71. All water test results shall be in written form and kept on file (see *Posting Documents* in chapter 8 on p. 289), ready for immediate viewing by regulatory personnel, or copies submitted as required by the local authority that regulates safe water.

Some regulatory authorities prefer to have copies of water test results kept available for inspection on site, while others that do not provide on-site inspections may prefer to have the reports submitted to them.

FA72. Emergency safe drinking water shall be supplied during interruption of the regular approved supply. Bottled water shall be certified as chemically and bacteriologically potable by the state or local health department or its designee.

This provision ensures a supply of safe drinking water at all times.

STANDARDS	RATIONALE	COMMENTS

Sewage

FA73. Sewage facilities shall be provided and inspected in accordance with state and local regulations. Whenever a public sewer is available, the facility shall be connected.

This standard is for health protection and aesthetic reasons.

FA74. Where public sewers are not available, a spectic tank system or other method approved by the state or local health department or its designee shall be installed.

See rationale for standard FA73.

FA75. Raw or treated wastes shall not be discharged on the surface of the ground.

See rationale for standard FA73.

FA76. The exhaust vent from a wastewater or septic system and drainage field shall not be located within the children's outdoor play area.

See rationale for standard FA73.

Waste and diaper storage and disposal

FA77. Garbage and rubbish shall be removed from rooms occupied by children, staff, parents, or volunteers on a daily basis and removed from the premises at least twice weekly or at other frequencies approved by the local health authority.

This practice provides proper sanitation and protection of health; prevents infestations by rodents, insects, and other pests; and prevents odors and injuries.

Compliance can be tested by checking for evidence of infestation.

FA78. Garbage and rubbish shall be kept in containers constructed of durable metal or other types of material approved by the local health authority that do not leak and do not absorb liquids. Plastic garbage bag liners shall be used in such containers.

This practice provides good sanitation and pest and odor control.

FA79. Waste containers shall be provided with tight-fitting lids or covers and shall be kept covered when stored or not in continuous use.

This practice provides pest control and prevents children from having access to disease-bearing body fluids.

FA80. Soiled diapers shall be stored in containers separate from other waste. Conveniently located, washable, plastic-lined, tightly covered receptacles, operated by a foot pedal, shall be provided within arm's reach of diaper-changing tables for soiled diapers. Separate containers shall be used for disposable diapers, cloth diapers (if used), and soiled clothes and linens.

Fecal material and urine should not be allowed to be comingled and disposed of as regular trash and thereby contaminate ground water and spread disease. These waste receptacles prevent the children from coming into contact with disease-bearing body fluids.

STANDARDS	RATIONALE	COMMENTS

FA81. Each waste and diaper container shall be labeled and kept clean and free of buildup of soil and odor. Waste water from such cleaning operations shall be disposed of as sewage.

This standard prevents noxious odors and the spread of disease.

FA82. There shall be a sufficient number of waste and diaper containers to hold all of the garbage and diapers that accumulate between periods of removal from the premises.

See rationale for standard FA81.

FA83. Exterior garbage containers shall be stored on an easily cleanable surface. If a compactor is used, the surface shall be graded to a suitable drain, as approved by the local health authority.

This standard ensures proper sanitation and pest control.

FA84. Infectious and toxic wastes shall be stored separately from other wastes and disposed of in a manner approved by the local health authority.

This practice provides for safe storage and disposal.

FA85. Children shall not be allowed access to refuse storage areas. Such areas shall be free of litter and uncontained waste.

This standard prevents injury and disease.

FA86. Child play areas shall be kept free of animal wastes, insects, rodents, or other pest infestations, and shall not provide shelter to pests.

An uncovered sandbox is an invitation for a cat or other animal to defecate or urinate and, therefore, is a source for disease transmission.[21] This standard also helps ensure pest control.

For additional information on waste and diaper storage and disposal, see also standard HP38 in chapter 3 on p. 75.

Pest control

FA87. Each foundation, floor, wall, ceiling, roof, window, exterior door, and basement and cellar hatchway shall be free from openings.

This standard prevents access to the interior by rodents.

FA88. Basement or cellar windows used or intended to be used for ventilation, and all other openings to a basement or cellar, shall not permit the entry of rodents.

See rationale for standard FA87.

Heavy-duty steel mesh screen (such as ¼-inch hardware cloth or similar, equally effective protective device) can be used to protect such entry points from access by rodents.

FA89. Openings to the outside shall be protected against the entrance of flies or other flying insects by outward-opening, self-closing doors; closed windows; screening; air curtains; or other effective and approved means.

FA90. Whenever the regulatory agency determines that the presence of pests in the area constitutes a health hazard, the facility shall take the necessary actions to exclude, exterminate, or otherwise control such pests on its premises.

For additional information on pest control, see also *Openings*, on p. 143 and *Insect Breeding Hazards*, on p. 193.

EXTERMINATION

FA91. All extensive extermination shall be provided by a licensed or certified pest control operator.

FA92. Pesticides shall be of a type applied by a licensed exterminator in a manner approved by the Environmental Protection Agency. Application shall be directly observed by a member of the child care staff to be sure toxic chemicals applied on surfaces do not constitute a hazard to the children or staff. Pesticides shall be used in strict compliance with the label instructions or as otherwise directed or approved by the regulatory authority. No pesticide shall be applied while children are present.

FA93. If toxic chemicals are used, only those that are registered with the Environmental Protection Agency shall be used. Use shall be in compliance with the directions. In addition, pesticides shall be applied only in such a manner as to prevent skin contact and other exposure to children or staff and to minimize odors in occupied areas. Following the use of pesticides, herbicides, fungicides, or other potentially toxic chemicals, the treated area shall be ventilated for the period recommended on the

See rationale for standard FA87.

To prevent contamination and poisoning, the consumer must be sure that these chemicals are applied by individuals who have been certified as competent to use them. Direct observation of pesticide operations by child care staff is essential to guide the exterminator away from surfaces that can be touched or mouthed by children.

The time of toxic risk exposure is a function of skin contact, the efficiency of the ventilating system, and the volatility of the toxic substance. The long-term effects of toxic substances are unclear.

The consumer should ask to see the license of the exterminator and should be certain that the individual who applies the toxic chemicals has personally been trained and licensed. In some states only the owner of an extermination company is required to have such training, and he/she may then employ unskilled workers to spread poison in the environment. Contact

Environmental Protection Agency
401 M St., S.W.
Washington, D.C. 20460

Manufacturers of such products usually provide product warnings that exposure to these chemicals can be poisonous. After the chemicals are applied, these warnings still apply. Contact the Environmental Protection Agency as specified above.

product label or by a nationally certified regional poison control center before being reoccupied. Tests shall be taken to determine safe levels before reoccupancy.

FA94. Pesticides shall be stored in their original containers and in a secure site accessible only to authorized staff. No restricted-use pesticide shall be stored or used on the premises except by properly licensed persons.

Children must be protected from exposure to poisons.

FA95. Right-of-way pesticide or herbicide spraying shall be prohibited on the grounds of a facility.

FA96. If the facility has been treated with a termiticide or any restricted- or prohibited-use pesticide in the last 10 years, ambient measurements shall be taken and tested by an organization certified to make such tests according to Environmental Protection Agency instructions to ensure that chlordane or other toxic chemicals are not present in unsafe levels. If unsafe levels are found, children shall not be allowed to use such areas until effective corrective measures have been taken to achieve safe levels.

This standard is to prevent contamination and poisoning.

Names of certified organizations that perform such tests can be obtained by contacting the regional office of the EPA through

Environmental Protection Agency
401 M St., S.W.
Washington, DC 20460

Additional Location, Layout, and Construction Requirements for Facilities Serving Children with Special Needs

See *Access* and *Space for Services*, on pp. 257–258.

GENERAL FURNISHINGS AND EQUIPMENT REQUIREMENTS

Facility Furnishings and Equipment

FA97. Equipment, materials, and furnishings shall be sturdy and free of sharp points or corners, splinters, protruding nails or bolts, loose rusty parts, hazardous small parts, or paint that contains lead or other poison-

This standard helps to reduce injuries.

Freedom from sharp points, corners, or edges shall be judged according to the Code of Federal Regulations, Title 16, Section 1500.48 and Section 1500.49.

STANDARDS	RATIONALE	COMMENTS

ous materials. The area shall be kept free from small parts that may become detached during normal use or reasonably foreseeable abuse of the equipment and that present a choking, aspiration, or ingestion hazard to a child.

Freedom from small parts should be judged according to the Code of Federal Regulations, Title 16, Part 1501.

To obtain these publications, contact

> Superintendent of Documents
> U.S. Government Printing Office
> Washington, DC 20402

Contact the United States Consumer Product Safety Commission (CPSC) for assistance in interpretation of the federal regulations:

> Office of the Secretary
> Consumer Product Safety
>   Commission
> Washington, DC 20207

The CPSC also has regional offices.

FA98. Durable furniture shall be child-sized or adapted for children's use.

Tables should be at waist height and the child's feet should reach a firm surface while the child is seated.

FA99. Equipment, furnishings, toys, and play materials shall be easy to clean.

FA100. Equipment shall be placed so as to help prevent collisions and accidents while still permitting freedom of action by the children.

This standard provides for the children's welfare and stimulation, which are essential to development, and helps prevent collisions and injury.

FA101. Floors, walls, and ceilings shall be smooth, in good repair, and easy to clean.[2]

FA102. Floors shall be free from cracks, bare concrete, dampness, splinters, sliding rugs, drafts, and uncovered telephone jacks or electrical outlets.

This standard promotes and accommodates good sanitation and safety.

FA103. Carpeting shall be clean, in good repair, nonflammable, and nontoxic.

Obtain ASTM D 2859 Pile Floor Coverings—Test for flammability of finished materials from

> American Society for Testing and
>   Materials
> 1916 Race St.
> Philadelphia, PA 19103

Ask the local fire marshal for fire safety code requirements.

FA104. The child care setting shall reduce risks of back injuries for adults.

Back strain can occur from adult use of child-sized furniture. Analysis of workers' compensation claims[22] shows that employees in the service

Some risk reduction approaches include
a) Adult-height changing tables.
b) Small, stable stepladders, stairs, or

industries, including child care, suffer an injury rate as great as or greater than that of workers employed in factories. Back injuries are the leading type of injury. Most back injuries can be prevented by appropriate design of work activities and training of workers.

The principles to support these recommendations (see Comments) are standard principles of ergonomics, in which jobs and workplaces are designed to eliminate biomechanical hazards.

other similar equipment to enable children to climb to the changing table or other places to which they would otherwise be lifted, without creating a fall hazard.

c) Convenient equipment for moving children, reducing the necessity of carrying them.

d) Adult furniture that eliminates awkward sitting or working positions in all areas where adults work. Caregivers shall not routinely be required to use child-sized chairs, tables, or desks.

This standard is not intended to interfere with child-adult interactions or to create hazards for children. Modifications can be made in the environment to minimize hazards and injuries for both children and adults. Adult furniture needs to be available at least for break times, staff meetings, and so forth.

FA105. High chairs, if used, shall have a wide base and a T-shaped safety strap. They shall be labeled or warranted by the manufacturer in documents provided at the time of purchase or verified thereafter by the manufacturer as meeting the American Society for Testing Materials (ASTM) Standard F-404 (Consumer Safety Specifications for High Chairs).

This standard is to help prevent falls.

ASTM F-404 covers sharp edges, locking devices, drop tests of tray, disengagement of tray, load and stability of chair, protection from coil springs and scissoring, maximum size of holes, restraining system tests, labeling, and instructional literature.

The Juvenile Products Manufacturers Association has a testing and certification program for high chairs, play yards, carriages, strollers, walkers, gates, and expandable enclosures. Consumers can look for labeling that certifies that these products meet the standards when purchasing such equipment.

Contact ASTM at the following address:

1916 Race St.
Philadelphia, PA 19103

FA106. Cribs shall be made of wood, metal, or approved plastic and have secure latching devices. They shall have slats spaced no more than 2⅜ inches apart, with a mattress fitted so that no more than two fingers can fit between the mattress and the crib side. The minimum height from the top of the mattress to the top of the crib rail shall be 36 inches. Drop-side latches shall securely hold sides in the raised position and shall not be reachable by the child in the crib. Cribs shall not be used with the drop side down. There shall be no corner post extensions (over 1/16 inch) or cut-outs in headboards on the crib.

Children have strangled because their shoulders or necks became caught in too wide a gap between slats or between mattress and crib side. Corner posts present a potential for clothing entanglement and strangulation.[23] Asphyxial crib death due to wedging of the head or neck in parts of the crib, and accidental hanging by a necklace or clothing over a corner-post have been well documented.[1, 2] CPSC crib safety standards went into effect in 1974 and were upgraded in 1982. More recently there have been voluntary standards regarding corner posts. However, there are thousands of older cribs still in use or in attic storage that could be used by the next generation of children.

Refer to ASTM F-966-90-Specification for Crib Corner Post Extensions.

To obtain this information, contact

American Society for Testing and Materials
1916 Race St
Philadelphia, PA 19103.

Cribs with big wheels (8 inches wide) are preferred in child care settings with ramps, as they are advantageous during fire evacuation of children.

Cribs should not be used with the side down as children may fall out.

FA107. Each carriage, stroller, gate, enclosure, and play yard used shall meet the corresponding ASTM standard and shall be so labeled on the equipment:

    Carriages/strollers—ASTM F833
    Gates/enclosures—ASTM F406
    Play yards—ASTM F406

The presence of a certification seal placed on Juvenile Products Manufacturers Association products ensures that the product is in compliance with the requirements of the current safety standard for that product at the time of manufacture. ASTM standards are, by congressional act, accepted as federal safety standards.

For more information, contact

    Juvenile Products Manufacturers
      Association, Inc.
    66 East Main St.
    Morristown, NJ 08057

    American Society for Testing and
      Materials
    1916 Race St.
    Philadelphia, PA 19103

FA108. Infant walkers shall be prohibited.

There is no indication that infant walkers are beneficial. A study of twins found that the twin not using the walker walked slightly earlier than did the sibling using the walker.[24] Infant walkers used with high-risk infants and young children with cerebral palsy perpetuated undesirable reflexes and precluded development.[24] Infant walkers are the cause of more injuries than any other baby product; in 1984, 15,100 children under the age of 1 were treated in emergency rooms for injuries related to infant walkers.[24] Because of increased mobility, a child in an infant walker is at high risk if left unwatched.[24]

Resources on infant safety are available from the

    American Academy of Pediatrics
    P.O. Box 927
    141 Northwest Point Blvd.
    Elk Grove Village, IL 60009-0927

FA109. The facility shall provide one working non-pay telephone for general and emergency use. (See also *Posting Documents*, on p. 296.)

A telephone must be available in an emergency.

Play Equipment

FA110. Play equipment and materials shall be provided that meet the standards of the Consumer Product Safety Commission and the American Society for Testing and Materials for juvenile products. Play equipment and materials shall be found to be appropriate to the developmental needs, individual interests, and ages of the children by a person with at least a master's degree in early childhood education, psychology, or psychiatry, or identified as age-appropriate by a label provided by the manufacturer on the product package. There shall be enough play equipment and materials that excessive competition and long waits are avoided.

Toys must be safe, sufficient in quantity for the number of children, and age-appropriate.

Measure compliance by structured observation.

STANDARDS

FA111. All play equipment shall be constructed and installed in such a manner as to be safe for use by children (e.g., height shall not be excessive; the equipment shall not be a potential source of entrapment). There shall be no pinch, crush, or shear points on or underneath such equipment that would be accessible by children.

FA112. Any hazardous play equipment shall be made inaccessible to children by barriers or removed until rendered safe or replaced. The barriers shall not pose any hazard.

FA113. Projectile toys shall be prohibited.

FA114. Water play tables shall be prohibited.

FA115. Tricycles and other riding toys used by the children shall be spokeless, steerable, and of a size appropriate for the child, and shall have low centers of gravity. All such toys shall be in good condition and free of sharp edges or protrusions that may injure the children. Helmets shall be worn by all riders. Plastic liners shall be used so children can share helmets. When not in use, such toys shall be stored in a location where they will not present a physical obstacle to the children and caregivers. Riding toys shall be inspected at least monthly for protrusions or rough edges that can lead to injury.

For additional special play equipment requirements for infants, toddlers, and preschoolers, see *Additional Indoor Requirements for Infants, Toddlers, and Preschoolers*, on p. 181. See also *Sanitation, Disinfection, and Maintenance of Toys and Objects*, on p. 178.

Supplies

FA116. Two readily available first aid kits shall be maintained by each facility, one to be taken on field trips and outings away from the site. Each

RATIONALE

Moving parts of play equipment must be designed so that no exposed joints or parts crush or hurt children's body parts when play equipment is being operated.

Contamination of hands, toys, and equipment in the room has appeared to play a role in the transmission of diseases in child care settings.[25, 26]

Riding toys can provide much enjoyment for children, but because of their high center of gravity and speed, they can often produce injuries in young children.

In facilities, an emphasis must be placed on safeguarding each child and ensuring that the staff are able to handle emergencies. In a recent

COMMENTS

Examples of barriers to play equipment that pose a safety hazard are prickly bushes and standing bodies of water.

Spokeless tricycles and other riding toys are recommended over those with spokes.

kit shall be a closed container for storing first aid supplies, accessible to child care staff members at all times but out of reach of children. First aid kits shall be restocked after use, and inventory shall be conducted at least monthly.

The first aid kit shall contain at least the following items:
a) Disposable nonporous gloves.
b) Sealed packages of alcohol wipes or antiseptic.
c) Scissors.
d) Tweezers.
e) Thermometer.
f) Bandage tape.
g) Sterile gauze pads.
h) Flexible roller gauze.
i) Triangular bandages.
j) Safety pins.
k) Eye dressing.
l) Pen/pencil and note pad.
m) Syrup of ipecac.
n) Cold pack.
o) Current American Academy of Pediatrics or American Red Cross standard first aid text or equivalent first aid guide.
p) Coins for use in a pay phone.
q) Insect sting preparation.
r) Poison control center telephone number.
s) Water.
t) Small plastic or metal splints.
u) Soap.

study that reviewed 423 injuries, first aid was sufficient treatment for 84.4 percent (357) of the injuries.[27] The supplies needed for pediatric first aid, including rescue breathing and first aid for choking, must be available to be used.

FA117. Combs, hairbrushes, toothbrushes, personal clothing, bedding, and towels shall never be shared and shall be labeled as to ownership

Respiratory, gastrointestinal, and skin infections (e.g., lice infestation, scabies, and ringworm) are among the most common infectious diseases in child care. These diseases are transmitted by direct skin-to-skin contact or by the sharing of personal articles such as combs, brushes, towels, clothing, and bedding. Prohibiting the sharing of personal articles and providing space so that personal items may be stored separately help prevent the spread of these diseases.

FA118. Unless shared use of cloth towels can be prevented, disposable towels or tissues shall be used and properly discarded.

Many communicable diseases can be prevented through appropriate hygiene, sanitation, and disinfection methods.

FA119. Bathrooms and handwashing sinks shall be adequately supplied with soap, hand lotion, and paper

Cracks in the skin and excessive dryness from frequent handwashing deter staff from compliance with

Bar or liquid soap can be used by staff, but children need to use liquid soap. Children's hands are too small

STANDARDS

towels or other hand-drying devices approved by the local regulatory or health agency, within arm's reach of the user of each sink, and supplied with toilet paper within arm's reach of the user of each toilet.

For additional information on supplies, see also *Sinks*, on p. 170; *Emergency Plan*, on p. 280, on first aid kits; and standards HP9 and HP10 in chapter 3 on p. 67 on toothbrushes.

Additional Furnishings and Equipment Requirements for Facilities Serving Children with Special Needs

See *Special Equipment*, on p. 259.

TOXIC SUBSTANCES

FA120. Cleaning materials, detergents, aerosol cans, pesticides, health and beauty aids, poisons, and other toxic materials shall be stored in their original labeled containers and shall be used according to the manufacturer's instructions and for the intended purpose. They shall be used only in a manner that will not contaminate play surfaces, food, or food preparation areas, and that will not constitute a hazard to the children. When not in actual use, such materials shall be kept in a place inaccessible to children and separate from stored medications and food.

FA121. The poison control center and/or physician shall be called for advice about safe use of any toxic products (e.g., pesticides, plants, rat poison) or in any ingestion emergency, and their advice shall be documented in the facility's files. The poison information specialist and/or physician shall be told the child's age and sex, the substance swallowed and the estimated amount, and the condition of the child.

RATIONALE

necessary hygiene and may lead to increased bacterial accumulation on hands. The availability of hand lotion to prevent dryness encourages staff to wash hands more often.

See also rationale for standard FA114, on p. 161.

Supplies must be within arm's reach of the user to prevent contamination of the environment with waste, water, or excretion.

This standard will prevent injury and poisoning. There were 1,368,748 human poison exposures reported in 1988 by 64 poison control centers nationwide that represented an estimated 63 percent of the U.S. population.[28] Children under age 6 accounted for the following number of exposures:[28]

Poisons	Exposures
Chemicals	16,215
Industrial and home cleaning products	87,393
Cosmetics and personal care products	92,560
Deodorizers	9,557
Rodenticides	9,406
Insecticides	22,136
with repellents	4,475

Toxic substances, when ingested, inhaled, or in contact with skin, may react immediately or slowly, with serious symptoms occurring much later. These symptoms may vary with the type of substance. Some common symptoms include dermatitis, nausea, vomiting, diarrhea, and congestion.

COMMENTS

and lack the dexterity to handle bar soap and provide adequate detergent action. Antibacterial soap is not necessary.

Any question on possible risks for exposures should be referred to professionals for proper first aid and treatment. Regional poison control centers have access to the latest information on emergency care of the poison victim.

STANDARDS	RATIONALE	COMMENTS

FA122. Employers shall provide child care workers with hazard information, as required by the Occupational Safety and Health Administration (OSHA), about the presence of toxic substances such as asbestos or formaldehyde. Such information shall include the identification of the ingredients of art materials and disinfectants.

These precautions are essential to the health and well-being of both the staff and the children.

The EPA and OSHA have stated that the quality of indoor air is, in general, poorer than that of outdoor air. Indoor air pollution is thus a potential occupational health hazard for child care workers, particularly since there is the concurrent potential for exposure to infectious and chemical agents. In addition, many cleaning products and art materials contain hazardous ingredients. Recent regulations make the complete identity of these materials known to users. Since nontoxic substitutes are available for virtually all necessary products, their substitution for toxic products should be required.

Employers may contact the local building safety inspection authority for information about toxic subtances in the building.

Protection of workers by the Occupational Safety and Health Administration is administered by the U.S. Department of Labor, which is listed in the phone books of all large cities and is headquartered at

200 Constitution Ave., N.W.
Washington, DC 20210

Standards change frequently and the latest standards should be sought from EPA. Information on toxic substances in the environment is available from

Environmental Protection Agency
401 M St., S.W.
Washington, DC 20460

For information on art materials, contact

Center for Safety in the Arts
5 Beekman St.
New York, NY 10038

FA123. When the manufacturer's Material Data Safety Sheet shows the presence of any toxic effects, these materials shall be replaced with non-toxic substitutes. If no substitute is available, the product shall be eliminated.

See rationale for standard FA122.

For guidance about hazardous and toxic materials, contact

Environmental Protection Agency
401 M St., S.W.
Washington, DC 20460

FA124. Radon concentrations shall be less than 4 picocuries per liter of air.

FA125. Any asbestos that is friable or in a dangerous condition found within a facility shall be removed by a contractor certified to remove asbestos, encapsulated, or enclosed in accordance with existing regulations of the Environmental Protection Agency, the federal agency responsible for asbestos abatement.

This action is taken to protect the staff and children and is based on the National Asbestos School Hazard Abatement Act of 1984 and CPSC guidelines.

Contact as follows:

Environmental Protection Agency
401 M St., S.W.
Washington, DC 20460

U.S. Consumer Product Safety Commission
Washington, DC 20207

FA126. Pipe and boiler insulation shall be sampled and examined in an accredited laboratory for the presence of asbestos in a friable or potentially dangerous condition.

This standard prevents unnecessary exposure to asbestos.

Contact regional offices of the EPA through

Environmental Protection Agency
401 M St., S.W.
Washington, DC 20460

STANDARDS	RATIONALE	COMMENTS

FA127. Nonfriable asbestos shall be identified to prevent disturbance and/or exposure during remodeling or future activities.

See rationale for standard FA126.

See comment for standard FA126.

FA128. Chemicals used in lawn care treatments shall be limited to those listed as nonrestricted use. All chemicals used inside or outside shall be stored in their original containers in a safe and secure manner, accessible only to authorized staff. They shall be used only according to manufacturers' instructions, and in a manner that will not contaminate play surfaces or articles.

The EPA has a list of restricted chemicals that are unsuitable for use in a child care environment. Contact

Environmental Protection Agency
401 M St., S.W.
Washington, DC 20460

FA129. All arts and crafts materials used in the facility shall be nontoxic. There shall be no eating or drinking by children or staff during use of such materials. Use of old or donated materials with potentially harmful ingredients shall be prohibited.

This standard prevents contamination and injury.

New federal government safety requirements for arts and crafts materials are being issued. Meanwhile, state government agencies such as the California Department of Health have listings of approved children's art materials presently considered safe. For information, contact

California Department of Health
Environmental, Epidemiology
  and Toxicology Section
5900 Hollis St., Building E
Emeryville, CA 94608

A list of unsafe art supplies is contained in Appendix VI.5 of *Health in Day Care: A Manual for Health Professionals*. To order this publication, contact

American Academy of Pediatrics
141 Northwest Point Blvd.
P.O. Box 927
Elk Grove Village, IL 60009-0927

FA130. Poisonous or potentially harmful plants on the premises shall be inaccessible to children. All plants accessible to children shall be identified and checked by name with the local poison control center to determine safe use.

Plants are among the most common household substances ingested by children. It is difficult to determine every commercially available household plant's toxicity. A more reasonable approach is to keep these and other potentially poisonous substances out of reach of children. All outside plants and their leaves, fruit, and stems should also be considered potentially toxic.[29]

See Appendix N, on p. 357 for a description of poisonous plants from the American Red Cross *Child Care Course.*

For more information about the American Red Cross *Child Care Course*, telephone the local chapter of the American Red Cross or write to

American Red Cross
National Headquarters,
  Health and Safety
18th and F Streets, N.W.
Washington, DC 20006

Lists of poisonous plants, safe plants, and ways to avoid plant poisoning are contained in Appendix VI.4 in *Health in Day Care: A Manual for*

STANDARDS	RATIONALE	COMMENTS

Health Professionals. To order this publication, contact

American Academy of Pediatrics
141 Northwest Point Blvd.
P.O. Box 927
Elk Grove Village, IL 60009-0927

FA131. The use of incense, moth crystals or moth balls, and chemical air fresheners that contain ingredients on the Environmental Protection Agency's toxic chemicals lists and those not approved as safe by the state or local regulatory agency shall be prohibited.

Contact the EPA Regional offices listed in the federal agency section of the telephone directory for assistance, or contact any nationally certified regional poison control center. Or contact

Environmental Protection Agency
401 M St., S.W.
Washington, DC 20460

FA132. Carpets made of nylon, orlon, wool and/or silk, and other materials that emit highly toxic fumes when they burn shall not be used.

Some materials emit highly toxic fumes when they burn; poisoning can occur even during evacuation. Polypropylene and cotton emit only carbon dioxide, carbon monoxide, and acrolein, which are safer than the fumes emitted by nylon, orlon, wool, or silk.[30]

FA133. Areas that have been recently carpeted or paneled using an adhesive that may contain toxic materials shall be well-ventilated and shall not be used by a facility for at least 7 days after such installation, or until there is no perceptible odor. Ambient testing in compliance with testing requirements of the Environmental Protection Agency shall be conducted if recommended by the local health department or building inspector before occupancy to ascertain that no unsafe levels of toxic substances (e.g., formaldehyde) resulting from the materials or their installation exist.

This standard is based on national, state, and local codes.

Much research is being done to establish "safe" levels of home indoor air pollutants.

The EPA should be contacted for details:

Environmental Protection Agency
401 M St., S.W.
Washington, DC 20460

FA134. Insulation or other materials that contain elements that may emit toxic substances (e.g., formaldehyde) over recommended levels in the child care environment shall not be used in facilities. If existing structures contain such materials, the facility shall be monitored regularly to ensure a safe environment as specified by the regulatory agency.

Exposure to toxic substances must be prevented.

EPA regional offices can be contacted for advice. Contact

Environmental Protection Agency
401 M St., S.W.
Washington, DC 20460

STANDARDS

FA135. Any surface painted before 1978 shall be tested for excessive lead levels.

a) In all centers, both exterior and interior surfaces covered by paint with lead levels of 0.06 percent and above and accessible to children shall be removed by a safe chemical or physical means or made inaccessible to children, regardless of the condition of the surface.

b) In large and small family-child-care homes, flaking or deteriorating lead-based paint on interior or exterior surfaces, equipment, or toys accessible to preschool-age children shall be removed or abated according to health department regulations.

c) Where lead paint is removed, the surface shall be refinished with lead-free paint or nontoxic material. Sanding, scraping, or burning of high-lead surfaces shall be prohibited.

FA136. No paint containing lead in excess of 0.06 percent shall be used when surfaces are repaired or when any new surfaces accessible to children are painted.

FA137. Construction, remodeling, or alterations of structures during child care operations shall be done in such a manner as to prevent hazards or unsafe conditions (e.g., fumes, dust, safety hazards).

For additional information on toxic substances, see also standard HP64 in chapter 3 on p. 80.

RATIONALE

Ingestion of lead paint made years ago or applied years ago can result in the leaching out of lead, which is a toxic substance that affects the central nervous system and can cause mental retardation.[31]

See rationale for standard FA135.

COMMENTS

Paints made before 1978 may contain lead. If there is any doubt about the presence of lead in existing paint, contact the health department for information regarding testing. Lead is prohibited in contemporary paints.

Paint and other surface coating materials should comply with lead content provisions of the Code of Federal Regulations, Title 16, Part 1303.

To obtain this publication, contact

Superintendent of Documents
U.S. Government Printing Office
Washington, DC 20402

Maximum lead content is 0.06 percent of the weight of the total non-volatile content of the paint.

5.2 Requirements for Indoor Space and Equipment by Area

STANDARDS

RATIONALE

COMMENTS

PLAY INDOORS

FA138. The designated area for children's activities shall contain a minimum of 35 square feet per child, 50 square feet measured on the inside, wall-to-wall dimensions.[32] These spaces are exclusive of food preparation areas of the kitchen, bathrooms, toilets, areas for the care of ill children, offices, staff rooms, corridors, hallways, stairways, closets, lockers, laundry, furnace rooms, cabinets, and storage shelving spaces.[1, 2]

Child behavior tends to be more constructive when sufficient space is organized to promote the practice of developmentally appropriate skills. Crowding has been shown to be associated with an increased risk of developing upper respiratory infections.[33]

The 35 square feet of available play space per child should be free of furniture and equipment. With a usual furnishing load, this space usually amounts to 50 square feet measured wall-to-wall.

FA139. The floor area beneath ceilings less than 7 feet 6 inches above the floor shall not be counted in determining compliance with the above space requirements. Areas not inhabited and used by children shall not be counted in determining compliance with the above space requirements.

Ceiling height must be adequate, in addition to floor dimensions, to provide a volume of air that does not quickly concentrate infectious disease or noxious fumes.

See *Additional Indoor Requirements for Special Groups or Ages of Children*, on p. 180. For additional indoor play requirements, see also *General Requirements for Toilet, Diapering, and Bath*, on location of toilets and sinks near indoor play areas and standard FA221, on p. 117 on indoor space being used to meet outdoor play space requirements.

TOILET, DIAPERING, AND BATH AREAS

General Requirements for Toilet, Diapering, and Bath

FA140. There shall be visibly clean toilet and handwashing facilities accessible to all indoor and outdoor play areas used by children.

Young children must be able to get to toilet facilities quickly. If pediatric first aid, including rescue breathing and first aid for choking, is required, rapid access to running water is essential.

TOILETS AND TOILET TRAINING EQUIPMENT

FA141. Toilets shall be located in rooms separate from those used for cooking or eating. If toilets are not on the same floor as the child care area, an adult shall accompany children less than 5 years of age to and from the toilet area.

This standard is to prevent contamination of food and to eliminate unpleasant odors from the food areas. Supervision and assistance are necessary for young children.

Monitor compliance by observation.

STANDARDS	RATIONALE	COMMENTS

FA142. In centers, separate and private toilet facilities shall be provided for males and females who are 6 years of age or older.

Although cultural differences in need for privacy exist, sex-separated toileting among nonrelatives is the norm for adults. Children should be allowed the opportunity to practice modesty when independent toileting behavior is well established among the majority. By age 6, most children can use the toilet by themselves.[34]

FA143. Chemical toilets are prohibited.

This standard provides injury control and sanitation.

FA144. Toilets and sinks, easily accessible for use and supervision, shall be provided in the following ratios: Toilets, urinals, and handsinks shall be apportioned at a ratio of 1:10 for toddlers and preschool-age children and 1:15 for school-age children. Maximum toilet height shall be 11 inches and maximum handsink height shall be 22 inches. Urinals shall not exceed 30 percent of the total required toilet fixtures. When the number of children in the ratio is exceeded by one, an additional fixture shall be required.

Young children toilet frequently and cannot wait long when they perceive the need to toilet.

The ratio of 1:10 is based on best professional experience of early childhood educators who are facility operators. This ratio also limits the group that will be sharing facilities (and infections).

A ratio of one toilet to every 10 children may be insufficient if only one toilet is accessible to each group of 10, so a minimum of two toilets per group is preferable when the group size approaches 10. However, a large toilet room with many toilets used by several groups is less desirable than several small toilet rooms, because of the opportunities such a large room offers for commingling of infectious disease agents.

These numbers shall be subject to the following minimums:
a) A minimum of one sink and one flush toilet for 10 or fewer toddlers and pre-school age children using toilets.
b) A minimum of one sink and one flush toilet for 15 or fewer school-age children using toilets.
c) A minimum of two sinks and two flush toilets for 16 to 30 children using toilets.
d) A minimum of one sink and one flush toilet for each additional 15 children.

FA145. Toilet training equipment shall not be counted as toilets in the toilet:child ratio.

FA146. Toilet training equipment shall be provided for children being toilet trained. Child-sized toilets or safe and cleanable step aids and modified toilet seats (where adult-sized toilets are present) shall be used in facilities; the use of potty chairs

Child-sized toilets, steps, and modified toilet seats provide for easier maintenance. Sanitary handling of potty chairs is very difficult. Flushing toilets are superior to any type of device that exposes staff to contact with feces or urine.

Low toilets with appropriate seats are preferable to training chairs.

See "sanitize" in the Glossary for solutions and methods to sanitize potty chairs.

STANDARDS	RATIONALE	COMMENTS

shall be discouraged. If child-sized toilets, step aids, or modified toilet seats cannot be used, potty chairs that are easily cleaned and sanitized shall be provided for toddlers, preschoolers, and children with disabilities who require them. Toilet training equipment shall be accessible to children only under direct supervision.

Many communicable diseases can be prevented through appropriate hygiene, sanitation, and disinfection methods. Surveys of environmental surfaces in child care settings have demonstrated evidence of fecal contamination. Fecal contamination has been used to gauge the adequacy of sanitation, disinfection, and hygiene.

FA147. Toilet rooms shall have at least one waste receptacle with a pedal-operated lid.

This standard prevents the spread of disease and filth.

For additional information on general requirements for toilet, diapering, and bath, see also *Sanitation, Disinfection, and Maintenance of Toilet Training Equipment, Toilets, and Bathrooms,* on p. 76.

Sinks

FA148. A handwashing sink shall be accessible without barriers, such as doors, to each child care area. In areas for infants, toddlers, and preschoolers, the sink must be located so that the caregiver may visually supervise the group of children while he/she washes his/her hands or has a child wash.

Many communicable diseases can be prevented through appropriate hygiene, sanitation, and disinfection methods.

Foot-operated handwashing sinks are preferable because they minimize hand contamination after handwashing.

FA149. Handwashing sinks shall be provided adjacent to diaper-changing tables in centers. There shall be a minimum of one handwashing sink for every two changing tables.

These sinks are needed to wash hands of staff and children and to help prevent the spread of contaminants and disease.

See comment for standard FA148.

FA150. Handwashing sinks shall be supplied in large and small family-child-care homes as specified in standard FA149, *except* that they need not be adjacent to changing tables.

See rationale for standard FA149.

See comment for standard FA148.

FA151. Handwashing sinks shall be within the caregiver's arm's reach of each toileting area.

FA152. Handwashing sinks shall not be used for rinsing soiled clothing or for cleaning toilet training equipment.

FA153. Centers with more than 30 children shall have a mop sink. Large and small family-child-care homes shall have a means of drawing clean mop water and disposing of it in a toilet or sink used only for such purposes.

Handwashing and food preparation sinks must not be contaminated by dumping of waste water. Contamination of hands, toys, and equipment in the room has appeared to play a role in the transmission of diseases in child care settings.[25, 26]

For additional information on sinks, see also standard FA69, on p. 153 on the use of a water supply when plumbing is unavailable, and *Kitchen and Equipment*, on p. 127.

Diaper-changing areas

FA154. The changing area shall never be located in food preparation areas and shall never be used for temporary placement or serving of food.

The separation of diaper-changing areas and food preparation areas prevents disease transmission.

FA155. Handwashing sinks shall be provided as specified in Sinks, on p. 170.

FA156. Changing tables shall have impervious, nonabsorbent surfaces. Tables shall be sturdy, shall be adult height, and shall be equipped with railings. Safety straps on changing tables shall not be used.

This standard is to prevent disease transmission and accidental falls and to provide safety measures during diapering. Safety straps are difficult to clean, may harbor contaminants, and decrease staff/child interaction.

An impervious surface is defined as a smooth surface that does not absorb liquid or retain soil.

While changing a child, it is necessary to hold onto the child at all times. This should also be seen as an opportunity for adult interaction with the child.

FA157. Soiled diapers shall be stored as specified in *Waste and Diaper Storage and Disposal*, on p. 170.

FA158. If cloth diapers are used, a toilet shall be easily accessible so that waste contents may be disposed of by dumping before placing the diapers in the waste receptacle.

Use of a toilet provides safe disposal of feces, which may carry disease-producing organisms.

FA159. Conveniently located, washable, plastic-lined, tightly covered receptacles, operated by a foot pedal, shall be provided for soiled burping cloths and linen.

These receptacles prevent the children from coming into contact with disease-bearing body fluids.

STANDARDS	RATIONALE	COMMENTS

For additional information on diaper-changing areas, see *Waste and Diaper Storage and Disposal*, on p. 150, and *Toileting, Diapering, and Toilet Training*, on p. 68.

Waste Containers

See *Waste and Diaper Storage and Disposal*, on p. 150.

Bathrooms

FA160. Every toilet room door shall be easily opened by children from the inside.

Doors that are easily opened will prevent entrapment.

FA161. Every toilet room door used by preschool children shall be openable from the outside.

See rationale for standard FA160.

FA162. Toilet rooms shall have barriers that prevent unattended toddler entry. Toddlers shall be supervised.

This standard ensures accident prevention and good sanitation.

FA163. Each bathroom, toilet room, and shower room floor and wall, up to a height of 5 feet, shall be impervious to water and capable of being kept in a clean and sanitary condition.

The use of impervious surfaces for floors and walls prevents deterioration and mold and ensures clean and sanitary surfaces.

See comment for standard FA156.

Bathtubs and Showers

FA164. Bathtubs and showers, when required or used, shall be located within the facility or in an approved building immediately adjacent to it.

This standard provides proper, safe personal hygiene for overnight care.

FA165. Bath and toilet rooms shall be located on the same floor as and adjacent to the sleeping areas. Bathtubs and showers need not be located in the same room as toilets.

FA166. Bath and toilet rooms shall be easily accessible to sleeping areas.

FA167. There shall be one bathtub or shower for every six children in overnight care. If infants are being cared for, there shall be age-appropriate bathing facilities for them.

Enough tubs must be available to permit separate bathing for every child.

Assuming each bath takes 10 to 15 minutes, a ratio of one tub to six children with time to wash the tub between children means bathing would require about 1½ hours.

STANDARDS

FA168. All bathing facilities shall have a conveniently located grab bar. Nonskid surfaces shall be provided in all tubs and showers.

For additional information on bathtubs and showers, see also *Hot Water* and standards HP110 and HP111 in chapter 3 on p. 96.

KITCHEN

See *Kitchen and Equipment*, on p. 127, and *Access to Kitchen*, on p. 129.

Hot Water

FA169. Facilities shall have water heating facilities that are properly connected to the water supply system. These facilities shall be capable of heating water to at least 120°F and shall deliver an adequate amount of hot water at every required fixture. Where a dishwasher is utilized, means shall be provided to heat water supplied to such equipment to at least 140°F.

FA170. All gas and oil appliances shall be properly vented as required by the regulatory agency.

FA171. Food preparation, handwashing, and bathing facilities shall be provided with hot and cold or temperate running water. Where such water will be in direct contact with children, the temperatures shall not exceed 120°F. Scald prevention devices such as special faucets or thermostatically controlled valves shall be permanently installed to provide this temperate water. These temperature limitations do not apply to water supplying dishwashers or laundry equipment where there is no direct exposure to children.

RATIONALE

Drowning and falls in bathtubs are a significant cause of injury for the young and children with disabilities. Falls in tubs are a well-documented source of injury in the National Electronic Injury Surveillance System (NEISS) data collected by the Consumer Product Safety Commission. Grab bars and nonslip surfaces reduce this risk.

This standard ensures the availability of hot water to facilitate cleaning, sanitation, and disinfection. Hot water is needed to clean and disinfect food utensils adequately and sanitize laundry.

Hot water is needed to remove soil properly. Water temperature must be controlled to prevent injury.

A review of hospital discharge summaries and emergency room log books implicates hot liquids as the major cause of nonfatal burns. Children under 5 are the most frequent victims.[8, 35, 36] Tap water burns are a leading cause of nonfatal burns.[37, 38] At 120°F the time for thermal injury is 2 minutes, and at 130°F the time is 30 seconds.[38]

COMMENTS

For further information on NEISS, contact

Consumer Product Safety Commission
Washington, DC 20207

Scald prevention devices marketed for home use can be installed by tenants using a central water heater on the lines that come into an apartment. Large and small family home caregivers in apartments can also adjust water temperature by having scald prevention devices installed at each sink or bathing fixture. Consult a plumbing contractor for details. These devices are not expensive.

STANDARDS	**RATIONALE**	**COMMENTS**

Drinking Water

FA172. Drinking water, dispensed in drinking fountains or by single-service cups, shall be accessible to children while indoors and outdoors.

Access to water provides for fluid maintenance essential to body health. The water must be protected from contamination to avoid the spread of disease.

FA173. Drinking fountains shall have an angled jet and orifice guard above the rim of the fountain. The pressure shall be regulated so the water stream does not contact the orifice or splash on the floor, but shall rise at least 2 inches above the orifice guard.

See rationale for standard FA172.

For further information, contact

Environmental Protection Agency
401 M St., S.W.
Washington, DC 20460

FA174. Drinking fountains shall be checked to ensure that they are not contributing high levels of lead to the water, as defined by the Code of Federal Regulations, Parts 141–143, and the 1988 Lead Contamination Control Act as amended.

For further guidance on drinking water, contact

Environmental Protection Agency
401 M St., S.W.
Washington, DC 20460

To obtain the Code of Federal Regulations, Parts 141–143, contact

Superintendent of Documents
U.S. Government Printing Office
Washington, DC 20402

FA175. Single-service cups shall be dispensed by staff or in a cup dispenser approved by the local health department.

FA176. At least 18 inches of space shall be provided between a drinking fountain and any sink or towel dispenser.

Space between a drinking fountain and sink or towel dispenser helps prevent contamination of the drinking fountain by organisms being splashed or deposited during handwashing.

Sinks

See *Sinks*, on p. 170, and *Kitchen and Equipment*, on p. 127.

LAUNDRY

FA177. Each center shall have a mechanical washing machine and dryer on site or shall contract with a laundry service. Where laundry

Bedding and towels that are not thoroughly cleaned pose a health threat to users of these items.

equipment is utilized in a large or small family-child-care home (or the large or small family home caregiver uses a laundrymat), the equipment shall comply with standard FA178.

FA178. Laundry equipment shall be located in an area separate and secure from the kitchen and child care areas. The water temperature for the laundry shall be maintained above 140°F unless (1) an approved disinfectant is applied in the rinse cycle, in which case the temperature used shall be specified by the manufacturer of the chemical, or (2) a dryer is used that the manufacturer attests heats the clothes above 140°F, or unless the clothes are completely ironed.[39] Dryers shall be vented to the outside.

With disinfectant, temperature is dependent on the chemical. Ironing or heating the clothing above 140°F will disinfect.

FA179. If a commercial laundry service is used, its performance shall at least meet or exceed the requirements in standard FA178.

See rationale for standard FA178.

SLEEPING

FA180. Play, dining, and napping may be carried on in the same room (exclusive of bathrooms, kitchens, hallways, and closets), provided that
a) The room is of sufficient size to have a defined area for each of the activities allowed there at the time when the activity is under way;
b) The room meets other building requirements; and
c) Programming is such that use of the room for one purpose does not interfere with use of the room for other purposes.

Measure compliance by direct observation.

FA181. Facilities shall have a crib, cot, sleeping bag, bed, mat, or pad for each child who spends more than 4 hours a day at the facility. Cribs, cots, sleeping bags, beds, mats, or pads shall be placed at least 3 feet apart, unless separated by screens.

This standard ensures sanitation, comfort, and adequate temperature.[2]

Since respiratory infections are transmitted by large droplets of respiratory secretions, a minimum distance of 3 feet should be maintained between cots or cribs used for resting or sleeping. It has been demonstrated that maintaining a distance of 3 feet between cots in military barracks limits the transmission of *Streptococcus pyogenes* infections.[40] It is reasonable to assume that this intervention would reduce the likelihood of transmission of other respiratory disease agents spread by large droplets and would be effective in the child care environment, but these points have not been demonstrated.

FA182. If used, mats and cots shall have nonabsorbent, cleanable coverings.

FA183. Pads and sleeping bags shall not be placed directly on concrete, linoleum, hardwood, or tile floors when children are resting. When pads are used, they shall be enclosed in washable covers, shall be used only over carpeting, and shall be long enough so the child's head or feet do not rest off the pad.

See rationale for standard FA183.

FA184. Regardless of age group, bed linens shall not be used as rest equipment in place of cots, beds, pads, or similar approved equipment.

See rationale for standard FA183.

FA185. Sleeping mats shall be stored so that there is no contact with the sleeping surface of another mat.

Lice infestation, scabies, and ringworm are among the most common infectious diseases in child care. These diseases are transmitted by direct skin-to-skin contact or by the sharing of personal articles such as combs, brushes, towels, clothing, and bedding. Providing space so that personal items may be stored separately helps prevent the spread of these diseases.

FA186. Child-sized futons may be used only if they are not on a frame, are easily cleanable, are encased in a tight-fitting waterproof cover, and meet all other standards in *Sleeping/ Napping*, on p. 175.

Frames pose an entrapment hazard. Futons that are easy to clean can be kept sanitary. Supervision is necessary to ensure that adequate spacing of futons is maintained and that bedding is not shared, thus reducing transmission of infectious diseases and keeping children out of traffic areas.

FA187. Stacked cribs shall not be used.

When cribs are stacked, the lower cribs can be contaminated with body fluids (saliva, urine, vomit) from the upper cribs.

FA188. The upper levels of double-deck beds shall not be used by children under 9 years of age.

Falls from bunk beds are a well-documented cause of injury for young children.

Consult the CPSC, the manufacturer's label, or the consumer safety information provided by the Juvenile

STANDARDS	RATIONALE	COMMENTS

Products Manufacturers' Association for advice.

Juvenile Products Manufacturers'
Association
66 E. Main St.
Morristown, NJ 08057

U.S. Consumer Product Safety
Commission
Washington, DC 20207

FA189. Children shall be provided individual sleeping arrangements (see standard FA181 on p. 175) with clean linen. No children shall share beds, even with family members.

Separate sleeping and resting, even for siblings, reduces the spread of disease from one child to another.

See also rationale for standard FA181 on p. 175.

FA190. Each item of sleep equipment (sheets, blankets, etc.) shall be assigned to a child and shall be used only by that child while he/she is enrolled in the facility. Children shall not share bedding. For children over 1 year of age, each mat, cot, or crib mattress shall be covered with the child's individual sheet for exclusive use by that child. No child shall sleep on a bare, uncovered surface. Seasonally appropriate covering, such as sheets or blankets that are sufficient to maintain adequate warmth, shall be available and shall be used by each child below school age. Pillows shall not be used for infants.

This standard provides comfort and minimizes transmission of disease via fomites. Lice infestation, scabies, and ringworm are among the most common infectious diseases in child care. These diseases are transmitted by direct skin-to-skin contact or by the sharing of personal articles such as combs, brushes, towels, clothing, and bedding. Prohibiting the sharing of personal articles helps prevent the spread of these diseases.

Appropriate hygiene and warmth are required.

Pillows pose a suffocation risk for infants.

Caregivers may ask parents to provide bedding that will be sent home weekly for washing.

Pillows need not be used for older children.

FA191. Bed linens used under children on cots, cribs, futons, and playpens shall be tight-fitting.

The use of tight-fitting bed linens prevents suffocation and strangling.

FA192. Substances of animal origin other than wool (such as feathers and animal hair) shall not be used in bedding.

These substances of animal origin commonly cause allergic reactions.

For additional information on sleeping, see also *Storage of Clothing and Supplies*, on p. 178, *Supervision Policy*, on p. 272, *Sanitation, Disinfection, and Maintenance of Bedding*, on p. 79 and *Sleep*, on p. 66.

AREAS FOR INJURED OR ILL CHILDREN

FA193. Each facility shall be provided with a separate room or designated area within a room for the temporary or ongoing care of a child who needs to be separated from the group due to injury or illness. This room or area shall be located so the child may be supervised. Toilet and lavatory facilities shall be readily accessible. If the child under care is suspected of having a communicable disease, all equipment used by the child shall be cleaned and disinfected after use. This room or area may be used for other purposes when not needed for the separation and care of a child or if the uses do not conflict.

For additional information on areas for injured or ill children, see also *Care of Ill Children*, on p. 274 and *Space*, on p. 102.

Children who are injured or ill may need to be separated from other children to provide for rest and to minimize spread of potential infectious disease.[2] Toilet and lavatory facilities must be readily available to permit frequent handwashing and provide rapid access in the event of vomiting or diarrhea to avoid contaminating the environment. Handwashing sinks should be stationed in each room not only to provide the opportunity to maintain cleanliness, but to permit the caregiver to maintain continuous supervision of the other children in care.

Some facilities have established separate areas or rooms that they call "get well rooms."

STORAGE OF CLOTHING AND SUPPLIES

FA194. Separate storage areas shall be provided for each child's and staff member's personal effects and clothing. Personal effects and clothing shall be labeled with the child's name. Bedding shall be labeled with the child's name and stored separately for each child. (See also *Sleeping*, on p. 175.)

This standard prevents the spread of insects and soil and provides for organization. Lice infestation, scabies, and ringworm are among the most common infectious diseases in child care. Lice can crawl from one collar or hood to another when hooks allow children's clothing to touch. These diseases are transmitted by direct skin-to-skin contact or by the sharing of personal articles such as combs, brushes, towels, clothing, and bedding. Providing space so that personal items may be stored separately helps prevent the spread of these diseases.

FA195. Mats for sleeping shall be stored as specified in standard FA185, on p. 176.

FA196. Coat hooks shall be spaced so coats will not touch each other, or individual cubicles or lockers of child's height shall be provided for

See rationale for standard FA195.

---

storage of children's clothing and personal possessions.

FA197. Space shall be provided and used for the storage of play and teaching equipment, supplies, records and files, cots, mats, and bedding.

This practice enhances safety and provides a good example of an orderly environment.

FA198. Facilities shall be provided for separate storage of soiled linen and clean linen.

This practice precludes contamination of clean areas and children with soiled and contaminated linen.

FA199. Where individual cloth towels used for bathing purposes, toothbrushes, washcloths, or combs are used by children, they shall be stored in separate, clean, closeable containers and shall be labeled with the child's name.

See rationale for standard FA194.

FA200. Closet doors accessible to children shall have an internal release for any latch so that the door can be opened by a child inside the closet.

Closet doors that can be opened from the inside prevent entrapment.

FA201. Matches and lighters shall be inaccessible to children.

Two percent of residential fire deaths are attributed to children playing with matches, cigarette lighters, and other ignition sources.[41]

FA202. Gasoline and other flammable materials shall be stored away from the children in a separate building.

Gasoline is involved in most non-housefire flash burn admissions to burn units among boys 6 to 16 years old.[8]

FA203. Thin plastic bags, whether intended for storage, trash, diaper disposal, or any other purpose, shall be stored out of reach of children.

Plastic bags have been recognized for many years as a cause of fatal suffocation. Warnings regarding this risk are printed on diaper pail bags, dry cleaning bags, and so forth. Baker and Fisher[42] found that 4 of 22 suffocation deaths in Maryland between 1970 and 1978 involved plastic bags; plastic bags were the most frequent cause of childhood suffocation in their study. Preliminary CPSC estimates for 1987 indicate 549 emergency room visits for injuries (not necessarily suffocation) caused by plastic bags in the 0–4 age group.[43]

FA204. Strings and cords (e.g., those that are parts of toys, or those that are found on window shades) long enough to encircle a child's neck (6 inches or more) shall not be accessible to children in child care.

Among 498 strangulation deaths of children ages 0 to 14 in California between 1960 and 1981, 93 were due to the child's neck becoming caught in a cord or rope (pacifier cords, high chair straps, venetian blind cords, etc.), and 116 were due to hangings, virtually all of which were uninten-

This standard should apply to toddlers and preschoolers as well as infants. It is unclear how important or practical it would be for older children. The length of a cord that would encircle a child's neck varies. There is a voluntary toy standard that sets cord lengths at a maximum of 12

STANDARDS

RATIONALE

COMMENTS

tional and occurred during play.[44] A CPSC study of 300 strangulations of children less than 5 years old revealed 41 deaths due to drapery and blind cords and 28 deaths from strings attached to pacifiers.[43]

inches.[45] For infants, A CPSC staff report has recommended 6 inches, which is 25 percent below the 50th percentile for neck circumference of 4–6-month-olds.[46]

This hazard is covered in ASTM F-963 section 5.4, which covers only labeling of the cords and their use by age. For information, contact

American Society for Testing and Materials
1916 Race St.
Philadelphia, PA 19103

FA205. Environmental hazards such as pits, abandoned wells, and abandoned appliances, which present a risk for entrapment or inhumation (burial), shall be covered or made inaccessible to children.

Among 471 childhood suffocation deaths in California between 1960 and 1981, 111 were caused by burial beneath earth, sand, or other material.[44] Some occurred at construction sites where children were playing, but others occurred at beaches and other remote areas. Children can also fall into wells, pits, and other excavations and can become trapped in refrigerators.

FA206. The center shall not have any firearms, pellet or BB guns (loaded or unloaded), darts, or cap pistols within the premises at any time. Such materials, if present in a small or large family-child-care home, must be unloaded and kept under lock and key in areas inaccessible to the children.

There is increasing awareness of the injury potential of firearms to young children. Such materials shall not be accessible to children in a facility.[47-50]

Monitor compliance via inspection.

FA207. Medications shall be stored as specified in HP85 in chapter 3 on p. 89.

ADDITIONAL INDOOR REQUIREMENTS FOR SPECIAL GROUPS OR AGES OF CHILDREN

Additional Indoor Requirements for Infants

In addition to the general indoor play requirements outlined in *Play Indoors,* on p. 168, see the following special requirements.

FA208. Infants and toddlers younger than age 2 shall be cared for in separate rooms, as specified in *Program Activities from Birth to 35 Months*, on p. 46.

FA209. When play and sleep areas for infants are in the same room, a minimum of 50 square feet of space per child shall be provided.

This requirement helps to prevent injury and provides sufficient space for activities.

See comment for standard FA138 in chapter 5 on p. 168.

FA210. Separate sleeping rooms for infants shall have a minimum of 30 square feet of space per child.

See rationale for standard FA209.

See *Additional Indoor Requirements for Infants, Toddlers, and Pre-schoolers*.

Additional Indoor Requirements for Infants, Toddlers, and Preschoolers

In addition to *Play Equipment*, on p. 160, see the following special requirements.

FA211. Small objects, toys, and toy parts available to infants and toddlers shall meet the federal small parts standards for toys. Toys or objects that have diameters of less than 1¼-inch, objects with removable parts that have diameters of less than 1¼-inch, toys with sharp points and edges, plastic bags, and styrofoam objects shall not be accessible to children under 4 years of age.

According to the federal government's small parts standard on a safe size toy for children under 3, a small part should be at least 1¼ inches in diameter and 2¼ inches long. Any part smaller than this is a potential choking hazard.

Injury and fatality due to aspiration of small parts is well documented.[1, 2, 51] Elimination of small parts from the environment of children will greatly reduce the risk.

Toys that do not meet the "small parts standard" are sometimes labeled "intended for children ages 3 and up." Since chokings on small parts occur throughout the preschool years, it is prudent to keep small parts away from children at least up to age 4. Also, children have occasionally choked on toys or toy parts that meet federal standards, so caregivers must constantly be vigilant.

The federal standard that applies is Code of Federal Regulations, Title 16, Part 1501, which defines the method for identifying toys and other articles intended for use by children under 3 years of age that present choking, aspiration, or ingestion hazards because of small parts. To obtain this publication, contact

> Superintendent of Documents
> U.S. Government Printing Office
> Washington, DC 20402

Also note ASTM F963-86 Specifications for Toy Safety. To obtain this publication, contact

> American Society for Testing and
>   Materials
> 1916 Race St.
> Philadelphia, PA 19103

Practically speaking, objects should not be small enough to fit entirely into a child's mouth

FA212. Crib gyms shall not be used for children who are able to push up on their hands and knees.

The presence of such toys presents a potential strangulation hazard for infants who are able to lift their heads above the crib surface.

Generally, children over 5 months should not have crib gyms.

FA213. Coins, rubber balloons, safety pins, marbles, and similar small objects shall not be available to children under 4 years old.

These objects represent aspiration hazards and are exempt from the small parts standard.[51]

FA214. Infants, toddlers, and preschool children shall not be permitted to inflate balloons, nor shall they have access to uninflated or under-inflated balloons.

Balloons are an aspiration hazard.[42] The CPSC reported at least 11 deaths from balloon aspiration in 1986 and 1987.

Additional Indoor Requirements for Toddlers and Preschoolers

In addition to the general indoor play requirements outlined in *Play Indoors*, on p. 168, see the following special requirements.

FA215. Where play and sleep areas are in the same room for toddlers and preschoolers, the following shall apply:
a) If stackable cots are used, there shall be 35 square feet of free floor space per child.
b) If cribs are used, there shall be a minimum of 65 square feet of space per child.

Toddlers need more room than infants because of their high activity level, which is associated with increased injury and infection risk in this age group. When cribs are used, 30 square feet will be used up by the cribs, leaving only 35 square feet.

The 35 square feet of available play space per child should be free of furniture and equipment. With usual furnishing load, this space usually amounts to 50 square feet measured wall-to-wall.

FA216. Sleep areas for toddlers and preschoolers in separate rooms shall have a minimum of 30 square feet of space per child.

FA217. Toddler and crawling areas shall be protected from general walkways and areas used for older children.

Additional Indoor Requirements for School-Age Children

In addition to the general indoor play requirements outlined in *Play Indoors*, on p. 168, see the following special requirements.

FA218. When school-age children are in care for periods that exceed 2 hours after school, a separate area away from areas for younger children shall be available for school-age children to do homework. Areas used for this purpose shall have table space, chairs, adequate ventilation, and lighting of 40–50 footcandles in the room and 50–100 footcandles on the surface used as a desk. (See *Lighting*, on p. 148.

School-age children need a quiet space to do homework so they are not forced to work against the demands for attention distractions posed by younger children.[7]

Children with Special Needs

In addition to the general requirements outlined in *Play Indoors*, on p. 168, see *Transportation*, on p. 256, *Access*, on p. 257, and *Space for Services*, on p. 258.

5.3 Playground and Outdoor Areas of the Facility

LAYOUT, LOCATION, AND SIZE OF PLAYGROUND AND OUTDOOR AREAS

FA219. The facility shall be equipped with an outdoor play area that directly adjoins the indoor facilities or that can be reached by a route "free of hazards" and is no farther than 1/8 mile from the facility. The playground shall comprise a minimum of 75 square feet for each child using the playground at any one time.

This standard is based on best professional experience.[1,2,52]

FA220. The following exceptions to the space requirements shall apply:
a) A minimum of 33 square feet of accessible outdoor play space is required for each infant.
b) A minimum of 50 square feet of accessible outdoor play space is required for each child from age 18 to 24 months.

These exceptions are based on best professional experience.[1,2,52,53,54]

STANDARDS	RATIONALE	COMMENTS

FA221. If there is less than 75 square feet of accessible outdoor space per child, a large indoor activity room that meets the 75-square-feet-per-child requirement may be used if it provides for types of activities equivalent to those performed in an outdoor play space; if the area is ventilated with fresh, temperate air at a minimum of 5 cubic feet per minute per occupant when open windows are not possible; and if the surfaces and finishes are resilient, as required for outdoor installations in standard FA245 in chapter 5 on p. 188.

This standard provides facilities located in inner-city areas with an alternative that allows gross motor play when outdoor spaces are unavailable. Such gross motor play must provide an experience like outdoor play, with safe and healthful environmental conditions that match the benefits of outdoor play as closely as possible. Such spaces may be interior if ventilation is adequate to prevent undue concentration of organisms and odors.

Every ventilating contractor has a meter to measure the rate of air flow. Before indoor areas are used for gross motor activity, such a heating and air conditioning contractor should be called in to make air flow measurements.

FA222. The total outdoor play area shall accommodate at least 33 percent of the licensed capacity at one time.

Staggered scheduling can be used to accommodate all the children over the course of 2 to 3 hours. Every young child should have the opportunity for gross motor play at least once and preferably twice a day.

FA223. A rooftop used as a play area shall be enclosed with a fence not less than 6 feet high and designed to prevent children from climbing it. An approved fire escape shall lead from the roof to an open space at the ground level that meets the safety standards for outdoor play areas. (See also *Exits*, on p. 144.)

This standard is to prevent injury.

FA224. The outdoor play area shall be arranged so that all areas are visible to staff at all times.

This arrangement allows prevention of injury and abuse.

Compliance can be ascertained by inspection.

FA225. There shall be at least one toilet and handwashing sink located within 40 feet inside the facility door that opens out onto the outdoor play area.

Young children must be able to get to toilet facilities quickly. If pediatric first aid, including rescue breathing and first aid for choking, is required, rapid access to running water is essential.

FA226. The playground site shall be free of hazards and not less than 30 feet from hazards such as electrical transformers, high-voltage power lines, electrical substations, air conditioner units, railroad tracks, or sources

This measure is essential for preventing access to streets (e.g., unsupervised retrieval of a ball from a busy street).

of toxic fumes or gases. Fencing or another form of barrier such as a hedge or other plants (at least 4 feet high) must be provided around the play area. Fencing twist wires and bolts shall face away from the playground.

FA227. Playgrounds shall be laid out to ensure ample clearance space for the use of each item: 9 feet around fixed items and 15 feet around any moving part. Equipment shall be situated so that clearance space allocated to one piece of equipment does not encroach on that of another piece of equipment.

This standard ensures ample space to enable movement around and use of equipment and also helps to restrict the number of pieces of equipment within the play area, thus preventing overcrowding.

FA228. Swings shall have a clearance area of 9 feet in all directions beyond swing beam.

A clear space area is needed to avoid body contact with children in swings.[55]

FA229. All fixed play equipment shall have a minimum of 9 feet clearance space from walkways, buildings, and other structures that are not used as part of play activities.

This standard is based on recommendations of the Consumer Product Safety Commission.

For further information on playground equipment clearance, contact

Consumer Product Safety
Commission
Washington, DC 20207

FA230. Metal equipment (especially slides) shall be placed in the shade when possible or shall be oriented in a north-south direction.

This placement prevents buildup of heat in metal.

FA231. All equipment shall be arranged so that children playing on one piece of equipment will not interfere with children playing on or running to another piece of equipment.

This standard ensures that preventable collisions between children utilizing different pieces of equipment do not occur.[56-58]

FA232. Moving equipment, such as swings and merry-go-rounds, shall be located toward the edge or corner of a play area or shall be designed in such a way as to discourage children from running into the path of the moving equipment.

This standard prevents collisions among children using different pieces of equipment. Placing movable equipment around the perimeter of the play area will enhance the spacing distance between such equipment.

It is assumed that the play spaces discussed above are those at the site and are thus the responsibility of the facility. Those facilities that do not have on-site play areas, but that use playgrounds and equipment in adjacent parks and/or schools, may not be able to ensure that children in their facility are playing on equipment or in play space in absolute conformance with the standards presented here. However, it should be clear that playgrounds designed for older children may present intrinsic hazard to preschool-age children. Facility management/parents should seek to ensure that using such facilities does not pose undue hazards.

STANDARDS	RATIONALE	COMMENTS

FA233. Outside play areas shall be free from unprotected swimming and wading pools, ditches, quarries, canals, excavations, fish ponds, or other bodies of water.

Drowning is the third leading cause of unintentional injury in children under 5 years.[19] In some parts of the United States, including the South, the Southwest, and California, drowning is the leading cause of death in children under 5 years of age.[13]

For additional information on layout, location, and size of playground and outdoor areas, see also standard FA76, on the sewage exhaust vent on p. 154 and standard FA140 on p. 168 on location of toilets and sinks near outdoor play areas.

EQUIPMENT, ENCLOSURES, COVERINGS, AND SURFACING OF PLAYGROUND AND OUTDOOR AREAS

FA234. Sunlit areas and shaded areas shall be provided by means of open space and tree plantings or other cover in outdoor spaces.

Exposure to sun is needed, but children must be protected from excessive exposure.

A tent, awning, or other simple shelter from the sun should be available.

FA235. The outdoor play area shall be enclosed with a fence or natural barriers. The barrier shall be at least 4 feet in height and the bottom edge shall be no more than 3½ inches off the ground. There shall be at least two exits from such areas, with at least one remote from the buildings. Gates shall be equipped with self-closing and positive self-latching closure mechanisms. The latch or securing device shall be high enough or of such a type that it cannot be opened by small children. The openings in the fence shall be no greater than 3½ inches. The fence shall be constructed to discourage climbing.

This standard helps to ensure proper supervision and protection, injury prevention, and area control. Small openings in the fence (3½ inches or less) prevent entrapment and discourage climbing.

Fences that prevent the child from obtaining a proper toehold, such as chain link fences, discourage climbing.

FA236. The soil in play areas shall not contain hazardous levels of any toxic chemical or substances. The facility shall have soil samples and analyses performed by the local health department, extension service, or environmental control testing laboratory, as required, where there is good reason to believe a problem may exist.

This standard ensures a safe play area.

STANDARDS	RATIONALE	COMMENTS

FA237. The soil in play areas shall be analyzed for lead content initially. It shall be analyzed at least once every 2 years where the exteriors of adjacent buildings and structures are painted with lead-containing paint. Lead in soil shall not exceed 500 ppm. Testing and analyses shall be in accord with procedures specified by the regulating health authority.

This standard helps to prevent lead poisoning.[59,60]

FA238. Sandboxes shall be constructed to permit drainage, shall be covered tightly and securely when not in use, and shall be kept free from cat or other animal excrement.

This standard is to eliminate contamination and disease from animal feces and to prevent insects from breeding in sandboxes. An uncovered sandbox is an invitation for a cat or other animal to defecate or urinate, and therefore is a source for disease transmission.[21]

FA239. Sand used in sandboxes shall not contain toxic or harmful materials.

FA240. Outdoor storage shall be available for equipment not secured to the ground, unless indoor storage space is available.

FA241. Anchored play equipment shall not be placed over, or immediately adjacent to, hard surfaces.

FA242. Outdoor play equipment shall be of safe design and in good repair. Climbing equipment and swings shall be set in concrete footings located below ground surface (at least 6 inches). Swings shall have soft and/or flexible seats. Access to play equipment shall be limited to age groups for which the equipment is developmentally appropriate.

This standard is based on guidelines of the Consumer Product Safety Commission.[52–54]

Reference for all playground standards: Home Playground Equipment ASTM F1148–88; Public Playgrounds ASTM F15.29 (Entrapment, Installation & Maintenance, Materials, Terminology, Falls, Environmental). Contact

American Society for Testing and Materials
1916 Race St.
Philadelphia, PA 19103

FA243. All pieces of playground equipment shall be designed to match the body dimensions of children. (See Appendix O-1, on p. 358, and Appendix O-2 on p. 361.)

This standard helps to ensure consideration of equipment and its construction and maintenance in the overall pursuit of injury reduction. Anthropometric considerations are critical for the prevention of age-specific injuries.[56–58,61,62]

FA244. All pieces of playground equipment shall be installed so that an average adult will not be able to cause a fixed structure to wobble or tip.

See rationale for standard FA243.

STANDARDS	RATIONALE	COMMENTS

FA245. All pieces of playground equipment shall be surrounded by a resilient surface (e.g., fine, loose sand; wood chips; wood mulch) of an acceptable depth (9 inches), or by rubber mats manufactured for such use, consistent with the guidelines of the Consumer Product Safety Commission and the standard of the American Society for Testing and Materials, extending beyond the external limits of the piece of equipment for at least 4 feet beyond the fall zone of the equipment. These resilient surfaces must conform to the standard stating that the impact from falling from the height of the structure will be less than or equal to peak deceleration 200G.[63] Organic materials that support colonization of molds and bacteria shall not be used. (See Appendix O-3, on p. 362.)

Head impact injuries present a significant danger to children. Falls into a resilient surface are less likely to cause serious injury, since the surface is yielding, and peak deceleration and force are reduced.[63]

The critical issue of playground surfaces, both under equipment and in general, should receive the most careful attention.[58,64,65]

See ASTM F-355, Shock-Absorbing Properties of Playing Surface Systems and Materials. Contact

American Society for Testing and Materials
1916 Race St.
Philadelphia, PA 19103

For guidelines on playground equipment and surfacing, contact

Consumer Product Safety Commission
Washington, DC 20207

Children should not dig in sand used under swings. It is not necessary to cover sand used in this manner.

FA246. All pieces of playground equipment shall be designed so that moving parts (swing components, teeter-totter mechanism, spring-ride springs, etc.) will be shielded or enclosed.

This standard is to prevent pinching, catching, or crushing of body parts or catching of scarves, mittens, hood strings, and so forth.

Because of the wide range of different types of equipment found in different facilities, standards for specific types of equipment are listed separately in Appendices O-4 through O-10, on pp. 363–370. For each type of equipment relevant to a specific playground or intended to be placed in a facility playground, please refer to these appendices for specific standards on dimensions and other characteristics as follows:

List of Playground Equipment Types:
a) Sandboxes and sand play areas, Appendix O-4, on p. 363.
b) Swings, Appendix O-5 on p. 364.
c) Teeter-totters and spring rides, Appendix O-6, on p. 365.
d) Slides and sliding surfaces, Appendix O-7, on p. 366.
e) Climbing equipment, Appendix O-8, on p. 368.
f) Platforms and other raised standing surfaces, Appendix O-9, on p. 369.
g) Fixed play elements, Appendix O-10, on p. 370.

FA247. All pieces of playground equipment shall be free of sharp edges, protruding parts, weaknesses, and flaws in material construction.

Any sharp or protruding surface presents a potential for laceration and contusions to the child's body.

STANDARDS	RATIONALE	COMMENTS

Sharp edges in wood, metal, or concrete shall be rounded to a minimum of ½ inch wide on all edges. Wood materials shall be sanded smooth and shall be inspected regularly for splintering.

FA248. All pieces of playground equipment shall be designed to guard against entrapment or situations that may cause strangulation by being made too large for a child's head to get stuck or too small for a child's head to fit into. Openings in exercise rings shall be smaller than 4¼ inches or larger than 9 inches in diameter. There shall be no openings in a play structure with a dimension between 4⅝ inches and 9⅛ inches. In particular, side railings, stairs, and other locations where a child might slip or try to climb through shall be checked for appropriate dimensions. Protrusions such as pipes or wood ends that may catch a child's clothing are prohibited. Distances between vertical infill, where used, must be 4⅝ inches or less to prevent entrapment of a child's head. No opening shall have a vertical angle of less than 55 degrees. To prevent finger entrapment, no opening larger than ⅜ inch and smaller than 1 inch shall be present.

Any equipment opening between 4-⅝ inches and 9⅛ inches in diameter presents the potential for head entrapment. Similarly, small openings can cause entrapment of the child's fingers.

See Appendices O–1 and O–2, on pp. 360–361, for guidelines on anthropometry and children's body dimensions in playground equipment.

FA249. All bolts, hooks, eyes, shackles, rungs, and other connecting and linking devices of all pieces of playground equipment shall be designed and secured to prevent loosening or unfastening except by authorized individuals with special tools.

These devices must be securely installed in order to avoid physical injury to children.

FA250. Crawl spaces of all pieces of playground equipment, such as pipes or tunnels, shall be securely anchored to the ground to prevent movement, and shall have a minimum diameter that permits easy access to the space by adults in an emergency or for maintenance.

Playground equipment components must be secure to prevent sudden falls by children. Adequate access space permits adult assistance and first aid measures.

FA251. The maximum height of any piece of playground equipment shall be no greater than 5½ feet if children up to the age of 6 are given access to it, and no higher than 3 feet if the maximum age of children is 3 years.

The greater the height, the greater the potential for serious injury. In a recent prospective study in Georgia, falls from equipment higher than 6 feet were associated with more serious injuries.[66]

FA252. All paved surfaces shall be well drained to avoid water accumulation and ice formation.

This standard prevents both injury and deterioration of the surface.

FA253. All walking surfaces, such as walkways, ramps, and decks, shall have a nonslip finish.

This standard prevents injury during nonplay activities of children and adults.

An example of a nonslip finish is asphalt.

FA254. All walking surfaces and other play surfaces shall be free of holes and sudden irregularities in the surface.

This standard prevents injury during play and nonplay activities among children and adults.

FA255. Space used for wheeled vehicles shall have a flat, smooth, and nonslippery surface. There shall be a physical barrier separating this space from traffic, streets, parking, delivery areas, driveways, stairs, hallways used as fire exits, balconies, and pools and other areas containing water.

Physical separation from environmental obstacles is necessary to prevent potential collision, injuries, falls, or drowning.

For additional information on equipment, enclosures, coverings, and surfacing of playground and outdoor areas, see also *Playground and Equipment Records*, on p. 294, *Play Equipment*, on p. 160, and *Additional Indoor Requirements for Special Groups or Ages of Children*, on p. 180.

MAINTENANCE OF PLAYGROUND AND OUTDOOR AREAS

FA256. All outdoor activity areas shall be maintained in a clean and safe condition by removing debris, dilapidated structures, broken or worn play equipment, building supplies, glass, sharp rocks, twigs, toxic plants, and other injurious material. The play areas shall be free from anthills, unprotected ditches, wells, holes, grease traps, cisterns, cesspools, and unprotected utility equipment. Holes or abandoned wells within the site shall be properly filled or sealed. The area shall be well drained with no standing water.

This standard is to prevent accidents and injury.

FA257. Outdoor play equipment shall not be coated or treated with, nor shall it contain, toxic materials in hazardous amounts that are accessible to children.[67]

FA258. The center director and the large and small family home caregiver shall conduct inspections of the

Regular inspections are critical for preventing deterioration of equipment and accumulation of hazardous playground area and the playground as specified below.

FA259. The general playground surfaces shall be checked every day for broken glass, trash, and other foreign materials (e.g., animal excrement).

FA260. The playground area shall be checked on a daily basis for areas of poor drainage and accumulation of water and ice.

FA261. Any particulate resilient material beneath playground equipment shall be checked at least monthly for packing due to rain or ice and, if found compressed, shall be turned over or raked up to increase resilience capacity. All particulate resilient material, particularly sand, shall be inspected daily for glass and other debris, animal excrement, and other foreign material. Loose fill surfaces shall be hosed down for cleaning and raked or sifted to remove hazardous debris as often as needed to keep the surface free of dangerous, unsanitary materials.

FA262. The playground equipment shall be checked on a monthly basis (as specified in *Safety Plan*, on p. 281, and *Playground and Equipment Records*, on p. 294) for the following:
a) Visible cracks, bending or warping, rusting, or breakage of any equipment.
b) Deformation of open hooks, shackles, rings, links, and so forth.
c) Worn swing hangers and chains.
d) Missing, damaged, or loose swing seats.
e) Broken supports or anchors.
f) Cement support footings that are exposed, cracked, or loose in the ground.
g) Accessible sharp edges or points.
h) Exposed ends of tubing that require covering with plugs or caps.
i) Protruding bolt ends that have lost caps or covers.
j) Loose bolts, nuts, and so forth that require tightening.
k) Splintered, cracked, or otherwise deteriorating wood.
l) Lack of lubrication on moving parts.

materials within the play site, and for ensuring that appropriate repairs are made as soon as possible.[58, 61]

These materials may cause injuries or infections in children.

Pools of water may cause children to slip and fall.

Surfaces should be resilient. Cold temperatures may cause "packing," which leads to loss of resiliency in the surface material. The presence of other materials, such as glass, debris, and animal excrement, presents potential sources of injury or infection.

Maintenance of loose fill surfaces provides for proper sanitation.

The presence of these conditions may lead to serious injuries in children. Periodic monitoring using a checklist ensures that these hazards are either removed or corrected.

m) Worn bearings or other mechanical parts.

n) Broken or missing rails, steps, rungs, or seats.

o) Worn or scattered surfacing material.

p) Hard surfaces, especially under swings, slides, and so forth (e.g., places where resilient material has been shifted away from any surface underneath play equipment). (See also standard FA245 on p. 188.)

q) Chipped or peeling paint.

r) Pinch or crush points, exposed mechanisms, juncture, and moving components. (See *Equipment, Enclosures, Coverings, and Surfacing of Playground and Outdooor Areas*, on p. 119. on playground equipment specifics.)

See *Playground and Equipment Records*, on p. 294 and standard FA86, on p. 155 on keeping play areas free of animal waste.

5.4 Swimming, Wading, and Water

FENCING AND POOL COVERS

FA263. All water hazards, such as pools, swimming pools, stationary wading pools, ditches, and fish ponds, shall be enclosed with a fence that is at least 5 feet high and comes within 3½ inches of the ground. Openings in the fence shall be no greater than 3½ inches. The fence shall be constructed to discourage climbing. Exit and entrance points shall have self-closing, positive latching gates with locking devices a minimum of 55 inches from the ground. The child care building wall shall not constitute one side of the fence unless there are no openings in the wall.

This standard is to prevent injury and drowning.[68] Most drownings take place in fresh water, often in home swimming pools.[69, 70] Most children drown within a few feet of safety and in the presence of a supervising adult.[71]

Small fence openings (3½ inches or less) prevent entrapment.

See Appendix O-11, on p. 371, for standards on water play areas.

Although some standards recommend that fences be at least 6 feet high, 5 feet is safe and adequate and is used in many state and local codes.

See U.S. CPSC standards and ASTM standards for pool safety.

Contact
  U.S. Consumer Product Safety
    Commission
  Washington, DC 20207

  American Society for Testing and
    Materials
  1916 Race St.
  Philadelphia, PA 19103

FA264. Above-ground pools shall have nonclimbable sidewalls that are 4 feet high or shall be enclosed with an approved fence as specified in standard FA263. When the pool is not in use, steps shall be removed from the pool or otherwise protected

This standard is based on best professional experience.

STANDARDS	RATIONALE	COMMENTS

to ensure that they cannot be accessed.

FA265. Sensors or remote monitors shall not be used in lieu of a fence or the proper supervision.

A temporary power outage negates the protection of sensors.

FA266. When not in use, in-ground swimming pools shall be covered with a safety cover that meets or exceeds the standards of the American Society for Testing and Materials (Above-ground pools shall be covered wien not in use with a secured cover that does not permit rainwater to accumulate.

Fatal injuries have occurred when water has collected on top of a secured pool cover. The depression caused by the water, coupled with the smoothness of the cover material, has proven to be a deadly trap for some children.[72] ASTM standards now define a safety cover "as a barrier for swimming pools, spas, hot tubs, or wading pools (intended to be completely removed before water use), which will—when properly labeled, installed, used and maintained in accordance with the manufacturer's published instructions—reduce the risk of drowning of children under five years of age, by inhibiting their access to the contained body of water, and by providing for the removal of any substantially hazardous level of collected surface water."[73]

Facilities should check whether the manufacturers warrant their pools as meeting ASTM standards.

See ASTM Emergency Standard ES-13 on Covers for Pools, Spas, Hot Tubs. Contact

American Society for Testing and Materials
1916 Race St.
Philadelphia, PA 19103

Fence heights are a matter of local ordinance. They can be 4, 5, or 6 feet high (6 feet is preferred, but 5 feet is frequently all that is required). A house exterior wall can constitute one side of a fence if the corners of the house are tight to the fence. A fence should be 5 feet high at a minimum. (See standard FA263 on p. 192.)

INSECT BREEDING HAZARD

FA267. No facility shall maintain or permit to be maintained any receptacle or pool, whether natural or artificial, containing water in such condition that insects breeding therein may become a menace to the public health.

DECK AREAS

FA268. A 4-foot, nonskid surface surrounding the pool perimeter shall be provided.

This standard is to prevent slipping and injury.

For additional information on deck areas, see also standard HP114 in chapter 3 on p. 97 on water safety and toys on the pool deck.

POOL AND SAFETY EQUIPMENT

FA269. Where applicable, swimming and built-in wading pool equipment and materials shall meet the health effects and performance standards of the National Sanitation

This standard facilitates proper pool operation and maintenance and minimizes injuries.

Contact

National Sanitation Foundation
3475 Plymouth Rd.
Ann Arbor, MI 48106

STANDARDS	RATIONALE	COMMENTS

Foundation, as determined by a local health department inspection.

FA270. All pool drain grates shall be in good repair and in place when children are swimming/wading.

There have been instances when children have died as a result of being disemboweled by the suction power of draining water.

FA271. When children are in the pool, there shall be an adult present who is aware of the location of the pump and is able to turn it off in the event a child is caught in the drain.

The power of suction of a pool drain is often such that the pump must be turned off before a child can be removed.

FA272. Electrical safety equipment shall be installed and inspected at and around the pool as required by the local electrical inspector.

Safety equipment prevents electrical hazards that could be life threatening.

The swimming pool manufacturers trade assoociation has a safety code. For electrical safety a ground fault interrupter is mandatory.

FA273. Each swimming pool more than 6 feet in width, length, or diameter shall be provided with a ring buoy and rope and/or a throwing line and a shepherd's hook. Such equipment shall be of sufficient length to reach the center of the pool from the edge of the pool and shall be safely and conveniently stored for immediate access.

This lifesaving equipment is essential.

Drowning is an injury with a higher rate of death than illness.[74]

FA274. Pool equipment and chemical storage rooms shall be locked and ventilated.

FA275. No electrical wires or unprotected electrical equipment may be located over or in the pool area.

FA276. Children shall not be permitted in hot tubs, spas, or saunas.

This precaution is to prevent injury and drowning. See also rationale in standards FA277 and FA278.

UNFILTERED WATER IN CONTAINERS

FA277. Bathtubs, buckets, and pails of water shall be emptied immediately after use.

In addition to home swimming and wading pools, young children also drown in bathtubs. Bathtub drownings are equally distributed among both sexes and the average age at the time of death is 11 months.[72] Any body of water, including hot tubs, pails, and toilets, presents a drowning risk to young children.[24,68,73,74,75]

FA278. Small, portable wading pools shall not be permitted.

Small, portable wading pools do not permit adequate control of sanitation and safety and provide a superior means of transmission of infectious diseases.[2]

Sprinklers, hoses, or individual water buckets are safe alternatives as a cooling or play activity.

STANDARDS	RATIONALE	COMMENTS

INSPECTION OF SWIMMING/ WADING POOLS

FA279. If swimming pools or built-in wading pools are on the premises and are used by children, they shall be constructed, maintained, and used in accordance with applicable state or local regulations and shall be regularly inspected (at least once every 7 to 10 days) by local health authorities to ensure compliance.

This standard is based on state and local regulations and the American Public Health Association (APHA) model codes on swimming places.[76]

To obtain the APHA publication, contact

American Public Health
  Association
1015 15th St., N.W.
Washington, DC 20005

SAFETY RULES FOR SWIMMING/WADING POOLS

FA280. Legible safety rules for the use of swimming and built-in wading pools shall be posted in a conspicuous location and shall be read and reviewed often enough by each caregiver responsible for the supervision of children that he/she is able to cite the rules when asked. An emergency plan shall be developed and reviewed as specified in *Emergency Plan*, on p. 280.

For additional information on safety rules for swimming/wading pools, see *Water Safety*, on p. 96.

See rationale for standard FA279.

Compliance can be assessed by interviewing caregivers to determine if they know the rules.

See comment for standard FA279.

WATER QUALITY OF SWIMMING/WADING POOLS

FA281. Water in swimming and built-in wading pools used by children shall be maintained between pH 7.2 and pH 8.2. The water shall be disinfected by available free chlorine greater than 0.4 ppm, or by an equivalent disinfectant as approved by the local health authority. The pool shall be cleaned daily and the chlorine level and pH level shall be tested every 2 hours during use periods.

This practice provides bacterial and algae control and enhances swimmer comfort and safety. Maintaining the pH and disinfectant level within the prescribed range suppresses bacterial growth to tolerable levels.

FA282. Water temperatures shall be maintained at no less than 82°F and no more than 93°F while the pool is in use.

Water temperature for swimming and wading should be warm enough to prevent excess loss of body heat and cool enough to prevent overheating. Because of their relatively larger surface area to body mass, young children can lose or gain body heat more easily than adults.

STANDARDS	RATIONALE	COMMENTS

FA283. Water shall be sampled and a bacteriological analysis conducted to determine absence of fecal coliform, *Pseudomonas aeruginosa,* and *Giardia lamblia* at least every 6 months or at intervals required by the local regulatory health agency.

Bacteriologic water safety must be ensured to prevent the spread of disease via ingestion of pool water.

FA284. Equipment shall be available to test for and maintain a measurable residual disinfectant content in the water and to check the pH of the water.

See rationale for FA 279, on p. 195 and rationale for standard FA 283.

5.5 Interior and Exterior Walkways, Steps, and Stairs

FA285. Safe pedestrian crosswalks, pick-up and drop-off points, and bike routes in the vicinity of the facility shall be identified, written in the facility's procedures (see *Safety Plan,* on p. 281), and communicated to all children, parents, and staff.

This procedure reduces the potential of accidents due to children's darting into traffic.

FA286. Inside and outside stairs, ramps, porches, and other walkways to the structure shall be constructed for safe use as required by the local building code and shall be kept in sound condition, well lighted, and in good repair.

The purpose of this standard is injury prevention.

FA287. For preschoolers and school-age children, bottom guardrails that are no more than 2 feet above the floor shall be provided for all porches, landings, balconies, and similar structures. For infants and toddlers, bottom guardrails shall be no more than 6 inches above the floor as specified above.

This standard is to prevent falls from children climbing under the guardrail.

FA288. Protective handrails and guardrails shall have balusters placed at intervals of less than 3½ inches or shall have sufficient protective material to prevent a 3½-inch sphere from passing through.

This standard is to prevent entrapment of a child's head.

FA289. Handrails at children's height shall be provided on both sides of stairways that consist of three or more steps, and shall be securely attached to the walls or stairs.

The majority of the population is right-handed, but some people are left-handed. Railings on both sides ensure a readily available handhold in the event of a fall down the stairs. Since right-handed people tend to carry packages in their left hand and keep their right hand free (if either hand is free), a right-hand descending handrail reduces the risk of falling on the stairs.

FA290. Landings shall be provided beyond each interior and exterior door that opens onto a stairway.

FA291. Securely installed, effective guards (e.g., gates) shall be provided at the top and bottom of each open stairway. Basement stairways shall be separated by a full door at the main floor level. This door shall be self-closing and shall be kept locked when the basement is not in use.

For additional standards on paved and walking surfaces, see standards FA252, FA253, and FA 254, on pp. 189–190. See also *Exterior Maintenance.*

5.6 Maintenance for Safety

EXTERIOR MAINTENANCE

FA292. Porches, steps, stairs, and walkways shall be maintained free from accumulations of water, ice, or snow; shall have a nonslip surface; and shall be in good repair.

This standard is to prevent injury.

FA293. Outside walkways shall be kept free of loose objects and in good repair.

See rationale for standard FA 292.

FA294. Outdoor areas shall be kept free of excessive dust, weeds, brush, high grass, and standing water.

This standard is to prevent injury and control allergen producers.

FA295. A cleaning schedule shall be developed and assigned to appropriate staff.

See rationale for standard FA292.

INTERIOR MAINTENANCE

For additional information on interior maintenance, see also *Sanitation, Disinfection, and Maintenance,* on p. 76, daily hygiene activities for the bathroom, diaper-changing areas, handwashing sinks, surfaces, carpets, rugs, floors, storage areas, bedding, and toys.

Furnace/Boiler Maintenance

FA296. Furnace and boiler maintenance shall comply with local building codes, as warranted in writing by the local building or fire inspector.

Kitchen Maintenance

See *Maintenance*, on p. 133.

Storage Area Maintenance

FA297. Storage areas shall be kept clean.

General Maintenance

FA298. The structure shall be kept in good repair and safe condition.

FA299. Each window, exterior door, and basement or cellar hatchway shall be kept in sound condition and in good repair.

Children's environments must be protected from exposure to moisture, dust, and excessive temperatures.

FA300. Electrical fixtures and outlets shall be maintained in safe condition and good repair.

FA301. Each gas pipe, water pipe, gas-burning fixture, plumbing fixture and apparatus, or any other similar fixture, and all connections to water, sewer, or gas lines (see standard FA67, on p. 152), shall be maintained in good, sanitary working condition.

This standard is to prevent accidents and hazardous and unsanitary conditions.

FA302. Humidifiers, dehumidifiers, and air-handling equipment that involves water shall be cleaned and disinfected at least once each week.

For additional information on general maintenance, see also standard FA286, on p. 196 on maintenance of interior and exterior walkways, steps, and stairs.

5.7 Transportation

| **STANDARDS** | **RATIONALE** | **COMMENTS** |

VEHICLES

FA303. A caregiver who provides transportation for children or contracts to provide transportation shall license the vehicle according to the laws of the state.

Motor vehicle accidents are the leading cause of death of children in the United States.[77] It is therefore necessary for the safety of children to require that the caregiver comply with minimum requirements governing the transportation of children in care, in the absence of the parent.[15]

It is reasonable that children be transported in vehicles that meet basic state standards for licensure and registration.

FA304. Each vehicle must be equipped with a first aid kit (see FA116, on p. 161 on first aid kits) and emergency identification and contact information for all children being transported.

This requirement is necessary so caregivers can respond to the needs of children in the event of injury or emergency. Because no environment is totally injury-proof, it is necessary to require that adequate supplies and emergency information be available and that staff be knowledgeable in their use.

FA305. Vehicles operated by the facility to transport children shall be air-conditioned whenever the temperature exceeds 75°F. The drivers shall be so instructed and the requirement shall be posted in each vehicle.

This requirement is necessary for basic health and safety. Some children also have problems with temperature regulation.

Compliance can be measured by interviewing drivers of vehicles and checking that the requirement is posted in each vehicle.

FA306. When vehicles operated by the facility are transporting children, such vehicles shall be heated whenever the temperature drops below 50°F. Drivers shall be so instructed, and these instructions shall be posted in each vehicle.

Keeping vehicles heated is necessary for basic health and safety.

FA307. When vehicles are transporting children, a backup vehicle shall always be available and shall be dispatched immediately in case of emergency. Documentation of these arrangements shall be included in the facility's written transportation plan. (See *Safety Plan*, on p. 281.)

Children cannot be left sitting in a disabled vehicle. A backup vehicle must be dispatched and the children transferred immediately.

Transportation contracts are best arranged with this provision.

FA308. Vehicles operated by the facility shall be cleaned and inspected inside and out at least weekly.

This standard is a general guideline for good health, as well as for pride and self-image for the children and families. Weekly cleaning and inspection help to ensure that the vehicle will be kept free of visible accumulation of soil and litter inside and that signs, lights, and other safety features on the exterior of the vehicle are operating effectively.

QUALIFICATIONS OF DRIVERS

In addition to the general staff quali-fications in *General Qualifications for All Staff,* on p. 16, drivers shall meet the following standards.

FA309. The vehicle shall be driven by a person who holds a current state driver's license that authorizes the driver to operate the vehicle driven.

Operators of vehicles must be appropriately licensed to operate them.

See also rationale for standard FA303, on p. 199.

FA310. The criminal record file in the state and the child abuse registry in the state shall be checked as speci-fied in *Individual Licensure/Certifi-cation*, on p. 301. No person recorded in the state child abuse registry as having abused children or with a criminal record of crimes of violence or sexual molestation shall be allowed to transport children.

TRANSPORTATION TRAINING

FA311. All drivers, passenger moni-tors, and assistants shall be required to receive instructions in child pas-senger safety precautions, including the use of safety restraints, handling of emergency situations, route train-ing, defensive driving, and child supervision responsibilities. Such instructions shall be documented in the personnel records of any paid staff or volunteer who provides transportation for the facility.

See also rationale for standard FA303, on p. 199.

FA312. All drivers, passenger moni-tors, and assistants shall be certified in pediatric first aid, including rescue breathing and first aid for choking, as specified in *First Aid and CPR*, on p. 22.

STANDARDS	RATIONALE	COMMENTS

PROHIBITED SUBSTANCES, INCLUDING ALCOHOL AND DRUGS, AND TRANSPORTATION

FA313. There shall be no smoking in the vehicles used by the facility at any time. A "NO SMOKING" sign shall be posted in each vehicle.

Children with respiratory problems will have increased difficulties if they are exposed to smokers' fumes.

Compliance can be measured by interviewing drivers and inspecting vehicles for evidence of smoking.

FA314. Drivers shall not have used alcohol within 12 hours prior to transporting children. The use of illegal drugs by drivers shall be prohibited. Drivers shall ensure that any prescription drugs taken will not impair their ability to drive. The center director shall require drug testing when noncompliance is suspected.

Adults must not be impaired in any way that can endanger the children.

The health care provider, at the time of prescription, should be advised by the driver of his/her job and questioned as to whether it is safe to drive children while on the medication.

Compliance can be measured by measurement of blood or urine levels of drugs. Refusal to permit such testing should preclude continued employment.

For additional information on prohibited substances, including alcohol and drugs, and transportation, see also *Smoking and Prohibited Substances Plan*, on p. 285.

TRANSPORTATION AND RADIO PLAYING

FA315. There shall be no loud radio playing or use by the driver of earphones to listen to music or other distracting sounds while the children are in the vehicles operated by the facility. A sign that says "NO LOUD RADIOS OR TAPES" shall be posted in each vehicle.

Loud noise may be especially disturbing to some children with central nervous system abnormalities, as well as being distracting to the driver and the passenger monitor or assistant attending the children in the vehicle.

Portable radios and recorders with earphones used by the driver are obviously also unacceptable from a safety point of view.

TRANSPORTATION CHILD:STAFF RATIOS

FA316. Child:staff ratios shall be used for transporting children as described in standard ST3 in chapter 1 on p. 3.

SEAT RESTRAINTS

FA317. When children are driven in a motor vehicle other than a bus or school bus operated by a common carrier, the following shall apply:

The use of restraint devices while riding in a vehicle reduces the likelihood of a passenger's suffering serious injury or death if the vehicle is

When school buses are used that meet current standards for the transport of school-age children, containment design features help protect

a) A child shall be transported only if the child is fastened in an approved safety seat, seat belt, or harness appropriate to the child's weight, and the restraint is installed and used in accordance with the manufacturer's instructions; each child must have an individual seat belt.

b) A child under the age of 4 shall be transported only if the child is securely fastened in a child passenger restraint system that meets the federal motor vehicle safety standards contained in the Code of Federal Regulations, title 49, section 571.213, and this compliance is so indicated on the safety restraint device.

c) If small buses or vans have safety belts installed, the belts shall be used by the children.

involved in an accident. *Accident Facts,* 1985, states that children under the age of 4 who were not using child safety seats were 11 times more likely to be killed in a motor vehicle accident than children using child safety seats.[77] It is reasonable to require that the license holder ensure that the child be placed in restraint devices that conform to state and federal laws. The provision does not apply when children are being transported in vehicles not routinely or commonly equipped with restraints. However, the provision does clarify that it is the responsibility of the caregiver to ensure that children are fastened in a restraint system. Federal law applies only to vehicles equipped with factory-installed seat belts after 1967. The provision of mandatory restraints, regardless of driver or age of the vehicle, is necessary to ensure the health and safety of the children.

children from injury, although the use of seat belts would provide additional protection.

To obtain the Code of Federal Regulations, contact

Superintendent of Documents
U.S. Government Printing Office
Washington, DC 20402

TRANSPORTATION PLAN

Transportation Emergency Preparedness Plan

FA318. All drivers shall know and keep in the vehicle the quickest route to the nearest hospital from any point on their route.

Knowledge of where to obtain emergency care is essential.

Travel Time Plan

FA319. Children shall not be transported for more than 1 hour per one-way trip.

The limitation of travel time to 1 hour per one-way trip is necessary because it is unreasonable to expect very young children to remain confined and seated in a transportation device for a period exceeding 1 hour. The limitation of 1 hour is recommended by the American Academy of Pediatrics in *Health in Day Care: A Manual for Health Care Professionals.*[2] Commuting is tiring in general, and particularly so given the long child care hours.

Pick-Up and Drop-Off Plan

FA320. A designated plan shall be developed for safe pick-up and drop-off points and pedestrian crosswalks in the vicinity of the facility. This plan shall be communicated to staff and parents. The plan shall include

Between 1980 and 1984, nearly 83 percent of pedestrian fatalities were to pupils either approaching or leaving a loading zone. Planning and communicating safe drop-off and pick-up points and adequate super-

Compliance can be measured by interviewing or surveying a sample of parents.

pick-up and drop-off of children only at the curb or at an off-street location protected from traffic. Children shall be supervised during boarding and exiting all vehicles by an adult who ensures that the child is buckled into a seat restraint after boarding and is clear of the path of the vehicle after exiting.

vision during these times can decrease pedestrian injuries.

Bicycles and Bike Routes

FA321. For facilities providing care for school-age children and permitting bicycling as an activity, bike routes allowed shall be reviewed and approved in writing by the local police and taught to the children in the facility.

School-age children who use bicycles for transportation should use bike routes that present the lowest potential for injury. Review and approval of bike routes by the local police minimizes the potential danger.

FA322. All children and adults shall wear approved safety helmets while riding bicycles. Approved helmets shall meet either the American National Standards Institute (ANSI) Z 90.4 or Snell Memorial Foundation Standard.

Bicycle injuries represent a leading cause of death and injury in children.[78] Every year over 600 children are killed by bicycle-related injuries.[79] Few children and adults currently use safety helmets.[80] Use of safety helmets has shown reduction in both death and illness.

Contact for information

American National Standards
  Institute
1430 Broadway
New York, NY 10018

Snell Memorial Foundation
P.O. Box 493
St. James, NY 11780

Child Transportation Instruction Plan

FA323. Children, as both passengers and pedestrians, shall be instructed in safe transportation conduct with terms and concepts appropriate for their age and stage of development.

Teaching passenger safety to children is a method suggested by Hoadley et al. to reduce injury from auto accidents to young children.[81] Several other authors support this method and state that young children need to develop skills that will aid them in assuming responsibility for their own health, and that these skills develop through health education implemented during the early years.[82-84]

Curricula and materials to be used can be obtained from state departments of transportation, the American Automobile Association, the American Academy of Pediatrics, the American Red Cross, and the National Association for the Education of Young Children. For information, contact

American Automobile Association
1000 AAA Drive
Heathrow, FL 32746-5063

American Academy of Pediatrics
141 Northwest Point Blvd.
P.O. Box 927
Elk Grove Village, IL 60009-0927

American Red Cross
18th and E Sts., N.W.
Washington, DC 20006

National Association for the
  Education of Young Children
1834 Connecticut Ave., N.W.
Washington, DC 20009

References

1. National Association for the Education of Young Children. *Planning Environments for Young Children.* Washington, DC: National Association for the Education of Young Children; 1977.

2. Deitch S, ed. *Health in Day Care: A Manual for Health Professionals.* Elk Grove Village, Ill: American Academy of Pediatrics; 1987.

3. *NFPA 101 Life Safety Code.* Quincy, Mass: National Fire Protection Association; 1988.

4. ASHRAE Standard 55. *Thermal Environmental Conditions for Human Occupancy.* Atlanta, Ga: American Society of Heating, Refrigerating and Air-conditioning Engineers; 1981.

5. *Fact Sheets: Stoves, Wood and Coal-Burning, and Space Heaters.* Washington, DC: US Consumer Product Safety Commission; 1985.

6. Spiller JA. Carbon monoxide exposure in the home: science and epidemiology. *Vet & Human Toxicol.* 1987;29:383–386.

7. *Safe Home Checklist.* Boston, Mass: Massachusetts Department of Public Health; 1987.

8. McLoughlin E, Crawford JD. Burns. *Pediatr Clin North Amer.* 1985;32:61–75.

9. US Dept of Health, Education and Welfare, Office of the Secretary. HEW day care regulations. *Federal Register,* March 19, 1980;45(55):17870–17885.

10. Feck J, Baptiste MS. The epidemiology of burn injury in New York. *Public Health Rep.* 1979;94:312–318.

11. Federal Day Care Center Requirements Draft. Washington, DC: US Dept of Health, Education and Welfare; April 3, 1972.

12. Headstart Program Performance Standards (45-CFR 1304). Washington, DC: US Dept of Health and Human Services; Nov 1984;12.

13. American Academy of Pediatrics. *Injury Prevention Program.* Elk Grove Village, Ill: American Academy of Pediatrics; 1989.

14. McLoughlin E, Vince CJ, Lee AM, et al. Project burn prevention: outcomes and implications. *Amer J Public Health.* 1982;82:241–247.

15. Pizzo P, Aronson SS. *Concept Paper on Health and Safety Issues in Day Care.* A portion of the study of the appropriateness of the Federal Interagency Day Care Requirements. Washington, DC: US Dept of Health, Education and Welfare; Sept 1976.

16. Reisinger KS. Smoke detectors: reducing deaths and injuries due to fire. *Pediatrics.* 1980;65:718–724.

17. Rossignol AM, Boyle CM, Locke JA, et al. Hospitalized burn injuries in Massachusetts: an assessment of incidence and product involvement. *Amer J Public Health.* 1986;76:1341–1343.

18. American National Standards Institute/Illuminating Engineers Society Standards. Table 1 Illuminance, category D & E. New York, NY: American National Standards Institute; 1990;10–12.

19. Baker SP, O'Neill B, Karph RS. *The Injury Fact Book.* Washington, DC: Lexington Books; 1984.

20. Safe Drinking Water Act–Federal Public Law 93-523; 1988.

21. Peterson DR, Tronca E, Bonin P. Human toxoplasmosis prevalence and exposure to cats. *Amer J Epidemiol.* 1972;96:215–218.

22. Klein BP, Jensen RC, Sanderson LM. Assessment of workers' compensation claims for back strains/sprains. *J Occup Med.* 1984;26:443–448.

23. Juvenile Products Manufacturers' Association. *Be Sure It's Safe for Your Baby* [brochure]. Philadelphia, Pa: American Society for Testing and Materials; 1990.

24. McIntire MS, ed. *Injury Control for Children and Youth.* Elk Grove Village, Ill: American Academy of Pediatrics Committee on Accident and Poison Prevention; 1987.

25. Weniger, BG, Ruttenber AJ, Goodman RA, et. al. Fecal coliforms on environmental surfaces in two day care centers. *Appl Environ Microbiol.* 1983;45:733–735.

26. Ekanem EE, DuPont HL, Pickering LK, et al. Transmission dynamics of enteric bacteria in day care centers. *Amer J Epidemiol.* 1983;118:562–572.

27. Chang A, Lugg MM, Nebedum A. Injuries in preschool children enrolled in day care centers. *Pediatrics.* 1989; 83:272–277.

28. 1988 Annual Report of the American Association of Poison Control Centers: National Data Collection System. *Amer J Emerg Med.* 1989;7:495–545.

29. Steele P, Spyker DD. Symposium on injuries and injury prevention. Poisonings. *Pediatr Clin North Amer.* 1985;32:77–85.

30. National Materials Advisory Board, National Research Council. *Report of the national committee on fire safety aspects of polymeric materials.* Westport, Conn: Technomic Publishing Co Inc; 1979. Publication No. NMAB–318, vol 5.

31. Agency for Toxic Substances and Disease Registry. *The Nature and Extent of Lead Poisoning in Children in the United States.* A Report to Congress. Atlanta, Ga: US Dept of Health and Human Services, Public Health Service; Jul 1988.

32. Prescott E. Concept paper published as part of the study of the appropriateness of the Federal Interagency Day Care Requirements. US Dept of Health, Education and Welfare, Sept 1976.

33. Fleming DW, Cochi SL, Hightower AW, et al. Childhood upper respiratory tract infections: to what degree is incidence affected by day-care attendance? *Pediatrics.* 1987;79:55–60.

34. Schmidt B. Daytime wetting (diurnal enuresis). *Pediatr Clin North Amer.* 1982;29(1):9–20.

35. Chatterjee BF, Barancik JI, Fratianne RB, et al. Northeastern Ohio trauma study: burn injury. *J Trauma.* 1986;26:844–847.

36. Feldman KW, Schaller RT, Feldman JA, et al. Tap water scald burns in children. *Pediatrics.* 1978; 62:1–7.

37. Baptiste MS, Feck G. Preventing tap water burns. *Amer J Public Health.* 1980;70:727–729.

38. Katcher M. Scald burns from hot tap water. *JAMA.* 1981;246:1219–1222.

39. Witt CS, Warden J. Can home laundries stop the spread of bacteria in clothing? *Textile, Chemist and Colorist.* 1971;3(7):55–57.

40. Wannamaker LW. The epidemiology of strepto-coccal infections. In: McCarty M, ed. *Streptococcal Infections.* New York, NY: Columbia University Press; 1954.

41. Merky MC, Baker SP. Fatal house fires in an urban population. *JAMA.* 1983;249:1466–1468.

42. Baker SP, Fisher RS. Childhood asphyxiation by choking and suffocation. *JAMA.* 1980;244:1343–1346.

43. US Consumer Product Safety Commission. *Preliminary National Electronic Injury Surveillance System—Estimates of National Injuries, 1987.* Washington, DC: US Consumer Product Safety Commission, National Injury Information Clearinghouse; 1988.

44. Kraus JF. Effectiveness of measures to prevent unintentional deaths of infants and children from suffocation and strangulation. *Public Health Reports.* 1985; 100:231–240.

45. Rutherford GW, Kelly S. Accidental strangulations (ligature) of children less than 5 years of age. Washington, DC: US Consumer Product Safety Commission; May 1981.

46. Deppa SW. *Human Factors Evaluation of Provisions Which Address Crib Toy Strangulations in the Toy Safety Voluntary Standard.* Washington, DC: US Consumer Product Safety Commission; Jul 1987.

47. Rivara F, Stapleton F. Handguns and children: a dangerous mix. *Dev Behav Pediatr.* 1982;3:35–38.

48. Christoffel K, Christoffel T. Handguns as a pediatric problem. *Pediatr Emerg Care.* 1986;2:75–81.

49. Wintemute G, Teret S, Kraus J, et al. When children shoot children—88 unintended deaths in California. *JAMA.* 1987;257:3107–3109.

50. Harris W, Luterman A, Curreri P. BB and pellet guns—toys or deadly weapons. *J Trauma.* 1983;23:566–569.

51. Rutherford GW, Beale SP, Friedman JI. *Hazard Analysis: Injuries Associated with Small Parts.* Washington, DC: US Consumer Product Safety Commission; May 1978.

52. US Consumer Product Safety Commission. *Playground Hazards.* Washington, DC: US Consumer Product Safety Commission; Jul/Aug 1978.

53. Taloff P. Playground safety enhanced in New York. *J Env Health.* Sept/Oct 1978;41(2).

54. Fisher L, Goddard-Harris V, Van Buren J, et al. Assessment of a pilot child playground injury prevention project in New York State. *Amer J Public Health.* Sept 1980;70(9).

55. Dango D, Fukui F. *Playground Perspective. A Curriculum Guide for Promoting Playground Safety.* Salt Lake City, Utah: Utah Department of Health; 1988. Publication M88.

56. *A Handbook for Public Playground Safety: Vol I. General Guidelines for New and Existing Playgrounds.* Washington, DC: US Consumer Product Safety Commission; 1981.

57. *A Handbook for Public Playground Safety: Vol II. Technical Guidelines for Equipment and Surfacing.* Washington, DC: US Consumer Product Safety Commission; 1981.

58. Hendriks B, ed. *A Safe Place to Play: Guidelines for Safe Public Playgrounds.* Vancouver, BC, Canada: The Playground Network; 1986.

59. Billick IH. Sources of lead in the environment. In: Rutter H, Jones RR, eds. *Lead vs Health: Sources and Effects of Low Level Lead Exposure.* Chichester, Engl: John Wiley and Sons Ltd; 1983.

60. Mielke HW, Anderson JC, Barry JK, et al. Lead concentration in inner-city soils as a factor in the child lead problem. *Amer J Public Health.* Dec 1983;73(12).

61. Zuckerman BA, Duby JC. Developmental approach to injury prevention. In: Alpert JJ, Buyer GB, eds. Symposium on injury and injury prevention. *Pediat Clin North Amer.* 1985;32:17–29.

62. Brink S, ed. Play safe guideline recommendations for safe children's play spaces and equipment. Ottawa, Ont: Canadian Institute of Child Health; Aug 1985.

63. US Consumer Product Safety Commission. *Playground Surfacing. Technical Information Guide.* Washington, DC: US Government Printing Office; 1990.

64. Greensher J, Mafenson HC. Injuries at play. In: Alpert JJ, Guyer GB, eds. Symposium on injuries and injury prevention. *Pediatr Clin North Amer.* 1985;32:127–139.

65. Wensel J, Growe B, eds. School safety checklist. Vancouver, BC, Canada: The Canadian Red Cross; 1983.

66. Sacks JJ, Smith JD, Kaplan KM, et al. The epidemiology of injuries in Atlanta day care centers. *JAMA.* 1989;262:1641–1645.

67. US Consumer Product Safety Commission. Treat pressure-treated wood with caution. *CPSC Newsletter.* Jul/Aug 1985; 3:(4).

68. Walker S, Middlekamp JN. Pail immersion accidents. *Clinical Pediatrics.* 1981;20:5.

69. Rowe MI, Abelardo A, Allington G. Profile of pediatric drowning victims in a water-oriented soociety. *J Trauma.* 1977;17:8.

70. Plueckhahn VD. Drowning: community aspects. *Med J Aust.* 1979;2:226–228.

71. *Save a Child's Life!* [brochure]. Elk Grove Village, Ill: American Academy of Pediatrics; 1988.

72. US Consumer Product Safety Commission. Medical examiners and coroners alert project. *MECAP News.* Aug 1987;12(3):13–15.

73. Emergency Standard (ES) 13. Standard performance specification for safety covers and labeling requirements for pools, spas, and hot tubs. Philadelphia, Pa: American Society for Testing and Materials; Apr 1989.

74. Stitt VJ. Drowning in North Carolina. *North Carolina Med J.* 1982;43:6.

75. Tron VA, Baldwin VJ, Pirie GE. Hot tub drownings. *Pediatrics.* 1985; 75:4.

76. American Public Health Association. *Public Swimming Pools: Recommended Regulations for Design and Construction, Operation and Maintenance.* Washington, DC: American Public Health Association; 1981.

77. *Accident Facts.* Chicago, Ill: National Safety Council; 1985.

78. Fife D, David J, Tate L, et al. Fatal injuries to bicyclists. The experience of Dade County, Florida. *J Trauma.* 1983;23:745–755.

79. Weiss B. Childhood bicycle injuries. What can we do? *Amer J Dis Child.* 1987;141:135–136.

80. Tompson RS, Rivara FP, Thompson DC. A case-control study of the effectiveness of bicycle safety helmets. *New England J Med.* 1989;320:1361–1367.

81. Hoadley M, Macrina D, Peterson F. Child safety programs: implications affecting use of child restraints. *J Sch Health.* 1981;51:352–355.

82. Parcel GS, Tiernank K, Nader PR, et al. Health education for kindergarten children. *J Sch Health.* 1979;49(3):129–131.

83. Brooks CH, Kirkpatrick M, Howard DJ. Evaluation of an activity centered health curriculum using the health belief model. *J Sch Health.* 1981;58(8):565–569.

84. Chang A, Dillman AS, Leonard E, et al. Teaching car passenger safety to preschool children. *Pediatrics.* 1985;76:425–428.

CHAPTER 6

Infectious Diseases

CHAPTER 6
INFECTIOUS DISEASES

6.1 Respiratory Infections

STANDARDS

RATIONALE

COMMENTS

TUBERCULOSIS

Please note that if a staff member has no contact with the children, or with anything that the children come into contact with, these standards do not apply to that staff member.

ID1. Tuberculosis (Tb) infection shall be controlled by requiring staff to have their Tb status assessed prior to beginning employment. Persons with positive screening skin test reactions shall be evaluated with the intradermal PPD (5TU) skin test followed by chest x-rays for those with positive PPD reactions (10+ mm induration).

Young children acquire tuberculosis infection from infected adults or, occasionally, adolescents. Infection is spread as a small-particle aerosol in indoor environments.

Infants and young children with tuberculosis do not transmit the infection to other children or adults.

ID2. Tuberculosis screening by skin testing of staff members with previously negative skin tests shall be repeated systematically (at least every 2 years or as dictated by the state or local health department). Staff members with previously positive skin tests shall be under management of a physician.

HAEMOPHILUS INFLUENZAE TYPE B

Please note that if a staff member has no contact with the children, or with anything that the children come into contact with, these standards do not apply to that staff member.

ID3. The facility shall require that all children attending provide evidence of immunization against *Haemophilus influenzae* type b (Hib) infection within the age limits specified by the U.S. Public Health Service Advisory Committee on Immunization Practices (ACIP) and the American Academy of Pediatrics (AAP),[1,2] as specified in *Vaccine-Preventable Diseases*, p. 219.

H. influenzae type b (Hib) is the most important cause of severe bacterial infection, particularly meningitis, in infants and young children in the United States.[3] Children in child care are at increased risk of Hib infection compared with children in the general population.[4]

Protection of children in child care from Hib infection is an important

---

🍎 applies to a small family-child-care home   Ⓐ applies to a large family-child-care home   🪜 applies to a center. If no symbol appears, the standard applies to all three.

goal. Primary prevention of Hib disease by immunization is presently available for children 2 months of age and older.[1,2] All children in child care should provide evidence of age-appropriate immunization for Hib infection. As ACIP and AAP guidelines for Hib immunization are modified, state and local regulations regarding Hib vaccination should be amended.

It is not known whether the primary risk of Hib infection associated with child care attendance can be reduced by any control measure other than immunization. However, hygienic principles related to limitation of spread of respiratory infections in general should be practiced.

ID4. If there has been an exposure, the facility shall inform parents of other children who attend the facility, in cooperation with the local health department, that their children may have been exposed to the Hib bacteria and may be at increased risk of developing serious Hib disease.

The risk of occurrence of secondary cases of Hib disease among child care child contacts does not appear to be uniform. Two recent prospective studies of child care contacts of children with Hib disease have not identified an increased risk of Hib disease in this setting.[5,6] Two other prospective studies did show an increased risk.[7,8] Geographic differences in child care may explain these differences.

In general, the risk of secondary Hib disease is probably lower for child care contacts than it is for household contacts. The risk of secondary cases of Hib disease among child care attendees, when it occurs, is greatest among, and may be limited to, children younger than 2 years of age.[8] In multiclassroom settings, increased risk has been shown only for children in the classroom of the index child.[8-9]

Sample letters of notification to parents that their child may have been exposed to an infectious disease are contained in the NAEYC publication *Healthy Young Children.* To order, contact

National Assocation for the Education of Young Children 1834 Connecticut Ave., N.W. Washington, DC 20009

ID5. When recommended by the responsible health department to prevent secondary Hib disease in the facility, an antibiotic taken to prevent an infection shall be given to children and staff. (See standard APP13 in Appendix I-1 on p. 343.)

Since the risk of secondary cases of Hib disease among child care Hib disease contacts appears to be variable, there are different opinions about the most appropriate guidelines for the use of rifampin taken to prevent an infection in the child care setting. Current guidelines of the ACIP and the AAP differ.

Rifampin treatment of children exposed to a child with Hib disease can reduce the prevalence of Hib respiratory tract colonization in treated children and reduce the subsequent risk of invasive Hib infection, particularly in children under 2 years of age.[8] However, rifampin taken to prevent an infection is not uniformly effective in preventing secondary cases of Hib disease;[10] when rifampin is employed as a disease-control strategy, consistent compliance with its use must be carefully monitored.

ID6. When the antibiotic taken to prevent Hib infection is indicated for child care contacts, children and staff shall be excluded from attending the facility until the antibiotic treatment has been initiated.

See rationale for standard ID5.

ID7. Children newly admitted to a facility during a separation of an ill child from non-ill classmates to prevent secondary cases of Hib infection shall be managed with respect to inclusion and the antibiotic taken to prevent an infection as are all other children currently enrolled in the facility.

See rationale for standard ID5.

For additional information on *Haemophilus influenzae* type b, see also Appendix I-1, on p. 343.

NEISSERIA MENINGITIDIS (MENINGOCOCCAL)

Please note that if a staff member has no contact with the children, or with anything that the children come into contact with, these standards do not apply to that staff member.

ID8. If there has been an exposure, the facility shall inform parents of other children who attend the facility, in cooperation with the local health department, that their children may have been exposed to the meningococcal bacteria and may be at increased risk of developing serious meningococcal disease.

N. meningitidis is one of the three most important causes of bacterial meningitidis in childhood.[11] The infection is spread from person to person by contact with respiratory secretions and by the spread of large droplets.

For a sample letter of notification to parents, see comment for standard ID4, on p. 208.

ID9. When recommended by the responsible health department to prevent secondary meningococcal infection in the facility, an antibiotic to prevent an infection shall be administered to children and staff. (See Appendix I-2, on p. 346.)

Children in child care who are exposed to a child or adult with meningococcal infection should receive an antibiotic to prevent an infection as soon as possible, preferably within 24 hours of diagnosis of the primary case.[12] Rifampin is usually employed; however, sulfonamide can be effective if the primary case is known to be caused by a sulfonamide-susceptible organism. The antibiotic taken to prevent an infection stops the disease-producing capabilities of the nose and throat and reduces the likelihood of developing invasive meningococcal disease.

ID10. When the antibiotic taken to prevent an infection for *Neisseria meningitidis* (meningococcal) is indicated for child care contacts, children and staff shall be excluded from attending the facility until such measures have been initiated.

ID11. Children newly admitted to a facility during separation of an ill child from non-ill classmates to prevent secondary cases of meningococcal infection shall be managed with respect to inclusion and the antibiotic taken to prevent infection as are all other children currently enrolled in the facility.

See rationale for ID9.

For additional information on *Neisseria meningitidis* (meningococcal), see also *Notification of Parents,* on p. 90, and Appendix I-2, on p. 346.

PERTUSSIS

Please note that if a staff member has no contact with the children, or with anything that the children come into contact with, these standards do not apply to that staff member.

ID12. The facility shall require that all children attending child care shall provide evidence of immunization against pertussis within the age limits specified by the ACIP and the AAP, as specified in Appendices P-1 and P-2, on pp. 372–374.

Bordetella pertussis is the most important cause of whooping cough. Infants and young children should be protected from pertussis because the rate of illness among infants and toddlers is extremely high, and mortality during the first 6 months of life is 1 percent.[13] Primary protection is provided by active immunization with diphtheria-tetanus-pertussis (DTP) vaccine. Evidence of age-appropriate immunization for pertussis should be provided for children in out-of-home care.

ID13. If there has been an exposure, the facility shall inform parents of other children who attend the facility, in cooperation with the local health department, that their children

While child-care-related outbreaks of pertussis have not been reported, it is likely that children who attend out-of-home care will occasionally con-

For a sample letter of notification to parents, see comment for standard ID4, on p. 208.

may have been exposed to pertussis and may be at increased risk of developing it. Guidelines for use of preventive antibiotics and vaccines for people who have been in contact with children who have pertussis shall be implemented also in cooperation with the local health department. (See Appendix I-3, on p. 349.)

tract pertussis. The spread of infection to incompletely immunized contacts can be reduced by treatment of the primary case and susceptible contacts with erythromycin.[14]

ID14. Children newly admitted to a facility during separation of an ill child from non-ill classmates to prevent secondary cases of pertussis shall be managed with respect to inclusion and the antibiotic taken to prevent infection as are all other children currently enrolled in the facility.

See rationale for standard ID13.

ID15. Children and adults shall be excluded from attending the facility until disease-prevention measures (including the administration of erythromycin) have been initiated.

For additional information on pertussis, see also *Notification of Parents*, on p. 90, and Appendix I-3, on p. 349.

STREPTOCOCCAL INFECTION

ID16. Children with streptococcal respiratory infections shall be excluded from child care until 24 hours after antibiotic treatment has been initiated and until the child has no fever (see Glossary) for 24 hours.

Streptococcal respiratory infections and scarlet fever have not been reported to be major problems for children in child care. However, a recently published investigation[15] and two unpublished experiences[16] suggest there is a definite potential for outbreaks of streptococcal disease in child care. Group A streptococcal upper respiratory infections can be benign, and many resolve with or without treatment. However, streptococcal respiratory infections can be complicated by development of more severe acute diseases, such as pneumonia, arthritis, rheumatic fever, and glomerulonephritis. In recent years, the incidence of rheumatic fever, which had been very low for more than a decade, has increased.[17]

Identification and treatment of streptococcal infections of the respiratory tract are central to prevention of rheumatic fever. Therefore, an awareness of the occurrence of streptococcal infection in child care is important. Adult child care staff are not immune to streptococcal infections and may be carriers of germs that cause disease in children in facilities. When outbreaks of streptococcal disease occur, interventions are available to limit transmission of streptococcal infection. Health department consultation is advised when high rates of streptococcal infection occur in facilities.

ID17. Caregivers shall be informed within 24 hours by a parent or legal guardian who knows his/her child is infected with group A beta-hemolytic *Streptococcus pyogenes,* has strep throat, or has scarlet fever.

See rationale for standard ID16.

ID18. If there has been an exposure, caregivers shall inform the parents of other children who attend the facility, in cooperation with the local health department, that their children may have been exposed to strep infection.

See rationale for standard ID16.

This information could be useful to the exposed child's health care provider if the exposed child develops illness.

For a sample letter of notification to parents, see comment for standard ID4, on p. 208.

For additional information on streptococcal infections, see also standard HP68 in chapter 3 on p. 80, on child inclusion/exclusion/dismissal, *Notification of Parents,* on p. 90, and Appendix I-4, on p. 351.

UNSPECIFIED RESPIRATORY INFECTION

Please note that if a staff member has no contact with the children, or with anything that the children come into contact with, these standards do not apply to that staff member.

ID19. A child without fever who has symptoms of mild or moderate severity associated with the common cold, sore throat, croup, bronchitis, pneumonia, or otitis media shall not be denied admission to or sent home from child care; nor shall such a child be separated from other children in the facility unless his/her illness is characterized by one or more of the following conditions:
a) The illness has a specified cause that requires exclusion as deter-

The incidence of acute respiratory diseases, including the common cold, croup, bronchitis, pneumonia, and otitis media, is high in infants and young children, whether they are cared for at home or attend out-of-home facilities.[18,19] Several recent studies suggest that children who attend facilities have a significantly increased risk of upper and lower respiratory tract infections compared with children who are cared for at home.[20-22] Available data suggest

Uncontrolled coughing, difficult or rapid breathing, and wheezing (if associated with difficult breathing or if there is no history of asthma) may represent severe illness or even a life-threatening condition (e.g., pneumonia, bronchitis, asthma, allergic reaction, pertussis, or upper airway obstruction). Exclusion in these cases is for the child's safety. Medical care should be obtained before the child is allowed to return to the facility.[24, 25]

mined by other specific performance standards in *Child
Inclusion/Exclusion/Dismissal*,
on p. 80.

b) The illness limits the child's comfortable participation in child care
activities.

c) The illness results in a need for
greater care than can be provided
by the staff without compromising the health and safety of other
children.

ID20. Child care staff shall not be
excluded from work for mild respiratory illness unless their illness is
characterized by one or more of the
following conditions:

a) The illness has a specified cause
that requires exclusion as determined by other specific performance standards in *Staff Exclusion*,
on p. 84.

b) The illness limits the staff's ability
to provide an acceptable level of
child care and compromises the
health and safety of the other
children.

For additional information on unspecified respiratory infection, see also
*Child Inclusion/Exclusion/Dismis-
sal*, on p. 80, and *Staff Exclusion*, on
p. 84.

that infants and young children in
child care have a higher incidence of
these infections when they first begin
to attend child care.[19] If children begin child care as infants, the highest
rates of disease occur during infancy.

Children experience an average of
5–10 illnesses each year.[20,21] Most of
these are common respiratory or
gastrointestinal infections, which are
not severe, and are caused by respiratory and intestinal viruses.

There is no evidence that the incidence of acute common respiratory
disease can be reduced among children in child care by any specific
intervention, including exclusion
from the facility. Controlling the
spread of viral respiratory infections
even in children on hospital wards
has proved difficult.[23] Most children
with respiratory viral infections remain infectious for at least 5 to 8
days. Frequently, infected children are
shedding viruses before it is obvious
that they are ill, and some infected
children never become overtly ill.
Therefore, it is unlikely that exclusion
of children with acute respiratory
disease from child care for the first 2
or 3 days of illness will limit transmission of respiratory infections in
the child care setting.

6.2 Enteric (Diarrheal) and Hepatitis A Virus Infections

STANDARDS

Please note that if a staff member has no contact with the children, or with anything that the children come into contact with, these standards do not apply to that staff member.

ID21. The following staff educational policies shall be employed by facilities to prevent and control infections of the intestines (often with diarrhea) or liver:

a) Continuing education for staff shall be conducted at least annually, to include the following:

   1) Methods of transmission of the hepatitis A virus and diarrheal bacteria that cause disease.

   2) Recognition and prevention of diarrhea and disease produced by hepatitis A virus. Education and monitoring shall be given on handwashing and cleaning of environmental surfaces more frequently than once a week. (See *Handwashing*, on p. 72.)

b) Weekly monitoring by the center director shall ensure that handwashing and cleaning procedures are followed as specified in the plan of the facility. (See *Handwashing*, on p. 72.)

c) All procedures relating to prevention of infections of the intestines (often with diarrhea) or liver and hepatitis A infections shall be in writing, with age-specific criteria for inclusion and exclusion of children who have a diarrheal illness or hepatitis A virus infection. (See *Child inclusion/Exclusion/Dismissal*, on p. 80.)

ID22. If there has been an exposure, parents of other children who attend the facility shall be informed, in cooperation with the local health department, that their child may have been exposed to the hepatitis A virus and may be at increased risk of developing hepatitis A. Guide-

RATIONALE

Staff training and monitoring have been shown to reduce the spread of infections of the intestine (often with diarrhea) or liver.[26–29] In a study of four centers, staff training in hygiene combined with close monitoring of staff compliance was associated with a significant decrease in infant-toddler diarrhea.[26] In another study, periodic evaluation of trained staff members was associated with significant improvement in the practices under study. Training combined with the evaluation process was associated with additional significant improvement.[27] In another study of 12 centers, continuous surveillance without training was associated with a significant decrease in diarrheal illness during the course of the longitudinal study. One-time staff training without subsequent monitoring did not result in additional decreases.[28] A similar decline in diarrhea rates during the course of surveillance without training was observed in a longitudinal study of 60 centers.[29] These studies suggest that training combined with outside monitoring of child care practices (when available) can modify staff behavior as well as disease occurrence.

COMMENTS

For a sample letter of notification to parents, see comment for standard ID4, p. 208.

lines on the administration of immune globulin given to prevent an infection in contacts of children with hepatitis A disease shall be implemented also in cooperation with the local health department.

For additional information on enteric (diarrheal) and hepatitis A virus infections, see *Training*, on p. 18, and *Notification of Parents*, on p. 90.

CHILD-SPECIFIC PROCEDURES FOR ENTERIC (DIARRHEAL) AND HEPATITIS A VIRUS INFECTIONS

ID23. The following child-specific procedures, in addition to those stated in *Inclusion/Exclusion/Dismissal*, on p. 80 shall be employed by facilities to prevent and control infections of the intestines (often with diarrhea) or liver and diarrheal diseases:

a) Any child who develops uncontrolled diarrhea (i.e., an increased number of stools compared with the child's normal pattern, with increased stool water and/or decreased form that cannot be contained by the child's diaper or use of the toilet) while attending child care shall be removed from the facility by calling his/her parent or legal guardian. Pending arrival of the parent/legal guardian, the child shall not be permitted to have contact with other children in the facility. This shall be accomplished by removing the ill child to a separate area away from contact with other children. When moving a child to a separate area creates problems with supervision of the other children, as in small family-child-care homes, the ill child shall be kept as comfortable as possible with the group, with minimal contact between the ill and well children, until the parent/legal guardian arrives.

The child with diarrhea shall be separated from the group with the onset of the uncontrolled diarrhea; separation shall not be deferred pending health assessment

Intestinal germs, including the hepatitis A virus, cause disease in children, child care staff, and close family members.[30-34] The primary age groups involved are children younger than 3 years who wear diapers. Disease has occurred in outbreaks within centers and as sporadic episodes. Although many intestinal agents can cause diarrhea in children in child care, rotavirus, *Giardia lamblia, Shigella,* and Cryptosporidium have been the main organisms implicated in outbreaks. In addition, excretion of intestinal agents, particularly *G. lamblia* and rotavirus, has been shown to occur in asymptomatic children.[35,36] The significance of this phenomenon in transmission is unknown. Surveillance of well children for signs of disease and of ill children by caregivers must be undertaken to permit early detection and permit implementation of control measures.

or laboratory testing to identify an intestinal agents.

b) A child who develops jaundice while attending child care shall be separated from other children and the child's parent/legal guardian shall be called to remove the child. The child shall remain separated from the others until the parent/legal guardian arrives.

c) Exclusion for acute uncontrolled diarrhea shall continue until diarrhea stops, and exclusion for hepatitis A shall continue for 1 week after onset of illness or until immune globulin has been given to appropriate children and staff at the facility. (See also standard HP68 in chapter 3 on p. 80 inclusion/exclusion of children with diarrhea.)

d) Alternate care for children with diarrhea or hepatitis A in special facilities for ill children shall be provided only in facilities that can provide separate care for children with infections of the intestine (often with diarrhea) or liver. (See also *Special Facilities for Ill Children*, on p. 100.)

e) Children who excrete intestinal agents but do not have diarrhea usually do not need to be excluded from the facility or to receive care in a separate area within the facility unless there are specific public health indications, as described by the responsible health department.

f) The local health department shall be informed within 24 hours of the occurrence of a hepatitis A virus infection or an increased frequency of diarrheal illness.

g) If there has been an exposure, caregivers shall inform parents of other children in the facility, in cooperation with the health department, that their children may have been exposed to hepatitis A virus infection or to an increased frequency of diarrheal illness.

Local health department consultation should be sought to determine whether the increased frequency of diarrheal illness requires public health intervention.

For a sample letter of notification to parents, see comment for standard ID4, on p. 208.

ENVIRONMENTAL STANDARDS AND HYGIENE FOR ENTERIC (DIARRHEAL) AND HEPATITIS A VIRUS INFECTIONS

Please note that if a staff member has no contact with the children, or with anything that the children come into contact with, these standards do not apply to that staff member.

ID24. The environmental and personal hygiene standards given in the following chapters shall be employed by facilities to prevent and control infections of the intestines (often with diarrhea) or liver:

Chapter	
8.2.D	Care of Ill Children
5.2.B	Toilet, Diapering, and Bath
3.1.F.1.	Handwashing
3.1.F	Hygiene
3.1.G	Sanitation, Disinfection, and Maintenance
3.1.G.6	Bedding
3.1.G.5	Toys and Objects
4.8	Food Safety
3.1.L	Animals
8.7.8	Child Records
5.6.B	Interior Maintenance
8.2.K	Food-Handling and Feeding Policy

The most important characteristic of child care associated with increased frequencies of infections of the intestines (often with diarrhea) or liver and hepatitis A is the presence of young children who are not toilet-trained.[29, 33]

Contamination of hands, communal toys, and other classroom objects is common and plays a role in the transmission of intestinal agents in outbreaks of diarrhea in facilities. Studies commonly find that fecal contamination of the environment is frequent in centers and is highest in infant and toddler areas, where infections of the intestines (often with diarrhea) or liver and hepatitis A problems are known to occur most often.[37–41] Limited studies indicate that the risk of diarrhea is significantly higher for children in centers than in age-matched children cared for at home or in small family-child-care homes.[34, 35]

The spread of infection from non–toilet-trained children in centers to their families is common, particularly when *Shigella*, rotavirus, *G. lamblia*, or hepatitis A virus are the causative agents.[36] To decrease diarrheal disease in child care, staff and parents must be kept aware of modes of transmission as well as practical methods of prevention and control. Staff training in handwashing and hygiene, combined with close monitoring of staff compliance, was associated with a significant decrease in infant/toddler diarrhea.[26] However, staff training on a single occasion, without close staff monitoring, did not result in a decrease in diarrhea rates; this finding emphasizes the importance of monitoring as well as education.[28] Therefore, good hygienic practices, as well as hygiene monitoring, are very important in limiting infections of the intestines (often with diarrhea) or liver in child care.

DISEASE SURVEILLANCE OF ENTERIC (DIARRHEAL) AND HEPATITIS A VIRUS INFECTIONS

ID25. Specific disease surveillance policies shall be used to prevent and control infections of the intestine (often with diarrhea) or liver and diarrheal diseases in facilities.

Disease surveillance and reporting to local health authorities are critical to the prevention and control of diseases in the child care setting. A major purpose of surveillance is to allow early detection of disease problems and prompt implementation of control measures. Ascertaining whether a child who attends a facility is ill is important when evaluating childhood illnesses; ascertaining whether an adult who works in a facility or is a parent of a child attending a facility is ill is important when considering a diagnosis of hepatitis A or other diseases transmitted by the route of infections of the intestines (often with diarrhea) or liver. Causes of such infections in household contacts may necessitate questioning about illness in the child attending child care and testing the child for infection. Information concerning communicable disease in a child care attendee, staff member, or household contact should be communicated to public health authorities, to the child care director, and to all parents.

ID26. Each facility shall have a written policy for reporting certain communicable infections of the intestines (often with diarrhea) or liver to the responsible public health authorities and for notifying parents.

See rationale for standard ID25.

For additional information on disease surveillance of enteric (diarrheal) and hepatitis A virus infections, see also chapter 8, *Administration*, on pp. 269–287, on additional policies, *Reporting Illness*, on p. 87, *Notification of Parents*, on p. 90, and *The Health Department's Role*, on p. 310.

6.3 Vaccine-Preventable Diseases

STANDARDS

RATIONALE

COMMENTS

Please note that if a staff member has no contact with the children, or with anything that the children come into contact with, these standards do not apply to that staff member.

ID27. Infants and children shall be immunized as specified in Appendix P-1, on p. 372.

ID28. All children younger than 7 years who were not immunized at the recommended times in infancy shall be immunized as specified in Appendix P-2, on p. 374.

ID29. The facility shall require that all children enrolling in child care provide written documentation of satisfactory immunization appropriate for age, which shall be retained on the child's record. Specifically, children shall demonstrate the following:

a) Diphtheria-tetanus-pertussis (DTP) vaccine: one dose by 3 months of age, two doses by 5 months of age, three doses by 7 months of age, and four doses by 2 years of age.

b) Trivalent poliomyelitis vaccine, either oral polio vaccine (OPV) or inactivated polio vaccine (IPV): one dose by 3 months of age, two doses by 5 months of age, and three doses by 19 months of age.

c) Combined measles-mumps-rubella (MMR) vaccine: one dose by 16 months of age.

d) *Haemophilus influenzae* type b conjugate vaccine (HbCV): one dose by 2 months of age, two doses by 4 months of age, and three doses by 1 year of age.

e) The facility shall require that children who have not been immunized in an age-appropriate manner prior to enrollment show evidence of an appointment for immunizations, and that they have their immunization series initiated within 1 month and completed according to Schedule 2 (see Appendix P-2, on p. 374).

Routine immunization at the appropriate age is the best means of averting vaccine-preventable diseases. Laws requiring the age-appropriate immunization of children attending licensed facilities exist in almost all states.[42] Surveys show that children in licensed child care have higher immunization levels than children of the same age who are not in child care. Therefore, parents of children who attend unlicensed child care should be encouraged to comply with the recommended schedule of immunization for infants and children. Immunization is particularly important for children in child care because preschool-aged children currently have the highest age-specific incidence of measles, pertussis, rubella, and *Haemophilus influenzae* type b disease.

Many cases of vaccine-preventable disease occur in unimmunized and underimmunized infants and children.[43] Of the 1,225 children ages 16 months to 4 years with measles reported to the Centers for Disease Control (CDC) in 1986, 83 percent were unimmunized.[44] An additional 1,229 measles cases occurred in children too young for measles immunization (i.e., less than 15 months of age).

Vaccine-preventable disease in young children is of great concern because younger children are at higher risk than older children for complications of their illnesses. For example, during

ID29. *continued*

the period 1984–85, a total of 5,865 pertussis cases were reported to the CDC.[13] Nearly three-fourths (74 percent) occurred in infants younger than 6 months of age, and 18 of 19 pertussis deaths were in this youngest age group. Of 1,504 pertussis cases in children 7 months through 6 years of age with known immunization status, 70 percent were underimmunized; 55 percent had not received at least three doses of vaccine—the minimum number considered necessary for adequate vaccine protection against pertussis. Thirty-one percent had not received any doses. Additionally, 51 percent of the 795 patients 3 to 6 months of age with known immunization status were underimmunized. Therefore, strict adherence to pertussis immunization recommendations would be expected to have a significant impact on the overall incidence of the disease among children and on childhood pertussis mortality.

The introduction of live mumps vaccine in 1967 and recommendations for its routine use in 1977 led to a steady decrease in reported mumps cases in the United States. However, since the record low number of cases in 1985 (2,982 cases), there has been a steady increase in the incidence of mumps, with 12,848 cases reported in 1987. Although most (55 percent) mumps disease occurs in school-aged children (5 to 14 years), 804 cases (7 percent) occurred in preschool-aged children during 1987; although this rate was low, it represented a 137 percent increase in the rate of mumps disease in preschool children between 1985 and 1987.[45]

Because of near-universal use of vaccines against diphtheria, tetanus, and polio, these diseases have become rare in the United States.

Two expert advisory groups—the Advisory Committee on Immunization Practices (ACIP) of the U.S. Public Health Service and the Committee on Infectious Diseases of the American Academy of Pediatrics — recommend a national immunization policy for U.S. children, and both have established similar standards for routine immunization of infants and preschool children.[46–48] Because these policies are updated regularly, immunization standards may change with respect to children in out-of-home care and their families.

ID30. Children who do not have age-appropriate immunization status or who have documented medical or personal exemptions from routine childhood immunization shall be allowed to attend child care unless there is a vaccine-preventable disease to which they are susceptible in the facility. In such a situation, all under-immunized children shall be excluded for the duration of possible exposure or until they have completed their immunizations.

See rationale for standard ID29.

ID31. Staff shall be current for all immunizations routinely recommended for adults.
a) All staff shall have completed a primary series for tetanus and diphtheria, and shall receive boosters every 10 years.
b) All staff shall have been immunized or certified immune by a health care provider against measles, mumps, rubella, and poliomyelitis, following guidelines of the ACIP.[49]

For additional information on vaccine-preventable diseases, see also *Child Health Services*, on p. 276, for additional immunization standards, *Preemployment Staff Health Appraisal, Including Immunization*, on p. 35, and *Immunizations and Preventive Health Care*, on p. 86.

6.4 Herpes Simplex Virus, Varicella-Zoster (Chicken Pox) Virus

STANDARDS

RATIONALE

COMMENTS

Please note that if a staff member has no contact with the children, or with anything that the children come into contact with, these standards do not apply to that staff member.

STAFF EDUCATION AND POLICIES ON HERPES SIMPLEX AND CHICKEN POX VIRUSES

ID32. Caregivers shall be instructed in the importance of handwashing and other measures aimed at limiting the transfer of infected material (e.g., saliva, tissue fluid, or fluid from a skin sore).

Although the risk of transmission of herpes simplex virus in the child care setting has not been defined, spread of infection within families has been reported and is thought to require direct contact with infected secretions.[50, 51]

With chicken pox, the virus appears to be present at times in respiratory secretions and to be shed from the mouth and throat as well as from sores; spread from oral or respiratory secretions to susceptible contacts is very likely. With shingles, the virus is present only in small, fluid-filled blisters, and spread is unlikely without direct contact. Sores that are covered appear to pose little risk to susceptible persons.

For additional information on staff education and policies on herpes simplex and chicken pox viruses, see also *Training*, on p. 18, and *Hygiene*, on p. 72.

DISEASE RECOGNITION AND CONTROL OF HERPES SIMPLEX AND CHICKEN POX VIRUSES

ID33. Children who develop chicken pox while attending child care shall be excluded until 6 days after onset of the rash, or until all sores have dried and crusted over. In mild cases with only a few sores and rapid resolution, an otherwise healthy child may be able to return sooner with permission of the child's physician. Children whose immune

Exclusion of children infected with herpes simplex virus and varicella-zoster virus may not control these illnesses in child care, but exclusion may help control disease caused by these viruses in some individuals (e.g., adults, immunocompromised children and adults, newborns, and fetuses). Both herpes simplex virus and varicella-zoster virus can be

Initial viral infection with varicella-zoster produces an acute fever and the appearance of chicken pox blisters; reactivation of the virus results in shingles.

systems do not function properly and children with longer cases of chicken pox shall be excluded from child care until blisters stop erupting.

transmitted from mother to fetus or newborn. However, maternal herpes infections that are a threat to off-spring are sexually transmitted genital infections; therefore, maternal exposure to herpes simplex in a child care setting will carry little, if any, risk for the fetus. Around 5 percent to 10 percent of adults will be susceptible to varicella-zoster virus; susceptible child care staff who are pregnant and are exposed to children with chicken pox should be referred to qualified physicians or other professionals for counseling within 24 hours after the exposure is recognized.[52]

See also rationale for standard ID32, on p. 222.

ID34. All staff members and parents shall be notified when a case of chicken pox occurs; they shall be informed concerning the greater likelihood of serious infection in susceptible adults and of the potential for fetal damage if infection occurs during pregnancy.

See rationale for standard ID33.

For a sample letter of notification to parents, see comment for standard ID4, on p. 208.

ID35. Staff members or children with shingles (herpes zoster) shall keep sores covered by clothing or a dressing until sores have crusted. The need for excluding an infected person shall be decided based on the recommendations of the person's health care provider.

See rationale for standard ID32, on p. 208.

See comment on standard 34.

ID36. Children with herpetic gingivostomatitis, an infection caused by the herpes simplex virus, who do not have control of oral secretions shall be excluded from child care. In selected situations, a child with mild disease who is in control of his/her mouth secretions may not require exclusion; consult the child's health care provider.

Initial herpes simplex virus disease in children often produces a sudden illness of short duration characterized by fever and sores around and within the mouth. Illness and viral excretion may persist a week or more; severe open skin sores may prevent oral intake and necessitate hospitalization.[50] Oral herpes is manifest as small, fluid-filled blisters on the lips and entails a much shorter period of virus shedding from sores. Adults and children also can shed the virus in oral secretions in the absence of identifiable sores.

See also rationale for standard ID32, on p. 208.

For additional information on disease recognition and control of herpes simplex and chicken pox viruses, see chapter *Inclusion/Exclusion/Dismissal,* on p. 80, and *Notification of Parents,* on p. 90.

6.5 Cytomegalovirus (CMV)

Please note that if a staff member has no contact with the children, or with anything that the children come into contact with, these standards do not apply to the staff member.

STAFF EDUCATION AND POLICIES ON CMV

ID37. Caregivers shall be instructed in hygienic measures (e.g., handwashing and avoiding contact with urine, saliva, and nasal secretions) aimed at reducing acquisition of cytomegalovirus (CMV). (See *Training* on p. 18, and *Hygiene*, on p. 72.

Transmission of CMV appears to require direct contact with virus-containing secretions. Therefore, careful attention to hygiene has been recommended to prevent infection in child care workers.[53] However, the effectiveness of hygiene (handwashing and avoiding contact with secretions) in an environment where CMV is very prevalent has not been measured.

ID38. Facilities that employ women of childbearing age shall educate these workers with regard to the following:
a) The increased probability of exposure to CMV in the child care setting.
b) The potential for fetal damage when CMV is acquired during pregnancy.

CMV is the leading cause of congenital infection in the United States, with approximately 1 percent of live-born infants infected prenatally.[54] Fortunately, most infected fetuses escape resulting illness or disability, but 10 percent to 20 percent will have hearing loss, mental retardation, cerebral palsy, or vision disturbances. Although it is well known that maternal immunity does not prevent congenital CMV infection, evidence indicates that initial acquisition of CMV during pregnancy (primary maternal infection) carries the greatest risk for resulting illness or disability of the fetus.[55]

Children enrolled in facilities are more likely to acquire CMV than are children cared for at home. There is also strong evidence that shows child-to-child transmission of CMV in the child care setting.[56–60] Rates of CMV excretion have varied among facilities and even between class groups within a facility. Children between 1 and 3 years of age have the highest rates

ID38. *continued*

of excretion; published studies report rates between 20 percent and over 80 percent in this age group. Studies in Birmingham, Alabama, have on several occasions revealed classes of 10 to 15 toddlers with excretion rates of 100 percent.[57] Children who acquire CMV from a maternal source or in a facility will continue to excrete the virus for years.[61] Thus, it is reasonable to conclude that child care staff are more likely to come into contact with CMV-excreting children than are individuals in any other known situation or occupation.

Epidemiologic and other data have shown that young children can transmit CMV to their parents and other caregivers. Epidemiologic data, as well as restriction endonuclease tracking of viral strains, has provided strong evidence for child-to-child transmission of CMV in the child care setting.[59, 62–65.]

Epidemiologic data and a restriction enzyme study of CMV strains have shown that premature newborns who acquire CMV in the nursery can and often do transmit the virus to their parents.[66, 67] Moreover, parents of children attending centers have a higher rate of development of antibodies to CMV than parents of children kept at home.[68] Parental development of antibodies to CMV is clearly related to CMV excretion by the child.[68] A restriction endonuclease study of viral strains also has provided strong laboratory data supporting child-to-parent transmission.[59, 68] Finally, with regard to child-to-staff transmission, two studies, each involving over 30 centers and about 500 adult staff, have revealed a high rate of development of antibodies to CMV among child care workers.[69, 70] Studies in Birmingham, Alabama, have shown an annualized development of antibodies to CMV rate of 19.9 percent.[69] Adler reported an annualized development of antibodies to CMV rate of 14 percent in child care staff in Richmond, Virginia.[70] Thus, there is substantial evidence that young preschool children can transmit CMV to classroom and household contacts, and that child care staff are at increased risk of CMV infection.

STANDARDS

ID38. *continued*

RATIONALE

The two most important identifiable sources of CMV infection in women of childbearing age appear to be young children and sexual contacts. There is no reason to believe that either one of these routes is more or less likely to lead to fetal infection when primary infection occurs during pregnancy. There is in fact indirect evidence from analysis of DNA from CMV strains that young children can be a source of maternal infection that is transmitted to the fetus.[71] Therefore, the exposure to CMV with increased rate of acquisition that occurs in child care staff will most likely lead to an increased rate of gestational CMV infection in staff without antibodies to CMV and an increased rate of congenital CMV infection in their offspring.

Data from several prospective studies of pregnant women have shown that the risk of fetal infection after primary maternal gestational CMV infection is around 40 percent.[54, 72–74] About 10 percent of infected offspring are symptomatic at birth; about 90 percent of these develop resulting illness or disabilities. Of the 90 percent who are asymptomatic at birth, 10 percent to 20 percent develop disabilities. Thus, of every 100 primary CMV infections during pregnancy, 7 to 11 infants develop disabilities due to congenital CMV infections. These estimates address only the outcome of primary infection during pregnancy. Women who are immune prior to conception also can have children with congenital CMV infection.[54, 75] Although recurrent maternal infections are thought to be due to reactivation of endogenous virus, there are limited data on the role of reinfection in congenital CMV. Regardless of source, congenital CMV infection occurs in 0.2 percent to 2 percent of offspring of women immune prior to conception; fortunately, these infections are not usually associated with fetal damage. It is not possible to estimate accurately the risk of resulting illness or disability in a baby with congenital CMV due to a maternal recurrence; only a few cases have been reported in the world literature. Therefore, women who have

COMMENTS

antibodies to CMV can be reassured that their risk of having a baby damaged by congenital CMV infection is extremely low—too small to estimate.

For additional information on staff education and policies on CMV, see also recommendation REC39 in chapter 9 on p. 312.

RISK MANAGEMENT AND DISEASE CONTROL OF CMV

ID39. Female employees of childbearing age shall be referred to their personal health care providers or to the responsible health department for counseling as to the risk of CMV infection in their specific situation. This counseling may include testing for serum antibody to CMV to determine the employee's immunity against CMV infection.

With current knowledge on the risk of CMV infection in child care staff and the potential consequences of gestational CMV infection, child care staff should be counseled regarding risks.

See also rationale for standard ID38, on p. 224.

Serologic testing for CMV is available in nearly all communities in the United States. Kits for measuring immunoglobulin gamma G antibody to CMV are available from major biotechnical companies and seem to perform well enough when used by qualified laboratories. They are accepted for screening blood products, transfusion recipients, and organ donors and recipients.

ID40. Testing of children to detect CMV excretion, or exclusion of children known to be CMV infected, shall not be recommended.

CMV testing is expensive and is likely to be misleading, as excretion status may change.

For additional information on risk management and disease control of CMV, see also recommendation REC39 in chapter 9 on p. 312.

6.6 *Hepatitis B Virus Infection*

Please note that if a staff member has no contact with the children, or with anything that the children come into contact with, these standards do not apply to that staff member.

DISEASE RECOGNITION AND CONTROL OF HEPATITIS B VIRUS INFECTION

ID41. Facilities shall have written policies for inclusion/exclusion of children known to be infected with hepatitis B virus (HBV).

Transmission of hepatitis B virus (HBV) in the child care setting is of increasing concern to public health authorities due to the increasing number of children known to be HBV carriers (particularly international adoptees from HBV-endemic areas) who require child care. However, the risk of disease transmission in child care is theoretically small, because blood or infected body fluid must get inside another body in order to transmit HBV infection. Data that quantify the risk of transmission in this setting are limited.

ID42. Children who carry HBV chronically and who have no behavioral or medical risk factors, such as unusually aggressive behavior (e.g., biting, frequent scratching), generalized dermatitis, or bleeding problems, shall be admitted to the facility without restrictions.

One instance of HBV transmission in a center in the United States has been recognized; this involved a known aggressive 3-year-old HBV carrier (biter and scratcher) who transmitted HBV to one child in the center, causing acute hepatitis B in the child.[76] Thorough investigation revealed no other disease transmission from the index HBV carrier or newly infected child to other children and staff at this center. Investigations of three other HBV carrier children in child care settings, including one child considered at high risk due to severe generalized dermatitis, failed to document HBV transmission in the facilities.[76, 77] Based on these data and the absence of other cases of HBV transmission in child care, the risk of disease transmission from an HBV carrier child or staff with normal behavior and without generalized dermatitis or bleeding problems is considered very low. This extremely low risk does not justify exclusion of such an HBV carrier child from out-of-home care, nor does it justify the routine screening of children for HBV carriage prior to admission to child care.

ID43. Admission of HBV carrier children with the above risk factors shall be assessed on a case-by-case basis by the child's health care provider, the center director or large or small family home caregiver, the facility's health consultant (see *Health Consultants*, on p. 33) and the responsible public health authorities.

HBV transmission in a child care setting is most likely to occur through direct exposure via bites or scratches that break the skin and introduce blood or body secretions from the HBV carrier into the victim. Indirect transmission via blood or saliva through environmental contamination may be possible but has not been documented. Saliva contains much less virus (1/1000) than blood; therefore, the potential infectivity of saliva is lower. In gibbons and chimpanzees, saliva has been shown to be infectious only when inoculated through the skin; it has not caused infection when administered by aerosol through the nose or mouth, by ingestion through the mouth, or by toothbrush on the gums.

Existing data in humans suggest a small risk of HBV transmission from the bite of an HBV carrier. Several single episodes and one outbreak have been reported in which the most likely pathway of HBV transmission was through bites of HBV carriers. The absolute risk of transmission from a bite, however, has not been quantified, nor is it likely that studies can be done to quantify the risk. Based on the evidence above, some experts recommend giving hepatitis B immune globulin disease-prevention measures to victims of bites by HBV carriers.

There are no data to indicate the risk of transmission if a susceptible person bites an HBV carrier. A theoretical risk exists if hepatitis B surface-antigen-positive blood enters the oral cavity of the biter. There are no reported cases of transmission in this manner, however, and animal studies in which infectious material was applied to the oral mucosa showed that transmission occurred only under circumstances of oral manipulation or trauma, such as toothbrushing. Since these data are limited, a firm recommendation cannot be made about management of such a situation.

When the HBV statuses of both the biting child and the victim are unknown, the risk of HBV transmission would be extremely low because of the expected low incidence of HBV carriage by children of preschool age and the low efficiency of disease transmission by bite exposure. Because it is extremely unlikely that a bite in this situation would involve an HBV carrier child, screening and disease-prevention measures are not warranted.

ID44. Testing children for HBV infection or carriage shall not be performed as a prerequisite for admission to facilities.

See rationale for standards ID42 and ID43.

ID45. When an HBV carrier child is admitted to a facility, the facility director or large or small family home caregiver and attendants usually responsible for the child shall be informed

See rationale for standards ID42 and ID43.

to allow proper precautions and assessment of behavioral problems.

ID46. The primary caregiver shall observe the child and the other children in the group for development of aggressive behavior, as outlined in standard ID42 above, that might facilitate HBV transmission. When such behavior occurs, the need for immediate disease-prevention measures with hepatitis B immune globulin shall be evaluated by the child's health care provider and/or the responsible public health authority; additionally, the continuing attendance of the child in the facility shall be reevaluated.

Regular assessment of behavioral risk factors and medical conditions of enrolled HBV carrier children is necessary, and requires that the center director and primary caregivers be informed about a known HBV carrier child. At present hepatitis B vaccination is not considered necessary for children or staff in contact with HBV carriers in child care unless high risk factors, stated in standard ID42 are present.

ID47. Information regarding an HBV carrier child shall be available to those caregivers who need to know because they regularly provide care to the child. This need to know, however, does not require that parents of other children cared for in the facility be informed of the attendance of an HBV carrier child.

See rationale for standard ID46.

ID48. All facility staff shall receive regular training on prevention of transmission of bloodborne diseases. (See also *Continuing Education*, on p. 24, on staff training and *Hygiene*, on p. 72.)

Efforts to reduce the risk of disease transmission in child care through hygienic and environmental standards in general, and particularly when a known HBV carrier child is enrolled, should focus primarily on blood precautions and limiting potential contamination of the environment by saliva as much as is practical.

ID49. Staff members known to have acute or chronic HBV shall not be restricted from work, but shall receive training on how to prevent transmission of bloodborne diseases. (See also *Continuing Education*, on p. 24, and *Hygiene*, on p. 72.)

See rationale for standard ID41.

ID50. Cases of acute HBV in any child or employee of a facility shall be reported to the responsible public health authorities for a determination of the need for further investigation or preventive measures. (See *Reporting Illness*, on p. 87, and *Notification of the Health Department*, on p. 92.)

See rationale for standard ID41.

For additional information on disease recognition and control of hepatitis B virus infection, see also *Management and Prevention of Illness*, on p. 80, on additional exclusion standards.

STANDARDS	RATIONALE	COMMENTS

HYGIENE FOR HEPATITIS B VIRUS INFECTION

ID51. Injuries that lead to bleeding by the HBV carrier child shall be handled promptly in the manner recommended for any such injury (see standard HP38 in chapter 3 on p. 75).

See rationale for ID48.

ID52. Caregivers shall adopt universal precautions as outlined in *Prevention of Exposure to Blood*, on p. 74.

ID53. Toothbrushes shall be individually labeled so that sharing of the same toothbrush among different children does not occur.

Saliva may contain viable HBV.

ID54. Toys and objects that are mouthed by young children (infants and toddlers) shall be cleaned and disinfected as stated in standard HP50 in chapter 3 on p. 78.

See rationale for ID53.

For additional information on hygiene for hepatitis B virus infection, see also standard FA117 in chapter 5 on p. 162.

6.7 Human Immunodeficiency Virus (HIV) Infection

Please note that if a staff member has no contact with the children, or with anything that the children come into contact with, these standards do not apply to that staff member.

ADMINISTRATIVE POLICIES ON HIV INFECTION

ID55. Human Immunodeficiency Virus (HIV)-infected children shall be admitted to child care providing their health, neurological development, behavior, and immune status are appropriate as determined on a case-by-case basis by qualified persons, including the child's health care provider, who are able to evaluate whether the child will receive optimal care in the specific facility being considered and whether an HIV-infected child poses a potential threat to others.

No reported cases of HIV infection are known to have resulted from transmission in out-of-home child care. Although the risk of transmission of HIV infection to children in the child care setting appears to be extremely low, data do not exist that directly address this issue. Guidelines can most reasonably provide methods to reduce the risk of transmission of HIV infection to caregivers in out-of-home child care.

ID56. Information regarding a child whose immune system does not function properly to prevent infection, whatever the cause, shall be

Since there are most likely HIV-infected children attending child care whose status is unknown, universal precautions should be adopted in

available to those caregivers who need to know to protect the child against other infections. Accordingly, illnesses that occur among other children and staff in the facility shall be brought to the prompt attention of the parent of the child whose immune system does not function properly to prevent infection; such parent may elect to seek medical advice regarding continued participation of the child in the facility.

For additional information on administrative policies on HIV infection, see also *Confidentiality and Access to Records*, on p. 288.

PREVENTING TRANSMISSION OF HIV INFECTION

ID57. Child care personnel shall adopt universal precautions as outlined in *Prevention of Exposure to Blood*, on p. 74.

ID58. Caregivers shall be knowledgeable about routes of HIV transmission and about prevention of transmission.

ID59. HIV-infected adults with no symptoms of illness may care for children in facilities provided they do not have open skin sores or other conditions that would allow contact of their body fluids with children or other adults.

caring for children in out-of-home child care.[78] The caregivers' need to know, however, does not require knowledge of the child's HIV status, since children whose immune systems do not function properly to prevent infections due to other acquired and congenital causes may also be in the facility.

See rationale in standard ID56, on p. 231.

Studies examining transmission of HIV support the concept that HIV is not a highly infectious agent.[79] The major routes of transmission are through sexual contact, through contact with blood, and from mother to child during the birth process. Several studies have shown that HIV-infected persons do not spread the HIV virus to other members of their households except through sexual contact. HIV has been isolated in very low volumes in saliva and urine. Transmission of hepatitis B virus (a virus very similar to HIV but more infectious) through saliva appears to be very uncommon. Isolated cases suggest that contact with blood from an HIV-infected individual is a possible mode of transmission. In these situations, the transmission appears most likely to have occurred through contact between nonintact skin and blood or blood-containing fluids.

On the basis of available data, there is no reason to believe that HIV-infected adults will transmit HIV in the course of their normal child care duties. Therefore, asymptomatic HIV-infected adults who do not have open, uncoverable skin sores or other conditions that would allow contact with

Any child whose immune system does not function properly to prevent infection, however, will be suspected of having HIV and universal precautions will be implemented.

their body fluids may care for children in facilities. However, immunosuppressed adults with acquired immunodeficiency syndrome (AIDS) may be more likely to acquire infectious agents from children and should consult with their own health care providers regarding the advisability of their continuing to work in a facility.[80]

PROTECTING HIV-INFECTED CHILDREN

ID60. Parents of an HIV-infected child shall be notified immediately if the child has been exposed to chicken pox, Tb, or measles through other children in the facility.

Children who are infected with HIV often have immune systems that do not function properly to prevent infections. Children with immunosuppression for multiple other reasons are at increased risk for severe complications from infections with chicken pox, CMV, Tb, and measles virus.[81] Available data indicate that measles infection is a more serious illness in HIV-infected children than in noninfected children. The first deaths due to measles in the United States reported to the CDC after 1985 were in HIV-infected children.[82.]

ID61. A child whose immune system does not function properly to prevent infection and who is exposed to measles or chicken pox shall be referred immediately to his/her health care provider to receive the appropriate preventive measure (immune globulin) following exposure.

See rationale for standard ID60.

ID62. The decision to readmit the exposed child to the facility shall be made jointly by the center director or large or small family home caregiver, the family, and the child's health care provider.

See rationale for standard ID60.

ID63. Caregivers known to be HIV-infected shall be notified immediately if they have been exposed to chicken pox, Tb, or measles through children in the facility; they shall receive an appropriate preventive measure (immune globulin) after exposure if exposed to measles or chicken pox; and their return to work after exposure shall be determined jointly by the center director or large or small family home caregiver and the health care provider for the HIV-infected caregiver.

See rationale for standard ID60.

References

1. Recommendations of the Immunization Practices Advisory Committee (ACIP). Update: prevention of *Haemophilus influenzae* type b disease. *MMWR.* 1988;37:13–16.

2. American Academy of Pediatrics Committee on Infectious Disease: *Haemophilus influenzae* type b conjugate vaccine. *Pediatrics.* 1988;81:908–911.

3. Schlech WF, Ward JI, Band JD, et al. Bacterial meningitis in the United States, 1978 through 1981. *JAMA.* 1985;253:1749–1754.

4. Cochi SL, Fleming DW, Hightower AW, et al. Primary invasive *Haemophilus influenzae* type b disease: a population-based assessment of risk factors. *J Pediatr.* 1986;108:887–896.

5. Osterholm MT, Pierson LM, White KE, et al. The risk of a subsequent transmission of *Haemophilus influenzae* type b disease among children in day care. *N Engl J Med.* 1987;316:1–5.

6. Murphy TV, Clements JF, Breedlove JA, et al. Risk of subsequent disease among day-care contacts of patients with systemic *Haemophilus influenzae* type b disease. *N Engl J Med.* 1987;316:5–10.

7. Band JD, Fraser DW, Ajello G, et al. Prevention of *Haemophilus influenzae* type b disease. *JAMA.* 1984;253:2381–2386.

8. Makintubee S, Istre GR, Ward JI. Transmission of invasive *Haemophilus influenzae* type b disease in day care settings. *J Pediatr.* 1987;111:180–186.

9. Fleming DW, Leibenhaut MH, Albanes D, et al. Secondary *Haemophilus influenzae* type b in day-care facilities: risk factors and prevention. *JAMA.* 1985;254:509–514.

10. Murphy TV, McCracken GH, Moore BS, et al. *Haemophilus influenzae* type b disease after rifampin prophylaxis in a day care center: possible reasons for its failure. *Pediatr Infect Dis.* 1983;2:193–198.

11. Fraser DW, Geil CC, Feldman RA. Bacterial meningitis in Bernalillo County, New Mexico. A comparison with three other American populations. *Amer J Epidemiol.* 1974;100:29–34.

12. Jacobson JA, Felice GA, Holloway JT. Meningococcal disease in day-care centers. *Pediatrics.* 1977;59:299–300.

13. Centers for Disease Control. Pertussis surveillance—United States, 1984 and 1985. *MMWR.* 1987;36:168–171.

14. Bass JE. Pertussis: current status of prevention and treatment. *Pediatr Infect Dis.* 1985;4:614–619.

15. Smith TD, Wilkinson V, Kaplan EL. Group A streptococcus-associated upper respiratory tract infections in a day-care center. *Pediatrics.* 1989;83:380–384.

16. Kaplan EL. Personal communication, March 21, 1989.

17. Kaplan EL, Hill HR. Return of rheumatic fever: consequences, implications, and needs. *J Pediatr.* 1987;111:244–246.

18. Denny FW, Collier AM, Henderson FW. Acute respiratory infections in day care. In: Osterholm MT, Klein JO, Aronson SS, Pickering LK, eds. *Infectious Diseases in Child Care: Management and Prevention.* Chicago, Ill: University of Chicago Press; 1987; 15–20.

19. Dingle JH, Badger GF, Jordan WS. *Illness in the Home: A Study of 25,000 Illnesses in a Group of Cleveland Families.* Cleveland, Ohio: Press of Case Western Reserve University; 1964.

20. Fleming DW, Cochi SL, Hightower AW, Broome CV. Childhood upper respiratory tract infections: to what degree is incidence affected by day-care attendance? *Pediatrics.* 1987;79:55–60.

21. Wald ER, Dashefsky B, Byers C, et al. Frequency and severity of infections in day care. *J Pediatr.* 1988;112:540–546.

22. Anderson LJ, Parker RA, Stricas RS, et al. Day-care attendance and hospitalization for lower respiratory tract illness. *Pediatrics.* 1988;82:300–308.

23. Gala CL, Hall CB, Schnable KC, et al. The use of eye-nose goggles to control nosocomial respiratory syncytial virus infection. *JAMA.* 1986;256:2706.

24. St. Gene J, Pickering L, Granoff D. Symposium—Day care diseases: does day care make respiratory illness worse? *Contemp Pediatr.* 1986;3:22–42.

25. Trumpp C. Management of communicable diseases in day care centers. *Pediatr Annals.* 1983;12(3).

26. Black RE, Dykes AC, Anderson KD, et al. Handwashing to prevent diarrhea in day care centers. *Am J Epidemiol.* 1981;113:445–451.

27. Aronson SS, Aiken LS. Compliance of child care programs with health and safety standards: impact of program evaluation and advocate training. *Pediatrics.* 1980;65:318–325.

28. Bartlett AV, Jarvis BA, Ross V, et al. Diarrheal illness among infants and toddlers in day care centers: effects of active surveillance and staff training without subsequent monitoring. *Amer J Epidemiol.* 1988;127:808–817.

29. Sullivan P, Woodward WE, Pickering LK, et al. A longitudinal study of the occurrence of diarrheal disease in day care centers. *Amer J Public Health.* 1984;74:987–991.

30. Pickering LK, Evans DG, DuPont HL, et al. Diarrhea caused by *Shigella,* rotavirus, and *Giardia* in day care centers: prospective study. *J Pediatr.* 1981;99:51–56.

31. Bartlett AV, Moore M, Gary GW, et al. Diarrheal illness among infants and toddlers in child day care centers. *J. Pediatr.* 1985;107:495–502.

32. Pickering LK, Hadler SC. Management and prevention of infectious diseases in day care. In: Feigin RD, Cherry JD, eds. *Textbook of Pediatric Infectious Diseases.* Philadelphia, Pa: WB Saunders Co; 1987. 2343–2361.

33. Hadler SC, Erben JJ, Francis DP, et al. Risk factors for hepatitis A in day care centers. *J Infect Dis.* 1982;145:255–261.

34. Hadler SC, Webster HM, Erben JJ, et al. Hepatitis A in day care centers: a community-wide assessment. *N Engl J Med.* 1980;302:1222–1227.

35. Pickering LK, Woodward WE, DuPont HL, et al. Occurrence of *Giardia lamblia* in children in day care centers. *J Pediatr.* 1984;104:522–526.

36. Pickering LK, Bartlett AV, Reves RR, Morrow A. Asymptomatic rotavirus before and after rotavirus diarrhea in children in day care centers. *J Pediatr.* 1988; 112:361–365.

37. Keswick BH, Pickering LK, DuPont HL, et al. Survival and detection of rotavirus on environmental surfaces in day care centers. *Appl Environ Microbiol.* 1983;46:813–816.

38. Kim K, DuPont HL, Pickering LK. Outbreaks of diarrhea associated with *Clostridium difficile* and its toxin in day care centers: evidence of person-to-person spread. *J Pediatr.* 1983;102:376–382.

39. Petersen JJ, Bressler GK. Design and modification of the day care environment. *Rev Infect Dis.* 1986; 8:618–621.

40. Weniger BG, Ruttenber J, Goodman RA. Fecal coliforms on environmental surfaces in two day care centers. *Appl Environ Microbiol.* 1983;45:733–735.

41. Pickering, LK, Bartlett AV, Woodward WE. Acute infectious diarrhea among children in day care: epidemiology and control. *Rev Infect Dis.* 1986; 8:539–547.

42. Hinman AR. Vaccine-preventable diseases and child day care. *Rev Infect Dis.* 1986; 8:573–583.

43. Markowitz LE, Preblud SR, Orenstein, WA. Patterns of transmission in measles outbreaks in the United States, 1985–1986. *N Engl J Med.* 1989;320:75–81.

44. Centers for Disease Control. Measles—United States, 1986. *MMWR.* 1987;36:301–305.

45. Centers for Disease Control. Mumps—United States, 1985–1988. *MMWR.* 1989; 38:101–105.

46. Recommendations of the Immunization Practices Advisory Committee (ACIP). General recommendations on immunization. *MMWR.* 1989;38:205–227.

47. American Academy of Pediatrics. *Report of the Committee on Infectious Diseases.* 21st edition. Elk Grove Village, Ill: American Academy of Pediatrics; 1988.

48. Centers for Disease Control. Rubella and congenital rubella syndrome—United States, 1985–1988. *MMWR.* 1989;38:173–178.

49. Recommendations of the Immunization Practices Advisory Committee (ACIP). Adult immunizations. *MMWR.* 1984;33S:1S–68S.

50. Kohl S. Postnatal herpes simplex virus infections. In: Feigin RD, Cherry JD, eds. *Textbook of Pediatric Infectious Diseases.* Philadephia, Pa: WB Saunders Co; 1987:1577–1601.

51. Juretic M. Natural history of herpetic infection. *Helv Paedatr Acta.* 1966;21:356–368.

52. Paryani SG, Arvin AM. Intrauterine infection with varicella-zoster virus after maternal varicella. *N Engl J Med.* 1986;314:1542–1546.

53. Prevalence of cytomegalovirus excretion from children in five day care centers—Alabama. *MMWR.* 1985;34:49–51.

54. Stagno S, Pass RF, Dworsky ME, Alford CA. Maternal cytomegalovirus infection and perinatal transmission. In: Knox GE, ed. *Clinical Obstetrics and Gynecology.* 1982:25:563–576.

55. Stagno S, Pass RF, Dworsky MD, et al. Congenital cytomegalovirus infection: the relative importance of primary and recurrent maternal infection. *N Engl J Med.* 1982;306:945–949.

56. Pass RF, August AM, Dworsky M, et al. Cytomegalovirus infection in a day care center. *N Engl J Med.* 1982;307:477–479.

57. Hutto C, Ricks RE, Pass RF. Prevalence of cytomegalovirus excretion from children in five day care centers. *JAMA.* 1985;253:1236–1240.

58. Hutto C, Ricks R, Garvie M, Pass RF. Epidemiology of cytomegalovirus infections in young children: day care vs. home care. *Pediatr Infect Dis.* 1985; 4:149–152.

59. Adler SP. The molecular epidemiology of cytomegalovirus transmission among children attending a day care center. *J Infect Dis.* 1985;152:760–769.

60. Pass RF, Hutto SC, Reynolds DW, et al. Increased frequency of cytomegalovirus infection in children in group day care. *Pediatrics.* 1984;74:121–126.

61. Pass RF, Hutto C. Group day care and cytomegaloviral infections of mothers and children. *Rev Infect Dis.* 1986;8:599–605.

62. Adler SP. Molecular epidemiology of cytomegalovirus: evidence for viral transmission to parents from children infected at a day care center. *Pediatr Infect Dis.* 1986;5:315–318.

63. Grillner L, Strangert K. Restriction endonuclease analysis of cytomegalovirus DNA from strains isolated in day care centers. *Pediatr Infect Dis.* 1986;5:184–187.

64. Hutto C, Little A, Ricks R, et al. Isolation of cytomegalovirus from toys and hands in a day care center. *J Infect Dis.* 1986;154:527–530.

65. Murph JR, Bale JF, Murray JC, et al. Cytomegalovirus transmission in a midwest day care center: possible relationship to child care practices. *J Pediatr.* 1986;109:35–39.

66. Yeager AS. Transmission of cytomegalovirus to mothers by infected infants: another reason to prevent transfusion-acquired infections. *Pediatr Infect Dis.* 1983;2:295–297.

67. Spector SA, Spector DH. Molecular epidemiology of cytomegalovirus infection in premature twin infants and their mother. *Pediatr Infect Dis.* 1982;1:403–409.

68. Pass RF, Hutto C, Ricks R, Cloud GA. Increased rate of cytomegalovirus infection among parents of children attending day care centers. *N Engl J Med.* 1986;314:1414–1418.

69. Pass RF, Hutto C, Cloud G. Day care workers and cytomegalovirus infection. *Clin Res.* 1988;36:65A.

70. Adler SP. Risk of cytomegalovirus infection among women employed at day care centers. *Pediatr Res.* 1988;23:362A.

71. Stagno RF, Little EA, Stagno S, et al. Young children as a probable source of maternal and congenital cytomegalovirus infection. *N Engl J Med.* 1987;316: 1366–1370.

72. Stagno S, Pass RF, Cloud C, et al. Primary cytomegalovirus infection in pregnancy: incidence, transmission to the fetus and clinical outcome in two populations of different economic backgrounds. *JAMA.* 1986;256:1904–1908.

73. Ahlfors K, Ivarson SA, Harris S, et al. Congenital cytomegalovirus infection and disease in Sweden and the relative importance of primary and secondary maternal infections. Primary findings from a prospective study. *Scand J Inf Dis.* 1984;16:129–137.

74. Griffiths PD, Baboonian C. A prospective study of primary cytomegalovirus infection during pregnancy: final report. *Br J Obstet Gynecol.* 1984;91:307–315.

75. Stagno S, Reynolds DW, Huang E-S, et al. Congenital cytomegalovirus infection. *N Engl J Med.* 1977; 296:1254–1258.

76. Shapiro CN, McCaig LF, Genesheimer KF, et al. Hepatitis B virus transmission between children in day care. *Pediatr Infect Dis.* 1989;8:870–875.

77. Shapiro ED. Lack of transmission of hepatitis B in a day care center. *J Pediatr.* 1987;110:90–92.

78. Task Force on Pediatric AIDS. Pediatric guidelines for infection control of human immunodeficiency virus (acquired immunodeficiency virus) in hospitals, medical offices, schools and other settings. *Pediatrics.* 1988;82:801–808.

79. MacDonald KL, Danila RN, Osterholm MT. Infection with human T-lymphotrophic virus type III/lymphadenopathy-associated virus: considerations for transmission in the child day care setting. *Rev Infect Dis.* 1986;8:606–612.

80. Centers for Disease Control. Education and foster care of children infected with human T-lymphotrophic virus type III/lymphadenopathy-associated virus. *MMWR.* 1985;34:517–521.

81. Immunization of children infected with human immunodeficiency virus—supplementary ACIP statement. *MMWR.* 1988;37:181–183.

82. Measles in HIV-infected children, United States. *MMWR.* 1988;37:183–186.

CHAPTER 7

Children with Special Needs

CHAPTER 7
CHILDREN WITH SPECIAL NEEDS

7.1 Introduction and Background

Historically, children with special needs*—including developmentally disabled, mentally retarded, and emotionally disturbed children; those with sensory or motor impairments; and chronically ill children—have been provided preschool, after-school, and child care programs in segregated settings, separate and apart from other children receiving these services or care. However, the past two decades have witnessed an unequivocal trend toward integrating those with disabilities into the mainstream of society. In this context, deinstitutionalization, normalization, and services in the "least restrictive environment" are terms that have been developed, espoused, utilized, and translated into the goals of achieving integration of persons with special needs into all aspects of social and community life.

In the area of child care, when available at all, separate facilities and programs for children with special needs have been the dominant mode of service delivery. Any philosophical or attitudinal biases that hindered more integrated programmatic approaches have been bolstered by realistic concerns about how best to service children with disabilities who may require special equipment, special programs, special handling, and specially trained staff to care for them.

A major thrust toward the development and implementation of services for children with special needs was the result of landmark legislation passed in 1976—P.L. 94-142 (the Education for All Handicapped Children Act[1]) and reauthorized in 1990 as P.L. 101-476 (the Individuals with Disabilities Education Act[2]). This legislation mandated a free, appropriate public education for all children with disabilities and special needs, irrespective of the degree of disability, with the aim of offering services to as many children as possible in "the least restrictive environment." The latter refers to incorporating children with special needs in the same schools with children without disabilities, and, if at all possible, in the same classrooms. As a result, school programs—both separate and integrated—have expanded for children with special needs, and an increasing number of children (currently around 4.3 million) are receiving specialized services, predominantly in public school programs. P.L. 94-142 included a provision for services to preschool-age children from ages 3 to 5 years. Many states decided to provide early intervention services for younger children, including, in some instances, those identified soon after birth as being disabled.

Of major importance was the passage of P.L. 99-457,[3] the Early Intervention Amendment to P.L. 94-142, which mandates services for all 3-to-5-year-old children with disabilities and provides in Part H of the legislation the option, through federal funding incentives, for states to offer early intervention services for children from 0 to 2 years (or 0 to 3 years) of age with disabilities and their families. States define the populations eligible for services, and have the option to serve the "at risk" populations within their definitions of eligibility.

Clearly, P.L. 99-457 is of major importance to the future of child care services, since it will provide fiscal incentives and will result in regulations that will affect how care and services are provided to young children with identified disabilities, plus those defined in each state as being in the "at risk" category. It is obvious, given the thrust of P.L. 99-457 to develop services to meet the needs of both the child and family (through what is called an Individualized Family Service Plan—IFSP), that child care services for the population of children with special needs must be a developmental program, as it should be for all children, with specialized therapeutic or multidisciplinary services a required element to be provided to the children with special needs when attending either separate or integrated programs, whether they are home-based or center-based.

A review of the development of national child care standards, the history of which was described in the Introduction to this document, indicates that these standards have been generic and have paid little attention to the unique requirements of children with special needs. Various sections of the 1972 draft Federal Day Care Requirements[4] emphasized the need to "develop mental abilities," to "contribute to physical development and health," and to ensure that "each child receives psychological and mental health evaluations and treatment for significant problems identified." However, specific programmatic issues for children with special needs are not mentioned. The 1980 Department of Health, Education and Welfare Day Care Regulations,[5] published in the Federal Register, require the state agency overseeing child care to implement a statewide plan for training caregivers, including training in "day care for handicapped children," but provide no specific guidance as to how specialized care, services, and provider training should be offered to ensure that children with disabilities and other special needs are to be satisfactorily served. Therefore, the current guidelines for children with special needs must

---

*The term *children with special needs* refers to those children with developmental disabilities, mental retardation, emotional disturbance, sensory or motor impairment, or significant chronic illness who require special health surveillance or specialized programs, interventions, technologies, or facilities.

draw heavily on the principles and practices used in high-quality child care programs and in the implementation of the federal special education legislation.

In principle, we encourage complete mainstreaming of children with special needs into the general child care setting with the least restrictive environment. For the convenience of the reader, the adaptations needed by facilities serving children with special needs are consolidated into this one chapter. However, these standards are applicable across all settings as appropriate. The standards in chapters 1, 2, 4, 5, 6, 8, and 9 reflect basic principles of care for all children and are the foundation to which the standards in chapter 7 should be added. All of these components are essential if the individual needs of the children are to be addressed. This also applies to the Guiding Principles enumerated in the Introduction. The Technical Panel on Children with Special Needs (see Introduction), however, wishes to emphasize the importance of Guiding Principles 6 and 28–33 on pp. xxv and xxvii.

7.2 Integration of Children with Special Needs Into the Child Care Setting

STANDARDS

CSN1. Facilities shall integrate children with disabilities and children without disabilities.

CSN2. Integration shall be assisted by the preparation of children without disabilities, parents, and staff to facilitate having the children with special needs participate at their facility.

RATIONALE

The goal is care in the least restrictive environment (P.L. 94-142 and P.L. 99-457).[1,3]

Mainstreaming without adequate preparation may lead to failure.

COMMENTS

It is recognized that some children—such as those with severe disabilities, including the technology-dependent child, and children with serious and severe chronic medical problems—may be difficult to integrate fully into child care settings. However, every attempt should be made to achieve integration.

There are many available funding mechanisms to supplement funding for services in the facility that should all be pursued. These sources could include Medicaid (Title XIX), private insurance, or state/federal funds for Children with Special Health Care Needs (Title V). Contracts help define the responsibilities of all parties.

The utilization of age-appropriate resources (including, but not limited to, puppet shows, brochures, books, guest speakers, and parents of the children with special needs) should be a component of any education program. Methods may vary with need and availability.

Opportunities should be provided to discuss the similarities as well as the differences among all the children enrolled. Such discussions are useful preparatory exercises that can be assisted by including parents in the group discussions.

It is helpful to have presentations and discussions about the special equipment that the children with special needs may require and use. The children without disabilities should be given the opportunity to explore and learn about these items.

applies to a small family-child-care home   [A] applies to a large family-child-care home   applies to a center.
If no symbol appears, the standard applies to all three.

7.3 Evaluation Process Prior to Enrolling at a Facility

STANDARDS	RATIONALE	COMMENTS

THE INITIAL ASSESSMENT

CSN3. A written multidisciplinary evaluation of the child and family shall be conducted before the child starts in the facility. This evaluation shall consist, at a minimum, of results of medical and developmental examinations, assessments of the child's cognitive functioning or current overall functioning, and evaluations of the family's needs, concerns, and priorities, as well as other evaluations as needed.

The definitive characteristic of services for children with special needs is the necessity of individualizing their care to meet these needs. Therefore, individual assessments must precede services.

This comprehensive assessment need not be carried out by the facility itself, but could be done largely by an outside center, clinic, or professional who conducts such evaluations. However, this evaluation forms the basis of planning for the child's needs in the child care setting and for the pertinent information available to the facility staff.

CSN4. The family assessment shall focus only on those aspects of family functioning that are relevant to the provision of services to the child and that optimize the child's development.

The family's needs, values, and child rearing practices are highly relevant to the provision of care to the child; however, the special needs of the child continue to be the central focus of intervention.

Seeking services for their children should not expose families to unwarranted intrusion into their lives.

CSN5. The initial assessment shall indicate how often and by whom the identified services will be provided. The facility shall involve parents in this process. (See standard CSN13, on p. 242 on informing parents.)

In order to serve children with varying types and severity of disability, a flexible approach in combining and delivering services is desirable.

In facilities that are not primarily designed to serve a population with special needs, the additional therapeutic services may be obtained through consultants or arrangements with outside programs for special needs.

INFORMATION EXCHANGE PROCEDURES

CSN6. The facility shall develop a written procedure, prior to initiating services, for obtaining necessary medical information to meet health standards (e.g., immunizations) and for implementing the program. (See *Child Health Services*, on p. 276, and *Information Exchange*, on p. 248.) This information includes the background diagnostic information and health and social history. (See Appendix C, item B, on p. 331.)

The facility needs accurate, current information on the medical status and treatment of the child in order to determine the facility's capability to provide needed services or to obtain them elsewhere.

The written procedure should adhere to general standards for child care and include additional relevant information for children with special needs.

CSN7. Information shall be sought on all therapies and treatments being provided to the child along with the anticipated length and frequency of expected services.

See rationale for standard CSN6.

Records of evaluations, follow-ups, and contacts with service providers are vital for children with special needs.

STANDARDS	RATIONALE	COMMENTS
CSN8. To document the requirements in standards CSN6 and CSN7, the facility shall obtain and keep records of the child's immunization and health history, treatments, prescribed medications, and any special procedures or precautions that the child may require. (See Appendix C, item B, on p. 331.)	This record must be available to staff at the facility so that they may both appropriately care for the child and deal with special therapeutic needs, including those required on an emergency basis.	Appropriate files of information, including medical records, should be maintained on all children.

PROCEDURES TO ENSURE CONFIDENTIALITY

See *Confidentiality and Access to Records*, on p. 288.

PARENTAL PARTICIPATION

CSN9. Parental participation in the process of evaluating the child and making decisions about services shall be required by the facility and shall be documented. Parents shall be explicitly invited to participate in all such decision-making activities and their presence at these meetings or invitations to attend shall be documented in writing.	Parental observations and reports about the child and expectations for the child must be recognized, as well as the family's need for child care services, in order to provide services effectively.	Parental participation in the planning of the developmental and educational program for the child should be integral to the process of evaluation by professionals and in the formulation of any plans for the child. Parental participation is basic to the development and implementation of IFSPs. A marked discrepancy between professional and parental observations of, or expectations for, a child necessitates further discussion and development of a consensus on a plan of action.
CSN10. Parental participation shall include caregivers' learning about parental expectations and goals and integrating this information into the IFSP.	See rationale for standard CSN9.	
 CSN11. Parent association groups and parent support mechanisms shall be established. These shall be documented and shall include, when possible, intraagency activities; if necessary, these activities shall be coordinated with those offered by other community support groups. Parental participation in such activities shall be recorded in the child's facility record. (See Appendix C, item F, on p. 335.)	Parental involvement at every level of program planning and delivery and parent support groups are elements that are usually beneficial to the children, parents, and staff of the facility. The parent association group facilitates mutual understanding between the center and parents. Parental involvement also helps to broaden parents' knowledge of administration of the facility and develop and enhance advocacy efforts.	Parent meetings and group counseling are useful means of communication within a facility that supplement mailings and indirect contacts.

STANDARDS

CSN12. Parents shall be informed about programs and sources of information that will improve their capability as advocates; they shall be referred to local advocacy training groups or workshops, if available, particularly if the caregiver does not directly offer these services. Such referrals shall be documented in writing.

For additional information on parental participation, see also *Parental Involvement*, on p. 58, and *Health Information Sharing*, on p. 59.

THE INFORMING PROCESS

CSN13. When an evaluation is done at the facility, the parents shall be informed of the results and given an opportunity to discuss and present alternative perspectives. The exchange must be documented.

CSN14. The formulation of an action plan for each child shall be based on this informing process (see standard CSN5, on p. 240). Such a plan shall be written and shall be maintained as a part of each child's record.

For additional information on the informing process, see also *Parental Involvement*, on p. 58.

RATIONALE

Such referrals will make parents more effective advocates.

Parents need to have accurate information about their child's disability.

An evaluation of a child is completed only when the information has been discussed with the parent.

Results must be sensitively and honestly explained to parents without using technical jargon.[6]

COMMENTS

Advocacy training can be provided by a service provider or an outside agency.

Parents need to be included in the process of shaping decisions about their children. They have both the motive and the legal right to be included in the decision-making process and to seek other opinions. (See report language of P.L.99-457[3] on parents' role in the IFSP and the regulations published in the *Federal Register*, June 22, 1989.[7])

Parents who contest or disagree with the results of an evaluation should have the information weighed and considered in future planning for the child. A second independent opinion can also be offered to the family to confirm the original evaluation, though extensive "shopping" for a more desirable or favorable opinion should be discouraged.

7.4 Developing a Service Plan for a Child with Special Needs

STANDARDS

RATIONALE

COMMENTS

DEVELOPMENT OF THE PLAN

CSN15. Each child and family identified shall have an IFSP developed within 45 days of eligibility determination and/or admission to the facility. The plan can be developed through local agencies (such as the state's designated lead agency for P.L.99-457, the Department of Human Services, the Department of Health, or the Area Education Agency), with child care services and goals being addressed.

The IFSP is necessary to ensure that the child and family receive appropriate services in a timely fashion and that the delivery of services is organized in such a way as to maximize benefits received from the resources used.[3]

Without a comprehensive plan of care, the child may experience preventable setbacks in health and/or developmental status. Similarly, without a comprehensive plan of care, resources may be used inefficiently and facility administrators will not be able to allocate and plan for the resources necessary to meet the service needs of eligible children and families.

To be most effective, as recommended in P.L. 99-457, the plan must include components that help the parent and the child.[3, 7]

The child care facility need not be the agency that develops and implements all components of the plan, but it clearly should participate in its development and in the child care component of the implementation. Assessments may be the financial responsibility of a state agency, such as the Department of Education or the Department of Health. It is hoped that funding available through the implementation of P.L. 99-457 will provide resources to assist in implementing the IFSP.

CSN16. The IFSP shall be developed in collaboration with the family, representatives from disciplines and organizations involved with the child and family, the child's health care provider, and the staff of the facility, depending on the family's wishes and the resources of the agency.

For the IFSP to provide systematic guidance of the child's developmental achievement and to promote efficient service delivery, service providers from all of the involved disciplines/settings must be familiar with the overall multi- or interdisciplinary plans and work toward the same goals for the child.

To be optimally effective, one comprehensive IFSP is developed and one care coordinator is designated to oversee the implementation of the plan (see *Documentation* and *Case Management*, on p. 246). Further, to foster and enhance the family's role and participation, and to obtain the best possible evaluation and plan, the parents or legal guardian (or other family caregivers) should be partners in the development and implementation of the IFSP.

The IFSP's development and implementation is a team effort.

Components of the IFSP may include those developed to meet service needs (i.e., Individualizeed Education Plan or health service plan) developed elsewhere, when applicable in the child care setting.

Note again that the child care facility should be involved in the process, but this does not mean that it is in charge of the process, unless it is so designated and provided the necessary resources by the lead agency for P.L. 99-457.

See also the comment for standard CSN15.

CSN17. One person shall be designated in the child care setting who shall be responsible for coordinating care in the facility and with any caregiver or coordinators in other service settings in accordance with the written IFSP.

It is most effective when one staff member is responsible for coordinating all elements of services. This avoids confusion and allows easier and more consistent communication with the family.

See also the comment for standard CSN15.

STANDARDS

CSN18. To ensure carryover to the home environment, there shall be a plan for the family to observe, participate in, and be trained in the aspects of care the family must provide and must carry over into the home environment.

CS19. Facilities shall have a *Program of Activities*, on p. 286, including special interventions for children with special needs and any special restriction(s) of activities.

For additional information on development of the plan, see also *Program of Activities*, on p. 286.

MEASURABLE OBJECTIVES IN THE PLAN

CSN20. The IFSP shall include long-range service plans that are based on measurable outcome objectives for the child's health and developmental achievement. Services, along with the designated responsibility for provision and financing, shall be delineated for each outcome objective.

CSN21. Each measurable outcome objective in the IFSP shall include a specific date when the objective is to be reassessed.

RATIONALE

This plan will help achieve the important goal of carryover of facility components from the child care setting to the child's home environment. The child's learning of new skills is a continuous process occurring both at home and in child care.

When measurable outcome objectives form the basis for the IFSP, the family and service providers jointly formulate the expected and desired outcomes for the child and family.

By using measurable outcome objectives rather than service units, all interested parties can concentrate on how well the child is achieving the outcome objectives. Thus, for example, the progress toward speech development assumes more importance than the number of hours of speech therapy provided. Further, measurable outcome objectives constitute an individualized approach to meeting the needs of the child and family, and as such can be integrated into, but are not solely dependent upon, the array of services that happen to be available in a particular geographic area.

The measurable outcome objectives will provide the facility with a meaningful framework for enhancing the child's health and developmental status on an ongoing basis.

Regularly scheduled reassessments of the outcome objectives provide the family and service providers with a framework for anticipating changes in the kind of services that may be needed, the financial requirements for providing the services, and identification of the appropriate service provider.

COMMENTS

There is reason to have a mutual exchange of information about child care techniques that may also involve parents instructing staff about special techniques they use at home for their children.

The defining of measurable goals provides a useful structure for facility staff and aids in the assessment of the progress of the child and the appropriateness of the components of the IFSP.

Though this principle should apply to all children in all settings, the implementation, especially in small and large family-child-care homes, will require ongoing assistance from, and the participation of, specialists, including those connected with programs outside of the child care setting, in order to provide the needed services.

See the comment on sources of training and technical assistance in standard CSN44, o n p. 252. See also the comment for standard CSN15, on p. 243.

Many facilities that provide treatment review the child's progress at least every 3 months (see *Program Review*, on p. 245). This is not a comprehensive review, but an analysis of the progress toward meeting objectives.

Generally, the entire plan and the child's progress receive a comprehensive review annually.

STANDARDS	RATIONALE	COMMENTS

It is likely that caregivers will need training on development of goals and the means of assessing progress (see the second and third comments for standard CSN20 above).

PROGRAM REVIEW

CSN22. There shall be a review of treatment and the child's progress every 3 months, with a full case review each year and documentation of this review. Treatment reviews shall involve the staff or persons providing the intervention and supervision, the parents, and independent observers.

Such reviews are mandated for programs serving the developmentally disabled and are also applicable here.

See the comment for standard CSN20 concerning the role of outside specialists in assisting small family-child-care homes.

CSN23. The interim dates for monitoring ongoing progress toward achievement of the objective shall also be included in the plan.

This practice ensures regular scheduling of reviews.

See comment on standard CSN22.

CSN24. Persons responsible for the monitoring shall be designated for each objective.

This practice ensures assignment of responsibility and continuity.

CONTRACTS AND REIMBURSEMENTS

CSN25. Arrangements shall be made with health, education, social services, and mental health agencies or providers to offer required specialized services when the personnel or staff needed to provide such services are not regular members of the facility's staff.

To achieve maximum benefit from services, those services should be provided in the setting most convenient for the child and family.

Whenever possible, the services should be provided by treatment specialists (e.g., therapists) in the facility where the child receives daytime care. Further, funding through public and private payers should be available to child care centers to reimburse the services delineated in the IFSP.

Such arrangements can be made by the agency that has evaluated the child and/or is planning the entire IFSP, or by the facility.

Different arrangements may be applicable in different settings. This principle is difficult to implement outside of centers, but would apply to some situations in large and small family-child-care homes. Specialists could be made available in any child care setting without requiring the facility to have a formal contractual relationship with the provider. However, in order to document such a relationship, a written confirmation of an arrangement would be useful. Contractual relationships are the optimal means of ensuring these relationships.

Families may also make their own formal or informal arrangements with other agencies for such services.

See also the second comment for standard CSN1 on p. 239.

7.5 Coordination of Services

DOCUMENTATION

CSN26. The facility shall be an integral component of the child's overall service plan. Services for all children shall be coordinated in a systematic manner so that the facility can document all of the services the child is receiving inside of the facility and is aware of the services the child is receiving outside of the facility.

Coordination of services is a fundamental component in the implementation of a plan for care of a child with special needs. This is particularly true of the need to coordinate the medical care with specialized developmental services, therapies, and child care procedures in the facility.

One of the most problematic areas in special education has been coordination of "related services" with the educational components.[8] In child care for children with special needs, such coordination is essential.

CASE MANAGEMENT

CSN27. A care coordinator from the facility staff shall be assigned for each child with special needs attending a facility. This individual shall be responsible for internal coordination of the child's and family's program and for ensuring a liaison with outside agencies or care providers.

There must be a single locus of responsibility for coordination; therefore, each child should have a care coordinator assigned at the time the IFSP is developed.

This requirement does not preclude outside agencies or care providers from having their own care coordinator or case manager. The intent is to ensure communication and coordination among different care providers for the child, both in the facility and elsewhere in the community.

The person who coordinates care within the facility will usually not be the person assigned to coordinate care or provide overall case management for the child and family. However, the facility may assume both roles if it so chooses.

A format and framework should be established for case management activities. The components and the role may vary; they will be determined by each facility and may depend on the roles and responsibilities of the staff member in the facility and those responsibilities assumed by the family and care providers in the community.

CSN28. The care coordinator shall have documented qualifications and experience to indicate that he/she has experience and training in coordinating services. This individual shall work in a cooperative or collaborative manner with an assigned care coordinator from another agency or may, in some instances, be designated as the care coordinator (or case manager) for the child and family, depending on both the family's wishes and the facility's resources.

It is expected that facilities serving children with special needs have professional staff who will be assigned to service coordination roles.

Standards for developmental disability (DD) programs have assigned this role to qualified DD specialists who include licensed or certified professionals in social work, special education, and so forth. Specialists to assume this role have also been defined by other programs including Title V (Children with Special Health Care Needs) and educational facilities.

The assignment of the care coordinator (or case manager) may vary depending on the skills of the individual and the specific needs of the child and family; different expertise may be needed in different situations (see standard CSN16 on p. 243). The specific care coordinator may vary from case to case, depending on the child's and the family's needs (e.g., a family with social problems, as opposed to one with other major problems, might benefit from more social work input and coordination).

Small and large family home caregivers may utilize a care coordinator from outside of their facility. (See second and third comments for

STANDARDS	RATIONALE	COMMENTS

standard CSN20 on p. 244 concerning the use of outside specialists.)

Training in care coordination (or case management) is a useful preparation for this role.

This care coordinator is not the same as the IFSP care coordinator. However, the facility may assume this role if it so chooses.

CSN29. Caregivers in small and large family-child-care homes shall be fully informed about the entire IFSP and the plans for its implementation. The IFSP shall be a component of the child's record (see Appendix C, on p. 330) in the facility.

A responsible person at these child care settings must be in a position to coordinate and/or participate in the plans.

This standard permits coordination with outside providers (see standard CSN28).

CSN30. The facility's care co-ordinator shall be responsible for ensuring that the components of the IFSP relevant to the facility are implemented.

The care coordinator does not have responsibility for directly implementing all program components, but is accountable for checking on whether the plans in the facility are being carried out.

The care coordinator functions as an advocate to encourage the implementation of the service plan and to help obtain or gain access to services.

The care coordinator (or case manager) may have a programmatic role for the child and family, but is assigned the responsibility for the coordination of care in the facility, and for establishing liaison with outside agencies that provide components of the IFSP and the adjunctive services that may be required (see standard CSN28 above).

Care coordination outside of the facility is likely to be handled by another person or agency, as specified by the lead agency for P.L. 99-457 or its designee (this may vary from state to state). This care coordinator is not the same as the IFSP care coordinator. However, the facility may assume this role if it so chooses.

COORDINATION WITH OUTSIDE AGENCIES

CSN31. Services must be coordinated not only within the facility but with service providers outside of the child care setting, and documentation for this coordination shall be available. (See also standard CSN30 on the facility's care coordinator.)

A responsible person at these child care settings must be in a position to coordinate and/or participate in the plans. This is the role of the care coordinator.

A role is outlined that a specific person is designated to fill. Specific forms, format, and procedures are the purview of the regulatory agency and/or the individual program.

CSN32. Components and services that require direct contacts between the caregiver and other service programs for all children shall include
a) Sources of regular medical care— the child's health care provider and medical facility.
b) Source of emergency services, when required.
c) Special clinics the child may attend, including sessions with medical specialists and registered dietitians.
d) Special therapists for the child (e.g., occupational, physical, speech, nutrition). Written documentation of the services provided shall be obtained from all care providers or therapists.
e) Counselors, therapists, or mental health service providers for parents (e.g., social workers, psychologists, psychiatrists). "Direct" contact between the caregiver and these service providers is not required.

Knowing who is treating the child and coordinating services with these individuals is vital to program implementation.

Every child should have a health care provider and/or medical facility that provides primary care.

Every child care facility should have emergency medical backup.

There should be a liaison with special clinics for specific disabilities and illnesses when children are seen for consultation at these units.

There must be coordination between services provided on site at the facility and those offered at another site.[8]

Sharing of information is best in writing, but telephone contacts are also helpful.

Regular contacts between professionals working with the child and family served by the child care facility can only improve coordination of care, minimizing confusion for the family and avoiding duplication. However, strict adherence to guidelines concerning confidentiality must be observed.

Documentation of special therapy is necessary for monitoring purposes.

These therapies may be provided by private therapists or by clinics or centers specializing in offering such services.

There may also be a need to share some social and psychological data, within the limits of discretion and confidentiality.

CSN33. Written mechanisms shall be established to communicate with other care providers for the child in order to ensure a coordinated, coherent service plan. Shared information may include, but is not limited to, information about staff conferences, written reports, consultations and other services provided.

Other care providers include babysitters, grandparents, or neighbors— those who spend considerable time with the child and who need to know and understand the aims and goals of the treatment plan.

With more than half of all mothers in the work force, it is common for caretakers other than the parents to spend considerable time with the children. These caretakers must know what special procedures are required; otherwise, there will be no carryover of program approaches to the home environment.

For additional information on coordination with outside agencies, see also chapter *Consultants and Technical Assistance for Children with Special Needs,* on p. 315. For transportation services, see the standards in *Transportation,* on p. 199.

INFORMATION EXCHANGE

CSN34. Written reports shall be available on ISFP's, conferences, and treatments provided, as confidentiality allows.

Written documentation ensures better accountability.

CSN35. Conference reports, IFSP's, and follow-up reports shall be shared, as needed, with other service providers, including specialized agencies providing services, as confidentiality guidelines or state laws permit.

This sharing of information is essential to service coordination.

For additional information on information exchange, see also *Confidentiality and Access to Records,* including obtaining written releases, on p. 288.

COORDINATION WITH AND AMONG PARENTS

See *Parent Relationships*, on p. 55.

7.6 Implementation of Service Plans

This section focuses primarily on services to be provided in centers with optimally integrated programs for children with and without disabilities. The Technical Panel on Children with Special Needs (see the Introduction) would prefer to see that all caregivers working with children with special needs meet all of the qualifications and standards listed below. However, these standards are most clearly applicable to centers with a significant number of children attending. (To assist in clarifying the questions of what is applicable to children with special needs in small family-child-care homes, see *Small Family-Child-Care Homes*, on p. 254.)

Financial resources may be obtained from the state's mechanism to implement P.L. 99-457, Medicaid (Title XIX), and state/federal funding for Children with Special Health Care Needs (Title V).

CENTER-BASED ADMINISTRATION

CSN36. The director of a center that includes children with special needs shall have the following qualifications, in addition to those general qualifications described in *Qualifications of Directors*, on p. 4.

The administrative responsibilities in directing a center serving children with special needs are substantial; given the complexities of the system of services for children with special needs and legislative requirements, this section attempts to outline the types of training and expertise required to administer such a facility.

The general APHA/AAP standards, as well as state and local regulations for facility administrators in regular child care, may apply but may need supplementation due to the special requirements of the populations of children with special needs.

a) Coursework or experience in administration as specified in *Qualifications of Directors of Centers,* on p. 4.

These are general qualificatons for leading a center. Running a center requires appropriate business skills.

A knowledge of a computerized accounting system is a desirable skill but may not be necessary in all cases. This knowledge should include the use of a personal computer and spreadsheet, balance and income statements, and billing options.

b) A knowledge of community resources that are available to children with special needs and the ability to utilize these resources for the purpose of making referrals or achieving interagency coordination. (See also *Use of Community Health Resources*, on p. 59.)

This special requirement is necessary if a facility director is to be effective.

The center is but one component in a network of services for children with special needs in most communities.

Every state participating in Part H of P.L. 99-457 is required to have a statewide Directory of Services for use. Having a Directory of Services available is useful and could fulfill part of the requirement. Many communities have agencies, such as local resource and referral agencies, that gather such information and publish directories that could be used.

STANDARDS

c) Coursework in child development and early childhood education, as specified in standard ST6 in chapter 1 on p. 4. A special education degree is useful but not mandatory.

d) A valid certificate in pediatric first aid, including rescue breathing and first aid for choking, as specified in *First Aid and CPR*, on p. 22.

e) Valid certification in infant and child cardiopulmonary resuscitation (CPR) as specified in *First Aid and CPR*, on p. 22.

f) Demonstrated life experience skills in working with children in any setting.

For additional information on center-based administration, see also *Qualifications of Directors,* on p. 4, on additional director qualifications.

DIRECT CARE AND PROVISIONAL STAFF

CSN37. In addition to the staffing requirements in *Child:Staff Ratio and Group Size*, on p. 1, centers enrolling children with special needs must have full-time equivalent staff to ensure a ratio of one staff member for every three children with special needs attending the facility.

RATIONALE

Basic knowledge of child development is a prerequisite for the care of all children. The presence of a degree in special education can add weight but is not seen as a requirement for administering a center serving children with special needs.

An understanding of the principles of early childhood education is essential to the leader of a center.

It is essential that the child:staff ratio allow the needs of the children enrolled to be met.

The facility should have sufficient direct care and professional staff to provide the required programs and services.

COMMENTS

Life experience may include experience raising one's own children or previous personal experience acquired in any child care setting. Work as a hospital aide or at a camp for children with special needs would qualify, as would experience in school settings. However, this experience must be supplemented by competency-based training (see *Preservice, Orientation, and Training Standards* and *Continuing Education* on pp. 252 and 254) to determine and provide whatever new skills are needed to care for children with special needs in child care settings.

These ratios do not include other personnel (e.g., bus drivers) necessary for specialized functions (e.g., transportation).

Integrated facilities with fewer resources may be able to serve children who need fewer services, and the staffing levels may vary accordingly. This is a minimum standard and does not preclude lower ratios of children with special needs to staff in cases that may require such ratios.

This ratio allows for the flexibility needed regarding the child's type of special need and degree of disability. The center may wish to increase the number of staff if the child has a severe disability(ies) or requires special assistance.

CSN38. In addition to *Qualifications of Teaching/Caregiving Staff*, on p. 8, and Appendix A, on p. 323, facilities serving children with special needs shall have one licensed/certified teacher (see *Individual Licensure/Certification*, on p. 301) who is certified in special education. Compliance is met if one caregiver is certified in special education and meets the requirements for a teacher or lead teacher as described in Appendix A, on p. 8.

A background in early childhood education is viewed as an essential requirement for a group of this age.

Both early childhood and special educational experience are required in a center, especially an integrated one.

CSN39. In order to deal with nutritional issues and special feeding procedures, a center shall have support staff including food service staff as specified in Appendix M, on p. 356 and a child care Nutrition Specialist (see Appendices B-1 and B-2, on pp. 328–329) or a registered nurse with training and/or experience in dietary and feeding requirements of children with special needs.

Having a cook on the staff ensures that the teachers have time to work with the children and need not leave the classroom to prepare food.

Integrated facilities with fewer resources may be able to serve children who need fewer services, and the staffing levels may vary accordingly. The support staff may not necessarily consist of full-time or regular staff members, but may include some personnel hired on a consulting or contractual basis.

CSN40. If medically fragile children are included in the facility, a registered nurse shall be employed on a full- or part-time basis to provide staff training and ongoing supervision of staff as well as children and to administer medication.

An on-site health care professional must be available to assess and manage the needs of medically fragile children.

CSN41. Staff or documented consultants shall include professionals knowledgeable in the field of developmental disabilities. These professionals shall include, but shall not be limited to, a physician, a registered dietitian, a registered nurse or pediatric nurse practitioner, a psychologist, a physical therapist, an occupational therapist, a speech pathologist, a social worker, and a parent of a child with special needs.

Consumer input is a valuable component of all such facilities.

The range of professionals needed may vary with the facility, but the listed professionals should be available as consultants when needed.

As noted earlier, such professionals need not be actual staff members of the facility, but may simply be available when needed through a variety of arrangements, including contracts, agreements, and affiliations.

For additional information on direct care and provisional staff, see *Special Procedures*, on p. 261, for additional requirements on nurses.

For qualifications of other staff, see Appendix A, on p. 8, and the follow-

STANDARDS	RATIONALE	COMMENTS

ing chapters: *Qualifications of Assistant Teachers and Associate Teachers*, on p. 12; *Qualifications of Aides*, on p. 12; *Qualifications of Health Advocates*, on p. 13.

See also *Health Consultation*, on p. 278, *Consultation Records*, on p. 295, and *Health Consultants*, on p. 33, on health consultant qualifications, responsibilities, visits, and plans.

See standard CSN45 on pediatric first aid certification and standard CSN46 on infant and child CPR certification requirements on p. 253.

PRESERVICE, ORIENTATION, AND TRAINING STANDARDS

CSN42. When centers and large family-child-care homes enroll children with special needs, the director shall ensure that staff have been oriented in understanding children with special needs and in ways of working with these children in group settings (in addition to *General Training*, on p. 18, and *Orientation Training*, on p. 19.)

A basic understanding of developmental disabilities and special care requirements is a fundamental part of any orientation for new employees.

See the comment for standard CSN44.

CSN43. Caregivers in small family-child-care homes who offer care for one or more children with special needs shall participate in an orientation about the child's special needs and how these needs may affect his/her developmental progression or play with other children (in addition to *General Training*, on p. 18, and *Orientation Training*, on p. 19.)

This preservice requirement is necessary to ensure that knowledgeable personnel are caring for the child.

See the comment for standard CSN44.

CSN44. In addition to *General Training, Preservice Qualifications,* and *Orientation Training*, on pp. 18–19, staff in facilities serving children with special needs shall have orientation training based on the special needs of children in their care. This training may include, but is not limited to, the following topics:
a) Positioning for feeding and handling techniques of children with physical disabilities.

A comprehensive curriculum is required to ensure quality services.

Training is an essential component to ensure that staff develop and maintain the needed skills.

These training topics are generally applicable to all staff serving children with special needs, and apply to such staff in facilities. The curriculum may vary depending on the type of facility, types of disabilities of the children in the facility, and the ages of the children.

It is assumed that staff will have the training described in *General Training, Preservice Qualifications,* and *Orientation Training*, on pp. 18–19, including child growth and development, and that these topics will

b) How different disabilities affect the child's ability to participate in group activities.

c) Methods of helping the child with special needs to participate in the facility's programs.

d) Role modeling, peer socialization, and interaction.

e) Behavior modification techniques, positive rewards for children, and promotion of self-esteem.

f) Grouping of children by skill levels.

g) Intervention for children with special health care problems.

CSN45. Facilities that serve children with special needs shall have at least one caregiver certified in infant and child CPR present whenever children with special needs are in care, as specified in *First Aid and CPR*, on p. 22.

CSN46. All staff involved in the provision of direct care shall be certified in pediatric first aid, including rescue breathing and first aid for choking, as specified in *First Aid and CPR*, on p. 22.

For additional information on preservice, orientation, and training standards, see also *Preservice Qualifications*, on p. 18, standard CSN75, on p. 262 on preservice training about adaptive equipment; and *Training*, on p. 316, on state and local training and technical assistance.

extend their basic knowledge and skills to help them work more effectively with children with special needs and their families.

Caregivers should have a basic knowledge of special needs, supplemented by specialized training for children with special needs. The type(s) of children with special needs served should influence the selection of the specialized training.

The number of hours offered in any in-service training program should be determined by the experience and professional background of the staff.

Training and other technical assistance can be obtained from the American Academy of Pediatrics; the American Nurses' Association; national therapy associations; local resource and referral agencies; and federally funded, university-affiliated programs for individuals with developmental disabilities, or other colleges and universities with expertise in training others to work with children with special needs. Additional help may be provided by the state-designated lead agency responsible for implementing P.L. 99-457.

STANDARDS	RATIONALE	COMMENTS

CONTINUING EDUCATION

CSN47. In addition to the continuing education outlined in *General Training*, on p. 18, *First Aid and CPR*, on p. 22, *Continuing Education*, on p. 24, and *Preservice, Orientation, and Training Standards*, on p. 252, continuing education and support for the staff shall be a component of all facilities, based on individual competency needs and the special needs of children in their care, and may include

Training is an essential component to ensure that staff develop and maintain the needed skills.

See the comment for standard CSN44 on p. 252.

a) Topics related to children with special needs in child care settings.
b) The provision of a list of caregivers in the community who work with children with special needs.
c) The provision of monthly opportunities for the staff to share their experiences and concerns with other caregivers.

Such continuing education keeps staff updated on current issues.
It is important to know the available community resources.

See the comment for standard CSN44 on p. 252.

This is best achieved through a regular staff conference mechanism.

For additional information on continuing education, see also standards CSN45 and CSN46 on p. 253 above on certification in infant and child CPR and in pediatric first aid, including rescue breathing and choke saving.

See also standard CSN72, on p. 262 on training for special medical procedures; standard CSN75, on p. 262 on continuing education about adaptive equipment; and *Training*, on p. 316, on state and local training and technical assistance.

COMPETENCY OF PERSONNEL

See *Performance Evaluation*, on p. 41.

SMALL FAMILY-CHILD-CARE HOMES

CSN48. A small family home caregiver who mainstreams a child with special needs into his/her facility shall meet the following standards, in addition to *Qualifications of Large and Small Family Home Caregivers*, on p. 14:

Service plans in small family-child-care homes may require a different implementation plan. The option of small family-child-care homes for children with special needs, if it is to be offered, must include special requirements. A modified set of standards in some areas are applicable to small family-child-care homes.

STANDARDS	RATIONALE	COMMENTS
a) Shall have a minimum of 2 years' experience as a caregiver.	This period of time allows the caregiver to become familiar with the multiple demands involved in providing care for these children in a home care setting.	
b) Shall be a high school graduate or hold an equivalency diploma.	The caregiver must demonstrate an ability to accomplish difficult tasks through persistence.	
c) Shall have three letters of recommendation from other caregivers, parents, or professionals in the field of child development.		
d) Shall operate a registered or licensed small family-child-care home in his/her local community, as specified in *The Regulatory Policy*, on p. 299, and shall be a member of the Family Day Care Association, as specified in *Qualifications of Large and Small Family Home Caregivers*, on p. 14. (See also *Networking for Small Family-Child-Care Homes*, on p. 316.)		
e) Shall have a working knowledge of community resources that provide services to children with special needs.	It is important to know the available community resources.	This qualification is difficult to measure, but use and/or ownership of a Directory of Services and membership in an association are indications of compliance.
f) Shall avail him- or herself of consultation services from professionals who work with children with special needs. These professionals shall include, but shall not be limited to, a physician, a registered nurse, a physical therapist, an occupational therapist, a speech pathologist, a social worker, a registered dietitian, and a psychologist.		The range of professionals needed may vary with the facility, but the listed professionals should be available as consultants when needed. The assitance of outside specialists, as needed, is an important facility component and could be arranged for in a variety of ways (see second and third comments in standard CSN20 on p. 244).
g) Shall have a documented plan for involving a substitute in the event that consultation time between the caregiver and other adults occurs during the facility's hours of operation. (See *Substitutes*, on p. 31.)	A backup caregiver is essential.	
h) Shall have valid infant and child CPR certification, as specified in *First Aid and CPR*, on p. 22.		
i) Shall have valid pediatric first aid certification that includes training in rescue breathing and first aid for choking, as specified in *First Aid and CPR*, on p. 22.		

STANDARDS	RATIONALE	COMMENTS

For additional information on small family-child-care homes, see also *Qualifications of Large and Small Family Home Caregivers*, on p. 14, and Appendix A, on p. 323, on additional general qualifications for small family home caregivers, standard CSN43 on p. 252 on orientation requirements, and *Consultants and Technical Assistance for Children with Special Needs*, on p. 315.

7.7 Special Requirements and Equipment

TRANSPORTATION

In addition to the following requirements, see *Transportation*, on p. 199.

CSN49. In vehicles used to transport children with special needs, there shall be at all times a working two-way radio, which can communicate to a dispatcher, in the vehicles operated by a facility.

The ability to radio for help to a central dispatcher is critical, as is the ability to call for help for a child.

This is a good general principle of emergency backup.

CSN50. In addition to the safety training specified in *Transportation Training*, on p. 200, when the facility arranges the transportation, all drivers, passenger monitors, and assistants involved in daily transportation of children with special needs to and from facilities shall receive a minimum of 6 hours' training in child development, developmental disabilities, and procedures to ensure safety of all children, including children with special needs, when they are transported.

It cannot be assumed that adults are knowledgeable about the various developmental levels or special needs of children.

Six hours of training is the minimum needed to cover this information in the most basic way.

It is advisable for all staff in contact with children with disabilities to have training, but this is the minimal level for staff who are trained.

CSN51. Vehicles shall accommodate the placement of wheelchairs with four tie-downs affixed according to manufacturer's instructions. The wheelchair occupant shall be secured by the wheelchair restraining belt during transport.

At all times vehicles should be ready to transport children who must ride in wheelchairs.*

Although restraint systems for children in wheelchairs do not exist, each wheelchair has a restraining belt that can be used to hold the child.

*Richards, A. *The Challenge of Transporting Children with Special Needs*. Elk Grove Village, IL: American Academy of Pediatrics, Safe Ride News, Spring 1987.

CSN52. All drivers, passenger monitors, and assistants involved in transportation of children with special needs shall be certified in infant/child CPR, as specified in *First Aid and CPR*, on p. 22.

There are enough children with respiratory, cardiac, and/or seizure disorders to necessitate competency in CPR for those accompanying the children to and from facilities.

It is advisable for all staff in contact with children with disabilities to have this basic training. It is especially necessary when staff are responsible for children with cardiac or respiratory disorders.

State agencies may provide such training for caregivers.

ACCESS

CSN53. Children who use wheelchairs or have ambulatory difficulties shall be located on the ground floor of the center.

Children who have ambulatory difficulties must be able to exit the building quickly and easily in case of emergency.

CSN54. The center shall be accessible for children who use wheelchairs and for other children with several motor disabilities, in accordance with Section 504 Guidelines.[9] Accessibility includes access to buildings, toilets, sinks, drinking fountains, and all classroom and therapy areas. Special provisions shall also be made, as needed, for the child with health, vision, or hearing impairment.

Accessibility has been detailed in full in Section 504 of the Guidelines of the Rehabilitation Act of 1973.[9]

It is clear that any facility accepting children with significant motor disabilities will need to be accessible to all children served. Small family home caregivers may be limited in their ability to serve such children, but are not precluded from doing so if there is a reasonable degree of compliance with this standard. It must be recognized that not all children with severe motor disabilities live at home with their families in fully physically accessible accommodations, and that special provisions are made to meet their needs at home.

If toilet training is a relevant activity, adapted equipment may result in a requirement for availability of toilets and toilet training equipment in addition to those specified in *Toilets and Toilet Training Equipment,* on p. 168.

CSN55. In facilities that include children with physical disabilities, all exits and steps necessary for evacuation shall have ramps approved by the local building authority.

For additional information on access, see also *General Location, Layout, and Construction of the Facility,* on p. 141, for additional access requirements.

SPACE FOR SERVICES

CSN56. The minimum allowance of space for children 0 to 2 years old with special needs in a classroom/playroom shall be 35 square feet of usable floor space. The minimum allowance of space for children 2 to 12 years old with special needs in a classroom/playroom shall be 40 square feet of usable floor space.

Federal requirements recommend 35 square feet per child. Experience has demonstrated that children with special needs, especially children ages 2 to 12, need additional space.

CSN57. In addition to accessible classrooms, there shall be separate rooms or private areas as follows:
a) One physical therapy/occupational therapy room for each 15 children in need of these services.
b) One speech therapy room for each 20 children in need of individual speech therapy.

Special therapeutic interventions shall, whenever possible, be provided to children within their integrated instructional groups, with primary caregivers assisting with, observing, or implementing therapies or activities. Therapists and specialists shall provide or arrange services with typical peers present and participating whenever possible, especially if services must be provided in space separate from regular classroom or playground space.

Quiet, private space is necessary for physical, occupational, and speech therapies.

Most caregivers also indicate that it is less disruptive to the other children in the facility if the therapies are provided in a separate area. For speech therapy, it is especially important to be able to work with a child in a quiet location.

Privacy is better for the child and the therapist, and this arrangement is also less distracting to the other children. However, we encourage that therapeutic principles be incorporated into the child's general child care activities to achieve maximum benefit.

CSN58. Small family-child-care homes and facilities integrating fewer than three children with special needs shall have a separate and private space available for such services to be provided to children who require therapies when such services are provided.

See rationale for standard CSN57.

See comments for standard CSN57.

CSN59. There shall be storage space for all adaptive equipment (e.g., equipment for physical therapy, occupational therapy, adaptive physical education) separate and apart from classroom floor space. The storage space shall be easily accessible to staff. Equipment shall be stored safely and in an organized way.

Storage of adaptive equipment is frequently a problem in centers. This equipment needs to be stored outside of classroom space in order to maximize floor space and minimize distracting clutter.

STANDARDS	RATIONALE	COMMENTS

For additional information on space for services, *Requirements for Indoor Space and Equipment*, on p. 168.

SPECIAL EQUIPMENT

CSN60. The facility shall have therapeutic and recreational equipment to enhance the educational and developmental progress of children with special needs.

Children with special needs require special equipment of various types.

For the individual child, the equipment should be available to meet the goals and methods outlined in the IFSP.

See Appendix Q, on p. 375, for a sample list of such equipment. The list in Appendix Q is comprehensive, but may not be entirely applicable in all facilities. A measure of compliance would be to see if the equipment and materials required for children's IFSP's are available. Caregivers in small and large family-child-care homes could make arrangements to borrow equipment that is not otherwise available.

7.8 Dealing with Children's Special Needs

SPECIAL FEEDING TECHNIQUES, NUTRITION, AND DIETS.

CSN61. Children with special needs due to chronic illness or disabilities shall have their feeding planned. This planning requires the expertise of the child care team, including the child care Nutrition Specialist (see Appendices B-1 and B-2, on pp. 328–329), to address ongoing dietary and feeding issues related to individual health conditions such as allergies, food idiosyncrasies, and other identified feeding problems.

As a safety and health precaution, staff should know in advance whether a child has food allergies, has tongue thrust, is medically fragile, and/or requires nasogastric or gastrostomy feedings or special positioning.[10-12]

See comments for standard CSN63.

CSN62. A written history of any special nutrition or feeding needs of the child shall be obtained before the child enters the facility. This history shall be reviewed by the staff with the child care Nutrition Specialist (see Appendices B-1 and B-2, on p. 328–329) or in consultation with a registered nurse.

As noted in standard CSN61, children with special needs may have individual problems relating to diet, swallowing, and so forth that require the development of an individual plan prior to their entry into the facility.

CSN63. The histories described in standard CSN62 above shall be used to develop individual feeding plans and, collectively, to develop facility menus. Disciplines related to special nutrition needs, including nursing, speech, and occupational and physical therapy, shall participate when needed and/or when they are available to the facility. With the exception of those children on special diets, the general nutrition guidelines for facilities in *General Requirements*, on p. 115, *Nutrition for Infants*, on

Many children with special needs evidence difficulty in the area of feeding, including delayed attainment of basic swallowing, chewing, and independent feeding skills. Food, utensils, and equipment, including furniture, may have to be adapted to meet the developmental and physical needs of individual children.

Close collaboration between the home and the facility will be needed for those children on special diets. Parents may have to provide food on a temporary or permanent basis if the facility, after exploring all community resources, is unable to provide the special diet.

STANDARDS

p. 117, *Nutrition for Toddlers and Preschoolers,* on p. 120, and *Nutrition for School-Age Children,* on p. 121, shall be applied.

CSN64. The feeding plan shall include steps to take when problems occur that require rapid response on the part of the staff (e.g., when a child chokes during mealtime). The completed plan shall be on file and accessible to staff.

For additional information on special feeding techniques, nutrition, and diets, see also chapter 4, *Nutrition and Food Service,* on p. 115.

TOILETING

CSN65. Toilet training shall be introduced for each child. The training shall be based not on the child's age, but on his/her developmental level.

CSN66. Toilet training, when initiated, shall follow a prescribed, sequential plan that is developed and coordinated with the parent's plan for implementation in the home environment.

For additional information on toileting, see also standard PR20 on toilet training in chapter 2 on p. 50.

SEIZURES

CSN67. The child's medical report (see Appendix C, item B, on p. 323) shall indicate whether there is a history of seizures and whether the child is currently taking medication to control the disorder.

RATIONALE

Staff must know ahead of time what procedures to follow, as well as their designated roles during an emergency.

The achievement of motor and intellectual/developmental skills may be delayed, depending on the child's primary disability or combination of disabilities.

The child may not be socially or emotionally ready to be toilet trained, despite the emergence of other skills.

The family may not be prepared, at the time, to extend training into the home environment.

Training is achieved more rapidly once a child is toilet-scheduled and demands are consistent from adults and across environments.

This information is essential for management of the child in the facility and coordination of care both inside the facility and with outside service providers.

COMMENTS

The area of toilet training for children with special needs is difficult because there are no age-related, disability-specific rules to follow. In general, before a program is initiated, the child should demonstrate:
a) An understanding of the concept of cause and effect;
b) An ability to communicate; and
c) The physical ability to remain dry for up to 2 hours.

Some children with multiple disabilities do not demonstrate any requisite skills other than being dry for a few hours. Establishing a toilet routine may be the first step toward toilet training and concomitantly improving hygiene and skin care.

Children with special needs will demonstrate variability in the amount of time needed to achieve independence in this area. As a result, support and counseling for parents and caregivers are required to help them deal with this issue.

A close and continuing liaison with the child's health care provider is necessary, especially if the seizure disorder is not well controlled.

It is possible to monitor the medication prescribed to control seizures through measurement of blood sam-

STANDARDS	RATIONALE	COMMENTS
		ples; dosage may have to be adjusted to reduce side effects.
CSN68. Staff shall be trained in and shall be prepared to utilize the procedures that must be followed when a child has a seizure. These procedures include proper positioning, keeping the airway open, and knowing when and whom to call for medical assistance. Telephone numbers for emergency care shall be posted as specified in item (o) in Appendix W, on p. 386.	These procedures are essential to provide emergency care.	The general guidelines for management of such situations apply here for children with special needs as for others. Training can be achieved through initial and ongoing inservice efforts (see *Continuing Education*, on p. 254.
CSN69. The child's facility health record (see Appendix C, item B, on p. 331) shall denote the type and frequency of both reported seizures and those observed in the facility.	This information is essential for management of the child in the facility and for coordination of care both inside the facility and with outside service providers.	
CSN70. All staff shall be instructed about the side effects of anticonvulsant medications and how to observe and report them. (See *Medications*, on p. 88.)	Anticonvulsant medication may affect a child's health and behavior.	Changes in health and behavior that may be due to medication should be reported to the parents. It would be useful to have a medical textbook available as a reference concerning seizures and medication side effects, particularly if a child begins a new medicine while attending the facility.

MEDICATIONS

STANDARDS	RATIONALE	COMMENTS
See *Medication Policy*, on p. 279; standard APP7 in Appendix C, item E, on p. 335; and *Medications*, on p. 88.		The policy applicable for medication administration in all facilities will apply here. However, children with special needs may have problems swallowing medications or need specific medications that present special risks.

SPECIAL PROCEDURES

STANDARDS	RATIONALE	COMMENTS
CSN71. A facility that enrolls children who require suctioning, oxygen, postural drainage, or catheterization on a daily basis (unless the children requiring catheterization can perform this function on their own) shall include a nurse as a consultant for the facility. (See *Direct Care and Provisional Staff*, on p. 250, on the requirements for a nurse.)	The specialized skills needed to implement these procedures are not traditionally taught to educators or educational assistants as part of their academic or practicum experience.	Specific equipment (see Appendix Q, on p. 375) is obviously also necessary at the facility, along with staff trained to use it. The implication of this standard is that facilities serving children with complex medical problems need special staffing; therefore, other facilities may not be able to serve these children. Thus this standard is most practicable for centers rather than for smaller facilities. However, smaller facilities, if they are adequately funded, can meet the standard.

STANDARDS	RATIONALE	COMMENTS

CSN72. Staff shall be provided special training to manage the care of children who require the special procedures listed in standard CSN 71. (See *Continuing Education*, on p. 254.)

See rationale for standard CSN71.

Training may be both generic and specific to the individual child's needs.

PROSTHETIC DEVICES

CSN73. Special adaptive equipment for children with special needs shall be provided or arranged for by the facility. (See also Appendix Q, on p. 375.)

If a facility serves one or more children with special needs, adaptive equipment necessary for the child's participation in all activities is needed.

CSN74. Prosthetic devices, including hearing aids, eyeglasses, braces, and wheelchairs, shall be checked by a designated staff member daily to ensure that these appliances are in good working order.

Battery-driven devices such as hearing aids require close monitoring because they have a short life and young children require adult assistance to replace the batteries. Eyeglasses scratch and break, as do other assistive appliances.

Parents should be asked to supply extra batteries or the facility should keep a small supply of batteries for hearing aids on hand. Facilities should make certain that the batteries are stored and discarded in such a manner that ingestion by children can be avoided.

Staff can perform minor repairs on equipment, but should not attempt major repairs.

CSN75. Staff and caregivers shall be given information and an orientation about the use of the individual child's adaptive equipment. This shall be part of the preservice and inservice training program (see *Preservice, Orientation, and Training Standards*, on p. 252).

This information and orientation prepare the staff to help the child use the equipment properly.

There is a large variety of adaptive equipment in use; staff need to understand how and why various items are used and what to look for to check for malfunctions.

CSN76. If staff identify defective equipment, the parent shall be notified.

The parent is responsible for notifying the health care or equipment provider about a problem, unless the parents request the staff to do this directly.

7.9 *Periodic Reevaluation*

THE REEVALUATION PROCESS

CSN77. The care coordinator shall ensure that formal reevaluations of the child's functioning and the family's needs are conducted at least yearly, or as often as is necessary to deal with changes in the child's or family's circumstances. This reevaluation shall occur at a conference in which the parent is invited to participate. Such conferences and lists of participants shall be documented in

The changing needs of children with developmental disabilites do not follow a predictable course. A regular, thorough process of reevaluation is essential to identify appropriate goals and services for the child.

Ad hoc reevaluations may be necessitated by changes in circumstances; regular treatment services are recommended for review at 3-month intervals (see standard CSN22, on p. 245).

STANDARDS

the child's facility health record (see Appendix C, item F, on p. 335).

CSN78. These reevaluations shall be performed by either the caregiver and/or an outside clinic, center, or professional. If the reevaluation is performed by ·an outside clinic or center, the caregiver shall be invited to participate in the case review. If this participation is not possible, then the caregiver shall be invited to provide a report about the child's progress. (See also *Evaluation Process Prior to Enrolling at a Facility*, on p. 240.)

CSN79. The reevaluation conference shall result in a new statement of program needs and therapeutic plans on which agreement has been reached with parents.

For additional information on the reevaluation process, see also recommendation REC64 in chapter 9 on p. 316 on coordination of reevaluation by the regulating body.

THE PARTICIPATING STAFF

CSN80. When the evaluators are not part of the child care staff, a formal mechanism shall be developed for coordinating reevaluations and program revisions. A staff member from the facility shall routinely be included in the evaluation process, team conferences, and so forth.

CSN81. Providers of special services who come into the facility to give intervention to a child must also communicate at each visit with the caregiver at the facility who is responsible for sharing information with the parent. Such providers may include,

RATIONALE

It is clearly in the child's and family's best interest if communication between providers of services, including evaluation and treatment services, is an inherent part of the plan and delivery of services.

Continued collaboration and coordination among all involved parties are essential.

These guidelines are intended to be useful to facilities and to be fully comprehensive. Children with developmental disabilities may be served in "special needs" facilities that have a full range of evaluation and therapy services, or in facilities that obtain evaluations and therapies from outside sources.

However, any facility assuming responsibility for serving children with developmental disabilities, mental illness, or chronic health impairments must develop mechanisms for identifying the needs of the children and families and obtaining the appropriate services.

Therapeutic services must be coordinated with the child's regular educational program and with the parents and caregivers so that everyone understands the child's needs.

To be optimally useful, the therapeutic techniques must be shared

COMMENTS

Again, parental participation in the entire process is urged.

See comment for standard CSN80.

Coordination between facilities and outside clinical resources is necessary. (See *The Reevaluation Process*, on p. 262 and standard CSN27, on p. 246.

Circumstances may vary in different communities. For example, there may be a specialized clinic or center that evaluates children with special needs, or this may be done by staff related to a local or county public agency. In other circumstances, private professionals may assess the child. However, in all of these situations, there should be input from and an exchange of information with the caregiver.

It is the intent of this standard to help both child and family. Again, maximum family participation is urged.

See the comment above in standard CSN80. See also *Developing a Service Plan for a Child with Special Needs*, on p. 243.

but are not limited to, physicians, registered nurses, occupational therapists, physical therapists, speech therapists, educational therapists, and registered dietitians. Such discussions shall be documented in the child's written record (see Appendix C, on p. 330).

For additional information on the participating staff, see also recommendation REC64 in chapter 9 on p. 316 on the role of the regulatory agency in this coordination.

with the caregivers and parents and utilized at times other than therapy sessions. Requiring the caregivers to share information with the parents ensures communication.

7.10 Discharge and Transition Process

REVIEW OF RECORDS

CSN82. Prior to a child's discharge from the facility or transfer to another facility, the facility or designated care coordinator shall collect and review the child's records.

Families in transition benefit when support and advocacy are available from a facility representative who is aware of their needs and of the community's resources.

Some families are capable of advocating effectively for themselves and their children; others require help negotiating the system outside of the facility.

REVIEW OF CHILD'S PROGRESS AND FUTURE PLANNING

CSN83. The staff at the facility, in partnership and collaboration with other service providers for the child and family, shall review and summarize the progress the child has made and make recommendations in a written plan for the future.

This process is an essential component of the process of planning for discharge.

An interdisciplinary process is encouraged. However, in small and large family-child-care homes where an interdisciplinary team does not exist, the caregivers shall participate in the planning and preparation process along with other care or treatment providers.

EXCHANGE OF REPORTS

CSN84. The discharge process shall also involve sharing and exhange of progress reports with other care providers for the child and the parents or legal guardian of the child within the realm of confidentiality guidelines. (See *Confidentiality and Access to Records*, on p. 288.)

There is a continuing need for information sharing as part of discharge planning.

See standard CSN78, on p. 263 on reevaluations.

It is important for all providers of care to coordinate their activities and referrals; otherwise the family may not be well informed.

FORMAT FOR THE TRANSITION PLAN

CSN85. Each service agency or caregiver shall have a format and timeline for the process of developing a transition plan to be followed when each child leaves the facility. The plan shall include the following components:

Many factors contribute to the success or failure of a transition. These concerns can be monitored effectively when a written plan is developed and followed to ensure that all steps in a transition are included and are

It is best if the process of planning begins at least 3 months and, in some cases, 6 to 9 months prior to anticipated transitions, since finding the proper facility for a child can be a complex and time-consuming process in some communities.

a) Review and final preparation of the child's records.

b) A child and family needs assessment.

c) Identification of potential child care, educational, or programmatic arrangements.

d) Plan and timetables for selection of the future care providers.

e) Identification of the next care or service arrangement.

f) Transition responsibilities and timelines for the family, the sending agency, and the receiving agency.

FOLLOW-UP

CSN86. Each service agency or caregiver shall have a mechanism for following up the transition plan, timelines for the process, a means of documenting current and future care and service arrangements, and an approach for addressing changes.

undertaken in a timely, responsive manner.

Families will benefit when they are provided support and services from the receiving agency.

Sending agencies need a means of tracking families beyond the next receiving agency, as moves can be quick and contact can be lost.

A final step in a transition plan should include a means of tracking a family to ascertain that the child is enrolled in a satisfactory facility and that the family is receiving the help it needs.

Each agency can adapt the format to its own needs. However, consistent formats for planning and information exchange in localities would be useful to both caregivers and families.

The use of outside consultants for small and large family-child-care homes is especially important in meeting this type of standard. (See second and third comments in standard CSN20, on p. 244 on technical assistance.)

The family may have a continuing need to consult trusted or familiar providers of services in the future, and these providers have a responsibility to ensure that the child is placed in an appropriate facility in the future.

This case management issue applies primarily to centers. However, it is important under all circumstances that the child with special needs is transitioned properly into another facility, and that the staff at the facility the child previously attended assist the family with the process and remain a resource for the family if problems in transitioning arise.

7.11 Formal and Informal Assessment of Facilities for Children with Special Needs

CAREGIVER RESPONSIBILITIES

CSN87. Each caregiver who cares for children with special needs shall have a written plan developed in consultation with an expert multidisciplinary team of professionals experienced in the care and education of children with special needs. (See *Parental Participation*, on p. 241, and *Written Plan*, on p. 266, for the specific requirements of the plan.)

This standard would engage each caregiver who plans to care for children with special needs in a self-assessment, to be conducted with assistance from a multidisciplinary team. The self-assessment would stimulate thought about both the present capabilities that this particular caregiver has and the medical and educational particularities of a range of special needs, from mild to severe disabilities.

This standard serves as a measure of protection for both children and

Caregivers thus have the opportunity to decide for themselves, in consultation with experts in the field, where, along the range of disability, they can comfortably and confidently take care of children and where they would feel equipped and skilled at any particular moment in time. This plan may be written by another agency, but a copy shall be maintained in the child's facility health care file (see Appendix C, on p. 330). Caregivers seeking to care for children with more challenging difficulties can gradually acquire the

caregivers, as caregivers cannot and should not be pressured into accepting children they have not been assessed as qualified to handle. Parents would also know, from the record of the written plan (which need not be more than a page or two), that a particular facility is well-prepared to handle children with, for example, mild retardation or hearing impairment, but is not the place for a child with more complex medical problems. However, this decision should be based upon a facility's capability and clearly not on any discriminatory policy or actions.

training that would equip them to do so.

This plan is for the facility as a whole, separate from the plan made for individual children.

Since the scope of the assessment is dicated by the range of children with special needs for whom the caregiver is considering offering services, caregivers seeking to care for one child with, for example, a seizure disorder could use this assessment to learn quickly what that child and only that child needs. This might be the case at either small or large family-child-care homes.

See also the comment on training and technical assistance in standard CSN44, on p. 252.

WRITTEN PLAN

CSN88. The facility's written plan (see *Caregiver Responsibilities*, on p. 265) shall
a) Describe the types of disabilities or medical needs of children that this caregiver is prepared to respond to, as assessed jointly by both the caregiver and the multi-disciplinary team.
b) Be used as the basis for decisions about enrollment of children with special needs in the facility.
c) Be reviewed and, where desired by the caregiver, revised every 2 years, unless the caregiver requests revisions more frequently.

See rationale for standard CSN87.

See comments for standard CSN87.

CSN89. The caregiver shall seek technical assistance in developing and formulating the plan for future services for children with special needs. (See recommendation REC60 on state technical assistance in chapter 9 on p. 315.)

This type of assistance is needed where caregivers lack specific capabilities.

Documentation of the caregiver's request and of the regulating agencies' responses in offering or providing assistance furnishes evidence of compliance.

State regulatory agencies should be in a position to provide such assistance to facilities (see *Consultants and Technical Assistance for Children with Special Needs*, on p. 315).

CSN90. The plan shall be reviewed at least annually to see if the caregiver is achieving the overall objectives for the agency or facility.

See also *Parental Participation*, on p. 241.

An annual review by caregivers is a cornerstone of any quality assurance procedure.

STANDARDS	RATIONALE	COMMENTS

STATE REGULATORY RESPONSIBILITIES

See *Consultants and Technical Assistance for Children with Special Needs*, on p. 315.

EMERGENCY PREPAREDNESS PLAN

CSN91. Facilities providing services to children with special needs shall have a written plan for emergency medical backup and medical procedures. This plan shall
a) Describe for each child with special needs the special emergency procedures that will be used if required by the caregiver or by a physician or registered nurse available to the caregiver.
b) Note any special medical procedures, if required by the child's condition, that will be used with the child while he/she is in the care of the caregiver.

The medical aspect of caring for children with special needs is likely to be the aspect of care that caregivers are most poorly equipped to carry out, since their training is usually in early childhood education.

The preparation of a written plan (a brief one would suffice) prepares caregivers to deal with routine and emergency medical needs.

See the comment about sources of technical assistance in standard CSN44, on p. 252.

CSN92. A copy of the plan shall be made available to the parents of each child with special needs. The plan shall be revised each time a new child with special needs enters the care of the caregiver, or when any child's medical condition changes.

Children's needs change and revisions are required to deal with the changes. Parental involvement in the process is essential.

This plan may be brief and it may be developed in partnership with a registered nurse, experienced special educator, or physician.

For additional information on an emergency preparedness plan, see also *Emergency Plan*, on p. 280, *Emergency Procedures*, on p. 95, and recommendation REC62 in chapter 9 on p. 316.

OPPORTUNITIES FOR PARENT ASSESSMENT OF CHILD CARE ARRANGEMENTS

See *Parental Involvement,* on p. 58, for these standards.

References

1. The Education for All Handicapped Children Act of 1976. PL 94-142.
2. The Individuals with Disabilities Education Act of 1990. PL 101-476.
3. The Early Intervention Amendments to the Education for All Handicapped Children Act of 1986. PL 99-457.
4. *Draft Federal Day Care Requirements.* Washington, DC: US Dept of Health, Education and Welfare, 1972.
5. US Dept of Health, Education and Welfare. HEW day care regulations. *Federal Register.* March 19, 1980;45(55):17870–17885.
6. Kaminer R, Cohen HJ. Informing parents about their child's mental retardation. *Contemp Pediatr.* 1988;5:36–49.
7. Regulations for PL 99-457. *Federal Register.* June 22, 1989.
8. American Academy of Pediatrics' Committee on Children with Disabilities. Provision of related services for children with chronic disabilities. *Pediatrics.* 1985;75:796–797.
9. The Rehabilitation Act of 1973. PL 93-112, Section 504.
10. Springer NS. *Nutrition Casebook on Developmental Disabilities.* Syracuse, NY: 1982.
11. Pipes P. *Nutrition in Infancy and Childhood.* St. Louis, Mo: Times, Mirror/Mosby, 1989.
12. Deitch S, ed. *Health in Day Care: A Manual for Health Professionals.* Elk Grove Village, Il: American Academy of Pediatrics; 1987.

The following references are provided for individuals who want to read further on issues presented here or who need further guidance on caring for children with special needs.

1. Bricker D. *Early Education of At-Risk and Handicapped Infants, Toddlers and Preschool Children.* Glenview, Ill: Scott, Foresman and Co; 1986.
2. Bourland B, Lillie D. *Special Things for Special Kids.* Chapel Hill, NC: Frank Porter Graham Child Development Center; 1985.
3. Cook R, Armbruster V. *Adapting Early Childhood Curricula: Suggestions for Meeting Special Needs.* St. Louis, Mo: CV Mosby and Co; 1983.
4. Cook R, Tessier, Armbruster V. Adapting early childhood curricula for children with special needs. Columbus, Ohio: Merrill Publishing Company; 1987.
5. Deinier PD. *Resources for Teaching Young Children With Special Needs.* New York, NY: Harcourt Brace Jovanovich, Inc; 1983.
6. Finnie N. *Handling the Young Cerebral Palsied Child at Home.* New York, NY: EP Dutton; 1974.
7. Guralnick M, ed. *Early Intervention and Integration of Handicapped and Non-Handicapped Children.* Baltimore, Md: University Park Press; 1978.
8. Hanson M. Teaching the Infant with Down's Syndrome. Austin, Tex: *Pro-Ed;* 1987.
9. Hanson M, Lynch E. Early Intervention. Implementing Child and Family Services for Infants and Toddlers Who Are At Risk or Disabled. Austin, Tex: *Pro-Ed;* 1989.
10. *Journal of Early Intervention.* Reston, Va: Division of Early Childhood, Council for Exceptional Children; 1988.
11. *The More We Get Together. Adapting the Environment for Children with Disabilities.* New York, NY: The Nordic Committee on Disability in cooperation with the World Rehabilitation Fund Inc; 1985.
12. Peterson N. *Early Intervention for Handicapped and At-Risk Children.* Denver, Colo: Love Publishing Co; 1987.
13. Topics in Early Childhood Special Education. *Pro-Ed.* 1991;10:4 (Austin, Tex.)
14. Safford P. *Integrating Teaching in Early Childhood.* White Plains, NY: Longman Inc; 1989.
15. Segal M. *In Time of Love: Caring for the Special Needs Baby.* New York, NY: Newmarket Press; 1988.
16. Souweize J, Crimmins S, Mazel C. *Mainstreaming: Ideas for Teaching Young Children.* Washington, DC: National Association for the Education of Young Children; 1981.
17. Stray-Gundersen K. *Babies with Down's Syndrome.* Kensington, Md: Woodbine House; 1986.

C H A P T E R 8

Administration

CHAPTER 8
ADMINISTRATION

8.1 Identifiable Governing Body/Accountable Individual

STANDARDS

AD1. The facility shall have an identifiable governing body or person with the responsibility for and authority over the operation of the center. The governing body shall appoint or employ one person who is responsible for the facility's day-to-day management. Responsibilities shall include, but shall not be limited to, the following:

a) Ensuring compliance with all applicable rules, regulations, and facility standards.

b) Developing and ensuring stable and continuing adherence to all policies and procedures for the facility and ensuring that policies are in writing, as described in this chapter.

c) Hiring, firing, assigning roles to, and supervising personnel.

d) Providing orientation of all new parents, employees, and volunteers to the physical structure, policies, and procedures of the facility. (See *Orientation Training*, on p. 19.)

e) Notifying all staff, volunteers, and parents of any changes in the facility's policies and procedures.

f) Providing for continuous supervision of visitors and all non-facility personnel providing repair, maintenance, supplemental education, or other services at the facility when children are present.

g) Providing inservice training (see *Continuing Education*, on p. 24) for staff and volunteers, based on the needs of the facility and qualifications of staff and volunteers.

h) Recommending an annual budget and managing the finances of the facility.

i) Maintaining required records for

RATIONALE

These standards are based on accepted personnel management practices. General administrative management starts with acceptance of the principle of "unity of command" and with role definition. For any organization to function effectively, lines of responsibility must be clearly delineated, with someone designated to have ultimate responsibility.

COMMENTS

Management to ensure that policy is carried out includes providing staff and parents with written handbooks; training; supervising with frequent feedback; and monitoring with a checklist.

In a national survey of model health and safety practices in facilities (see Introduction), the APHA/AAP project found exemplary facilities that had effective surveillance procedures. For example, in one of these facilities, a checklist was developed covering every area of the facility from parking lot to classrooms. Two individuals were assigned to walk around the center noting whether all items on the checklist were in good order. The two individuals were a parent and a staff member, or the director and a staff member. When any deficiencies were found, the process included identifying a person responsible for correcting the problem and a date for its correction.

🍎 applies to a small family-child-care home   Ⓐ▣ applies to a large family-child-care home   🛝 applies to a center. If no symbol appears, the standard applies to all three.

personnel and children at the facility.

j) Providing for parent involvement, including parent education. (See *Parent Relationships*, on p. 55.)

k) Reporting to the governing board on a regular basis as to the status of the facility's operation.

l) Providing oversight of research studies conducted at the facility and joint supervision of students using the facility for clinical practice.

AD2. The administrator of a facility shall see to it that policies that promote the achievement of quality child care are developed, and shall also ensure stable and continuing adherence to all policies. When problems are identified, the administrator shall be responsible for a follow-up plan to be sure that corrective action was taken and assign a person to correct the problem by a specified date.

Management principles of quality improvement in any human service require identification of goals and leadership to ensure that all those involved (those with authority, those with experience, and those affected) participate in working toward those goals. Problem-solving approaches that are effective in other settings also work in early childhood programs.

See comment on standard AD1.

AD3. There shall be written delegation of administrative authority, designating the person in charge of the facility and the person(s) in charge of individual children, for all hours of operation.

Caregivers are responsible for the protection of the children in care at all times. Children should not be placed in the care of unauthorized family members or other individuals.

AD4. The designated person in charge shall have access to the records necessary to manage the facility and shall grant access to the facility and records to regulatory staff.

Those with responsibility must have access to the information required to make reasonable decisions.

For additional information on the identifiable governing body/accountable individual, see also standard ST77 in chapter 1 on p. 37 on the director's role in work release.

8.2 Management Plan and Statement of Services

STANDARDS

RATIONALE

COMMENTS

AD5. The facility shall have a management plan to specify how the caregiver addresses the needs of children of different ages and with disabilities who can be served by the facility. This plan shall include, but need not be limited to, the items described below in *Admission Policy, Supervision Policy, Discipline Policy, Care of Ill Children, Health Plan, Medication Policy, Emergency Plan, Evacuation Plan and Drills, Safety Plan, Sanitation Plan, Nutrition Plan and Policy, Evening and Night Care Plan, Smoking and Prohibited Substances Plan,* and *Review and Revision of Policies, Plans, and Procedures,* on pp. 271–285. For centers, all of these items shall be included in a written plan.

Facility policies should vary according to the ages and disabilities of the children enrolled to accommodate special needs. Program planning should precede, not follow, the enrollment and care of children at different developmental levels and with different disabilities.

AD6. At enrollment, the facility shall provide parents and the regulatory agency with a statement of services that shall include the items specified in Appendix X, on p. 389. Parents shall sign this statement of services.

For additional information on management plan and statement of services, see also Appendix C, on p. 330.

ADMISSION POLICY

AD7. The facility's written admission policy shall be nondiscriminatory in regard to race, color, sex, religion, national origin, ancestry, or disability except insofar as the child's needs cannot be met by the facility (see chapter 7, *Children with Special Needs,* on p. 237). A copy of the policy and definitions of eligibility shall be available for review on demand.

A democratic pluralistic society rests on valuing cultural diversity.[1,2]

Facilities should be able to accommodate all children except those whose needs require extreme facility modifications beyond the capability of the facility's resources.

AD8. Arrangements for enrollment of children shall be made by the parents or legal guardians. The facility shall advise the parents/legal guardians of their responsibility to provide

Parents or legal guardians must be fully informed about the facility's services before delegating responsibility for care of the child. The facility and parents must exchange information to the facility regarding their children.

For additional information on admission policy, see also standard reccommendation REC38 in chapter 9 on p. 311.

SUPERVISION POLICY

AD9. Each facility's supervision policy shall specify
a) That no child shall be left alone or unsupervised while under the care of the child care staff. Caregivers shall supervise children at all times, even when the children are sleeping (a caregiver must be able to both see and hear infants while they are sleeping). Caregivers shall not be on one floor while children are on another floor. School-age children shall be permitted to participate in activities and visit friends off premises as approved by their parents and by the caregiver(s). (See also *Sleep*, on p. 66.)
b) That developmentally appropriate child:staff ratios shall be met during all hours of operating, including field trips. (See *Child: Staff Ratio and Group Size*, on p. 1, and *Field Trips*, on p. 52.)

The policy shall include specific procedures governing supervision of the indoor and outdoor play spaces that describe the child:staff ratio, precautions to be followed for specific areas and equipment, and staff assignments for high-risk areas.

The supervision policies of centers and large family-child-care homes shall be written policies.

AD10. All young children shall be supervised while using bathroom facilities as specified in *Supervision*, on p. 52.

DISCIPLINE POLICY

AD11. Each facility shall have a discipline policy that encompasses the specifics described in this section and in *Discipline*, on p. 52. Centers and large family-child-care homes shall have written discipline policies.

information necessary for the safety and health of the child.

Children who are supposedly sleeping can be awake and in need of adult attention. In the event of fire, caregivers separated from children by stairs may be blocked from reaching the children by smoke, which tends to quickly fill stairways. Risk-taking behavior must be detected and illness, fear, or other night behaviors managed. Children should be protected against sexual abuse by limiting situations in which a caregiver is left alone with children without another adult present.

See rationales for standards AD12–14.

Planning must include advance assignments to maintain appropriate staffing. Sufficient staff to evacuate the children safely must be maintained.

Compliance should be measured by structured observation, by counting caregivers and children in each group at varied times of the day. Compliance can also be measured by reviewing written policies.

AD12. The caregiver shall implement a policy that prohibits corporal punishment, emotional abuse, humiliation, abusive language, and the withdrawal of food and other basic needs. The specifics are outlined in standard PR35 in chapter 2 on p. 54.

Corporal punishment may be physical abuse or may become abusive very easily. Emotional abuse can be extremely harmful to children, but, unlike physical or sexual abuse, it is not adequately defined in most state child abuse reporting laws. Corporal punishment is clearly prohibited in small family-child-care homes in 32 states, and is prohibited in centers in 39 states.[3] Research links corporal punishment with negative effects such as later criminal behavior and impairment of learning.[3]

Primary factors supporting the prohibition of certain methods of punishment include current child development theory and practice; legal aspects (namely that a caregiver is not acting in loco parentis with regard to the child); and increasing liability suits.

AD13. The facility's discipline policy shall outline methods of guidance (described in *Discipline, on p. 52)* appropriate to the ages of the children enrolled; it shall explicitly describe positive, nonviolent, nonabusive methods for achieving discipline. All caregivers shall sign a facility agreement to implement this discipline policy.

Caregivers are more likely to avoid abusive practices if they are well informed about effective, nonabusive methods for managing children's behaviors.

Positive methods of discipline create a constructive and supportive social group and reduce incidents of aggression.

Examples of appropriate alternatives to corporal punishment for infants and toddlers include brief, verbal expressions of disapproval; for preschoolers, "time out" (i.e., out-of-group activity) under adult supervision; for school-age children, denial of privileges.

AD14. The facility shall have policies for dealing with acts of aggression and fighting (e.g., biting, hitting) by children. These policies shall include separation of the children involved; immediate attention to the individual children or caregiver involved; notification to parents of children involved in the incident, if an injury requires first aid or medical attention as specified in *Incidence Logs of Illness, Injury, and Other Problems,* on p. 290; review of the adequacy of the caregiver supervision and appropriateness of facility activities; and administrative policy for dealing with recurrences.

Aggressive acts, both intentional and unintentional, occur in out-of-home care settings.[4–6] Administrative guidelines are necessary for the management of recurrent acts of aggression and should be developed within the facility based on the resources and structure of the facility. Potential injuries and infections that may be incurred when caring for young children are health and safety hazards for caregivers. Little training and few educational materials on these risks are available to caregivers.

In general, reducing child:staff ratios and child group sizes, having training for caregivers, and using positive discipline will help to decrease acts of aggression, such as biting.

For additional information on discipline policy, see also *Discipline,* on p. 52.

CARE OF ILL CHILDREN

AD15. The facility's plan for the care of ill children and caregivers shall include the following. Centers and large family-child-care homes shall have written policies for the care of ill children and caregivers.

a) Standing orders (see Glossary for definition) for emergency care.

b) Admission and inclusion/exclusion policies. Conditions that require that a child be excluded and sent home are specified in *Child Inclusion/Exclusion/Dismissal*, on p. 80.

c) A description of illnesses common to children in child care, their management, and precautions to protect the health of other children and caregivers. (See chapter 6, *Infectious Diseases*, on p. 207.)

d) A procedure for documenting the date and time of illness, the person affected, a description of symptoms, the response of the caregiver to these symptoms, who was notified (e.g., parent, legal guardian, nurse, physician, health departments), and their response.

e) The standards described in *Reporting Illness*, on p. 87 and *Notification of Parents*, on p. 90.

The policy for the management of ill children should be developed in consultation with health care providers to address technical issues of contagion and other health risks. The policy should focus on the needs and behavior of the ill child. The policy should address the circumstances under which separation of the ill child from the group is required; the circumstances under which the caregiver, parents, legal guardian, or other designated persons need to be informed; and the procedures to be followed in these cases. The policy should take into consideration

• the physical facility

• the number and qualifications of facility's personnel

• the fact that children do become ill frequently and at unpredictable times

• the fact that working parents often are not given leave for children's illnesses.[7]

Infectious diseases are a major concern of parents and caregivers. The focus needs to be on the child and on the health and well-being of caregivers and other children exposed to the ill child. Since children are a reservoir for many infectious agents and since caregivers come into close and frequent contact with children, caregivers are at risk for developing a wide variety of infectious diseases. The infection control standards are recommended to protect both children and caregivers from communicable disease.

Recording the occurrence of illness in a facility and the response to the illness characterizes and defines the frequency of the illness, suggests whether an outbreak has occurred, may suggest an effective intervention, and provides documentation for administrative purposes.

Facilities may comply by adopting a model policy provided by the licensing agency, resource and referral agency, or health department.

Little training and few educational materials on these infectious disease risks are available at present to caregivers.

See sample symptom record in Appendix G, on p. 341.

A sample symptom record is also provided in *Healthy Young Children*. To obtain this publication, contact

National Association for the Education of Young Children
1834 Connecticut Avenue, N.W.
Washington, DC 20009

AD16. Policies shall be used to prevent and control infections of the intestines (often with diarrhea) or liver and diarrheal diseases as specified in *Disease Surveillance of Enteric (Diarrheal) and Hepatitis A Virus Infection*, on p. 218.

STANDARDS

AD17. At the caregiver's discretion, children who are ill shall be permitted to receive care in their usual child care setting if

a) Their care poses no increased risk to them or to other children in care;

b) They are able to participate fully in facility activities, or their limited participation can be accommodated by adjustments of the facility that the caregiver is willing to make; and

c) Their need for special attention (such as frequently offered fluids) can be met.

When children are not permitted to receive care in their usual child care setting and cannot receive care from a parent or relative, they shall be permitted to receive care in one of the following arrangements if the facility meets the applicable standards:

a) Care in the child's usual facility in a special area for care of ill children.[8]

b) Care in a separate small family-child-care home or center that serves only children with illness or temporary disabilities.[9] (See *Special Facilities for Ill Children*, on p. 100.)

c) Care by a child care worker in the child's own home.[10]

RATIONALE

Young children who are developing trust, autonomy, and initiative require the support of familiar caregivers and environments during times of illness in order to recover physically and avoid emotional distress.[11-13]

Young children enrolled in facilities experience a high incidence of mild illness (e.g., upper respiratory infections, otitis media) and other temporary disabilities (e.g., exacerbation of asthma, eczema) that may preclude their participation in the usual facility activities. Because many state regulations now require that children with these conditions be excluded from their usual care arrangement,[14] several alternative care arrangements have been established. Clearly, when children with possible communicable diseases are present in the alternative care arrangements, emphasis on preventing the further spread of disease is as important as in the usual facilities. Although most facilities claim to adhere to general principles of prevention and control of communicable disease, only one facility studied followed strict isolation procedures;[15] another facility demonstrated no additional transmission of communicable disease from the children served to the rest of the well children attending the usual child care facilities.[16]

Prevention of additional cases of communicable disease should be an important objective in these alternative care arrangements for children with minor illness and temporary disabilities.

COMMENTS

Working parents should be entitled to family sick leave days to care for their ill children. There is general agreement among professionals and the general public that when a child is seriously ill or when it is not yet clear that the illness is a mild one, the parent should have the right to be at home with the child. When a child is recuperating or has a cold or other mild illness, parents often need alternative arrangements. At a minimum, working parents should be able to use their own sick or personal days to care for their ill children. This is certainly the preferred arrangement.

However, children are ill frequently and some parents need help in making alternative arrangements for the days when the child is not very ill and the parents need to be at work. Facilities unable to care for ill children should be supportive and helpful to parents, giving them ideas for alternative arrangements. However, the responsibility for care cannot be transferred from the parent to the caregiver if the caregiver is unwilling to accept this responsibility. The decision to accept responsibiity for the care of ill children rests with the caregiver, who must weigh staffing and programmatic considerations that affect this decision and that may vary from one instance to another.

Sometimes a child can be included in the facility's regular group of children, with modified activities. Sometimes a center can set up a "get-well room" where ill children not able to be in the regular group can be cared for. Some centers have set up satellite small family-child-care homes for their enrolled children, where the children know the caregiver because he/she works at the center when no child is ill. Similarly, a child's regular small or large family home caregiver could include the child in the regular group if appropriate, or might have a "get-well room," if adequate supervision can be provided. When necessary, alternative care arrangements may include a worker in the child's home, or other arrangements in a pediatric unit of a hospital, pediatric office, or other similar setting. Special facilities caring only for ill children should

STANDARDS	RATIONALE	COMMENTS

meet more specialized requirements (see *Special Facilities for Ill Children*, on p. 100).

AD18. Any facility that offers care for the ill child of any age shall[11]
a) Use a caregiver familiar to the child.
b) Be in a familiar place.
c) Involve a caregiver who has time to give individual care and emotional support, who knows of the child's interests and knows activities that appeal to the age group and to a sick child.
d) Offer a program planned in consultation with qualified health personnel and with ongoing medical direction.

For additional information on care of ill children, see *Reporting Illness*, on p. 87, and *Health Department Plan*, on p. 309.

Because children are most comfortable in a familiar place with familiar people, the preferred arrangement for ill children will be the child's regular facility, when the facility has the resources to adapt to the needs of such children.

Care provided in a child's home is a matter between the parents and the caregiver they select; it is not a situation that can be regulated or licensed, except by "personal" licensing/certification of caregivers (see *Individual Licensure/Certification*, on p. 301).

HEALTH PLAN

Child Health Services

AD19. Each facility shall develop and follow a procedure that requires children to have immunizations (see immunization schedules in Appendices P-1 and P-2, on pp. 372–374) and periodic health assessments (see Appendix F, on p. 340), and shall encourage parents/legal guardians to schedule these as recommended by the American Academy of Pediatrics. Documentation of an age-appropriate health assessment shall be completed within 6 weeks of admission (see Appendix C, item B, on p. 331). The facility shall not exclude a child for failure to obtain these assessments unless the health of others at the facility may be jeopardized and resources for the assessments are accessible and available. Centers shall have written procedures on immunizations and periodic health assessments of children. (See chapter 6, *Infectious Diseases*, on p. 207.)

Health assessments are important to ensure prevention, early detection of remediable problems, and planning for adaptations needed so that all children can reach their potential. When health assessments are promoted through child care (among other settings), children enrolled in child care will have increased access to immunizations and other preventive services.[17,18]

The facility should expect and encourage regular health assessments. Assistance for caregivers and low-income parents can be obtained through the local Medicaid Early Periodic Screening and Diagnostic Treatment (EPSDT) program.

AD20. The facility shall require medical reports prior to admission and shall review the information about the child's health. (See Appendix C, item B on p. 351.) Questions raised shall be directed to the family

Facilities cannot accept responsibility for a child whose health needs are unclear. Although up to 6 weeks may be allowed to obtain complete information, parents must provide sufficient information to allow the care-

The minimum acceptable medical report is a history obtained from the parents and documentation of an appointment to obtain the remaining immunizations. A child's entrance into the facility need not be delayed

or (with parental permission) to the child's health care provider for explanation and implications for child care.

giver to plan for care of the child.

if an appointment for health supervision is scheduled. Appointments for well-child care must often be scheduled several weeks in advance.

A sample consent form for accessing a child's medical records is shown in Appendix II.6 of *Health in Day Care: A Manual for Health Professionals*. To obtain a copy of this publication, contact

American Academy of Pediatrics
141 Northwest Point Blvd
P.O. Box 927
Elk Grove Village, IL 60009-0927

AD21. There shall be written policies and procedures that comply with local and state regulations for filing and regularly updating each child's immunization records, according to the recommended schedule, prior to admission. A child's immunizations shall be up to date for age on admission or shall be initiated before admission and updated according to the recommended schedule after admission. (See the recommended immunization schedules in Appendices P-1 and P-2, on pp. 372–374.)

Immunizations must be up to date for children in child care to reduce the incidence of diseases preventable by immunization. Involving large numbers of our youngest children, who are now enrolled in facilities, in updating immunizations is an opportunity to improve significantly the health of our nation. National surveys document the fact that child care has a positive influence on protection from vaccine-preventable illness.[19] Immunizations should be required for all children in child care settings, should be documented, and should follow the recommendations in the most current report of the Committee for Infectious Disease, American Academy of Pediatrics, Elk Grove Village, Illinois, and the Advisory Committee on Immunization Practices of the U.S. Public Health Service.

Facilities should require immunizations at the level of the most comprehensive current standards. Resources must be provided by state and local health departments so that families can obtain immunizations. Local public health staff (the staff of immunization units, EPSDT programs, etc.) should provide assistance to caregivers in the form of record-keeping materials, educational materials, and on-site visits for education and help with surveillance activities. It is helpful to transcribe data to a simple form that contains guidelines for updating. (Samples may be obtained from California Immunization Unit, Dept. of Health Services, 2151 Berkeley Way, Room 712, Berkeley, CA 94704.) Such a form should be provided by a public health agency to caregivers and should be standard nationwide.

AD22. The facility shall allow 3 months for parents to obtain the required immunizations on admission to the facility. A child whose immunizations are not kept up to date shall be dismissed after three written reminders to parents over a 3 month period. If more than one immunization is needed in a series, time shall be allowed for the immunizations to be obtained at the appropriate intervals. (See the recommended immunization schedules in Appendices P-1 and P-2, on pp. 372–374).

See rationale for standard AD21.

AD23. The facility shall require that the parent or legal guardian provide documentation that the child has received immunizations (see Appendix P-1, on p. 372) and health supervision

This requirement encourages continuity of the child's health care and helps to ensure that the child does not develop conditions that impair the child's development or increase

STANDARDS	RATIONALE	COMMENTS

to correct any omissions in immunizations and/or health assessments (see Appendix C, item B, on p. 331), based on the AAP's recommended schedule (see Appendix F, on p. 340), prior to admission to the facility.

the risk of illness from child care participation.

AD24. As part of the enrollment of a child, the caregiver shall ask the family to identify the child's health care providers and to provide written consent (see *Confidentiality and Access to Records*, on p. 288) to enable the caregiver to establish communication with those providers. (See standard PR52 in chapter 2 on p. 59.)

Pediatricians (and other health care providers) are involved not only in the medical care of the child but in the ecological system in which the child exists.[20] A major barrier to productive working relationships between child care and health care providers is inadequacy of communication channels.[21]

A source of health care may be a well-child clinic, a public health department, or a private physician. Families should also know the location of the hospital emergency room nearest to their home. (The emergency room is not an appropriate place for routine care, but may properly be used in an emergency.) Education and information for caregivers about community resources is a good topic for staff training.

AD25. Nutrition assessment data (i.e., growth and anemia screening) shall be an integral part of the routine health supervision documented in the health record. Children found at risk shall have additional assessments, follow-ups, and recommendations for facility management as needed. (See standards PR42 in chapter 2 on p. 56 and HP5 in chapter 3 on p. 66.)

Children who need special intervention or modification of child care feeding routines because of growth problems must be identified so that preventive health/nutrition care can be provided at a critical time during growth and development.

AD26. Families shall be asked to share information about family health (i.e., chronic diseases) that might affect the child's health.

A family history of chronic disease is an important component of any health history, particularly where inherited diseases are identified.

Information on family health can be gathered by simply asking parents to tell the caregiver about any chronic health problems that the child's parents, siblings, or household members have.

Family management of chronic illness may require additional support services.

Health Consultation

AD27. Every facility shall utilize the services of a health consultant to provide ongoing consultation to the facility and to assist in the development of written policies relating to health and safety, as specified in *Health Consultants*, on p. 33.

Caregivers are rarely trained health professionals. Health consultants can help develop and implement written policies for the prevention and management of injury and disease. Advance planning in this area can reduce stress for caregivers, parents, and health professionals.

Unless provided through a public health system, the health consultant's services are very difficult to obtain—particularly for small family-child-care homes. Caregivers should seek the volunteer services of a health consultant through state and local professional organizations, such as local chapters of the American Academy of Pediatrics, the American Nurses' Association, the Visiting Nurse Association, the American Academy of Family Physicians, the National Association of Pediatric Nurse Associates and Practitioners, the National Association for the Education of Young Children, and the National Association for Family Day Care, or through state and local health departments (especially the public health nursing departments and the state communicable disease specialist's or epidemiologist's office). Caregivers should not overlook health professionals who are parents of children enrolled in their facilities.

The specific policies for an individual facility depend on the resources available to that facility.[22] To be effective, a health consultant should know what resources are available in the community and should involve caregivers and parents in setting policies. Setting policies in cooperation with both caregivers and parents will better ensure successful implementation.[23]

Licensing requirements for facilities increasingly require that facilities make specific arrangements with a health consultant to assist in the development of written policies for the prevention and control of disease.

For additional information, see also *Health Consultants*, on p. 33 for qualifications and responsibilities of the health consultant; *Health Consultants in Special Facilities for Ill Children*, on p. 106; and *Consultants*, on p. 314, on state and local consultants.

MEDICATION POLICY

AD28. Written policies shall specify the requirements detailed in *Medications*, on p. 88, and in Appendix C, item E, on p. 335. There shall be a written policy for the use of any commonly used nonprescription medication for oral or topical use kept on hand by the facility to be used for any child, with parental consent, for whom the medication may be indicated.

Caregivers need to be aware of what medication the child is receiving and when, who prescribed the medicine, and what the known reactions or side effects may be in the event that a child has a negative reaction to the medicine.[24] A child's reaction to medication may occasionally be extreme enough to initiate the protocol developed for emergencies. This medication record is especially important if medications are frequently prescribed or if long-term medications are being used.

A sample medication administration policy is provided in Appendix II.2 of *Health in Day Care: A Manual for Health Professionals*. To order, contact

American Academy of Pediatrics
141 Northwest Point Blvd.
P.O. Box 927
Elk Grove Village, IL 60009-0927

STANDARDS	RATIONALE	COMMENTS

EMERGENCY PLAN

AD29. The facility shall have an emergency plan as specified in Appendix R, on p. 377.

AD30. The facility's written emergency plan shall be reviewed with each employee upon employment and family member residing in the facility to ensure that policies and procedures are understood and followed in the event of an emergency.

See rationale for standard AD29.

For additional information on emergency plan, see also *Evacuation Plan and Drills*, and *Emergency Procedures*, on p. 95.

EVACUATION PLAN AND DRILLS

AD31. The facility shall have a written plan for reporting and evacuating in case of fire, flood, tornado, earthquake, hurricane, blizzard, power failure, or other disaster that could create structural damages to the facility or pose health hazards. The facility shall also include procedures for staff training on this emergency plan.

Emergency situations are not conducive to calm and composed thinking. Drafting a written plan provides the opportunity to prepare and to prevent poor judgments made under the stress of an emergency.

An organized, comprehensive approach to injury prevention and control is necessary to ensure that a safe environment is provided children in child care. Such an approach requires written plans, policies, procedures, and record-keeping so that there is consistency over time and across staff and an understanding between parents and caregivers about concerns for, and attention to, the safety of children.

Diagrammed evacuation procedures are easiest to follow in an emergency. Floor plan layouts that show two alternate exit routes are best. Plans should be clear enough that a visitor to the facility could easily follow the instructions.

A sample emergency evacuation plan is provided in *Healthy Young Children*. To obtain this publication, contact

National Association for the Education of Young Children 1834 Connecticut Avenue, N.W. Washington, DC 20009

AD32. Evacuation drills shall be practiced as follows in areas where natural disasters occur: for tornadoes, on a monthly basis in tornado season; for earthquakes, every 6 months; and for hurricanes, annually.

Regular evacuation drills constitute an important safety practice in areas where these natural disasters occur.

AD33. The center director shall use a daily class roster in checking the evacuation and return to a safe indoor space of all children in attendance during an evacuation drill. Small and large family home caregivers shall count to be sure that all children are safely evacuated and returned to a safe indoor space during an evacuation drill.

Use of a roster ensures that all children are accounted for.

STANDARDS	RATIONALE	COMMENTS

AD34. A fire evacuation procedure shall be approved by a fire inspector and shall be practiced at least monthly from all exit locations at varied times of the day and during varied activities, including naptime. (See also *Evacuation Drill Records*, on p. 293, and *Posting Documents*, on p. 296.)

The extensive turnover in child care necessitates this level of frequency. Practicing fire evacuation procedures on a monthly basis provides the frequency needed for this to become a routine procedure for children in the event of an emergency. Fires are responsible for the great majority of burn deaths.[25,26] The routine practice of emergency evacuation plans fosters calm, competent use of the plans in an emergency.

The facility should time the procedure and aim to evacuate all persons in a specific (approved) number of minutes.

AD35. A fire evacuation procedure shall be maintained by the caregiver and practiced at least monthly from all exit locations at varied times of the day and during varied activities, including naptime. (See also *Evacuation Drill Records*, on p. 293, and *Posting Documents*, on p. 296.)

See rationale for standard AD34.

Fire prevention programs for planning exit routes for the home are readily available. One such program is called "EDITH" ("Exit Drill In The Home"), which applies to one's own family. This program is available from local fire departments.

See also comment for standard AD34.

SAFETY PLAN

AD36. The safety plan for all facilities shall conform to the standards in this section. Centers shall have written safety plans. In centers, all caregivers shall be given a copy of the safety plan at the time of employment, and the plan shall be reviewed with each caregiver to ensure that the policies are understood and followed. This written plan shall be on file at the center for review.

See rationale for standard AD31 on p. 280.

AD37. Names, addresses, and telephone numbers of persons authorized to take the child under care out of the facility shall be maintained. Policies shall also address how the facility will handle the situation if a parent arrives who is intoxicated or otherwise incapable of bringing the child home safely, or if a noncustodial parent attempts to claim the child without the consent of the custodial parent.

Caregivers must not be unwitting accomplices in schemes to gain custody of children by accepting a telephone authorization provided falsely by a person claiming to be the child's custodial parent.

Local police should be consulted about their recommendations for how staff can obtain support from law enforcement authorities to avoid incurring increased liability by releasing a child into an unsafe situation or by improperly refusing to release a child.

AD38. The facility shall honor a telephone authorization to release a child only with prior written authorization from the custodial parent. (See standard AD37 above.)

See rationale for standard AD37.

The facility needs a mechanism for verifying the identification of a new person to whom the parents have given telephone authorization to pick up their child.

STANDARDS	RATIONALE	COMMENTS

AD39. Caregiving adults who bring the child to, or remove the child from, the facility (parents and staff) shall sign children in and out of the facility.

The keeping of accurate records of admission and release is of utmost importance to the caregiver in relation to establishing the amount (and date) of service for reimbursement and in case of possible legal sanctions or liability suits.

Time clocks and cards can serve as verification. This standard requires any adult who is in charge of the child at the time to note the child's coming to, and leaving, the facility. It does not require that the person receiving the child into care sign the child in.

AD40. Written policies shall address the safe transport of children by vehicle to or from the facility, including field trips or special outings. The following shall be provided for:
a) Licensing of vehicles and drivers. (See *Vehicles*, on p. 199, and *Qualifications of Drivers*, on p. 200.)
b) Maintenance of vehicles (See *Vehicles*, on p. 199.)
c) Operation of the vehicles.
d) Driver selection, training, and supervision. (See *Qualifications of Drivers* and *Transportation Training*, on p. 200.)
e) Child:staff ratio during transport. (See *Child:Staff Ratio and Group Size*, on p. 1.)
f) Permitted and prohibited activities during transport.
g) Backup arrangements for emergencies.
h) Seat belt and car seat use. (See *Seat Restraints*, on p. 201.)
i) Drop-off and pick-up. (See *Pick-Up and Drop-Off Plans*, on p. 202.)

Motor vehicle accidents are the leading cause of death in the United States.[27] Therefore it is necessary for the safety of children to require that the caregiver comply with minimum requirements governing the transportation of children in care, in the absence of the parent.[28]

Maintenance should include a pretrip inspection checklist for every trip, and vehicle maintenance service to be performed at least quarterly.

AD41. Written policies shall address the safe transport of children by vehicle to and from the small or large family-child-care home for any reason, including field trips or special outings (see *Field Trips*, on p. 52). The following shall be provided for:
a) Child:staff ratio during transport. (See *Child:Staff Ratio and Group Size*, on p. 1.)
b) Backup arrangements for emergencies.
c) Seat belt and car seat use. (See *Seat Restraints*, on p. 201.)
d) Licensing of vehicles and drivers. (See *Vehicles*, on p. 199, and *Qualifications of Drivers*, on p. 200.)

See rationale for standard AD40.

---

e) Maintenance of the vehicles. (See *Vehicles*, on p. 199.)

AD42. There shall be policies for the use of equipment for gross motor play, supervision of play spaces, and at least monthly maintenance checks of play equipment. For centers, these shall be written policies. (See *Playground and Equipment Records*, on p. 294.)

Properly laid out play spaces, properly designed and maintained equipment, installation of energy-absorbing surfaces, and adequate supervision of the play space by caregivers/parents help to reduce both the potential and the severity of injury.[29,30]

Written policies and procedures are essential for education of staff and may be useful in situations where liability is an issue.

The increasing number of children in out-of-home care, as well as an increasing awareness and understanding of issues in child safety, combine to highlight the importance of developing and maintaining safe play spaces for children in child care settings. Parents certainly expect that their child will be adequately supervised and that they will not be exposed to hazardous play environments, yet will have the opportunity for free, creative play.

AD43. The facility shall provide a telephone as specified in *Facility Furnishings and Equipment*, on p. 157, and post emergency telephone numbers and instructions as specified in Appendix N, on p. 357.

For additional information on safety plan, see also standard HP100 in chapter 3 on p. 94, standard FA285 in chapter 5 on p. 196 on safe pedestrian routes to be written into the facility's procedures, and *Transportation*, on p. 199.

SANITATION PLAN

AD44. The facility's sanitation plan shall include policies and procedures for the following items. Centers shall have written sanitation plans.

a) Maintaining equipment used for handwashing, toileting, and toilet training in a sanitary condition, as specified in *Toilet, Diapering, and Bath Areas*, on p. 168, and *Toileting, Diapering, and Toilet Training*, on p. 68.

b) Maintaining diaper-changing areas and equipment in a disinfected condition, as specified in *Diaper-Changing Areas*, on p. 171.

c) Maintaining toys in a disinfected condition in facilities, as specified in *Sanitation, Disinfection, and Maintenance of Toys and Objects*, on p. 78.

d) Managing pets or other animals in a safe and sanitary manner, as specified in *Animals*, on p. 97.

e) Proper handwashing procedures consistent with the method described in the publication *What*

Many communicable diseases can be prevented through appropriate hygiene, sanitation, and disinfection methods. Bacterial cultures of environmental surfaces in facilities have demonstrated evidence of fecal contamination, which has been used to gauge the adequacy of sanitation, disinfection, and hygiene practices. Contamination of hands, toys, and other equipment in the room has appeared to play a role in the transmission of diseases in child care settings.[31,32] Regular and thorough cleaning of rooms prevents transmission of illness.[33]

Animals, including pets, can be a source of illness for people, and people may be a source of illness for animals.[34]

The steps involved in effective handwashing (to reduce the amount of bacterial contamination) are easily

To order the publication *What to Do to Stop Disease in Child Day Care Centers*, write

STANDARDS

to *Do to Stop Disease in Child Day Care Centers,* by the Centers for Disease Control. The facility shall display handwashing instruction signs conspicuously. (See *Handwashing,* on p. 72.)

f) Personal hygiene of caregivers and children as specified in *Handwashing,* on p. 72.

g) Practicing environmental sanitation policies and procedures, as specified in *Interior Maintenance,* on p. 197.

NUTRITION PLAN AND POLICY

AD45. The facility shall have a nutrition plan that addresses kitchen layout; food procurement, preparation, and service; staffing; and nutrition education (see specifics in Chapter 4, *Nutrition and Food Service,* on p. 115) and delegates responsibility for each of these items. The nutrition plan of centers shall be a written plan and shall have input by the Nutrition Specialist (see Appendices B-1 and B-2, on pp. 328–329) and a food service expert.

AD46. The facility's policies and procedures for handling food shall include items specified in *Kitchen,* on p. 173, *Food Brought From Home,* on p. 126, *Kitchen and Equipment,* on p. 127, *Food Safety,* on p. 130, and *Maintenance,* on p. 133. Centers shall have written food-handling policies.

RATIONALE

forgotten. Posted signs provide frequent reminders to staff and orientation for new staff. Education of caregivers regarding handwashing and other cleaning procedures can reduce the occurrence of illness in the group of children with whom they work.[35]

Illnesses may be spread in a variety of ways, such as in human waste (urine, stool); in body fluids (drool, nasal discharge, open skin sores, eye discharge, and blood); by direct, skin-to-skin contact; by touching an object that has germs on it; and through the air, in droplets that result from sneezes and coughs. Since many infected people carry communicable diseases without symptoms, and many are contagious before they experience a symptom, caregivers need to protect themselves and the children they serve by carrying out, on a routine basis, sanitation and disinfection procedures that approach every potential illness-spreading condition in the same way.

Having a plan that clearly delegates responsibility and that encompasses the pertinent nutrition elements will ensure an adequate, appropriate, and effective nutrition unit.

Handling food in a safe and careful manner prevents the growth of bacteria, viruses, fungi, and parasites, and prevents contamination of the food by insects or rodents.

Outbreaks of foodborne illness have occurred in many settings, including facilities. Because large centers serve more meals on a daily basis than many restaurants, food handlers in these settings should practice appropriate food-handling procedures.

COMMENTS

Centers for Disease Control
1600 Clifton Road, N.E.
Atlanta, GA 30333

AD47. Policies about infant feeding shall be developed as specified in Appendix L, on p. 354.

For additional information on nutrition plans, see also standard NU1 in chapter 4 on p. 115, standards NU27 and NU28 in chapter 4 on p. 122, standard NU44 in chapter 4 on p. 125, and standards NU105 and NU106 in chapter 4 on p. 136.

EVENING AND NIGHT CARE PLAN

AD48. Facilities that provide evening and nighttime care shall have plans for such care that include the supervision of sleeping children as specified in *Supervision Policy*, on p. 272, and the management of sleep equipment as specified in *Sleeping*, on p. 175, and *Sanitation, Disinfection, and Maintenance of Bedding*, on p. 79. Centers shall have written plans for evening and night care.

Evening and night care routines are significantly different from those required for daytime and should be addressed in a planned way.

SMOKING AND PROHIBITED SUBSTANCES PLAN

AD49. Facilities shall have written policies specifying that smoking, use of alcohol, and use or possession of illegal substances or unauthorized potentially toxic substances are prohibited in the facility when children are in care.

The age, defenselessness, and lack of discretion of the child under care make this prohibition an absolute requirement.

The policies should be discussed via handouts or pamphlets that are given to parents, especially those who have children in small family-child-care homes or school-age-child care facilities, to inform them of the dangers of these prohibited substances.

REVIEW AND REVISION OF POLICIES, PLANS, AND PROCEDURES

AD50. The facility shall make policies, plans, and procedures available to all persons affected (including parents and staff) at least annually and when changes are made. When a child enters a facility, parents shall sign a statement that they have read and/or understand the content of the policies.

State-of-the-art information changes. A yearly review encourages child care administrators to keep information and policies current. Current information on health and safety practices that is shared and developed cooperatively among caregivers and parents invites more participation and compliance with health and safety practices.

This standard assumes that all disciplines that support and inform child care services—such as health, public safety, emergency preparedness, and regulatory agencies—have systems for disseminating current and accurate information that affects the health of all people in child care settings. Illiterate parents will need to have the policies presented orally to them.

AD51. The facility shall obtain review of the policies by a health consultant (see *Health Consultants*, on p. 33) at least annually and when changes are made.

For additional policies to review, see standards AD30, on p. 280, AD36, on p. 281, *Sanitation Plan*, on p. 283, and *Personnel Policies*, on p. 287.

8.3 Program of Activities

AD52. The facility shall have a written program of activities (as specified in *Management Plan and Statement of Services*, on p. 271) that sets out the basic elements from which the daily plan is to be built. The program of activities shall

a) Address each age group served, that is, infants, toddlers, preschoolers, and/or school-age children.

b) Cover the elements specified in *Program of Developmental Activities*, on p. 45.

c) Maintain the child:staff ratios described in *Child:Staff Ratio and Group Size*, on p. 1.

d) Provide for incorporation of specific health and safety education activities into the curriculum on a daily basis throughout the year. Topics of health education shall include physical, oral, mental, and social health, and shall include items specified in *Nutrition Learning Experiences and Education*, on p. 136, and Appendix E, on p. 338.

e) Include a parent education plan to educate parents about child health. Such plan shall have been reviewed and approved by a licensed health profesional, who may also serve as the facility's health consultant (see *Health Consultants*, on p. 33). This plan shall primarily involve personal contacts with parents by knowledgeable caregivers. The parent education plan shall include topics identified in Appendix E, on p. 338, and *Health Education for Parents*, on p. 62.

AD53. Small family-child-care-homes shall have schedules of activities and educational progams as specified in *Management Plan and Statement of Services*, on p. 271.

Those who provide child care and education must themselves be clear about their program.

Child care is a "delivery of service" involving a contractual relationship between provider and consumer. A written plan helps to particularize the service and contributes to specific and responsible operations that are conducive to sound child development and safety practices and to positive consumer relations.

Early childhood specialists agree on the inseparability of cognitive and emotional/social development; the influence of the child's health on all areas; the central importance of continuity of affectionate care; the relevance of the phase or stage concept; and the importance of action (including play) as a mode of learning.[36]

Young children learn better by experiencing an activity and observing behavior than through didactic training.[37] There may be a "reciprocal relationship" between learning and play, so that play experiences are closely related to learning.[38]

Parental behavior can be modified by education.[39,40] Parents should be involved closely with the facility.[41] The concept of parent control and empowerment is key to successful parent education in the child care setting.[39] It has not been documented that a child's eventual success in education or in society is related to parent education, but support and education for parents lead to better parenting abilities.[39]

See rationale for standard AD52.

The process of preparing plans promotes thinking about programming for children. Plans also allow for monitoring and for accountability.

Suggestions for topics and methods of presentation are widely available, for example, in the NAEYC publication *Healthy Young Children* and in the AAP publication *Health in Day Care: A Manual for Health Professionals*. To order these publications contact

National Association for the Education of Young Children
1834 Connecticut Avene, N.W.
Washington, DC 20009

and

American Academy of Pediatrics
141 Northwest Point Blvd.
P.O. Box 927
Elk Grove Village, IL 60009-0927

Examples of health education activities include the verbal explanation of principles of personal hygiene and discussions about the food value of snacks, the importance of buckling up seat belts, and the value of exercise.

Parents and staff can experience mutual learning in an open, supportive setting.

(See *Program of Developmental Activities*, on p. 45, for specifics)

AD54. Transition contacts (e.g., contacts at time of dropping off or picking up) and other interactions with parents shall be the responsibility of the large or small family home caregiver or the designated center or school-age-child care facility caregiver on each shift. These caregivers shall be trained in health and development and shall observe each assigned child's physical condition, behavior, and personality factors during the day. When several staff shifts are involved, information about the child shall be exchanged between caregivers assigned to each shift.

Personal contact on a daily basis between the child care staff and parents is essential to ensure the transfer of information required to provide for the child's needs. Information about the child's experiences and health during the interval when an adult other than the parent is in charge should be provided to parents because they may need such information to deal with the child's later behavior.

This designated caregiver could be the health advocate (see *Qualifications of Health Advocates*, on p. 13).

8.4 Personnel Policies

AD55. The facility shall have and follow personnel policies as specified in Appendix S, on p. 379.

For additional information on personnel policies, see also *Staff Benefits*, on p. 40.

8.5 Written Statement of Services

AD56. The facility shall provide parents with a statement of services that contains the items specified in *Management Plan and Statement of Services*, on p. 271. Parents shall sign this statement of services.

8.6 Special Needs Plan

See *Caregiver Responsibilities*, on p. 265, *Written Plan*, on p. 266, and *Emergency Preparedness Plan*, on p. 267 for the specific contents of a plan for children with special needs.

8.7 Records

CHILD RECORDS

AD57. The facility shall maintain a file for each child as specified in Appendix C, on p. 330.

CONFIDENTIALITY AND ACCESS TO RECORDS

AD58. The facility shall have policies and procedures that cover the exchange of information among parents, the facility, and other professionals or agencies that are involved with the child and family before the child enters the facility, during the time the child is cared for in the facility, and after the child leaves the facility. Parental consent, confidentiality, and the sharing of information useful in the provision of service to the child and family shall be addressed. For centers, these shall be written policies and procedures.

The child's record shall be available to the parents for inspection at all times. The exchange of information about the child and family among providers of service can greatly enhance the effectiveness of child and family support, and should be accomplished with sensitivity to issues of confidentiality and the need to know. Procedures should be developed and a method established to ensure accountability and to ensure that the exchange is being carried out.

The responsibiity for a child's health is shared by all those responsible for the child: parents, health professionals, and caregivers. Caregivers should expect parents to transfer to them health information about the child given to and by health professionals. Such transfer of information is often facilitated by the use of forms, but telephone communication, with parental consent, is also appropriate to clarify concerns about a specific child. If a parent does not give permission, caregivers can use state override procedures when it is in the child's best interest to do so. Caregivers should also expect health professionals to provide their expertise for the formulation and implementaton of facility policies and procedures.

AD59. The facility shall establish and follow a written policy on confidentiality of the records of staff and children that ensures that the facility will not disclose material in the records without the written consent of parents (with legal custody) or legal guardian for children, or of staff for themselves.

Confidentiality must be maintained to protect the child and family[42] and is defined by law.[19]

Parental trust in the caregiver is the key to the caregiver's ability to work toward health promotion and to obtain needed information to use in decision making and planning for the child's best interest. Assurance of confidentiality fosters this trust. When custody has been awarded to only one parent, access to records must be limited to the custodial parent. In cases of disputed access, the facility may need to request that the parents supply a copy of the court document that defines parental rights.

Operational control to accommodate the health and safety of individual children requires basic information regarding each child in care.

AD60. Caregivers shall not disclose or discuss personal information regarding children and their relatives with any unauthorized person. Confidential information shall be seen by and discussed with only staff who need the information in order to provide services.

See rationale for standard AD59.

STANDARDS	RATIONALE	COMMENTS

AD61. The director of the facility shall decide who among the staff may have confidential information shared with them. Clearly, this decision must be made selectively, and all caregivers must be taught the basic principles of all individuals' rights to confidentiality.

Someone in each facility must be authorized to make decisions about the sharing of confidential information, and the director is the logical choice. However, the decision about sharing information must also involve the parent(s) or family. Sharing of confidential information shall be selective and shall be based on a need to know and on the parent's authorization for disclosure of such information.

AD62. Written releases shall be obtained from the child's parent or legal guardian prior to forwarding information and/or the child's records (see Appendix C, on p. 330) to other service providers.

Requiring written releases ensures confidentiality.

Continuity of care and information is invaluable during childhood when growth and development are rapidly changing.

Release formats may vary from state to state and within facilities. It may be helpful if user-friendly forms are furnished for all caregivers to facilitate the exchange of information.

AD63. Each child's records (see Appendix C, on p. 330) shall be copied for the child's parents on request. The originals shall be given to the child's parents on request.

The facility must retain the records in the event of a requirement for legal defense, but parents have the right to know and have the full contents of the records.

An effective way to educate parents on the value of maintaining the child's developmental and health information is to have them focus on their own child's records. Such records should be used as a mutual education tool by parents and caregivers.

AD64. The content of the written procedures for protecting the confidentiality of medical and social information shall be consistent with federal, state, and local guidelines and regulations and shall be taught to caregivers. Confidential medical information pertinent to safe care of the child shall be provided to facilities within the guidelines of state or local public health regulations. However, under all circumstances, confidentiality about the child's medical condition and the family's status shall be preserved unless such information is released at the written request of the family, except in cases where abuse or neglect is a concern. In such cases, state laws and regulations apply.

Serving children and families involves significant facility responsibilities in obtaining, maintaining, and sharing confidential information.

Each caregiver must respect the confidentiality of information pertaining to all families served.

This standard may also apply to the sharing of any other personal information.

STANDARDS	RATIONALE	COMMENTS

AD65. Where these standards require the facility to have written policies, reports, and records, these records shall be available to the licensing agency for inspection and proof of compliance.

The licensing agency must have access to required documents to monitor compliance effectively.

PERSONNEL RECORDS

AD66. Individual files for all staff, including volunteers, shall be maintained as specified in Appendix T, on p. 381.

ATTENDANCE RECORDS

AD67. The facility shall keep daily attendance records, including the times of arrival and departure of each child enrolled, for 90 days.

Operational control to accommodate the health and safety of individual children requires basic information regarding each child in care. This standard ensures that the facility knows which children are receiving care at any given time. It aids in the surveillance of child:staff ratios and provides data for program planning.

See sample enrollment/attendance/symptom record, Appendix G, on p. 341.

AD68. Centers shall keep daily attendance records of the names of each caregiver in attendance.

See rationale for standard AD67.

INCIDENCE LOGS OF ILLNESS, INJURY, AND OTHER PROBLEMS

AD69. For illnesses with onset while a child is attending (or a staff member is working in) a facility that potentially require exclusion (see *Inclusion/Exclusion/Dismissal*, on p. 80), the facility shall record the date and time of the illness, the person affected, a description of the symptoms, the response of the staff to these symptoms, who was notified (e.g., parent, legal guardian, nurse, physician), and their response.

Recording the occurrence of illness in a facility and the response to the illness characterizes and defines the frequency of the illness, suggests whether an outbreak has occurred, may suggest an effective intervention, and provides documentation for administrative purposes.

Surveillance for symptoms can be accomplished easily by using a combined attendance and symptom record. Any symptoms can be noted when the child is signed in, with added notations made during the day when additional symptoms appear. Simple forms that record data for the entire group for a weekly or monthly period help caregivers spot patterns of illness for an individual child or among the children in the group or center.

See sample enrollment/attendance/symptom record, Appendix G, on p. 341.

Multicopy forms can be used to make copies of an injury report simultaneously for the child's record, for the

STANDARDS	RATIONALE	COMMENTS

COMMENTS

parent, for the folder that logs all injuries at the facility, and for the regulatory agency.

AD70. When an injury occurs in the facility that requires first aid or medical attention for a child or adult, the facility shall complete a report form that provides the following information:

a) Name, sex, and age of the injured.
b) Date and time of injury.
c) Location where injury took place.
d) A description of how the injury occurred.
e) Part of the body involved.
f) Description of any consumer product involved.
g) Name of staff member responsible for the care of the injured person at the time of the injury.
h) Actions taken on behalf of the injured following the injury.
i) Name of person who completed the report.
j) Name and address of the facility.

The injury report form shall be completed in triplicate. One copy shall be given to the child's parent or legal guardian (or to the injured adult). The second copy shall be kept in the child's (or adult's) folder at the facility, and the third copy shall be kept in a chronologically filed injury log. This last copy shall be kept in the facility for the period required by the state's statute of limitations.

Injury patterns useful for injury prevention and recognition of child abuse can be discerned from such records.[43] A report form is also necessary for providing information to the child's parents and health care provider and other appropriate health agencies.

See also rationale for standard AD69.

See Appendix U, on p. 383, for a sample injury report form.

Samples of injury report forms can be found in Appendix VI.7 of *Health in Day Care: A Manual for Health Professionals* and *Healthy Young Children*. Order *Health in Day Care: A Manual for Health Professionals* from

> American Academy of Pediatrics
> 141 Northwest Point Blvd.
> P.O. Box 927
> Elk Grove Village, IL 60009-0927

Healthy Young Children may be obtained from

> National Association for the Education of Young Children
> 1834 Connecticut Avenue, N.W. Washington, DC 20009

See also comment for standard AD69.

AD71. When an injury occurs in the small or large family-child-care home that requires first aid or medical attention for a child or staff member, the caregiver shall complete a report form that provides the following information:

a) Name, sex, and age of the injured.
b) Date and time of injury.
c) Location where injury took place.
d) A description of how the injury occurred.
e) Part of the body involved.
f) Actions taken on behalf of the injured following the injury.

See rationale for standard AD70.

See comment for standard AD70.

STANDARDS	RATIONALE	COMMENTS

AD72. The facility shall document that a child's parent or legal guardian was notified immediately of an injury or illness that required professional medical attention.

See rationale for standard AD70.

See comment for standard AD70.

AD73. The completed injury and illness report forms (see above) shall be made available to health care providers and other appropriate health agencies for review and analysis. In addition to maintaining a record for documentation of liability, forms shall be used to identify patterns of injury and illness amenable to prevention. The injury and illness log shall be reviewed by caregivers at least semi-annually and inspected by licensing staff (*Inspections*, on p. 306) and health consultants (see *Health Consultants*, on p. 33) at least annually.

See rationale for standard AD70.

See comment for standard AD70.

AD74. The required form shall be sent to the licensing agency or health department within 5 working days in the event of the death of a child, hospitalization of a child for an injury that occurred in child care, or hospitalization for a reportable communicable disease.

See rationale for standard AD70.

See comment for standard AD70.

AD75. The facility shall also record other events relating to health and safety, such as a lost child.

See rationale for standard AD70.

See comment for standard AD70.

LICENSING AND LEGAL RECORDS

AD76. Every facility shall hold a valid license or registration.

Licensing/registration provides recognition that the facility meets regulatory requirements.

AD77. The facility shall maintain and display in one central area within the facility current copies of applicable inspection reports and documentation that all required corrections have been completed. Such reports and documentation may include
a) Licensing/registration reports.
b) Fire inspection reports.
c) Sanitation inspection reports.
d) Building code inspection reports.
e) Plumbing, gas, and electrical inspection reports.
f) Zoning inspection reports.
g) Results of all water tests. (See *Water Testing*, on p. 153.)

Facility safeguarding is not achieved by one agency carrying out a single regulatory program. Total safeguarding is achieved through a multiplicity of regulatory programs and agencies. Licensing staff, consumers, and concerned individuals benefit from having documents of regulatory approval and legal action in one central location.

Parents, staff, consultants, and visitors should be able to assess the extent of evaluation and compliance of the facility with regulatory and voluntary requirements.

h) Evacuation drill records. (See *Evacuation Plan and Drills*, on p. 280.)
i) Any accreditation certificates.

AD78. When deficiencies are identified during annual policy and performance reviews by the licensing department, funding agency, or accreditation organization, the director or small or large family home caregiver shall follow a written plan for resolution, outlined with the regulatory agency. This plan shall include the following: a description of the problem; a proposed timeline for resolution; designation of responsibility for correcting the deficiency; and a description of the successful resolution of the problem. For centers, this shall be a written plan.

AD79. Reports of legal actions against the facility shall be maintained in one central area.

For additional information on licensing and legal records, see also standard AD65, on p. 290 on access to records by the licensing agency.

FIRE EXTINGUISHER RECORDS

AD80. A report of inspection and maintenance of fire extinguishers shall be available for review and shall be renewed every 3 months.

EVACUATION DRILL RECORDS

AD81. A record of evacuation drills shall be kept on file. (See *Evacuation Plan and Drills*, on p. 280.)

For additional information on evacuation drill records, see also *Posting Documents*, on p. 296, on posting fire evacuation procedures.

Accreditation documentation provides additional information about surveillance and quality improvement efforts of the facility.

A written plan or contract for change is more likely to achieve the desired change.

A fire extinguisher may lose its effectiveness over time. It should work properly at any time when needed to put out a small fire or to clear an escape path.[44]

Routine practice of emergency evacuation plans fosters calm, competent use of the plans in an emergency.

Simple problems amenable to immediate correction do not require extensive documentation. For these, a simple notation of the problem and that the problem was immediately corrected will suffice. However, a notation of the problem is necessary so that recurring problems of the same type can be addressed by a more lasting solution.

Many fire extinguishers are equipped with gauges that can easily be read by caregivers who can do the inspection themselves. Since chemicals tend to separate within these canisters, maintenance instructions (e.g., ''Invert containers at least semiannually'') should be followed.

STANDARDS

INSURANCE RECORDS

AD82. A center shall carry the following insurance. Small and large family home caregivers shall carry this insurance if available.
a) Accident insurance on children.
b) Liability insurance.
c) Vehicle insurance on any vehicle owned or leased by the facility and used to transport children.
d) Property insurance.

PLAYGROUND AND EQUIPMENT RECORDS

AD83. The facility shall maintain all information and records pertaining to the manufacture, installation, and regular inspection of facility playground equipment.

AD84. Report forms shall be used to record the results of monthly maintenance checks of play equipment and surfaces (see *Safety Plan,* on p. 281, *Maintenance of Playground and Outdoor Areas*, on p. 190). These forms shall be reviewed by the facility annually and shall be retained for the number of years required by the state's statute of limitations.

For additional information on playground and equipment records, see also *Maintenance of Playground and Outdoor Areas*, on p. 190.

RATIONALE

With the current increase in litigation, reasonable protection against liability action through proper insurance is essential for reasons of economic security, peace of mind, and public relations.

Requiring insurance reduces risks because insurance companies stipulate compliance with health and safety regulations before issuing or continuing a policy.

The costs of adverse events occurring at a facility can easily cause a financial disaster that can disrupt care for the children. Protection, via insurance, must be secured to provide stability and protection for both the individuals and the facility.

Liability insurance carried by the facility provides a recourse for parents of children enrolled in the event of negligence.

Information regarding manufacture, installation, and maintenance of playground equipment is essential to provide appropriate instructions regarding repair and maintenance procedures.

Written records of monthly maintenance checks and appropriate corrective action are necessary to reduce the risk of potential injury. Annual review of such records provides a mechanism for periodic monitoring and improvement.

COMMENTS

The liability insurance should include coverage for administration of medications, as well as for unintentional injuries, illnesses, and so forth.

Individual health injury coverage may be documented by evidence of personal health insurance coverage as a dependent. Workman's compensation covers adult injuries in case of an accident.

Notwithstanding these guidelines, individual jurisdictions may have specific regulations regarding information, records, equipment, policies, and procedures.

A sample playground safety checklist is provided in *Healthy Young Children*. To obtain this publication, contact

National Assocation for the
Education of Young Children
1834 Connecticut Ave., N.W.
Washington, DC 20009

STANDARDS	RATIONALE	COMMENTS

CONSULTATION RECORDS

AD85. Documentation of health consultation/training visits shall be maintained in the facility's files. Copies of personal training experience shall be provided to caregivers, if certification is available, or as arranged with the local health department. (See *Health Plan*, on p. 276, and *Health Consultants*, on p. 33 on health consultant responsibilities and qualifications.)

Health consultants, licensing agents, health departments, and fellow caregivers should act as reinforcers of appropriate health behavior. Documentation of consultation provides the opportunity to evaluate the use of recommendations and training provided by the consultant.

Documentation can take the form of a list of recommendations and training topics addressed.

FOOD SERVICE RECORDS

AD86. The facility shall maintain records covering the nutrition services budget, expenditures for food, numbers and types of meals served daily with separate recordings for children and adults, inspection reports made by health authorities, and recipes. Copies shall be maintained in the facility files for at least 1 year.

For additional information on food service records, see also Appendix W, item 1, on p. 387.

Food service records permit efficient and effective management of the facility's nutrition component and provide data from which a child care Nutrition Specialist (see Appendices B-1 and B-2, on pp. 328–329) can develop recommendations for program improvement.

COMMUNITY RESOURCE FILE

AD87. The facility shall obtain or have access to a community resource file, updated at least annually, which shall be available to share with parents as needed for child or parent needs. For non-English-speaking families, community resource information shall be available in the parents' language or through the use of interpreters.

Since staff and time are often limited, caregivers should have access to consultation on available resources in a variety of fields (physical and mental health care, nutrition, safety, oral health care, developmental disabilities, etc.).[41,20,45]

When physical, mental, or social health concerns are raised for the child or for the family, they should be addressed appropriately, often by referring the family to resources available in the community.

Facilities with a significant number of non-English-speaking families need to provide materials in the parents' native language.[42]

In many communities, community agencies (e.g., resource and referral agencies) offer community resource files and may be able to supply updated information or service directories to local caregivers. Even small family home caregivers will be able to maintain a simple list of phone numbers of human services such as that published in the telephone directory.

If a resource file is maintained, it must be updated regularly and should be used by a caregiver knowledgeable about health and the community.

STANDARDS	RATIONALE	COMMENTS

LARGE AND SMALL FAMILY-CHILD-CARE HOME RECORDS

AD88. Large and small family home caregivers shall maintain records as specified in Appendix V, on p. 384.

For additional information on large and small family-child-care home records, see also Appendix W, on p. 386.

8.8 Posting Documents

AD89. Each facility shall post documents as specified in Appendix W, on p. 386.

8.9 Contracts

AD90. When the facility contracts for services, the contracted services must meet the specifics of the contract and must meet the same standards applicable to the facility.

Whether the caregiver performs the services directly or arranges for them to be performed, children's interests must be equally well protected.

The contract language should not only specify the requirement for compliance, but should also define methods for monitoring and for redress.

An example of such a contract is a food service contract.

8.10 Drop-in Care

AD91. Facilities that provide drop-in care (see Glossary) shall comply with all of the APHA/AAP standards except for those in *Health Plan*, on p. 276, and *Records*, on p. 287. In addition, at the time of enrollment, parents shall provide evidence that the child is up to date with recommended immunizations as specified in *Vaccine-Preventable Diseases*, on p. 219.

Except for the time of participation at the facility, the needs for staff, equipment, and policies and procedures to protect children are the same for children receiving brief child care as for children in continuous care.

If drop-in care is used repeatedly over extended periods of time, requirements for communication about the child's progress over time are relevant. Parent/caregiver conferences (see *Regular Communication*, on p. 56) and maintenance and review of records will be simplified, but remain necessary.

References

1. Ramsey PG. Multicultural education in early childhood. *Young Children*. 1982;37(2):13–24.

2. Saracho O, Spodek B, eds. Understanding the multicultural experience in early childhood education. *Children's Environmental Quarterly*. 1983;1–2.

3. Morgan G. *The National State of Child Care Regulation 1986*. Boston, Mass: Work/Family Directions Inc; 1987.

4. Solomons HC, Lakin JA, et al. Is day care safe for children? Accident reports reviewed. *Children's Health Care*. 1982;10:90–93.

5. Chang A, Lugg MM, Nebedum A. Injuries in preschool children enrolled in day care centers. *Pediatrics*. 1989;83:272–277.

6. Garrard J, Leland N, Klein-Smith D. Epidemiology of human bites to children in a day care center. *Amer J Dis Child*. 1988;142:643–650.

7. Shapiro ED, Kuribby J, Potter J. Policies for the exclusion of ill children from group day care: an unresolved dilemma. *Rev Infect Dis*. 1986;8(4).

8. Chiles DW. Help sick kids? We had to beat the bureaucracy first. *Medical Economics*. 1981; 133–142.

9. Chang A, Zeledon-Friendly A, Britt A, et al. Management of illness and temporary disability in children enrolled in day care centers. *Amer J Dis Child*. 1988;142:651–655.

10. Wilson DA, Bess CR. Establishing a community-based sick child center. *Pediatr Nurs*. 1986;12: 439–441.

11. Fredericks B, Hardman R, Morgan G, et al. *A Little Bit Under the Weather: A Look at Care for Mildly Ill Children*. Boston, Mass: Work/Family Directions Inc; 1986.

12. Sterne G. Day care for sick children. *Pediatrics*. 1987;79(3):445–446.

13. Langbaum T. What's happening with day care for sick children? *Contemp Pediatr*. 1987;4(2):127–132.

14. Morgan GG, Stevenson CS, Fiene R, et al. Gaps and excesses in the regulation of child day care: report of a panel. In: Osterholm MT, Klein JO, Aronson S, et al., eds. *Infectious Diseases in Child Day Care: Management and Prevention*. Chicago, Ill: University of Chicago Press; 1987:122–131.

15. Tauxe RV, Johnson KE, Boase JC, et al. Control of day care shigellosis: a trial of convalescent day care in isolation. *Amer J Public Health*. 1986;76: 627–630.

16. McDonald KL, White KE, Heiser JL, et al. Lack of detected increased risk of subsequent illness for children attending a sick-child day care center. *Pediatr Infect Dis J*. 1991;9:15.

17. Blank H. The special needs of single-income families. *Group Care for Young Children*, Pediatric Round Table 12. 1986;12:25–35.

18. Haskins R, Kotch J. Day care and illness: evidence, costs and public policy. *Pediatrics* 1986;77 (suppl) (6), pt 2:951–982.

19. Aronson S. Maintaining health in child care settings. *Group Care for Young Children*, Pediatric Round Table 12. 1986; X.214:224.

20. Policy Statement of the American Academy of Pediatrics Committee on Early Childhood, Adoption, and Dependent Care. The pediatrician's role in promoting the health of a patient in day care. *Pediatrics*. 1984;74(1).

21. Goodman RA, Lie LA, Deitch SR, et al. Relationship between day care and health providers. *Rev Infect Dis*. 1986;8(4).

22. Aronson SS, Gildorf JR. Prevention and management of infectious diseases in day care. *Pediatr in Rev*. 1986;7:259–268.

23. Hadler SC, Erben JJ, Francis DP, et al. Risk factors for hepatitis A in day care centers. *J Infect Dis*. 1982; 145:255–261.

24. Aronson S, Smith H. Medication administration in child care. *Exchange*. 1985;41:27–29.

25. Baker SP, O'Neill B, Karpf RS. *The Injury Fact Book*. Lexington, Mass: Lexington Books; 1984.

26. McLaughlin E, Crawford JD, Burns. *Ped Clin North America*. 1985;32:61–75.

27. *Accident Facts*. Chicago, Ill: National Safety Council; 1985.

28. Aronson SS, Pizzo P. Concept paper on health and safety issues in day care. Washington, DC: US Dept of Health, Education and Welfare; Sept 1976.

29. *A Handbook for Public Playground Safety Vol 1: General Guidelines for New and Existing Playgrounds*. Washington, DC: US Consumer Product Safety Commission; 1981.

30. *A Handbook for Public Playground Safety Vol 2: Technical Guidelines for Equipment and Surfacing*. Washington, DC: US Consumer Product Safety Commission; 1981.

31. Ekanem EE, Dupont HL, Pickering LK. Transmission dynamics of enteric bacteria in day care centers. *Amer J Epidemiol*. 1983;118:562–572.

32. Weniger BG, Ruttenber AJ, Goodman RA. Fecal coliforms on environmental surfaces in two day care centers. *Appl Environ Microbiol*. 1983;45:733–735.

33. Taylor MRH, Keane CT, Kerrison IM. Simple and effective measures for control of enteric cross-infection in a children's hospital. *Lancet*. 1979;1:865–867.

34. Benenson A. *Control of Communicable Diseases in Man*. Washington, DC: American Public Health Association; 1985.

35. Black RE, Dykes A, Anderson K. Handwashing to prevent diarrhea in day care centers. *Amer J Epidemiol*. 1981;113:445–451.

36. *Head Start Program Performance Standards*. Washington, DC: US Dept of Health and Human Services; November 1984.

37. Kendrick AS, Kaufmann R, Messenger KP, eds. *Healthy Young Children: A Manual for Programs*. Washington, DC: National Association for the Education of Young Children; 1991.

38. Chance P. *Learning Through Play.* New Brunswick, NJ: The Company; 1979.

39. Yogman M. Child care as a setting for parent education. *Group Care for Young Children,* Pediatric Round Table 12. 1986; XV.184:123.

40. Caldwell B. Education of families for parenting. In: Yogman M, Brazelton TB. *Stress and Coping in Families: A Systems Perspective.* Boston, Mass: Harvard University Press; 1986:229–241.

41. Introduction of S-1885. *Congressional Record.* November 19, 1987.

42. Aronson S. Health concerns for caregivers. *Exchange.* 1987;54:33–37.

43. Deitch S, ed. *Health in Day Care: A Manual for Health Professionals.* Elk Grove Village, Ill: American Academy of Pediatrics; 1987.

44. *Safe Home Checklist.* Boston, Mass: Massachusetts Department of Public Health; 1987.

45. *Accreditation and Criteria Procedures of the National Academy of Early Childhood Programs.* Washington, DC: National Association for the Education of Young Children; 1984.

CHAPTER 9

Recommendations
for Licensing and
Community Action

CHAPTER 9
RECOMMENDATIONS FOR
LICENSING AND COMMUNITY ACTION

INTRODUCTION

This chapter differs from the preceding chapters in that it contains recommendations for the responsibilities of agencies, organizations, and society, and not for the individual caregiver. These recommendations are not standards per se. They are being made to provide the support systems necessary for the implementation of the standards in the preceding chapters. Although some of these recommendations have implications beyond health and safety alone, they significantly affect the ability of caregivers to ensure the health and safety of children in out-of-home child care settings.

The guidelines for health and safety were initially formulated by ten technical panels of experts (see

Introduction). The process employed was consensus development. Over 130 ethnically and geographically diverse individuals with professional backgrounds in medicine, nursing, social work, health education, nutrition, sanitation, psychology, early childhood education, law, and other related fields were involved in the development of the guidelines.

This chapter's content, unlike that of the previous chapters, is organized into two columns: the first contains the recommendation, and the second a discussion of the way the recommended action affects health and safety in child care and how the recommendation might be implemented.

9.1 The Regulatory Agency

RECOMMENDATIONS

THE REGULATORY POLICY

REC1. We recommend that every state should have a statute that identifies the regulatory agency and mandates the licensing and regulation of all regular full-time and part-time out-of-home care of children, regardless of setting, except that provided by parents or legal guardians, grandparents, siblings, aunts, or uncles.

REC2. We recommend that the licensing agency should regulate and issue permits of operation to all facilities that comply with standards. Anyone (except parents or legal guardians, grandparents, siblings, aunts, or uncles) who provides child care in any type of facility should have obtained an individual license/certificate to provide such care. (See *Individual Licensure/Certification*, on p. 301.)

DISCUSSION

A state statute gives government the authority to protect children as vulnerable and dependent citizens and to protect families as consumers of child care service. Because licensing is unknown to the common law, it must have a statutory basis; the statute must address the administration and location of the responsibility. Fifty states have child care regulatory statutes. The laws of 20 of these states exempt part-day centers, whereas other states exempt other categories of care provided outside the family, such as school-age child care, care provided by religious organizations, or care provided in small or large family-child-care homes. These exclusions and gaps in coverage expose children to unacceptable risks.

Because the standards are directed toward the protection of children, every child has a right to care that meets the standards, regardless of the child care setting in which the child is enrolled. Public and private schools, nurseries, preschools, centers, child development programs, babysitting centers, early childhood observation centers, small and large family-child-care homes, and all other settings where young children receive care by individuals who are not close relatives should be regulated. Facilities have been able to circumvent rules and regulations in some states by calling themselves by names not covered under existing licensing statutes. Nothing in the educational philosophy, religious orientation, or setting of an early childhood program inherently protects children from health and safety risks or provides assurance of a level of

applies to a small family-child-care home applies to a large family-child-care home applies to a center.
If no symbol appears, the standard applies to all three.

Caring for Our Children   299   Chapter 9 Licensing and Community Action

RECOMMENDATIONS

Facility Licensing

REC3. We recommend that states should adopt uniform categories and definitions for their licensing requirements. Every state should have individual standards that are applied to the following categories of facilities, at a minimum, as defined below:

a) Small family-child-care home: A facility providing care and education of one to six children, including preschool children of the caregiver, in the home of the caregiver.

b) Large family-child-care home: A facility providing care and education of 7 to 12 children, including preschool children of the caregiver, in the home of the caregiver, with one or more qualified adult assistants to meet child:staff ratio requirements.

c) Center: A facility providing care and education of any number of children in a nonresidential setting if open on a regular basis (i.e., if it is not a drop-in facility).

DISCUSSION

quality of child care. Any exemptions for care provided outside the family may place children at risk.

In addition to the basic protection afforded by stipulating requirements and inspecting for licensing, requiring that facilities be authorized to operate gives states a mechanism by which to identify facilities and individuals who are providing child care as potential targets for training, technical assistance, and consultation services. Currently, many church-run nurseries, nursery schools, group play centers, and home-based programs operate incognito in the community because they are not required to notify any centralized agency that they care for children.

The lead agency for licensing of child care in most states is the social welfare agency. However, the state public health agency has proven to be an appropriate licensing authority for safeguarding children in some states. The education system is increasingly involved in providing services to children in early childhood. The standards should be equally stringent no matter what agency assumes the responsibility for regulating child care.

In-home care, which is the care of a child in his/her own home by someone whom the parent has employed, is not care within the family. This type of care should not be licensed as a facility. Because the relationship between the parent and caregiver is that of employer and employee rather than that of purchaser and provider of care, licensing/certification of the individual who provides such care, rather than of the service itself, is desirable and recommended. (See *Individual Licensure/Certification*, on p. 301.)

A good resource on enforcement issues related to child care is *Health of Children in Day Care: Public Health Profiles*[1] (P. Schloesser, editor), published by the Kansas Department of Health and Environment in 1986 and supported by a grant from the Bureau of Maternal and Child Health of the Department of Health and Human Services and the Head Start Bureau, Department of Health and Human Services.

Lack of standard terminology hampers the ability of citizens and professionals to compare rules from state to state or to apply national guidance material to upgrade the quality of care.[2] For example, the term for child care for 7 to 12 children in the residence of the caregiver is *family day care*, *group day care home*, and *mini-center* in different states. The recommended terminology would help to distinguish this type of care from care provided for six or fewer children by one caregiver in his/her home, and from community facilities for the mentally retarded, the elderly, and other adults and teenagers who need supervised care.

d) Drop-in facility: A facility providing care and education of one or more children in a residential or nonresidential setting for less than 10 hours per day, less than once a week, to any child.

e) School-age-child care facility: A facility offering activities to school-age children before and after school and/or during vacations.

f) Facility for children with special needs: A facility providing care and education in a residential or nonresidential setting of one or more children with developmental disabilities, mental retardation, mental illness, sensory or motor impairment, or significant chronic illness who require special health surveillance, therapy, or interventions (see chapter 7, *Children with Special Needs*, on p. 237).

g) Facility for ill children: A facility providing care of one or more ill children who are temporarily excluded from care in their regular child care setting (see *Special Facilities for Ill Children*, on p. 100).

  1) Integrated or small group care for ill children: A facility that has been approved by the licensing agency to care for well children and to include up to six ill children.

  2) Special facility for ill children: A facility that cares only for ill children, or a facility that cares for more than six ill children at a time (see *Special Facilities for Ill Children*, on p. 100).

h) Facility for abused children: A facility providing care and education in a residential or nonresidential setting of one or more children who have been physically or emotionally abused.

REC4. We recommend that a center, small family-child-care home, large family-child-care home, or school-age-child care facility should be permitted to care for ill children with symptoms requiring exclusion (see standard HP151 in chapter 3 on p. 108) and should be permitted to mainstream a child with special needs, provided that the licensing authority has approved the facility's written plan describing the symptoms or disabilities to be cared for, justification for inclusion, and procedures for daily care. Facility types should be specific to the child's developmental level and health condition (see standard HP129 in chapter 3 on p. 99).

See rationale for standard HP68 in chapter 3 on p. 80 and *Introduction and Background*, on p. 237.

Individual Licensure/Certification

REC5. We recommend that all persons who provide child care or who may be responsible for children or alone with children in a facility should be individually licensed, certified, or credentialed by a state licensing agency or credentialing body recognized by the state regulatory agency. The license, certificate, or credential should be granted to individuals who meet age, education, and experience qualifications; are in good health; and have no record of conviction for criminal offenses against persons, especially children, or founded child abuse claims (see recommendation REC6 on p. 303. The state should establish qualifications for differentiated roles

Individual licensing/credentialing will enhance child health and development and protect children by ensuring that the staff who care for children are healthy and are qualified for their roles. The current system, in which the details of staff qualifications and ongoing training are checked as part of facility inspection, is cumbersome for child care administrators and licensing staff alike. Child care administrators must gather and have on file records from all staff about their educational experiences, criminal records checks, and character references. A licensing inspector must determine on each visit that each staff member is qualified for the role in which he/she func-

RECOMMENDATIONS

in child care and a procedure for verifying that the individual who is authorized to perform a specified role meets the qualifications for the role. (See *Qualifications by Role*, on p. 4, *General Qualifications of All Staff*, on p. 16, *Training*, on p. 18, *Staff Health*, on p. 35, and Appendix A, on p. 323.)

DISCUSSION

tions, by checking back even on the content of courses he/she may have taken. When staff members change jobs, the whole checking process must be repeated by a new licensing inspector. If staff qualifications were established as part of a separate, more central process, these tasks would become less burdensome overall. The licensing agency staff could check center records of character references and whether staff members have licenses for the roles for which they are employed.

Successful completion of education should be verified by requiring the individual to submit evidence of completion of credit-bearing courses that have been previously approved as meeting the state's requirements. Criminal records and child abuse registries should be checked by state licensing agency staff for evidence of behavior that would disqualify an individual for work in specified child care roles. Evidence of a recent health examination indicating ability to care for children can be submitted at the same time. The center director then knows whether job applicants are qualified at the time they apply for the job, without lengthy waiting for background checks of a prospective employee and without having to hire before background checks have been completed. By this means, children are not exposed to health and safety risks from understaffing, or to care by unqualified or even dangerous individuals employed provisionally because the results of a check are not yet available to the director.

Individual certification, credentialing, qualifying, or licensing (whichever term is consistent with the state's approach to authorizing legal professional activity) should be centralized to improve control over quality, encourage a career ladder with increasing qualifications, and reduce the risk of abuse. Such a process is analogous to that provided for other professions in which consumer protection is needed, even those involving less potential for harm than is involved in caring for children. The qualifications of health professionals and teachers are generally approved by such a process.

One state, Massachusetts, has adopted such a system. The cost of individual certification, credentialing, or licensure is expected to be offset by the benefits to consumers of reliable and consistent qualifications of child care personnel. Cost savings should be experienced by program administrators, licensors, and child care personnel, who will not have to undertake the tedious process of verification of each portion of an individual's credentials each time a site is licensed or an individual applies for a new position or moves to a new locale.

Periodic renewal of the license, certificate, or credential should be required, and should be related to requirements for continuing education and the absence of founded claims of child abuse or criminal convictions. The requirement for renewable certification is likely to deter people from applying for work in child care as a way of gaining access to children for sexual purposes,[3] since the process would include a check of the child

RECOMMENDATIONS

REC6. We recommend that before granting a license/certificate, the licensing agency should check as specified below for a record of a physical examination and for educational qualifications, and should check criminal record files and the child abuse registry for all adults who are permitted to be alone with children in a facility. The licensing agency should also check the criminal record files and child abuse registry, as specified below, for all adults who live in a small or large family-child-care home where child care is provided.

a) Staff health appraisals as specified in *Preemployment Staff Health Appraisal, Including Immunization*, on p. 35.

b) Educational requirements as specified in *Qualifications by Role*, on p. 4, *General Qualifications of All Staff*, on p. 16, and *Training*, on p. 18.

c) Criminal record files for crimes of violence against persons, especially children, within the state of residence; and for personnel who have moved into the state within the past 5 years, federal or out-of-state criminal records of the other state(s) where the individual has resided in the past 5 years.

d) The child abuse registry for a known history of child abuse or neglect in the state of residence; and for personnel who have moved into the state within the past 5 years, the other states(s) where the individual has resided in the past 5 years.

DISCUSSION

abuse registry. While there is value in checking criminal records, not all criminal records represent hazards for children so serious as to prohibit the individual from working in a child care setting. States should specify which crimes defined in the state's criminal code will prohibit licensure/certification and whether any other crimes should limit the ability of the individual to be licensed/certified for certain roles. Individuals who have been convicted of violent and/or sexual crimes should not work in child care settings.

States should be careful not to rely entirely on criminal record checks to prevent abuse. This method is expensive and does not result in a high number of "hits" as records are checked, because many abusers have not yet been convicted of a crime. States should rely on other, less costly measures as well if children are to be protected. The Federal Bureau of Investigation, 10th and Pennsylvania Avenue, N.W., Washington, DC 20535, maintains a central criminal file.

If caregivers are all licensed/certified, and if they are required to carry their licenses/certificates while working, their identity, background, and competence can be documented. Checking compliance with the recommendation requires simple inspection of the license/certificate and verification by contacting the state agency that maintains the computerized registry of qualified individuals. Precautions against forgery should be built into the system.

For information on individual staff qualifications, see *Qualifications by Role*, on p. 4 and *General Qualifications of All Staff*, on p. 16.

See discussion for recommendation REC 5.

RECOMMENDATIONS

REC7. We recommend that no personnel recorded in a state child abuse registry as having abused children, or with a record or conviction for criminal offenses of violence against persons, especially children, or sexual molestation, and no personnel with household members having such records, should be licensed/certified or permitted to reside in a facility.

Waivers

REC8. We recommend that waivers should be granted for state licensing requirements only when the intent of the requirement is being met by alternative means not foreseen in the writing of the requirement.

REC9. We recommend that the licensing law shall specify that waivers or exemptions from certain licensing regulations may be granted to care for children who are ill or for children with special needs, in particular for outdoor play, meals, grouping by age category, and program activities, provided that the care of such children requires these exemptions according to the plan for care approved by the child's source of routine health care.

THE REGULATION-SETTING PROCESS

REC10. We recommend that the state regulatory agency should formulate, implement, and enforce regulations that reduce risks to children in out-of-home child care.

REC11. We recommend that state licensing laws should require a citizen review process to reexamine the entire text of the child care licensing requirements no less often than once every 5 years. The process should be carried out by a review committee on which are represented parents; caregivers from all relevant types of facilities; and experts and practitioners in the field of child development, in the field of health and safety, and from relevant state agencies. Regulations formulated through a representative citizen process should come before the public at well-publicized public hearings held at convenient times and places in different parts of the state.

DISCUSSION

See discussion in recommendation REC6.

Flexibility in applying licensing regulations should be permitted to the extent that children's need for protection is met.

Flexibility will be necessary in applying licensing requirements to care for children who are ill or who have disabilities, or to special circumstances not foreseen when the requirements were written. State requirements should not stand as a barrier to the mainstreaming of children with special needs who could benefit from the facility. Modifications in arrangements and facilities may be necessary to match the health conditions of individual children.[4] At least one state has specified waivers for facility modifications in its licensing requirements for facilities for ill children.[5]

Regulations should describe the minimum performance required of a facility. They should be understandable to any reasonable citizen; specific enough that any person knows what is to be done and what is not to be done; enforceable, in that they are capable of measurement; and consistent with new technical knowledge and changes in public views to offer necessary protection.

Licensing has been described by experts as essentially a community organizational service to protect families as consumers of child care for forms of care available in the community. Licensing permits one who meets the regulatory requirements to engage in an activity otherwise prohibited by statute (a "status movement" operation). In a democratic society, widespread community participation should be involved in licensing.

The legal principle of broad-interest representation has long been applied to the formulation of regulations for child care. The review committee could be an ad hoc task force created specifically to write one set of requirements, such as care for ill children, or it can be a standing advisory committee. Changes in regulation can be implemented only with broad support from the different interests affected. Public review is required by state administrative laws and constitutional principles. The interests of the child must take precedence over all other interests.

RECOMMENDATIONS

REC12. We recommend that local and state health departments, licensing agencies, health professionals, attorneys, and caregivers should work together to develop licensing requirements and guidelines for facilities for ill children. These licensing requirements and guidelines should be reviewed not less often than once in 5 years by such a group, and revised if necessary. (See also *Management and Prevention of Illness*, on p. 80.)

ADMINISTRATION OF THE LICENSING AGENCY
General

REC13. We recommend that there should be authorization, funding, and staffing of all phases of regulatory administration, that is, formulation, implementation, and enforcement of licensing standards and training of licensing staff.

REC14. We recommend that the agency should be funded to engage in a variety of caregiver and consumer training and support services as integral components of its mission to reduce risks to children in out-of-home child care.

REC15. We recommend that licensing staff should receive competency-based training to monitor compliance with health and safety requirements. Competency should be initially and periodically assessed by simultaneous, independent monitoring by a skilled inspector until the trainee attains the necessary skills.

Staffing Capability

REC16. We recommend that the workload of a licensing inspector should be such that not less than two-thirds of his/her time is spent visiting and inspecting facilities.

DISCUSSION

Local and state health departments have the legal responsibility to control communicable diseases in their jurisdictions.[6] To meet this responsibility, health departments generally have the expertise to provide leadership and technical assistance to licensing authorities, caregivers, parents, and health professionals in the development of licensing requirements and guidelines for the management of communicable diseases for special facilities providing care for ill children. The heavy reliance on the expertise of local and state health departments in the establishment of facilities to care for ill children has fostered a new partnership in many states among health departments, licensing authorities, caregivers, and parents for the adequate care of ill children in child care settings.

Funds for all phases of the licensing process should be provided, or faulty administrative operations may result, such as formulation of irresponsible standards, inadequate investigations, and insufficient and unfair enforcement.

Licensing agencies do not, as a matter of course, have the resources to carry out the work that is expected of them. The licensure process will be meaningless without resources and expertise sufficient to give the agency respectability.

Objective assessment of compliance is a learned skill that can be fostered by classroom and self-teaching methods but should be mastered through direct practice and apprenticeship. To ensure consistent protection of children, licensing inspectors should undergo periodic retraining and reevaluation to assess their ability to recognize sound and unsound practices.[7]

Licensing centers and large family-child-care homes should require at least one prelicensing visit, and at least one more visit after granting of the provisional license and after children are in attendance to determine that all requirements are being met and that a full license can be granted. In addition, licensing inspectors should follow up on all complaints of noncompliance made by parents and the general public. They should make routine unannounced visits at least annually to determine continued compliance, and they should study compliance at length at the time of relicensing. The most effective way of ensuring compliance with standards is through the licensors' presence in facilities, identifying deficiences and giving consultation to bring about compliance. Workloads should be designed so that the licensing inspectors' time is not consumed by in-office tasks.

RECOMMENDATIONS

REC17. We recommend that licensing inspectors should be prequalified by education and experience to be knowledgeable about the form of child care they are assigned to inspect. They should receive no less than 40 clock hours of orientation training upon employment. In addition, they should receive no less than 24 clock hours of continuing education each year, covering the following topics and other such topics as necessary based on competency needs:
a) The rules and regulations for child care.
b) Child development and child care programming, scheduling, and design of space.
c) Law enforcement and the rights of licensees.
d) Center and large or small family-child-care home management.
e) Child and staff health in child care.
f) Detection, prevention, and management of child abuse.
g) Practical techniques for mainstreaming children with special needs.
h) Exclusion/inclusion of ill children.
i) Health, safety, and nutrition.
j) Recognition of hazards.

For additional information on licensing agency staffing capability, see also Appendices B-1 and B-2, on pp. 328–329, on state and local nutrition staff requirements.

Inspections

REC18. We recommend that the state regulatory agency should ensure that on-site inspections of facilities are conducted as authorized by state statute. These inspections should be performed by staff trained to make licensing inspections.

REC19. We recommend that the licensing agency should adopt issuance and monitoring strategies that ensure confirmed compliance with licensing requirements. When these strategies do not include annual review of all licensing requirements, the agency should review the policies and performance areas in each facility at least annually and should have procedures and staffing in place to increase the level of compliance monitoring for any facility found in significant noncompliance.

REC20. We recommend that the licensing inspector should make an initial announced inspection visit upon receipt of the application for license, and at least one annual unannounced inspection visit to each center and large family-child-care home. The method of regulating small family-child-care homes should consist of an initial announced visit from the licensing office, followed by unannounced visits conducted on a schedule dependent on the quality of the facility as measured by an objective assessment (e.g., accreditation or an instrument based on objective assessment), with no less than one unannounced visit for each small family-child-care home every 5 years.

DISCUSSION

Licensing inspectors are a point of contact and linkage for caregivers and sources of technical information needed to improve the quality of child care. This is particularly true for areas not usually within the network of early childhood professionals, such as health and safety expertise. Unless the licensing inspector is competent and able to recognize areas where facilities need to improve their health and safety provisions, the opportunity for such linkages will be lost.

See discussion for *Staffing Capability*, on p. 305. Unannounced visits provide the opportunity to see care as it functions from day to day, without the "best face" preparation that inevitably accompanies an announced visit. Ongoing monitoring at some level is necessary to ascertain that facility performance does not slip below levels that are safe for children. A requirement for at least an annual policy review by the caregiver helps to focus the caregiver's attention on facility performance and encourages self-evaluation and correction. Evaluation alone has been shown to be associated with improved performance of health and safety in child care.[8]

Because small family-child-care homes serve fewer children, the requirements are less formal. Some states have not visited homes in the past, and this lack of visiting has been associated with low compliance with the requirements. It is desirable to achieve good compliance and also to achieve full regulatory coverage of all small family-child-care homes—an enormous number of facilities.

Often the initial inspection and consultation leads to full compliance with health and safety standards. See also the discussion for recommendation REC16, on p. 305.

RECOMMENDATIONS

The number of inspection visits should not include those visits conducted for the purpose of investigating complaints. Parents should be given a summary list of requirements and a telephone number for reporting violations, and should be encouraged to observe the facility for compliance.

REC21. We recommend that inspectors and administrators in licensing agencies and state-supported resource and referral agencies should receive 16 hours of training about child abuse with emphasis on how child abuse occurs in child care.

REC22. We recommend that licensing staff should inspect the injury log as specified in *Incidence Logs of Illness, Injury, and Other Problems*, on p. 290.

Procedures for Complaints and Reporting

REC23. We recommend that each licensing agency should have a procedure for receiving complaints from parents and the public regarding noncompliance with the regulations. Such complaints should be recorded and followed up, and appropriate action should be taken. The telephone number for complaints should be included on the child care license, which should be posted in a conspicuous place at all facilities. (See also standard APP37, item o, on filing complaints in Appendix X on p. 391 and standard APP33, item a, in Appendix W on p. 386 on posting the license.)

REC24. We recommend that state law should ensure that caregivers and child care staff who report noncompliance with licensing requirements in the settings where they work are immune from discharge, retaliation, or other disciplinary action for that reason alone, unless it is proven that the report was malicious.

REC25. We recommend that licensing agencies should publicize the requirements for reporting and methods of reporting child abuse, and should develop procedures for evaluating allegations of physical and emotional abuse. (See *Posting Documents*, on p. 296, *Continuing Education*, on p. 24, and standard ST40 in chapter 1 on p. 19.)

DISCUSSION

Although some states are relying on self-assessment and random inspections, this does not provide adequate protection to children in out-of-home care.

It is estimated that 30 percent of the children in out-of-home child care are in small family-child-care homes. Support provided through licensing inspections can help diminish the isolation that a small family home caregiver may experience as a professional in a home setting.

In regulated homes, the complete immunization status for preschoolers is close to 95 percent, whereas for preschoolers in their own homes the complete immunization status is 60–70 percent.

The incidence of unintentional injury is higher for young children in their own homes than in regulated child care settings.

Licensing and resource and referral persons should be as well informed about child abuse issues as caregivers, or better.

States should establish inspection procedures to ensure compliance of their agency personnel.

Monitoring patterns of injuries is helpful in identifying injuries that are potentially preventable and in identifying possible signs of child abuse.

The telephone number for filing complaints should be listed on material about licensing that is given to parents by the state licensing agency or the resource and referral agency. At a minimum, the licensing agency has responsibility for consumer protection. Complaints serve as an early warning before more serious adverse events occur. A fair and equitable process for handling complaints is essential to protect both the complainer and the target of the complaint from harassment.

See recommendation REC23.

To prevent child abuse, child care staff and parents should be aware of the reporting requirements and the procedures for handling reports of child abuse. State requirements may differ, but those for whom reporting abuse is mandatory usually include child care personnel. Information on how to call and how to report should be posted so it is readily available to parents and staff. Emotional abuse can be extremely harmful to children, but, unlike physical or sexual abuse, it is not adequately defined in most state child abuse reporting laws. States need to develop procedures for handling allegations of all types of abuse.

RECOMMENDATIONS

Enforcement

REC26. We recommend that there should be a strong commitment to suppression of illegal operations and to enforcement of child care regulations and statutes by the governor, the attorney general, the legislature, and the licensing agency.

Advisory Group

REC27. We recommend that states should have an official state advisory body assigned to the regulatory agency. It should be composed of public and private agency personnel, child development and health professionals, caregivers, parents, and citizens.

DISCUSSION

Without proper enforcement, especially the suppression of illegal operations, licensing could become a ritual and lose its safeguarding intent.

Some state laws lack adequate provisions for enforcement.

A child care advisory board is needed to review overall rules and regulations for the operation and maintenance of facilities and the granting, suspending, and revoking of both provisional and regular licenses; to recommend administrative policy, including the review of 3-year policy issuances; and to propose legislation related to child care licensing.

The advisory group may include representatives from the following agencies and groups: the governor's office; the legislature; state agencies with regulatory responsibility or an interest in child care (social welfare, public health, fire marshal, education, human resources, attorney general); private organizations with a child care emphasis; caregivers; professionals with expertise in pediatrics, nutrition, mental health, oral health, or early childhood education; parents who represent ethnic and cultural diversity; and citizens. The advisory group should actively seek citizen participation in the development of child care policy and standards.

9.2 The Health Department's Responsibility

REC28. We recommend that state and local health departments should be responsible for extending assistance to caregivers in planning and operating facilities that prevent and control the spread of disease. Similar assistance should be made available to the licensing agency during the promulgation and enforcement of the facility standards. These services should be in addition to the health agency's assigned responsibilities for enforcement of the state's health laws and regulations.

State and local health departments are legally required to control certain communicable diseases within their jurisdictions. All states have laws that grant extraordinary powers to public health departments during outbreaks of communicable disease.[6] Since communicable disease is likely to occur in child care settings, a plan for the control of communicable diseases in these settings is important and is often legally required. Early recognition and prompt intervention will reduce the spread of infection. Outbreaks of communicable disease in child care settings can have great implications for the general community.[9] Programs administered by local health departments have been more successful in controlling outbreaks of hepatitis A than those that rely primarily on private physicians. Programs coordinated by the local health department also provide reassurance to caregivers, staff, and parents, and thereby promote cooperation with other disease-control policies.[10]

Communicable diseases in child care settings pose new epidemiologic considerations. Never before has it been so common for very young children to spend most of their days together in groups. Given the opportunity, public health authorities could expand their role in studying this situation and designing new preventive health measures.[4]

RECOMMENDATIONS

DISCUSSION

See discussion in *The Regulatory Policy*, on p. 299, for a good resource on the role of health departments in child care.

HEALTH DEPARTMENT PLAN

REC29. We recommend that local and state health departments should have written plans for the prevention and control of reportable and nonreportable communicable diseases in facilities.

See discussion for recommendation REC28.

REC30. We recommend that the child care licensing authority should require all facilities under its regulatory jurisdiction to make such reports (see recommendation REC29) to the health department.

See discussion for recommendation REC28.

REC31. We recommend that the health department plan should describe the responsibilities of those community agencies and organizations involved in the prevention and control of communicable disease in facilities and should identify child-care-related diseases and provide guidance for disease prevention and control.

Collaboration is necessary to utilize limited resources most effectively. In small states, a state-level task force might be sufficient. In larger or more populous states, local task forces may be needed to ensure the most effective use of resources. The collaboration should focus on establishing the role of each agency in ensuring that necessary services and systems exist to prevent and control communicable diseases in facilities. Activities to be coordinated should include reporting and surveillance systems; guidance in managing outbreaks; training and consultation; and education of parents, physicians, public health workers, licensing inspectors, and employers as to their role in preventing and controlling communicable diseases in child care.

REC32. We recommend that the health department plan should specify outbreak control activities, including methods for notifying parents, caregivers, and health care providers of the problem; appropriate actions; policies for exclusion or isolation of infected children; and a source and method for the administration of needed medication.

Effective control and prevention of infectious diseases in child care settings depends on affirmative relationships among parents, caregivers, public health authorities, and primary health care providers. The major barriers to productive working relationships between caregivers and health care providers are inadequate channels of communication and uncertainty of role definition. Public health authorities can play a major role in improving the relationship between caregivers and health care providers by disseminating information regarding disease-reporting laws, prescribed measures for control and prevention of diseases, and resources that are available for these activities.[11]

REC33. We recommend that the health department plan should be developed in collaboration with the licensing agency, health care providers, caregivers, and parents to ensure the availability of sufficient community resources for successful implementation.

See discussion for recommendation REC32.

RECOMMENDATIONS

REC34. We recommend that the health department plan should be based on one or more of the following current guidelines:

a) Guidelines provided by the Centers for Disease Control (including *What to Do to Stop Disease in Child Day Care Centers*).

b) Guidelines from the American Academy of Pediatrics (including the *Report of the Committee on Infectious Diseases* and *Health in Day Care: A Manual for Health Professionals*).

c) Guidelines from the American Public Health Association (including *Control of Communicable Diseases in Man*).

d) Guidelines from the U.S. Public Health Service's Advisory Committee on Immunization Practices (as reported periodically in *Morbidity and Mortality Weekly Report*).

e) State and local regulations and guidelines regarding communicable diseases in facilities.

THE HEALTH DEPARTMENT'S ROLE

REC35. We recommend that the responsible local or state health department should require that all facilities, regardless of licensure status, and all health care providers report certain communicable diseases to the responsible local or state public health authority.

a) The child care licensing authority should require such reporting by facilities under its regulatory jurisdiction and should collaborate fully with the health department when the latter is engaged in an enforcement action with a licensed authority.

b) Guidelines should be developed and provided to facilities that provide a list of reportable diseases, including descriptions of these diseases.

c) The list should specify where diseases are to be reported and what information is to be provided.

d) Reports of communicable diseases received from facilities should be verified against the assessment and diagnosis of the disease made by a health care provider and/or the local or state health department.

(See also *Reporting Illness*, on p. 87.)

REC36. We recommend that when a communicable disease of public health importance to child care is reported by a physician or other health care provider, the responsible local or state health authority should determine whether the disease represents a potential health risk to children in out-of-home child care, and should conduct the epidemiologic investigation necessary to initiate public health interventions.

DISCUSSION

The specific policies for an individual facility depend on the resources available to that facility.[12]

To obtain these publications, write to the addresses below:

Centers for Disease Control
1600 Clifton Road, N.E.
Atlanta, GA 30333

American Academy of Pediatrics
141 Northwest Point Blvd.
P.O. Box 927
Elk Grove Village, IL 60009-0927

American Public Health Association
1015 15th Street, N.W.
Washington, DC 20005

Morbidity and Mortality Weekly Report
Centers for Disease Control
1600 Clifton Road, N.E.
Atlanta, GA 30333

See also discussion in *The Health Department's Responsibility*, on p. 308.

See discussion for recommendation REC28, on p. 308.

See discussion for recommendation REC31, on p. 308.

RECOMMENDATIONS

REC37. We recommend that when children attending a facility are exposed to a specific infectious agent, the responsible local or state health department should recommend a disease-prevention or control strategy that is based on sound public health and clinical practices, such as the use of vaccine, immunoglobulin, or antibiotics taken to prevent an infection. The health department should take the following actions to seek compliance with the recommendation:

a) Obtain support for the recommendations from the facility by explaining the need and reason for the recommendation.

b) Prepare written handouts that explain the recommendations. Include the telephone number of the responsible health department so that concerned parents and health care providers can call to discuss the recommendations. Distribute the handouts to parents so they may give the information to their child's health care providers, if appropriate.

c) If health care providers object to or question the recommendations, the health department should discuss the need and reasonableness of the recommendations with these health care providers and seek consensus by expanding the discussion to include other health care providers, if necessary.

d) If no consensus can be achieved among parents or health care providers and the recommendations cannot otherwise be successfully implemented, the responsible local or state public health agency should act within its legal authority to ensure that recommendations are implemented.

(See also standard HP92 in chapter 3 on p. 91, standard ID18 in chapter 6 on p. 212, and standard ID23 in chapter 6 on p. 215.)

REC38. We recommend that the local or state health department should prepare prototype parent fact sheets on common illnesses associated with child care. These sheets should

a) Contain the following information:
   1) Disease (case or outbreak) to which the child was exposed.
   2) Signs and symptoms of the disease that the parent should watch for in the child.
   3) Mode of transmission of the disease.
   4) Period of communicability.
   5) Disease-prevention measures recommended by the public health department (if appropriate).
   6) Control measures implemented at the facility.

b) Emphasize mechanisms of transmission of respiratory disease and infections of the intestines (often with diarrhea) and liver, common methods of infection control (e.g., handwashing—see *Hygiene*, on p. 72), and specific diseases that may be asymptomatic in the child but have important consequences for a parent contact (e.g., hepatitis A virus, CMV—see chapter 6, *Infectious Diseases*, on p. 207).

DISCUSSION

See discussion for recommendation REC31, on p. 308.

Education is a primary method for providing information to physicians and parents about the incidence of communicable diseases in child care settings.[13] Education of child care staff and parents on the recognition and transmission of various communicable diseases is important to any infection control policy.[14] Training of child care staff has improved the quality of their health-related behaviors and practices. Training should be available to all parties involved, including caregivers, public health workers, health care providers, parents, and children. Good quality training, with imaginative and accessible methods of presentation supported by well-designed materials, will facilitate learning. The number of studies evaluating the importance of education of child care staff in the prevention of disease is limited. However, data from numerous studies in hospitals illustrate the important role of continuing education in preventing and minimizing the transmission of communicable disease.[14]

The provision of fact sheets on communicable childhood diseases at the time their child is admitted to a facility helps educate parents as to the early signs and symptoms of these illnesses and the need to inform caregivers of

RECOMMENDATIONS

c) Be provided to parents when their child is first admitted to the facility and when communicable disease notification is recommended.

REC39. We recommend that educational materials specific to CMV transmission, exposure, and fetal risk for women providing child care should be developed by the Centers for Disease Control or responsible state or local health departments (see *Staff Education and Policies on CMV*, on p. 224).

REC40. We recommend that local and state health departments should design systems and forms for use by special facilities for ill children to document the surveillance of illnesses cared for and problems that arise in the care of children in such child care settings.

REC41. We recommend that the responsible public health department should monitor each special facility for ill children by visiting the facility and reviewing illness documentation records at least every 6 months.

REC42. We recommend that local and state health departments should assist in the development of orientation and annual training programs for caregivers in facilities that include ill children, as well as those in special facilities that serve only ill children. This training should focus on communicable disease control and the recognition and management of childhood illnesses (see *Training*, on p. 104.)

REC43. We recommend that public health nurses or epidemiologists in local and state health departments should assist the licensing authority in the licensure and periodic review of special facilities for ill children by performing the following activities:
a) Reviewing written policies developed by the facility regarding inclusion/exclusion/dismissal criteria and plans for health care, emergency care, and reporting and managing children with communicable disease.
b) Assisting with periodic compliance reviews for those requirements relating to inclusion/exclusion/dismissal, daily health care, emergency care, and reporting and management of children with communicable disease.

DISCUSSION

their existence. Illness information sheets can be assembled in a convenient booklet for this purpose.

CMV is the leading cause of congenital infection in the United States, with approximately 1 percent of live-born infants infected prenatally.[15] Fortunately, most infected fetuses escape resulting illness or disability, but 10 to 20 percent will have hearing loss, mental retardation, cerebral palsy, or vision disturbances. Although it is well known that maternal immunity does not prevent congenital CMV infection, evidence indicates that initial acquisition of CMV during pregnancy (primary maternal infection) carries the greatest risk for resulting illness or disability.[16]

With current knowledge about the risk of CMV infection in child care staff and the potential consequences of gestational CMV infection, child care staff should be counseled regarding risks. However, it is unlikely that many facility directors have access to the information needed to counsel employees, and many health care providers also may lack sufficient knowledge in the area. Therefore, educational materials should be developed by the Centers for Disease Control and distributed by state and local health departments.

See discussion for recommendation REC12, on p. 305.

See discussion for recommendation REC12, on p. 305.

See discussion for recommendation REC12, on p. 305.

See discussion for recommendation REC12, on p. 305.

RECOMMENDATIONS

REC44. We recommend that health care personnel, such as qualified public health nurses, pediatric and family nurse practitioners, and pediatricians, should serve as health consultants or members of advisory boards for facilities serving ill children (see also *Health Consultants in Special Facilities for Ill Children* on p. 106).

For additional information on the health department's role, see also *Reporting Illness*, on p. 87; Appendices I-1 through I-4 on pp. 343–351; *Special Facilities for Ill Children*, on p. 100; recommendation REC48 on p. 316 providing health materials; and *Training*, on p. 316.

DISCUSSION

See discussion for recommendation REC12, on p. 305.

9.3 Technical Assistance and Consultation to Caregivers and Families

GENERAL

REC45. We recommend that private and public authorities should maintain mechanisms for technical assistance to states, localities, and child care agencies.

This administrative practice is designed to enhance the overall quality of child care that meets the social and developmental needs of children.

The chief sources of technical assistance are the licensing agency (on ways to meet the regulations), the health department (on health-related matters), and resource and referral agencies (on ways to achieve quality, how to start a new facility, supply/demand data, how to get licensed, and what parents want).

TECHNICAL ASSISTANCE FROM THE LICENSING AGENCY

REC46. We recommend that the state regulatory agency should provide technical assistance to all caregivers on ways to meet the licensing/certification requirements (see *Individual Licensure/Certification*, on p. 301).

If an adequate supply of good-quality child care is to be developed and maintained, the state agency has a continuing responsibility to assist applicants in qualifying for a license/certificate and to help licensees improve and maintain the quality of their facility.

Regulations should be available to parents and interested citizens on request.

Licensing representatives throughout the state should be required to offer assistance and consultation as a regular part of their duties.

REC47. We recommend that state agencies should provide centers and networks of small or large family-child-care homes with guidelines and information on establishing a program of care that meets the developmental needs and respects the cultural diversity of children.

This initiative is intended to promote appropriate programs of activities.

Child care staff are rarely trained health professionals. Since staff and time are often limited, caregivers should have access to consultation on available resources in a variety of fields (physical and mental health care, nutrition, safety, oral health care, developmental disabilities, etc.).[17, 18]

Almost everything that goes on in a center and almost everything about the center itself affects the health of the children it serves.[19]

REC48. We recommend that the local or state health department and licensing/regulatory agency should produce handouts or pamphlets on specific health-related issues that should be discussed with parents (see *Health Education for Parents*, on p. 62).

See discussion for recommendation REC47.

RECOMMENDATIONS

REC49. We recommend that child abuse prevention materials for staff, parents, and children should be provided by the licensing agency.

REC50. We recommend that the licensing agency should assist parents and caregivers in developing the written legal agreements that are required to be in the files at the time of inspection visits by developing standard contract language for agreements and distributing them at no charge to caregivers.

REC51. We recommend that the state licensing agency should develop any forms and instructions needed by caregivers to comply with requirements implemented by the state, and should furnish this information without charge.

REC52. We recommend that the state regulatory agency should develop or have access to a surveillance system for collecting data relative to the incidence of illness, injuries, confirmed child abuse and neglect, and death of children in facilities.

For additional information on technical assistance from the licensing agency, see also *Child Abuse and Neglect*, on p. 93.

CONSULTANTS

REC53. We recommend that state agencies should subsidize the expense of a program consultant from the local community to provide technical assistance for program development and maintenance. The consultant should be chosen on the basis of his/her training and experience in early childhood education and ability to help establish links between the facility and community resources.

REC54. We recommend that the state regulatory agency should have available an identified child health consultant who has expertise in child health and child development and is knowledgeable about the special needs of children in out-of-home care settings. A regional plan to make consultants accessible to facilities should be developed.

REC55. We recommend that each community should have access to an identified child health consultant who can provide consultation and technical assistance on health issues to facilities. The health consultant should have expertise in child health and child development and knowledge about the special needs of children in out-of-home care settings. A registry of consultants in other fields, such as child development, nutrition, oral health, mental health, and safety, within the community should be maintained.

DISCUSSION

Centers and small and large family-child-care homes are locations in which to distribute materials for the prevention of abuse.

States will need to learn to select from the many available media that can be employed in child abuse prevention activities.

Provision of these agreements by the licensing agency will relieve parents and caregivers of the expense of producing them, and will ensure that abuse of children in care is prevented with a minimum of difficulty for the parties involved.

The licensing agency has the resources to develop such materials.

Sound public policy planning in respect to health and safety in facilities starts with the collection of epidemiologic data.

Securing the expertise is acceptable by whatever method is most workable at the state/local level (e.g., consultation could be provided from a resource and referral agency).

See also discussion for recommendation REC47, on p. 313.

Optimally this individual should be based in the state public health department and should be a pediatrician, certified pediatric or family nurse practitioner, or a public health nurse. This individual should be available for consultation and technical assistance to the community-based child care health consultants.

See also discussion for recommendation REC53.

Optimally, the health consultant should be a physician, certified pediatric or family nurse practitioner, or public health nurse. The health consultant should work closely with the local public health agency and should have direct access to the state child care health consultant. See also discussion for recommendation REC53.

RECOMMENDATIONS

REC56. We recommend that every state regulatory agency should employ or contract with a nutrition agency that employs at least one qualified Nutrition Specialist (see Appendices B-1 and B-2 on pp. 328–329) full-time on its staff to be responsible for the development of policies and procedures and for the implementation of nutrition standards to provide high-quality meals and nutrition education programs; to provide service standards statewide; and to provide consultation to agency personnel, including licensing staff.

REC57. We recommend that the state mental health agency should require community mental health agencies and child guidance clinics to assist centers, large family-child-care homes, and networks of small family-child-care homes in meeting the emotional needs of particular children and families, and should provide funding for this assistance.

REC58. We recommend that the local regulating agency should provide centers and small and large family-child-care homes with a list of community agencies available to provide needed health and social services to families.

REC59. We recommend that the local regulating agency should ensure that all facilities receive the names and addresses of at least three licensed providers of dental services who have agreed to accept referrals of children in need of emergency treatment and to give advice regarding dental emergencies.

For additional information on consultants, see also *Health Consultants*, on p. 33.

Consultants and Technical Assistance for Children with Special Needs

REC60. We recommend that state regulatory agencies and oversight bodies should provide technical assistance to caregivers or make referrals to sources of assistance to enable the caregiver for children with special needs to develop and formulate a plan for future services for such children. (See standard CSN89 in chapter 7 on p. 266.)

REC61. We recommend that the state regulatory agency (or council of such agencies) responsible for overseeing child care for children with special needs should

DISCUSSION

Consultation with a Nutrition Specialist (see Appendices B-1 and B-2, on pp. 328–329) is necessary to plan meals and food service for young children.

A review of state licensing agencies' regulations (see Introduction) points to a need for more comprehensive and detailed nutrition standards, including the need for a Nutrition Specialist on the state licensing agency staff or one who is accountable for assisting the state licensing agency with staff work. The Nutrition Specialist should have experience as a nutritionist in a health program, including services to infants and preschool children. (See Appendices B-1 and B-2, on pp. 328–329.)

See also discussion for recommendation REC53.

This initiative is intended to enhance staff qualifications and support and a nurturing environment.[20] In order for the facility to have as comprehensive a program as possible to meet the individual needs of the family, community resources should be tapped.

In communities where the mental health system has viewed its role as supportive to the facilities in the catchment area, this support has enabled facilities to better help enrolled families.

See also discussion for recommendation REC53.

See discussion for recommendation REC53.

Early intervention may save a tooth.[21]

See also discussion for recommendation REC53.

This type of assistance is needed where caregivers lack specific capabilities.

The state licensing agency, the state agencies responsible for implementation of P.L. 94-142 and 99-457 (see *Introduction and Background*, on p. 237), and other state regulatory agencies should be in a position to provide such assistance to facilities.

The state agency requirement makes it more likely that these assessments will occur by providing reimbursement for them.

compensate the hours of time spent by the multidisciplinary team and the caregiver in developing the assessment defined in *Caregiver Responsibilities* and *Written Plan*, on pp. 265–266.

REC62. We recommend that the state agency or council of agencies responsible for child care for children with special needs should ensure that a nurse, special educator, and physician are available to provide consultation (if needed) to caregivers who are writing plans for backup medical and emergency services. (See *Emergency Preparedness Plan*, on p. 267.)

This recommendation lifts from the caregiver the burden of locating and reimbursing health consultants to facilities for children with special needs. For the purposes of this recommendation, such consultation is limited to the preparation of this emergency plan and its subsequent revisions. General health consultation is required elsewhere in these standards (see *Health Consultation*, on p. 278, and *Health Consultants*, on p. 33).

Some of the public schools mainstreaming children with special needs in centers and nursery schools that serve the community are already providing centralized consultation to enable these facilities to adapt to and meet the needs of children with special needs.

REC63. We recommend that the state agency or council of agencies responsible for child care services for children with special needs should provide printed and audiovisual information to parents about assessment of facilities.

Parents should participate in facility evaluation, both formally and informally.

REC64. We recommend that the child care regulating body should be responsible for ensuring that coordination of special services providers, caregivers, parents, and the regular educational program takes place in the reevaluation process (see *The Reevaluation Process*, on p. 262, and *The Participating Staff*, on p. 263).

This coordination will vary from state to state in some localities and should be a component reviewed in any quality assurance mechanism.

This coordination requires good record keeping and may require a log of coordinating activities and documentation of communications that have occurred.

Networking for Small Family-Child-Care Homes

REC65. We recommend that states and municipalities should develop neighborhood-based networks of small family-child-care homes to attract, train, support, and monitor those caregivers who would like to be a part of an organized system. In addition, local health departments, licensing agencies, and resource and referral agencies should provide training and technical assistance to independently licensed/certified caregivers (see *Individual Licensure/Certification*, on p. 301).

This recommendation is an initiative to enhance staff qualifications and support and a nurturing environment.[20] Individual small family home caregivers vary widely in educational background and experience. Participation in a network provides access to education and support for individual caregivers.

These networks should, when possible, include a central facility for enrichment activities for groups of children and support and in-service programs for caregivers.

Small family-child-care homes are particularly appropriate for infant, toddler, and school-age-child care.

9.4 Training

REC66. We recommend that state regulatory agencies should establish and implement a statewide plan for providing or purchasing in-service training for staff in all centers and small and large family-child-care homes. This plan should specify the nature and extent of training for caregivers and should address the need to cover at least the following subjects:

This initiative is intended to enhance staff qualifications and support nurturing environment.[20]

It is appropriate that the state regulatory agency should be the lead agency for a training plan. Training should relate to requirements and should specifically qualify caregivers to move into new roles in the child care system.

RECOMMENDATIONS

a) Child growth and development.
b) Child care programming and activities.
c) Health and safety practices and infection control.
d) Cultural diversity.
e) Nutrition and eating habits.
f) Parent education.
g) Design and use of physical space.
h) The care and education of children with special needs.

DISCUSSION

Caregivers in centers and in large and small family-child-care homes must, by the nature of their caregiving tasks, attain knowledge and skills that are multifaceted. Child health and employee health are integral parts of any education/training curriculum and program management plan.

Training needs should be based on *knowledge* needs rather than on a required number of hours. The training recommended here reflects the focus of caregivers on *child development*, supplemented by health and safety. The total of 24 clock hours of annual training is used by leading organizations in child care and early childhood education. The National Association for the Education of Young Children (NAEYC) recommends that every early childhood professional complete a minimum of 24 clock hours of in-service training annually, and that this training include training in child growth and development, curriculum, discipline, communication with parents, health, safety, nutrition, multicultural aspects, and professional issues.[22] Twenty-four hours of continuing education were recommended in early legislation proposed (although not passed in the final approved legislation of the Child Care and Development Block Grant) by the Alliance for Better Child Care, as well as in NAEYC's *Accreditation and Criteria Procedures of the National Academy of Early Childhood Programs.*[23] The American Red Cross has a 27-hour course on health issues specific to child care for entry-level caregivers in its *Child Care Course.*[24] For more information about this course, telephone the local chapter of the American Red Cross or write to

American Red Cross
National Headquarters
Health and Safety
18th and F Streets, N.W.
Washington, DC 20006

In addition to low child:staff ratio, group size, age mix of children, and stability of caregiver, the training/ education of caregivers is a specific indicator of child care quality.[25]

Most states require training for child care staff depending on their functions and responsibilities. Staff who are better trained are more able to prevent, recognize, and correct health and safety problems.

There are very few illnesses for which children need to be excluded from child care. Decisions about management of illness are facilitated by the caregiver's increased skill in assessing the child's behavior that suggests illness.[26] The American Red Cross *Child Care Course* requires 3 hours of training in preventing infectious diseases.[24]

Nutrition education and information are among the recommendations of the U.S. Department of Health and Human Services for improving the health of the nation.[27]

All caregivers should be trained to prevent, assess, and treat injuries common in child care settings and to comfort an injured child.

RECOMMENDATIONS

REC67. We recommend that private and public agencies should create mechanisms and provide funding for training of prospective child care staff (including supervised experience on-site) prior to their assuming responsibility for the care of children.

REC68. We recommend that Child Development Associate (CDA) certification programs for caregivers at centers and large and small family-child-care homes should be made available at community colleges, vocational schools, and high schools.

REC69. We recommend that local or state health departments should provide training, written information, and/or technical consultation in coordination with other community resources to facilities, including staff, parents, licensing personnel, and health consultants, in each of the following subject areas:
a) Immunization.
b) Surveillance and reporting of communicable diseases.
c) Techniques for the prevention and control of communicable diseases.
d) Exclusion guidelines.
e) General hygiene and sanitation.
f) Food handling precautions.

For additional information on training, see also *Continuing Education*, on p. 24, and *The Health Department's Role*, on p. 310.

DISCUSSION

There is a community responsibility to see that resources exist to protect children. This does not necessarily mean that government agencies should provide such resources —it simply means that they should see that such resources are available. See also the discussion above.

CDA training should be offered in ways that are feasible for staff who are employed full-day in facilities to attend.

See also the discussion for recommendation REC66.

See the discussion for recommendation REC38, on p. 311.

9.5 Program Development

REC70. We recommend that technical assistance and incentives should be provided by state and municipal, public and private agencies to encourage facilities to address cultural and socioeconomic diversity in child care settings.

Children who are exposed to cultural and socioeconomic diversity beginning in early childhood are more likely to value and accept differences between their own backgrounds and those of others as they move through life. This attitude results in improved self-esteem and mental health in children from all backgrounds. Facilities can attract participants from different income and cultural groups by locating in areas convenient to low-income families and accessible to middle- and upper-income parents, and by offering programs that are desirable to a range of parents. Possible locations include sites close to the edges of, rather than deep within, low-income areas; sites near worksites and schools that serve a mix of families; and sites in mixed-income housing.

REC71. We recommend that public and private agencies should foster collaboration among public, private, and parochial schools and local child care networks, caregivers, youth organizations, small family-child-care home networks, centers, large and small family-child-care homes, and resource and referral agencies to establish mechanisms for school-age child care facilities for children aged 5 to 12. Such care should be designed to meet the social and developmental needs of children who receive care in any setting.

School-age children who are undersupervised ("latch-key children") are exposed to considerable health and safety risks. Bringing them into supervised, quality child care is a societal responsibility.

RECOMMENDATIONS

REC72. We recommend that state and regional agencies should establish mechanisms and provide funding to facilitate the care of ill children in the following settings:

a) A separate area in the child's own facility or in a specialized center.

b) A child's own small family-child-care home.

c) A space within the small family-child-care home network's central place that would serve children from participating small family-child-care homes.

d) The child's own home under the supervision of an adult known to parents and child.

DISCUSSION

This initiative is intended to make possible the appropriate care of ill children.

These guidelines parallel those in *Health in Day Care: A Manual for Health Professionals*, published by the American Academy of Pediatrics.[28]

9.6 Regulatory Coordination

REC73. We recommend that the state health department, regulatory agencies, child protection agencies, law enforcement agencies, community service agencies, and local government should collaborate to coordinate activities related to the prevention and control of communicable diseases, injury, and child abuse in facilities. The child care licensing, building, fire safety, and health authorities, as well as any other regulators, should work together as a team to evaluate applications for licensing of new facilities and applications for renewal of licenses of previously licensed facilities.

We recommend that activities to be coordinated should include inspection, reporting and surveillance systems, guidance in managing outbreaks of infectious diseases, preventing exposure of children to hazards, reporting child abuse, and training and technical consultation. In addition, agencies should collaborate to educate parents, health care providers, public health workers, licensors, and employers about their roles in ensuring health and safety in child care settings.

Collaboration is necessary to utilize limited resources effectively, avoid contradictions in regulatory codes, simplify inspection procedures, and reduce bureaucratic disincentives to the provision of safe and healthy care for children.

Collaboration should focus on establishing the role of each agency in ensuring that necessary services and systems exist to prevent and control health and safety problems in facilities. Caregivers are frequently burdened by complicated procedures required to obtain clearance from various authorities to operate. When regulatory authorities work as a team, each member of the team gains opportunities to learn about the responsibilities of other team members so that close working relationships can be established, conflicts can be resolved, and decisions can be reached.

In small states, a state-level task force may be sufficient. In larger or more populous states, local task forces may be needed to promote effective use of resources.

9.7 Public Policy Issues and Resource Development

REC74. We recommend that each state should establish a state-level commission on child care or charge an existing commission with the responsibility for developing a child care plan and facilitating cooperation among government, human services agencies, schools, employers, and caregivers to ensure that the health, safety, and child development needs of children are met by child care services provided in the state. The commission should include both parents and representatives of agencies and organizations affecting child care. The commission should be mandated by law, and should report to the legislature, to the governor, and to all agencies and organizations represented on the commission no less frequently than once a year. Larger communities should have a local child care advisory body charged with the responsibility of overseeing the development and provision of child care to meet the needs of the particular community with the same broad representation recommended for the state-level commission.

Policy-making for child care is fragmented at the state level, despite the fact that interagency coordination has been shown to be effective in other service areas for children (e.g., services for children with special needs). Especially when young children are in care, coordination among public and private sources of health, social service, and education services is essential. Some states have separate groups that advise the health agency, the social service agency, the education agency, the licensing agency, the governor, and the legislature. Other states have some, but not all, of these advisory bodies—each of which has some relevance to child care, but often with different focuses. Time-limited task forces could be created for specific purposes, but there is a need for one standing commission that addresses child care as its primary responsibility. Mandating the commission by law will reduce the likelihood that the commission will be victimized by changes in political leadership or dissolved when its recommendations are not in agreement with a

---

RECOMMENDATIONS

DISCUSSION

current administration. Large municipalities with a similarly diverse group of agencies, authorities, and public and private resources should also have a group to coordinate child care activity.

Participation of parent representatives in planning and implementing child care initiatives at the state and local levels promotes effective partnerships between parents and caregivers.

REC75. We recommend that states should encourage the use of public and private resources in local communities to develop resource and referral agencies. The functions of these agencies should include the following:

a) Helping parents find developmentally appropriate child care that protects the health and safety of children.

b) Giving parents consumer information to enable them to know about, evaluate, and choose among available child care options.

c) Helping parents maintain a dialogue with their caregivers.

d) Recruiting new potential caregivers.

e) Providing training, technical assistance, and consultation to new facilities, and to all caregivers.

f) Compiling data on supply and demand to identify community needs for child care.

g) Providing information to employers on options for their involvement in meeting community child care needs.

Resource and referral agencies provide a locus in the community to assist parents in fulfilling their child-rearing responsibilities, a mechanism to coordinate and provide the resources and services that supplement and facilitate the functions of the family, and a mechanism for the coordination of services that helps keep children safe and healthy.

REC76. We recommend that public and private policymakers should use financial and other incentives to help caregivers meet licensing/certification (see *Individual Licensure/Certification*, on p. 301) and funding requirements. They should also coordinate public and private resources to ensure that all families have access to affordable, safe, and healthful child care for their children. To the extent possible, they should coordinate multiple funding streams of child care.

Quality cannot be attained by merely applying standards to caregivers; resources are necessary to meet the cost of quality care at a price that parents can afford. Currently, the low wages and benefits earned by child care staff result in high staff turnover, which adversely affects the health and safety of children. Frequently replaced, untrained, barely oriented, poorly compensated, and overworked staff cannot maintain sanitation routines, be prepared for emergencies, or meet the mental health needs of children for constancy in relationships.

Child care is a labor-intensive service. Staff wages make up the largest cost in providing care, and caregiver wages in the United States are currently too low to attract and retain qualified staff. Countries that successfully recruit and retain good child care staff pay salaries and benefits equal to those paid to elementary school teachers. The cost of child care in the United States is currently subsidized by the low wages and benefits of caregivers, who leave their jobs at an astonishingly high rate.

Research provides clear evidence that a well-qualified and stable staff is essential to the provision of good care for children. Quality care requires not only lower child:staff ratios and smaller group sizes, but also well-trained staff to reduce the spread of infectious diseases and provide for safe evacuation and management of emergency situations. Facilities cannot benefit from training provided to staff if the staff leave their jobs before the training is implemented.[20]

RECOMMENDATIONS

REC77. We recommend that public and private mechanisms should be developed to support the ability of parents to choose to take temporary leave from work after the birth or adoption of a child, or to care for an ill child for whom out-of-home child care is not as safe and healthful as parental care.

DISCUSSION

Good, quality care costs more than the majority of middle- and low-income families can afford, leaving no alternative for many parents but to purchase substandard, hazardous, and unhealthful arrangements for their children. Financing of safe and healthful child care must come from a combination of public and private subsidies for the cost of care that exceeds the reasonable ability of parents to pay for care themselves. Coordination of funding should be achieved by parties other than the caregiver so that administrators of child care can focus on ensuring the quality of care rather than on raising funds for facility survival.

Safe and healthful child care at times when a child is significantly ill or when the child is a newborn or newly adopted child is usually best provided by parents. These are times when the interests of the child are best served by parental care in the child's own home. The United States is currently debating parental leave policies and how the cost of parental leave can be borne at times when parents choose, in the best interest of the child, to provide care for the child themselves. Development of societal policy in this area is essential so that parents are not forced to put their child at risk physically and emotionally because of economic necessity.

References

1. Schloesser P., ed. *Health of Children in Day Care: Public Health Profiles.* Topeka, Kan: Kansas Department of Health and Environment; 1986.

2. Morgan G. *The National State of Child Care Regulation.* Washington, DC: National Association for the Education of Young Children; 1986.

3. Finkelhor D, William LM, Burns N. *Nursery Crimes: Sexual Abuse in Day Care.* Beverly Hills, Calif: Sage Publications; 1988.

4. Fredericks B, Hardman B, Morgan G, et al. *A Little Bit Under the Weather: A Look at Care for Mildly Ill Children.* Boston, Mass: Work/Family Directions, Inc; 1985.

5. *Proposed Rules for Sick Care Programs.* Minneapolis, Minn: Dept of Human Services; Dec 1987.

6. Haskins R, Kotch J. Day care and illness: evidence, costs, and public policy. *Pediatrics.* 1986; 77 (suppl):977.

7. Colorado Dept of Health. Colorado child care survey (unpublished); 1986.

8. Aronson S, Aiken L. Compliance of child care programs with health and safety standards: impact of program evaluation and advocate training. *Pediatrics.* 1980;65:318–325.

9. Hadler SC, McFarland L. Hepatitis in day care centers: epidemiology and prevention. *Rev Infect Dis.* 1986; 8:548–557.

10. Bartlett AV, Broome CV, Hadler SC. Public health considerations of infectious diseases in child day care centers. *J Pediatr.* 1984;105:683–701.

11. Goodman RA, Lie LA, Deitch SR, et al. Relationship between day care and health care providers. *Rev Infect Dis.* 1986;8:669–671.

12. Aronson SS, Gilsdorf JR. Prevention and management of infectious diseases in day care. *Pediatr in Rev.* 1986;7:259–268.

13. Aronson SS, Osterholm MT. Infectious diseases in child day care: management and prevention, summary of the symposium and recommendation. *Rev Infect Dis.* 1986;8:674.

14. Pickering LK, Bartlett AV, Woodward WE. Acute infectious diarrhea among children in day care: epidemiology and control. *Rev Infect Dis.* 1986;8:545.

15. Stagno S, Pass RF, Dworsky ME, et al. Maternal cytomegalovirus infection and perinatal transmission. In: Knox GE, ed., *Clinical Obstetrics and Gynecology* 1982;25:563–576.

16. Stagno S, Pass RF, Dworsky ME, et al. Congenital cytomegalovirus infection: the relative importance of primary and recurrent maternal infection. *N Engl J Med.* 1982;306:945–949.

17. Committee on Early Childhood, Adoption and Dependent Care. Pediatrician's role in promoting the health of a patient in day care. *Pediatrics.* 1984; 74:157–158.

18. Introduction of S-1885. *Congressional Record.* November 19, 1987.

19. Aronson SS. Health and safety in child care. In Chehrazi S, ed., *Psychosocial Issues in Day Care.* Washington, DC: American Psychiatric Press; 1990.

20. Whitebook M, Howes C, Phillips D. *Who Cares: Child Care Teachers and the Quality of Care in America.* Oakland, Calif: Child Care Employee Project; 1989.

21. Bogert JA. The American Academy of Pediatric Dentistry: its scope and function. *NYS Dent J.* Feb 1988.

22. *Don't Shortchange America's Future: The Full Cost of Quality Must Be Paid.* Washington, DC: National Association for the Education of Young Children; 1990.

23. *Accreditation and Criteria Procedures of the National Academy of Early Childhood Programs.* Washington, DC: National Association for the Education of Young Children; 1984.

24. American Red Cross. *American Red Cross Child Care Course.* Washington, DC: American Red Cross; 1990.

25. Ruopp R, Travers J, Glantz F, et al. *Children at the Center. Final Report of the National Day Care Study. Vol. 1.* Cambridge, Mass: Abt Assoociates; 1979.

26. *Protocol for Management of Infections in Child Care Facilities.* Charlotte, NC: Mecklenberg County Health Department; 1983.

27. *Promoting Health/Preventing Disease: Objectives for the Nation.* Washington, DC: US Dept of Health and Human Services; 1980.

28. Deitch S, ed. *Health in Day Care: A Manual for Health Professionals.* Elk Grove Village, Ill: American Academy of Pediatrics; 1987.

APPENDICES

Appendix A

Qualifications and Responsibilities of Caregivers
by Age Groups of Children

TITLE / ROLE RESPONSIBILITY	AGE	EDUCATION	SKILLS / EXPERIENCE
Children Aged 0–35 Months			
Director	21	Undergraduate degree in early childhood education, child development, social work, nursing, or other child-related field, OR a combination of college course-work and experience and 2 or more years' experience as a teacher of infants and toddlers. Coursework in business administration or business-related experience. Preservice training in child development, early childhood education, and health management in child care. Directors of large centers meet more stringent qualifications.	• Knowledge of, and competence in dealing with, infant/toddler skills and behavior. • Administrative and management skills in facility operations. • Capability in curriculum design. • Knowledge of community resources. • Verbal and written communication skills. • Ability to communicate with parents. • Pediatric first aid, including rescue breathing and first aid for choking.
Lead Teacher	21	Undergraduate or master's degree in early childhood education, child development, social work, nursing, or other child-related field. Licensed as lead teacher, teacher, or associate teacher. Education and experience related to infant and toddler development and caregiving. One or more years' experience in child care under qualified supervision.	• Knowledge of, and competence in dealing with, infant/toddler skills and behavior. • Ability to respond appropriately to these children's needs. • Verbal and written communication skills. • Recognition of signs of illness and safety hazards. • Pediatric first aid, including rescue breathing and first aid for choking. • Ability to communicate with parents.
Early Childhood Teacher	21	Undergraduate degree in early childhood education, child development, social work, nursing, or other child-related field, OR a combination of college coursework and experience. Also, 1 year's experience, OR one semester practicum, OR associate degree and 1 year's experience, OR CDA credential, 2 years' experience, and one additional course in early childhood education, OR four courses in child development.	• Competence in the care and education of young children.
Early Childhood Associate Teacher	18	CDA credential or associate degree in early childhood education or child development. Six or more months' experience in child care.	• Competence in the care and education of young children.
Early Childhood Teacher Assistant	18	High school diploma or GED. Participation in ongoing training.	• Competence in assigned tasks. • Ability to respond appropriately to young children's needs.
Aide	18	On-the-job training.	• Ability to nurture children, as attested to by a qualified educator who has observed the caregiver caring for children. • Sound judgment. • Ability to follow instructions. • Ability to carry out assigned tasks under supervision of another staff member.

TITLE / ROLE RESPONSIBILITY	AGE	EDUCATION	SKILLS / EXPERIENCE
Health Advocate	18	Health training related to infant and toddler development and caregiving. Licensed as lead teacher, teacher, or associate teacher, or shall be a health professional or social worker employed by and at the facility.	• Knowledge of, and competence in dealing with, infant/toddler skills and behavior. • Ability to respond appropriately to these children's needs. • Verbal and written communication skills. • Recognition of signs of illness and safety hazards. • Pediatric first aid, including rescue breathing and first aid for choking.
Large Family Home Caregiver	21	High school diploma or GED. CDA credential, associate or undergraduate degree in early childhood education or child development, OR coursework in child growth and development plus 1 year's experience in a facility or as a licensed small family home caregiver. Preservice training in health management in child care.	• Knowledge of, and competence in dealing with, infant/toddler skills and behavior. • Ability to respond appropriately to these children's needs. • Verbal and written communication skills. • Recognition of signs of illness and safety hazards. • Ability to communicate with parents. • Pediatric first aid, including rescue breathing and first aid for choking.
Small Family Home Caregiver (See Levels 1 and 2 described in *Qualifications of Large and Small Family Home Caregivers*, on p. 14)	21	Preservice training in health management in child care. Ongoing training courses related to care specific to this age group.	• Knowledge of, and competence in dealing with, infant/toddler skills and behavior. • Ability to respond appropriately to these children's needs. • Verbal communication skills. • Recognition of signs of illness and safety hazards. • Ability to communicate with parents. • Pediatric first aid, including rescue breathing and first aid for choking.
Children Aged 3–5 Years			
Director	21	Undergraduate degree in early childhood education, child development, social work, nursing, or other child-related field, OR a combination of college coursework and experience and 2 or more years' experience as a teacher of preschoolers. Coursework in business administration or business-related experience. Preservice training in child development, early childhood education, and health management in child care. Directors of large centers meet more stringent qualifications.	• Knowledge and understanding of child development. • Administrative and management skills in facility operations. • Capability in curriculum design. • Verbal and written communication skills. • Knowledge of community resources. • Ability to communicate with parents. • Pediatric first aid, including rescue breathing and first aid for choking.
Lead Teacher	21	Undergraduate or master's degree in early childhood education, child development, social work, nursing, or other child-related field. Licensed as lead teacher, teacher, or associate teacher. Education in child development and early childhood education and supervised experience with preschoolers. One or more years' experience working in child care under qualified supervision.	• Knowledge and understanding of developmental characteristics of 3- to 5-year-olds. • Independence and competence in assigned tasks. • Ability to respond appropriately to preschoolers' needs. • Verbal and written communication skills. • Recognition of signs of illness and safety hazards. • Pediatric first aid, including rescue breathing and first aid for choking. • Ability to communicate with parents.

TITLE / ROLE RESPONSIBILITY	AGE	EDUCATION	SKILLS / EXPERIENCE
Early Childhood Teacher	21	Undergraduate degree in early childhood education, child development, social work, nursing, or other child-related field, OR a combination of college coursework and experience under qualified supervision. Also, 1 year's experience, OR one semester practicum, OR associate degree and 1 year's experience, OR CDA credential, 2 years' experience, and one additional course in early childhood education, OR four courses in child development.	• Competence in the care and education of young children.
Early Childhood Associate Teacher	18	CDA credential or associate degree in early childhood education or child development. Six or more months' experience in child care.	• Competence in the care and education of young children.
Early Childhood Teacher Assistant	18	High school diploma or GED. Participation in ongoing training.	• Competence in assigned tasks. • Ability to respond appropriately to young children's needs.
Aide	18	On-the-job training.	• Ability to nurture children. • Sound judgment. • Ability to follow instructions. • Ability to carry out assigned tasks under supervision of another staff member.
Health Advocate	18	Health training related to development and care for 3- to 5-year olds. Licensed as lead teacher, teacher, or associate teacher, or shall be a health professional or social worker employed by and at the facility.	• Knowledge and understanding of developmental characteristics of 3- to 5-year-olds. • Ability to respond appropriately to these children's needs. • Verbal and written communication skills. • Recognition of signs of illness and safety hazards. • Pediatric first aid, including rescue breathing and first aid for choking.
Large Family Home Caregiver	21	High school diploma or GED. CDA credential, associate or undergraduate degree in early childhood education or child development, OR coursework in child growth and development plus 1 year's experience in a facility or as a licensed small family home caregiver. Preservice training in health management in child care.	• Knowledge and understanding of child development. • Ability to respond appropriately to the needs of 3- to 5-year olds. • Verbal and written communication skills. • Recognition of signs of illness and safety hazards. • Ability to communicate with parents. • Pediatric first aid, including rescue breathing and first aid for choking.
Small Family Home Caregiver (See Levels 1 and 2 described in *Qualifications of Large and Small Family Home Caregivers*, on p. 14)	21	Preservice training in health management in child care. Ongoing training courses related to care specific to this age group.	• Knowledge and understanding of child development. • Ability to respond appropriately to the needs of 3- to 5-year-olds. • Verbal communication skills. • Recognition of signs of illness and safety hazards. • Pediatric first aid, including rescue breathing and first aid for choking. • Ability to communicate with parents.

TITLE / ROLE RESPONSIBILITY	AGE	EDUCATION	SKILLS / EXPERIENCE
		School-Age Children	
Director	21	Undergraduate degree in early childhood education, elementary education, child development, recreation or other child-related field, OR a combination of college coursework and experience under qualified supervision and 2 years' experience working with school-age children. Coursework in business administration or business-related experience Preservice training in child development, early childhood education, and health management in child care. Directors of large centers meet more stringent qualifications.	• Knowledge and understanding of child development. • Administrative and management skills. • Verbal and written communication skills. • Capability in curriculum design. • Knowledge of community resources. • Pediatric first aid, including rescue breathing and first aid for choking.
Group Leader	21	Undergraduate or master's degree in early childhood education or child development (covering ages 0 to 8 or 3 to 8), elementary education, recreation, or a related field. Licensed as lead teacher, teacher, or associate teacher. Education in child development and programming specific to school-age children and supervised experience specific to this age group. Training in child development and education appropriate for school-age children. One or more years' experience in child care under qualified supervision.	• Knowledge and understanding of developmental characteristics of 5- to 12-year-olds. • Independence and competence in assigned tasks. • Verbal and written communication skills. • Recognition of signs of illness and safety hazards. • Pediatric first aid, including rescue breathing and first aid for choking.
Aide	18	On-the-job training.	• Ability to nurture children. • Sound judgment. • Ability to follow instructions. • Ability to carry out assigned tasks under supervision of another staff member.
Health Advocate	18	Health training related to development and care of school-age children. Licensed as lead teacher, teacher, or associate teacher, or shall be a health professional or social worker employed by and at the facility.	• Knowledge of the social and emotional needs and developmental tasks of 5- to 12-year-olds. • Verbal and written communication skills. • Recognition of signs of illness and safety hazards. • Pediatric first aid, including rescue breathing and first aid for choking.
Large Family Home Caregiver	21	High school diploma or GED. CDA credential, associate or undergraduate degree in early childhood education or child development, OR coursework in child growth and development plus 1 year's experience in a facility. Preservice training in health management in child care.	• Knowledge of, and competence in dealing with, school-age children's skills and behavior. • Ability to respond appropriately to these children's needs. • Verbal and written communication skills. • Recognition of signs of illness and safety hazards. • Ability to communicate with parents. • Pediatric first aid, including rescue breathing and first aid for choking.

TITLE / ROLE RESPONSIBILITY	AGE	EDUCATION	SKILLS / EXPERIENCE
Small Family Home Caregiver (See Levels 1 and 2 described in *Qualifications of Large and Small Family Home Caregivers,* on p. 14)	21	Preservice training in health management in child care. Ongoing training courses related to care specific to this age group.	• Knowledge of, and competence in dealing with, school-age children's skills and behavior. • Ability to respond appropriately to the needs of 5- to 12-year-olds. • Verbal communication skills. • Recognition of signs of illness and safety hazards. • Ability to communicate with parents. • Pediatric first aid skills, including rescue breathing and first aid for choking.
All Children (for very large centers, chains, or systems)			
Child Care Nutrition Specialist*	21	Registered Dietitian designation. Undergraduate and master's degrees in nutrition. Supplemental courses in child growth and development. Two or more years' related experience.	• Expertise in nutrition consultation and training. • Experience in food budgeting.
Child Care Food Service Manager*	18	High school diploma or GED. Food-handler class certification; relevant nutrition coursework; 2 years' food service experience.	• Supervisory skills in food service.
Child Care Food Service Worker (Cook)*	18	High school diploma or GED. Food-handler class certification; basic menu planning coursework; 1 or more years' experience in food service.	• Experience in menu planning. • Experience in food preparation and service.
Child Care Food Service Aide	18	High school diploma or GED. Food-handler class certification within 1 to 2 months of employment.	
Transportation Staff			
Drivers/ Other Attendants**	18	Training in child passenger safety precautions.	• Pediatric first aid, including rescue breathing and first aid for choking.
Maintenance Staff	18		

*See Appendices B-1 and B-2 on pp. 328–329 for a full description of qualifications and experience.
**See *Transportation*, on p. 199, for a full description of qualifications and experience.

Appendix B-1

A Model for State and Community Nutrition Services

STANDARDS

APP1. The state Department of Education's Nutrition Bureau or the licensing agency shall employ at least one child care Nutrition Specialist full time on staff or contract with an agency that employs at least one qualified child care Nutrition Specialist. The child care Nutrition Specialist shall assist in locating local nutrition resources for facilities in need of consultation and guidance in nutrition education, for the food service unit, and for parents of children with special problems or conditions requiring diet or feeding modifications.

APP2. Minimum qualifications for a child care Nutrition Specialist are a bachelor's and master's degree in nutrition; current registration with the Commission on Dietetic Registration of the American Dietetic Association (or eligibility for the next scheduled examination); and course(s) in child growth and development plus at least 2 years of related experience as a nutritionist in a health program including services to infants and children. A master's degree (MPH or MS) from an approved program in public health nutrition may be substituted for registration with the Commission on Dietetic Registration. The state child care Nutrition Specialist with licensure/certification must conform to these minimum requirements.

APP3. The state child care Nutrition Specialist shall implement a policy on recommended minimum qualifications for nutrition personnel (see Appendix B-2, on p. 329) and shall develop the children's food plan as specified in standard NU1 in chapter 4 on p. 115.

See also *Staffing*, on p. 122.

RATIONALE

The expertise of the child care Nutrition Specialists on the state level is needed in the determination of appropriate placement of the local-level child care Nutrition Specialist. The size and complexity of local facilities and programs vary considerably, so assistance from the state agency is imperative.

A review of state licensing agencies' regulations (see Introduction) indicates the need for a child care Nutrition Specialist on the state agency staff who has experience as a nutritionist in a health program, including services to infants and preschool children.

The Technical Panel on Nutrition (see Introduction) was unanimous in its opinion that each state should be required to have at least one full-time child care Nutrition Specialist on its staff. This standard was meant to ensure that a person qualified in nutrition has input into and monitors the nutrition component for the state agency responsible for licensing child care.

COMMENTS

The following are resources to contact to locate a child care Nutrition Specialist: Nutrition Specialists with state maternal and child health departments and divisions of children with special health care needs; local health departments; university and college nutrition departments; home economists at utility companies; and groups such as the American Home Economics Association, state affiliates of the American Dietetic Association, and state and regional affiliates of the American Public Health Association.

The designation of Registered Dietitian (RD) is granted by the Commission on Dietetic Registration to persons who meet defined academic and supervised practice requirements and who have successfully completed an examination administered by the Commission.

See also comment for standard APP1.

See comment for standard APP2.

Appendix B-2

Nutrition Specialist and Child Care Food Service Staff Qualifications

TITLE	LEVEL OF PROFESSIONAL RESPONSIBILITY	EDUCATION AND EXPERIENCE
Child Care Nutrition Specialist (state level)	Develops policies and procedures for implementation of nutrition food standards statewide and provides consultation to state agency personnel, including staff involved with licensure.	Current registration with the Commission on Dietetic Registration of the American Dietetic Association or eligibility for registration, with minimum qualifications (see Appendix B-1, on p. 328) including or supplemented by course(s) in child growth and development, plus at least 2 years of related experience as a nutritionist in a health program including services to infants and children.
Child Care Nutrition Specialist (local level)	Provides expertise to child care center director and provides ongoing guidance, consultation, and in-service training to facility's nutrition personnel in implementing and evaluating all aspects of the nutrition component. The number of sites and facilities for one child care Nutrition Specialist will vary according to size and complexity of local facilities.	Registered Dietitian, as above. At least 1 year of experience as described above.
Child Care Food Service Manager	Has overall supervisory responsibility for the food service unit at one or more facility sites.	High school diploma or GED. Successful completion of a food-handler class. Coursework in basic menu-planning skills, basic foods, introduction to child feeding programs for managers, and/or other relevant courses (offered at community colleges). Two years of food service experience.
Child Care Food Service Worker (Cook)	Under the supervision of the Food Service Manager, carries out food service operations including menu planning, food preparation and service, and related duties in a designated area.	High school diploma or GED. Successful completion of a food-handler class. Coursework in basic menu-planning skills and basic foods (offered through adult education or a community college). One year of food service experience.
Child Care Food Service Aide	Works no more than 4 hours a day, under the supervision of an employee at a higher level in food service unit.	High school diploma or GED. Must pass the food-handler test within 1 to 2 months of employment. No prior experience is required for semi-skilled persons who perform assigned tasks in designated areas.

See also *Staffing*, on p. 122.

Appendix C
Child Records

STANDARDS

APP4. The facility shall maintain a file for each child in one central location within the facility. This file shall be kept in a confidential manner (see *Confidentiality and Access to Records*, on p. 288) but shall be immediately available to the child's caregivers, parents or legal guardians, and the licensing authority upon request.

APP5. The file for each child (see standard APP4) shall include the following:
A) *Pre-admission enrollment information* including the following:
   1) The child's name, address, sex, and date of birth.
   2) The full names of the child's parents or legal guardians, and their home and work addresses and telephone numbers. Telephone contact numbers shall be confirmed by a call placed by the facility during its hours of operation. Names, addresses, and telephone numbers shall be updated at least quarterly.
   3) The names, addresses, and telephone numbers of at least two additional persons to be notified in the event that the parents or legal guardians cannot be located. Telephone information shall be confirmed and updated as specified in item 2 above.
   4) The names and telephone numbers of the child's primary sources of medical care, emergency medical care, and dental care.
   5) The child's health payment resource.
   6) The emergency information in items 1 through 5 above shall be obtained in duplicate with original parent/legal guardian signatures on both copies, and one copy shall be easily accessible at all times. This information shall be updated quarterly and as necessary. The duplicate card must accompany the child to all off-site excursions.

RATIONALE

Operational control to accommodate the health and safety of individual children requires that information regarding each child in care be kept and made available on a need-to-know basis.

These records and reports are necessary to protect the health and safety of children in care. An organized, comprehensive approach to injury prevention and control is necessary to ensure that a safe environment is provided for children in child care. Such an approach requires written plans, policies, procedures, and record-keeping so that there is consistency over time and across staff and an understanding between parents and caregivers about concerns for, and attention to, the safety of children.

Emergency information is the key to obtaining needed care in emergency situations.[1] Caregivers must have written permission to allow them to respond quickly to emergency problems.[2] Contact information must be verified for accuracy.

Health payment resource information is usually required before any non–life-threatening emergency care is provided.

COMMENTS

Phone numbers provided for emergency contacts should never include an answering-machine phone number.

Duplicate records are easily made using multiple-copy forms, carbon paper, or photocopying.

STANDARDS

7) Written instructions of the parent, legal guardian, or child's health care provider for any special dietary needs or special needs due to a health condition, or any other special instructions from the parent.

8) Scheduled days and hours of attendance.

9) In the event that one parent is the sole legal guardian of the child, legal documentation evidencing his/her authority.

10) Enrollment date, reason for entry in child care, and fee arrangements.

11) Signed permission to act on parent's behalf for emergency treatment and for use of syrup of ipecac. (See *Emergency Procedures*, on p. 95, and *Emergency Plan*, on p. 281.)

12) Authorization to release child to anyone other than the custodial parent. (See *Safety Plan*, on p. 281.)

APP6.

B) A *medical report* completed and signed by the child's health care provider, preferably *prior to enrollment or no later than 6 weeks after admission*. The medical report shall include the following medical and developmental information:

1) Records of the child's immunizations.

2) A description of any disability, sensory impairment, developmental variation, seizure disorder, or emotional or behavioral disturbance that may affect adaptation to child care (include previous surgery, serious illness, history of prematurity, etc., only if relevant).

3) An assessment of the child's growth based on height, weight, and head circumference and the percentile for each, if the child is younger than 24 months.

RATIONALE

The requirement of a medical report for each child reflecting completion of health assessments and immunizations is a valid way to ensure preventive care for children who might not otherwise receive it[3,4] and can be used in decision making for admission.[5]

Quality child care requires a preadmission physical examination and the initiation of immunizations that might not be received if care were provided by a caregiver not knowledgeable about mechanisms for the prevention of disease.[6]

The objective of early evaluation is to permit detection and counseling for improved oral, physical, mental, and emotional/social health.[7]

The health care provider's chronological account of a child's health is a valuable source of data on illness and wellness. The medical report can give the documentation needed for decisions on management of health prob-

COMMENTS

The purpose of a medical report is to

a) Give information about a child's abilities, special needs, and health status to allow the caregiver to provide a safe setting and healthful experience for each child.

b) Promote individual and collective health by fostering compliance with approved standards for health care assessments and immunizations.

c) Document compliance with licensing standards.

d) Serve as a means to ensure early detection of health problems and a guide to steps for remediation.

e) Serve as a means to facilitate and encourage communication and learning among caregivers, health care providers, and parents.

Ideally, the medical report should be updated every year, rather than every 2 years for school-age children, at contract time (see *Management Plan and Statement of Services*, on p. 271).

STANDARDS

4) A description of health problems or findings from an examination or screening that need follow-up.
5) Results of screenings—vision, hearing, dental, nutrition, developmental, tuberculosis, hemoglobin, urine, lead, and so forth.
6) Dates of significant communicable diseases (e.g., chicken pox).
7) Prescribed medication(s), including information on recognizing, documenting, and reporting potential side effects.
8) A description of current acute or chronic health problems under or needing treatment.
9) A description of serious injuries sustained by the child in the past that required medical attention or hospitalization.
10) Special instructions for the caregiver.

The medical report shall include space for additional comments about the management of health problems and for additional health-related data offered by the health care provider or required from the facility.

The medical report shall be updated as follows:
- No later than 6 weeks after admission to the facility.
- Every 6 months for children under 2 years of age.
- Every year for children ages 2 to 6.
- Every 2 years for school-age children.

For additional information on the medical report, see also standard AD20 in chapter 8 on p. 276 for review of the medical report, standard AD23 in chapter 8 on p. 277 for procedure to correct omissions in assessments, and standard PR42 in chapter 2 on p. 56.

RATIONALE

lems, exclusion, and so forth. It is a positive means of communication, via a parent or directly, between the health care provider and the caregiver.[8]

COMMENTS

This report will provide an update on contagious diseases, new or changed prescribed medications, new or changed special concerns, and so forth.

The medical report should indicate that the American Academy of Pediatrics (AAP) or Medicaid's Early Periodic Screening and Diagnostic Treatment (EPSDT) guidelines for assessments have been followed in evaluating the child.[1, 4]

Health data should be presented in a form usable by caregivers to identify any special needs for care. Local EPSDT programs should be called upon to help with liaison and education activities. In some situations, screenings may best be performed at the facilities. There are still many physicians who do not fill out forms completely enough to assist the caregiver in understanding the significance of health assessment findings or the unique characteristics of a child.

A sample medical report is provided in Appendix II.2 of *Health in Day Care: A Manual for Health Professionals.* To order this publication, contact

American Academy of Pediatrics
141 Northwest Point Blvd.
P.O. Box 927
Elk Grove Village, IL 60009-0927

Samples of a physician's exam form, chronic-illness health record, and asthma record, as well as facility considerations for children with health impairments, are provided in *Healthy Young Children.* To obtain this publication, contact

National Association for the
Education of Young Children
1834 Connecticut Ave., N.W.
Washington, DC 20009

The AAP recommends vision and hearing screenings at every health supervision visit, and recommends that all children have their first dental exam at 3 years of age. An authorized health care provider could examine the mouth of a child up to 3 years of age. After 3 years, the child should visit a dentist for examinations at in-

STANDARDS

RATIONALE

COMMENTS

tervals prescribed by the dentist. Children with suspected oral problems should see a dentist immediately, regardless of age or interval. These guidelines are described in "A Guide to Children's Dental Health," a brochure published by the American Academy of Pediatrics (see address above).

C) *Signed parent agreement at enrollment,* including the following:

1) Admission agreement (see *Management Plan and Statement of Services,* on p. 271) or contract stating the rule prohibiting corporal punishment (see *Discipline Policy,* on p. 272, and *Discipline,* on p. 52).

Corporal punishment may be physical abuse or may become abusive very easily.

2) Admission agreement (see *Management Plan and Statement of Services,* on p. 271) or contract stating that all parents may visit the site at any time when their child is there, and that they will be admitted immediately. (See standard PR41 and *Management Plan and Statement of Services,* on p. 271.)

The open-door policy may be the single most important method of preventing the abuse of children in child care.[1] When access is restricted, areas observable by the parents may not reflect the care the children actually receive.

3) Documentation of written consent (see Appendix X, on p. 389) signed and dated by the parent or legal guardian for
   a) Emergency transportation.
   b) All other transportation provided by the facility. (See *Child:Staff Ratio and Group Size,* on p. 1, and *Transportation,* on p. 199.)
   c) Planned or unplanned activities off-premises. Such consent shall give specific information about where, when, and how such activities shall take place, including specific information about walking to and from activities away from the facility. (See *Field Trips,* on p. 52.)
   d) Phone authorizations for release of the child. (See *Safety Plan,* on p. 281.)
   e) Swimming/wading, if the child will be participating. (See *Child:Staff Ratio and Group Size,* on p. 1, *Water Safety,* on p. 96, and *Swimming, Wading, and Water,* on p. 192.

These records and reports are necessary to protect the health and safety of children in care.

STANDARDS

RATIONALE

COMMENTS

f) Any health service obtained for the child by the facility on behalf of the parent. Such consent shall be specific for the type of care provided to meet the tests for "informed consent" to cover on-site screenings or other services provided.

g) Release of any information to agencies, schools, or providers of services. (See *Confidentiality and Access to Records*, on p. 288.)

h) Authorization to release the child to anyone other than the custodial parent. (See *Safety Plan*, on p. 281.)

i) Emergency treatment. (See *Emergency Procedures*, on p. 95, and *Emergency Plan*, on p. 280.)

j) Administration of medications (standing orders and short-term). (See *Medications*, on p. 88, and *Medication Policy*, on p. 280.)

4) Statement that parent has received and discussed a copy of the state child abuse reporting requirements.

These consents would be needed by the person delivering the medical care. Advance consent for emergency medical or surgical service is not legally valid, since the nature and extent of injury, proposed medical treatment, risks, and benefits cannot be known until after the injury occurs.

The parent/child care partnership is vital. Participation of parents in decisions concerning children is a primary goal of Head Start.[4]

D) A *health history* completed by the parent *at admission*, preferably with staff involvement. This history shall include the following:

1) Developmental variations, sensory impairment, or a disability that may need consideration in the child care setting.

2) Description of current physical, social, and language developmental levels.

3) Current medications. (See *Medications*, on p. 88, and *Medication Policy*, on p. 280.)

4) Special concerns—allergies, chronic illness, pediatric first aid information needs.

5) Specific diet restrictions, if the child is on a special diet.

6) Individual characteristics or personality factors relevant to child care.

7) Special family considerations.

8) Dates of communicable diseases.

A health history is the basis for meeting the child's needs in health, mental, and social areas in the child care setting.

A sample developmental health history is provided in *Healthy Young Children*. To obtain this publication, contact

National Association for the
Education of Young Children
1834 Connecticut Ave., N.W.
Washington, DC 20009

STANDARDS

RATIONALE

COMMENTS

APP7.

E) A *medication record* maintained on an *ongoing basis* by designated staff that shall include the following:

1) Specific, signed parent consent for the caregiver to administer medication.
2) Prescription by a health care provider, if required.
3) Administration log.
4) Checklist information on medication brought to the facility by the parents.

For additional information on medication record, see *Medications*, on p. 88.

See rationale for standard HP82 in chapter 3 on p. 88.

The medication record contents and format, as well as policies on handling of medications, are provided in the AAP publication *Health in Day Care: A Manual for Health Professionals*. See samples of medication checklist, consent form, and administration log in Appendices II.3 and II.4 of this publication. To order, contact

American Academy of Pediatrics
141 Northwest Point Blvd.
P.O. Box 927
Elk Grove Village, IL 60009-0927

A sample medication administration log is provided in *Healthy Young Children*. To obtain this publication, contact

National Association for the
    Education of Young Children
1834 Connecticut Ave., N.W.
Washington, DC 20009

APP8.

F) A *facility health record* maintained on an *ongoing basis* by designated staff that shall include the following:

1) Staff and parent observations of the child's health status and physical condition.
2) Response to any treatment provided while the child is in child care, and any observable side effects.
3) Notations of health-related referrals and follow-up action.
4) Notations of health-related communications with parents or the child's health care providers.
5) Staff observations of the child's learning and social activity.
6) Documentation of planned communication with parents. (See *Regular Communication*, on p. 56.)
7) Documentation of parent participation in health education. (See *Health Education for Parents*, on p. 62.)

The facility health record to be kept by caregivers can document caregivers' observations and concerns that may lead to intervention decisions.

See sample symptom record, Appendix G, on p. 341.

The facility health record is a confidential, chronologically oriented location for the recording of staff observations. Patterns of illness, parent concerns, and so forth can be followed and can become guidelines for intervention, if needed.

Facility observation records provide useful information over time on a child's unique style. Parents and caregivers can use these records in planning for the child's needs. On occasion, the child's health care provider can use them as an aid in diagnosing a health condition.

"Hands-on" opportunities for parents to work with their own child or others in the company of caregivers should be documented.

Appendix C continued

STANDARDS

RATIONALE

COMMENTS

Staff notations on communications with parents can be in a "parent log" separate from the child's health record, or there can be one "parent log" for all children's parents (such as one with a calendar format).

G) A *record of injury or illness* maintained on an *ongoing basis* by staff as specified in *Incidence Logs of Illness, Injury, and Other Problems*, on p. 290.

Appendix D

Major Occupational Health Hazards in Child Care

Infectious Diseases*

Hepatitis
Cytomegalovirus (CMV)
Chicken pox
Rubella
Polio
Influenza
Tuberculosis
Shigellosis

Giardia
Meningitis
Streptococcus
Ringworm
Scabies, lice
Herpes
Cryptosporidium
Rotavirus

Injuries and Noninfectious Diseases

Back injuries
Bites

Dermatitis

Stress

Undervaluing of work (in both monetary
    compensation and status)
Inadequate break time, sick leave, and
    personal days
Working alone

Responsibility for children's welfare
Inadequate training
Inadequate facilities
Fear of liability

Environmental Exposure

Art materials
Formaldehyde (indoor air pollution)

Noise
Disinfecting solutions

*See chapter 6, *Infectious Diseases*, on p. 207 and the Glossary, on p. 395, for further details on these diseases.

Appendix E

Health Education Plan

STANDARDS	RATIONALE	COMMENTS

APP9. Health education for children and staff shall include physical, mental, oral, and social health and shall be included daily in the program of activities (see standards PR57 and PR60, on p. 61 in chapter 2). Health education shall be integrated with other curricular activities to include topics such as body awareness, families (including cultural heritage), personal/social skills, expression of feelings, self-esteem, nutrition, personal hygiene, safety (home, vehicular car seats and belts, playground, bicycle), physical health, handwashing, awareness of special needs, importance of a healthful environment, importance of rest and sleep, fitness, oral health, taking medications, and dialing 911 for emergencies. (See also *Health Education for Children*, on p. 61.)

APP10. Specific health-related issues shall be discussed with parents via handouts or pamphlets (see standard PR63 in chapter 2 on p. 62). Written material shall address the most important health and safety issues for all age groups served and may include the following topics:
a) Safety (home, vehicular, bicycle, etc.).
b) Oral health promotion and disease prevention.
c) Value of wellness care and components of wellness care (e.g., exercise, nutrition, avoidance of substance abuse).
d) Child development.
e) Parental health (pregnancy care, drugs, alcohol, AIDS, stress, etc.).
f) Prevention and management of infectious disease, including the need for parents with infants in child care to adopt some handwashing and diapering procedures (as done in child care) for the parents' protection as well as for the protection of the other children and adults in the family.

Parental behavior can be modified by education. Parents should be involved closely with the facility. Didactic teaching, although it can be valuable if done well, has not been shown to be the most effective technique for educating parents.[1, 2]

The concept of parent control and empowerment is key to successful parent education in the child care setting. It is not documented that a child's eventual success in education or in society is related to parent education, but support and education for parents lead to better parenting abilities.[1]

Community resources could provide written health-related materials. Small and large family home caregivers can cover these areas on an informal basis, as the small size of the homes and the varied ages of the enrollees preclude a "curriculum" per se. School-age child care facilities do not need to incorporate child health education into their programs, as enrollees receive this information in school.

STANDARDS	**RATIONALE**	**COMMENTS**

g) Child behavior (normal and problematic).

h) Handling emergencies/first aid.

i) Child advocacy skills.

j) Special needs.

See also *Health Education for Parents*, on p. 62.

AMERICAN ACADEMY OF PEDIATRICS
Practice and Ambulatory Care

RECOMMENDATIONS FOR PREVENTIVE PEDIATRIC HEALTH CARE
Committee on Practice and Ambulatory Medicine

Each child and family is unique; therefore these **Recommendations for Preventive Pediatric Health Care** are designed for the care of children who are receiving competent parenting, have no manifestations of any important health problems, and are growing and developing in satisfactory fashion. **Additional visits may become necessary** if circumstances suggest variations from normal. These guidelines represent a consensus by the Committee on Practice and Ambulatory Medicine in consultation with the membership of the American Academy of Pediatrics through the Chapter Presidents. The Committee emphasizes the great importance of **continuity of care** in comprehensive health supervision and the need to avoid **fragmentation of care.**

A prenatal visit by the parents for anticipatory guidance and pertinent medical history is strongly recommended.

Health supervision should begin with medical care of the newborn in the hospital.

	INFANCY						EARLY CHILDHOOD					LATE CHILDHOOD					ADOLESCENCE[1]			
AGE[2]	By 1 mo.	2 mos.	4 mos.	6 mos.	9 mos.	12 mos.	15 mos.	18 mos.	24 mos.	3 yrs.	4 yrs.	5 yrs.	6 yrs.	8 yrs.	10 yrs.	12 yrs.	14 yrs.	16 yrs.	18 yrs.	20+ yrs.
HISTORY Initial/Interval	•	•	•	•	•	•	•	•	•	•		•	•	•	•	•	•	•	•	•
MEASUREMENTS Height and Weight	•	•	•	•	•	•	•	•	•	•		•	•	•	•	•	•	•	•	•
Head Circumference	•	•	•	•	•	•														
Blood Pressure	•	•							•	•		•	•	•	•	•	•	•	•	•
SENSORY SCREENING Vision	S	S	S	S	S	S	S	S	S	S	O	O	O	O	S	O	O	S	O	O
Hearing	S	S	S	S	S	S	S	S	S	S	O	O	S[3]	S[3]	S[3]	O	S	S	O	S
DEVEL./BEHAV.[4] ASSESSMENT	•	•	•	•	•	•	•	•	•	•		•	•	•		•	•	•	•	•
PHYSICAL EXAMINATION[5]	•	•	•	•	•	•	•	•	•	•		•	•	•	•	•	•	•	•	•
PROCEDURES[6] Hered./Metabolic[7] Screening	•																			
Immunization[8]		•	•	•			•	•	•			•					•			
Tuberculin Test[9]						•			•									•		
Hematocrit or Hemoglobin[10]				•					•				•					•		
Urinalysis[11]			•						•									•		
ANTICIPATORY[12] GUIDANCE	•	•	•	•	•	•	•	•	•	•		•	•	•	•	•	•	•	•	•
INITIAL DENTAL[13] REFERRAL										•										

1. Adolescent related issues (e.g., psychosocial, emotional, substance usage, and reproductive health) may necessitate more frequent health supervision.
2. If a child comes under care for the first time at any point on the schedule, or if any items are not accomplished at the suggested age, the schedule should be brought up to date at the earliest possible time.
3. At these points, history may suffice; if problem suggested, a standard testing method should be employed.
4. By history and appropriate physical examination: if suspicious, by specific objective developmental testing.
5. At each visit, a complete physical examination is essential, with infant totally unclothed, older child undressed and suitably draped.
6. These may be modified, depending upon entry point into schedule and individual need.
7. Metabolic screening (e.g., thyroid, PKU, galactosemia) should be done according to state law.
8. Schedule(s) per Report of Committee on Infectious Disease, *1986 Red Book.*

9. For low risk groups, the Committee on Infectious Diseases recommends the following options: (1) no routine testing or (2) testing at three times—infancy, preschool, and adolescence. For high risk groups, annual TB skin testing is recommended.
10. Present medical evidence suggests the need for reevaluation of the frequency and timing of hemoglobin or hematocrit tests. One determination is therefore suggested during each time period. Performance of additional tests is left to the individual practice experience.
11. Present medical evidence suggests the need for reevaluation of the frequency and timing of urinalyses. One determination is therefore suggested during each time period. Performance of additional tests is left to the individual practice experience.
12. Appropriate discussion and counselling should be an integral part of each visit for care.
13. Subsequent examinations as prescribed by dentist.

N.B.: **Special chemical, immunologic, and endocrine testing** are usually carried out upon specific indications. Testing other than newborn (e.g., inborn errors of metabolism, sickle disease, lead) are discretionary with the physician.

Key: • = to be performed; S=subjective, by history; O=objective, by a standard testing method.

September 1987

ENROLLMENT / ATTENDANCE / SYMPTOM RECORD

Classroom _____

MONTH [   ] 19__

FOR EACH CHILD, EACH DAY CODE TOP BOX "+" = PRESENT or "O" = ABSENT, N=NOT SCHEDULED
CODE BOTTOM BOX "O"=WELL or " "= SYMPTOM CODE FROM BOTTOM OF PAGE.

NAME	AGE IN MOS.	DAILY HOURS IN CARE	1	2	3	4	5	6	7	8	9	10	11	12	13	14	15	16	17	18	19	20	21	22	23	24	25	26	27	28	29	30	31

NUMBER OF DAYS FACILITY WAS OPEN

TOTAL PLACED ON REGISTER

Symptom Codes: 1 = ASTHMA, WHEEZING,   2 = BEHAVIOR CHANGE WITH NO OTHER SYMPTOM,   3 = DIARRHEA,   4 = FEVER,   5 = HEADACHE,   6 = RASH,   7 = RESPIRATORY (COLD, COUGH, RUNNY NOSE, EARACHE, SORE THROAT, PINK EYE),   8 = STOMACHACHE,   9 = URINE PROBLEM,   10 = VOMITING,   11 = OTHER (SPECIFY ON BACK OF FORM)

Development of this record was supported in part by Project #MCJ-426025 from the Bureau of Maternal and Child Health, Department of Health and Human Services.

For some conditions, you need to get medical help immediately. When this is necessary, and you can reach the parent without delay, tell the parent to come right away. You may also have to have the parent tell the doctor that you will be calling because you are with the child. If the parent or the child's doctor is not immediately available, contact the facility's health consultant or EMS for immediate medical help.

Tell the parent to come right away and get medical help immediately when any of the following things happen:

- An infant under 4 months of age has an axillary tempeature of 100 degrees Fahrenheit or higher or a rectal temperature of 101 degrees Fahrenheit or higher.

- A child over 4 months of age has a temperature of 105 degrees Fahrenheit or higher.

- An infant under 4 months of age has forceful vomiting (more than once) after eating.

- Any child looks or acts very ill or seems to be getting worse quickly.

- Any child has neck pain when the head is moved or touched.

- Any child has a stiff neck or severe headache.

- Any child has a seizure for the first time.

- Any child acts unusually confused.

- Any child has uneven pupils (black centers of the eyes).

- Any child has a blood-red or purple rash made up of pinhead-sized spots or bruises that are not associated with injury.

- Any child has a rash of hives or welts that appears quickly.

- Any child breathes so fast or hard that he or she cannot play, talk, cry, or drink.

- Any child has a severe stomachache that causes the child to double up and scream.

- Any child has a stomachache without vomiting or diarrhea after a recent injury, blow to the abdomen, or hard fall.

- Any child has stools that are black or have blood mixed through them.

- Any child has not urinated in more than 8 hours; the mouth and tongue look dry.

- Any child has continuous clear drainage from the nose after a hard blow to the head.

Note for programs that provide care for sick children: If any of the conditions listed above appear after the child's care has been planned, medical advice must be obtained before continuing child care can be provided.

This appendix is copied with permission from the *American Red Cross Child Care Course 1990.* For information about the course, telephone the local chapter of the American Red Cross or write to the American Red Cross, National Headquarters, Health and Safety, 18th and F Streets, N.W., Washington, DC 20006.

Appendix I-1

Recommended Practices for Haemophilus Influenzae Type B

STANDARDS	RATIONALE	COMMENTS

APP11. The local health department shall be informed within 24 hours of the occurrence of a serious Hib infection (e.g., an infection associated with bacteremia or meningitis) by the physician who diagnosed the illness, in accordance with local and state health department rules for reportable diseases. The report to the health department shall specify whether the child attends a facility.

Haemophilus influenzae type b (Hib) is the most important cause of severe bacterial infection, particularly meningitis, in infants and young children in the United States.[1] Children who attend child care are at increased risk of Hib infection compared with children in the general population.[2]

APP12. The local health department shall inform the director of the ill child's facility that an attendee has a serious Hib infection (see standard APP11 above).

See rationale for standard APP11.

APP13. When recommended by the responsible health department to prevent secondary Hib disease in the facility, rifampin shall be administered orally in a dose of 20 mg per kg body weight (maximum dose 600 mg) given once daily for 4 consecutive days.
a) The dose for adults is 600 mg given orally as a single dose on 4 consecutive days.
b) Pregnant women shall not receive the antibiotic to prevent an infection because rifampin is contraindicated during pregnancy.
c) When an antibiotic is indicated for child care contacts to prevent an infection, children and staff shall be excluded from attending the facility until the antibiotic to prevent an infection has been initiated.
d) If possible, health department representatives shall supervise the administration of rifampin to all child contacts in the facility. This supervision ensures that the same policy described in Appendix I-1 will be followed by all attendees and that the disease-prevention measure will be administered to all contacts simultaneously (see standards ID5 and ID6 on pp. 208–209).

Rifampin treatment of children exposed to a child with Hib disease can reduce the prevalence of Hib respiratory tract colonization in treated children and reduce the subsequent risk of invasive Hib infection, particularly in children under 2 years of age.[3] However, rifampin taken to prevent an infection is not uniformly effective in preventing secondary cases of Hib disease;[4] when rifampin is employed as a disease control strategy, consistent compliance with administration of rifampin must be carefully monitored.

STANDARDS

APP14. Local health departments shall develop specific guidelines for responding to the occurrence of a case of Hib disease in a child who attends child care. These guidelines shall include a position on the use of the antibiotic to prevent an infection in child care Hib disease contacts. These guidelines shall be consistent with the most current recommendations of the ACIP and the AAP. Presently, the AAP recommendations, detailed in the 1988 Report of the Committee on Infectious Disease,[5] can be summarized as follows (see standards ID3 on p. 207 and ID4–ID7 on pp. 208–209 in chapter 6):

a) Careful observation of child care Hib disease contacts is essential. Children who develop illnesses with fever shall receive prompt medical evaluation.

b) When there is exposure to a child with Hib infection in a group of children less than 2 years of age, and the group members are in close contact for 25 or more hours a week (thus simulating household contact), rifampin taken to prevent infection shall be given.

c) Rifampin taken to prevent infection is not required in facilities where all contacts are older than 2 years.

d) Rifampin taken to prevent an infection is indicated in all facilities when two or more cases of serious Hib disease have occurred among attendees within a 60-day period.

e) When rifampin taken to prevent an infection is employed, all facility attendees and staff shall receive rifampin treatment. In multiclassroom settings, only classroom contacts need the disease prevention measure.

f) Because therapy for systemic Hib disease does not reliably eradicate respiratory carriage of Hib bacteria, a child recently treated for Hib disease shall be given rifampin treatment before returning to the facility, if rifampin taken to prevent an infection has been given to his/her child care contacts.

g) Representatives of the local health department shall supervise the ad-

RATIONALE

In general, the risk of secondary Hib disease is probably lower for child care contacts than it is for household contacts. The risk of secondary cases of Hib disease among child care attendees, when it occurs, is greatest in, and may be limited to, children younger than 2 years of age. In multiclassroom settings, increased risk has been shown only for children in the classroom of the index child.[3, 6]

Since the risk of secondary cases of Hib disease among child care Hib disease contacts appears to be variable, there are different opinions about the most appropriate guidelines for the use of rifampin taken to prevent an infection in the child care setting. Current guidelines of the U.S. Public Health Service Advisory Committee on Immunization Practices (ACIP) and the American Academy of Pediatrics (AAP) differ. Local health department guidelines for rifampin taken to prevent an infection should be compatible with the most recent statements of the ACIP or the AAP. Current recommendations of the AAP are provided in these performance standards.[6] The ACIP recommends that the antibiotic be taken to prevent an infection following a single case of Hib disease in a facility in which children younger than 2 years of age have been exposed.[7-10]

See also the rationale for standard APP13 above.

COMMENTS

STANDARDS	RATIONALE	COMMENTS

ministration of the antibiotic when child care exposure to Hib has occurred and the antibiotic to prevent the infection is indicated.

See also chapter *Haemophilus Influenzae Type b*, on p. 207.

Appendix I-2

Recommended Practices *for* Neisseria Meningitidis

STANDARDS

APP15. The local health department shall be informed within 24 hours of the occurrence of a serious meningococcal infection (e.g., an infection associated with bacteremia or meningitis) by the physician who diagnosed the illness, in accordance with local and state health department rules for reportable diseases. The report to the health department shall specify whether the child attends a facility.

APP16. The local health department shall inform the director of the ill child's facility that an attendee has a serious *Neisseria meningitidis* (meningococcal) infection (see standard APP15).

APP17. When recommended by the responsible health department to prevent secondary meningococcal infection in the facility, an antibiotic to prevent an infection shall be administered. Rifampin is usually the drug of choice; sulfisoxazole can be used when the organism causing disease in the primary case is known to be susceptible to sulfonamides. Duration of the disease-prevention measure is 2 days.
a) Rifampin is administered orally in a dose of 10 mg per kg body weight (maximum dose 600 mg), given every 12 hours for four consecutive doses. (Adults receive the maximum dose.)
b) Sulfisoxazole is administered orally in a dose of 500 mg once daily for children less than 1 year old, 500 mg twice daily for children 1 to 12 years old, and 1 gm twice daily for children older than 12 years and for adults.
c) When an antibiotic to prevent meningococcal infection is indicated for child care contacts, children and staff may be excluded from attending the facility until the antibiotic taken to prevent the infection has been initiated.

RATIONALE

Neisseria meningitidis is one of the three most important causes of bacterial meningitis in childhood. The infection is spread from person to person by contact with respiratory secretions and by large-droplet spread.[1] Children in child care who are exposed to a child or adult with meningococcal infection should receive an antibiotic to prevent infection as soon as possible, preferably within 24 hours of diagnosis of the primary case.[2]

See rationale for standard APP15.

Children in child care who are exposed to a child or adult with meningococcal infection should receive an antibiotic to prevent an infection as soon as possible, preferably within 24 hours of diagnosis of the primary case. The antibiotic taken to prevent an infection terminates nasopharyngeal carriage and reduces the likelihood of developing invasive meningococcal disease.[2]

COMMENTS

STANDARDS	RATIONALE	COMMENTS

d) If possible, health department representatives shall supervise the administration of the antibiotic to child care contacts to prevent a meningococcal infection. This ensures that the same policy described in Appendix I-2 will be followed by all attendees and that the disease-prevention measure will be administered to all contacts simultaneously (see standards ID9 and ID10 in chapter 6 on pp. 209–210).

APP18. Because systemic antibiotic therapy of meningococcal disease does not reliably eradicate nasopharyngeal carriage of meningococcal bacteria, a child treated for meningococcal disease shall be given rifampin treatment before returning to the facility.

APP19. Local health departments shall develop specific guidelines for responding to the occurrence of a case of meningococcal disease in a child who attends child care. These guidelines shall include a position on the use of the antibiotic to be taken to prevent an infection in child contacts of children with meningococcal disease. These guidelines shall be consistent with the most current recommendations of the American Academy of Pediatrics (AAP)[3] and the U.S. Public Health Service Advisory Committee on Immunization Practices.[4] Presently, the AAP recommendations, detailed in the 1988 Report of the Committee on Infectious Disease,[3] can be summarized as follows (see standards ID8–ID11 in chapter 6 on pp. 209–210):

a) Careful observation of child contacts of children with meningococcal disease is essential. Children who develop illnesses with fever shall receive prompt medical evaluation.

b) Child care contacts (children of all ages and adults) shall receive the antibiotic to prevent an infection as soon as possible, preferably within 24 hours after the diagnosis of the primary case.

See rationale for standard APP17.

STANDARDS   **RATIONALE**   **COMMENTS**

c) Child care contacts (children and adults) shall be excluded from attending the facility until the antibiotic, taken to prevent an infection has been initiated.

d) Representatives of the local health department shall supervise the administration of the antibiotic to be taken to prevent an infection when child care exposure to meningococcal disease has occurred.

See also *Neisseria Meningitidis (Meningococcal), on p. 209*.

Appendix I-3

Recommended Practices for Pertussis

STANDARDS	RATIONALE	COMMENTS

APP20. The local health department shall be informed within 24 hours of the occurrence of a case of pertussis by the physician who diagnosed the illness, in accordance with local and state health department rules for reportable diseases. The report to the health department shall specify whether the child attends a facility.

Infants and young children should be protected from pertussis because the rate of illness among infants and toddlers is extremely high, and mortality during the first 6 months of life is 1 percent.[1]

The incidence of pertussis in the United States has increased substantially in recent years.[1] Although child-care-related outbreaks of pertussis have not been reported, it is likely that children who attend out-of-home care will occasionally contract pertussis.

APP21. The local health department shall inform the director of the ill child's facility that an attendee has pertussis (see standard APP20).

See rationale for standard APP20.

APP22. Local health departments shall develop specific guidelines for responding to the occurrence of a case of pertussis in a child who attends child care. These guidelines shall include a position on the use of antibiotics and vaccines to prevent an infection in contacts of children with pertussis. These guidelines shall be consistent with the most current recommendations of the U.S. Public Health Service Advisory Committee on Immunization Practices[3] and the American Academy of Pediatrics (AAP).[4] Presently, the AAP recommendations, detailed in the 1988 Report of the Committee on Infectious Disease,[4] can be summarized as follows (see standards ID12 on p. 210 and ID13–15 on pp. 210–211 in chapter 6):

a) Children younger than 7 years who received four doses of diphtheria-tetanus-pertussis (DTP) vaccine but whose last dose was given 3 or more years before exposure shall have a booster dose of DTP vaccine unless a booster dose is contraindicated.

The spread of infection to incompletely immunized contacts can be reduced by treatment of the primary case and susceptible contacts with erythromycin.[2] If a case of pertussis occurs in a facility, contact children and adult staff should be treated with erythromycin to prevent an infection.[3]

STANDARDS   **RATIONALE**   **COMMENTS**

b) Children who have received 3 doses of DTP vaccine and whose last dose was given 6 or more months before exposure shall be given a booster dose of DTP vaccine unless a booster dose is contraindicated.

c) Children who do not meet the criteria outlined in items a or b above shall continue to receive DTP vaccine doses at the regularly scheduled intervals.

d) Erythromycin, 40 to 50 mg per kg body weight per day, shall be administered to all child care contacts (children and adults) for 14 days.

e) Children and adults shall be excluded from attending the facility until erythromycin to prevent an infection has been initiated.

f) Children shall be observed for the development of respiratory symptoms for 14 days after contact is terminated.

g) Symptomatic children shall be excluded from child care until evaluated by a physician. If the illness is diagnosed as possible pertussis, the child shall be excluded from care until erythromycin has been taken for at least 5 days.

h) Children with proven cases of pertussis shall return to child care if their medical condition permits, and if they have received at least 5 days of erythromycin treatment.

i) Representatives of the local health department shall supervise the administration of the antibiotic and vaccine to prevent an infection when child care exposure to pertussis has occurred.

See also *Pertussis*, on p. 210.

Appendix I-4

Recommended Practices for Streptococcal Infection

STANDARDS	RATIONALE	COMMENTS
APP23. The local health department shall develop guidelines for responding to reports of outbreaks of streptococcal disease among children in facilities.		When outbreaks of streptococcal disease occur, interventions are available to limit transmission of streptococcal infection. Health department consultation is advised when high rates of streptococcal infection occur in child care.
See also *Streptococcal Infection*, on p. 211.		

Appendix J

Food Components for Infants[1-5]

0–3 MONTHS	4–7 MONTHS	8–11 MONTHS
	MORNING	
4–6 fluid oz. breast milk or iron-fortified formula	4–8 fluid oz. breast milk or iron-fortified formula	6–8 fluid oz. breast milk, iron-fortified formula, or whole cow's milk
	0–3 tablespoons dry, iron-fortified infant cereal (optional before 6 months, but introduce by 6 months)	1–4 tablespoons fruit of appropriate consistency
		2–4 tablespoons dry, iron-fortified infant cereal
	MID-DAY	
4–6 fluid oz. breast milk or iron-fortified formula	4–8 fluid oz. breast milk or iron-fortified formula	6–8 fluid oz. breast milk, iron-fortified formula, or whole cow's milk
	0–3 tablespoons dry, iron-fortified infant cereal (optional—see above)	1–4 tablespoons fruit *and/or* vegetable of appropriate consistency
	0–3 tablespoons strained fruit and/or vegetable (optional, but if introduced, introduce as close to 6 months as possible)	2–4 tablespoons dry, iron-fortified infant cereal *and/or* 1–4 tablespoons fish, lean meat,* poultry, or cooked dry beans or peas (all of appropriate consistency), *or* ½ to 1½ oz. cheese *or* 1–3 oz. cottage cheese *or* 1 egg yolk (introduce at 11 months of age)
	SUPPLEMENT SNACK	
4–6 fluid oz. breast milk or iron-fortified formula	4–6 fluid oz. breast milk or iron-fortified formula	2–4 fluid oz. breast milk, iron-fortified formula, or whole cow's milk, *or* 2 oz. full-strength fruit juice
		0–½ slice hard toast or 0–2 crackers or teething biscuits (optional) suitable for infants, made from whole-grain or enriched flour

Note—On the infant's arrival at the facility, the caregiver must ascertain what foods and/or formula the infant was fed at home in order to determine the infant's nutritional needs.

*Lean meat is beef, pork, or veal without visible fat. Luncheon meats and frankfurters are high in fat and are *not* considered lean meat.

Appendix K

Food Components for Toddlers, Preschoolers, and School-Age Children[1-6]

	1–2 years	3–5 years	6–12 years
Breakfast			
Milk, fluid	½ cup	¾ cup	1 cup
Juice (full-strength) *or* fruit or vegetable	¼ cup	½ cup	½ cup
Bread *and/or* cereal (whole-grain or enriched)			
Bread	½ slice	½ slice	1 slice
Cereal			
Cold/dry *or*	¼ cup	⅓ cup	¾ cup
Hot/cooked	¼ cup	¼ cup	½ cup
Lunch or Supper			
Milk, fluid	½ cup	¾ cup	1 cup
Lean meat* *or* meat alternate			
Lean meat, fish, or poultry, cooked			
(lean meat without bone)	1 ounce	1½ ounces	2 ounces
or Cheese	1 ounce	1½ ounces	2 ounces
or Egg	1	1	1
or Cooked dry beans or peas	¼ cup	⅜ cup	½ cup
or Peanut butter (smooth)	2 tablespoons	3 tablespoons	4 tablespoons
or Nuts and/or seeds**	½ ounce**	¾ ounce**	1 ounce**
Fruit and/or vegetable			
(two or more total)	¼ cup	½ cup	¾ cup
Bread or bread alternate			
(whole-grain or enriched)	½ slice	½ slice	1 slice
Supplement (Snack)—Select two of the four components (midmorning or midafternoon supplement)			
Milk, fluid	½ cup	½ cup	1 cup
Lean meat* or meat alternate	½ ounce	½ ounce	1 ounce
(see above) *or* yogurt	¼ cup	¼ cup	½ cup
Juice (full strength) *or* fruit *or* vegetable	½ cup	½ cup	¾ cup
Bread *and/or* cereal (whole-grain or enriched)			
Bread	½ slice	½ slice	1 slice
Cereal			
Cold/dry *or*	¼ cup	⅓ cup	¾ cup
Hot/cooked	¼ cup	¼ cup	½ cup

Note—On the child's arrival at the facility, the caregiver must ascertain what food was fed at home in order to determine the child's nutritional needs.

*Lean meat is beef, pork, or veal without visible fat. Luncheon meats and frankfurters are high in fat and are *not* considered lean meat.

**This portion can meet only one-half of the total serving of the meat/meat alternate requirement for lunch or supper. Nuts or seeds must be combined with another meat/meat alternate to fulfill the requirement. For determining combinations, 1 ounce of nuts or seeds is equal to 1 ounce of cooked lean meat, poultry, or fish. *CAUTION:* Children under 5 are at the highest risk of choking. Any nuts and/or seeds must be served to them in a prepared food and be ground or finely chopped.

Appendix L

Infant Feeding Policies

APP24. Written policies about infant feeding shall be developed with the input and approval of the child's health care provider and the child care Nutrition Specialist (see Appendices B-1 and B-2, on p. 328–329), and shall include the following:

a) Storage and handling of expressed breast milk. (See *Requirements for Special Groups of Children*, on p. 117.)

b) Determination of the kind and amount of commercially prepared formula to be prepared for infants, as appropriate. (See *Requirements for Special Groups of Children*, on p. 117.)

c) Preparation, storage, and handling of formula. (See *Requirements for Special Groups of Children*, on p. 117.)

d) Use and proper disinfection of feeding chairs and of mechanical food preparation and feeding devices, including blenders, feeding bottles, and food warmers. (See *Maintenance*, on p. 133.)

e) Whether formula or baby food shall be provided from home, and if so, how such food will be transported, stored, and handled.

f) A prohibition against bottle propping or prolonged feeding. (See *Requirements for Special Groups of Children*, on p. 117.)

g) A prohibition against allowing children to have their bottles at times other than when they are held or while seated for feeding. (See *Requirements for Special Groups of Children*, on p. 117.)

h) Specification of the number of children who can be fed by one adult at one time. (See *Meal Service, Seating, and Supervision*, on p. 123.)

i) Handling of food intolerance or allergies (e.g., to cow's milk, orange juice, eggs, or wheat). (See *General Requirements*, on p. 115.)

Growth and development during infancy require that nourishing, wholesome, and developmentally appropriate food be provided, using safe approaches to feeding. Because individual needs must be accommodated and improper practices can have dire consequences for the child's health, the policies for infant feeding should be developed with professional nutrition expertise.

STANDARDS	RATIONALE	COMMENTS

j) Responding to infants' need for food in a flexible fashion to approximate demand feedings. (See *Requirements for Special Groups of Children*, on p. 117.)

APP25. Written policies for each infant about infant feeding shall be developed with each individual infant's parents and shall include all of the items specified in standard APP24 except item h.

See rationale for standard APP24.

For additional information on infant feeding policies, see also Appendix J, on p. 352.

Appendix M

Child Care Food Service Staff Requirements

Setting	Food Service Staff
Small and large family-child-care homes	Caregiver
Centers serving up to 30 children	Full-time child care Food Service Worker (cook)*
Centers serving up to 50 children	Full-time child care Food Service Worker (cook) and part-time child care Food Service Aide*
Centers serving up to 125 children	Full-time child care Food Service Manager or full-time child-care Food Service Worker (cook) and full-time child care Food Service Aide
Centers serving up to 200 children	Full-time child care Food Service Manager and full-time child care Food Service Worker (cook) and one full-time plus one part-time child care Food Service Aide
Vendor food service	One assigned staff member or one part-time staff member, depending on amount of food service preparation needed after delivery

*These staff perform under the professional guidance of a child care Food Service Manager or local child care Nutrition Specialist (see Appendices B-1 and B-2, on pp. 328–329).

Appendix N

About Poisonous Plants

TIPS ABOUT POISONOUS PLANTS

- Keep **all** plants away from small children. Teach children never to eat unknown plants.

- Different parts of plants are poisonous. Phone the Poison Control Center before treating a child who has eaten a plant. Follow their directions. Keep an unexpired bottle of syrup of ipecac in a locked place if your policy allows. Use it only if the Poison Control Center tells you to make a child vomit.

POISONOUS PLANTS (not a complete list)

Flower Garden Plants
Autumn Crocus
Bleeding Heart
Chrysanthemum
Daffodil
Foxglove
Hyacinth
Iris
Jonquil
Lily of the Valley
Morning Glory
Narcissus

House Plants
Bird of Paradise
Castor Bean
Dumbcane (Dieffenbachia)
English Ivy
Holly
Jequirty Bean (Rosary Pea)
Jerusalem Cherry
Mistletoe
Mother-in-Law
Oleander
Philodendron
Rhododendron

Trees and Shrubs
Black Locust
Boxwood
Elderberry
English Yew
Horse Chestnut
Oak Tree

Vegetable Garden Plants
Sprouts and green parts of potato
Rhubarb leaves
Green parts of tomato

Wild Plants
Bittersweet
Buttercups
Jack-in-the-Pulpit
Jimson Weed
Mushroom (certain ones)
Nightshade
Poison Hemlock
Poison Ivy, Oak, Sumac
Skunk Cabbage

This appendix is copied with permission from the *American Red Cross Child Care Course*. For more information about the course, telephone the local chapter of the American Red Cross or write to the American Red Cross, National Headquarters, Health and Safety, 18th and F Streets, N.W., Washington, DC 20006.

Appendix O-1

From the Viewpoint of a Preschooler

Source: Hendricks, Barbara, ed. "A Safe Place To Play: Guidelines for Safe Public Playgrounds." Vancouver, BC, Canada: The Playground Network; May 1986. (Reprinted from the Playground Network News.)

When was the last time you took an 18-month-old or 2-year-old child to the park to play? Remember how you had to hold the child as he or she climbed up and slid down? You probably also remember the bumps and bangs you received helping the child move through and explore the play structure. The visit probably ended because you were tired of carrying and catching the child. A common experience—but it need not be. It is possible to design good, safe play opportunities for this age group. And, considering the numbers of them in our midst these days, all local playgrounds should have some items oriented to the younger preschool child.

Playground design for this age group—like all good design—must be designed according to the anthropometry of the child. Tables 1 and 2 and Figures 1 and 2 summarize and illustrate some critical dimensions that must be considered when designing a play area and selecting equipment and furnishings for such an area.

Well-designed, preschool-scale play areas are not only more fun—they are safer. The childen will play longer and accidental scrapes and bumps are less likely to occur. Equally important is the development of a sense of independence because the child can do things "by myself" without needing assistance from Mom and Dad. Your car, your workspace and your personal computer are all designed based on ergonomics to ensure health, safety and comfort. These same design rules should apply to children's play spaces for the same reasons.

Ergonomic design for preschool children means, among other things, that hand rails should be at hand height and graspable by small hands—a height of 60–70 cm (23⅝ to 27⅞ inches) and a diameter of 40–45 mm (1⅝ to 1¾ inches); the distance between, 40–50 cm (15¾–19¾ inches) apart—so that the child can securely grasp both rails. A handrail or guardrail at 96.5 cm (38 inches)—a standard for school-age child playground apparatus—is quite useless to a 93.4 cm (26¾ inch) tall child.

Steps and climbing distances between platforms should be between 15 and 25 cm (5⅞–9⅞ inches) with the space between steps or platforms enclosed or filled in to prevent the child slipping through. Ladder rungs should be between 23–30 cm (9⅛–11¾ inches) on center and ladders should be at about a 75 degree angle. Comfortable seat height is around 24 to 30 cm (9½–11¾ inches), counter tops at 40–45 cm (15¾–17¾ inches) and table tops at 45 to 50 cm (17¾–19¾ inches).

When designing for this age group, the designer should remember that these children are still learning a lot about how their bodies run and walk as well as many other things. This means that young children do not have good recovery when unbalanced or tripping. Decks, ground spaces, and other surfaces such as slide entries must be smooth and free of tripping edges and foot catchers (see Figure 2). The average foot length of a 2–3½ year old is 14.7 cm (5⅞ inches), while that of a 20-month toddler is around 12.5 cm (4⅞ inches long and 4.1 to 5.2 cm (1⅝–2 inches) wide (see Table 1). Decking and steps should give adequate footing. Round logs used for a deck create an uneven surface and have gaps into which the child's foot slips—causing many falls. At the same time, the deck and all walking surfaces should be non-slip.

In summary, design for preschool children should be based on the scale of the preschool child or rather the range of scales of these children, as there are significant differences between the size and abilities of a 20-month-old child and a 5-year-old. The toddlers of 14 to 20 months who will be making their first visits to the park to use the playground should find it a place where they are welcome. Let's give them a good start to childhoods of safe fun.

Appendix O-1 continued

TABLE 1
PRESCHOOL CHILDREN—SELECTED BODY DIMENSIONS
(Males and females)

Age	a* Average Height	Average Vertical Reach	b* Average Chest Height	Average Hip Height	Average Hand Length	Average Knee Height
2–3½	93.4 (36¾)	107.3 (42¼)	65.2 (25⅝)	40.4 (15⅞)	10.5 (4⅛)	22.3 (8¾)
3½–4½	101.4 (39¹⁵⁄₁₆)	116.6 (45⅞)	72.0 (28⅜)	46.2 (18³⁄₁₆)	11.4 (4½)	24.0 (9⁷⁄₁₆)
4½–5½	108.3 (42⅝)	126.1 (49⅝)	78.2 (30¹⁵⁄₁₆)	50.5 (19⅞)	12.0 (4¾)	26.4 (10⅜)

Note—Dimensions are given in centimeters and (in parentheses) inches.
a*, b*—see Figure 1.

TABLE 2
TODDLERS—SELECTED BODY DIMENSIONS

Age	Average Height	Average Hip Height	Average Knee Height	Average Hand Length	Average Foot Length	Average Foot Width
12–15 mo	76.5 (30⅛)	35.4 (13⅞)	20.8 (8⅛)	9.2 (3⅝)	11.7 (4⅝)	4.9 (1¹⁵⁄₁₆)
16–19 mo.	79.2 (31¼)	37.5 (14¾)	12.6 (8½)	9.3 (3¹¹⁄₁₆)	11.9 (4¾)	5.0 (2)
20–23 mo	82.6 (32½)	40.5 (16)	23.0 (9⅛)	9.5 (3¾)	12.5 (4¹⁵⁄₁₆)	5.2 (2⅛)

Note—Dimensions are given in centimeters and (in parentheses) inches.

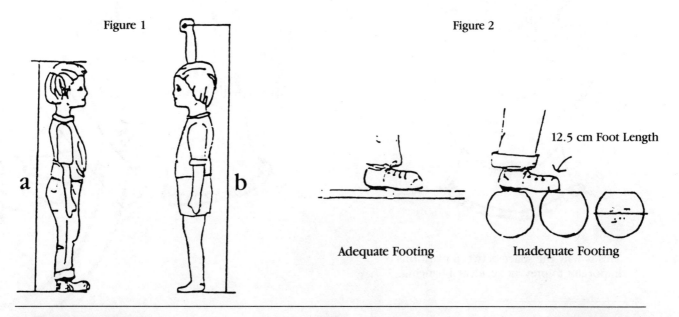

Figure 1

a
b

Figure 2

12.5 cm Foot Length
Adequate Footing
Inadequate Footing

USING ANTHROPOMETRY TO ELIMINATE HAZARDS

Source: "Anthropometry of Infants, Children, and Youths at Age 18 For Product Safety Design." Society of Automotive Engineers.

GRIPPING: A safe, secure handhold for a preschool child is very important to his or her safety when climbing or undertaking new body movements. The child's hand should be able to enclose more than ⅔ of the gripping surface to be effective, i.e., handholds, handrails, bannisters, climbing rungs and anywhere else a secure handhold is important for the safety of the child. A gripping item for a preschool child should have a diameter of 35 mm to 44 mm (1½ inch to 1¾ inch).

Handrails, guardrails, ladder rungs, etc., should also be located so that they can be conveniently grasped by the child when necessary. Handrails and guardrails should be mounted at a height of 60–70 cm (23½–27½ inches) for children between the ages of 3 and 5. NEVER USE TWO HANDRAILS PARALLEL TO EACH OTHER TO SERVE CHILDREN OF DIFFERENT HEIGHTS UNLESS DESIGNED TO PREVENT CLIMBING AND POSSIBLE FALLS OVER THE TOP OF THE RAILING.

HEAD ENTRAPMENT: A child's body may be able to slip through certain openings but the head could be caught. These are openings with a dimension between 11 cm and 23 cm (4¼–9⅛ inches). Avoid openings which are large enough for a child's body to get through and with one or more dimensions between 11 cm and 23 cm (4¼ and 9⅛ inches). Watch for these openings on chairs, cribs, open stairs, balcony railings, sides on play platforms, spaces between furniture, spaces between components on play equipment and so forth.

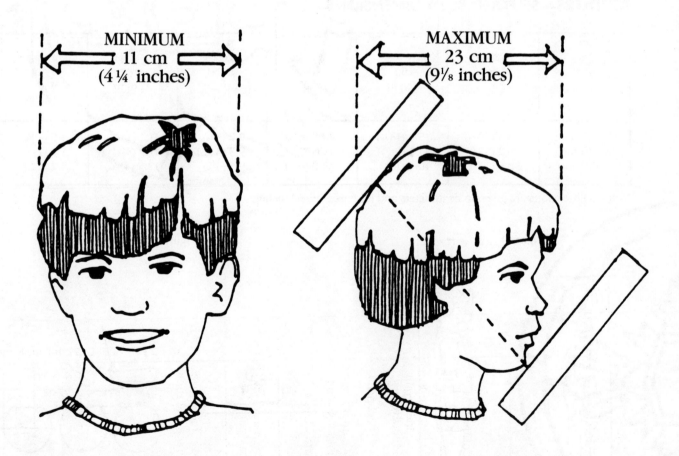

MINIMUM
11 cm
(4 ¼ inches)

MAXIMUM
23 cm
(9⅛ inches)

This is why the space between platforms is important to prevent accidental hanging.

Appendix O-2

Selected Critical Dimensions for Safety of Playground Users

Source: Hendricks, Barbara, ed. "A Safe Place to Play: Guidelines for Safe Public Playgrounds." Vancouver, BC, Canada: The Playground Network. May 1986.

Component	Age/Ability				
	1–3 yrs	3–6 yrs	6–9 yrs	9–14 yrs	With Disabilities
Equipment height with guardrail required and protective surfacing beneath	Less than 1 meter	0–1.5 m	0–2.5 m	0–3 m	Vary with disability
Guardrail height	600–700 mm	700–800 mm	800–900 mm	up to 1 m[1]	600–900 mm
Maximum diameter of gripping component	35 mm	40 mm	45 mm	45 mm	35–45 mm
Maximum slide exit height (from surfacing)	120 mm	200 mm	250 mm	350 mm	Ground level
Openings—where children can gain access			Less than 110 mm or greater than 230 mm		
Maximum space between horizontal rungs	Don't use	300 mm	400 mm	450 mm	300 mm
Minimum width of mobility device access	90 cm	90 cm	90 cm	1 m	90–100 cm
Passing width—wheelchair/pedestrian	112 cm	122 cm	150 cm	180 cm	122–180 cm
Parking area for wheelchair and mobility devices	90 × 150 cm	90 × 150 cm	90 × 150 cm	90 × 150 cm	90 × 150 cm

[1]This height is acceptable only if assured that preschool children will not be using the structure and the structure is clearly labeled for age appropriateness.

Appendix O-3

Critical Heights (in Feet) of Tested Materials Used for Surfaces Under and Around Playground Equipment

Material	Uncompressed Depth			Compressed Depth
	6 inches	9 inches	12 inches	9 inches
Wood Mulch	7	10	11	10
Double Shredded Bark Mulch	6	10	11	7
Uniform Wood Chips	6	7	>12	6
Fine Sand	5	5	9	5
Coarse Sand	5	5	6	4
Fine Gravel	6	7	10	6
Medium Gravel	5	5	6	5

This table reflects the results of tests to determine the relative shock-absorbing properties of seven loose-fill materials commonly used for surfaces under and around playground equipment. The table provides the *critical height* (expressed in feet) for each of the surface materials tested.

The table should be read as follows: If, for example, uncompressed wood mulch is used to a minimum depth of 6 inches, the critical height is 7 feet. If 9 inches of uncompressed wood mulch is used, the critical height is 10 feet. It should be noted that, for some materials, the critical height decreases when the material is compressed.

Critical height may be considered as an approximation of the maximum fall height from which a life-threatening injury may not be expected to occur.

These values represent the relative rather than absolute performance of the surface materials tested and may be used as a guide in selecting the type and depth of loose-fill material providing the greatest degree of safety for equipment of various heights. The shock-absorbing properties of some surfaces, such as sand and mulch, may vary due to moisture, long-term use, or lack of continued maintenance. The depth of any loose-filled surface could be reduced during use, resulting in different shock-absorbing properties. For these reasons, a margin of safety should be considered in selecting a type and depth of material for a specific use.

Reproduced (with permission) from *Playground Surfacing Technical Information Guide,* by the Consumer Product Safety Commission, Washington, D.C. 20207

Appendix O-4

Standards for Sandboxes / Sand Play Areas

PERFORMANCE STANDARD

1) Sand play areas must be distinct from landing areas for slides or other equipment.

2) Sandboxes, if less than 10 feet by 10 feet, shall be lidded or covered when not in use. Covers must allow light and air circulation to allow natural cleansing of sand (attached but loose-fitting plywood is recommended).

3) Sand-play-area covers must be adequately secured when they are lifted or moved to allow children to play in sandbox.

4) Sand in the box shall be washed, free of organic materials, and fine enough to be shaped easily.

5) Sand in sandboxes and sand play areas shall be turned over to a depth of 460 mm (18 inches) annually. Sand in such areas shall be completely replaced every 2 years.

6) Sandboxes shall be regularly cleaned of foreign matter and disinfected with a safe disinfectant.*

*Recipe for sandbox sand disinfectant:

1. Materials and equipment required: fluid chloride of lime, water, 2-gallon watering can, stir stick.

2. Measure sandbox area and determine depth of sand.

3. Determine volume of sand in the box.

4. For each 5 cubic meters (175 cubic feet) of sand, fill the watering can with water and add 110 cm (4 fluid ounces) fluid chloride to the watering can. Stir well.

5. Using the watering can, evenly distribute the solution over the sandbox sand. Refill the watering can and make additional cleaning solution if required, depending on the size of the sand area.

6. Hose down the area to allow solution to penetrate into the sand.

7. The sand shall be turned over one shovelful deep (17 cm or 7½ inches) before the children use it again.

Appendix O-5

Standards for Swings, Cable Rides, and Other Swinging Devices

PERFORMANCE STANDARD

1) Swing seats shall be made of rubber or approved impact-absorbing material and design. Wood or metal seats must not be used.

2) Triangular support systems employed where the seat is attached to the chain shall have an opening of 30 mm (1½ inches). If these openings are larger, they must be enclosed or have an insert.

3) Bearing hangers on swings shall be spaced a minimum of 60 cm (24 inches) apart to prevent twisting of chains and to ensure that the swings move parallel to each other.

4) Swing seats providing adequate support and safety for very young children (baby seats) shall be available at the site. These seats shall be on a separate frame.

5) Swings shall have a clearance (no encroachment) area of 3 m (10 feet) beyond the swing beam extending in all directions of swinging.

6) Swing seats shall be no higher than 400 mm (16 inches) above the ground.

7) To-and-fro swings shall have a minimum clearance of 700 mm (27½ inches) from the frame and the same clearance between swings.

8) Swing frames with two seats per frame are preferred.

9) All swings shall be suspended by linked chains with small links. Fiber rope shall not be used for suspension of swings.

10) Swing support frames shall be A-frames for stability and they shall be designed so that children cannot climb up beside the A-frame.

11) Tire swings shall have a minimum clearance of 1000 mm (38 inches) between swing seat and supports.

12) For tire swings in which the tire is horizontal (parallel to the ground), the distance between the bottom of the tire and the ground shall not exceed 400 mm (16 inches).

13) For tire swings in which the tire is vertical (at a right angle to the ground), the bottom of the tire shall be no more than 400 mm (16 inches) from ground level.

14) In all tire swings, whether hung vertically or horizontally, holes shall be drilled in the most dependent part of the tire to ensure adequate drainage.

RATIONALE

The use of impact-absorbing materials helps to reduce injuries, particularly head injuries, caused by being struck by a swing seat.

This standard is intended to prevent children from slipping their hands or feet into the opening.

This standard reduces the possibility of collision due to reckless play.

The use of chains eliminates the problem of fraying.

Appendix O-6

Standards for Teeter-Totters and Spring Rides

Ensuring safety on teeter-totters and spring rides while maintaining play value is a complex task. This complexity stems from the ability of young children to gain maximum benefit from the play piece. The value of these rides lies in giving toddlers and preschool-age children opportunities to develop balancing skills and a sense of independence by being able to create motion without the assistance of adults. Thus general considerations regarding spring rides and teeter-totters must include features allowing children to get on and off the ride by themselves and create the motion of the ride while being able to control the speed. Teeter-totters that are high in the air or springs that won't move under the body weight of a toddler or preschool-age child not only are potentially dangerous, but they do not have play value.

PERFORMANCE STANDARD

1) Conventional teeter-totters shall have blocks or part of a rubber tire secured below the seats.

2) The fulcrum of the teeter-totter shall be enclosed.

3) Teeter-totters shall be designed to preclude the possibility that a child on one end will be dropped too hard against the ground or dangled unwillingly high in the air. Teeter-totters for preschool-age children shall have a maximum height of no more than 4 feet 6 inches (1.5 m).

4) Coil springs on spring rides must be covered or otherwise designed to prevent pinching of body parts.

5) Spring rides and teeter-totters shall be designed so that small children can seat themselves on the ride.

6) Spring rides and teeter-totters shall have good handholds and footrests that allow and encourage the child to be comfortably seated with good posture.

7) Spring or motion mechanisms shall respond to the weight of preschool-age children, and must allow the child to have control over the speed of motion.

8) There shall be clearance of at least 1 m (39 inches) in all directions around the perimeter of the ride.

9) Any spring ride shall be designed to minimize the risk of a child's banging his/her face into handholds or other parts of the ride.

RATIONALE

This standard is intended to prevent feet from catching and being crushed under the board.

This standard is intended to prevent children's fingers from being caught in the mechanism.

Appendix O-7

Standards for Slides/Sliding Surfaces

PERFORMANCE STANDARD

1) Generally, the maximum height for slides for preschool-age children shall not exceed 2 m (6 feet 6 inches); ideally slides shall be 1.5 m (4 feet 6 inches) or less. For those slides higher than 1.5 m, adequate enclosures at the top of the slide are required. (See standard 5 below.)

2) Slide entrances for slides over 1.5 m in length shall permit only single-file access to the slide.

3) The entry to the slide shall be smooth, with a guardrail and handholds. Guardrail height above the platform shall be 60–70 cm (23½–27 inches) for preschool-age children.

4) The opening to the slide entry must be no wider than the width of the sliding surface. On a platform wider than the slide bed, the sides of the platform shall have side rails and infill to prevent a child's falling off the platform. There shall be no gaps or openings in which a body part or clothing, such as a scarf or strings, can be trapped or caught as the child begins to descend the slide.

5) Slides higher than 1.5 m shall have protective sides at the top of the slide.

6) Sliding surfaces accommodating 2 or more children at the same time shall be no longer than 3.6 m (12 feet).

7) Overall slide incline shall not exceed 40 degrees to the horizontal. In general, the slide bed shall be approximately twice as long as the slide height.

8) The slide bed must be installed flush with the entrance platform to the slide.

9) Raised slide edges must provide comfortable hand grips for children. Such hand grips shall be a minimum of 75 mm (3 inches) above the slide bed surface throughout the entire length of the slide.

10) All slide exits must have a smooth run off (such as a length of slide) parallel to the ground for a minimum distance of 300 mm (12 inches) and no greater than 400 mm (16 inches).

11) The raised, run off section of slide exit shall be between 100 mm (7 inches) to 305 mm (12 inches) above the surface.

12) An unobstructed area of at least 3.3 m (11 feet) shall be provided beyond the exit of all slides.

13) There shall be a clear space of 1.8 m (6 feet) along both sides of the slide measured from the inner edge of the safety side rail. Such a clear space must be free of obstruction, such as upright pipes, support posts, or other elements that could catch clothing or body parts in sliding motion.

RATIONALE

Guardrails and handholds help to prevent a child from accidentally falling or being pushed down the slide.

PERFORMANCE STANDARD

14) A freestanding slide accessed by a ladder with steps or a stairway shall have enclosed steps.

15) Metal is the recommended material for slides. However, a wooden slide may be used if it is sanded smooth and not subject to splintering. Wooden slides shall be inspected frequently for deterioration.

RATIONALE

Enclosed steps prevent a child from falling through or being pulled off the stairs.

Appendix O-8

Standards for Climbing Equipment/Devices

PERFORMANCE STANDARD

1) The maximum height of climbing equipment shall be no greater than 2 m (6.6 feet).

2) Large nets, climbing chains, or similar devices must be securely fixed.

3) Vertical climbing ropes shall be secured at both base and top.

4) Space between horizontal bars of climbing equipment, steps, ladders, and so forth shall be consistent throughout and should be 225–300 mm (8½–12 inches). Smaller spaces [those less than 230 mm (9⅛ inches)] shall be enclosed.

5) Handholds on climbing equipment/devices shall be 35–45 mm (1⅜–1¾ inches) and shall never be less than 25 mm (1 inch) in outside diameter.

6) Rungs on ladders shall be no less than 35–45 mm (1⅜ inches) in outside diameter. The rungs of vertical ladders in which rungs serve as both handhold and tread shall be 42 mm (1⅝ inches).

7) Ladders with rungs shall have a positive angle of incline no greater than 75 degrees, ladders with steps shall have a positive angle of incline between 50 and 75 degrees, and stairways shall have a positive angle of incline of 35 degrees or less.

8) Rungs or bars on ladders must be secured to prevent rolling or other unanticipated movement.

9) Climbing ropes shall be attached to support structures by I splice with thimble and shackle. Ends of rope must not be clamped.

10) There must be no intrusion into the climbing zone by protruding pipes, log ends, or other obstacles.

11) The space underneath climbing structures shall be free of rungs, bars, protrusions, or other hard objects in areas where children may fall.

12) All net and ladder chains shall be of a size that will not trap fingers.

13) All connecting points within nets must be adequately secured to reduce wear and movement in the net.

RATIONALE

This spacing prevents a child from falling through and prevents head entrapment.

Clamped rope ends will eventually shred and fall out.

Appendix O-9

Standards for Platforms and Other Raised Standing Surfaces

PERFORMANCE STANDARD

1) Platforms and other surfaces shall have a maximum height of 2 m (6 feet 6 inches); if higher than 1.5 m (4½ feet), they must have guardrails around the perimeter.

2) Surfaces of a height of 2 m (6 feet 6 inches) must be fully enclosed to a height of 1 m (39 inches) or higher, and infill below a top rail must not be horizontal or offer footholds to allow climbing.

3) Guardrails on structures must be at a height between 600 mm (23½ inches) and 800 mm (31½ inches).

4) At fall heights over 1.2 m (47 inches), there must be infill between the platform back and the top rail. Infill shall be vertical and openings between infill bars shall be less than 110 mm (4⅝ inches).

5) Double parallel horizontal hand- and guardrails on raised equipment are not allowed.

6) Suspended bridges shall be designed to support 10 kN/m² (kilonewtons per square meter) anywhere on the bridge surface.

7) Suspended bridges shall have handrails at convenient heights, and the handrails shall be designed for comfortable gripping.

8) Play structures shall offer more than one way of access and exit.

9) Access stairs to structures shall have steps with risers between 150 mm (6 inches) and 250 mm (10 inches). The distance between stepped platforms must be no greater than 305 mm (12 inches).

10) If the space between platforms and stair risers is greater than 110 mm (4⅝ inches), the space must be filled in.

11) All stairs to reach the height of a platform must be of uniform rise and run throughout.

RATIONALE

These types of hand- and guardrails encourage children to use railings as play elements for climbing, and thus increase the danger of falling off the equipment.

These requirements are intended to prevent a child from slipping through, and particularly from getting his/her head caught.

Appendix O-10

Fixed Play Elements

Child care and preschool facilities frequently have the opportunity to employ a variety of industrial artifacts or other kinds of equipment as play elements on playgrounds. This equipment may include old machinery, vehicles, and so forth. It is essential that the general principles indicated in Appendices O-4 through O-9, on pp. 363–369, be applied to these pieces of equipment as well as to equipment specifically designed for playground use. In particular, it is important to ensure that the equipment is well anchored; that there are no sharp or protruding points; that the material is in good condition and that it is not deteriorating; that any moving parts have been made inoperable; that the overall height of the object does not exceed 2 meters (6 feet 6 inches); and that there are no chemical or other contaminants contained within the object. Specifically, asbestos, oils and other lubricants should be removed prior to the item's use as play equipment.

Appendix O-11

Standards for Water Play Areas

PERFORMANCE STANDARD

1) Water play areas must conform to all state and local health regulations.

2) Water play areas must not include hidden or enclosed spaces.

3) Spray areas and water-collecting areas must have a nonslip surface, such as asphalt.

4) Water play areas, particularly those in which there is standing water, must not have sudden changes in depth of water.

5) Drains, streams, water spouts, and hydrants shall not create strong suction effects or water-jet forces.

6) All toys and other equipment used in and around the water play area shall be made of sturdy plastic. No glass shall be permitted.

7) Water play areas in which standing water is maintained for more than 24 hours shall be inspected for glass, trash, animal excrement, and other foreign material.

RATIONALE

All areas must be visible to allow adequate supervision.

This standard will prevent accidental falls into deeper water.

Appendix P-1

Immunization Schedule

STANDARDS

APP26. The following immunization schedule, or a similar schedule as may be modified in the future by the Advisory Committee on Immunization Practices (ACIP) of the U.S. Public Health Service and the American Academy of Pediatrics (AAP), or as may be modified by local health departments to control disease outbreaks (e.g., measles vaccine at 6 months of age in outbreak control), shall be used routinely for all infants, beginning at the age of 2 months.

SCHEDULE 1: RECOMMENDED SCHEDULE OF IMMUNIZATIONS FOR INFANTS AND CHILDREN	
Recommended Age	**Vaccine(s)***
2 months	DTP-1, OPV-1[a] or IPV-1, HbCV-1[b]
4 months	DTP-2, OPV/IPV-2, HbCV-2[b]
6 months	DTP-3, HbCV-3[b]
15 months	MMR-1[c], HbCV-4[b]
15–18 months	DTB-4, OPV/IPV-3
4–6 years	DTP-5, OPV/IPV-4
4–14 years	MMR-2

*DTP=diphtheria and tetanus toxoids with pertussis vaccine; OPV=oral poliovirus vaccine containing attenuated poliovirus types 1, 2, and 3; IPV=inactivated poliovirus vaccine containing killed type 1, 2, and 3 polioviruses; MMR=attenuated measles, mumps, and rubella viruses in a combined vaccine; HbCV=*H. influenzae* type b conjugate vaccines.

[a]Trivalent oral polio virus (OPV) vaccine is currently the vaccine of choice for immunization of children in the United States.[1, 2]

RATIONALE

Routine immunization at the appropriate age is the best means of averting vaccine-preventable diseases. Laws requiring the age-appropriate immunization of children attending licensed facilities exist in almost all states.[3] Surveys show that children in licensed child care have higher immunization levels than children of the same age who are not in child care. Therefore, children who attend unlicensed child care should be encouraged to comply with the recommended schedule of immunization for infants and children. Immunization is particularly important for children in child care because preschool-age children currently have the highest age-specific incidence of measles, pertussis, rubella, and *Haemophilus influenzae* type b disease.

Vaccine-preventable disease in young children is of great concern, because younger children are at higher risk than older children for complications of their illnesses. For example, during the period 1984–85, a total of 5,865 pertussis cases were reported to the Centers for Disease Control (CDC).[4] Nearly three-fourths (74 percent) occurred in infants younger than 6 months of age, and 18 of 19 pertussis deaths were in this youngest age group. Of 1,504 pertussis cases in children 7 months through 6 years of

[b]Presently (May 1991) there are two Hib conjugate vaccines (HbCV) licensed for administration to children younger than 15 months of age. One or the other shall be given to all children at age 8 weeks, and can be given as early as 6 weeks of age. The two vaccines have different dosing schedules. For routine immunization of infants younger than 7 months of age, either a 3-dose series of HbOC (HibTITER™) or a 2-dose series of PRP-OMP (PedvaxHIB™) shall be given at 2 month intervals. A booster dose is required at 12 months if using the PRP-OMP series or at 15 months if using the HbOC series. For doses given to children 15 months of age and older, any licensed conjugate vaccine—HbOC, PRP-OMP, or PRP-D (ProHIB-IT™)—is acceptable.

COMMENTS

[c]The initial dose of MMR vaccine may be given at 12 months of age in areas with recurrent measles transmission, and at younger ages with specific direction from the responsible health department. The second dose of MMR vaccine shall be given at or after school entry (ideally, between age 4 and 14 years); policies of the responsible local health department shall be followed with respect to the timing of this second dose.

Appendix P-1 continued

STANDARDS

APP26. *continued*

RATIONALE

age with known immunization status, 70 percent were underimmunized; 55 percent had not received at least three doses of vaccine—the minimum number considered necessary for adequate vaccine protection against pertussis. Thirty-one percent had not received any doses. Additionally, 51 percent of the 795 patients 3–6 months of age with known immunization status were underimmunized. Therefore, strict adherence to pertussis immunization recommendations would be expected to have a significant impact on the overall incidence of the disease among children and on childhood pertussis mortality.

The introduction of live mumps vaccine in 1967 and recommendations for its routine use in 1977 led to a steady decrease in reported mumps cases in the United States. However, since the record low number of cases in 1985 (2,982 cases), there has been a steady increase in mumps, with 12,848 cases reported in 1987. Although most mumps cases (55 percent) occur in school-age children (5–14 years), 804 cases (7 percent) occurred in preschool-age children during 1987; although this rate was low, it represented a 137 percent increase in the rate of mumps in preschool children between 1985 and 1987.[5]

Because of near-universal use of vaccines against diphtheria, tetanus, and polio, these diseases have become rare in the United States.

Two expert advisory groups—the Advisory Committee on Immunization Practices of the U.S. Public Health Service and the Committee on Infectious Diseases of the American Academy of Pediatrics—recommend a national immunization policy for children in the United States, and both have established similar standards for routine immunization of infants and preschool children.[1,2,6] Because these policies are updated regularly, immunization standards may change with respect to children in out-of-home care and their families.

COMMENTS

Immunization Schedule for Children Younger Than 7 Years Not Immunized in Infancy

STANDARDS

APP27. The following immunization schedule, or a similar schedule as may be modified in the future by the Advisory Committee on Immunization Practices (ACIP) of the U.S. Public Health Service and the American Academy of Pediatrics (AAP), shall be used routinely for all children younger than 7 years who were not immunized at the recommended time in infancy.

SCHEDULE 2: RECOMMENDED SCHEDULE OF IMMUNIZATIONS FOR INFANTS AND CHILDREN UP TO THEIR 7th BIRTHDAY, NOT IMMUNIZED AT THE RECOMMENDED TIME IN EARLY INFANCY

Age at First Visit	Vaccine(s)
2–14 mos.	DTP-1, OPV-1 or IPV-1, HbCV[b]
15–24 mos.	DTP-1, OPV/IPV-1, and MMR[a] and HbCV[b]
18 mos. of age or older	DTP-1, OPV/IPV, MMR, and HbCV[b]
2 mos. after DTP-1, OPV/IPV-1	DTP-2, OPV/IPV-2
2 mos. after DTP-2	DTP-3
6–12 mos. after DTP-3	DTP-4, OPV/IPV-3
Preschool[c] (4–6 yrs. of age)	DTP-5, OPV/IPV-4
Preschool (4–6 years) or school-age (4–14 years) and at least 1 month after MMR-1	MMR-2

RATIONALE

Many cases of vaccine-preventable diseases occur in unimmunized and underimmunized infants and children.[1] Of the 1,225 children ages 16 months to 4 years with measles reported to the Centers for Disease Control (CDC) in 1986, 83 percent were underimmunized.[2] An additional 1,229 measles cases occurred in children too young for measles immunization (i.e., less than 15 months of age).

See also rationale for standard APP26 in Appendix P-1 on p. 372.

COMMENTS

---

[a] MMR—shall be given on first visit after child reaches 15 months of age.

[b] HbCV—Presently (May 1991) there are two Hib conjugate vaccines [HbOC (HibTITER™), and PRP-OMP (PedvaxHIB™)] licensed for administration to children younger than 15 months of age, and a third vaccine [PRP-D (ProHIBIT™)] licensed for administration to children 15 months of age and older. When immunization is initiated between 7 and 11 months of age, 3 doses are required, and the dosing schedules for HbOC and PRP-OMP vaccines are identical: the first 2 doses are given at 2-month intervals, and the third dose at 15 to 18 months of age. When immunization is initiated between 12 and 14 months of age, 2 doses of either vaccine are required given at 2 month intervals. When immunization is initiated between 15 and 60 months of age, a single dose of vaccine is required. For doses given to children 15 months of age and older, any licensed conjugate vaccine—HbOC, PRP-OMP, or PRP-D (ProHIBIT™)—is acceptable. HbCV is not generally recommended for children older than 60 months of age.

[c] The preschool dose is not necessary if DTP-4 and OPV/IPV-3 are given after the 4th birthday.

Appendix Q

Adaptive Equipment for Children with Special Needs

PHYSICAL THERAPY/OCCUPATIONAL THERAPY EQUIPMENT

INFANTS, AGE 0–2

Equipment

2- to 3-inch floor mats (medium to firm)
Therapy ball: 37-inch diameter
Wedges: 4-inch, 6-inch, 8-inch, 12-inch
Inflatable mattress
Air compressor (for inflatables)
Therapy rolls
Platform swing
Cube chairs or bumper seats
Nesting benches (varying heights)
Infants or tumble form seat
Wooden weighted push cart

Feeding

Scoop bowls
"Mothercare" spoons
Coated spoons

Toys

Rattles
Squeeze toys
Tracking toys
Toys for pushing, swiping, cause and effect
See-through inflatable toys

PRE-K, AGE 2–5

Equipment

2-inch mats (firm)
Therapy balls: 37-inch diameter
    24-inch diameter
    20-inch diameter
    16-inch diameter
Suspended Equipment: Platform swing
    Net swing
    T-bar
Therapy rolls: 8-inch diameter
    10-inch diameter
    12-inch diameter
Toddler gym with slide
Small chair and table

Toys

Tricycles
Ride-on scooters
Wagon
Wooden push cart
Nesting benches
Manipulative toys (puzzles, beads, pegs and
    pegboard, nesting toys, etc.)
Fastening boards (zipper, snaps, laces, etc.)
Paper, crayons, chalk, markers
Adaptive equipment as needed for individual
    children (walkers, sidelyers, proneboards, adapted
    chairs)

SPEECH AND LANGUAGE EQUIPMENT

INFANTS, AGE 0–2

Equipment

Mirrors, wall and hand-held
Assorted spoons, cups, bowls, plates
Mats and sheets
Preston feeding chairs
High chairs

Toys

Dolls (soft with large features)
Rattles (noisemakers and easy to grasp)
Manipulative toys (for pulling, pushing, shaking,
    cause and effect)
Assorted picture books (large pictures, one to a page)
Building blocks
Balls/bells
Telephone
Stacking rings
Shape sorters
Xylophone
Drum

Assessments and Books

Small Wonder Activity Kit
Pre-Feeding Skills by Suzanne Morris
Parent-Infant Communication
Bayley Scales of Infant Development
Movement Assessment of Infants (S. Harris and L.
    Chandler)
RIDES
HAWAII HELP
Early Learning Accomplishments Profile and Kit
    (Kaplan)

PRE-K, AGE 2–5

Equipment

Mirrors, wall and hand-held
Tongue depressors
Penlight
Stopwatch
Tape recorder and tapes

Assessments and Books

Sequenced Inventory of Communication Development
Peabody Picture Vocabulary Test
Zimmerman Pre-School Language Scale
Test of Auditory Comprehension of Language
Goldman Fristore Test of Articulation

Toys

Dolls (with movable parts and removable clothing)
Manipulative toys (cars and toys for pushing, stacking, cause and effect)
Building blocks
Dollhouse
Assorted story books (few, if any, words and large pictures)
Pretend play items: Dress-up clothes, dishes, sink, foods, telephone
Play-Doh or clay
Puzzles (individual pieces or minimal interlocking parts)
Picture cards (nouns, actions, etc.)
Puppets
Animals

ADAPTIVE PHYSICAL EDUCATION EQUIPMENT

BALANCE/GROSS MOTOR COORDINATION

Incline mat
4-inch-wide balance beam
12-inch-wide balance beam
2-inch floor mats
Bolsters
Rocking platforms
Scooters (sit-on ones)
Tunnel (accordion style)
Training stairs
Hurdles (adjustable height)

EYE-HAND COORDINATION

Balls (to hit, throw, catch)
Beanbags
Hula hoops
Lightweight paddles/rackets
Lightweight bats
Traffic cones or batting tees
Targets for beanbags
Beachballs

EYE-FOOT COORDINATION

Balls for kicking
Foot placement ladder
Footprints or ''stepping stones''
Horizontal ladder

Appendix R

Emergency Plan

STANDARDS

APP28. The facility shall have a written plan for reporting and managing any incident or unusual occurrence that is threatening to the health, safety, or welfare of the children or staff. The facility shall also include procedures for staff training on this emergency plan.

The following *incidents*, at a minimum, shall be addressed in the emergency plan.
a) Lost or missing child.
b) Sexual or physical abuse or neglect of a child (as mandated by state law).
c) Injuries requiring medical or dental care.
d) Serious illness requiring hospitalization, death of a child enrolled in the facility, or death of a caregiver, including deaths that occur outside of child care hours.

The following *procedures*, at a minimum, shall be addressed in the emergency plan.
e) Provision for a caregiver to accompany a child to the emergency care source and remain with the child until the parent or legal guardian assumes responsibility for the child. (See also Appendix X, on p. 389.) Provision for a backup caregiver or substitute (see *Substitutes*, on p. 31) for large and small family-child-care homes to make this feasible. Child:staff ratios must be maintained at the facility during the emergency (see *Staff Health*, on p. 35).
f) The source of emergency medical care—a hospital emergency room, clinic, or other constantly staffed facility known to caregivers and acceptable to parents.
g) Ensure that first aid kits are resupplied following each first aid incident, and that required contents are maintained in a serviceable condition, by a periodic review of the contents. (See FA116 in chapter 5 on p. 161.)

RATIONALE

Emergency situations are not conducive to calm and composed thinking. Drafting a written plan provides the opportunity to prepare and to prevent poor judgments made under the stress of an emergency.

An organized, comprehensive approach to injury prevention and control is necessary to ensure that a safe environment is provided for children in child care. Such an approach requires written plans, policies, procedures, and record-keeping so that there is consistency over time and across staff and an understanding between parents and caregivers about concerns for, and attention to, the safety of children.

Routine restocking is necessary to ensure supplies are available at the time of an emergency.

COMMENTS

Because kits may not be used for long periods of time, a procedure for periodic review is necessary.

STANDARDS

h) The names and addresses of at least three licensed providers of dental services who have agreed to accept emergency dental referrals of children and to give advice regarding a dental emergency. (See recommendation REC59 in chapter 9 on p. 315.)

RATIONALE

Management within the first hour or so following a dental injury may save a tooth.[1]

COMMENTS

Parents may also have on file their preferred provider of dental services in case of emergency. Parents should be notified, if at all possible, before dental services are rendered, but emergency care should not be delayed because the child's own dentist is not immediately available.

Appendix S

Personnel Policies

STANDARDS	RATIONALE	COMMENTS

APP29. The facility shall have and follow written personnel policies. All written policies shall be reviewed and signed by the employee affected by them on hiring and annually thereafter. These policies shall address the following items. For centers, these shall be written policies.
a) A wage scale with merit increases.
b) Sick leave.
c) Vacation leave.
d) Educational benefits.
e) Health insurance.
f) Social Security or other retirement plan.
g) Holidays.
h) Workers' compensation.
i) A break of at least 15 minutes every 4 hours, with a total 30-minute break, at a minimum, during an 8-hour period.
j) Maternity benefits/parental leave.
k) Overtime/compensatory time policy.
l) Probation period.
m) Grounds for termination.
n) Training of new caregivers and substitute staff (see *Substitutes*, on p. 31.), including written documentation of training completion as specified in *Training Record*, on p. 30.
o) Personal/bereavement leave.
p) Disciplinary action.
q) Periodic review of performance. (See *Performance Evaluation*, on p. 41.)
r) Exclusion policies pertaining to staff illness. (See *Staff Exclusion*, on p. 84.)
s) Staff health appraisal. (See *Staff Health*, on p. 35.)

Written personnel policies provide a means of staff orientation and evaluation essential to the operation of any organization. Caregivers who are responsible for compliance with policies must have reviewed them.

See also the rationale for standard ST 80 in *Staff Benefits*, on p. 40.

Staff benefits may be appropriately addressed in center personnel policies and in state and federal labor standards. Not all the material in such policies is necessarily appropriate for state child care licensing requirements.

Although the business plan of the caregiver will determine the scope of benefits the caregiver can offer, this standard outlines the types of benefits that must be offered to control staff turnover and reduce stress, which decreases caregiver performance.

A policy of encouraging sick leave, even without pay, or of permitting a flexible schedule will allow the caregiver to take time off when needed for illnesss. An acknowledgment that the facility does not provide paid leave but does give time off will begin to address workers' rights to these benefits and improve quality of care. There may be other nontraditional ways to achieve these benefits.

Costs of staff benefits will need to be subsidized for child care to be affordable to parents.

See also the comments for standard ST80 in *Staff Benefits*, on p. 40.

APP30. Large family-child-care homes shall have and follow written personnel policies. All written policies shall be reviewed and signed by the employee affected by them on hiring and annually thereafter. These

See rationale for standard APP29.

See comment for standard APP29.

STANDARDS   **RATIONALE**   **COMMENTS**

policies shall address the following:

a) Sick leave.

b) Vacation leave.

c) Educational benefits.

d) Health insurance.

e) A break of at least 15 minutes every 4 hours, with a total 30-minute break, at a minimum, during an 8-hour period.

f) Overtime/compensatory time policy.

g) Probation period.

h) Training of new caregivers and substitute staff (see *Substitutes*, on p. 31), including written documentation of training completion as specified in *Orientation Training*, on p. 19.

Appendix T

Personnel Records

STANDARDS	RATIONALE	COMMENTS

APP31. Individual files for all staff, including volunteers, shall be maintained in a central location within the facility and shall contain the following:

a) The individual's name, birth date, address, and telephone number.

b) The position application, which includes a record of work experience and work references; verification of reference information, education, and training; and records of any checking for criminal record, and so forth. (See *Individual Licensure/Certification*, on p. 301, *Qualifications*, on p. 4, and *Training*, on p. 18.)

c) The health assessment record, a copy of which, having been dated and signed by the employee's health care provider, shall be kept in a confidential file in the facility. This record shall be updated at least annually with the staff member and shall be updated by another health appraisal when recommended by the staff member's health care provider or supervisory or regulatory/certifying personnel.[1,2] (See *Staff Health*, on p. 35, and *Ongoing Staff Health Appraisals*, on p. 37.)

d) The name and telephone number of the person, physician, or health facility to be notified in case of emergency.

e) The job description or the job expectations for staff and substitutes. (See *General Qualifications for All Staff*, on p. 16.)

f) Required licenses, certificates, transcripts, and so forth (See *Individual Licensure/Certification*, on p. 301.)

g) The date of employment or volunteer assignment.

h) A daily record of hours worked.

i) A record of continuing education for each staff member and volunteer. (See *Continuing Education*, on p. 24.)

Complete identification of staff, paid or volunteer, is an essential step in safeguarding children in child care.

Emergency contact information for staff, paid or volunteer, is needed in child care in the event an adult becomes ill or injured at the facility.

Appendix T continued

STANDARDS **RATIONALE** **COMMENTS**

j) Written performance evaluations. (See *Performance Evaluation*, on p. 41.)

k) A record of benefits. (See *Staff Benefits*, on p. 40.)

l) A signed statement of agreement that the employee understands and will abide by the following:

  1) Regulations and statutes governing child care.

  2) Personnel policies and procedures. (See *Personnel Policies*, on p. 287.)

  3) Discipline policy. (See *Discipline Policy*, on p. 272, and *Discipline*, on p. 52.)

  4) Guidelines for reporting suspected child abuse, neglect, and sexual abuse.

Appendix U
Injury Report Form

NAME OF INJURED _____

SEX _____

AGE _____

DATE WHEN INJURY OCCURRED _____

TIME WHEN INJURY OCCURRED _____

LOCATION WHERE INJURY OCCURRED _____

_____

DESCRIPTION OF HOW INJURY OCCURRED _____

_____

_____

_____

DESCRIPTION OF PART OF BODY INVOLVED _____

NAME OF CONSUMER PRODUCT INVOLVED (IF ANY) _____

ACTION TAKEN ON BEHALF OF THE INJURED _____

_____

_____

_____

WAS PARENT/LEGAL GUARDIAN SPECIFICALLY ADVISED OF INJURY? _____

WAS PARENT/LEGAL GUARDIAN SPECIFICALLY ADVISED TO OBTAIN MEDICAL ATTENTION? _____

NAME OF INDIVIDUAL(S) INVOLVED IN SUPERVISION AT TIME OF INJURY _____

_____

NAME OF PERSON COMPLETING THIS REPORT FORM _____

DATE OF COMPLETION OF FORM _____

Appendix V

Large and Small Family-Child-Care Home Records

STANDARDS	RATIONALE	COMMENTS

APP32. Large and small family home caregivers shall maintain the following records:

a) A copy of the facility's license or registration, all inspection reports, correction plans for deficiencies, and any legal actions. (See *Licensing and Legal Records*, on p. 292, and *Posting Documents*, on p. 296.)

b) Physical health records for any adult regularly giving care, and for family members who are present when the children are in care. (See *Preemployment Staff Health Appraisal, Including Immunization*, on p. 35, and *Ongoing Staff Health Appraisals*, on p. 37.)

c) Training records of the caregiver and any assistants. (See *Training*, on p. 18.)

d) Results of the search for a criminal history record of any person living or working in the large or small family-child-care home; child abuse record of any person living or working in the large or small family-child-care home. (See *Licensure/Certification of Qualified Individuals*, on p. 4, *Qualifications by Role*, on p. 4, and *Individual Licensure/Certification*, on p. 301.)

e) Results of well-water tests where applicable. (See *Licensing and Legal Records*, on p. 292.)

f) Results of lead paint tests. (See specifics in standard FA135 in chapter 5 on p. 167.)

g) Insurance records. (See *Insurance Records*, on p. 294.)

h) Child records. (See *Child Records*, on p. 287.)

i) Attendance records. (See *Attendance Records*, on p. 290.)

j) List of reportable diseases. (See *Incidence Logs of Illness, Injury, and Other Problems*, on p. 290.)

k) Injury report form. (See *Incidence Logs of Illness, Injury, and Other Problems*, on p. 290.)

Operational control to accommodate the health and safety of individual children requires that information regarding each child in care be kept and made available on a need-to-know basis. These records and reports are necessary to protect the health and safety of children in care.

An organized, comprehensive approach to injury prevention and control is necessary to ensure that a safe

Appendix V *continued*

STANDARDS

l) Fire extinguisher records. (See *Fire Extinguisher Records*, on p. 293.)

m) Evacuation drill records. (See *Evacuation Drill Records*, on p. 293.)

RATIONALE

environment is provided for children in child care. Such an approach requires written plans, policies, procedures, and record-keeping so that there is consistency over time and across staff and an understanding between parents and caregivers about concerns for, and attention to, the safety of children.

COMMENTS

Appendix W

Posting Documents

STANDARDS

APP33. Each center shall post the following in a conspicuous public place clearly visible to parents, caregivers, and visitors:

a) The center's license or registration (which also includes the telephone number for filing complaints with the regulatory agency), as specified in *Licensing and Legal Records*, on p. 292.

b) A statement informing parents/legal guardians about how they may obtain a copy of the licensing or registration requirements from the regulatory agency.

c) Information on procedures for filing complaints with the regulatory authority.

d) Inspection and any accreditation certificates, as specified in *Licensing and Legal Records*, on p. 292.

e) Reports of any legal sanctions, as specified in *Licensing and Legal Records*, on p. 292.

f) A notice that inspection reports, legal actions, and compliance letters are available for inspection in the facility.

g) Evacuation plan, as specified in standard AD31 in chapter 8 on p. 280.

h) Fire evacuation procedures. (These shall be posted in each room of the center.)

i) Procedures for the reporting of child abuse consistent with state law and local law enforcement and child protective service contacts.

RATIONALE

Since licensing is a "status movement" operation whereby the state gives official permission to certain persons to operate by virtue of their compliance with standards, documents relating to investigations, inspections, and approval to operate should be generally accessible to consumers, caregivers, concerned persons, and the community.

Consciousness of the child abuse reporting requirements and procedures is essential to the prevention of child abuse. State requirements may differ, but those for whom the reporting of child abuse is mandatory usually include child care personnel. Information on how to call and how to report should be readily available to parents and caregivers. Therefore, posting of these instructions is necessary.

COMMENTS

Compliance can be measured by looking for posted documents.

Parents have a right to see any reports and notices of any legal actions taken against the facility that have been sustained by the court. Since unfounded suits may be filed, knowledge of which could undermine parent confidence, only actions that result in corrections or judgments need to be made accessible.

STANDARDS

RATIONALE

COMMENTS

j) A notice announcing the "open-door policy" (that parents may visit at any time and will be admitted without delay) and action the facility will take to handle a visitor's request for access if the caregiver is concerned about the safety of the children. (See Appendix X, on p. 389, for statement of services.)

The open-door policy may be the single most important method for preventing the abuse of children in child care.[1] When access is restricted, areas observable by the parents may not reflect the care the children actually receive.

The caregiver and parents need to know how an unstable (e.g., intoxicated) parent who wants admittance but whose behavior presents a risk to children will be handled.

k) A class roster in each facility room that lists the names of all children assigned to that room and the name of the caregiver primarily responsible for each child.

Identification of primary caregiver responsibility helps foster and channel communication between parents and caregivers. A posted roster also helps parents see how facility responsibility is assigned and know which children receive care in their child's group.

l) A current weekly menu for parents and caregivers. The facility shall provide copies to parents, if requested. Copies of menus served shall be kept on file for 1 year. (See also *Food Service Records*, on p. 295.)

In order to ensure that children receive the minimum daily requirements of nutrients, parents need to know the daily menu provided by the facility.

Menus filed should reflect last-minute changes so that a nutrition consultant who reviews these documents can get an accurate picture of what was actually served.

m) A copy of the policy and procedures for discipline, including the prohibition of corporal punishment. This requirement also applies to school-age child care facilities. (See also *Discipline Policy*, on p. 272.)

Parents and caregivers must have a common basis of understanding about what disciplinary measures are to be used to avoid conflict and promote consistency in approach between caregivers and parents. Corporal punishment may be physical abuse or become very abusive easily.

n) Legible safety rules for the use of swimming and built-in wading pools. (See also *Safety Rules*, on p. 195, and *Water Safety*, on p. 96.)

Safety rules shall be posted conspicuously on the pool enclosure.[2]

o) Phone numbers and instructions for contacting the fire department, police, emergency medical services, physicians, dentists, rescue and ambulance services, and the poison control center; the address of the facility; and directions to the facility from major routes north, south, east, and west. This information shall be conspicuously posted adjacent to the telephone.

In an emergency, phone numbers must be immediately accessible.

A sample telephone emergency list is provided in *Healthy Young Children*. To obtain this publication, contact

National Association for the Education of Young Children 1834 Connecticut Ave., N.W. Washington, DC 20009

p) A list of reportable communicable diseases as required by the state and local health authorities. (See *Reporting Illness*, on p. 87.)

See also *Procedures for Complaints and Reporting*, on p. 307.

STANDARDS

APP34. Large and small family home caregivers shall post the following in a conspicuous place:
q) The facility's license or registration (which also includes the telephone number for filing complaints with the licensing agency, if applicable), as specified in *Licensing and Legal Records*, on p. 292.
r) Inspection and any accreditation certificates, as specified in *Licensing and Legal Records*, on p. 292.
c) Fire evacuation procedures.

For records required in small and large family-child-care homes, see *Large and Small Family-Child-Care Home Records*, on p. 296.

RATIONALE

See rationale for standard APP33.

COMMENTS

See comment for standard APP33.

Appendix X

Management Plan and Statement of Services

STANDARDS

APP35. At the time of enrollment, the facility shall provide parents with a statement of services that shall include the following information. Parents shall sign this statement of services. The facility shall have the statement of services available for review by the regulatory agency.

APP36. For centers and large and small family-child-care homes, the following items shall be in writing:
a) The names, ages, and number of children in care.
b) Services offered to children. Any special requirements for a child shall be clearly defined in writing before enrollment.
c) Hours and days of operation.
d) Vacation, leave, and holidays (see *Staff Benefits*, on p. 40).
e) Policies for termination and notice by the parent or the facility.
f) Policies regarding payment of fees, deposits, and refunds.
g) Evacuation procedures for fire, natural disasters, and injuries. (See *Emergency Procedures*, on p. 95, *Emergency Plan*, on p. 280, and *Evacuation Plan and Drills*, on p. 280.)
h) Schedule of meals and snacks. (See *General Requirements*, on p. 115, *Requirements for Special Groups or Ages of Children*, on p. 117, and *Nutrition Plan and Policy*, on p. 284.
i) Policy for food brought from home. (See *Food Brought From Home*, on p. 126.)
j) Policies for helpers or substitutes. (See *Substitutes*, on p. 31.)
k) Nonemergency transportation policies. (See *Transportation*, on p. 199.)
l) Presence of any pets in the home. (See *Animals*, on p. 97.)
m) Policy on health assessments and immunizations. (See *Child Health Services*, on p. 276.)

RATIONALE

So that they may be responsible for the proper care of their children, parents are entitled to have full and ready knowledge of the service operations of the facility where they have placed their children, and they must understand the scope and limit of services provided by the facility. Having parents sign the statement of services reflects the contractual arrangement that is needed when parents place their children in out-of-home child care.

Caregivers must have clear-cut policies about their day-to-day operations to define for parents what type of service they and their children will receive. Written policies help avoid later misunderstandings and complaints.

The facility and parents must exchange information necessary for the safety and health of the child.

COMMENTS

Model written policies can be provided by regulatory agencies and voluntary organizations of caregivers to ease the burden of drafting such policies for each small family home caregiver.

STANDARDS

RATIONALE

COMMENTS

n) Policy regarding care of ill children, including exclusion or dismissal from the facility. (See *Child Inclusion/Exclusion/Dismissal*, on p. 80, and *Care of Ill Children*, on p. 274.)

o) Emergency plan. (See Appendix R, on p. 377.)

p) Policy on infant feeding. (See *Nutrition for Infants*, on p. 117, and *Nutrition Plan and Policy*, on p. 284.)

q) Policy on administration of medications. (See *Medications*, on p. 88.)

r) Policy on smoking and prohibited substances. (See *Smoking and Prohibited Substances Plan*, on p. 285.)

s) Emergency transportation plan. (See Appendix R, on p. 377.)

A sample emergency transportation permission form for parents is provided in *Healthy Young Children*. To obtain this publication, contact

National Association for the Education of Young Children 1834 Connecticut Avenue, N.W. Washington, DC 20009

APP37. For centers and large family-child-care homes, the following policies and information shall be in writing. These items need not be in writing for the small family-child-care home; however, the small family home caregiver shall be able to discuss competently all of the following as they relate to his/her service. Parents shall sign this statement of services.

a) The policy of free admittance of a parent or legal guardian immediately at any time when his/her child is at the facility, except when the parent's or legal guardian's behavior poses a risk to the children.

b) Admission requirements (see *Admission Policy*, on p. 271).

c) Philosophy of the facility.

d) Qualifications and results of credential checks of caregivers who provide child care directly, as well as persons in the facility who provide auxiliary services (e.g., drivers or family members residing in the facility who serve as

The open-door policy may be the single most important method for preventing the abuse of children in child care.[1] When access is restricted, areas observable by the parents may not reflect the care the children actually receive.

Parents can be interviewed to see if the open-door policy is enthusiastically implemented.

Caregivers need to know how to handle unstable (e.g., intoxicated) parents who want admittance to the facility but whose behavior poses a risk to the children.

STANDARDS	RATIONALE	COMMENTS

assistants). (See *Qualifications*, on p. 4, and *Substitutes*, on p. 31.)

e) Routines and program of activities. (See *Program of Developmental Activities*, on p. 45, and *Program of Activities*, on p. 286.)

f) Supervision policy and child:staff ratios. (See *Child: Staff Ratio and Group Size*, on p. 1, and *Supervision Policy*, on p. 272.)

g) Policy on daily arrival and departure of children. (See *Safety Plan*, on p. 281.)

h) Safety plan. (See *Safety Plan*, on p. 281.)

i) Discipline policies. (See *Discipline Policy*, on p. 272.)

j) Ability of the facility to adjust or modify routines to accommodate the individual needs of children.

k) A description of off-premise activities and any necessary transfer of medical records (such as emergency contact information described in standard APP5 in Appendix C, item A on p. 330). (See Appendix C, item C.3.c, on p. 333.)

l) Responsibilities and expected involvement of parents in facility activities. (See *Parent Relationships*, on p. 55.)

m) Accident and liability insurance carried by the facility. (See *Insurance Records*, on p. 294.)

n) Policy on immunizations. (See *Vaccine-Preventable Diseases*, on p. 219.)

o) The telephone number for filing complaints with the licensing agency.

p) Whether religious training is included in the program.

q) Policy on use of swimming or built-in wading pools. (See *Child: Staff Ratio and Group Size*, on p. 1, *Water Safety*, on p. 96, and *Swimming, Wading, and Water*, on p. 192.)

r) Daily health assessment of children. (See *Daily Health Assessment*, on p. 65.)

s) Notification to parents of the posted documents specified in *Posting Documents*, on p. 296.)

Parents must be informed if their children will be provided religious training so that they can decide whether the facility's teaching is desirable for their children.

STANDARDS

RATIONALE

COMMENTS

t) Policy regarding each child's personal belongings, and the provision of diapers, clothing, formula, and baby food if the facility is licensed/registered for infant and/or toddler care.

See also Appendix C, item C on p. 333 for parental consent items to include in the child's record.

References for Appendices

APPENDIX C

1. Deitch S, ed. *Health in Day Care: A Manual for Health Care Professionals.* Elk Grove Village, Ill: American Academy of Pediatrics; 1987.
2. Kendrick AS, Kaufmann R, Messenger KP, eds. *Healthy Young Children: A Manual for Programs.* Washington, DC: National Association for the Education of Young Children; 1991.
3. Haskins R, Kotch J. Day care and illness: evidence, costs and public policy. *Pediatrics.* 1986;77(6) (suppl) (pt 2).
4. Collins R. Head Start research: a new chapter. *Children Today.* Jul/Aug 1983;15–19.
5. Aronson S. Maintaining health in child care settings. Group Care for Young Children, Pediatric Round Table 12. Skillman, NJ: Johnson & Johnson; 1986.
6. Sterner GG, Hinam A, Schmid S. Potential health benefits of child day care attendance. *Infect Dis.* Jul/Aug 1986;660–662.
7. Reyes RE. Prevention in pediatric dentistry. *NYS Dent J.* 1988;54(2):34–35.
8. American Academy of Pediatrics Committee on Early Childhood, Adoption, and Dependent Care. The pediatrician's role in promoting the health of a patient in day care. *Pediatrics.* 1984;74(1):157–158.

APPENDIX E

1. Yogman M. Child care as a setting for parent education. Group Care for Young Children. Pediatric Round Table 12. Skillman, NJ: Johnson & Johnson; 1986.
2. Caldwell B. Education of families for parenting. In: Yogman M, Brazelton T, eds. *Stress and Coping in Families: A Systems Perspective.* Boston, Mass: Harvard University Press; 1986:229–241.

APPENDIX I-1

1. Schlech WF, Ward JI, Band JD, et al. Bacterial meningitis in the United States, 1978 through 1981. *JAMA.* 1985;253:1749–1754.
2. Cochi SL, Fleming DW, Hightower AW, et al. Primary invasive *Haemophilus influenzae* type b disease: a population-based assessment of risk factors. *J Pediatr.* 1986;108:887–896.
3. Fleming DW, Leibenhaut MH, Albanes D, et al. Secondary *Haemophilus influenzae* type b in day-care facilities: risk factors and prevention. *JAMA.* 1985;254:509–514.
4. Murphy TV, McCracken GH, Moore BS, et al. *Haemophilus influenzae* type b disease after rifampin prophylaxis in a day care center: possible reasons for its failure. *Pediatr Infect Dis.* 1983;2:193–198.
5. *Report of the Committee on Infectious Disease of the American Academy of Pediatrics.* Elk Grove Village, Ill: American Academy of Pediatrics; 1988:204–210.
6. Makintubee S, Istre GR, Ward JI. Transmission of invasive *Haemophilus influenzae* type b disease in day care settings. *J Pediatr.* 1987;111:180–186.
7. Recommendation of the Advisory Committee on Immunization Practices (ACIP). Update: Prevention of *Haemophilus influenzae* type b disease. *MMWR.* 1986;35:170–177, 179–180.
8. Broome CV, Mortimer EA, Katz SL, et al. Use of chemoprophylaxis to prevent the spread of *Haemophilus influenzae* type b in day care facilities. *N Engl J Med.* 1987;316:1226–1228.
9. Broome CV, Mortimer EA, Katz SL, et al. More on rifampin prophylaxis against *Haemophilus influenzae* type b in day care facilities. *N Engl J Med.* 1988;318:48–49.
10. Osterholm MT, Murphy TV. More on rifampin prophylaxis against *Haemophilus influenzae* type b in day care facilities. *N Engl J Med.* 1988;318:49.

APPENDIX I-2

1. Fraser DW, Geil CC, Feldman RA. Bacterial meningitis in Bernalillo County, New Mexico: a comparison with three other American populations. *Amer J Epidemiol.* 1974;100:29–34.
2. Jacobson JA, Felice GA, Holloway JT. Meningococcal disease in day-care centers. *Pediatrics.* 1977;59:299–300.
3. *Report of the Committee on Infectious Disease of the American Academy of Pediatrics.* Elk Grove Village, Ill: American Academy of Pediatrics; 1988;289–292.
4. Recommendation of the Advisory Committee on Immunization Practices (ACIP). Meningococcal vaccines. *MMWR.* 1985;34:255–259.

APPENDIX I-3

1. Centers for Disease Control. Pertussis—United States, 1984 and 1985. *MMWR.* 1987;36:168–171.
2. Bass JE. Pertussis: current status of prevention and treatment. *Pediatr Infect Dis.* 1985;4:614–619.
3. Recommendation of the Advisory Committee on Immunization Practices (ACIP). Diphtheria, tetanus and pertussis: guidelines for vaccine prophylaxis and other preventive measures. *MMWR.* 1985; 34:1–17.
4. *Report of the Committee on Infectious Disease of the American Academy of Pediatrics.* Elk Grove Village, Ill: American Academy of Pediatrics; 1988;315–325.

APPENDIX J

1. *Feeding Infants—A Guide for Use in the Child Care Food Program.* Washington, DC: US Dept of Agriculture; 1988. Food and Nutrition Service publication FNS-258.
2. Code of Federal Regulations Part 226.20. *Federal Register.* July 6, 1988;53:129.
3. *Head Start Program Performance Standards.* Washington, DC: US Dept of Health and Human Services; Nov 1984.
4. Marotz LR, Rush J, Cross MZ. *Health, Safety and Nutrition for the Young Child.* Albany, NY: Delmar Publishers Inc; 1989.
5. *Pediatric Nutrition Handbook.* Elk Grove Village, Ill: American Academy of Pediatrics; 1985.

APPENDIX K

1. *Head Start Program Performance Standards.* Washington, DC: US Dept of Health and Human Services; Nov 1984.
2. *Pediatric Nutrition Handbook.* Elk Grove Village, Ill: American Academy of Pediatrics; 1985.
3. *Minimum Standards for Licensed Child Care Centers.* Richmond, Va: Virginia Department of Social Services; Apr 1986.
4. *Child Care Food Program. Manual for Child Care Providers.* Albuquerque, NM. Child Care Food Program, Health and Environment Department; 1986.
5. *Handbook for Food Service Standards and Nutrition Education for Group Care of Preschool Children with Recommendations for Older Children.* New York, NY: New York City Department of Health, Bureau of Nutrition; 1986.
6. *A Planning Guide for Food Service in Child Care Centers.* Washington, DC: US Dept of Agriculture; revised July 1989. Food and Nutrition Service publication FNS-64.

APPENDIX P-1

1. Advisory Committee on Immunization Practices (ACIP). General recommendations on immunization. *MMWR.* 1989;38:205–227.
2. American Academy of Pediatrics. *Report of the Committee on Infectious Diseases.* 21st edition. Elk Grove Village, Ill: American Academy of Pediatrics; 1988.
3. Hinman AR. Vaccine-preventable diseases and child day care. *Rev Infect Dis.* 1986;8:573–583.
4. Centers for Disease Control. Pertussis surveillance—United States, 1984 and 1985. *MMWR.* 1987;36:168–171.
5. Centers for Disease Control. Mumps—United States, 1985–1988. *MMWR.* 1989;38:101–105.
6. Centers for Disease Control. Rubella and congenital rubella syndrome—United States, 1985–1988. *MMWR.* 1989;38:173–178.

APPENDIX P-2

1. Markowitz LE, Prebuld SR, Orenstein WA. Patterns of transmission in measles outbreaks in the United States, 1985–1986. *N Engl J Med.* 1989;320:75–81.
2. Centers for Disease Control. Measles—United States, 1986. *MMWR.* 1987;36:301–305.

APPENDIX R

1. Bogert JA. The American Academy of Pediatric Dentistry: its scope and function. *NYS Dent J.* Feb 1988.

APPENDIX T

1. Aronson S. Health policies and procedures. *Child Care Information Exchange.* Sept/Oct 1983;14–16.
2. Aronson S. Coping with the physical requirements of caregiving. *Child Care Information Exchange.* 1987;55:39–43.

APPENDIX W

1. Deitch S, ed. *Health in Day Care: A Manual for Health Professionals.* Elk Grove Village, Ill: American Academy of Pediatrics; 1987.
2. *Public Swimming Pools: Recommended Regulations for Design and Construction, Operation and Maintenance.* Washington, DC: American Public Health Association; 1981.

APPENDIX X

1. Deitch S, ed. *Health in Day Care: A Manual for Health Professionals.* Elk Grove Village, Ill: American Academy of Pediatrics, 1987.

Glossary

Note: Many of the items in this glossary are reprinted with permission from *Infectious Diseases in Child Care Settings: Information for Directors, Caregivers, and Parents or Guardians*. Prepared by the Epidemiology Departments of Hennepin County Community Health, St. Paul Division of Public Health, Minnesota Department of Health, Washington County Public Health, and Bloomington Division of Health.

AAP—Abbreviation for the American Academy of Pediatrics, a national organization of pediatricians founded in 1930 and dedicated to the improvement of child health and welfare, headquartered at 141 Northwest Point Blvd., P.O. Box 927, Elk Grove Village, IL 60009-0927.

ACIP—Abbreviation for the U.S. Public Health Service Advisory Committee on Immunization Practices, which provides general recommendations on immunization against certain communicable diseases.

AIDS—See **Human immunodeficiency virus (HIV) disease.**

ANSI—Abbreviation for the American National Standards Institute, an organization that acts as a clearinghouse for standards, ensuring that any standard that comes out is created by a consensus process. ANSI is located at 1430 Broadway Street, New York, NY 10018.

Anthropometric—Relating to physical measurements of the human body, for example, height, weight, or head circumference.

Anthropometry—The study of human body measurements.

Antibody—A protein substance produced by the body's immune defense system in response to something foreign. Antibodies help protect against infections.

Antigen—Any substance that is foreign to the body. An antigen is capable of causing a response from the immune system.

Antisiphon ballcock—An automatic valve in the toilet tank, the opening and closing of which is controlled by a spherical float at the end of a lever. The antisiphon ballcock does not allow dirty water to be admixed with clean water.

APHA—Abbreviation for the American Public Health Association, a national organization of health professionals, which protects and promotes the health of the public through education, research, advocacy, and policy development. APHA's offices are located at 1015 15th Street, N.W., Washington, DC 20005.

Aseptic technique—The use of procedures that prevent contamination of an object, fluid, or person with infectious microorganisms.

Asphyxial crib death—Death attributed to an item within the crib that caused deprivation of oxygen or obstruction to normal breathing of an infant.

Asphyxiation—Death or unconsciousness due to inadequate oxygenation, the presence of noxious agents, or other obstructions to normal breathing.

Assessment—An in-depth appraisal conducted to diagnose a condition or determine the importance or value of a procedure.

ASTM—Abbreviation for the American Society for Testing and Materials, an organization that provides voluntary standards through a consensus process for materials, products, systems, and services. ASTM is located at 1916 Race Street, Philadelphia, PA 19103.

Asymptomatic—Without symptoms. For example, a child may not have symptoms of hepatitis infection, but may still shed hepatitis A virus in the stool and may be able to infect others.

Bacteria—Plural of bacterium. Bacteria are organisms with a cell wall that can survive in and out of the body. They are much larger than viruses and can usually be treated effectively with antibiotics.

Bacteriostatic—Having the ability to inhibit the growth of bacteria.

Bleach solution for disinfecting environmental surfaces—One-quarter (¼) cup of household liquid chlorine bleach (sodium hypochloride) in 1 gallon of water, prepared fresh daily. See also **Disinfect.**

Body fluids—Urine, feces, saliva, blood, nasal discharge, eye discharge, and injury or tissue discharge.

Bronchitis—An inflammation or swelling of the tubes leading into the lungs, often caused by a bacterial or viral infection.

Campylobacter—The name of a bacterium that causes diarrhea.

Campylobacteriosis—A diarrheal infection caused by the *campylobacter* bacterium.

Capture velocity—Airflow that will collect the pollutant (e.g., dust or fumes) that you want removed.

Cardiopulmonary resuscitation (CPR)—Emergency measures performed by a person on another person whose breathing or heart activity has stopped. Measures include closed-chest cardiac compressions and mouth-to-mouth ventilation in a regular sequence.

Care coordinator—This term is used by some agencies or caregivers in place of, or in association with, the term **case manager.** The term *care coordinator* implies that someone is assigned to work with the child's family or alternative caretaker to assist in coordinating services, either internally within an agency directly providing services or with other service providers for the child and family. The term *care coordinator* is usually preferred these days over the term *case manager,* since the latter implies management of a case rather than assistance in ensuring coordinated care.

Caregiver—Used here to indicate the primary staff who work directly with the children, that is, director, teacher, aide, or others in the center and the child care provider in small and large family-child-care homes.

Carrier—A person who carries within his/her body a specific disease-causing organism, who has no symptoms of disease, and who can spread the disease to others. For example, some children may be carriers of *Haemophilus influenzae* or giardia and have no symptoms.

Case manager—See **Care coordinator.**

Catheterization—The process of inserting a hollow tube into an organ of the body, either for an investigative purpose or to give some form of treatment (e.g., to remove urine from the bladder of a child with neurologic disease).

CCFP—Abbreviation for the U.S. Department of Agriculture's Child Care Food Program, a federally sponsored program whose child care component provides nutritious meals to children enrolled in centers and family child-care-homes throughout the country. It is located at 3101 Park Center Drive, Room 1006, Alexandria, VA 22023.

CDA—Abbreviation for Child Development Associate, a credential awarded by a program that trains workers in Head Start, centers, and small and large family-child-care homes to help them achieve professional status in the child care field. The CDA credential is based on the caregiver's ability to work with young children, rather than on formal academic credits. This program is implemented by the Council for Early Childhood Professional Recognition, 1718 Connecticut Avenue, N.W., Washington, DC 20009.

CDC—Abbreviation for the Centers for Disease Control, which is responsible for monitoring communicable diseases, immunization status, and congenital malformations, and for performing other disease surveillance activities in the United States. Its offices are located at 1600 Clifton Road, N.E., Atlanta, GA 30333.

Center—A facility that provides care and education for any number of children in a nonresidential setting and is open on a regular basis (i.e., it is not a drop-in facility).

Child abuse—For the purposes of this set of standards, its definition is considered to be that contained in the laws of the state in which the standards will be applied. While these differ somewhat, most of them contain basic elements as follows:

> **Emotional abuse**—Acts that damage a child in psychological ways, but do not fall into other categories of abuse. Most states require for prosecution that psychological damage be very definite and clearly diagnosed by a psychologist or psychiatrist; this category of abuse is rarely reported and even more rarely a cause of protective action.

> **Neglect**

>> **General neglect**—Failure to provide the common necessities, including food, shelter, a safe environment, education, and health care, but without resultant or likely harm to the child.

>> **Severe neglect**—Neglect that results or is likely to result in harm to the child.

> **Physical abuse**—An intentional (nonaccidental) act affecting a child that produces tangible physical harm.

> **Sexual abuse**—Any sexual act performed with a child by an adult or by another child who exerts control over the victim. (Many state laws provide considerable detail about the specific acts that constitute sexual abuse.)

Child:staff ratio—The maximum number of children permitted per caregiver.

Children with special needs—Children with developmental disabilities, mental retardation, emotional disturbance, sensory or motor impairment, or significant chronic illness who require special health surveillance or specialized programs, interventions, technologies, or facilities.

Chlordane—An insecticide that has been used successfully against flies and mosquitoes that are resistant to DDT, and for the control of ticks and mites. Chlordane requires special handling, as it is toxic to humans when applied to the skin.

Chronic—Adjective describing an infection or illness that lasts a long time (months or years).

Clean—To remove dirt and debris (e.g., blood, urine, and feces) by scrubbing and washing with soap and water.

CMV—See *Cytomegalovirus.*

Cohorting toys—Keeping toys used by a group of children together for use only by that group of children.

Communicable disease—A disease caused by a microorganism (bacterium, virus, fungus, or parasite) that can be transmitted from person to person via an infected body fluid or respiratory spray, with or without an intermediary agent (e.g., louse, mosquito) or environmental object (e.g., table surface).

Communicable period—The period of time when an infected person is capable of spreading infection to another person.

Compliance—The act of carrying out a recommendation, policy, or procedure.

Congenital—Existing from the time of birth.

Conjunctivitis (pink eye)—Inflammation (redness and swelling) of the delicate tissue that covers the inside of the eyelids and the eyeball.

Contamination—The presence of infectious microorganisms in or on the body, on environmental surfaces, on articles of clothing, or in food or water.

Contraindication—Something (as a symptom or condition) that makes a particular treatment or procedure inadvisable.

Corporal punishment—Pain or suffering inflicted on the body (e.g., spanking).

CPR—See **Cardiopulmonary resuscitation.**

CPSC—Abbreviation for the U.S. Consumer Product Safety Commission, created in 1972 and charged with the following responsibilities: (1) to protect the public against unreasonable risks of injury associated with consumer products; (2) to assist consumers in evaluating the comparative safety of consumer products; (3) to develop uniform safety standards for consumer products and to minimize conflicting state and local regulations; and (4) to promote research and investigation into the causes and prevention of product-related deaths, illnesses, and injuries. The CPSC is located at 5401 Westbard Avenue, Bethesda, MD 20207.

Croup—Spasms of the airway that cause difficult breathing and a cough sounding like a seal's bark. Croup can be caused by various bacteria and viruses.

Cryptosporidium—A parasite that causes cryptosporidiosis, a diarrheal illness.

Cytomegalovirus **(CMV)**—A very common virus, which often infects young children. In most cases, CMV causes no symptoms. When symptoms are experienced, they typically consist of fever, swollen glands, and fatigue. CMV can infect a pregnant woman who is not immune and damage the fetus, leading to mental retardation, hearing loss, and other nervous system problems. in the unborn child.

Decibel—The unit of measure of the loudness of sounds; one decibel is the lowest intensity of sound at which a given note can be heard. The decibel level is the number of decibels of noise perceived or measured in a given place.

Deinstitutionalization—The process by which persons with mental retardation or mental illness have been removed from large residential facilities and placed in various forms of community-based care.

Dermatitis—An inflammation of the skin due to irritation or infection.

Diarrhea—An increased number of abnormally loose stools in comparison with the individual's usual bowel habits.

Diphtheria—A serious infection of the nose and throat caused by the bacterium *Corynebacterium diphtheriae,* producing symptoms of sore throat, low fever, chills, and a grayish membrane in the throat. The membrane can make swallowing and breathing difficult and may cause suffocation. The bacteria produce a toxin (a type of poisonous substance) that can cause severe and permanent damage to the nervous system and heart.

Disease surveillance—Close observation for the occurrence of a disease or infection. Surveillance is performed to discover a disease problem early, to understand a disease problem better, and to evaluate the methods used to control the disease.

Disinfect—To eliminate virtually all germs from inanimate surfaces through the use of chemicals (e.g., products registered with the U.S. Environmental Protection Agency as "disinfectants") or physical agents (e.g., heat). In the child care environment, a solution of ¼ cup household liquid chlorine bleach added to 1 gallon of tap water and prepared fresh daily is an effective disinfectant for environmental surfaces and other inanimate objects that have been contaminated with body fluids (see **Body fluids**), provided that the surfaces have first been cleaned (see **Clean**) of organic material before disinfecting. To achieve maximum disinfection with bleach, the precleaned surfaces should be left moderately or glistening wet with the bleach solution and allowed to air dry. A slight chlorine odor should emanate from this solution. If there is no chlorine smell, a new solution needs to be made, even if the solution was prepared fresh that day. The solution will contain 500–800 parts per million (ppm) chlorine. Solutions much less concentrated than the recommended dilution have been shown in laboratory tests to kill high numbers of blood-borne viruses, including HIV and hepatitis B virus. This solution is not toxic if accidentally ingested by a child. However, since this solution is moderately corrosive, caution should be exercised in handling it and when wetting or using it on items containing metals, especially aluminum. DO NOT MIX UNDILUTED BLEACH OR

THE DILUTED BLEACH SOLUTION WITH OTHER FLUIDS, ESPECIALLY ACIDS (E.G., VINEGAR), AS THIS WILL RESULT IN THE RAPID EVOLUTION OF HIGHLY POISONOUS CHLORINE GAS. A disinfecting agent that is at least as effective as the chlorine bleach solution and is approved by the state or local health department may be used as a disinfectant in place of the bleach solution. Disinfection is commonly used for toys, children's table tops, diaper-changing tables, food utensils, and any other object or surface that is significantly contaminated with body fluids. Disinfection of food utensils can be accomplished by using a dishwasher or equivalent process, as described in *Maintenance*, on p. 133.

Drop-in care—Sporadic care for less than 10 hours per week and no more than once a week.

DTP—Abbreviation for the immunization against diphtheria, tetanus, and pertussis.

Dyspnea—Difficulty in breathing or shortness of breath.

Ectoparasite—An organism that lives on the outer surface of the body.

Endonuclease tracking—The laboratory process of examining the genetic material of viruses and bacteria, often used to determine similarities and differences among viruses or bacterial strains that appear to be the same.

Emergency response practices—Procedures used to call for emergency medical assistance, to reach parents or emergency contacts, to arrange for transfer to medical assistance, and to render first aid to the injured person.

Encapsulated asbestos—Asbestos fibers that are coated with a material that makes them not easily inhaled.

Encephalitis—Inflammation (redness and swelling) of the brain, which can be caused by a number of viruses, including mumps, measles, and varicella.

Enteric—Describing infections of the intestines (often with diarrhea) or liver.

EPA—Abbreviation for the U.S. Environmental Protection Agency, established in 1970, which administers federal programs on air and water pollution, solid waste disposal, pesticide regulation, and radiation and noise control. The EPA is headquartered at 401 M Street, S.W., Washington, DC 20201.

Epidemiology—The scientific study of the occurrence and distribution of diseases.

Epiglottis—Tissue lid of the voice box. When this organ becomes swollen and inflamed (a condition called *epiglotitis),* it can block breathing passages. *Haemophilus influenzae* is a common cause of epiglotitis.

EPSDT—Abbreviation for Medicaid's Early Periodic Screening and Diagnostic Treatment program, which provides health assessments and follow-up services to income-eligible children.

Erythromycin—An antibiotic medication used to treat many upper respiratory illnesses. It is often prescribed for people exposed to pertussis.

Evaluation—Impressions and recommendations formed after a careful appraisal and study.

Exclusion—Denying admission of an ill child or staff member to a facility. (See *Inclusion/Exclusion/Dismissal,* on p. 80.)

Excretion—Waste material that is formed and not used by the body, such as feces and urine.

Facility—A legal definition. The buildings, the grounds, the equipment, and the people involved in providing child care of any type.

Failure-to-thrive syndrome—Failure of a child to develop mentally and physically. This syndrome may be due to a variety of causes, but often is associated with a disturbed mother/child relationship.

Fecal coliforms—Bacteria in stool that normally inhabit the gastrointestinal tract and are used as indicators of fecal pollution. They denote the presence of intestinal pathogens in water or food.

Fecal-oral transmission—Transmission of a germ from an infected person's stool (bowel movement) into another person's mouth to infect him/her. This transmission usually occurs when the infected person fails to wash his/her hands after having a bowel movement and then handles things (e.g., food or toys) that other people subsequently put in their mouths. Many diseases are spread this way, including hepatitis A, campylobacteriosis, shigellosis, and salmonellosis.

Fever—An elevation of body temperature. The body temperature can normally be as high as 99.3° oral, 100° rectal, or 98° axillary. A fever exists when the body temperature is higher than these numbers. The amount of temperature elevation varies at different body sites, and the height of the fever does not indicate a more or less severe illness. The method chosen to take a child's temperature depends on the need for accuracy, available equipment, the skill of the person taking the temperature, and the ability of the child to assist in the procedure. Oral temperatures should not be taken on children younger than 4 years. Rectal temperatures should be taken only by persons with specific health training in performing this procedure. Axillary temperatures are only accurate in young infants. (See *Child Inclusion/Exclusion/Dismissal* on p. 80 regarding fever criteria for inclusion/exclusion purposes.) Electronic devices for measuring temperature in the ear canal give temperature results similar to rectal temperature, but these devices require specific training and are not widely available in child care settings.

First aid—See **Pediatric first aid.**

Fomites—Environmental surfaces or objects that may serve as reservoirs for spreading disease from person to person.

Foodborne pathogen—A germ contained in a food product that is transmitted to persons eating the food.

Fungi (singular **fungus**)—Plant-like organisms, such as yeasts, molds, mildews, and mushrooms, which get their nutrition from other living organisms or from dead organic matter.

Gestational—Occurring during or related to pregnancy.

Giardia lamblia—A parasite that causes giardiasis, a diarrheal illness.

Ground fault circuit interrupter—A piece of equipment in an electrical line that offers protection against electrocution if the line comes into contact with water.

Group size—The number of children assigned to a caregiver or team of caregivers occupying an individual classroom or well-defined space within a larger room. (See *Child:Staff Ratio and Group Size*, on p. 1.)

Haemophilus influenzae **type b (Hib)**—The most frequent cause of bacterial infections (i.e., meningitis, blood infections, pneumonia, arthritis) in infants and young children in the United States.

HbCV—Abbreviation for the *Haemophilus b* Conjugate Vaccine, one of the vaccines available against *Haemophilus influenzae* type b (Hib).

HBIG—Abbreviation for hepatitis B immunoglobulin, preventive treatment for those that have been exposed to hepatitis B virus carriers.

HBV—An abbreviation for hepatitis B virus (see **Hepatitis**).

Health care provider—A health professional licensed to write prescriptions (e.g., a physician, nurse practitioner, or physician's assistant).

Health consultant—A physician, certified pediatric or family nurse practitioner, or registered nurse who has pediatric or child care experience and is knowledgeable in child care, licensing, and community resources. The health consultant provides guidance and assistance to child care staff on health aspects of the facility. (See *Health Consultation*, on p. 278, *Consultation Records*, on p. 295, *Health Consultants*, on p. 33, and *Health Consultants*, on p. 106.)

Health plan—A written document that describes emergency health and safety procedures, general health policies and procedures, and policies covering the management of mild illness, injury prevention, and occupational health and safety.

Hepatitis—Inflammation of the liver caused by viral infection. There are five types of infectious hepatitis: type A; type B; non-A, non-B; C; and delta hepatitis. Hepatitis type A infection has been documented as a frequent cause of hepatitis in child care settings and is often asymptomatic in children. Chronic carriers of hepatitis B may be found in child care settings. Non-A, non-B, and C hepatitis are associated with blood transfusions and intravenous drug abuse, and have not been identified as a problem in child care settings. Delta hepatitis occasionally accompanies hepatitis B infections.

Herpetic gingivostomatitis—Inflammation of the mouth and lips caused by the herpes simplex virus.

Hib—see *Haemophilus influenzae* **type b.**

HIV—see **Human immunodeficiency virus disease.**

Human immunodeficiency virus (HIV) disease—HIV disease leads to a failure of the human immune system, leaving the body unable to fight infections and cancers. It is characterized by a relatively long (up to 10 years) asymptomatic stage and a brief acute stage. Gradually, an HIV-infected person develops multiple symptoms and infections that progress to the end stage of the disease, called acquired immunodeficiency syndrome (AIDS). HIV is transmitted by sexual contact or blood-to-blood contact, or from an infected mother to her baby during pregnancy, labor, delivery, or breast-feeding.

Hygiene—Protective measures taken by individuals to promote health and limit the spread of infectious diseases. These measures include (1) washing hands with soap and running water after using the toilet, after handling anything contaminated, and before eating or handling food; (2) keeping hands, hair, and unclean items away from the mouth, nose, eyes, ears, genitals, and wounds; (3) avoiding the use of common or unclean eating utensils, drinking glasses, towels, handkerchiefs, combs, and hairbrushes; (4) avoiding exposure to droplets from the noses and mouths of other people, such as the droplets spread by coughing or sneezing; (5) washing hands thoroughly after caring for another person; and (6) keeping the body clean by frequent (at least daily) bathing or showering, using soap and water.

IFSP—see **Individualized Family Service Plan.**

Immune globulin (Gamma globulin, immunoglobulin)—An antibody preparation made from human plasma. It provides temporary protection against diseases such as hepatitis type A. Health officials may wish to give doses of immune globulin to children in child care when cases of hepatitis appear.

Immunity—The body's ability to fight a particular infection. For example, a child acquires immunity to diseases such as measles, mumps, rubella, and pertussis after natural infection or by immunization. Newborn children initially have the same immune status as their mothers. This immunity usually disappears within the first 6 months of life.

Immunizations—Vaccines that are given to children and adults to help them develop protection (antibodies) against specific infections. Vaccines may contain an inactivated or killed agent or a weakened live organism. Childhood immunizations include protection against diphtheria, pertussis, tetanus, polio, measles, mumps, rubella, and *Haemophilus influenzae* type b. Adults need to be protected against measles, rubella, mumps, polio, tetanus, and diphtheria.

Immunocompromised—The state of not having normal body defenses (immune responses) against diseases caused by microorganisms.

Immunosuppression—Inhibition of the body's natural immune response, used especially to describe the action of drugs that allow the surgical transplantation of a foreign organ or tissue by inhibiting its biological rejection.

Impervious—Adjective describing a smooth surface that does not become wet or retain soil.

Incubation period—Time between exposure to an infectious microorganism and beginning of symptoms.

Individualized Family Service Plan—This term, which is formalized in P.L. 99–457, The Early Intervention Amendments to The Education for All Handicapped Children Act, refers to a plan formulated in collaboration with the family to meet the needs of a child with a developmental disability or delay, to assist the family in its management of the child, and to deal with the family's needs to the extent to which the family wishes assistance.

Infant—A child between the time of birth and the age of ambulation, usually one aged 0 to 12 months.

Infection—A condition caused by the multiplication of an infectious agent in the body.

Infectious—Capable of causing an infection.

Infested—Having parasites (such as lice or scabies) living on the outside of the body.

Influenza ("flu")—An acute viral infection of the respiratory tract. Symptoms usually include fever, chills, headache, muscle aches, dry cough, and sore throat.

Influenza should not be confused with *Haemophilus influenzae* infection caused by bacteria, or with "stomach flu," which is usually an infection caused by a different type of virus.

Injury, intentional—Physical damage to a human being resulting from an intentional event (one done by design) including a transfer of energy (physical, chemical, or heat energy).

Injury, unintentional—Physical damage to a human being resulting from an unintentional event (one not done by design) involving a transfer of energy (physical, chemical, or heat energy).

IPV—Abbreviation for inactivated polio virus, as in the inactivated (Salk-type) polio virus vaccine.

Isolation—The physical separation of an ill person from other persons in order to prevent or lessen contact between other persons and the isolated person's body fluids.

Jaundice—Yellowing of the eyes or skin.

Large family-child-care home—Usually, care and education for 7 to 12 children (including preschool children of the caregiver) in the home of the caregiver, who employs one or more qualified adult assistants to meet the child:staff ratio requirements. This type of care is likely to resemble center care in its organization of activities. Applicable terms are abbreviated here to *large family home* or *large family home caregiver.*

Lethargy—Unusual sleepiness.

Lice—Parasites that live on the surface of the human body (in head, body, or pubic hair). Louse infestation is called *pediculosis.*

Listeriosis—A term applied to the diseases caused by *Listeria* bacterium. *Listeria* can cause meningitis, blood infections, heart problems, and abscesses, and can cause a pregnant woman to miscarry. These diseases are usually acquired by eating or drinking unpasteurized milk or milk products.

Longitudinal study—A research study in which patients are followed and examined over a period of time.

Mainstreaming—A widely used term that describes the philosophy and activities associated with providing services to persons with disabilities in community settings, especially in school programs, where such children or other persons are integrated with persons without disabilities and are entitled to attend programs and to have access to all services available in the community.

MD—Abbreviation for Doctor of Medicine. An MD is a health practitioner who has received a degree from a college of medicine.

Measles (red measles, rubeola, hard measles, 8- to 10-day measles)—A serious viral illness characterized by a red rash, high fever, light-sensitive eyes, cough, and cold symptoms.

Medically fragile—A term applied to children with substantial, life-threatening medical problems who require very close supervision and attention to their medical needs.

Meninges—The tissue covering the brain and spinal cord. When this tissue becomes infected and inflamed, the disease is called **meningitis.**

Meningitis—A swelling or inflammation of the tissue covering the spinal cord and brain. Meningitis is usually caused by a bacterial or viral infection.

Meningococcal disease—Pneumonia, arthritis, meningitis, or blood infection caused by the bacterium *Neisseria meningitidis.*

Midinfancy—The middle of the infancy period or the first year of life, that is, about 6 to 7 months of life.

MMR—Abbreviation for the vaccine against measles, mumps, and rubella.

Monilia—A type of fungus, also know as *Candida albicans.* The infection may occur in the mouth, lungs, intestine, vagina, skin, or nails. If found in the mouth, it is known as oral thrush.

Mucocutaneous—Involving the skin and mucous membranes, such as the eye conjunctiva or the mouth.

Mumps—A viral infection with symptoms of fever, headache, and swelling and tenderness of the salivary glands, causing the cheeks to swell.

NAEYC—Abbreviation for the National Association for the Education of Young Children, a membership-supported organization of people who share a desire to serve and act on the needs and rights of children from birth through age 8. Its offices are located at 1834 Connecticut Avenue, N.W., Washington, DC 20009-5786.

Nasogastric feeding—The administration of nourishment using a plastic tube that stretches from the nose to the stomach.

Nasopharyngeal—Pertaining to the pharynx and nose.

Neisseria meningitidis (meningococcus) (Nm)—A bacterium that can cause meningitis, blood infections, pneumonia, and arthritis.

NFPA—Abbreviation for the National Fire Protection Association, which provides specific guidance on public safety from fire in buildings and structures. The NFPA is located at Battery March Park, Quincy, MA 02269.

Nm—see *Neisseria meningitidis.*

Nutrition Specialist—As defined in these standards, a registered dietitian with 1 to 2 years' experience in infant and child health programs and coursework in child development, who serves as local or state consultant to child care staff. (See Appendices B-1 and B-2, on pp. 328–329, for a full description of qualifications and responsibilities.)

Occupational therapy—Treatment based on the utilization of occupational activities calculated to encourage the patient with physical or mental disabilities to contribute to his/her own recovery.

OPV—Abbreviation for oral polio virus, as in trivalent (Sabin-type) polio virus vaccine.

Organisms—Living things. Often used as a general term for germs (e.g., bacteria, viruses, fungi, or parasites) that can cause disease.

OSHA—Abbreviation for the Occupational Safety and Health Administration of the U.S. Department of Labor, which administers the Occupational Safety and Health Act, regulating health and safety in the workplace. Its headquarters are located at 200 Constitution Avenue, N.W., Washington, DC 20013.

Otitis media—Inflammation or infection of the middle part of the ear. Ear infections are commonly caused by *Streptococcus pneumoniae* or *Haemophilus influenzae.*

Parasite—An organism that lives on or in another living organism (e.g., ticks, lice, mites).

Pediatric first aid—Emergency care and treatment of an injured child before definite medical and surgical management can be secured. Pediatric first aid includes rescue breathing and first aid for choking. (See *First Aid and CPR,* on p. 22.)

Pertussis—A highly contagious bacterial respiratory infection, which begins with cold-like symptoms and cough and becomes progressively more severe, so that the person may experience vomiting, sweating, and exhaustion with the cough. Although most older children and adults with pertussis whoop with coughing spells (hence the common term *whooping cough*), infants with pertussis commonly do not whoop but experience apneic spells, during which the infant becomes blue and stops breathing. The cough and apnea may persist for 1 to 2 months.

Physical therapy—The use of physical agents and methods (e.g., massage, therapeutic exercises, hydrotherapy, electrotherapy) to assist in rehabilitation and restoration of normal bodily function after illness or injury.

Picocuries per liter of air—A measure of concentration of radiation in air.

Pneumonia—An infection of the lungs.

Poliomyelitis—A disease caused by the polio virus with signs that may include paralysis and meningitis, but often with only minor flu-like symptoms.

Postural drainage—Body positioning resulting in the gradual flow of mucous secretions from the edges of both lungs to the main airway so that they can be removed from the lungs by coughing.

Potable—Suitable for drinking.

PPD—Abbreviation for purified protein derivative, a substance used in intradermal tests for tuberculosis.

Preschooler—A child between the age of toilet training and the age of entry into a regular school; usually aged 36 to 59 months.

Prodromal—Pertaining to the earliest symptoms of a disease or those that give warning of its presence.

Pseudomonas aeruginosa—A type of organism that is commonly a contaminant of skin sores but that occasionally causes infection in other parts of the body and is usually hospital-acquired; the most serious infections occur in debilitated patients with lowered resistance due to other diseases and/or therapy.

Purulent—Containing pus, a thick white or yellow fluid.

Rescue breathing—The process of breathing air into the lungs of a person who has stopped breathing. This process is also called artificial respiration.

Respiratory syncytial virus—A virus that causes colds, bronchitis, and pneumonia.

Respiratory system—The nose, ears, sinuses, throat, and lungs.

Rhinovirus—A virus that causes colds.

Rifampin—An antibiotic often prescribed for those exposed to an infection caused by *Haemophilus influenzae* type b (Hib) or *Neisseria meningitidis* (meningococcus), or given to treat a person for a tuberculosis infection.

Rotavirus—A viral infection that causes diarrhea, vomiting, and cold symptoms.

Rubella (German measles, 3-day measles, light measles)—A mild viral illness with symptoms of red rash, low-grade fever, swollen glands, and sometimes achy joints. The rubella virus can infect and damage a fetus if the mother is not immune to the disease.

Salmonella—A type of bacteria that causes food poisoning (salmonellosis) with symptoms of vomiting, diarrhea, and abdominal pain.

Salmonellosis—A diarrheal infection caused by Salmonella bacteria.

Sanitize—To remove filth or soil and small amounts of certain bacteria. For an inanimate surface to be considered sanitary, the surface must be clean (see **Clean**) and the number of germs must be reduced to such a level that disease transmission by that surface is unlikely. This procedure is less rigorous than disinfection (see **Disinfect**) and is applicable to a wide variety of routine housekeeping procedures involving, for example, bedding, bathrooms, kitchen countertops, floors, and walls. Soap, detergent, or abrasive cleaners may be used to sanitize. A number of EPA-registered "detergent-sanitizer" products are also appropriate for sanitizing. Directions on product labels should be followed closely.

Scabies—A skin disease popularly called "the itch," caused by a tiny parasite that burrows into the skin, particularly on the front of the wrist, the webs and sides of the fingers, the buttocks, the genitals, and the feet, and that causes intense itching.

School-age child—A child who is enrolled in a regular school, including kindergarten; usually from 5 to 12 years of age.

School-age-child care facility—A center offering a program of activities before and after school and/or during vacations.

Screening—Mass examination of a population group to detect the existence of a particular disease (e.g., diabetes or tuberculosis).

Secretions—Wet material, such as saliva, that is produced by a cell or a gland and that has a specific purpose in the body.

Seroconversion—The increase in serum antibody

against a microorganism that occurs after an infection with the microorganism or after vaccination with all or a part of the microorganism.

Serologic—Pertaining to the study of blood serum.

Seronegative—Refers to the absence of serum antibodies against a specific microorganism.

Seropositive—Refers to the presence of serum antibodies against a specific microorganism.

Serum—The clear liquid that separates in the clotting of blood.

Shigella—A type of bacterium that causes bacillary dysentery or shigellosis, a diarrheal infection.

Shigellosis—A diarrheal infection caused by the *Shigella* bacterium.

SIDS—see **Sudden Infant Death Syndrome.**
Small family-child-care home—Usually, the care and education of one to six children (including preschool children of the caregiver) in the home of the caregiver. Caregivers model their programs either on a nursery school or on a skilled parenting model. Applicable terms are abbreviated here to *small family home* or *family home caregiver.*

Small family-child-care home network—A group of small-family-child-care homes in one management system.

Special facility for ill children—A facility that cares only for ill children or a facility that cares for more than six ill children at a time. (See *Special Facilities for Ill Children*, on p. 100 for specifics.) This is not the same as child care for ill children provided by the child's regular center, large family-child-care home, or small family-child-care home.

Stacked cribs—Cribs that are assembled like bunk beds and can be stacked three or four cribs high.

Staff—Used here to indicate all personnel employed at the facility, including both caregivers and personnel who do not provide direct care to the children (cooks, drivers, housekeeping personnel, etc.).

Standing orders—Orders written in advance by a health care provider that describe the procedure to be followed in defined circumstances.

Staphylococcus—A common bacterium found on the skin of healthy people that may cause skin infections or boils.

Streptococcus—A common bacterium that can cause sore throat, upper respiratory illnesses, pneumonia, skin rashes, skin infections, arthritis, heart disease (rheumatic fever), and kidney disease (glomerulonephritis).

Substitute staff—Caregivers (often without prior training or experience) hired for one day or for an extended period of time, who work under direct supervision of a trained, licensed/certified (see *Qualifications*, on p. 4) permanent caregiver. (See *Substitutes*, on p. 31, for a full description of qualifications and responsibilities.)

Suction—The use of a device (e.g., a pipe or tube) to exert a sucking or drawing force upon a solid, liquid, or gaseous substance (as from a body cavity) by reducing air pressure over part of its surface.

Sudden Infant Death Syndrome (SIDS)—The sudden and unexpected death of an apparently healthy infant, typically occurring between the ages of 3 weeks and 5 months and not explained by an autopsy.

Sulfa drugs—A group of antibiotics often prescribed to those exposed to an infection caused by *Neisseria meningitidis* (meningococcus).

Syrup of ipecac—A type of medicine that induces vomiting in a person who has swallowed a toxic or poisonous substance.

Systemic—Pertaining to a whole body rather than to one of its parts.

Tb—see **Tuberculosis.**

Toddler—A child between the age of ambulation and the age of toilet training, usually one aged 13 to 35 months.

Toxoplasmosis—A parasitic disease usually causing no symptoms. When symptoms do occur, swollen glands, fatigue, malaise, muscle pain, fluctuating low fever, rash, headache, and sore throat are reported most commonly. Toxoplasmosis can infect and damage an unborn child while producing mild or no symptoms in the mother.

Transmission—The passing of an infectious organism or germ from person to person.

Tuberculosis (Tb)—A disease caused by the bacterium *Mycobacterium tuberculosis* that usually causes an infection of the lungs.

Underimmunized—A person who has not received the appropriate number or types of immunizations for his/her age is said to be underimmunized.

Universal precautions—A term that describes the infectious control precautions recommended by the Centers for Disease Control to be used in all situations to prevent transmission of blood-borne germs (e.g., human immunodeficiency virus, hepatitis B virus). These precautions are described in the publication *Morbidity and Mortality Weekly Report* (Volume 38, No. S-6), June 23, 1989. See also **Disinfect** and **Sanitize** on handling body fluids not visibly contaminated with blood.

Vacuum breaker—A device put on a pipe containing liquid (e.g., drinking water) to prevent the liquid from being sucked backward within the pipe.

Virus—A microscopic organism, smaller than a bacterium, that may cause disease. Viruses can grow or reproduce only in living cells.

Volunteer—In general, a volunteer is a regular member of the staff who is not paid and is not counted in the child:staff ratio (see *Child:Staff Ratio and Group Size*, on p. 1). If the volunteer is counted in the child:staff ratio, he/she must be 16 years or older and preferably work 10 hours or more in the facility.

WIC—Abbreviation for the U.S. Department of Agriculture's Special Supplemental Food Program for Women, Infants and Children, which provides food supplements and nutrition education to pregnant and breastfeeding women, infants, and young children who are considered to be at nutritional risk due to their level of income and evidence of inadequate diet.

Index

Food service staff 122–123
  in centers for children with special
    needs 251–252
  qualifications 327, 329
Formaldehyde 164, 166
Formulas 354
Freezers 128, 132
Frozen foods 131
Fruits 131
Furnishings 157–160
Futons 176

G

Garbage 133, 154–155
Gasoline 179
Gates, interior 160, 197
Giardia lamblia diarrhea 91, 196
Gloves 76
  and diapering 71
  preventing exposure to blood 75
Governing body 269–270
Group size 1–4
Growth data 66
Guardrails 196
Guards
  fireplace 148
  heaters 148
  window 143
Guns 180

H

Haemophilus influenzae type b
    207–209
  notification of parents 85
  recommended practices 343–345
Haemophilus influenzae type b
    conjugate vaccine 219
Handrails 196
Handwashing 72–74
Handwashing sinks 127–128
  cleaning 77
  in diaper-changing areas 170–171
  number of sinks required 169
  supplies for 162–163
HbCV. *See Haemophilus influenzae*
    type b conjugate vaccine
HBV. *See* Hepatitis B virus infection
Head lice 82, 85
  notification of parents 91
Health advocates 13–14
  qualifications 324–326
Health assessments
  for children 56–57, 59
  daily 65–66
  policies 276–278
  for staff 36–37
Health care, preventive 340
Health consultants 33–35, 278–279
  documenting visits 295
  in facilities for ill children 106–107
  recommendations for 314–316
Health departments
  notification of illnesses 87–88, 92
  practices for disease occurrence
    343–351
  recommendations 308–313

Health education
  for children 60–61
  for parents 62
  plan 338–339
  for staff 61–62
Health hazards 337
Health history 334
Health plan policy 276–279
Health record 335
Health resources 59–60
Heaters, portable 147
Heating 146–148
Heating units, food 129
Heavy metals 129
Helmets 161
Hepatitis A virus infections
  causing exclusion or dismissal 82, 85
  notification of parents 92
  procedures 214–218
Hepatitis B immune globulin 230
Hepatitis B virus infection 227–231
Herbicides 157
Herpes simplex virus 222–224
Herpetic gingivostomatitis 83
Hib. *See Haemophilus influenzae* type b
High chairs 159
Hitting 273
HIV infection 231–233
Home-canned foods 131
Hospitalization 292
Hot liquids 123
  water 173
Human immunodeficiency virus
    infection. *See* HIV infection
Humidity 146, 148
Hurricanes, evacuation plan 280
Hygiene 72–76

I

IFSP. *See* Individualized family service
    plan
Ill children
  alternative care arrangements
    275–276
  policy for care of 274–276
  special area for 178
Ill children, facilities for 100–102
  child:staff ratio 105–106
  directors 103–104
  environmental space 102–103
  health consultants 106–107
  licensing 108
  procedures for care 108–110
  staffing 103–104
  training 104–105
Illnesses
  causing exclusion or dismissal 80–86
  levels of severity 99–100
  notification of health department
    87–88, 92
  notification of parents 90–92
  report forms 290, 292
  requiring immediate medical help
    342
  symptoms 81
Immune globulin 216

Immunization 86–87, 219–221
  of caregivers 36, 221
  diphtheria-tetanus-pertussis 349–350
  documentation 219–220
  Haemophilus influenzae type b 207
  measles-mumps-rubella 219
  policies 276–278
  schedules 372–374
Impetigo 82
Incense 166
Incidence logs 290–292
Inclusion, of ill children 108
Individualized family service plan
  coordination of services 246–248
  development 243–245
  implementation 249–256
Indoor play areas 168
Indoor space requirements
  for infants 181
  for preschoolers 182
  for school-age children 183
  for toddlers 182
Infants
  feeding policies 354–355
  food components for 352
  formula 118–119
  indoor space requirements 181
  nutrition 117–120
  program activities 44–49
  qualifications of caregivers 9,
    323–324, 327
Infection control 104–105
Infestation 82
Injured children 178
Injuries
  report forms 291–292, 383
  requiring immediate medical help
    342
Injury report form 383
Insects 133, 156
  breeding hazard 193
Inspections
  of pools 195
  recommendations 306–307
  reports 292–293
Insulation 166
Insurance records 294
Integration of children with special
    needs 239
Interior maintenance 197–198
Intestinal infections 91
Intoxication 281

J

Jaundice 216

K

Kitchens 127–129
  access by children 129–130
  for ill children 102

L

Language development 47, 50
Large family-child-care homes
  child:staff ratio 1-3

ORDER FORM

(Please print)

Please send me _____ copies of

Caring for Our Children

National Health and Safety Performance Standards: Guidelines for Out-Of-Home Child Care Programs ISBN 0-87553-205-5, (450 pages, softcover, Stock No. 054) at $50.00 each for nonmembers and $35.00 for APHA members.

U.S.—Add $7.00 per book for shipping and handling.
Non-U.S.—Add $9.50 per book for shipping and handling.
For orders over $200.00, call (202) 789-5667 for shipping and handling charges.

_____ **Total** dollars including shipping and handling.

☐ Payment enclosed (make check payable to APHA). All checks and money orders must be in US dollars and drawn on US banks.

☐ Visa   ☐ Mastercard

Credit Card No. _____ Expiration Date _____

Cardholder's Signature _____

Name _____

Member No. _____

Organization _____

Address _____

City/State/Zip _____

Country _____

Phone ( ) _____

Is this a business address? ___ Yes ___ No

___ Send me your publications catalog ___ Send me membership information

Mail order form to: **American Public Health Association**
Publication Sales
Department 5037
Washington, DC 20061-5037

To order or charge by phone, call (202) 789-5636. Prices subject to change without notice.